NATI N

NATURE AS REASON

A Thomistic Theory of the Natural Law

JEAN PORTER

William B. Eerdmans Publishing Company
Grand Rapids, Michigan / Cambridge, U.K.

Wm. B. Eerdmans Publishing Co.
255 Jefferson Ave. S.E., Grand Rapids, Michigan 49503 /
P.O. Box 163, Cambridge CB3 9PU U.K.

Printed in the United States of America

10 09 08 07 06 05 7 6 5 4 3 2 1

Library of Congress Cataloging-in-Publication Data

ISBN 0-8028-4906-7

www.eerdmans.com

For my mother and stepfather,
June and Henry Heidelberg,
with love and gratitude

Contents

Preface

About five years ago, I completed a study of the scholastic concept of the natural law, as developed by canon lawyers and theologians in the twelfth and thirteenth centuries. I concluded by observing that this concept is still fundamentally sound and theologically promising, and expressing a hope that others might take it up as a resource for contemporary theological ethics. Of course, I hoped to make an attempt to do so myself, and this book is the result. More specifically, in this book I develop a constructive theory of the natural law, taking the scholastic concept as my starting point. As I explain in the first chapter, I rely especially on the thought of Thomas Aquinas, seen however in its scholastic context. In order to do so, I follow the time-honored method of reflective interpretation, taking Aquinas and his interlocutors as conversation partners, and trying to think through central issues with them. I do not claim that the resulting theory is Aquinas's theory, or much less that of the scholastics more generally; but I do claim that it is Thomistic, in the sense that it takes his theory of the natural law as a starting point and develops in a way that is, I hope, faithful to his overall intent.

In what follows I presuppose, rather than attempting to defend, the interpretations of scholastic thought generally and of Aquinas's theory in particular set out in the earlier book. I provide references to that book for those who are interested in seeing a fuller defense of these interpretations, or who would like more extensive references than I can provide here. By the same token I do not attempt the kind of systematic textual study of Aquinas, or any other medieval author, that would be necessary to defend the readings I presuppose. With respect to Aquinas, I focus mostly on the *Summa theologiae*, which is cited in the text; I cite passages from other works when these seem to me to provide a fuller or clearer insight on a given point, and these are mostly incorporated in the footnotes. As far as possible, references for other medieval authors have been incorporated directly into the text. At a number of points, I draw on the texts collected by Odon Lottin, *Le droit naturel chez saint Thomas d'Aquin et ses prédécesseurs,* 2nd ed. (Bruges: Beyart, 1931), 105-25, and Rudolf Weigand, *Die Naturrechtslehre der Legisten und Dekretisten von Irnerius bis Accursius und von Gratian bis Johannes Teutonicus* (Munich: Max Hueber, 1967), 17-63 (the civilians) and 140-258 (the canonists). References to Lottin are given by name and page number, and to Weigand by name and paragraph number. All translations from both collections are my own, as are all other translations, except where otherwise noted.

Acknowledgments

First of all, I would like to thank the University of Notre Dame and the chair of the Theology Department, John Cavadini, for granting me a year's leave within which to finish this project. Thanks also to Jon Pott and his colleagues at Eerdmans for their encouragement and support, to Kevin Lowery and Paul Martens for assistance with bibliographic research in the early stages of this project, and to Charles Camosy for preparing the bibliography. I would also like to thank Celia Deane-Drummond, Paul Martens, William McDonough, William Mattison, Christopher Megone, and Charles Pinches for extensive and insightful comments on an earlier draft of this manuscript. Lenny Moss gave me much-needed guidance in contemporary genetic theory and the philosophy of biology, and also offered invaluable suggestions for further reading in this area. It probably goes without saying, but any errors that remain are due to my obtuseness and should not be attributed to my readers and conversation partners. My husband Joseph Blenkinsopp also read and commented on this manuscript, but my debts to him go well beyond that — for his patience and tolerance for my somewhat obsessive working style, and for his unflagging love and support.

Portions of the first and last chapters were drawn from two previously published articles: "A Tradition of Civility: The Natural Law as a Tradition of Moral Inquiry," *Scottish Journal of Theology* 56 (2003): 27-48; and "Natural Law as a Scriptural Concept: Theological Reflections on a Medieval Theme," *Theology Today* 59 (2002): 226-41. They are used here by the kind permission of the editors of these journals.

My mother recently retired after fifty years of teaching and academic administration, and moved back to the town where she spent much of her childhood and her early adult years. Shortly afterwards, she reestablished contact with a childhood friend, who, like my mother, had long been alone after the death of a spouse. What happened next is not uncommon, but when it happens in one's own life, or the lives of those one loves, it is always a cause for wonder and joy — they found a new love and began a new life together. This book is dedicated to my mother, and to the warm and generous man who has brought so much to both our lives.

CHAPTER ONE

Introduction

In this book, I will set out a theological account of the natural law, taking my starting points from medieval natural law theorists (especially, but not only, Aquinas) and developing them into a constructive moral theory within a context of contemporary perspectives and concerns. This will strike many readers as a paradoxical project. The natural law is usually regarded as a universal morality, accessible to all rational persons whatever their particular metaphysical or religious commitments (if any), and therefore most appropriately studied through philosophical analysis. This approach, in turn, reflects a more general philosophical commitment to purifying reason from the contingencies of history and particular cultural practices. As applied to the natural law in the early modern period, this commitment was expressed through ongoing efforts to detach the natural law from the matrix of particular beliefs and practices — especially, in this case, the theological beliefs and practices — with which it had historically been associated. In the words of Ernest Barker, "Allied to theology for many centuries . . . the theory of Natural Law had become in the sixteenth century, and continued to remain during the seventeenth and eighteenth, an independent and rationalist system, professed and expounded by the philosophers of the secular school of natural law."[1] The claim that a sound appraisal of our moral beliefs and practices might depend in some substantive way on particular theological beliefs or modes of inquiry would seem from this perspective to be antithetical to a natural law approach on any plausible construal of what the natural law is.

1. Ernest Barker, *Traditions of Civility,* quoted by Gerard Watson, "The Natural Law and Stoicism," in *Problems in Stoicism,* ed. A. A. Long (London: Athlone, 1971), 216. I have been unable to locate the original reference.

The most austere defenders of the philosophical approach do not try to show that their construal of the natural law is consonant with the earlier tradition of natural law reflection. After all, just as a purely rational morality does not depend on culturally specific beliefs and practices for its content or force, so the history of reflection on such a morality cannot condition its development in any substantive way. Nonetheless, evidence for the historical validity of the philosophical approach to the natural law is available — or so it would seem. Consider a frequently cited passage from Cicero's *Republic:*

> True law, however, is right reason corresponding to nature, diffused in all, unchanging, everlasting, which commanding, calls to duty, and forbidding, deters from wrongdoing. And indeed, it does not command or forbid the upright in vain, although neither its commands nor its prohibitions move the wicked. It is not permitted to alter this law, nor is it licit to attempt to derogate from it, nor can it be altogether abolished. Nor indeed can we be freed from it by the Senate or by the people. Neither need we seek for another to explain or interpret it for us. There will not be one law for Rome and another for Athens, nor will there be one law now, and another law in the future, but one everlasting and immutable law will govern all peoples at all times. And there will be one master and ruler common to all, God who is the author, the promulgator, and the judge of this law. And he who does not observe it is a fugitive from himself and rebellious against his own nature, and will thus suffer the worst penalties even if he evades what are commonly regarded as penalties.[2]

At first glance, these words appear to support a purely philosophical approach to the natural law. Cicero describes the natural law as a law that is universal in scope, identically the same in all times and places, and unalterable, in such a way as not to admit of abolition, exceptions, or dispensations. Moreover, if we were to continue with our survey of the natural law tradition, we would find that these characteristics are indeed generally regarded as marks of the natural law. In the words of an anonymous twelfth-century canon lawyer, "The natural law precedes others in dignity, as it precedes them in time; with respect to time, because it began with human nature; with respect to dignity, because while other laws may be changed, it remains immutable. Hence, justice also is defined as a constant and perpetual will rendering to each one his right. Furthermore, reasons of state can set aside

2. *De republica* III.XXII, 33. The translation is mine, but checked against the Loeb edition's translation. This text was transmitted to the scholastics by Lactantius, as the Loeb edition indicates (p. 210).

the civil laws, but not so, the natural law" (The *Cologne Summa,* excerpted in Lottin, 106).

Yet Cicero's remarks also hint at other ways of approaching the natural law. The natural law, he says, is "right reason corresponding to nature," and while the reference to "right reason" fits nicely with contemporary philosophical approaches, his reference to nature reminds us that historically, accounts of the natural law have frequently been associated with specific and contestable scientific and metaphysical accounts of nature — our own human nature, or the natural order more generally considered, or both together. What is more, he explicitly says it is God who is "the author, the promulgator, and the judge of this law," and in this way he links God's sovereignty over all peoples to the natural law. Presumably these remarks would not have the same meaning for Cicero that they came to have for later Jewish and Christian thinkers, but however they are to be understood, they do not fit comfortably with a purely philosophical approach to the natural law, at least as such an approach would be understood by most of our contemporaries.

In fact, reflection on the natural law comprises a rich and varied tradition, in which we find more than one way of construing what the natural law is and assessing its significance and practical force. Certainly, the philosophical approach to the natural law as sketched above represents one prominent strand of that tradition, emerging in the early modern period and dominating most discussions of the natural law up to the present day. But so long as we regard this as the only possible approach to the natural law, or consider it to represent the standard of clarity and rational adequacy by which other approaches should be evaluated, we will overlook or distort the alternative approaches this tradition also offers — approaches which are worthy of consideration in their own right, and which are in some ways, and from some perspectives, more promising than the currently dominant philosophical approach.

One such alternative is suggested by another text, taken from what came to be called the Ordinary Gloss. This is an early twelfth-century gloss, that is to say, a running commentary on Scripture, compiled out of patristic commentaries on individual passages; it is described as the "ordinary" gloss because it quickly became the standard such compilation for scholarly use in the medieval schools. As such, it offers a particularly valuable witness to Western Christian theological reflection, since it epitomizes earlier patristic views while at the same time anticipating the main lines of subsequent scholastic theology. Here is what it says about what later became a locus classicus for scholastic reflection on the natural law, Romans 2:14: "When Gentiles, who do not possess the law, do instinctively what the law requires, these, though not having the law, are a law to themselves":

> Paul said above that the Gentiles are damned if they act badly and saved if they act well. But since they do not have a law, as it were being ignorant of what is good or evil, it would seem that neither should be imputed to them. Contrary to this, the Apostle says: Even if one does not have the written law, one nonetheless has the natural law, by which one understands and is inwardly conscious of what is good and what is evil, what is vice insofar as it is contrary to nature, which in any case grace heals. For the Image cannot be so far extirpated from the human soul by the stain of earthly desires, that none of its lineaments should remain in it. For that is not altogether removed which was impressed there through the Image of God when the human person was created. Accordingly, when vice has been healed through grace, they naturally do those things which pertain to the law. Grace is not denied on account of nature, but rather nature is healed through grace; which being restored in the inner individual, the law of justice, which fault deleted, is reinscribed through grace.[3]

On a first reading, it might seem that these remarks reflect the same basic understanding of the natural law that we find in modern philosophical approaches. Certainly, there are important continuities between the two, insofar as both insist on Cicero's distinguishing marks of the natural law, including its antiquity, its imperishability, and its universal scope. At the same time, however, the Gloss construes these marks in a distinctive way. Most strikingly, the natural law is here treated unproblematically as a scriptural doctrine, insofar as Scripture provides both a warrant for affirming the existence of the natural law and a theological context within which it is rendered meaningful. The natural law is grounded in creation and represents one aspect of the human reflection of the divine Image; as such it provides both a benchmark for sin and a basis for the hope of restoration. At the same time, the Gloss emphasizes what we might describe as the noetic, rather than the substantive or lawlike, character of the natural law, insofar as it is described as a capacity or power for moral discernment rather than as essentially or primarily a set of rules of right conduct. As we will see, the scholastics do believe that the natural law also generates specific moral norms. Yet they do not regard these as central to the natural law in its most important senses; rather, they identify

3. I take this from Migne's *Patrologiae Cursus Completus* (1852), 114:475-76; I also checked the facsimile text published as the *Biblia Latina cum Glossa Ordinaria,* vol. 4 (Brepols: Turnhout, 1992). The Ordinary Gloss later came to be attributed, wrongly, to Walafrid Strabo (d. 849), and is published under his name in Migne. For a comprehensive account of the formation of the Gloss and its later significance, see Beryl Smalley, *The Study of the Bible in the Middle Ages* (Blackwell, 1952; reprint, Notre Dame: University of Notre Dame Press, 1964), 46-65.

the natural law in the primary sense with a capacity for moral discernment, or the fundamental principles through which such a capacity operates. This fact is significant because it points to an alternative way of construing Cicero's marks of the natural law, in terms of the universality of a capacity or power, rather than in terms of a universally accessible set of moral rules. Even so, the universally existing capacities and actions associated with the natural law call for theological interpretation, because they have been in some way damaged or obscured — otherwise, we would not need to be assured that they cannot be altogether extirpated and removed by sin, or told that they function properly when they have been healed by grace.

It is clear that this theological approach to the natural law would fit awkwardly, at best, with the modern and contemporary insistence on the universality and rationally compelling force of the natural law, considered as a set of moral norms. It is therefore not surprising to find that many modern and contemporary interpreters of the natural law have regarded their patristic and medieval forebears as confused, and have celebrated the modern emergence of the natural law as "an independent and rationalist system." But the modern approach to the natural law is not the only one possible, nor does it set the standard by which all other construals of the natural law should be judged. In particular, the distinctively theological approach exemplified by the Gloss should be of interest in its own right for theologians even today — that, at least, is an assumption underlying the current project.

In this book, I will develop a theological account of the natural law which takes its starting points and orientation from the concept of the natural law developed by scholastic jurists and theologians in the twelfth and thirteenth centuries. Admittedly, this is not an obvious starting point for developing a natural law ethic for the twenty-first century. As I hope to show in what follows, the scholastic approach to the natural law has much to offer, particularly seen from the standpoint of theological ethics. It suggests a way of thinking about the natural law that is distinctively theological, while at the same time remaining open to other intellectual perspectives, including those of the natural sciences. By the same token, it provides starting points for reflecting on the moral significance of prerational nature, seen in itself and in connection with the operations of human reason — and as we will see, the connection between the scholastics' approach to nature and their theological convictions is not adventitious. The natural law does not provide us with a system of ethical norms which is both detailed enough to be practical and compelling to all rational and well-disposed persons. However, there are good reasons to doubt whether any moral theory can provide us with such a system, and this approach to the natural law offers us something arguably more valuable, namely, a way of reflecting theologically on the phenomenon of human morality.

In developing this account, I will attempt to be mindful of the distance between the scholastics and ourselves. Nor do I want to suggest that the scholastic concept offers us a perfectly satisfactory account of the natural law, in comparison to which later approaches represent sheer decline. Reflection on the natural law comprises a living tradition in which later stages reflect the weaknesses as well as the strengths of their predecessors, and in this case, as we will see, later versions of the natural law reveal some of the ambiguities of the medieval approach. For both reasons, what I will offer should not be seen as an exposition of the scholastic concept of the natural law, but a contemporary theory of the natural law which draws freely on that concept.

At the same time, the distance between the scholastics and ourselves only extends so far. On certain key points the scholastics were right — or that, at least, will be a further assumption in what follows. They were right to insist on the distinctively theological significance of the natural law, as indicated by scriptural and doctrinal perspectives on nature. They were right to ground their accounts of the natural law in a robust concept of nature, including prerational components of human existence as well as human reason. And they were right to identify the natural law in its primary sense with fundamental capacities for moral discernment and action, rather than moral rules — without denying that the natural law, so understood, does yield determinate norms for conduct. My own approach to the natural law takes these insights as its starting points, and it is my hope that they will be vindicated by the developed account.

This project is motivated by the conviction that the scholastics offer us a cogent and attractive approach to the natural law. In developing a constructive theory out of this approach, my primary aim is not to solve contemporary problems or to correct the deficiencies of other approaches, to moral reflection generally or to the natural law in particular. Rather, I hope to develop what seem to me the key elements of the scholastic approach into a constructive theory, which will stand on its own merits as a theologically sound and cogent account of the moral life. But of course, this project does presuppose a background of problems to be solved and deficiencies to be remedied — otherwise, what would be the point of developing one's own views? I do not mean to imply that I can in fact address all the relevant questions about the natural law that might arise, but I do claim that the theory to be developed does advance an ongoing conversation in fruitful ways. At any rate, the point of this theory is to retrieve and develop what I take to be the characteristic features of the scholastic conception of the natural law, and so it behooves me to say more than I have done about what I take these characteristic features to be. Hence, in the first section of this chapter, I will attempt to indicate, in a necessarily summary form, what I take the scholastic concept of the natural law to be. I will then contrast it with subsequent modern and contemporary approaches. By doing so, I hope both to identify some of the ambiguities and points of incomplete development in the scholastic concept, and to indicate more clearly what I take to be its strongest and most distinctive features. Finally, in the last section I will return to the task at hand, offering an overview of the account of the natural law that I am proposing.

1. The Scholastic Concept of the Natural Law

As I have just indicated, I hope to develop a theory of the natural law in continuity with the historical tradition of natural law tradition, and in what follows I draw freely on one part of that tradition for starting points and insights. "Tradition" is of course a loaded term for many philosophers and theologians today, and so I should begin by making it clear that I do not intend to stake out a position on current debates over the meaning of tradition, or much less to suggest that the tradition of natural law reflection is valuable precisely *as* a tradition. Rather, I refer to the tradition of natural law reflection as a way of indicating that prior to self-reflective theorizing on the natural law we find an extended history of reflection and commentary on the natural law, mediated through texts and developed through a process of self-conscious appropriation, commentary, critique, and revision of earlier approaches.[4] We are justified in regarding this process of reflection as a unified tradition on both historical and substantive grounds. That is to say, we can trace a more or less continuous line of appropriation, critique, and revision, in which later

4. Over the past century, there has been a considerable amount of work on the history of reflection on the natural law. For a standard, and very useful, survey of the history of natural law thought, see A. P. d'Entreves, *Natural Law: An Introduction to Legal Philosophy,* rev. 2nd ed. (London: Hutchinson, 1970). Detailed treatments of scholastic discussions of the natural law up to Aquinas include M. Grabmann, "Das Naturrecht der Scholastik von Gratian bis Thomas von Aquin," in vol. I of *Mittelalterliches Geistesleben: Abhandlungen zur Geschichte der Scholastik und Mystik,* 3 vols. (Munich: Hueber, 1926), 65-103; Lottin (1931); Weigand (1967); and Michael Crowe, *The Changing Profile of the Natural Law* (The Hague: Martinus Nijhoff, 1977), 192-245. For further details, including a more extensive bibliography, see J. Porter, *Natural and Divine Law: Reclaiming the Tradition for Christian Ethics* (Ottawa: Novalis; Grand Rapids: Eerdmans, 1999), 66-75.

natural law thinkers refer explicitly to their forebears, or reflect the shape of earlier thought in implicit but identifiable ways — and at the same time, we can also trace the lines of a broad consensus on the natural law, and correlatively a set of recurring problems, informing natural law reflection throughout much of its history.[5]

It is especially important to keep these aspects of natural law reflection in mind when dealing with the scholastics, at least in the high medieval period. (Scholastics in the early modern period came increasingly to adopt the philosophical perspectives and methods characteristic of the time.) I do not mean to suggest that the scholastics themselves understood their reflections on the natural law in terms of our own understandings of tradition. Nonetheless, by framing their reflections in these terms, we underscore a point that is otherwise likely to be overlooked or misunderstood in considering scholastic reflection on the natural law. That is, one of the defining characteristics of scholasticism in this period is its reliance on texts, including both the supremely authoritative text of Scripture and a wide range of other texts, of Jewish, Islamic, and classical as well as Christian provenance, which were regarded as having lesser but still weighty authority.[6] These latter preserved fragments of the truth, while Scripture provided the interpretative key for reuniting these fragments into a systematic and comprehensible whole. To an extent that seems remarkable today, the scholastics were confident both in the reliability of textual authorities as mediators of truth, and in their own abilities to restore the integral truth which these texts preserved in fragmentary ways. They did not achieve this aim, but they did manage to construct more limited yet impressive and cogent systems out of the diverse perspectives mediated to them through authoritative texts.

This, I want to suggest, indicates the way to understand the scholastic concept of the natural law, at least in the period we are considering. The tradition of the natural law as the scholastics received it was mediated through a wide variety of texts, all of them considered authoritative, although only one of them, namely, Scripture, was taken to be supremely authoritative. In addition to Scripture, these included the writings of the church fathers, especially but not only Augustine, and a wide variety of classical authors, including Aristotle, the Roman jurists collected by Justinian, a number of other Roman and Hellenistic philosophers, and most importantly of all among the non-

5. Grabmann emphasizes the fundamental agreement of the early scholastics on the natural law, in spite of differences of detail, in "Das Naturrecht der Scholastik von Gratian bis Thomas von Aquin," 96-97.

6. I rely here especially on R. W. Southern, *Scholastic Humanism and the Unification of Europe*, vol. 1: *Foundations* (Oxford: Blackwell, 1995), 1-57 and 102-33.

Christian sources, Cicero.[7] This was not simply a heterogeneous collection of sources; it had already been shaped through an ongoing process of textual transmission and commentary, with later authors appropriating, expanding, and correcting their forebears. Hence, the unity of this tradition was provided first of all by a process of deliberate transmission, albeit a transmission of authoritative texts and the truths they were thought to contain, rather than a tradition as such.

At the same time, the scholastics were not simply the passive recipients and transmitters of a received textual tradition. The eleventh and twelfth centuries constituted a period of rapid social change and institutional reform, culminating in the flowering of intellectual life commonly known as the renaissance of the twelfth century.[8] The scholastics were the immediate heirs of these changes and were largely responsible for rationalizing and consolidating them. In order to develop a new social theology adequate to what was in many ways a new society, the scholastics drew heavily on earlier stages of the natural law tradition, while at the same time they reformulated it in such a way as to respond to the needs of their own day. Hence, scholastic reflection on the natural law was genuinely innovative, while at the same time its innovative character was expressed through reflection upon and reformulation of accepted sources. The scholastics speak in the language of their classical and patristic forebears — but it would be a mistake to assume that they always mean what these forebears meant. Ancient claims took on new meanings when they were asserted in the light of new social conditions, and different strands of thought were drawn together in ways that their originators could not have foreseen, much less intended.

Taken by itself, the textually informed character of scholastic reflection would not necessarily be incompatible with the modern ideal of constructing universally defensible philosophical systems — textual reflection might be regarded, for example, as a way of dialectically uncovering self-evident truths. Yet there is a further respect in which scholastic reflection on the natural law

7. The emphasis on Cicero may be surprising, in view of a widespread tendency to assume that the medieval conception of the natural law is fundamentally Aristotelian. However, Cary Nederman's work on medieval political theory has persuaded me that this assumption is mistaken. See his "Nature, Sin and the Origins of Society: The Ciceronian Tradition in Medieval Political Thought," *Journal of the History of Ideas* 49 (1988): 3-26, and "Aristotelianism and the Origins of 'Political Science' in the Twelfth Century," *Journal of the History of Ideas* 52 (1991): 179-94.

8. I rely here in particular on Southern's *Scholastic Humanism and the Unification of Europe;* for further details, including a more extensive bibliography, see my *Natural and Divine Law,* 34-41.

reveals its indebtedness to a text, and in taking note of this aspect, we do depart from the view that the natural law comprises a universally valid set of moral norms, accessible to all rational persons. That is, scholastic reflection on the natural law is grounded in, and fundamentally shaped by, a commitment to one particular text as the supremely authoritative source for reflection. That text is of course Scripture, and its status in scholastic reflection on the natural law gives that reflection a perspectival character that is not consistent with the theoretical view of the natural law held by most of its proponents today.

It would be misleading to say that Scripture is the sole source for scholastic reflection on the natural law, meaning that the scholastics started from scriptural texts taken in isolation from other sources and developed their account of the natural law accordingly. Such an approach would presuppose a distinctively modern and (typically) Protestant commitment to *sola Scriptura* which is foreign to the scholastics' openness to a wider textual tradition.[9] This openness disposed them to accept the natural law tradition in its broader form, including classical as well as Christian sources. Nonetheless, by the time the scholastics received it, the natural law tradition was already a Christianized tradition in which Scripture and other sources were inextricably intertwined. Moreover, in the process of appropriating and developing this tradition, the scholastics turned to Scripture both to justify appeals to the natural law and to guide them in appropriating and reformulating the tradition they received. It would likewise be misleading to assume that the relation between Scripture and the other sources of their received tradition was one-sided, in such a way that scriptural texts always determined the contours of the natural law as the scholastics understood it. Their reading of Scripture was itself shaped by wider assumptions about the natural law, which were in turn formed by a multifaceted tradition of reflection on the natural law. Nonetheless, in its warrants and in its overall contours, the scholastic concept of the natural law was profoundly shaped by their reading of Scripture as mediated through patristic commentary.

9. I do not know of anyone who attempts to develop an account of the natural law in precisely this way, but some of our contemporaries do argue that the normative significance of the natural law can only be established, or reliably established, on the basis of revelation as mediated through authoritative interpretation. This approach is at least suggested by the recent encyclical *Veritatis Splendor* (published in *Origins: CNS Documentary Service* 23, 14 October 1993); see in particular paragraphs 44, 53, and 117. Russell Hittinger takes a similar approach in *The First Grace: Rediscovering the Natural Law in a Post-Christian World* (Wilmington: ISI Books, 2003), 3-37. Stephen Pope discusses and critiques a similar approach in "Scientific and Natural Law Analyses of Homosexuality: A Methodological Study," *Journal of Religious Ethics* 25, no. 1 (1997): 89-126.

The last point should be underscored. While the scholastics did not place the theologians of the early church on a par with Scripture, they did regard patristic commentaries as providing the best possible guideline for understanding scriptural texts. At the same time, earlier theological (and for that matter, philosophical) reflections on the natural law tended to be brief and occasional. Writing in response to a variety of intellectual and social factors, and working within the broader tradition of reflection of the natural law, the scholastics developed key motifs from patristic comments on the natural law into a coherent concept, which provided a basis for further theoretical development. It would take us too far afield at this point to explore the circumstances which led the scholastics to develop this concept; suffice it to say that in its main lines, it incorporated the main lines of earlier theological reflection on the natural law, which it integrated into a more or less unified concept of the natural law (more or less, depending on which author we are considering).[10]

Because the scholastic concept of the natural law emerged out of reflection on an earlier tradition, we need to situate it within that tradition in order to appreciate its distinctive features. The tradition of reflection on the natural law had long embodied a set of distinctions which set the parameters within which distinctive theories of the natural law were developed. With very few exceptions, appeals to the natural law presupposed that we can meaningfully draw a distinction between human laws, customs, and practices — in short, social conventions of all kinds — and the preconventional givens of human life out of which those conventions emerge. Theorists of the natural law did not necessarily move directly from this distinction to a moral judgment, along the lines of "preconventional good, conventional bad." However, they did generally imply or claim that social conventions can be analyzed, in part at least, in terms of their preconventional origins, and that this line of analysis will be morally significant in some way.

Of course, a distinction between preconventional givens and social conventions can be drawn at any number of places and interpreted in light of a wide range of understandings of human nature.[11] Hence, it should be no surprise to find the tradition of the natural law accommodating a diversity of more or less well-developed theoretical accounts of the natural, its normative or lawlike character, and its relation to social conventions. At various times

10. For further details, see my *Natural and Divine Law,* 25-62.

11. For more details on the scholastic concept of natural law and its relation to medieval conceptions of nature, including further references, see my *Natural and Divine Law,* 66-75. I discuss patristic conceptions of the natural law on 124-29.

"nature" has been identified with the order displayed by the natural world or revealed through metaphysical analysis, with the regularities of human nature, including those aspects of it shared with other animals, and with the operations of human reason. The normative force of nature has been construed as one expression of an irresistible nexus of causal interrelationships, as a set of moral rules following more or less perspicuously from the natural order or from rational reflection, and as a power or capacity for moral discernment. Social conventions have been construed as the immediate and organic expressions of human nature, or as reflective constructions developed, perhaps in contingent and unpredictable ways, from naturally given starting points.

The flexibility of the natural law tradition left ample room for Christian theologians to appropriate and develop it in accordance with their distinctive commitments. Not only did this tradition allow ample room to introduce a Christian conception of God as the author and defender of the natural law (as Cicero's remarks illustrate); even more fundamentally, the distinction between the natural and the conventional opened the way to identify both revealed law and conscience with the "natural" in this context. After all, seen from a Christian perspective, both are clearly preconventional, and both give rise, albeit in different ways, to a range of social expressions. Hence we find, for example, that Origen identifies the law of nature with the law of God. Similarly, Ambrose identifies the natural law with the Mosaic law, explaining that the latter confirms and extends the former; he also takes Paul's reference to the inner law of the Gentiles (Rom. 2:14-15, cited above) to refer to the natural law. Jerome likewise identifies this inner law with the natural law, and in addition, he offers the much-quoted comment that synderesis, or reason, cannot be extinguished even in Cain. Augustine also identifies the natural law with the unwritten law of the Gentiles, and as such, he considers it to be universally binding, even though he sometimes adds that it has been almost entirely obscured through sin. He also associates the natural law with the Image of God, which he interprets as the rational soul; hence, on his view the natural law is innate, it is coeval with the creation of the first human beings, and it cannot be eradicated. Finally, in common with many other patristic authors, he connects the natural law to the Golden Rule and the Decalogue. The former, he says, is a basic moral norm known to all, and from this rule it would theoretically be possible to derive at least the fundamental principles of morality. At the same time, given the pervasive effects of sin, our moral knowledge is at best limited and corrupt. For this reason, God has mercifully formulated the fundamental precepts of the natural law in the Mosaic law, particularly in the Decalogue. Hence, the latter can be considered a written formulation of the natural law.

When the scholastics turned to the task of developing their own accounts of the natural law, they found that the complexity of the tradition they received offered them a wide variety of definitions of the natural law.[12] This complexity was both a problem and an opportunity. Their reverence for authoritative texts led them to try to incorporate the diverse interpretations of the natural law, as far as possible, into their own accounts, and they did not always integrate these perspectives into coherent theories. At the same time, however, the flexibility of the received tradition meant it could accommodate the newest findings of natural philosophy and systematic theology — both flourishing and widely influential disciplines at this point — as well as earlier perspectives on human nature and the natural order more generally. The scholastics quickly saw that almost any originating principle of human life can be regarded as "nature," corresponding to the "law" embodied — actually or ideally — in social conventions. As we would expect, these included both reason and the inclinations or orderly processes we share with nonrational creatures, as well as more general metaphysical principles and even widely shared social conventions. It was not always apparent that these diverse approaches could or should be brought within the ambit of one unified conception of the natural law, and indeed, the twelfth-century jurists generally spoke in terms of multiple natural laws. The jurists quickly began to attempt to bring some order to this multiplicity, and the theologians continued to work along these lines, but neither jurists nor theologians ever attempted to reduce it to the homogeneity of one and only one "proper" definition of the natural law.

In their efforts to systematize their accounts of the natural law, the scholastics did however move toward identifying a primary or central understanding of the natural law, to which other construals were related as secondary senses, expressions of the primary natural law, or derivations from it. As we would by now expect, they turned to Scripture in order to identify this primary sense, and in particular, they turned to Paul's reference to the unwritten law of the Gentiles, as interpreted through generations of patristic commentary. This led them to develop a view according to which the natural law is fundamentally a capacity or power to distinguish between good and evil; it is intrinsic to the character of the human soul as made in the Image of God, and therefore it cannot be altogether obliterated; and it is expressed or developed through moral precepts which are confirmed, as well as being completed and

12. Brian Tierney discusses this point in some detail in his *The Idea of Natural Rights: Studies on Natural Rights, Natural Law, and Church Law, 1150-1625* (Atlanta: Scholars Press, 1997), 43-77; also see my *Natural and Divine Law*, 76-98.

transcended, through the operation of grace. Even though the natural law understood in its primary sense does not consist of specific moral rules, it does find immediate expression in the fundamental precepts of the Golden Rule or the two great commandments of love of God and neighbor; these in turn yield the more specific norms of the Decalogue, which can be further specified as warranted by the circumstances of human life. Hence, the natural law more broadly understood does include specific moral norms as well as a fundamental capacity for moral judgment, although there is considerable room for both legitimate variation and sinful distortion at the level of particular norms.

We see a good example of both the complexity of the scholastic concept of the natural law and the way they attempted to bring order to this complexity, in the writings of the late twelfth-century canon lawyer Huguccio:

> And because different people have different views on the natural law, let us set forth its different meanings. Thus, the natural law is said to be reason, insofar as it is a natural power of the soul by which the human person distinguishes between good and evil, choosing good and rejecting evil. And reason is said to be a law [*jus*], because it commands [*jubet*]; also, it is said to be law [*lex*] because it binds [*ligat*] or because it compels one to act rightly [*legitime*]; it is said to be natural, because reason is one of the natural goods, or because it agrees supremely with nature, and does not dissent from it. Concerning this natural law, the Apostle says, "I see another law in my members, which opposes the law of the mind," that is to say, the reason, which is called law, just as has been said. Now in the second place, the natural law is said to be a judgment of reason, namely, a motion proceeding from reason, directly or indirectly; that is, any work or operation to which one is obliged by reason, as to discern, to choose, and to do good, to give alms, to love God, and those sorts of things. Commenting on the text of the Apostle, "For since the gentiles who do not have the law naturally do the things of the law, they are a law to themselves," Origen says, concerning this law, "He says naturally, that is, by a natural reason, namely, by a natural leading of reason." Concerning this same text, Hilary says, "the natural law is to do injury to no one, not to take anything belonging to others, to refrain from fraud and perjury, not to insinuate oneself into another marriage, and things of this sort, and if I may speak briefly, not to do to others what you do not wish done to yourself, which agrees with the evangelical teaching." But understood in this way, it is said to be natural law improperly; because any of the things which we have said to be contained in this understanding of the natural

law should rather be said to be an effect of the natural law, or should be said to derive from it, or to be something that one is bound to do by the natural law, rather than taking it as the natural law itself. Likewise, according to a third sense, the natural law is said to be an instinct and order of nature by which like things are propagated by their like, by which like things rejoice in their like, by which they are well suited to one another, by which they suckle newborn young, by which they seek peace, flee disturbance, and do other things which they have to do in accordance with sensuality, that is, a natural appetite. Concerning this law, the jurist says, "the natural law is that which nature teaches all animals;" this law is common to all animals, while in the aforesaid two senses, it is only appropriate to rational beings. Hence the jurist says, "we see that other animals, even wild animals, are considered to be learned in this law." Likewise, in a fourth sense, the natural law is said to be divine law, that is, what is contained in the law of Moses and the evangelical law; and this is said to be natural law, because the highest nature, that is, God, transmitted it to us and taught it through the law and the prophets and the gospel, or because natural reason leads and impels us even through extrinsic learning to those things which are contained in the divine law. Hence, if I may speak boldly, I say quite certainly that this law is called natural in an improper sense, because the natural law, that is, reason, compels one to do those things which are contained in it, and one is obliged to do those things by reason. (Lottin, 109-10)[13]

I quote this text at some length, because even though Huguccio self-consciously sets forth a distinctive and somewhat controversial position ("If I may speak boldly . . ."), his way of analyzing the natural law comes to dominate the scholastic approach in the twelfth and thirteenth centuries.[14] What

13. Huguccio of Ferrara is generally regarded as the best of the decretists, that is to say, commentators on Gratian's *Decretum;* this text dates from about 1188. The "jurist" to whom he refers is Justinian, and the actual passage quoted comes from Ulpian; "thus it is taken in the beginning" refers to the beginning of Gratian's *Decretum,* on which Huguccio is commenting. Almost nothing is known about Gratian himself, although we are reasonably sure he was a cleric and a legal scholar associated with Bologna. His analytic compendium of canon law, the *Concordia discordantium canonum,* or more commonly the *Decretum Gratiani,* dating from about 1140, represents the first attempt, so far as we know, to bring the canons of the church into a coherent system, and it exercised a far-reaching influence on subsequent theology, as well as canon law.

14. Tierney claims that Huguccio was in fact the first to identify the natural law in the primary sense with reason and to analyze other senses of the natural law accordingly; see *Idea of Natural Rights,* 64-65.

seems at first glance to be a catalogue of diverse senses of the natural law turns out on closer inspection to be informed by analysis, through which these diverse interpretations are related to a primary sense, usually identified with reason or with fundamental principles of moral discernment, and evaluated accordingly. Even more strikingly, what seems at first glance to be a rationalistic interpretation of the natural law turns out to be grounded in Scripture, and correlatively, the divine law revealed in Scripture is said to be congruent with natural reason.

This brings us to a point noted briefly above. That is, the scholastics were well aware of the pronounced strains of universalism in the natural law tradition, exemplified by the text from Cicero with which we began. Yet they did not seem to notice, or much less to address, the implied tension between the scriptural and the universal elements of the natural law as they understood it. This might seem to lend support to the view that the scholastics' approach to the natural law was simply confused, but such a judgment would be too quick. What appears to us to be a paradox, or an outright inconsistency, did not appear in the same light to them. In part, this is due to the specifics of the concept they developed. After all, it is easier to defend the universality of the natural law understood as a God-given capacity for moral judgment than to argue for the universality of a specific set of moral norms.

Huguccio's words suggest a still more fundamental reason why their approach did not strike them as paradoxical. For them, Scripture was the supreme and definitive expression of divine wisdom, but not the only such expression — natural processes and human reason were likewise reflections, albeit fragmented and ambiguous expressions, of God's wisdom.[15] The interpretation of Scripture presupposes innate capacities for reason and judgment which are themselves God-given. As Bonaventure says, we would not be able to understand the moral message of Scripture if it were not for the light of reason with which God has endowed us (*Collationes de decem praeceptis* I 2.2). Hence, the scholastics have no qualms about interpreting Scripture, in part, in light of explicit or implicit standards of reasonableness. But at the same time, the human faculty of reason is itself interpreted in theological and ultimately scriptural terms. That is why the scholastics did not attempt to derive a system of natural law thinking out of purely natural data or rationally self-evident intuitions, and that is also why they appealed to Scripture to establish specific points of natural law morality — for example, the wrongfulness of fornication, which they cheerfully admit could not easily be determined by

15. Southern emphasizes this point; see *Scholastic Humanism,* 1-57. I discuss the relevant issues in more detail in *Natural and Divine Law,* 129-46.

reason alone.[16] Although they would not have put it in these terms, the scholastics offered a perspectival interpretation of a universal phenomenon, namely, the functioning of God's wisdom through nature and human reason. Human reason and Scripture are complementary and mutually interpreting, in such a way that reason enables us to comprehend and interpret Scripture even as Scripture completes and corrects the deliverances of reason.

This brings me to a final point. It might appear from what has been said so far that the scholastics regarded the natural law as a theological concept, rather than a moral concept with practical consequences. And such an impression would not be entirely wrong. The scholastic concept of the natural law reflects the predominantly theological concerns informing its development, and we often find it employed in order to resolve a theological problem, rather than to defend a particular moral claim. Moreover, the scholastics did not attempt to derive a complete and comprehensive system of moral claims from first principles, nor did they even attempt to show how generally accepted moral norms might be systematically derived and developed into a comprehensive system. They did interpret existing norms in light of their natural law origins, but they did not always do so with the aim of drawing moral conclusions.

But this does not mean that their concept of the natural law had no practical significance. The twelfth and thirteenth centuries comprised a period of institutionalized conflict, as well as reform and development — between ecclesiastical and secular authorities, and among different elements within the church and civil society, at every level from the village to the (putative) empire.[17] The university system and correlatively scholasticism itself emerged out of this process, and over the next two centuries the practice of scholasticism as institutionalized in the emerging university system provided one centrally important institutional framework for assessing, critiquing, and developing these institutional changes. As Richard Southern observes,

> In the twelfth and thirteenth centuries, general acceptability was the product of protracted arguments in the schools. Scholastic arguments,

16. The relevant texts are assembled by John Dedek in his "Premarital Sex: The Theological Argument from Peter Lombard to Durand," *Theological Studies* 41 (1980): 643-67. At the same time, Dedek offers a good example of the assumptions that have kept us from fully appreciating the distinctiveness of the scholastic approach to the natural law, since on his view the scriptural arguments offered by the scholastics on this point cannot be genuine natural law arguments.

17. I am particularly indebted to Southern's analysis of the interconnection between these social and institutional developments and the emergence of scholasticism as an intellectual movement; see *Scholastic Humanism,* especially 198-231, and for further details and documentation, my *Natural and Divine Law,* 34-41.

> remote though they were in their terminology from everyday language, performed many of the functions of arguments in political assemblies today: they brought the issues of faith and behaviour before a continuing stream of men, many of whom would one day have to administer what today they discussed. Western society was not naturally conformist: the population was divided into too many semi-autonomous groups, and the inclination to oppose authority was too strong to be lightly disregarded. The arguments in the schools served the purpose of bringing to light the objections which would be raised outside the schools, so a congruity of outlook between schools and the outside world was an essential basis of practical success. Far more than the meetings of the royal council which came to be called "parlements," the schools were the parliaments of medieval Europe.[18]

The concept of the natural law played a central role in these processes of debate and legitimation. Western Europe was by now a predominantly Christian society, and these debates were cast in theological terms, with all sides claiming to represent the authentic voice of the Christian faith. In this context, the scholastic concept of the natural law, precisely because it represented a synthesis of scriptural, classical, and philosophical elements, provided a most useful framework for sorting out and adjudicating these competing claims. At the same time, this concept of the natural law, because of its strongly scriptural orientation, did tend to weight arguments in favor of theological and ecclesiastical claims — that (I believe) is why we find that a concept of the natural law plays a central role in the writings of canon lawyers and theologians but not secular jurists, for whom a concept of reason or equity provides the overarching framework for social critique.[19] (I should add that throughout this book, whenever I refer to the scholastics, unless otherwise indicated I am referring specifically to the theologians and canon lawyers of the twelfth and thirteenth centuries. I do this for convenience, but it is admittedly a somewhat imprecise usage, since the secular jurists were also scholastics.)

At the same time, the scholastics were aware — as many later natural law thinkers were not — that the practices and institutions of society cannot be regarded as organic expressions of nature, which emerge spontaneously from its exigencies and derive their authority from that fact. On the contrary, they never lost sight of the fact that social practices and institutions are always more or less conventional, and in some cases contrary to the law of na-

18. Southern, *Scholastic Humanism*, 144-45.

19. As Crowe points out in *Changing Profile*, 110; also see my *Natural and Divine Law*, 47-48.

ture, at least seen from some perspectives. In this respect they follow Cicero rather than Aristotle.[20] That is, rather than endorsing Aristotle's view that social conventions stem immediately from natural inclinations, in such a way as to reflect human nature directly, they appropriate Cicero's view that human society reflects a long-standing process of human reflection and invention, in which natural inclinations are given expression through negotiation, legislation, and the emergence of custom. (This, by the way, is why we cannot assume that Cicero's remarks quoted at the beginning of this chapter reflect a modern sense of the natural law as a universally accessible set of moral codes — Cicero is too conscious of the conventional character of social norms simply to endorse such a view without qualification.) To once again use a contemporary expression, they were aware that human nature underdetermines the social conventions and practices stemming from it.[21]

Yet the scholastics were convinced that social norms do stem from human nature, construed in some sense or other, in a way that is at least sometimes open to analysis and morally instructive. Hence, when they reflected on specific moral norms in the light of the natural law, they almost always took received norms and practices as their starting point, and proceeded by analyzing these in terms of the principles of the natural law from which they emerge. Here, for example, is Bonaventure's analysis of marriage, following on a remark that the virtue of conjugal chastity is

> in accordance with that very law of nature by reason of nature as originally constituted, which was formed in distinct sexes, according to the beginning of Genesis: "God created the human person in accordance with his image and likeness, male and female he created them." It is also in accordance with the law of nature remaining to this day by reason of a further precept, according to the beginning of Genesis: "God blessed them and said, 'Increase and multiply, fill the earth and subdue it,'" which indeed cannot legitimately be done except through the exercise of conjugal chastity. It is no less in accordance with the law of nature by reason of a revelation given from above. For Adam spoke prophetically after his sleep, when he said, "This then is bone of my bones and flesh of my flesh. For this reason, a man shall leave his father and mother and cleave to his wife, and the two shall be one flesh." . . . From the first of these, the union of man and woman is natural, from the second, it is moral, and from the

20. In general, see my *Natural and Divine Law,* 247-58; on the indebtedness of the scholastics to Cicero, see the articles by Nederman cited above, note 7.

21. For a particularly helpful discussion of this point, see John Kekes, "Human Nature and Moral Theories," *Inquiry* 28 (1985): 231-45.

> third, it is sacramental; and these are all consistent with one another in accordance with a determination of the law of nature, from which in the first instance the acts and practices of conjugal chastity are drawn. *(De perfectione evangelium* 3.1)[22]

Very often the scholastics were content simply to analyze existing norms and practices in terms of their natural origins. However, this line of analysis could also provide a basis for the legitimation of received practices and social institutions. Taking their orientation from the general principle of the goodness of nature seen as God's creation, they could claim that any institution that reflects a genuine aspect of human nature in a reasonable and legitimate way is by that token morally legitimate. Although it is not apparent from the quotation above, Bonaventure's analysis of marriage is in fact an example of this kind of argument, as the immediately preceding context makes clear; he is here defending the claim that conjugal chastity is a genuine virtue worthy of the Christian life, over against those who argued that sexual activity is always sinful, or at best a shameful necessity.

Of course, a great deal can be packed into qualifiers such as "reasonable" and "legitimate," and this raises the question whether the scholastics' concept of the natural law was capable of generating these qualifiers on its own terms — whether, that is to say, it depended on external principles for its moral force. It is difficult to answer this question in any definitive way, precisely because the basic concept is so capacious. Any preconventional principle for morality can be regarded as one type of natural law, or as an expression or manifestation of the natural law. This means that principles emerging from outside the scope of the natural law seen from one perspective could be regarded as themselves natural law principles seen from another perspective. As we have already noted, reason and even Scripture could thus be regarded as forms of natural law, completing and correcting the principles stemming from the natural law of our common animal nature, or our sensuality. For this reason, it is more fruitful to ask whether the scholastics were able to integrate this pluriform concept of the natural law into any kind of coherent unity, in such a way as to develop an account of the natural law capable of

22. The Franciscan Bonaventure and the Dominican Aquinas were almost exact contemporaries who were born within five years of each other (Bonaventure in 1221, Aquinas sometime around 1225) and died in the same year, 1274. Both were scholastic theologians who spent a significant part of their adult lives in the University of Paris, although Bonaventure, unlike Aquinas, also held ecclesial office, first assuming leadership of the Franciscans in 1257 as the minister general of the Franciscan Order and then assuming the position of cardinal bishop of Albano in 1273.

generating real normative force on its own terms. In general, we find the most developed and cogent accounts of the natural law among the thirteenth-century scholastic theologians, because their theological systems provided orienting frameworks within which to sort out the different senses of nature and to place them systematically in relation to one another.

It would take us too far afield to explore the specific accounts of the natural law developed by individual theologians in any detail. Without going further into these views, however, we can take note of other ways in which the scholastic concept of the natural law provided both a basis for moral critique of social practices and a basis for defending existing or innovative practices. We are accustomed to associate medieval natural law with a particular sexual ethic, which is developed in terms of a distinction between natural and unnatural forms of behavior, the latter being condemned under all circumstances. Certainly, the idea of unnaturalness played an important role in this context (and a few others as well), but the scholastics' repertoire of principles for critique and revision was broader than this example would suggest. In particular, they were well aware that not every practice that is nonnatural, in the sense of stemming from social conventions, is unnatural in a pejorative sense. For example, property was traditionally regarded as a nonnatural institution in this sense, yet no scholastic in this period doubted the legitimacy of property as an institution. Nonetheless, the concept of the natural law could still provide criteria, formulated in terms of overall purposes or legitimating justifications, in terms of which nonnatural institutions such as property could be subjected to some kind of moral critique. We find a good example of this approach in the early thirteenth-century theologian William of Auxerre. He notes that the community of possessions, that is to say, the condition that would exist apart from the institution of property

> was not a precept of the natural law simply speaking, but only in accordance with some qualification; for it was a precept in the state of innocence, or in the state of nature as well organized; but in the state of greed and corrupted nature it is not a precept, nor should it be, since if it were, public order would be dissolved, and the human race would destroy itself by mutual slaughter. It is nonetheless true that all things should be held in common in a time of extreme necessity, since natural reason directs that the well being of the neighbor is to be cherished in preference to one's worldly goods. (*Summa aurea* III 18.1)[23]

23. William of Auxerre was a secular theologian — that is to say, not a member of a religious order — whose *Summa aurea*, written around 1220, had a considerable influence on Aquinas's work.

Other theologians are prepared to say that property is not altogether contrary to the natural law, if the complexity of the latter is taken into account; by the same token, however, the complexity of the relevant aspects of the natural law provides resources for a richer moral critique and analysis. Here is Albert the Great on the same topic:

> The common possession of all things and the ownership of some things are both derived from the natural law, because the principles of the law are not the same, as we have already said. Hence according to that state in which there is neither robbery nor usurpation of that which is given over to common use, conscience and reason directed that nothing should be private property, but should be handed over to the common possession of everyone, as it was created in common. But with changing conditions, and the increase of malice and robbery and rancor, nature employs another principle, namely, that private property should be legitimated, for the provision of oneself and of the poor. And so from that point it is not contrary to the law of nature to have something of one's own, but this is to be shared in time of necessity. And so the law according to which unowned property is granted to the occupant is established, as are other similar edicts. (*De bono* V 1.3 *ad* 6)[24]

Aquinas takes Albert's analysis of property one step further, arguing that there is a collective (not individual) right to property:

> . . . exterior things can be considered in two ways. In one way, with respect to their nature, which is not subject to human power, but only to the divine power, which all things obey straightaway. In another way, with respect to the use of the thing itself. And so the human person has natural ownership [*dominium*] of exterior things, because through his reason and will he is able to make use of them for his benefit, as if they were made for him, for more imperfect things always exist for the sake of more perfect things. . . . And by this argument, the Philosopher proves in the first book of the *Politics* that the possession [*possessio*] of exterior things is natural to the human person. Furthermore, this natural ownership [*dominium*] over other creatures, which is appropriate to the human person on account of reason, in which consists the image of God, is manifested in the very creation of the human person, where it is said, "Let us

24. Albert the Great (also known as Albert of Cologne; 1200-1280) was a Dominican theologian who commented extensively on Aristotle's works and wrote on philosophy and natural science as well as theology.

> make the human person to our image and likeness, and let him have authority over the fishes of the sea," etc. [Gen. 1:26]. (*ST* II-II 66.1)

He then goes on to argue for constraints on the claim to property derived from the same natural principles from which the institution stems:

> Those things which are of human right cannot restrict natural right or divine right. Now according to the natural order instituted by divine providence, lower things are directed to this end, that human need is to be relieved by them. And therefore, the distribution and appropriation of things, which proceeds from human right, does not prevent human need from being relieved by things of this kind. . . . [He adds that ordinarily, human needs will be met through such practices as almsgiving.] Nevertheless, if the need be so urgent and evident that it is manifest that the immediate need must be relieved by whatever things occur . . . , then someone can licitly take another's things to relieve his need, whether openly or in secret. Nor does such an action properly have the character of theft or robbery. (II-II 66.7)

This last quotation provides a further example of the way this process of interpretation could provide a basis for normative critique, in such a way as practically to affect the development of social institutions. Aquinas does not quite say that in a situation of extreme need a poor person has a right to the goods of the rich person. But in effect, he does say that the poor person in this situation is immune from punishment if she takes the goods of the rich. That is already a fairly significant qualification on the claims generated by private ownership (which is considered by Aquinas to be conventional and not natural). And as we will see in chapter 5, some scholastics in the late thirteenth century went even further down this road than Aquinas, arguing that the claims of the poor for material necessities constituted a right which should be safeguarded by law, and generating new legal institutions for adjudicating and safeguarding these claims. This represents a further, most important way in which the scholastic concept of the natural law had concrete normative implications. That is, it generated social norms insofar as it provided a justification for the innovative social practices embodying those norms.

The scholastic concept of the natural law, together with the specific theories and moral arguments developed within the context it provided, constitute one of the great achievements of medieval theology. It is an impressive achievement in its own right, and offers a resource of permanent value for theology and moral reflection. The distinctive contours and the value of this achievement have been largely obscured, because the medieval scholastics did not attempt the one task that their immediate successors regarded as centrally important — that is to say, they did not attempt to derive a comprehensive set of moral precepts from one or a few first principles, regarded as compelling to all rational persons. It is difficult to appreciate this fact because we are so accustomed to thinking of the natural law in just this way. But this approach to the natural law is distinctively modern — more specifically, it is especially characteristic of those early modern philosophers regarded collectively as the "fathers" of natural law. Ever since, we have tended to assess the scholastics in terms of what they did not do, and given their own aims and assumptions, had no reason to attempt — rather than asking what we might learn from their own distinctive approach.

At the same time, it would be a mistake to assume that the transition from medieval to modern accounts of the natural law was simply a process of decline. The scholastic concept remained in some respects underdeveloped, and modern appropriations of, and reactions to, medieval natural law theories served to bring their ambiguities to light. For this reason, an examination of the subsequent development of the concept of the natural law will serve both to highlight what is distinctive about the scholastic concept, and to indicate some of the issues that a contemporary appropriation of that concept will need to address.

2. The Modern Approach to the Natural Law

Since we ended the last section by focusing on property as an example of an institution that was analyzed and developed through the concept of the natural law, it may be helpful to begin this section with an early modern perspective on the same topic. Consider these words of William Everard, Gerrard Winstanley, and other leaders of the so-called Diggers, writing in 1649:

> In the beginning of time, the great Creator, Reason, made the earth to be a common treasury. . . . For man had dominion given to him over the beasts, birds, and fishes. But not one word was spoken in the beginning, that one branch of mankind should rule over another. . . .
>
> But since human flesh . . . began to delight himself in the objects of the creation more than in the Spirit Reason and Righteousness . . . then he fell into blindness of mind and weakness of heart. . . .
>
> And here upon the earth, which was made to be a common treasury of relief for all, both beasts and men, was hedged into enclosures by the

> teachers and rulers, and the others were made servants and slaves. And that earth that is within this creation made a common storehouse for all, is bought and sold and kept in the hands of a few; whereby the great Creator is mightily dishonored; as if he were a respecter of persons, delighting in the comfortable livelihood of some, and rejoicing in the miserable poverty and straits of others. From the beginning it was not so. . . .[25]

The more radical thinkers in the English Civil War are not always considered as figures in the natural law tradition, or indeed as participants in the development of modern moral thought.[26] Yet in spite of their strangeness — perhaps, because of it — they foreshadow the development of the natural law tradition in the modern period. Consider the passage just quoted. On the one hand, we hear the distinctive voice of the scholastics here, not only in the affirmation of a renunciation of ownership, but also in the repetition of such medieval commonplaces as "the earth is a common treasury." Indeed, these comments show that the scholastics' appeal to an ideal or primeval natural state could be transformed into a platform for revolutionary social change, simply by being taken as an attainable program for social life here and now. The scholastics had themselves suggested this possibility through the Franciscans' defense of radical poverty, a state in which, as Bonaventure says, one lives in accordance with the natural state of the human person at birth and death, going about "poor and naked."[27] On the other hand, the scholastic account of the natural law is here reconfigured as a deliverance of reason, the "Spirit Reason and Righteousness" — even though it is also presented, correctly, as a scriptural doctrine!

25. William Everard, Gerrard Winstanley, et al., *The True Levellers' Standard Advanced* (1649), in *The Puritan Revolution: A Documentary History,* ed. Stuart E. Prall (New York: Doubleday/Anchor, 1968), 174-75.

26. Richard Tuck is a noteworthy exception, at least insofar as he considers the influence of these thinkers on moral thought. See *Natural Rights Theories: Their Origin and Development* (Cambridge: Cambridge University Press, 1979), 143-55. I do not want to imply that Tuck would agree with my interpretation, however. I should add that while the radical reformers reflect the transition from medieval to modern conceptions of natural law in a particularly telling way, they are of course not the earliest of the modern natural law theorists; they would have been active between about 1645 and 1650, thus earlier than John Locke but later than Hugo Grotius.

27. The phrase comes from *Quaestiones disputatae de perfectione evangelicum* 2.1. Bonaventure himself clearly did not intend to call the moral legitimacy of property into question, but the ideal of poverty he defended at least implied that the institution of property, together with the distinctions of rank that it implied, was not only conventional but dispensable as a basis for society. As Richard Tuck observes with respect to later developments of the Franciscan ideal, "if it was possible for some men to live in an innocent way, then it should be possible for all men to do so." See *Natural Rights Theories,* 22.

This pattern recurs throughout the more sober writings of the modern natural lawyers. Most of these authors identify themselves explicitly as Christian thinkers, and present their moral and political writings as efforts to draw out the implications of Christian thought for the changing social conditions of their time. Let me offer a few examples.

Near the middle of *Leviathan,* Thomas Hobbes declares that "I have derived the Rights of Sovereign power and the duty of subjects hitherto, from the Principle of Nature only. . . . But in that I am next to handle, which is the Nature and Rights of a Christian Commonwealth, whereof there depends much upon supernatural revelations of the will of God, the grounds of my discourse must be, not only the Natural word of God, but also the Prophetical."[28] He then goes on to make his claim good through an extended exegetical display of the scriptural grounds for a Christian political theory, which will extend and complete his general account of the natural law. Similarly, John Locke's natural law theory as set forth in the *Second Treatise of Government* is preceded by a *First Treatise* which argues through extensive scriptural exegesis that kings do not have an unlimited right of dominion over their subjects.[29] For a third example, consider Hugo Grotius, who after his famous remark that the natural law would have force even if God did not exist, immediately adds that "Hence it follows that we must without exception render obedience to God as our Creator, to Whom we owe all that we are and have; especially since in manifold ways, He has shown Himself supremely good and supremely powerful, so that to those who obey Him he is able to give supremely great rewards, even rewards that are eternal, since He himself is eternal."[30] There is some tendency to view these and similar remarks as insincere or self-protective posturing. I see no reason to regard them as such, but even if they were, that would not affect the point I am trying to make. That is, in the public discourse of the early modern period, there was no apparent incongruity between natural law and theological arguments; rather, these were seen as reinforcing and extending one another.

Nonetheless, there is a fundamental difference between modern natural

28. Thomas Hobbes, *Leviathan,* edited with an introduction by C. B. MacPherson (1651; reprint, Middlesex, U.K., and Baltimore: Penguin Books, 1968), 409.

29. John Locke, *Two Treatises of Government,* edited with an introduction and notes by Peter Laslett (Cambridge: Cambridge University Press, 1963; reprint, New York: Mentor, 1965; originally published 1690; 2nd ed. 1694; 3rd ed. 1698); the *First Treatise* comprises 175-298 in this volume.

30. Hugo Grotius, *On the Law of War and Peace* (1625), in *Moral Philosophy from Montaigne to Kant,* vol. 1, ed. J. B. Schneewind (Cambridge: Cambridge University Press, 1990), 90-110, here 92.

law thinkers and their medieval forebears. Knud Haakonssen refers to the "prima facie ambiguity" under which both Grotius and Hobbes labor: "On the one hand, they both write from a theistic standpoint, according to which life and morals are part of the divine dispensation. On the other hand, they intend to account for the moral aspect of this dispensation in such a way that it explains how people without theistic beliefs can have a moral life."[31] It seems to me that this ambiguity runs throughout early modern writings on the natural law. It is reflected in Hobbes's remark that "I have derived the Rights of Sovereign power . . . from the Principle of Nature only," as well as by Locke's way of structuring his two treatises and Grotius's claim that God's authority confirms what reason independently establishes.[32] In each case, what is operative is a particular account of reason and revelation, according to which these are two mutually compatible, complementary, but ultimately distinct sources for moral knowledge. Reason does its work, and *then* revelation steps in to confirm, correct, and supplement the moral code reason generates.

Here again, we see an innovative reading of a tradition being framed in traditional language, and so it is worth underscoring that this *is* an innovation. The scholastics had also said that the natural law is a product of reason. Yet at the same time, as we have seen, they interpreted reason itself in theological terms. That is why they did not hesitate to draw on Scripture as well as rational arguments in order to determine the concrete content of the natural law, and it is also why they did not attempt to construct theories of the natural law on the basis of purely rational — that is to say, nontheological — starting points and arguments.

In contrast, the modern natural lawyers attempted to do precisely that. Now for the first time we see the emergence of the ideal of a genuine scientific knowledge of morality, which in the words of Samuel Pufendorf "rests entirely upon grounds so secure, that from it can be deduced genuine demonstrations which are capable of producing a solid science. So certainly can its

31. Knud Haakonssen, *Natural Law and Moral Philosophy from Grotius to the Scottish Enlightenment* (Cambridge: Cambridge University Press, 1996), 31. More generally, his discussion of the development of natural law theories in the seventeenth century, 15-62, seems to confirm the main lines of this section. Further details on the authors mentioned can be found in *Natural Rights Theories*, 58-81 (Grotius) and 169-73 (Locke), and more recently, Jerome Schneewind's *The Invention of Autonomy: A History of Modern Moral Philosophy* (Cambridge: Cambridge University Press, 1998), 58-81 (Suarez and Grotius), 82-100 (Hobbes), 118-40 (Pufendorf), and 141-66 (Locke and Thomasius).

32. Thus, Locke follows his exegetical *First Treatise* with a philosophically argued *Second Treatise* on political authority, published as 299-478 in the Laslett edition; for Grotius's often-cited claim that the laws of nature can be derived from reason alone, and would therefore hold even if God did not exist, see Schneewind, ed., *Moral Philosophy from Montaigne to Kant*, 92.

conclusions be derived from distinct principles, that no further ground is left for doubt."[33] This is the point at which the natural law begins to be regarded as a system for deriving a comprehensive set of specific moral rules, or at least a framework for assessing existing rules, confirming them and placing them in systematic relation to one another. Correlatively, the natural law now begins to be identified primarily with that set of specific rules which can be so derived or justified. This further separates the modern appropriation of the natural law tradition from its medieval version, which identified the natural law in its primary sense with a natural capacity for moral judgment, or the very general principles through which this capacity operates.[34]

Hence, in the transition from the later Middle Ages to modernity, the tradition of the natural law was transformed from a theologically grounded interpretation of human morality into a philosophical framework for deriving, or at least testing and supplementing, determinate moral norms. This transformation left considerable room for disagreement at the level of theory, and so once again we see not one but many theories of the natural law emerging in this period, some of which give greater emphasis to prerational nature, others of which insist on the autonomous sufficiency of practical reason to generate moral norms. Nonetheless, these theories are united — and distinguished from the medieval scholastic approach — by their insistence that the natural law can ideally be expressed in terms of a set of moral norms derived from one or a few first principles, as given by nature in the wider sense, or by the exigencies of practical reason itself.

What are we to make of this transformation? Probably most defenders of the natural law today would claim that the modern natural lawyers were essentially right, at least in their basic aspirations. That is, most contemporary natural law theorists would agree that it is possible to establish a natural law morality through rational reflection alone, without any necessary refer-

33. Samuel Pufendorf, *The Law of Nature and of Nations* (1672), excerpted with notes in *Moral Philosophy from Montaigne to Kant,* 170-82, here 175. As Haakonssen observes, Pufendorf's "insistence on the scientific character of the natural law, inspired by Cartesianism and by Hobbes, was a renewal of Grotius's ambition to use mathematics as the guiding ideal for natural law, an ideal mostly submerged by his humanist learning" (*Natural Law,* 37).

34. Initially, at any rate. However, as Haakonssen observes, "The great questions which late seventeenth-century natural law theory, especially that of Pufendorf and Locke, had stated so forcefully were, in effect, the questions of in what sense, and to what extent, morals could be accounted for as a human construct without lapsing into 'scepticism,' that is, relativism" (*Natural Law,* 61), and as a result these theorists turned — I would say, returned — to the "moral powers in individual human nature," or to the "evidence for the collective effects of such moral powers in the moral institutions of humankind" (61) as a focal point for reflection on the natural law.

ence to particular religious or other traditional beliefs. Seen from this perspective, the scholastic account of the natural law would appear as an early, relatively unsophisticated presentation of principles which can be formulated and defended on rational grounds — tantamount, from this perspective, to nontheological grounds. Hence, the story of the natural law tradition is basically a story of more or less steady progress from obscurity to clarity through the progressive reformulation of the natural law as "an independent and rationalist system."[35]

I would disagree with this view on a number of grounds. In the first place, I do not in fact believe that modern attempts to defend a natural law ethic, which is at once both compelling to all rational persons and yet detailed enough to be practically significant, have been successful. I have serious doubts about whether such a defense is possible, for reasons to be considered in more detail in a subsequent chapter. More fundamentally, I would argue that the scholastics appear to us to be confused because we are evaluating them in terms of a conception of the natural law which is not their own, rather than trying to understand them in the light of their own aims and convictions. As we have already seen, the scholastics approach the natural law within the parameters of a scripturally informed theology, and while they bring considerable philosophical sophistication to bear in developing this concept, it always remains located within a framework of distinctively Christian commitments and concerns. Their approach will only appear confused or arational if we assume that rational inquiry must be purified of all historical and cultural contingencies. But as is well known, this assumption has been called into question from a number of perspectives, both by theologians and independently by philosophers and cultural critics of all stripes. We need not adopt the deep skepticism of some postmodernists in order to defend the possibility that rational inquiry can *only* take place within some context of culturally specific practices, mores, and traditions.[36] Seen from this perspective, the scholastic approach to the natural law once again appears plausible and attractive.

35. Ernest Barker, quoted above (see n. 1).

36. There is a very considerable literature on this point; as will soon be apparent, my main debt here is to Alasdair MacIntyre's extensive work on the rationality of traditions, although I do not agree with him on every point. His account is developed through numerous articles as well as through his longer writings, but in what follows I rely especially on the three books in which it is developed, namely, *After Virtue: A Study in Moral Theory* (Notre Dame: University of Notre Dame Press, 1981; 2nd ed. 1984); *Whose Justice? Which Rationality?* (Notre Dame: University of Notre Dame Press, 1988); and *Three Rival Versions of Moral Enquiry: Encyclopedia, Genealogy, and Tradition* (Notre Dame: University of Notre Dame Press, 1990).

This is one of those disputes that cannot be conclusively settled through an examination of the historical evidence, because it is precisely a dispute over the way in which that historical evidence is to be interpreted. And the interpretative task will inevitably be shaped by the evaluative presuppositions that we bring to it.[37] Nonetheless, the history of natural law reflection can at least suggest that one interpretation of the natural law is more plausible than another. To turn to the issue at hand, it will always be possible to argue that the history of natural law reflection consists in a sometimes confused yet progressive development of a purely rationalist, and therefore properly philosophical, theory of morality. The specific moral claims embodied in that reflection can almost always be construed as expressions of more universal principles, provided that one is prepared to move one's analysis to a sufficiently high level of abstraction. Appeals to particular warrants, for example Scripture, can be construed as early and confused efforts to establish what is later put on more solid rational foundations, or else they can be taken to illustrate the point that we sometimes arrive at valid conclusions by means of dubious and adventitious arguments. Yet the more closely we examine the development of natural law reflection in its rich particularity, the less plausible this kind of reductive analysis appears to be.[38]

At the same time, even if we conclude that the modern approach to natural law is problematic in some respects, we should resist the contrary temptation to regard it as a simple decline from a medieval ideal. Modern natural lawyers, like their medieval forebears, developed their concept of the natural law within a context of practical concerns generated by their own social and intellectual situation, and to the extent that we share that situation, these concerns must be ours as well. Just as we cannot interpret the medieval scholastics in modern terms, neither can we disregard the distinctive concerns informing modern approaches to the natural law — particularly since we ourselves share those concerns to a very considerable degree. What is more, the ambiguities inherent in the modern approach to the natural law can to some degree be traced to the scholastic concept from which that approach emerged. This is particularly so with respect to the ambiguities we have just been discussing concerning the rational status of the natural law.

Seen from the perspective of our own concerns, neither the modern natural lawyers nor their scholastic forebears were sufficiently clear about

37. The idea of an evaluative history has many antecedents, but I take it from MacIntyre, *After Virtue,* 2nd ed.; see in particular 1-5 and 265-72.

38. As I argue in more detail in "A Tradition of Civility: The Natural Law as a Tradition of Moral Inquiry," *Scottish Journal of Theology* 56, no. 1 (2003): 27-48.

whether, and to what extent, their fundamental commitments depended on specifically theological perspectives.[39] For the scholastics, this ambiguity was not recognized, and did not undermine their development of the concept, because the context in which they worked did not, so to say, force the issue. The twelfth and thirteenth centuries constituted a period of rapid social change and institutional development, but this development took place within a context of broad consensus on theological and moral commitments. In this context, the concept of the natural law provided a framework for analysis and critique of the practices and institutions emerging within one society. Correlatively, within this context natural law analysis consisted of displaying the relationship between existing social forms and the natural principles from which they stemmed, understanding "natural principles" in a very broad sense. The medieval natural lawyers simply did not need to appropriate the natural law as a basis for developing a systematic system of moral norms — the norms of morality were in place, at least in their main lines, and what was not in place could be developed through processes of critique and extension of existing ideals and practices.

In the early modern period, this situation changed. The rapid expansion of European societies meant that for the first time in some centuries, Europeans were brought into sustained contact with societies whose beliefs and ways of life were markedly different from their own.[40] At the same time, this was also the period in which the nation-state system emerged as the basis for social organization within Europe, even though the nation-state itself is medieval in origin.[41] Although this system eventually provided a basis for social stability and international law, in its earlier stages it was attended by considerable social upheaval, both within national communities (for example, the

39. Philippe Delhaye makes this point with respect to the medieval scholastics in his *Permanence du droit naturel* (Louvain: Editions Nauwelaerts, 1960), 66-84.

40. This contrast should not be overstated, since the scholastics and their contemporaries also had to deal with "the other" in the form of the non-Christian peoples of Europe and later the Muslims — not to mention the "outsiders within," the Jewish community. Nonetheless, there were very considerable continuities as well as differences among the diverse peoples of Europe, Asia Minor, and northern Africa — the "barbarians" and European Christians were after all more or less the same peoples, and Christians, Jews, and Muslims shared a common history and culture, at least to a considerable degree. The differences among the peoples of Europe, sub-Saharan Africa, and the Americas, in contrast, were far more marked, and those on all sides had to struggle to make sense of them. For further details, see Anthony Padgen, *The Fall of Natural Man: The American Indian and the Origins of Comparative Ethnology* (Cambridge: Cambridge University Press, 1982), 10-26; on the use of natural law arguments in this context, see 57-108.

41. I rely in particular here on Hendrik Spruyt, *The Sovereign State and Its Competitors* (Princeton: Princeton University Press, 1994).

English Civil War) and between nations and peoples. It is hardly surprising that men and women in this period felt the need for an overarching framework of universally acceptable moral norms, in terms of which they could make sense of the profoundly different societies they were encountering, and on the basis of which they could negotiate conflicts at home and abroad.

Moreover, it is hardly surprising that they would turn to the natural law tradition to provide them with this framework. After all, this tradition had long affirmed the existence of a law which is more fundamental than the law codes of particular societies, which is supremely authoritative and cannot be abrogated. What better touchstone could there be for evaluating the practices of other cultures, and what better basis for establishing domestic authority and international law? In addition, as Pufendorf's comments suggest, the emergence of modern science as a distinctive intellectual enterprise, with its own extraordinarily successful methods of inquiry, held out the promise that moral inquiry, too, might be placed on a new footing, on the basis of which it might attain the certainty and completeness that social conditions made so desirable.

I have already suggested that the modern aspiration toward defending an ethic that is both universally compelling and practically usable is not likely to be met, and I will return later to defend this claim in more detail. And yet, this does not mean that the modern aspirations toward universalism can simply be disregarded. To a very considerable extent, we still face the same challenges which gave rise to those aspirations, and to that extent we need to find an alternative way to address them. For this reason, if no other, we cannot simply retrieve the scholastic concept of the natural law as a basis for contemporary ethical reflection. What is needed, rather, is a reformulation of that concept that is responsive to the challenges of our own situation.

Let me turn now to a further trajectory in the development of the tradition of natural law reflection, one which will bring us still closer to the concerns of this project. That is, after the early modern enthusiasm for the natural law considered as an "independent and rationalist system," the credibility of the natural law among secular philosophers suffered a sharp decline. Nonetheless, the natural law tradition continued to be preserved and developed by Roman Catholic moral theologians, with the result that it came to be associated specifically with Catholic thought — an association that persists to this day. Considered in this context, the natural law has been the focus of sharp debates, as well as more recent reappraisals, among Catholic intellectuals and between Catholics and Protestants. Yet paradoxically, this theological contextualization has not led to much in the way of a reevaluation of the modern view of the natural law as a set of moral rules capable of being established through "pure" reason. Rather, throughout its later history, with only a few exceptions, the natural law has been regarded as a philosophical theory of morality to be either defended or rejected on nontheological grounds. We turn now to a closer examination of this trajectory.

3. The Later Trajectory of the Natural Law Tradition

The early modern natural lawyers included Protestant as well as Catholic philosophers and legal scholars, and arguably the Protestants were more influential.[42] At any rate, as we have seen, these theorists aspired to develop theories of a kind which, if successful, would have made their denominational commitments irrelevant. Nonetheless, after the eighteenth century natural law theories came to be associated primarily with the moral teachings of the Catholic Church, due both to the influence of Aquinas and his early modern interpreters within the Catholic Church, and to the fact that outside that community the idea of natural law was widely discredited.[43] It is important to realize, however, that the versions of the natural law preserved within Catholicism were in some respects quite different from the scholastic concept sketched above. Most importantly, Catholic versions of the natural law were shaped by the same presuppositions that we find operative in early modern discussions generally. When church officials and theologians appealed to the natural law, they usually did so with the explicit aim of setting forth moral arguments which are, or should be, rationally compelling for all men and women of good will.

At the same time, the terms of this appeal changed in significant ways as we move from the modern to the contemporary period. In its earlier forms, the modern Catholic account of the natural law was grounded in an account of the aims, and the overall order, manifested in prerational nature. This of course represented another point of continuity between the early modern

42. As Haakonssen points out, much of the early modern work on the natural law represented, among other things, a Protestant reaction to late scholastic natural law theories; see *Natural Law,* 24-26.

43. For more details on modern and contemporary Catholic theories of the natural law, and Protestant critiques and reapprasials of those theories, see my *Natural and Divine Law,* 29-33. Todd Salzman offers a good overview of contemporary debates over the natural law within the Catholic community in *What Are They Saying about Catholic Ethical Method?* (Mahwah, N.J.: Paulist, 2003), 17-47; for a more critical appraisal of current approaches, together with an extended discussion of *Veritatis Splendor,* see Hittinger, *The First Grace,* 3-37.

natural lawyers and their medieval forebears, since they too regarded prerational nature as morally significant. At the same time, however, the prerational origins of the natural law were not thought to obviate its fundamentally rational character, by either medieval or modern Catholic natural lawyers. And here we come to a second respect in which the modern adaption of a medieval concept generated problems. This difficulty cannot be traced in the same way to the scholastics, because their accounts of nature, while contested and diverse, were not particularly ambiguous. However, these accounts did presuppose specific philosophical and theological views of nature, which — unsurprisingly — were not in fact rationally compelling to all persons of good will. Given the modern commitment to universal cogency as the standard of rationality, Catholic theorists of the natural law found themselves increasingly forced to choose between the naturalness of the natural law and its rational character.

Almost without exception they chose to emphasize the rationality of the natural law, rather than its naturalness understood in an earlier sense according to which prerational nature has independent moral significance. By the beginning of the twentieth century, this conception of nature was widely regarded as untenable. For those Catholics trained in Anglophone moral philosophy, the modern Catholic approach to the natural law seemed vulnerable to arguments against the so-called naturalistic fallacy, according to which it is illegitimate to derive moral conclusions from metaphysical or factual premises. Even more importantly, the insistence on sharp divisions between natural and unnatural characteristic of this approach increasingly came to seem arbitrary and unreasonable. In a widely influential book published in the 1930s, the theologian Herbert Doms argued that the overall well-being of the person, rather than a biologically derived naturalness, should be the primary criterion for sexual ethics.[44] This line of argument was subsequently generalized and developed by some of the most influential Catholic theologians of the twentieth century, including both Karl Rahner and Bernard Lonergan, who argued that the traditional account of the natural law is inadequate because it represents a "static" or "classical" view of human nature. The more we become conscious of the ways in which the expression of our human nature is historically conditioned, the less we are prepared to draw moral conclusions from our own ideas of the "permanent" structures of that nature; or so the argument goes.[45]

44. For further details on the significance of Herbert Doms's work, see Lisa Cahill, *Sex, Gender, and Christian Ethics* (Cambridge: Cambridge University Press, 1996), 91.

45. For a helpful discussion of Rahner's reformulation of the natural law, with an exten-

3. The Later Trajectory of the Natural Law Tradition

Yet very few Catholics have been prepared to reject the idea of a natural law altogether. For this reason, when we examine early twentieth-century Catholic accounts of the natural law, we find that they agree, with few exceptions, on a construal of the natural law tradition which emphasizes the rational character of the natural law and minimizes or even denies the normative significance of nature, except insofar as human nature is simply equated with rationality. John Courtney Murray is typical in this respect. Murray does affirm the metaphysical foundations of the natural law in a teleological account of nature. However, he also appears to equate human nature more or less completely with the human capacity for rationality; hence, his explanations of the way the natural law functions emphasize the operations of practical reason, in such a way as to minimize or even deny the normative force of nature understood in any wider sense. Speaking of the natural law consensus informing public life, he says:

> The quality of being in accord with reason is the non-contingent element in the body of thought that constitutes the consensus [concerning the natural law]. Brute fact or sheer experience have no virtue to elaborate themselves into controlling rules of public conduct. The transcendence of experience and the transformation of fact into principle is the work of reason. The act whereby the doctrine of the consensus is formulated is not the act of inquiry into the facts, nor the act of reflection on the experience. It is an act of judgement, an exercise in moral affirmation or denial.[46]

---

sive bibliographic note, see James F. Bresnahan, "An Ethics of Faith," in *A World of Grace: An Introduction to the Themes and Foundations of Karl Rahner's Theology,* ed. Leo J. O'Donovan (New York: Crossroad, 1981), 169-84. Michael J. Himes offers a good overview and assessment of Lonergan's work on the natural law in "The Human Person in Contemporary Theology: From Human Nature to Authentic Subjectivity" (1983), reprinted in *Introduction to Christian Ethics: A Reader,* ed. Ronald R. Hamel and Kenneth R. Himes, O.F.M. (New York: Paulist, 1989), 49-62. Charles Curran offers a critique of "classical" natural law theory which incorporates the insights of both authors in his "Natural Law in Moral Theology" (1970), reprinted in *Readings in Moral Theology No. 7: Natural Law and Theology,* ed. Charles E. Curran and Richard A. McCormick (New York: Paulist, 1991), 247-95; more recently, he has offered a more sympathethic but still critical appraisal of natural law approaches to ethics in *The Catholic Moral Tradition Today: A Synthesis* (Washington, D.C.: Georgetown University Press, 1999), 35-45. For further, more recent critiques of natural law approaches developed along similar lines, see Josef Fuchs, "Natural Law or Nauralistic Fallacy?" in his *Moral Demands and Personal Obligations* (Washington, D.C.: Georgetown University Press, 1993; originally 1988), 30-51, and Edward Vacek, "Divine-Command, Natural-Law and Mutual-Love Ethics," *Theological Studies* 57 (1996): 633-53.

46. John Courtney Murray, *We Hold These Truths* (New York: Sheed and Ward, 1960), 122.

There is at least one major exception to this tendency in the years leading up to the Council, namely, the highly influential account of the natural law and natural rights put forward by Jacques Maritain, who asserts the metaphysical foundations of the natural law in no uncertain terms:

> What I am emphasizing is the first basic element to be recognized in natural law, namely, the *ontological* element; I mean the *normality of functioning* which is grounded on the essence of that being: man. Natural law in general, as we have just seen, is the ideal formula of development of a given being; it might be compared with an algebraical equation according to which a curve develops in space, yet with man the curve has freely to conform to the equation. Let us say, then, that in its ontological aspect, natural law is an *ideal order* relating to human actions, a *divide* between the suitable and the unsuitable, the proper and the improper, which depends on human nature or essence and the unchangeable necessities rooted in it.[47]

However, when we read further we find that even though Maritain grounds the natural law in a robustly metaphysical conception of nature, this conception has little direct normative significance. The reason is that Maritain, in contrast to most of his contemporaries, does not consider the natural law, considered as a source for moral norms, to be directly accessible to human reason: "At this point let us stress that human reason does not discover the regulations of natural law in an abstract and theoretical manner, as a series of geometrical theorems. Nay more, it does not discover them through the conceptual exercise of the intellect, or by way of rational knowledge."[48] How, then, do we come to know the regulations of natural law? Appealing to Aquinas, as Maritain interprets him, he goes on to explain that our practical knowledge of the natural law "is not rational knowledge, but knowledge *through inclination.* That kind of knowledge is not clear knowledge through concepts and conceptual judgement; it is obscure, unsystematic, vital knowledge by connaturality or congeniality, in which the intellect, in order to bear judgement, consults and listens to the inner melody that the vibrating strings of abiding tendencies make present in the subject."[49]

It is difficult to know what to make of a form of human knowledge that is neither conceptual nor rational (and more than difficult to ascribe such an

47. Jacques Maritain, *Man and the State* (Chicago: University of Chicago Press, 1951), 87-88, emphasis in original.

48. Maritain, *Man and the State,* 91.

49. Maritain, *Man and the State,* 91-92, emphasis in original.

idea to Aquinas), but at any rate it is clear that Maritain does not claim that moral precepts can be derived, in any straightforward way, from reflection on the normative significance of human nature. In this way, he is the exception to the general tendency that proves the rule. That is, he does construe the natural law in such a way as to preserve the connection between the natural law and a robust conception of human nature; but in order to do so, he denies that human nature has any direct, cognitively accessible normative force.

The approach to the natural law that emphasizes its rational character finds its most comprehensive expression in the "new theory of the natural law" developed by John Finnis, Germain Grisez, and their followers. We will have occasion to turn more than once to this influential theory of the natural law, and so it will be helpful to set out its main lines here. This theory has been subject to considerable development and intense debate over the more than thirty years since it was first suggested by Germain Grisez; the following summary relies on John Finnis's *Aquinas*, which represents one of the most recent and extensive formulations of the view.[50]

Finnis takes his starting point from an interpretation of Aquinas's remarks on the natural law, which on his view rests on a particular understanding of what is required for human action to be fully reasonable.[51] As Finnis reads him, Aquinas holds that we are directed by the inclinations mentioned in the *Summa theologiae* I-II 94.2 toward certain human goods, for example, life, knowledge, and practical reasonableness. Although knowledge of these goods is not innate, once experienced they are immediately grasped by the intellect as good in themselves, apart from their emotional appeal or their instrumental value. Hence, they can also be described as primary or basic human goods. Any action which aims at one of these goods is, to that extent at least, ipso facto intelligible, and for that reason the basic goods are said to

50. In addition to John Finnis, *Aquinas: Moral, Political, and Legal Theory* (Oxford: Oxford University Press, 1998), the main statements of the theory would include John Finnis, *Natural Law and Natural Rights* (Oxford: Clarendon, 1980); Germain Grisez, Joseph Boyle, and John Finnis, "Practical Principles, Moral Truth, and Ultimate Ends," *American Journal of Jurisprudence* 32 (1987): 99-151; and Germain Grisez, *The Way of the Lord Jesus 1: Christian Moral Principles* (Chicago: Franciscan Herald Press, 1983) and *The Way of the Lord Jesus 2: Living a Christian Life* (Chicago: Franciscan Herald Press, 1993). Robert George offers especially clear and helpful summaries of the theory in the course of defending it against various critics in the essays collected in *In Defense of Natural Law* (Oxford: Oxford University Press, 1999); see in particular 45-54 and 83-91. In addition, see the helpful summary provided in Rufus Black's introduction to the volume of essays edited by him and Nigel Biggar, "The New Natural Law Theory," in *The Revival of Natural Law: Philosophical, Theological, and Ethical Responses to the Finnis-Grisez School* (Aldershot: Ashgate Press, 2000), 1-28.

51. In *Aquinas*, 56-102.

provide intelligible ends or, alternatively, basic reasons for action.[52] As such, they provide content for the first principle of practical reason, "Good is to be done and pursued, and bad is to be avoided" (*ST* 94.2).[53]

This first principle, Finnis adds, does not by itself give rise to the "ought" of moral obligation. "Ought" in the moral sense is reached "when the absolutely first practical principle is followed through, in its relationship to all the other first principles, with a reasonableness which is unrestricted and undeflected by any subrational factor such as distracting emotion."[54] While no one can pursue every instantiation of every basic good, reason demands that we remain open to the fullest possible instantiation of every basic good, a demand Finnis describes as the integral directiveness of the first principles enjoining us to pursue the basic goods.[55] Hence, practical reasonableness rules out any act which is "immediately or mediately contrary to some basic good," as for example killing is contrary to the good of life, or adultery is contrary to the good of marriage.[56] There are other norms of morality, most notably other-regard and fairness, but these seem also to be analyzed in terms of what is implied by a genuinely unrestricted openness to all the basic goods.[57]

Finally, not only do the basic human goods provide intelligible reasons for action, they provide the only such reasons, considered precisely in abstraction from their particular instantiations. Hence, when I walk for the sake of my health (my example, not Finnis's), my action is intelligible and good insofar as it is aimed at preserving an instantiation of the basic good of life — not because it is aimed at preserving *my* life (by itself, that would be an egoistical motive), and not because I enjoy it (that would be an emotional, rather than a rational, reason for action).[58] This does not mean that an act is rendered morally bad by the presence of self-referential and emotional motives in addition to the rational pursuit of a basic good, but it is the latter sort of motivation which renders an action morally praiseworthy.[59]

I have argued elsewhere that this interpretation of the natural law does not accurately represent Aquinas's own understanding of the natural law, and in fact Grisez, unlike Finnis, no longer attempts to argue that their "new

52. Finnis, *Aquinas,* 60.
53. Finnis's translation, in *Aquinas,* 86.
54. Finnis, *Aquinas,* 87.
55. Finnis, *Aquinas,* 106.
56. Finnis, *Aquinas,* 140; see further 138-40, 163-70.
57. Finnis, *Aquinas,* 111-17, 123-29.
58. On the first point, see Finnis, *Aquinas,* 89, 111-17; on the second, see 73-78.
59. Finnis, *Aquinas,* 74-75.

natural law theory" is an accurate rendition of Aquinas's account.[60] Be that as it may, considered on its own terms, this is a formidable and widely influential theory of the natural law. And as the above summary indicates, it is very much a natural law theory in the modern mode, since it claims to derive a comprehensive system of moral precepts from an indubitable first principle, namely, the first principle of practical reason as specified through the apprehension of the basic goods. Admittedly, the process of derivation in question appears to be specification rather than deduction; that is, in experiencing the basic good of life (for example), we rationally apprehend that life is worthy of pursuit and should never be destroyed or prevented from coming into existence. Nonetheless, this process of specification does yield definite moral rules which can themselves approach, without fully attaining, the rationally compelling character of the first principle of practical reason and the basic goods.[61]

This interpretation of the natural law has generated considerable controversy among Catholic moral theologians, many of whom challenge the stringent prohibitions generated by the theory.[62] Nonetheless, by and large these critics agree with Grisez and Finnis in their fundamental approach to moral reasoning. They share the conviction that moral norms are to be analyzed in terms of the basic goods to be pursued through action, disagreeing primarily over what should count as "acting against" a basic good.[63] Most importantly, from our perspective, Catholic moral thinkers on both sides of this debate continue to hold that the natural law is to be understood as a morality of reason which can be grasped by all rational and well-disposed persons. In the words of Richard McCormick and Charles Curran, "From the viewpoint of moral theology or Christian ethics anyone who admits human reason as a source of moral wisdom adopts a natural law perspective."[64] Hence, in all its

60. Specifically, in my "Reason, Nature and the End of Human Life: A Consideration of John Finnis' *Aquinas*," *Journal of Religion* 80, no. 3 (July 2000): 476-84. Similar arguments are developed by Anthony J. Lisska, *Aquinas's Theory of the Natural Law: An Analytic Reconstruction* (Oxford: Clarendon, 1996), 139-65, and Ralph McInerny, *Aquinas on Human Action: A Theory of Practice* (Washington, D.C.: Catholic University of America Press, 1992), 184-92, and "Grisez and Thomism," in *The Revival of Natural Law*, 53-72.

61. As George points out, it is a mistake to assume that the specific conclusions of the natural law share in the same rational certainty as the first principle of practical reason and the norms through which it is specified; see *In Defense*, 45.

62. The main arguments are summarized in Salzman, *What Are They Saying?* 39-44; see also the sympathethic yet critical apprasial offered by Nigel Biggar in his conclusion to *The Revival of Natural Law*, 283-94.

63. As Salzman observes in *What Are They Saying?* 39-40.

64. Curran and McCormick, *Natural Law and Theology*, 1.

forms modern and contemporary Catholic natural law thinking reflects the assumptions and concerns of modern moral thought more generally. These include, above all, the need for a framework for dialogue within which "all people of good will" could reason together about matters affecting the public well-being, and a basis for the defense of moral boundaries, wherever precisely these are to be drawn.

We have not so far examined Protestant critiques and reappraisals of the idea of natural law. Yet these should also be considered part of the natural law tradition. The ongoing development of accounts of the natural law has been profoundly shaped both by Protestant natural law theorists and by engagement with Protestant critiques of a natural law approach to Christian ethics. Recently, Protestant reappraisals have retrieved aspects of the earlier tradition that many Catholic theologians have rejected, particularly its emphasis on prerational nature as a source for moral discernment. Finally, the criticisms and partial accommodations to the natural law on the part of Protestant thinkers point to further ambiguities and unexamined assumptions in the natural law tradition as developed so far.

The main lines of Protestant critiques of the natural law are well known. Since the Reformation, this doctrine has been seen as an expression of human pride, an effort to establish human righteousness apart from God's law and God's grace — a line of criticism powerfully expressed in the twentieth century by Karl Barth. Similarly, Reinhold Niebuhr forcefully argued for the classical Protestant view that the pervasive reality of human sinfulness has decisively undermined our knowledge of a natural moral order. More recently, Stanley Hauerwas has rejected the doctrine of the natural law on the grounds that it provides an insufficiently theological basis for a Christian ethic.[65]

Twentieth-century Catholic reappraisals of the idea of natural law did not forestall these criticisms. On the contrary, the extent to which Catholic and Protestant critiques resembled one another in this period is striking. For both sets of critics, earlier approaches to the natural law reflected an illegitimate

65. See Karl Barth, *Church Dogmatics* II/2, trans. G. W. Bromiley et al. (Edinburgh: T. & T. Clark, 1957), 528-35; Reinhold Niebuhr, "Christian Faith and Natural Law" (1940), reprinted in *Love and Justice: Selections from the Shorter Writings of Reinhold Niebuhr* (Louisville: Westminster/John Knox, 1957), 46-54; and Stanley Hauerwas, *The Peaceable Kingdom: A Primer in Christian Ethics* (Notre Dame: University of Notre Dame Press, 1983), 50-71. For a distinctively Lutheran perspective, see the nuanced and sympathetic critique of natural law as portrayed in *Veritatis Splendor* developed by Reinhard Hütter in "'God's Law' in *Veritatis splendor:* Sic et Non," in *Ecumenical Ventures in Ethics: Protestants Engage Pope John Paul II's Moral Encyclicals*, ed. Hütter and Theodor Dieter (Grand Rapids: Eerdmans, 1998), 84-114.

tendency to identify actually existing social practices with an unalterable natural law. As we have already noted, Catholic theologians throughout much of the twentieth century argued that the earlier approach reflects a static or classical worldview, which takes no account of the contingencies of history or the needs of individual men and women. Compare this with Reinhold Niebuhr's comment that "reason is not capable of defining any standard of justice which is universally valid or acceptable. Thus Thomistic definitions of justice are filled with specific details which are drawn from the given realities of a feudal social order and may be regarded as 'rationalizations' of a feudal aristocracy's dominant position in society."[66] At the same time, however, Catholics have continued to insist on the possibilities for some kind of universal ethic, grounded in reason rather than in prerational nature, over against what appeared to them as the sectarian dangers of Protestant ethics.[67]

Yet we would have a one-sided view of Protestant approaches to the natural law if we considered nothing but these criticisms. Over the past thirty years Protestant theologians have increasingly turned to the natural law tradition as a source for their own moral reflection. Indeed, in English-speaking circles one of the most influential advocates for a reconsideration of the theological significance of nature has been the Reformed theologian James Gustafson. On his view, Catholics are right to insist that nature is an important theological category, and Protestant theologians have been wrong to try to understand all divine and human activity under the rubrics of freedom and history.[68] At the same time, however, he also insists that the fundamental assumptions of this theory cannot be sustained in the light of contemporary scientific perspectives on nature. Hence, he argues that for both Protestant and Catholic theologians, "the question to be addressed somewhat systematically is that of the status of nature in theological ethics."[69]

Gustafson himself addresses this question through an account of the

66. Reinhold Niebuhr, "Christian Faith and Natural Law," *Theology* 40 (February 1940): 86-94, here 87-88. Similarities between Protestant and Catholic critiques continue; compare Niebuhr's defense of an ethic of love as an alternative to, and corrective for, natural law ethics to Edward Vacek's very similar proposal in "Mutual-Love Ethics," 649-53.

67. For a good example from one of the most influential twentieth-century moral theologians, see Bernard Häring, *The Law of Christ: Moral Theology for Priests and Laity,* vol. I, trans. Edwin G. Kaiser (Westminster, Md.: Newman Press, 1965), 243. More recently, similar concerns have been expressed, although not by reference to the natural law specifically, by David Hollenbach, *The Common Good and Christian Ethics* (Cambridge: Cambridge University Press, 2002), 137-70, and Lisa Cahill, "Toward Global Ethics," *Theological Studies* 63 (2002): 324-44.

68. In particular, see James Gustafson, "Nature: Its Status in Theological Ethics," *Logos* vol. E (1982): 5-23.

69. Gustafson, "Nature," 6.

ways in which a fundamental Christian stance of piety can be nurtured and expressed in the context of reflection on the natural world, seen as one centrally important expression of divine power as it both sustains and ultimately destroys human life.[70] This approach has the advantage, from Gustafson's point of view, of not requiring a problematic theory of nature, or indeed, any systematic account of nature at all. Rather, he construes nature in terms of the nonhuman world as we experience and engage it, and he looks to discernment informed by piety to bring moral content to nature so understood.

Gustafson's emphasis on nature as a comprehensive context for human discernment and responsibility has had a wide appeal. And its appeal is by no means limited to Protestant scholars; the distinguished Catholic moral theologian Charles Curran, himself an influential critic of traditional Catholic versions of the natural law in earlier years, has recently developed a Catholic moral theology within the framework of an ethic of responsiveness along the lines sketched above.[71] Even more strikingly, we see similar ideas expressed in more recent Protestant retrievals of a natural law ethic, which on the surface are very different from Gustafson's liberal and pragmatic approach. Here, for example, is a summary of what is theologically valid and worthwhile in the natural law tradition, as seen by the Lutheran theologian Reinhard Hütter:

> This task [of moral discernment] is not a "theory" to be applied but a particular practice involving both theoretical and practical reasoning. It is bound to a way of theological thinking that presupposes (a) God the creator and redeemer who unmasks and judges human estrangement from the divine origin, from each other, and from creation and who calls humans into the communion of the divine life; (b) a created order and a "way of life" willed for all humans; and (c) a practical reason that is neither unimpaired nor fully transparent to itself but rather wounded and obscured by sinful desires, habits, and practices. Natural law is not "something out there" that we eventually "bump" into if we search long enough. Neither is it to be found "written" in our genes or in the stars. It does not mean that we have a priori access to the moral universal. While some principles of practical reason are accessible to all of us, the natural law in its fullness is not simply inscribed in our minds. Instead diverse practices and traditions that structure human society display a matrix of contingent and unpredictable resonances with God's purpose for hu-

70. Developed most extensively in his two-volume *Ethics from a Theocentric Perspective,* vol. 1: *Theology and Ethics* (Chicago: University of Chicago Press, 1981), and vol. 2: *Ethics and Theology* (Chicago: University of Chicago Press, 1984).

71. See Curran, *Catholic Moral Tradition Today,* 73-83.

> mankind as articulated in the narratives of Israel and Jesus. In particular structures of responsibility (their vocations), Christians have to discern and judge the resonances and dissonances in light of God's commandments. Where we recognize a significant and broadly based correspondence between God's law and traditions and patterns of human society, there "natural law" has been re(dis)covered.[72]

Hütter's overall theological orientation is very different from Gustafson's, in ways that cannot just be traced to classical differences between Reformed and Lutheran theology. Yet for that very reason, their points of agreement are striking. Like Gustafson, Hütter does not identify the natural law with a moral theory which could be expected to yield moral conclusions in advance of an encounter with a particular situation. Rather, the natural law is revealed through the believer's faithful response to a situation, in which some aspect of the ordering of human life is seen to be congruent with God's will. At that point — and apparently, not before — we recover, and rediscover, the natural law.

Hütter does not appear to develop his interpretation of the natural law in conversation with Gustafson. Their general similarity in approach reflects a more general tendency in Protestant theology, namely, the emphasis on responsiveness and discernment to God's will as expressed through the divine commandments mediated through Scripture. Of course, this theme runs throughout the history of Christian theology, but in the twentieth century it owes its most distinctive formulation, and its pervasive influence, to the work of Karl Barth, for whom responsiveness to God's command was the central task and privilege of the Christian life.[73] This fact helps to account for an aspect of recent Protestant theology which would otherwise be difficult to explain, given Barth's own views, namely, the openness to some appeal to naturalness as a moral standard among so many Protestant theologians influenced by Barth.[74] In a happy irony, Barth's influence thus provides an opening for a

72. Reinhard Hütter, "The Twofold Center of Lutheran Ethics: Christian Freedom and God's Commandments," in *The Promise of Lutheran Ethics,* ed. Karen Bloomquist and John Stumme (Minneapolis: Fortress, 1998), 31-54, here 51.

73. My interpretation of Barth's ethics relies on Nigel Biggar, *The Hastening That Waits: Karl Barth's Ethics,* paperback edition with new conclusion (Oxford: Clarendon, 1995).

74. I am thinking in particular of Oliver O'Donovan; see his *Resurrection and Moral Order: An Outline for Evangelical Ethics* (Grand Rapids: Eerdmans, 1986), 31-52. At the same time, however, he insists that he is not advocating a return to a "natural ethic"; see *The Desire of the Nations: Rediscovering the Roots of Political Theology* (Cambridge: Cambridge University Press, 1996), 19-20. Even Hauerwas has recently argued that Barth's theology provides an opening to natural theology in his *With the Grain of the Universe: The Church's Witness and Natural Theol-*

rapprochement between traditional Catholic and Protestant approaches to the natural law.

Although the following observations would need to be qualified, contemporary appropriations of the natural law tradition tend to divide along denominational lines. In recent years, Protestant theologians have begun to rethink the long-standing Reformed suspicion of the natural law, to the point of challenging Catholics to take their own natural law ethic more seriously. Nonetheless, for most Protestants the usable core of the natural law tradition is located in a certain attitude toward the natural givens which confront us, an attitude of pious acceptance or active discernment of God's will as mediated through the contingencies of nature. On this view, nature is seen as presenting a context for Christian reflection in its givenness, but not in its intrinsic orderliness or purposefulness. For most Catholics, in contrast, the natural law is identified more or less straightforwardly with the deliverances of moral reasoning, which takes account of the regularities of nature, to be sure, but not in such a way as to be bound by them. The Catholic emphasis on the reasonableness of morality reflects traditional Catholic concerns with the specificity and the general validity of a moral law, but by the same token, it leaves little scope for distinctively theological norms and ideals. Hence, recent Catholic versions of the natural law generate more normative content than most Protestant versions do, but at the same time, they offer less in the way of a specifically Christian perspective on the moral life.[75]

This assessment, taken together with the history of the modern development of the natural law tradition, points to recurring problematics that any theory of the natural law needs to address. In what sense can the natural law be understood to be "for all peoples and at all times, one law, perduring and unchangeable"? To what extent does a sound account of the natural law depend on particular theological (or other) perspectives, and how is this reflected in our interpretation of its universality? How are we to interpret the preconventional origins of morality and social practices, and in particular, what accounts of prerational nature and reason shall we presuppose? To what

ogy (Grand Rapids: Baker, 2001), 173-204. However, this line of argument does not include a reappraisal of the natural law; see the brief and disparaging reference at 134-35.

75. At least, this would generally be the case. However, as we have already noted, Hittinger's *The First Grace* seems to reflect a contrary trend toward de-emphasizing the possibilities for independent moral discernment grounded in the natural law. Similarly, Martin Rhonheimer argues that the authority of practical reason is grounded in divine authority, and not in the intelligibilities of nature as perceived by reason; see *Natural Law and Practical Reason: A Thomist View of Moral Autonomy,* trans. Gerald Malsbary (New York: Fordham University Press, 2000), 11-12.

extent, and in what ways, does the natural law function as a law, that is to say, a source for practicable moral norms? We will return to all of these issues in subsequent chapters.

4. The Natural Law and Theological Ethics: The Proposed Project

In the past two sections, we have taken note of the ambiguities and problematics of the natural law tradition. Yet these should not blind us to its continuing appeal, especially but not only for theologians. The recent reappraisals of the natural law tradition by Protestant as well as Catholic theologians testify to that fact. As Hütter's remarks remind us, the idea of a natural law has long served as a framework within which to draw out the moral implications of centrally important theological doctrines, including the goodness of creation and the status of the human person as a free participant in God's universal providence.

My aim in this book is to develop a fresh construal of the natural law tradition, taking the medieval scholastic concept as my starting point and attempting to develop a theory responsive to the questions identified above. I hope that by this point the motivation behind this approach is more apparent. Seen from our standpoint, the scholastic concept of the natural law has much to commend it. It offers a way to affirm the moral significance of human nature, including the prerational dimensions of that nature, without denying the central importance of reason for moral reflection and practice. As such, it suggests fresh lines of inquiry — fresh, at least, to us — into a whole range of topics. Most importantly, from our perspective, it offers a distinctively theological approach to these questions, which combines a scriptural and doctrinal approach with openness to other perspectives.

How, then, might we develop a concept of the natural law which is responsive to contemporary concerns while still preserving what is attractive in the scholastic approach? I will proceed by way of a selective retrieval of the natural law tradition as embodied in scholastic reflection in the twelfth and thirteenth centuries. More specifically, I will take what I regard as the key features of the scholastic concept of the natural law, reflect on them in the light of relevant contemporary thought, and develop them into a systematic account of the natural law which indicates both its place in a wider theological framework and its relevance for moral reflection. The resultant account of the natural law will not provide a basis for deriving moral norms from indubitable first principles. It will, however, provide a framework for analyzing, critiquing, and developing norms and practices and defending innovations within a context of practical concerns. Seen from our perspective, once again, the advantage of this particular framework lies in the specific way it enables us to bring theological perspectives systematically to bear on moral reflection.

While it would of course be anachronistic to describe this method as scholastic, I believe it is a friendly approach to the scholastics, one which starts from assumptions they would have shared. First and fundamentally, like scholasticism itself, this is a textually based approach to moral and theological reflection, in the straightforward sense that medieval texts will provide the basis, and much of the structure, for what follows. But secondly, this approach does not treat the relevant texts as constituting a self-contained system, to be interpreted through a process of intratextual commentary. Rather, the governing assumption, which must of course be confirmed through the study as a whole, is that these writings reflect a way of understanding the natural law that is fundamentally sound and widely defensible — not in its entirety to everyone, but in significant parts to a wide range of interlocutors. In other words, these texts are valuable precisely because they offer a valid and fruitful perspective on the world outside the texts, and for that very reason they can be interpreted and developed in the light of assumptions, beliefs, and concerns that are in some respects markedly different from the scholastics' own. This approach, too, reflects assumptions that the scholastics themselves would have shared, at least to some extent, since for them, too, texts are valuable because they contain truths about the world beyond the text, albeit in fragmentary and distorted forms.[76] Finally, I believe that the account of the natural law that I will be developing is an authentic expression of the scholastic concept, although admittedly an expression which they could not have developed in their own day. However, I will not attempt in this book to argue for the accuracy of my reading of the scholastics on this topic, and of course, I do not claim that my own account of the natural law represents the views of any one of the scholastic authors.

This brings me to another point. It will become apparent as this study proceeds that one of the scholastic authors plays a central role in the development of my own account of the natural law, namely, Thomas Aquinas. Indeed, I believe that my own theory of the natural law *is* in its essentials that of Aqui-

76. Of course, there are significant differences between the approach adopted here and the scholastics' own ways of working. Most significantly, they regarded textually based forms of inquiry as not just one, but the best, and very nearly the only way of conducting intellectual inquiry, although the processes of logical analysis and construction also played a role in their work. Here again I rely on Southern's *Scholastic Humanism*, 15-57.

nas, as developed and extended in a contemporary context, or at least that it is a development and extension of that theory within the spirit of his overall project. Of course, I am well aware that my own interpretations of Aquinas would be questioned at many points, and others have developed very different theories of the natural law on the basis of their readings of Aquinas. I do not attempt in this book to contest these alternative interpretations, except tangentially in the course of developing my own account, nor do I attempt to defend the following theory of the natural law as a reading of Aquinas.

Given this, some may wonder why I represent this study as a reformulation of the scholastic concept of the natural law, and not simply as a reformulation of Aquinas's own views. In the first place, Aquinas's account of the natural law cannot fully be understood, even on its own terms, unless it is placed in the context of the views of his own immediate forebears and contemporaries, nor is its significance for our own time fully apparent apart from this context.[77] Furthermore, no one author, not even Aquinas, can fully represent the richness of an extended discussion such as the scholastics' treatment of the natural law, and there is much of value there which is not included, or not given prominence, in Aquinas's own thought. For both of these reasons, I have developed my own account of the natural law by drawing on a range of twelfth- and thirteenth-century authors, although Aquinas's analysis provides the fundamental theoretical structure for developing their insights into a coherent account. This is of course one further reason why the account that follows should be regarded as a Thomistic account of the natural law, but not as a straightforward presentation of Aquinas's own views. I have tried to signal both my indebtedness to the scholastic concept generally, and my particular reliance on Aquinas, through the title and subtitle of the book, taking the title itself from a phrase which recurs throughout scholastic discussions of the natural law, while the subtitle signals the specific approach being taken here.

77. Although I am very much in sympathy with their overall approach, it seems to me that the interpretations of Aquinas's theory of the natural law offered by Anthony Lisska and Kevin Flannery are limited by their focus on the Aristotelian roots of that theory, to the neglect of Aquinas's other sources or his immediate intellectual context; see Lisska, *Aquinas's Theory of the Natural Law,* and Kevin L. Flannery, S.J., *Acts Amid Precepts: The Aristotelian Logical Structure of Thomas Aquinas's Moral Theory* (Washington, D.C.: Catholic University of America Press, 2001). As will be apparent, I take the Aristotelian naturalism of Aquinas's natural law theory very seriously indeed. At the same time, however, Aquinas appropriated Aristotle in order to develop a concept of the natural law that was not immediately Aristotelian in origin, but stemmed from the work of his own immediate predecessors and contemporaries. In my view we cannot understand even the most Aristotelian elements of Aquinas's natural law theory unless we keep this in mind.

The time has come to indicate, in a preliminary way, what I consider the natural law to be, and to offer some overview of the account to be developed in what follows.[78] I take my starting point from Aquinas's answer to the question whether there is a natural law within us:

> It is manifest that all things participate to some degree in the eternal law, insofar, that is to say, as they have from its impression inclinations to their own acts and ends. Among the others, however, the rational creature is subject to divine providence in a more excellent way, insofar as it is itself made a participant in providence, being provident for itself and others. Hence there is in it a participation in the eternal reason, through which it has a natural inclination towards a due act and end. And such participation in the eternal law by the rational creature is called the natural law. (*ST* I-II 91.2)

It is no mistake that Aquinas frames his account of the natural law in terms that are theologically specific but morally somewhat general. The concept of the natural law provides him with a way of locating human morality within a wider framework of theological concepts, in which creation and providence play a central role, while its generality allows him to incorporate the variety of ways in which the scholastics understood the natural law. At the same time, he is not content with an ad hoc appropriation of different accounts of the natural law. Rather, he integrates these into a system, under the governing idea of providence seen as action for an end.[79]

Aquinas's systematic account of the natural law presupposes a more

78. What follows is simply a summary of points to be developed later, and so I do not attempt to document the following claims in detail at this point.

79. Thanks here to Aaron Canty, who first called the link between providence and natural law in Aquinas to my attention. Hittinger likewise identifies the doctrine of providence as the key to understanding Aquinas's theory of the natural law, but he seems to conclude from this that men and women cannot reliably form moral judgments without the guidance of revelation, as authoritatively interpreted through church authorities; see *The First Grace,* 24-32. Yet Aquinas systematically connects the human person's subjection to providence with the distinctively human capabilities for independent judgment and action; in addition to the introduction to the introduction to the *prima secundae* of the *Summa theologiae,* see *ST* I-II 91.2 and the *Summa contra gentiles* III 111 and 113. Similarly, Hittinger argues that on Aquinas's view the natural law considered as a capacity for moral judgment has been so weakened by sin that it cannot function properly, citing a late text, *In duo praecepta* Prologue 1, in support of this view. In my own view, however, this line of interpretation cannot be sustained; even the text Hittinger cites is not quite so negative as he implies, and elsewhere Aquinas makes it clear that he does believe that our capacities for moral judgment can function, at least to some extent, even apart from revelation and grace. For further details, see my *Natural and Divine Law,* 173-76.

general scholastic understanding of nature, and the ways in which nature can be said to constitute a law, or to generate laws. This is one of the most controversial aspects of Aquinas's moral thought, and it has led some to argue that for him, morality depends on reason alone. Yet no scholastic would drive this kind of wedge between human reason and the intelligibility inherent in nature more broadly understood. The intelligibility of nature can be understood in more than one way, depending on what kind of nature is at stake — the primary options being nature considered as an ordered whole, and the nature proper to a given kind of creature. But for the scholastics, including Aquinas, reflection on the natural law always presupposes that human reason is one expression of a more general intelligibility proper to the natural world, and to the nonrational components of human nature itself.[80]

In this connection, it is important to recall a point made in the first section. That is, the scholastics, including Aquinas, do not regard actually existing social institutions and practices as the immediate expressions of prerational nature. Rather, following Cicero rather than Aristotle, they regard social practices as constructs of reason, which draw on prerational aspects of human nature and are shaped by them, but not in any one determinate way. Hence, the scholastics are aware of what we would describe as the underdetermination of human morality by human nature. Even though they insisted on the naturalness, in a comprehensive sense, of human norms and practices, they were also aware that something else must be brought into play, in order to move from human nature generally understood to human morality.

What is this "something else"? Seen on one level, the additional factor transforming natural inclinations into social practices is reasoned communal reflection, giving rise to the laws and customs appropriate to a society of rational men and women.[81] However, this process can be carried out well or badly, and so a further question arises, namely, what are the principles which ought to govern this process? Aquinas's most important contribution to the development of the scholastic concept of natural law lies in the fact that he answers this question in such a way as not to beg it. The norms of natural law, he says, are determined by the judgments of reason — and practical reason, in turn, is informed by the ends toward which it is directed. Hence, Aquinas's account of the natural law is essentially teleological — that is to say, it is developed and structured through reflection on the purpose, or end, of human

80. For details, see my *Natural and Divine Law,* 77-79.

81. This point is noted and developed in different ways by Pamela Hall, *Narrative and the Natural Law: An Interpretation of Thomistic Ethics* (Notre Dame: University of Notre Dame Press, 1994), especially at 38-43 and 45-64, and Flannery, *Acts Amid Precepts,* 167-94.

life, and the way this end incorporates and brings order to the diverse inclinations of our complex specific nature.

We should underscore the point that for Aquinas (unlike many subsequent Catholic thinkers), the end of action which informs and gives structure to the precepts of the natural law is the overall perfection, which is to say, the happiness of the acting person, and not the separate ends of organs or functions. These latter do have normative significance, to be sure, but they cannot be adequately understood or pursued except as seen in proper relation to one another, and to the overall well-being of the creature. Moreover, for Aquinas, terrestrial happiness is said to consist in the practice of virtue, which does not consist simply in good moral character, but more fundamentally in the full development and exercise — the perfection — of all the capacities of the human agent. Hence for Aquinas, the life of virtue provides the goal which informs and gives structure to the various precepts of the natural law. This may seem strange to us, accustomed as we are to drawing a sharp dichotomy between natural law and virtue as two approaches to moral reflection. But this dichotomy was unknown to the early scholastics, and as we will see, it reflects assumptions about the relation of virtue to law that we need not make our own.

Nonetheless, it is true that ideals of virtue, at least as commonly understood, do not provide a sufficient basis for moral reflection. Aquinas shared the general scholastic assumption that morality comprises a law, which is paradigmatically expressed through God's divine law as revealed in Scripture. Yet for them, divine law is not simply imposed on the formless contingencies of human existence; it draws on and completes imperatives which are already there, and which also reflect aspects of God's wisdom and will. The virtues themselves generate some of these imperatives, and more fundamentally, so do our species-specific tendencies toward certain patterns of behavior. The norms of divine law bring coherence and completion to these imperatives, but only after they themselves have been interpreted in the context set by the natural law generally construed, and by what we might call the pragmatics of moral responsibility, its scope and its limits. These processes of interpretation integrate the diverse aspects of natural and divine law into a system of precepts, appropriate to the way of life of rational creatures living in a particular time and place.

In the next three chapters of this book, I will examine these three components of the scholastic and Thomistic account of the natural law, developing them in the light of contemporary concerns. In the next chapter I will consider how far the scholastics' assumptions and beliefs about nature can be appropriated in light of contemporary scientific views about the origins and development of life. I will argue that, contrary to what is commonly assumed, the scholastics' views do not conflict with the doctrine of evolution, or more generally with contemporary biological sciences — although they do require us to make certain judgments regarding the philosophical implications of those sciences. The challenge posed by contemporary biological theories has to do, rather, with the question of whether we can speak of the natures of living things, as components of their existence having intelligibility and causal force. I believe we can do so, and I will try to make the case for this view in the second chapter. In the third chapter I will examine Aquinas's account of happiness, seen in relation to his overall theory of virtue — an account which will turn out to be more complex and fruitful than is sometimes recognized. Then in the fourth chapter I will take up the scholastics' claim that reason generates moral norms, another claim that will turn out to be more complex than we might at first suspect. In particular, I will focus on the way in which the exigencies of human action give rise to determinate moral rules, which are at one and the same time precepts of the virtue of justice and boundaries expressing and safeguarding a communal sense of the irreducible value of human persons. I will then turn to a closer look at the virtue of prudence, arguing that while this virtue does not generate moral norms directly, it plays an important, albeit indirect role in the development of moral knowledge at the individual and communal level. Correlatively, prudential reasoning within a Christian context opens up the possibility that moral norms are in some meaningful sense both rational and revealed, and this is why a Thomistic approach to the natural law allows for a distinctively theological natural law ethic, which is nonetheless not simply a projection of theological convictions onto the raw materials of nature and reason.

This brings us to the issues raised at the end of the second section of this chapter. That is, to what extent can or should we aspire to arrive at a system of moral precepts that is both rationally compelling and specific enough to be practically detailed? Aquinas's reservations about the idea of a moral science suggest that this goal cannot be attained, and recent work on the character of moral traditions would seem to confirm that insight — or so I will argue. However, this does not mean that moral traditions are impervious to rational critique, or completely opaque or unpersuasive to those standing outside them. We need a more nuanced account of the relationship between specific beliefs and practices, and the moral claims they generate. Because it focuses on the complex relation between social conventions and the natural principles from which those conventions stem, a Thomistic theory of the natural law is well suited to provide a starting point for developing such an account. Or so I will argue in the fifth chapter, focusing on the question of natural rights to provide a focal point and illustration for the argument.

Finally, at the end of the fifth chapter I will turn — necessarily briefly — to the complex question of nature and grace. The scholastics' positive attitudes toward the natural world, and their readiness to interpret it in theological terms, might suggest that they did not draw the sharp distinction between nature and grace that we find in later Catholic thought. Certainly, it would be a mistake to project the neo-scholastic dichotomy between natural and supernatural onto the early scholastics. Nonetheless, they did insist on a distinction between nature and grace. As I will argue, this distinction presupposes, and was called for by, the same attitudes toward nature that informed the concept of the natural law, namely, the scholastics' sense of the goodness of creation and their belief, particularly prominent in the later scholastics, that nature is best understood in terms of the intelligible natures of kinds of creatures. I will argue that this distinction is still valid, and in fact theologically indispensable. This does not mean that we need to interpret it in exactly the same way the scholastics did, any more than we can simply appropriate the scholastic concept of natural law without some systematic reformulation. But that will be a topic for another day.

CHAPTER TWO

Nature As Nature: The Roots of Natural Law

Near the beginning of his analysis of the natural law, Albert the Great remarks that "The natural law is nothing other than the law of reason or obligation, insofar as nature is reason. When, however, I say that nature is reason, it is possible to understand it more as nature, or more as reason, or equally as nature and reason" (*De bono* V 1.2). He speaks as one who begins a treatise with a commonplace, and this remark does indeed capture the general scholastic approach in the period that concerns us. In its primary sense, the natural law is identified with reason, which after all is the defining mark of human nature. But this way of construing the natural law does not imply that other aspects of human nature, including its prerational components, are empty of moral significance. On the contrary, "nature as nature" is freighted with independent moral significance, even though that significance must be discerned through rational reflection. Hence, the natural law reflects both the distinctiveness of the human creature and our more basic continuity with the rest of God's creation: distinctiveness, because only a rational creature can be said properly speaking to follow a law; continuity, because our participation in the natural law is one expression of the universal activity of God's provident wisdom, in which all things are created and through which all things are governed.

Similarly, Albert's pupil Aquinas remarks that "all those things to which the human person is inclined in accordance with his nature pertain to the law of nature. For everything whatever is naturally inclined to an operation appropriate to itself in accordance with its form; for example, fire is inclined to heat. Hence since the rational soul is the proper form of the human person, there is a natural inclination in each person to act in accordance with reason" (*ST* I-II 94.3). This might seem to reflect an approach according to which human nature, and by implication the natural law, are to be interpreted in terms of the exigencies of reason alone. But this is clearly not Aquinas's view; as he goes on to explain, "the nature of the human person can be said to be either that which is proper to the human person . . . or that which is common to the human person and to other animals," and both kinds of nature give rise to moral constraints, corresponding to distinctive kinds of sins (I-II 94.3 *ad* 2).

Until very recently, these and similar remarks would have seemed to our own contemporaries to reflect the most dated and least attractive aspects of the scholastic concept of the natural law. The suggestion that Albert, Aquinas, and their interlocutors might have been right, at least in general terms, would have been met with incredulity. On the contrary, until very recently most contemporary defenders of the natural law rejected the commitments to the moral significance of prerational nature that were long assumed to be central to any natural law theory. This observation would apply as much to Christian natural law thinkers as to any others. As we noted in the last chapter, throughout much of the preceding century Catholic theologians emphasized the historical and personal dimensions of the human person, while questioning the moral significance of prerational nature. At the same time, as we also noted, even the most sympathetic Protestant theologians have been reluctant to ascribe moral significance to what is natural, beyond construing it as a locus for responsiveness and discernment. In addition to these theological considerations, there are a number of well-known arguments against the moral significance of what is natural, and whatever we may think of their merits, they have had a profound effect on theological as well as philosophical ethics. Finally, many theologians are suspicious of any kind of appeal to naturalness on account of the role played by such appeals to justify what is widely seen as a problematic sexual ethic — although recently, some have attempted to defend a more traditional approach to sexual ethics in such a way as to avoid direct appeals to the moral significance of prerational nature.[1] For all of these reasons, the widespread rejection of the moral significance of prerational nature on the part of theologians, surprising though it might seem at first to be, is understandable.

Yet this stance has come with costs. It amounts to a comprehensive rejection of what was for centuries a central feature of Christian moral teaching, which served to connect ethical and doctrinal convictions in a variety of ways, as well as providing a foundation for much of the normative content of that teaching. It has left theologians with few resources out of which to bring

1. For example, see John Finnis, *Aquinas: Moral, Political, and Legal Theory* (Oxford: Oxford University Press, 1998), 143-54.

distinctive perspectives to contemporary debates over bioethics, environmental ethics, or natural rights — precisely the areas in which one might have expected a characteristically Christian voice to be heard. By the same token, it has kept us from engaging fully in contemporary philosophical and scientific efforts to retrieve a moral ideal of naturalness, and in this way it has obstructed what is potentially a most significant point of contact between Christian thought and other elements of the wider culture.

Recently, theologians have begun to reconsider the possibility that human nature, comprehensively considered, might be morally significant after all.[2] These explorations are motivated by a wide range of concerns and go in a number of different directions, but taken together, they reflect a sense that this aspect of historic Christian moral teaching might after all be important for the church's moral reflection and witness. Nor are theologians the only ones reconsidering the moral significance of nature; we are currently in the midst of a revival of interest in this topic among philosophers, political activists, physicians, and lawyers. Indeed, it would be impossible to do justice to all of the different aspects of this revival within the scope of a single book.[3] At the same

2. Among Catholics, Stephen Pope's sympathetic and nuanced explorations of the theological significance of evolutionary psychology have done a great deal to promote this reconsideration; see his *The Evolution of Altruism and the Ordering of Love* (Washington, D.C.: Georgetown University Press, 1994), and more recently, "The Evolutionary Roots of Morality in Theological Perspective," *Zygon* 33, no. 4 (December 1998): 545-56. In addition, Gustafson's call for a theological reappraisal of nature has been highly influential among both Protestant and Catholic theologians. In addition to the works of Gustafson and others discussed in the last chapter, further examples of this reconsideration, developed from a wide range of perspectives, would include Martin Cook, "Ways of Thinking Naturally," *Annual of the Society of Christian Ethics* (1988), 161-78; Ralph McInerny, *Aquinas on Human Action: A Theory of Practice* (Washington, D.C.: Catholic University of America Press, 1992); Philip Hefner, *The Human Factor: Evolution, Culture, and Religion* (Minneapolis: Fortress, 1993); Cynthia S. W. Crysdale, "Revisioning Natural Law: From the Classicist Paradigm to Emergent Probability," *Theological Studies* 56 (1995): 464-84; Anthony J. Lisska, *Aquinas's Theory of the Natural Law: An Analytic Reconstruction* (Oxford: Clarendon, 1996); Michael S. Northcott, *The Environment and Christian Ethics* (Cambridge: Cambridge University Press, 1996), 257-327; and Stephen Clark, *Biology and Christian Ethics* (Cambridge: Cambridge University Press, 2000). While some of these are professionally philosophers rather than theologians (Clark, Lisska, McInerny), all attempt to retrieve the moral significance of nature within the framework of explicitly Christian commitments.

3. As will become apparent, my primary philosophical interlocutors in this book are defenders of a naturalistic ethic of the virtues developed along the lines proposed by Philippa Foot, most recently in *Natural Goodness* (Oxford: Clarendon, 2001). Further references to this literature will be provided in the next chapter. Other examples include Mary Midgley, *Beast and Man: The Roots of Human Nature* (New York: Meridian, 1978), and more recently, *The Ethical Primate: Humans, Freedom, and Morality* (London: Routledge, 1994); Owen J. Flanagan, Jr., "Quinean Ethics," *Ethics* 93 (1982): 56-74 and *Varieties of Moral Personality: Ethics and Psycholog-*

time, the ideal of naturalness, which was never completely extirpated from Western culture, has once again become a dominant motif in industrialized societies. Given this context, a reconsideration of the scholastic approach to nature and the natural law is timely. Broadly construed, this would be one way of describing the task of this book. But clearly, this project presupposes that the scholastic conception of human nature is fundamentally defensible, since otherwise the project of retrieving their concept of the natural law cannot get off the ground. At least, it should be possible to show that the scholastics offer the elements for a plausible general account of human nature.

In this chapter I will try to show that the scholastics do indeed offer a defensible approach to human nature, albeit one which needs to be defended anew in light of our own intellectual context. I will do so by setting forth what I hope is a persuasive account of human nature, taking my starting points from scholastic thought and developing them in light of contemporary scientific and philosophical perspectives. I will not attempt in this chapter to show how this account is morally significant, except in a preliminary way — that is the task of subsequent chapters — but I do hope to prepare the ground to do so. This task will necessarily involve some selectivity, since it would be impossible, in the scope of a single chapter of one book, to identify and address every possible argument against the claim that there is such a thing as human nature, and we can know (more or less) what it is. My strategy is rather to attempt to set forth a plausible account of human nature, in the process arguing that this account is defensible in philosophical and scientific terms that would be widely, albeit not universally, accepted among our contemporaries. As I indicated at the end of the last chapter, this account will be theological rather than strictly philosophical, but I hope to avoid simply imposing theological claims onto recalcitrant material. I will attempt to offer an account which is responsive to the relevant scientific perspectives, even if it is not governed by these. And while no general account of human nature (theological or otherwise) can avoid choosing among competing scientific and philosophical perspectives at some points, I will argue that it is possible to defend a

---

ical Realism (Cambridge: Harvard University Press, 1991); Leon Kass, *Toward a More Natural Science: Biology and Human Affairs* (New York: Macmillan, 1985); Martha Nussbaum, "Non-Relative Virtues: An Aristotelian Approach," in *Midwest Studies in Philosophy XIII: Ethical Theory: Character and Virtue,* ed. Peter French, Theodore E. Uehling, Jr., and Howard K. Wettstein (Notre Dame: University of Notre Dame Press, 1988), 32-53, and more recently, *Women and Human Development: The Capabilities Approach* (Cambridge: Cambridge University Press, 2000); Allan Gibbard, *Wise Choices, Apt Feelings: A Theory of Normative Judgment* (Cambridge: Harvard University Press, 1990); and Larry Arnhart, *Darwinian Natural Right: The Biological Ethics of Human Nature* (New York: SUNY Press, 1998).

broadly scholastic approach to human nature without ruling out any of these perspectives on tendentious grounds.

The approach I will be defending is summed up in Albert's expression, "nature as nature" — implying, as we will see, that nature, in the sense relevant to moral reflection, is intelligible in its operations, and this intelligibility in turn reflects the goodness as well as the inherent reasonableness of the variety of forms of created existence which go to make up the world. In the second section of this chapter, I will examine this perspective in more detail; then in subsequent sections, I will attempt to develop it in the light of contemporary scientific and philosophical perspectives. Finally, in the last section of the chapter I will explore, in a preliminary way, what it might mean to say that human nature comprehensively considered is morally significant.

Before proceeding, however, we need to address an issue that has already come up in the first chapter, and which will recur in different contexts throughout this project. This is the issue of realism, in both its speculative and moral forms, and more particularly the relation between realism and the kind of particularism implied by a distinctively theological approach to the natural law. In the present context, this issue arises out of the commitment to developing an account of human nature responsive to contemporary philosophical and scientific perspectives. Given a professed aim of developing a theology of the natural law, why is it necessary to attend to nontheological perspectives such as these? And by the same token, given the rejection of universalism suggested in the last chapter, how can we claim to have a genuine knowledge of human nature in any case? In the first section of this chapter, I address these questions.

1. Speculative Realism and the Natural Law: A Preliminary Consideration

In this project I presuppose that we are able to attain genuine, albeit imperfect, knowledge of the world around us, and to formulate and express that knowledge through concepts which adequately correspond to the kinds of things they represent.[4] That is to say, I presuppose a kind of realism, at least

4. Thus, when I refer to "realism," what I have in mind is realism according to the current usage, which contrasts this term with "relativism" or "skepticism." "Realism" is also sometimes used as a contrast to "nominalism," and in this context it refers to a realism about universals. The scholastics in the period we are considering were realists in both senses, and I think an argument could be made that realism in the broader sense implies realism in this more specific sense — but that must be an argument for another day. For a useful survey of the relevant issues, see Marilyn McCord Adams, "Universals in the Early Fourteenth Century," in *The Cam-*

concerning our knowledge of the natural world. (I will also defend a kind of moral realism, but it would be premature to say which kind at this stage of the project.) To say the very least, this is a controversial position — current debates over realism and its alternatives have been going on for at least a century, and show little sign of being resolved. It would go well beyond the scope of a book on a different subject to offer a full-scale exposition and defense of a realist position. Nonetheless, I will attempt to say more clearly what I mean by realism, why I regard this as a plausible position, and why I believe that a theology of the natural law needs to presuppose such a view.

To many readers, this attempt will seem to be both unnecessary and wrongheaded. Unnecessary, because given the aim of developing a theology of the natural law, it might seem unnecessary to take account of other, nontheological views on the world around us. Wrongheaded, because a defense of realism might seem to be ruled out on both philosophical and theological grounds. Wouldn't it make more sense to ground a theology of the natural law in a theological construal of nature? In one sense, that is just what I intend to do. But I also want to argue that the theologian is committed, on her own grounds, to construing nature in a way that is responsive to our best speculative understanding of the world around us, which today comes to us largely, though not exclusively, through the natural sciences. And it is this commitment that will be challenged, on both philosophical and theological grounds.

In his *A Scientific Theology*, volume 1: *Nature*, Alister McGrath captures the spirit of this objection:

> "Nature" is thus not a neutral entity, having the status of an "observation statement;" it involves seeing the world in a particular way — and the way in which it is seen shapes the resulting concept of "nature." Far from being a "given," the idea of "nature" is shaped by the prior assumptions of the observer. One does not "observe" nature; one constructs it. And once the importance of socially mediated ideas, theories and values is conceded, it is impossible to avoid the conclusion that the concept of nature is, at least in part, a social construction. If the concept of nature is socially mediated — to whatever extent — it cannot serve as an allegedly neutral, objective or uninterpreted foundation of a theory or theology. *Nature is already an interpreted category.*[5]

---

bridge History of Later Medieval Philosophy from the Rediscovery of Aristotle to the Disintegration of Scholasticism, 1100-1600, ed. Norman Kretzman, Anthony Kenny, and Jan Pinborg (Cambridge: Cambridge University Press, 1982), 411-39.

5. Alister E. McGrath, *A Scientific Theology*, vol. 1: *Nature* (Edinburgh: T. & T. Clark; Grand Rapids: Eerdmans, 2001), 113, emphasis in original.

Given the constructed character and relative emptiness of the conception of nature, the theologian is free to interpret it in whichever way best suits her own perspectives and aims:

> Nature itself offers no ontology as a means of categorical justification. It is an interpreted and socially mediated category. For the theologian, this raises the critical question: given that "nature" is an interpreted and mediated notion, what interpretation is to be preferred? The Christian theologian will wish to explore another category as a means of reclaiming the concept of "nature" as an intellectually viable category, while at the same time interpreting it in a Christian manner. The category? Creation.[6]

I agree with much of what McGrath says here. We cannot derive clear and uncontroversial starting points for theological speculation, much less a whole ontology, from our observations of the natural world. Our ideas about nature stem out of social processes of inquiry and reflection, and if that is what McGrath means by saying that "nature" is an interpreted and socially mediated category, then he is certainly right. (I do have reservations about his way of making the point, however.) Moreover, I agree that the theologian should construe nature as creation, and I would add that this construal provides the theologian with the necessary interpretative key for integrating and making sense of a diversity of other perspectives on nature. At the same time, however, I also want to claim that a theological construal of nature must be answerable, at least to some extent and in some ways, to our best independently established accounts of the natural world. It is not clear to me that McGrath himself would disagree with this qualification, since he devotes a considerable part of the second volume of his *Scientific Theology* to defending the claims of scientific realism. What is the point of doing so, unless to argue that contemporary science can establish genuine knowledge of the natural world, knowledge which is important for the theologian as well as everyone else?

This brings me to the reservation about McGrath's comments signaled above. That is, he assumes that theological appeals to nature presuppose a single, unitary conception of nature, and furthermore presuppose what is often called naive realism — the view that the character of the natural world lies open to inspection, for all to see. These assumptions would not have been accepted in antiquity or the high Middle Ages, and there is no need for us to insist on them today. Our forebears were well aware that there are many different ways of understanding nature, at least some of which — more than one,

6. McGrath, *A Scientific Theology*, 133.

at any rate — are intellectually respectable. Correlatively, they saw that the plurality of defensible approaches to nature raises interesting and difficult intellectual problems. As we noted in the last chapter, the tradition of natural law reflection developed in a context of a diversity of approaches to nature, and its flexibility in accommodating this diversity goes a long way toward accounting for its endurance. Contemporary defenders of the natural law need not be any less sophisticated than our forebears. Seen from this perspective, the natural sciences offer us further ways of conceiving of the natural world, including ourselves as a part of that world — not the only such ways, to be sure, but valid and indispensable conceptions nonetheless.

For someone like McGrath, who objects to naïveté about the idea of nature but does not deny scientific realism, this line of argument may well be persuasive. But other theologians, to say nothing of many philosophers and cultural critics, would take McGrath's objections further, arguing that not only our concepts of nature but our (putative) knowledge of the natural world in general, including scientific knowledge of the world, are socially constructed.[7] If this is so, then we might as well go for a construction that makes sense within the ambit of our own intellectual community, and stop worrying about whether our claims will be persuasive to anybody else.

In order to assess this proposal, we need first to get clearer on what it means to say that knowledge, or anything else, is socially constructed. No one denies that our knowledge of the world, together with the congeries of inquiries, arguments, and speculations informing that knowledge, are socially mediated, at least to some extent and in some ways. After all, the relevant intellectual activities are mediated through language, which is in some sense a product of a particular society. The difficulties begin when we attempt to sort through the qualifiers — in what ways, and to what extent, does this social framework condition and constrain our knowledge of the world, and our attempts to formulate and communicate that knowledge? As Ian Hacking points out, the claim that knowledge is socially constructed can be construed

7. Although now somewhat dated, the collections of essays edited by Martin Hollis and Steven Lukes, *Rationality and Relativism* (Cambridge: MIT Press, 1982), and Michael Krauz, *Relativism: Interpretation and Confrontation* (Notre Dame: University of Notre Dame Press, 1989), provide a good introduction to the main lines of the relevant debates, at least among English-speaking philosophers. In particular, the introduction by Hollis and Lukes, *Rationality and Relativism*, 1-20, and their chapter "Relativism, Rationalism, and the Sociology of Knowledge," 21-47, and the introduction in Krauz, *Relativism*, 1-11, provide a helpful guide to the main issues. More recently, Ian Hacking has offered a comprehensive analysis of the wide variety of positions currently associated with the claim that reality is socially constructed in his *The Social Construction of What?* (Cambridge: Harvard University Press, 1999), 1-34.

in a wide variety of ways, not all of them tantamount to denying any possibility of knowledge of an external world or meaningful language about that world — on the contrary, these kinds of skepticism are fairly rare.[8] Nonetheless, there is considerable space between naive realism and outright skepticism, and defenses of the socially constructed character of knowledge or discourse can take a number of different forms.

Fortunately, it is not necessary for our purposes to sort through the relevant arguments in more detail. We can focus more clearly on what is at stake for us by means of a contrast, between claims for the social construction of knowledge and what many defenders of that claim take to be the alternative, namely, some form of foundationalism. Very often, arguments for some version of constructivism are motivated, not by generalized skepticism, but in opposition to the claim that we can only attain reliable knowledge on the basis of foundations which themselves cannot be questioned. What more exactly might this mean, and what does its rejection imply for the project at hand?

In the previous chapter, I noted that modern theories of the natural law reflect an ideal of a scientific morality which makes use of the methodologies of mathematics and the sciences to establish clear and certain moral conclusions. This ideal reflects one of the most striking differences between the early modern natural lawyers and their medieval forebears. We have already observed that the medieval scholastics identified the natural law with capacities for moral discernment, or with the very general principles through which those capacities operate. They did not expect to be able to derive certain and comprehensive systems of moral rules from these starting points; such a project would have seemed to them both unnecessary (since revelation has completed our knowledge of the natural law) and, given the inherent limitations of practical reason, most probably fruitless.

The early modern natural lawyers, in contrast, believed that the project of deriving a complete, definite, and certain system of moral norms is not only feasible, but an appropriate and necessary goal given the supreme importance of morality for human life. We have already remarked on the social conditions that made this project appear exigent, as well as feasible. At this point I want to call attention to another aspect of the modern natural lawyers' context, that is to say, the sea change in assumptions about the proper form and scope of intellectual inquiry associated with the Enlightenment. The modern natural lawyers' project of placing moral knowledge on certain foundations, compelling to all rational persons, was one part of what Alasdair

8. Hacking, *Social Construction of What?* 24-25.

MacIntyre has described as the Enlightenment project.[9] That is to say, the modern approach to the natural law reflected a more general ideal for intellectual inquiry, which aimed to develop or uncover standards of reasonableness which are both perspicuous and compelling to any rational human being, and substantive enough to resolve specific theoretical and moral disagreements.

This ideal is frequently described as foundationalism, and while this term can be misleading, taken as a shorthand way of expressing what early modern philosophers were after, it does no harm.[10] The men and women of the Enlightenment were chary of received traditions as a basis for knowledge, whether speculative or moral. The scholastics' respect for established authorities and their reliance on texts as a focus for inquiry were widely discredited, for both good and (arguably) bad reasons. In place of authoritative texts, philosophers and scientists attempted to establish perspicuous and universally accessible foundations for their claims, in the form of logical or mathematical principles, clear and certain ideas, empirical observations, or some combination of these. Moreover, these starting points were thought to be not only necessary but also sufficient to resolve theoretical disagreements, either taken by themselves or in conjunction with our general knowledge of the world around us. Rational certainty came to be seen as the ideal for knowledge, and correlatively, authentic knowledge was thought to be accessible to all rational persons, whatever their presuppositions might be.

This ideal, and the philosophical and scientific programs it inspired, dominated Western intellectual life throughout the modern period — in-

9. For a recent discussion of the "Enlightenment project" and its failures, see MacIntyre, *Three Rival Versions of Moral Enquiry: Encyclopedia, Genealogy, and Tradition* (Notre Dame: University of Notre Dame Press, 1990), 55-56.

10. Here again, one has to be cautious about terms. If "foundationalism" is taken to mean, simply, that thought is impossible without some starting points which stand in need of no justification — to put it another way, that justification is not an infinite regress — then the scholastics were foundationalists, too, as were many of the Greek philosophers. I agree with Robert Pasnau that Aquinas was a foundationalist in this sense; see *Thomas Aquinas on Human Nature: A Philosophical Study of "Summa theologiae" Ia 75-89* (Cambridge: Cambridge University Press, 2002), 308. However, among modern and contemporary philosophers, "foundationalism" has come to have a stronger meaning, according to which the starting points for knowledge, whatever they are taken to be, provide sufficient as well as necessary conditions for attaining knowledge. Hence, this form of foundationalism emphasizes certainty and universal cogency as the marks of true knowledge — if the proper foundations are in place, and one's perception and reasoning are sound, true knowledge should follow as a matter of course. It is quite possible to deny foundationalism in this strong sense while at the same time affirming a weaker classical or medieval version — as MacIntyre himself does (see section 4 below).

deed, many would take it to be one of the defining marks of modernity. It began to break down in the twentieth century under the cumulative weight of philosophical, cultural, and literary attacks on its central presuppositions. These critiques, and the stances they represent, are unsurprisingly known as postmodernity, and it is sometimes said that we are all postmodern now. This is perhaps an overstatement, but it does seem to be the case that Enlightenment foundationalism has been widely discredited, in favor of some account which takes seriously the elements of contingency and social conditioning to be found in all forms of intellectual inquiry.

The postmodern emphasis on contingency and social location has seemed to many to imply, if not outright skepticism, then at least a very considerable degree of modesty about our capacities for attaining any kind of knowledge. Yet it is not obvious that the denial of Enlightenment foundationalism need commit us to denying every form of robust realism. MacIntyre has argued that the postmodern penchant for skepticism is itself one of the implications of the "Enlightenment project":

> [It might be said that] if the only available standards of rationality are those made available by and within traditions, then no issue between contending traditions is rationally decidable. . . . There can be no rationality as such. Every set of standards, every tradition incorporating a set of standards, has as much and as little claim to our allegiance as any other. Let us call this the relativist challenge, as contrasted with a second type of challenge, that which we may call the perspectivist . . . the perspectivist challenge puts in question the possibility of making truth claims from within any one tradition.[11]

Hence, the plausibility of both relativism and perspectivism derives from the fact that these are inversions of the Enlightenment ideal of a universally perspicuous standard of rationality and truth. Since this cannot be attained (as MacIntyre himself would agree), the only alternative, it is said, is some form of relativism or perspectivism. On the contrary, MacIntyre responds, there is a third alternative, namely, the possibility that the development of traditions, both internally and in relation to one another, can itself be considered a genuinely rational process which, if it goes well, moves in the direction of an ever-fuller grasp of reality.[12] He goes on to develop this third alternative through an account of what he calls rationality as tradition-guided

11. MacIntyre, *Whose Justice? Which Rationality?* (Notre Dame: University of Notre Dame Press, 1988), 352.

12. MacIntyre, *Whose Justice? Which Rationality?* 353-54.

inquiry. On this view, "the standards of rational justification themselves emerge from and are part of a history in which they are vindicated by the way in which they transcend the limitations of and provide remedies for the defects of their predecessors within the history of that same tradition."[13] These standards are further tested and developed through a process of encounter with rival traditions, in the process of which the proponents of one tradition may come to see the rival as superior, judged in terms of their own problems and by their own best standards of justification. If all goes well, tradition-guided inquiry thus develops in such a way as to open up possibilities for rational critique, both of the tradition itself and other, competing traditions. By the same token, it provides a framework for truth claims which cannot simply be equated with whatever statements are warranted by the tradition itself, and which can meaningfully be regarded as mediating a correspondence between the intellect and extramental reality.

In my view, MacIntyre's theory of rationality as tradition-guided inquiry is persuasive, at least considered as an account of speculative rationality. However, my aim here is not to defend MacIntyre's theory, but to use it to illustrate a point. As we will see, MacIntyre himself believes (and I would agree) that tradition-guided inquiry can in some instances attain to a highly developed theoretical account of a given subject matter, of such a kind as to reveal proper divisions and causal connections within a field of inquiry. If this is so, then the contingencies inherent in the socially situated character of inquiry need not, by themselves, rule out a genuine, rationally articulated knowledge of the world. In this way, MacIntyre offers an example of a philosopher who rejects Enlightenment foundationalism, while at the same time affirming a robust form of realism according to which we are able to attain genuine knowledge and to express that knowledge in true and (I would add) meaningful speech.

We will have further occasions to return to the possibilities and limitations of speculative realism, and its implications for the natural law. Let me turn now, briefly, to the other question posed at the beginning of this section. That is, even granting the possibility of a robust realism, what stake does the theologian have in defending such a view? Let me attempt to address this question, again in a preliminary way, by asking what stake the scholastics would have had in affirming realism in the sense just indicated.

There is no doubt that the scholastics would have agreed with McGrath that nature should be understood most fundamentally through the theological categories of creation and (they would add) providence. I have argued

13. MacIntyre, *Whose Justice? Which Rationality?* 7.

elsewhere that the scholastic concept of the natural law represents one centrally important expression of this basic commitment.[14] The scholastics were of course not the first to interpret the natural law by reference to the doctrines of creation and providence. But for them, this connection was particularly important, and their development of the concept of the natural law reflects this fact.

In order fully to appreciate this point, we need to focus on one aspect of the historical context for scholastic reflection on the natural law. That is, by the thirteenth century this reflection was not only shaped by theological and practical considerations; it was also given an edge through controversies with various dissident groups, particularly the Cathar movement developing in southern France and Italy in this period.[15] It is difficult now to reconstruct the Cathars' views exactly, but it seems fairly clear that they were dualists who held that the visible world is more or less corrupt, imperfect, or downright evil. Hence, this world cannot be the creation of a good God, although there seems to have been some disagreement on its exact origins. Hence, they viewed the material world, the body, and the processes of reproduction as evil, and held that the Christian can only be saved by breaking with the material world as far as possible. By the same token, they rejected the authority of much of Scripture, including the Old Testament and parts of the New Testament (or at least, that is what the scholastics took them to be saying). The true God is revealed to us in the New Testament, and the God of the Old Testament is either a myth, or worse still, the evil principle responsible for the world as it now exists.

14. See my *Natural and Divine Law: Reclaiming the Tradition for Christian Ethics* (Ottawa: Novalis; Grand Rapids: Eerdmans, 1999), 164-77, and more recently, "Natural Law as a Scriptural Concept: Theological Reflections on a Medieval Theme," *Theology Today* 59, no. 2 (July 2002): 226-41. As McGrath's comments illustrate, the doctrine of creation and its relation to concepts of nature is once again receiving sustained theological attention; for a good overview of recent arguments, see Hans Schwarz, *Creation* (Grand Rapids: Eerdmans, 2002), 87-162. In addition, the Jewish theologian David Novak argues that Jewish reflections on the natural law should be grounded in a doctrine of creation and, correlatively, an appreciation for the wisdom of God; see *Natural Law in Judaism* (Cambridge: Cambridge University Press, 1998). His arguments suggest that a theological doctrine of the natural law is better understood as a theistic rather than a uniquely Christian doctrine. I have no stake in denying such a claim — I would only add that theistic arguments are also properly Christian arguments. Not everything that is properly Christian is uniquely Christian; it would be strange indeed if we Christians did not share a great deal theologically with the other great theistic religions, although it is not our place unilaterally to declare exactly what the areas of overlap will be.

15. For further details on the Cathar heresy, see Malcolm Lambert, *Medieval Heresy: Popular Movements from the Gregorian Reform to the Reformation*, 2nd ed. (Oxford: Blackwell, 1992), 33-61, 105-46; in addition, see my *Natural and Divine Law*, 74-80, for further details and references.

Over against this the scholastics asserted the unity and supremacy of God as Creator, the goodness of the visible and material world, and the unity of Scripture as God's self-revelation. In developing these responses, they drew extensively on their concept of the natural law.[16] They appealed to this concept to argue that none of the natural inclinations of the human person is bad in itself, and each has its proper mode of expression; hence, no food is sinful in itself, and more importantly, there is an appropriate place for sexual activity in human life.[17] Certainly, they were aware of the pervasive effects of human sinfulness, and did not always find it easy to distinguish what is natural to human life from these distortions. Nonetheless, they insisted that at the very least, whatever is necessary to the continuing life of the individual or the species cannot be bad in itself, whatever the distortions introduced by sin might be. Similarly, they appealed to the concept of the natural law to provide a hermeneutic for harmonizing the seemingly contradictory precepts of the Old and New Testaments.

Seen over seven hundred years later, these issues may seem to be of purely historical interest. I am not so sure this is the case; dualism is still very much a live option for many Christians. At any rate, the theological implications of the scholastic concept of the natural law go beyond its function as a way of answering various forms of dualism, important though that is. The larger significance of this concept lies in its implications for our understanding of God's revelation, and by implication, God's creative, providential, and redemptive activity. That is to say, what the scholastics presuppose in developing their concept of the natural law is the fundamental unity of God and of God's actions; correlatively, they presuppose that the different expressions of God's actions are mutually consistent, in such a way that each can be drawn on to cast light on the others. This unity is expressed first of all through the unity of Scripture itself, and for this reason they are careful to note that the basic natural law precept of the Golden Rule is found in both the Old and the New Testaments. It is also expressed in the fundamental unity between God's creative and redemptive work, as expressed in the congruity between the deliverances of the natural law and the divine law as revealed in both Testa-

16. Again, I defend these claims in detail in *Natural and Divine Law;* see in particular 63-98 and 187-206.

17. Both Bonaventure (*Collationes de decem praeceptis* 6.6) and Aquinas (*Summa contra gentiles* III 127) make the point that no food is illicit in itself, and Aquinas does so in the context of an extended discussion of the precepts of the natural law. Of course, this comment might be directed against Jewish or Muslim dietary restrictions, but Aquinas has just mentioned the errors of those who regard all sexual intercourse as sinful (III 126) — surely the Cathars — and Bonaventure explicitly says the view he is refuting comes from the Manichees, i.e., the Cathars.

ments of Scripture. And these fundamental commitments, to the unity of Scripture and the congruity between creation and revelation, carry the further implication that the intelligibility and goodness we perceive in the world around us are not illusory, but represent genuine, albeit limited and fragmentary, intimations of God's wisdom and creative will.

Commenting on the current controversy over creationism and evolution, Ernan McMullin remarks that "The entire notion of creation has been rendered suspect by an ill-advised literalism that would already have seemed out of place in Augustine's day."[18] As this remark suggests, the scholastics were not creationists in the modern sense, nor were they strongly committed to a literal interpretation of the first chapter of Genesis. On the contrary, creationism would be problematic to them for just the same reason that a radical rejection of realism would be problematic. On either view, the world can still be regarded as an expression of God's creative power, but in neither case can we depend on any reliable connection between aspects of creation and God's creative wisdom or will. Correlatively, there can be no possibility of arguing from some particular aspects of creation to some knowledge of God's character or God's will. This outcome would of course be fatal to the scholastic approach to the natural law, or to any other theological ethic which attempts to ground normative conclusions in God's will as expressed in creation. More seriously, it would imply that the world, while created by God, is wholly opaque to God — and from that point, it is only a short step back to some form of world-denying dualism.

Scholastic theologians have often been criticized for the attention they gave to metaphysical questions which might seem very far from the spirit and intent of a truly evangelical theology. But their metaphysical seriousness should be seen in this context. By and large, scholastic theologians did believe that human reason can establish God's existence and can determine some truths about God, albeit imperfectly. And they were aware of the value of these arguments, both for their intrinsic interest and as a point of contact with those (both living and dead) who did not accept Christian revelation. However, I believe that their primary interest in metaphysical speculation lay elsewhere — that is, it was essential to their overall theological project, because it provided the necessary context within which to discern God's wisdom and will through reflection on God's creatures.[19] We will see this illus-

18. Ernan McMullin, "Introduction: Evolution and Creation," in *Evolution and Creation*, ed. Ernan McMullin (Notre Dame: University of Notre Dame Press, 1985), 1-58, here 47.

19. Michel Bastit argues that Aquinas's appropriation of an Aristotelian approach to metaphysics, and his corresponding reinterpretation of Platonic categories of hierarchy and participation, serve the purposes of his overall theological project because they enable him to

trated when we examine the ways the scholastics construed nature, in the context of developing their concept of the natural law.

2. Nature and the Natural Law

We have already observed that the scholastics share in the general presupposition informing the natural law tradition, according to which almost any preconventional ground for social practices and moral norms can be regarded as a kind of nature. Seen from this perspective, "nature" may have little or nothing to do with nature as we usually understand it — it can be interpreted as equivalent to reason, as we have seen, or even to Scripture or to widely shared social conventions, all of which can be regarded in some contexts as giving rise to social conventions (or in the latter case, to more specific, as opposed to universal, social conventions).

At the same time, the scholastics also had a stake in defending the moral significance of nature, more specifically of human nature, understood comprehensively to include prerational as well as distinctively rational components. Moreover, they had the resources for such a defense, in the form of a rich and sophisticated philosophy of nature which began to emerge in the eleventh century, and which continued to develop throughout the period on which we are focusing.[20] Originally, philosophy of nature as a systematic field of thought developed out of attempts to harmonize the Genesis account of creation with Plato's (seemingly) parallel account in the *Timaeus,* and as a result it tended to

---

develop a science of theology which can make some positive affirmations about its proper object, namely, God. "Le thomisme est-il un aristotélisme?" *Revue Thomiste* 101 (2001): 101-16, 115-16. This seems right to me; I would only add that while Aquinas's metaphysical theology is distinctively his own, it reflects an aspiration shared more generally among scholastic theologians at this time.

20. For further details on the natural philosophy of the eleventh and twelfth centuries, and its impact on the scholastic concept of the natural law, see my *Natural and Divine Law,* 66-85. It is worth noting that the distinctively scholastic approach to nature does not survive the advent of experimental science, and the scholastics' indifference to direct observation and experiment was certainly one great weakness of the system. As Richard Southern observes: "All systems of thought have some pervasive weakness built into their structure, and the weakness is all the more ineradicable when it forms in some sense the strength of the system. The characteristic strength of medieval scholastic thought was its elaboration of the authoritative statements of the past. These were the bricks from which the system was formed; they provided the material for argument and the foundations for the most daring conclusions. But they also defined limits beyond which the system could not develop" (*Scholastic Humanism and the Unification of Europe,* vol. 1: *Foundations* [Oxford: Blackwell, 1995], 54).

be Platonic in its general orientation. Seen from this perspective, "nature" is identified with the world as a whole, regarded as a cosmos of intelligibly interrelated things. The early scholastics tended to personify nature, so understood, speaking of her (and "Nature" is almost always feminine) as an independent entity governing the manifest world of creatures in accordance with her wisdom. This way of understanding nature was widely regarded as only dubiously orthodox, however, and the rediscovery of Aristotelian philosophy offered later scholastics an alternative way of construing nature. On this view, which we find in both Albert and Aquinas, nature is understood primarily in terms of the natures of specific kinds of creatures, regarded as the intelligible principles of their existence and their causal powers. The orderly interrelationships of creatures are thus to be explained in terms of their causal interrelationships, stemming from the specific natures proper to each kind.

These different interpretations of nature did share one critical presupposition, however — they presupposed that nature, understood in most of the ways in which the term can be used, is intelligible, and as such can and should be analyzed in terms of its own proper principles of operation.[21] Of course, the scholastics did not deny God's ultimate sovereignty over the natural world, but unlike earlier medieval intellectuals, they were chary of appealing too readily to the miraculous as a means of explanation. They focused on God's wisdom, as manifested through the orderly processes of movement and change in the visible world, rather than on God's power as manifested in miraculous disruptions of that order. And by the same token, when they began to develop their distinctive concept of the natural law, they did so in terms of the ways in which the intelligibilities of nature inform and constrain human life.

As we might expect, this general approach gives scope to a wide range of accounts of nature and the natural, including various combinations of the two approaches (devoid, in the later scholastic period, of tendencies to personify nature). And many scholastics in the period we are considering did not bother to develop their own philosophy of nature, any more than most moral philosophers or theologians today attempt to master the details of contemporary scientific research, or to develop a fully worked-out philosophy of science. They simply presupposed the different accounts of nature available to them, each one of which could potentially give rise to a natural law. In the words of the Dominican theologian Roland of Cremona:

21. Most of the ways, because they did sometimes speak of one's individual constitution and temperament as one's nature — and likewise, the operations of sheer chance could be regarded as nature. But significantly, neither of these forms of nature was correlated with any kind of natural law. See my *Natural and Divine Law*, 77-78, for particulars.

I say that, just as nature is analyzed by the philosophers, just so, the manifold natural law ought to be analyzed. For there is a certain law or a certain universal nature, according to which it is said that all things naturally desire to be, or desire the good. Such a desire is universal nature, and the universal law of nature, and this is in all creatures, and perhaps this law or this nature proceeds from species, mode and order, of which enough has been said at the end of the second book. And there is a certain other nature, or particular law, which is in plants; for it belongs to the particular law of plants, that they should produce leaves and an abundance of fruits, just as Aristotle says in the book of trees and plants and vines. . . . There is another more particular law in animals, by which each and every animal is united to one similar to itself, as Boethius says; and certain other laws are particular to certain kinds of animals, as for example, it is by nature that the spider weaves that she might catch the flies that she eats. And there is a more particular law, that is synderesis, in the human person. (Lottin, 115)[22]

For the scholastics, human reason reflects the same intelligible structures of existence and action as are manifested in prerational nature, to which it brings understanding and the possibilities of deliberate, organized realiza-tion.[23] In particular, the scholastics gave special attention to those principles which appear to manifest themselves in other living creatures, as well as ourselves. They did not hold the view sometimes attributed to them, according to which human beings should simply imitate the behavior of nonhuman animals, because they were well aware that other animals engage in forms of behavior, for example, sexual promiscuity, which are not appropriate for human beings. Nonetheless, they placed greater weight on the continuities between the other animals and ourselves than contemporary philosophers have done, at least until very recently. While norms for human practices cannot be derived directly from animal behavior, there are nonetheless continuities between human morality and the behavioral norms which the other animals observe.

22. Together with Hugh of St. Cher, Roland of Cremona was one of the first two Dominican masters at Paris; he is writing between 1229 and 1230. "Synderesis" refers to the higher or superior component of reason, and as such is often associated but not identified with conscience. Both terms have a long and complex history; for further details, see Odon Lottin, "Syndérèse et conscience aux XIIe et XIIIe siècles," in *Psychologie et morale aux XIIe et XIIIe siècles,* vol. 2: *Problèmes de morale, première part* (Louvain: Abbaye du Mont César, 1948; six vols. published 1942-60), 103-350.

23. For further details on the scholastics' understanding of prerational nature as a source for natural law, see my *Natural and Divine Law,* 76-85.

Of course, for the scholastics these continuities are not the expressions of our biological kinship with nonrational animals, nor much less do they believe that human rationality is a product or epiphenomenon of biological processes, as some of our contemporaries have claimed. As I will argue below, the scholastics would have had no stake in denying the former claim, although they would certainly have rejected the latter claim. In any case, for them the continuities between animal and human inclinations are to be explained metaphysically and theologically. Every creature manifests certain orderly patterns of action, simply as such — to be, to maintain its existence — and in addition, every living creature manifests further, more complex patterns, for example, orderly growth and reproduction. Because we are both creatures and animals, we too manifest these orderly patterns of action. In this way, the intelligible structures of natural processes provide the basis for the properly rational activities of the human creature — and these rational activities, in turn, are given coherence and direction by the natural processes out of which they stem. "Nature is reason" in the sense that reason is itself a natural capacity, and in its functioning it is informed or mirrored by the intelligible order manifested in our own humanity, and in the world within which our lives are embedded.

The link between prerational nature and reason is thus constituted by the intelligibility of nature, rather than the naturalness (in our sense) of reason.[24] In virtue of its intelligibility, nature broadly construed is open to com-

24. In *Mind and World* (Cambridge: Harvard University Press, 1994), John McDowell offers an illuminating way of getting at the same point from within the parameters of contemporary philosophy (although his own perspective is clearly informed by Aristotle). He argues that we must find a way of affirming the naturalness of reason, if we are to allow for both the receptivity and the spontaneity of reason (3-23). And both must be affirmed, if we are to hold on to some version of realism. Without receptivity, our thought would not be subject to constraints from the outside world; yet these constraints must not function in such a way as to deprive human thought of some element of spontaneity, since otherwise they could not inform the processes of reasoning in the needed ways. Hence, he argues, even our most basic perceptions must necessarily include a conceptual component in order to inform our beliefs and rational reflection (24-65, especially 57-60). He goes on to argue that we can only hold receptivity and spontaneity together in the needed way by affirming the naturalness of human reason (66-86). This seems right to me, but he then goes on to spell this out in terms of what I think is an unilluminating appeal to Aristotle's idea of "second nature." It would be better, on McDowell's own terms, to retrieve the scholastic (and classical) insight that the capacities of the human mind are informed by the intelligibilities structuring the natural world as a whole, in such a way as to track these intelligibilities through their proper operations. In other words, our most basic processes of perception and reasoning attach to reality, because the natural operations of the mind are isomorphic with the fundamental metaphysical structures of reality. Janet Coleman makes this point with respect to Aquinas in "MacIntyre and Aquinas," in *After MacIntyre: Critical Perspectives on the Work of Alasdair MacIntyre,* ed. John Horton and Susan Mendes (Notre Dame: University of Notre Dame Press, 1994), 65-90.

prehension by human reason. Moreover, since intelligibility implies purposiveness, human nature in particular provides reason with aims which provide starting points and goals for its practical operations. In this sense, practical reason in its operations opens downward — although the metaphor is perhaps not ideal — drawing on the intelligibilities of prerational nature, which it extends and completes in a distinctively human fashion. More specifically, reason shapes our prerational inclinations into determinate social practices and institutions, through which natural aims and exigencies can be pursued. In addition, it introduces tendencies of its own, directed toward goods which cannot be attained by nonrational creatures, and it brings its own exigencies, grounded in requirements for proper functioning. Certainly, reason bestows distinctive meaning on behaviors we share with the other animals, and this in turn leads to distinctive moral precepts. Yet even in these aspects of its functioning, reason is not divorced from prerational nature.

It would be possible to cite any number of passages from the scholastics illustrating the interplay between prerational nature and reason. One of the clearest of these occurs in the writings of the secular theologian Philip the Chancellor (d. 1263):

> . . . since the natural law is so called from nature, that is, it is that which natural reason directs and that which is written in the natural reason, since according to this way of speaking, reason is itself nature, so in the same way, it is possible to take nature as nature, or nature as reason. Nature, insofar as it is nature, directs the rational creature, that is, the human person, to have sexual relations with another, that is, for the well-being of the species, that is, for the preservation of the well-being of the species itself; and for this purpose, there is the command, "do not commit adultery," and so on; just as for the preservation of the individual there is the command, "do not kill." Nature as reason directs that one have sexual relations with one and not many; but reason as reason directs that this be one who is united to oneself. For I say "united" as regards nature, insofar as it is reason. (Lottin, 112-13)

Hence, the basic animal inclination to reproduce one's kind directs the human person to unite with a member of the opposite sex. At the same time, this inclination is experienced by us as a human inclination, which is to say it is mediated through rational judgment and reflection, and reason qualifies it in such a way as to specify that it should be directed toward its proper object, namely, the one individual with whom one is mated. (Together with most of the other scholastics, Philip believes monogamy is a requirement of reason, albeit one that can be suspended in some circumstances.) Finally, this inclination is further qualified through reason as expressed through human institutions, which specifies in addition that the appropriate mate is one who is united to oneself through the distinctively human practice of marriage. Significantly, according to Philip, the prohibition against adultery stems from an aspect of our nature more basic than reason in either its primary or institution-generating operations, namely, the fundamental instinct to reproduce one's kind through union with another.

For obvious reasons, the ethics of sexuality and marriage lends itself to analysis in these terms. But sexuality is not the only aspect of human life which is so analyzed. Philip offers a very similar analysis of the prohibition against killing, claiming that it originates in prerational nature and is then specified through rational reflection to refer more narrowly to those who are innocent of crime. An anonymous canonical summa offers a similar analysis of the institution of inheritance:

> Here there is a discussion of the succession of heirs, which is introduced either from the natural law or the evangelical law, since it is written that "children should not lay up treasure for their parents, but parents for their children." Or from the law of reason: for reason directs the human person that it is better to designate one's child as the heir of one's property, than a stranger. Or from the law of sensuality: for a parent is moved by carnal affection more strongly towards his own children, than towards strangers. (*Summa Reginensis;* Weigand, no. 385)

It will be clear that when the scholastics attended to the prerational roots of human inclinations and practices, their intention was in part analytic.[25] The natural law had traditionally been formulated in terms of a distinction between the preconventional and the conventional, and here we see that distinction expressed through an analysis of human social conventions in terms of their origins in inclinations that we share with the other animals. At the same time, the scholastics also draw normative conclusions from this kind of analysis, and it is here that we find the most controversial, but also the

25. As Servais Pinckaers points out, Aquinas's sources for this language are Aristotle, the Stoics, and Cicero, rather than his own contemporaries; in fact, he appears to be the only scholastic who speaks explicitly in terms of inclinations. See *Les sources de la morale chrétienne: Sa méthode, son contenu, son histoire* (Fribourg: Editions Universitaires Fribourg, 1985), 411-14, for further details. The other scholastics prefer to speak, as Philip does, of the diverse laws of nature. But clearly these laws of nature are understood to stem from innate human tendencies directed toward particular ends — inclinations, in other words. Hence, I don't think the use of Thomistic terminology distorts their meaning.

most interesting, aspect of their concept of the natural law. Once again, Philip provides a helpful point of reference. We noted above that he associates the prohibition against adultery with the fundamental inclination, shared with all living creatures, to reproduce one's kind. Elsewhere he associates the prohibition against killing with another fundamental inclination, namely, to preserve one's life. This is likely to strike us as incongruous. How is it possible to derive moral norms, which presuppose relationships of mutual respect, from the prerational components of human nature?

In the first place, it should be noted that Philip does not *derive* prohibitions against adultery and murder from the inclinations in question, in the sense of establishing these norms through some argument based on a consideration of the inclinations taken by themselves. He notes that these prohibitions take their rationale and point from the inclinations in question, but that does not necessarily imply that we could arrive at these prohibitions solely by reflecting on our natural inclinations. This claim is at least consistent with a view according to which we receive these prohibitions in another way — for example, from social norms, or through God's commands — and only then, retrospectively, see their point through a reflection on human nature. And in general, the scholastics hold that practically speaking, moral knowledge depends in part — there is considerable room for debate over how large a part — on just this kind of special prompting, whether from God or from learned reflection on the part of "the wise."

Nonetheless, it is safe to assume that Philip does believe that the prohibition against adultery can be justified by reference to the inclination to reproduction, even if he leaves open the possibility that we might only come to realize this retrospectively, through reflection on the prohibition itself. And even this more restricted claim may seem incongruous. Today, we are more likely to associate the reproductive instinct with efforts to spread one's genes widely, through as many sexual contacts as possible — for males, anyway. Seen from this perspective, marriage and the prohibition against adultery would be viewed as social constructs which serve to channel and constrain the inclination to reproduce — at best, they would be associated with Philip's second level of analysis, at which rational considerations qualify the fundamental inclination to reproduce.

But in fact, Philip's analysis reflects a subtle but important difference between the scholastic approach to prerational human nature and our own. That is, when Philip associates the prohibition against adultery with the basic, prerational inclination to reproduce, he is not simply gesturing toward a theory of the origins of the prohibition. Rather, he presupposes an account, spelled out in the writings of other scholastics in this period, of the properly human form of reproduction. On this view, human reproduction is not simply a matter of making babies. Rather, it is naturally aimed toward bringing forth human children, who will mature into rational agents and members of society. Correlatively, the process of reproduction, considered in its properly human form, involves not only biological reproduction but also the care and nurture, and as we would say, the socialization, of the child. The specific ways in which this socialization takes place, and the ideals informing it, will of course be conventional, but the necessity for some kind of socialization stems from aspects of our nature, including, in this case, our fundamentally social way of life and the relative weakness and lack of development of human children. On the scholastics' view, this process of socialization requires a certain kind of family structure, built around some kind of stable marriage — although also they recognize that more than one kind of structure for marriage and family life will suffice for this purpose. Hence, because adultery transgresses and undermines the structures of marriage and kinship necessary for the formation of children into fully functioning adults, it can be said to be contrary to the inclination to reproduce — even considered prior to qualifications introduced by rational reflection and institutional formulation.

This brings us to a further point. While the scholastics hold that we can understand our fundamental inclinations by analogy with the inclinations exhibited by nonrational animals, they also recognize that even the most fundamental human inclinations are not experienced as the other animals would experience them.[26] Normal adults experience these inclinations in and through the mediation of some kind of rational reflection, and this experience is further qualified and shaped by the cultural forms through which the inclination is expressed.[27] In this way, even our most basic inclinations are inextricably bound up with the exigencies of our life as rational and social creatures, and we cannot adequately interpret them unless we see them within the context of human life considered as a whole. By the same token, the moral significance of the inclinations only becomes apparent when they are placed within wider contexts of philosophical and theological judgments.

This point should be underscored, because we so frequently assume that the scholastics derived moral conclusions from a simplistic analysis ac-

26. As McDowell observes, the fact that we share some capacities and inclinations with other animals does not mean that these take the same forms in us, or are experienced in the same ways, as their equivalents in other animals; see *Mind and World,* 63-65, 108-26.

27. What is more, even children experience the inclinations in rational form at second hand, so to speak, insofar as they experience them through the mediation of the direction and judgments of their caretakers and through institutionally formed practices — as we will see in more detail in the next chapter.

cording to which the functions of biological processes are indicated by the normal consequences of those processes. On this view, the scholastics' claim that sexual intercourse is oriented toward reproduction — for example — is refuted by the simple fact (which they somehow failed to notice) that most acts of sexual intercourse do not in fact result in reproduction. But their claims about the purpose of sexual intercourse did not depend on any such simplistic arguments from the effects of sexual intercourse. Rather, these claims depended on judgments about which of the effects of intercourse were good, and *therefore* natural in a positive sense. As Philip says: "To have sexual relations with another for the sake of the preservation of the species, and to have sexual relations with another on account of one's pleasure, are opposite ends; the first is in accordance with the intention of nature, and the second is against the intention of nature; and if the preservation of the species should come about by an act of this latter kind, nonetheless, it is not in accordance with the intention of nature, but of libidinous pleasure" (Lottin, 113).

Much less do the scholastics derive moral judgments from the structures or functions of organs; rather, the moral parameters for the use of one's body are derived from philosophical, and ultimately theological, considerations. Aquinas makes this point clearly:

> Nor should it be considered to be a light sin if someone procures the emission of semen apart from a justified purpose of generation and education, on account of the fact that it is either a light sin, or no sin at all, if someone should use a part of his body in some way other than that ordained by nature; for example, if someone should walk on his hands, or use his feet to carry out the operations of the hands. For through such inordinate activities as these, the good of the human person is not much hindered, but the inordinate emission of semen is inimical to the good of nature, that is, the conservation of the species. Hence after the sin of murder, through which human nature actually in existence is destroyed, this kind of sin, through which the generation of human nature is obstructed, would seem to have second place. (*SCG* III 122)

No doubt, there is much to criticize in the specifics of the scholastics' interpretation of the place of sexual intercourse in human life. But it is the structure of the argument that I want to underscore. The scholastics do not argue from observed effects of sexual intercourse, or from the structure and function of the sexual organs, to conclusions about the place of sexuality in human life.[28] Rather, they argue from judgments about the proper place of

28. This interpretation is defended in more detail in my *Natural and Divine Law,* 190-99.

sexuality in human life to a set of conclusions about the purpose of the sex act and the proper uses of one's sexual organs. Their analysis is teleological, in the sense that it presupposes some account of what human life considered as a whole should look like and what purposes the different inclinations and functions of human life serve within that context. But nothing in their analysis requires them to argue from the purposes of human functions or organs, considered in isolation from a context set by the overall well-being of the organism, or by a broader account of the proper shape of human life.

If this is so, we might question whether the scholastics really do derive moral knowledge from prerational nature in any interesting sense. That is, if the moral significance of the fundamental human inclinations can only be seen when they are placed within the context of wider claims about the proper shape of a human life, then it would appear that the prerational components of human nature provide, at most, raw materials for moral reflection. On this view, human inclinations toward reproduction, for example, are morally significant because they provide a very important field for human judgment and decision making, and of course, if we are to discern and act wisely in this sphere, we need accurate and complete information about our nature as sexual beings. But this does not imply that the exigencies of reproduction, or the inclinations structuring human sexuality more generally, have their own proper, morally significant intelligibility, which might in some way inform and constrain rational reflection. Rather, the realities of human sexuality would be regarded as the raw materials, as it were, to be shaped in accordance with rational judgments about the appropriate expressions of sexuality, in accordance with criteria for appropriateness which have nothing to do with sexuality in particular.

Many of our own contemporaries favor this approach, especially but not only in matters of sexual ethics. And the scholastics do sometimes incline toward this approach as well. However, when we examine their views more broadly, we find that their overall view is more complex. They do hold that fundamental human inclinations must be understood in the context of their place in human life, taken as a whole. This latter qualification can be spelled out in a straightforwardly moral sense, but it can also be interpreted in a more naturalistic way. Moreover, the scholastics' overall assumptions about nature predisposed them to believe that broadly recurring human tendencies do reflect human nature, and that they are, precisely as such, capable of being interpreted teleologically.

This brings us to a more general point.[29] The scholastics' approach to nat-

29. Further justification for what follows may be found in my *Natural and Divine Law*, 77-78 and 190-99.

ural law reasoning is given form and direction by the textual tradition they appropriate, but it is also shaped through their ongoing reflection on human inclinations as they are experienced and enacted in human life. In this very basic sense, their concept of the natural law is not simply imposed on the raw data of human experience; rather, that concept is itself informed by reflection on experience and practice. Admittedly, this reflection is also informed by theoretical judgments concerning nature and what is implied by describing something as natural. The scholastics are well aware that some human tendencies and conditions stem from natural causes and are nonetheless harmful or morally problematic — diseases would count as obvious examples of the former, innate character traits predisposing someone to some vice would count as examples of the latter. In order to count as a genuine expression of human nature on the scholastic view, an observed inclination must be not only innate and generally experienced, it must also be amenable to construal in terms of what is proper to, or at least characteristic of, human nature considered as such.

By the same token, as the scholastics reflected on their own observations and experiences, they did change their views about what should count as an expression of human nature, and they modified their conceptions of the natural law accordingly. Scholastic appraisals of reproduction and sexuality offer an especially clear example of this process. As Philip's remarks illustrate, the scholastics were heirs to a widespread patristic view that sexual desire is intrinsically sinful. In the twelfth century, the canon lawyers in particular were inclined to endorse this view, even though they stopped short of saying that sexual desire is in itself mortally sinful. But it was apparent even then that this position is incongruent, given a more general assumption that whatever stems from human nature must in some way be good. The scholastics soon began to modify their position accordingly, either by distinguishing between sinful and morally neutral forms of sexual desire or by simply asserting that sexual desire as such is morally neutral. Aquinas is the first of the scholastics to say clearly that sexual desire is in itself good, but this view was anticipated by his predecessor William of Auxerre, and we find it intimated, though not explicitly said, by his contemporary Bonaventure.[30]

In this way the scholastic concept of the natural law was built up through an ongoing process of reflection; basic human inclinations, needs, and desires were placed within wider contexts set by theological and philo-

30. While Aquinas's defense of the naturalness and neutrality of sexual pleasure (for example, at *ST* II-II 153.2, especially *ad* 2) has been shaped by his Aristotelian theory of nature, it also reflects the trajectory of scholastic thought on the topic; see my *Natural and Divine Law,* 195, for further details.

sophical considerations, while at the same time they also provided an experiential foundation for developing and modifying those considerations. It is important to realize that throughout this process no one component of this concept carries all the interpretative, much less moral, weight. The scholastics do not simply impose rational or theological ideals onto the raw materials of prerational human nature. These latter components of our nature carry independent significance. At the same time, the natural inclinations which play such a central role in their reflections do not carry decisive and overriding weight, such that it would be possible to move directly from reflection on one of these inclinations to moral conclusions. In order to be understood and rightly exercised, the inclinations must be seen within some wider context, indicating their place in human life.

This brings us to a critical difference between the scholastic approach to the natural law and most modern and contemporary approaches. As we observed in the preceding chapter, modern and contemporary natural law theorists have usually tried to avoid controversial metaphysical or theological claims, since these might otherwise undermine their claims to develop a universally cogent ethic. Given this constraint, it is difficult to develop an interpretation of basic human inclinations, desires, or needs in the light of their similarities or connections to other aspects of the natural world. Yet human inclinations, desires, and needs offer the most obvious starting points for developing an ethic based on human nature. Hence, theories of the natural law in the modern period tended to frame their analysis in terms of the purposes which are perspicuously displayed by human inclinations, or by the recurring functions of the organism, or even by the functions of specific organs. Richard McCormick quotes the influential Jesuit moral theologian Franciscus Hürth: "The will of nature was inscribed in the organs and their functions. . . . Man only has disposal of the use of his organs and faculties, with respect to the end which the Creator, in His formation of them, has intended. This end for man, then, is both the biological law and the moral law, such that the latter obliges him to live according to the biological law."[31] As this ap-

31. Quoted by Richard A. McCormick in "Human Sexuality: Towards a Consistent Ethical Method," in *One Hundred Years of Catholic Social Thought: Celebration and Challenge*, ed. John A. Coleman, S.J. (Maryknoll, N.Y.: Orbis, 1991), 189-97, here 191. The original reference is to "La fécondation artificielle: Sa valuer morale et juridique," *Nouvelle revue théologique* 68 (1946): 416. Although I would not want to overstate the similarities, it seems to me that Lisska's reconstruction of the natural law, which focuses on the inclinations seen as directed to a variety of disparate ends, likewise emphasizes the moral significance of diverse ends of human life, rather than the unitary end, that is to say, the overall perfection, of the human creature; see especially *Aquinas's Theory*, 82-115.

proach was increasingly discredited, contemporary natural law thinkers began to develop alternative lines of analysis, including most notably the "new natural law" discussed in the last chapter, which grounds the natural law in the self-evidently desirable quality of certain basic goods, as discerned by practical reason. Of course, these represent very different approaches to the natural law. Nonetheless, they share the fundamental assumption that whatever we take to be the starting point for the natural law must show itself to be such apart from any wider account of the proper shape of human life — otherwise, one's moral foundations would not be foundational at all.

In contrast, the scholastics do not hesitate to place the fundamental human inclinations, and the goods at which they aim, in wider metaphysical and theological contexts. They do believe that human persons naturally and spontaneously desire certain goods which are connatural to the human being in some way. Furthermore, they assume that these inclinations are normally qualified by rational reflection and instruction in such a way as to inform moral judgment, without the need of elaborate theological and metaphysical systems. Nonetheless, these assumptions are consistent with the view that basic human inclinations can only be fully understood, and their moral implications exhaustively developed, within the context of some theoretical account of what it is to be a human being. And this is the approach the scholastics do take — some of them through brief gestures toward the theological and philosophical discussions of the day, others through carefully developed accounts of the place of desire and discernment in overall human life. These accounts are not simply imposed on the relevant experiences, but they do bring order and coherence to these experiences — they are, in other words, theories proposing to illuminate the significance of human desires, needs, and tendencies, not simply observational reports. As such, they provide criteria for distinguishing between true and false inclinations, that is to say, between those inclinations which stem from basic needs and capacities of the human person as such, and those which reflect individual idiosyncrasies or pathologies. In addition, they provide a basis for placing true inclinations in some ordering. Most importantly, these theories provide the necessary framework within which to move from reflection on basic human inclinations to a developed account of moral norms.

What kinds of theories are in question? All the scholastics take their starting points from some consideration of the diverse senses of the natural law, including most importantly (in this context) a more general sense in which we may be said to share the natural law with other animals, and a more specific sense in which the natural law is identified with distinctively human capacities for rational judgment. This means that whatever the specifics of their particular theories, the scholastics offer some account of the ways in which these two aspects of the natural law are related. Generally, they do so by providing accounts, more or less developed, of the way in which human reason draws on, is informed by, extends and completes the inclinations we share with the other animals. This process, in turn, is placed within wider contexts, which may be more or less systematically developed. God's commands as mediated through Scripture and tradition provide one such context; ideals of virtue and perfection provide another. As we noted above, Philip's easy transition from the inclination to reproduce to a prohibition against adultery reflects a set of judgments about the place of the sexual instinct in human life, and the conditions under which it can best be expressed — judgments which go beyond simple observations but need not constitute a fully developed theory. These kinds of judgments provide a third important context within which basic human inclinations can be interpreted.

Not all the authors we are considering attempt to draw together their observations on the natural law into a systematic account of the natural law. But those who do are pressed by the logic of their own analysis to draw these diverse contexts together into some normative account of the overall shape and purpose of human life. For this reason, the scholastic approach to the natural law lends itself to a kind of eudaemonism. That is to say, it lends itself to interpretation in terms of some account of the ultimate purpose or overall goal of human life, understood in terms of happiness, blessedness, or flourishing. Not all the scholastics take their reflections in this direction, of course, and among those who do, the eudaemonism is more or less developed. The most developed such account is that of Aquinas, who organizes his account of morality in terms of the human desire for happiness, a desire which on his view allows for both natural and supernatural modes of fulfillment.

At the same time, when we examine Aquinas's own eudaemonism, it is striking to see how much of a place he gives to the basic human inclinations.[32] We would not have expected this from his general summary statements of what happiness is — the enjoyment of the vision of God, in supernatural happiness, or the practice of the intellectual and moral virtues, in terrestrial forms of happiness. Yet these claims must be seen in connection with his remark that everyone desires happiness, insofar as she desires that her will be fulfilled; and as we read a little further on, the will is naturally oriented toward certain natural goods. These remarks, in turn, suggest that whatever happiness involves, it must allow some place for the pursuit and at-

32. These comments anticipate the arguments of chap. 3, and references will be provided at that point.

tainment of natural goods, a suggestion reinforced by the fact that Aquinas structures the precepts of the natural law in accordance with our natural inclinations. My point is that Aquinas's more general remarks, especially concerning natural happiness, must be read in conjunction with his analysis of human desire and striving in terms of natural inclinations. In order to count as *human* happiness or flourishing, any state of affairs must provide for the appropriate and well-ordered pursuit and attainment of at least some of the natural human goods, even as it regulates and places constraints on their enjoyment. Whatever else it is, human happiness must be recognizable as a kind of flourishing appropriate to a creature that exists and lives and enjoys a distinctively animal life.[33]

In the next two chapters, we will further explore and develop these claims. But at this point, any such consideration would be premature. It will be apparent that the overall scholastic approach to the natural law raises philosophical and (broadly speaking) scientific questions, which need to be addressed before proceeding further. In the next two sections, I will attempt to identify and address what seem to me to be the most important such questions.

3. Defending a Teleological Conception of Human Nature

The scholastic concept of the natural law presupposes a teleological conception of human nature. That at least is the conclusion of the last section, and if it is sound, then any attempt to appropriate this conception for contemporary theological ethics will need, first of all, to defend the legitimacy of teleological analysis. That will be the aim of this section. Until very recently, this would have been regarded as very nearly a hopeless project, because we have tended to assume that any appeal to natural purposes is fundamentally inconsistent with contemporary scientific accounts of the evolutionary origins and development of living creatures. Recently, however, a number of biologists and philosophers of science, most of whom have no allegiance to theological perspectives on human life, have begun to argue for the legitimacy and indeed the necessity of incorporating certain kinds of teleological analysis into the biological sciences. As we will see, these arguments provide a point of contact between scholastic and contemporary perspectives on human nature.

33. This is strikingly illustrated in the *Summa contra gentiles*, in which Aquinas argues that the diverse kinds of desires for particular goods, such as honor or pleasure, will be fulfilled in a superlative way through the Beatific Vision; see *SCG* III 63.

Nonetheless, it is still the case that most educated people today would be surprised to hear that there are any points of continuity at all between medieval and contemporary perspectives on nature and human life. The scholastic approach to the natural law might attract more sympathetic attention today if there were not a general perception, among theologians as much as anyone else, that the theological presuppositions of this approach are inconsistent with contemporary theories about the origins of life. Indeed, there are many, including both practicing scientists and theologians, who assume that Christianity and the Darwinian theory of evolution are inconsistent tout court.[34] In response, there have recently been a number of attempts to defend the compatibility of Christianity with evolutionary perspectives, through appeals to some version of process theism, or to the evolutionary philosophy of Teilhard de Chardin, or to a reinterpretation of fundamental Christian doctrines as symbolic, or in a positive sense mythic.[35]

Seen from the scholastic perspective, these kinds of defenses are more damaging to Christian beliefs than the arguments they attempt to refute. Or at any rate, none of these arguments would be consistent with fundamental convictions about God and God's relation to the world shared by all the scho-

34. This is not universally the case, however, even among those who have no theological commitments. For example, in *Can a Darwinian Be a Christian? The Relationship between Science and Religion* (Cambridge: Cambridge University Press, 2001), the philosopher Michael Ruse offers a basically sympathetic overview and assessment of the supposed inconsistencies between Christianity and Darwinism. In response to Michael Dennett and Richard Dawkins, he argues that there is nothing in evolutionary theory per se, even taken in its strongest sense (as he does), that requires us to adopt their kind of reductive materialism: "No sound argument has been mounted showing that Darwinism implies atheism. The atheism is being smuggled in, and then given an evolutionary gloss. This is no good reason for giving a negative answer to our title question" (128).

35. In his widely influential *God after Darwin: A Theology of Evolution* (Boulder, Colo.: Westview Press, 2000), John Haught argues that the form of theism most appropriate to evolutionary theory would be a fusion of process thought with Teilhard de Chardin's theology of cosmic evolution, in such a way as to affirm that reality is developing in an autonomous and self-ordering way toward the lure of divine love. Thus he argues that if God is seen as "self-emptying, suffering love," then "The universe would . . . be spontaneously self-creative and self-ordering" (53). The main lines of his position are set out at 45-56; he argues for his appropriation of de Chardin at 81-104. Similarly, in *The Human Factor: Evolution, Culture, and Religion* (Minneapolis: Fortress, 1993), Philip Hefner argues that "Human beings are God's created cocreators whose purpose is to be the agency, acting in freedom, to birth the future that is most wholesome for the nature that has birthed us — the nature that is not only our own genetic heritage, but also the entire human community and the evolutionary and ecological reality in which and to which we belong. Exercising this agency is said to be God's will for humans" (27). At the same time, because Hefner explicitly disavows offering either a doctrine of God or a systematic analysis of nature, it is difficult to know how to interpret this claim.

lastics, whatever their specific views. No scholastic could have accepted a view which in effect denies that statements about God are truth claims, much less true. As for the first two approaches, they would have agreed with McMullin that "The God of evolutionary philosophy is, almost necessarily, an immanent one and thus not at all the transcendent Creator of traditional Christian belief."[36] Any appropriation of scholastic natural law thought which hopes to respect the integrity of their thought must do so in such a way as to respect what they themselves considered to be fundamental, that is to say, God's transcendence and God's status as sole and all-sufficient Creator of the world.

By the same token, the specificity of the scholastic approach to the natural law serves to focus what is all too often a somewhat imprecise discussion. That is, to what extent are contemporary theories of evolution compatible with the theism presupposed by the scholastics, and more specifically with their approach to the natural law? As I will argue, they are at any rate not fundamentally incompatible — that is, there is no inconsistency in affirming both a theory of evolution and a version of scholastic theism. Nonetheless, there are tensions between these two views, albeit not the tensions usually identified in discussions of evolution and religion. These tensions do not force us to give up either evolution or a theory of the natural law derived from scholastic thought. But they do require us to qualify our approach to both, and in that sense they are fruitful tensions, pressing us to consider both our scientific and our theological views more carefully.

Let me begin with what, in the minds of most of our contemporaries, will be the most obvious question about the scholastic approach to natural law reasoning. That is, to what extent does the scholastic concept of the natural law presuppose an untenable view of the origins of life and the formation of species? More specifically, must we embrace creationism in order to accept the scholastic approach to the natural law?

We have already noted that the scholastics affirmed a doctrine of creation — that is to say, they held that God is the sole, uncaused cause of everything that exists apart from God, having created the world, in the traditional phrase, "ex nihilo." Correlatively, everything that now exists must be attributed in some way, directly or indirectly, to God's creative activity. However, this view does not necessarily imply any particular account of the way God creates and sustains the world. Nor, more specifically, does the doctrine of creation rule out any role for secondary causes in the actual coming to be and development of the world as we now experience it. When I learned as a child that God made me, it would never have occurred to me (past a certain age,

36. McMullin, "Introduction," 43.

anyway) that my mother and father had no hand in the process. By the same token, a defense of the doctrine of creation need not be incompatible with a view according to which the original creation contained within it principles or potentialities for further development, which only unfold over time.

For this reason, the scholastic doctrine of creation need not commit us to creationism, in the sense of a distinctively modern view according to which the creation narrative of Genesis is to be taken more or less as a descriptive narrative of the processes of creation.[37] The twelfth-century theologians who fostered the revival of the philosophy of nature insisted on the intelligibility of natural processes, which should be understood in terms of the unfolding of intrinsic principles through mundane causes. Of course they did not deny the doctrine of creation, but they insisted that God created the world as an integral whole, with internal principles of action sufficient to generate the processes of growth and decay which sustain the created order. Subsequently the scholastics were more cautious about affirming the autonomy of nature, but they too held that nature has been created with the principles necessary to generate and direct its own operations. At least some of them acknowledged the possibility that God did not actually create the different kinds of living creatures mentioned in the opening chapter of Genesis in the primal creation, but rather, that God initially bestowed causal principles which eventually gave rise to these creatures.[38] Moreover, they recognized that the created order incorporates elements of contingency and fallibility; the goodness and intelligibility of the world does not imply that every aspect of it is good and intelligible tout court.

By the same token, the scholastics' affirmation of a doctrine of creation leaves room for considerable flexibility with respect to specific ways of understanding God's creative activity. For them, the exact mechanics of creation are less important than the central claim that God is in fact the Creator of everything that is not God, a doctrine which is compatible with a wide range of

37. For further details on developments in the philosophy of nature in this period, and their influence on the scholastic concept of the natural law, see my *Natural and Divine Law,* 66-75. Even in the modern period, theological reactions to evolutionary theory were by no means as uniformly negative as we sometimes assume. For a detailed and illuminating assessment of the issues at stake in early Reformed reactions to Darwin, see David N. Livingstone, "The Idea of Design: The Vicissitudes of a Key Concept in the Princeton Response to Darwin," *Scottish Journal of Theology* 37 (1984): 329-57. For a helpful analysis of the wider historical context of the reception of Darwin's work, see Lenn E. Goodman and Madeleine J. Goodman, "Creation and Evolution: Another Round in an Ancient Struggle," *Zygon* 18, no. 1 (March 1983): 3-43.

38. I am thinking especially of Augustine's interpretation of Genesis, according to which God endowed creation with "seed-principles" for further development, a view which Aquinas notes, without definitely endorsing (*ST* I 69.2; I 71, 72). McMullin provides an illuminating discussion of Augustine's position and Aquinas's reading of it in "Introduction," 11-21.

views concerning the manner in which God creates and sustains the world. This approach is startling to modern sensibilities, but it is also fully consistent with the classical Christian doctrine of creation. That is, precisely because the doctrine of creation postulates a transcendent God who is the sole and sufficient cause of all that is, this doctrine is compatible with a wide range of views about the temporal origins (or otherwise), the development, and the predicted end of the created universe. By the same token, because God's creative act is sui generis, it is, strictly speaking, unimaginable. This would seem to imply that we are free to represent creation to ourselves in a variety of ways, although the scholastics do not (to my knowledge) develop this point.[39] Hence, we are not tied to the imagery of Genesis in our representations of creation, although of course for Christians and Jews this imagery will always have pride of place, and much less are we bound to take it as a literal account of the origins of the cosmos or of human life more specifically. A strong doctrine of creation thus turns out to be not less, but more compatible with modern evolutionary theory than many contemporary theological options.

This aspect of scholastic thought has been obscured, to some extent at least, by an assumption that the scholastics were committed to some version of the argument from design, best known today through William Paley's famous argument for the existence of God from the supposed design of living creatures. This assumption gains credibility from the fact that at least some of the scholastics, Aquinas among them, endorse a teleological view of natural processes according to which these processes are directed toward specific ends. But on closer examination, it is apparent that Aquinas and Paley are not making the same argument. According to Paley, the design of living creatures proves the existence of God because no imaginable concatenation of natural causes could have designed or assembled the unimaginably complex components of living creatures. This is brought out by Paley's well-known comparison between a watch and a living creature. He begins with the observation that anyone can see that a watch, unlike a stone, must have been made by someone, because

> when we come to inspect the watch we perceive — what we could not discover in the stone — that its several parts are framed and put together for a purpose, e.g., that they are so formed and adjusted as to produce motion,

39. However, at least some scholars in this period were prepared to say that we need not take the language of Genesis literally; Tulio Gregory offers the example of the early twelfth-century philosopher William of Conches, who remarks that the Genesis story of the creation of Adam and Eve "must not be believed literally." For further details and citations, see Gregory, "The Platonic Inheritance," in *A History of Twelfth Century Western Philosophy,* ed. Peter Dronke (Cambridge: Cambridge University Press, 1988), 54-80, here 65.

and that motion so regulated as to point out the hour of the day; that if the different parts had been differently shaped from what they are, or placed after any other manner or in any other order than that in which they are placed, either no motion at all would have been carried on in the machine, or none which would have answered the use that is now served by it.[40]

The argument turns, in other words, on an analogy between artifacts and living creatures; just as artifacts cannot assemble themselves, so living creatures could not have come together spontaneously, apart from an agency working outside of the framework of natural causality as we know it. As Paley goes on to explain, once we realize what a watch is, "the inference we think is inevitable, that the watch must have had a maker — that there must have existed, at some time and at some place or other, an artificer or artificers who formed it for the purpose which we find it actually to answer, who comprehended its construction and designed its use."[41]

Aquinas's fifth proof for the existence of God is commonly regarded as if it were a version of this same argument. We should be suspicious of this interpretation, however, if only because Paley's argument turns on an analogy between artifacts and living creatures, whereas Aquinas, like Aristotle before him, insisted on the contrast between them. On their view, artifacts must be designed and assembled precisely because they do not possess their own intrinsic forms, or correlatively, their own internal orientation toward a purpose intrinsic to that form. Moreover, when we turn to Aquinas's specific argument, we see that it does not appeal to the design of living creatures, but rather to the goal-directed character of natural operations, including but not limited to the operations of living things:

> The fifth way is taken from the governance of things. For we see that those things which lack reason, such as natural bodies, operate by reason of an end, which is apparent from this, that always or most frequently they operate in the same way, in such a way as to attain what is best. Thus it is plain that they attain an end from intention, and not from chance. But those things which do not have cognition do not move towards an end unless they are directed by another having knowledge and understanding, just as the arrow is directed by the archer. Therefore, there is something with understanding, from which all natural things are ordained towards an end, and this we call God. (*ST* I 2.3)

40. "Natural Theology," in *The Works of William Paley* (London: William Orr, 1844), 25-28, quoted by McGrath, *A Scientific Theology,* vol. 1, 251.

41. "Natural Theology," quoted in *A Scientific Theology,* vol. 1, 251-52.

Taken by itself, this might seem to imply another kind of quasi-miraculous intervention into the processes of natural causality. But the language of governing, directing, and the like need not be understood in terms of discrete, quasi-miraculous interventions into the created order; they can also be taken as ways of understanding creation itself. As Aquinas elsewhere makes clear, God is said to direct the creature toward its end, by bestowing on it a particular nature with distinctive causal principles, in virtue of which it will naturally act in such a way as to attain its end — which is nothing other than the perfect realization of its form, that is to say, the fullest possible expression of the distinctive kind of creature that it is (I-II 93.5).[42] Whatever we may think of this argument as a proof for God's existence, it does not depend on an appeal to a quasi-miraculous intervention into the natural order of causality, but rather turns on an analysis of what is implied by the intelligibility inherent within that natural order.

At this point, however, we do come to a point of genuine tension between the scholastic approach to the natural law and some interpretations of evolution. That is, the scholastic approach presupposes the real existence of natures — presupposes, that is to say, that our concepts of universals or natural kinds correspond, at least roughly and in part, with the actual character of the world. And this kind of realism is fundamental to the theological account of the natural law that I am developing, because it provided the foundation for the teleological judgments that are central to this concept. For the scholastics, nature is normative to the extent that it is good, and it is good to the extent that it manifests intelligibility and purpose in its operations. This purpose, in turn, is to be interpreted by reference to the overall life and well-being of the creature. What this approach to the natural law presupposes, in other words, is the overall goodness or value of a specific kind of life, the form of life appropriate to a given kind of creature when it is flourishing in accordance with the intrinsic principles of its existence.

For many of our contemporaries, in contrast, evolutionary theory and

42. As we will see in the next chapter, he makes the same point in his commentary on the Neoplatonic treatise *On the Divine Names,* attributed to Dionysius the Areopagite; see *De divinis nominibus* X, 1.1, 857. Similarly, see *De veritate* 22.1, 2 and the *SCG* III 25. In this way Aquinas reinterprets the Platonic conceptions of hierarchy and participation in terms of direct divine causality, which is in turn interpreted in terms of an Aristotelian conception of natures; thus, on this view God's creative activity is interpreted as the constitution of the natures of things in and through intelligible principles of self-motion. By the same token, since effects reflect the intelligible principles of their cause, at least to some extent, we can move from knowledge of creatures to a limited yet genuine knowledge of God. I follow Bastit here; see "Le thomisme est-il un aristotélisme?" passim, for the full argument.

current biological science more generally have made it impossible to speak of natural teleologies of any kind. On this view, the processes of evolution are governed by sheer chance, in such a way as to rule out any claims to find order or direction in these processes, or much less to regard ourselves as their culminating achievement. It is not clear that this view, taken by itself, would necessarily rule out the kind of teleology presupposed by the scholastics, since this is a teleology grounded in norms of flourishing proper to kinds of creatures, and not (or at least, not directly and primarily) a kind of teleology manifest in the processes of evolution taken as a whole. However, this line of analysis is sometimes extended in a direction which would rule out the kind of teleology in question. That is, it is sometimes said that the theory of evolution implies not only that species emerge and develop over time, but also that the kinds which emerge out of this process have no real existence independently of the particular creatures that instantiate them. In other words, because the processes of evolution are construed as random interactions of chance events, therefore the products of evolution, namely, species, are likewise to be seen as sheerly contingent groupings.[43] And this view would of course rule out any kind of appeal to the norms of flourishing intrinsic to a kind of creature, for the simple reason that it denies that there are kinds of creatures, existing as such apart from our systems of classification. That, at least, is the interpretation of evolutionary theory favored by some of its exponents. Yet this interpretation is by no means universally held, nor, as I will argue, is it the most likely interpretation.

These debates take us beyond the implications of evolutionary biology, important as these may be, to include some of the oldest and most fundamental questions in the philosophy of biology.[44] That is to say, how are we to understand the kinds of order proper to living creatures? Can we provide a fully satisfactory account of biological order by analyzing it solely at the level of the most fundamental causal forces (chemical, or even atomic), or must we go to a higher level of description and interpretation in order to develop adequate interpretations of living creatures? It is critical to realize that this is not

43. For a good summary and defense of this view, see Richard Dawkins, "Accumulating Small Change," in *Philosophy of Biology,* ed. Michael Ruse (Amherst: Prometheus Books, 1998), 62-68, reprinted from *The Blind Watchmaker: Why the Evidence of Evolution Reveals a Universe without a Design* (New York: Norton, 1986, 1987, 1996).

44. See, for example, Richard Lewontin's explanation of the different approaches taken by the molecular biologist, who attempts to explain biological phenomena at the level of molecular interactions, and the organismic biologist for whom "it is the whole organism that matters"; *The Triple Helix: Gene, Organism, and Environment* (Cambridge: Harvard University Press, 2000), 76.

only or even primarily a question about the kinds of efficient causality that come into play in the life process. In particular, there is no question here of arguing for some kind of mysterious life force, or much less to a kind of ad hoc divine intervention, in order to account for the distinctive characteristics of living creatures.[45] Rather, the question here concerns the level of description at which a living creature can be rendered intelligible, at least sufficiently so to be the object of systematic description and fruitful hypothesizing. By implication, this question concerns the autonomy of biology as a science; could we, even in theory, analyze biological phenomena without remainder in terms of the operations of the most basic physical forces, or will an adequate biological science necessarily also require distinctive principles and modes of inquiry? As will be apparent by now, the view I am defending implies the latter position.

The first point to be noted is that the natural kinds of living creatures that we identify do seem to exist in nature; this much is defended by many biologists and philosophers of science who have no stake whatever in any particular version of metaphysical realism, or much less doctrines of the natural law. As Ernst Mayr points out, "As the naturalists, beginning with the seventeenth century, began to make increasingly careful studies of species of organisms in nature, evidence began to accumulate that these species were something different from so-called species of inanimate objects. These naturalists showed quite conclusively that biological species not only had reality in nature, but also that in many, if not most cases, they were sharply distinguishable from each other by a natural discontinuity."[46]

The same can be said of the higher levels of biological taxa; indeed, as Mayr says elsewhere, these "are defined by intrinsic characteristics. Birds is the class of feathered vertebrates. Any and all species that satisfy the definition of 'feathered vertebrates' belong to the class of birds. An essentialist definition is satisfactory and sufficient at the level of the higher taxa."[47]

45. On the view being defended, God is of course involved in these processes, and all other operations, insofar as God is the creative origin of the proper principles of the natures of things, and also in virtue of the fact that God sustains the continued existence and operation of all things. The point is that the processes of evolution stem from the operations and interactions of things (nonliving and living) in accordance with the principles proper to their natures; thus, we need not invoke any further distinctive kind of divine intervention, apart from God's "normal" creative and sustaining activities, to account for these processes.

46. Ernst Mayr, *Toward a New Philosophy of Biology: Observations of an Evolutionist* (Cambridge: Harvard University Press, 1988), 317-18.

47. Ernst Mayr, "Species Concepts and Their Application," in *Populations, Species, and Evolution* (Cambridge: Harvard University Press, 1963, 1970), 10-20, reprinted in *Philosophy of*

At the same time, while Mayr believes that species and higher taxa exist in nature, he denies that these represent essences in an Aristotelian (or presumably, scholastic) sense. While he grants that all the members of a species have properties in common, he denies that this is tantamount to saying that a biological species has an essence: "a property in common and an essence are two entirely different things. To be sure, every essence is characterized by properties in common, but a group sharing properties in common does not need to have an essence. The outstanding characteristic of an essence is its permanence, its immutability. By contrast, the properties that a biological group have in common may be variable and have the propensity for evolutionary change."[48]

But as I have argued elsewhere, this confuses the unchangeability proper to a concept with the supposed unchangeability of those entities which instantiate the concept.[49] If we do in fact have an adequate concept of a human being, such that we can identify those traits which are characteristic of human beings as such, then the *concept* will be timeless in two distinct senses: it will not stand in need of revision (on the supposition that it is adequate to its object), and it will not include within itself any intrinsic reference to time (hence, it can be applied to any human being existing at any time whatever). This does not mean that the reality to which the concept applies is unchanging. It is almost certainly the case that the category "human being" came into existence at the end point of a process of evolution extending over a considerable period of time, and it may well be the case that we will either evolve into something else or (more likely) cease to exist altogether. Therefore, there was a time when the concept of humanity had no application, and there may well be a time when it once again ceases to have application. Nonetheless, it does not follow that the concept itself is subject to time in the same way.

By the same token, if our concept of a bird reflects some reality in the world, over and above the individuals we happen to group together under this category, then that reality obtains even if it is, so to speak, temporally located. The existence of natural kinds in the required sense does not necessarily presuppose the existence of some entity, along the lines of a Platonic idea,

---

Biology, 136-45, here 140. As Mayr explains (139-41), biologists classify living creatures hierarchically, proceeding from less to more inclusive categories, including "species," "genus," "family," and "order." A "taxon" (plural "taxa") would refer to any group of populations distinct enough to have a definite category in this system of classification. Strictly speaking, "species" is not a taxon, but a particular species, such as "Robin," would be.

48. Mayr, *New Philosophy of Biology,* 345.

49. In *Natural and Divine Law,* 104-5.

existing over and above the realities instantiating it. Rather, it presupposes that the categories under which things are sorted — or more exactly, some of them — reflect real qualities or aspects of the things in question, in virtue of which they count as the kinds of things they are. It presupposes, in other words, that it is in some way meaningful to speak of the essential forms of things, which identify them in terms of the kinds of things they are. By the same token, this view presupposes that the forms of things can be grasped through concepts, albeit imperfectly, and moreover that these concepts are genuinely explanatory, that is to say, they help us make sense of the operations of natural things in ways that would otherwise be inaccessible to us.

In the Aristotelian-Thomistic terms that I am retrieving, these sorts of explanations would be described as appeals to the formal cause, but it is important not to be misled by this expression. A formal cause indicates the description under which something can be understood in terms of the kind of thing it is.[50] In this context, the language of "cause" does not necessarily imply efficient causality, but refers more broadly to any principle of intelligibility and explanation. It is a kind of category mistake to think of the forms of living creatures as among the kinds of things that can have independent existence, prior to specification in some individual; they are instantiated or they are not, and it is these instantiations, not the forms themselves, which come into being and pass away.[51] By the same token, the forms of living creatures do not exist over against the creatures in such a way as to exercise efficient causality on them. As James Lennox puts it, referring specifically to Aristotle's conception of form, "the form of a living thing is its soul, and Aristotle considers soul to be a unified set of goal-ordered capacities — nutritive, reproductive, locomotive, and cognitive."[52] As such, the form is manifested in and through the modali-

50. As Pasnau points out, for Aquinas the intelligibility of a given kind of thing stems from its form, which (together with the matter, where appropriate) is captured by its proper definition; hence, the "formal cause" refers to the principle of explanation in terms of which something is identified as the kind of creature it is. In the case of nonartificial substances, the formal and final causes are identical, since natural operations are directed toward sustaining or communicating some form. For further particulars, see *Thomas Aquinas*, 7-10, 21-22, 89-95. Coleman and Clark also offer illuminating discussions of these interconnections; see Coleman, "MacIntyre and Aquinas," 70-73, and Clark, *Biology and Christian Ethics*, 13-19.

51. I do not mean to deny here that the human soul is a substantive form, of such a kind as to survive the death of the body. However, even the human soul cannot exist prior to its instantiation in a human body, nor can it ever be understood except by reference to its individuation in matter — which is not to deny that it requires existence in matter at every point in order to continue to exist. See Pasnau, *Thomas Aquinas*, 45-57, for further details.

52. James Lennox, *Aristotle's Philosophy of Biology* (Cambridge: Cambridge University Press, 2001), 128; see more generally 127-30.

ties of efficient causality proper to the kind of creature in question. Seen from the perspective of biological science, the specific form of a given kind of creature often provdes a starting point for investigation — that is to say, the kinds of order proper to living creatures invite scientific inquiry, and provide a structured framework within which such inquiry can take place.

It might be said that the fact that species and higher levels of kinds really exist in nature, taken by itself, does not necessarily rule out the possibility that they are simply the products of chance developments. But if species and higher taxa actually do exist in nature — that is to say, if our concepts of kinds of creatures are not just projections, but reflect real features of the world — then species cannot be just random groupings of individuals.[53] The claim that species and higher taxa have real existence implies that recognizable kinds of creatures exhibit intelligible similarities, and relate to one another in orderly ways. Moreover, these ordered interactions take place not only within species, but between members of different species — diverse kinds of creatures are related to one another over time by relations of descent, and synchronously by a multitude of relations of competition and interdependence, in accordance with the capacities and limitations proper to their kinds. If this is so, then the diverse kinds of living creatures are not just a set of random groupings — they constitute an *ordered* set of natural kinds. And it is difficult to see how this ordering can be entirely the result of random chance. Nor need this conclusion imply that the process is being directed "from above," so to speak, by God or by some other external agency. Rather, it implies that the order reflected in living creatures reflects causal forces intrinsic to the creatures themselves which operate in directed and intelligible ways. This conclusion would not rule out some role for sheer chance, nor would it necessarily commit us to the view that we could predict the direction the process would go in advance — it would simply rule out an explanation according to which the only causal forces at work in the development of life are those which operate at such a basic level that they can only interact in random ways.

Admittedly, the differentiation of species, defined in the biological sense

53. I should add that I have no stake in arguing that the process of evolution, considered as a whole, manifests an internal directedness toward the production of specific kinds of creatures — namely, us. I agree with McMullin that the degree of contingency in the overall direction of evolutionary processes is a nonissue for the theologian; see his "Cosmic Purpose and the Contingency of Human Evolution," *Theology Today* 55 (1998): 389-414. Similarly, Ruse argues that the theory of evolution implies that the actual results of the evolutionary process are contingent, but adds that such a conclusion is not necessarily incompatible with Christianity (though I would reach this conclusion somewhat differently than he does); see *Can a Darwinian?* 82-93.

as interbreeding populations reproductively isolated from other such populations, does seem to reflect considerable chance. Species can be separated off from one another through any chance event that separates two populations. But the further we go through the biological taxa, the less room we seem to find for contingencies of this sort. The kinds of living creatures seem to reflect necessary stages or levels of biological organization, in terms of which the processes of evolutionary development are themselves ordered — they are replicated throughout the world, no matter how isolated different regions may be, and they seem to relate to one another in the same way. Mammals do not seem to evolve directly from fish, nor do they give rise to birds. An ordered progression seems to be respected throughout. None of this, I want to emphasize, requires direct divine intervention in the processes of evolution at any point, but it does suggest that the characteristics proper to given kinds of creatures operate in such a way as to place constraints on evolutionary processes, in such a way as to give them a directedness and consistency that cannot be accounted for through chance alone.

This brings us to a point noted above. The claim that evolution is a random process implies a claim about the level at which the causal processes operative in evolution should be analyzed. Those who defend the randomness of the process do so in terms of an account which analyzes evolutionary change in terms of interactions of genetic material, or even at a lower level of molecular and atomic interactions.[54] This claim, in turn, presupposes a more general account of biological processes, according to which these can be exhaustively analyzed at the level of genetic operations, or perhaps even at a more basic level of simple atomic interactions. On this view, there would indeed be no place for anything like a scholastic conception of formal causality. If we could account for the operations of living creatures at the level of genetic interactions, then we would never need to refer to the kind of creature in question in formulating a causal explanation for its operations.

However, there is considerable debate over whether biological processes can cogently be analyzed at this level alone. A number of biologists have recently pointed out that the genes by themselves do not even determine their expression in an individual creature (in other words, genotype underdetermines phenotype), and much less can they account for the processes through which kinds of creatures develop and evolve. As Richard Lewontin

54. Lenny Moss summarizes the issues at stake here, arguing for the irreducible complexity of living creatures, in *What Genes Can't Do* (Cambridge: MIT Press, 2003), 51-73. Similarly, Marjorie Grene argues that evolutionary theory itself calls for analysis in terms of a hierarchy of levels of causation too complex to be captured by a reductive analysis in "Hierarchies in Biology," *American Scientist* 75 (1987): 504-9.

observes, it is impossible to account for evolutionary change within the time frame that it operates through random genetic mutations alone:

> Genetic mutation depends on the process of mutation, and mutations are rare events. Any particular new DNA mutation will occur only once in about 100 million gametes. Moreover, when a single mutation occurs in a single newborn, even if it is a favorable mutation, there is a fair probability that it will not be represented in the next generation because its single carrier may not, by chance, pass it on to its few offspring. The time between the origin of a species and the time that a mutation of just the right sort occurs and reaches a high enough frequency to be significant in the selective process is of the same order as the total lifetime of the species, around ten million years. So most mutations that would have been selected if they had occurred are never seen. A species must make do with the variations that it actually has.[55]

Of course, Lewontin has no intention of denying that species emerge, develop, and cease to exist through a series of changes taking place over time. However, his point is that the relevant processes should be understood as occurring most frequently through the expression and development of potentialities already existing within the genotype, rather than through random changes which alter the phenotype in some stable way — even though such changes *do* occur, albeit rarely, and presumably do play some role in the evolutionary process. My point, in turn, is that this process presupposes ongoing interactions among creatures of a given kind in a changing environment, in which the potentialities of the kind of creature, expressed most immediately through its phenotype, provide it with a range of responses through which it can adapt to changing conditions. For this reason, explanations for the adaptive development of a given kind of creature cannot proceed without some reference to the kind of creature in question.

I should add that Lewontin himself would probably be uneasy about the direction in which I have taken his observations. He begins *The Triple Helix* by arguing against a Platonic view of species, according to which kinds of creatures develop in accordance with an inner program in a way that may be conditioned, but is not fundamentally shaped by external conditions.[56] However, the account of formal causality to which I am committed does not require the developmental determinism to which Lewontin objects. It certainly does not entail the view — which I take to be Lewontin's primary target — according to which

55. Lewontin, *The Triple Helix*, 91-92.

56. In particular, see Lewontin, *The Triple Helix*, 3-22.

the development of individual creatures reflects the unfolding of a determinate plan exhaustively programmed into the genetic code. On the contrary, the underdetermination of phenotype by genotype offers further support for the legitimacy of formal causes in biological explanation. That being said, what I am committed to holding is some account of development according to which the ways creatures engage their environment, and the lines of development they exhibit, are integrally connected to the kinds of creatures they are. Such a view would leave room for a great deal of indeterminacy and variability in the development of kinds of creatures, but it would of course not be consistent with a complete indeterminacy in this regard. Nor do I think that is what Lewontin means — otherwise, it is difficult to see how he could speak of individual creatures and kinds of creatures as realities distinct from their environment.[57]

Others have argued more explicitly that the processes of living creatures cannot be explained exhaustively in terms of the operations of genetic material. For example, Lenny Moss argues that these kinds of efforts reflect a fundamental confusion over what the gene is and what it can accomplish within the life of the organism. Most fundamentally, a gene is simply a template for producing proteins of a particular kind. In order for a creature's genetic structure to be expressed in a particular way, its genes must be activated in order to be expressed, and their expression must be directed in a particular way. And this process of activation and expression cannot be accounted for at the level of genetic operations alone:

> The empirical fruits of several decades of research in molecular, cell, and developmental biology have revealed that what distinguishes one biological form from another is seldom, if ever, the presence or absence of a certain genetic template but rather *when* and *where* genes are expressed, *how* they are modified, and into *what* structural and dynamic relationships their "products" become embodied. If genes are to be both molecules which function as physical templates for the synthesis of other molecules and determinants of organismic traits and phenotypes, then somehow genes would have to, in effect, provide their own instructions for use.[58]

But as he goes on to argue, genes cannot function as their own templates in this way. Rather, the activation and expression of the genes is determined by interactions at the cellular level: "Under the heading of 'organizational structure,' I have begun to marshal evidence on behalf of the idea that *cellular context* as a whole is basic to the nature and continuity of living be-

57. Lewontin, *The Triple Helix,* 41-68.

58. Moss, *What Genes Can't Do,* xvii, emphases in original.

ings and is irreducible to any of its constituent parts."[59] It is possible, as Moss shows, to describe the requisite cellular processes in some detail. At the same time, however, even this level of explanation is not sufficient to account for the intelligible phenotypic expression of genetic templates. Cancerous cells also reflect the activation of genetic information through a flourishing — all-too-flourishing — cellular development. What has gone wrong in such a case is the relationship of the aberrant cells to the organism as a whole; in the case of cancer, "the hallmark of pathology is an arrested or aberrant path of differentiation, in both cases an expression of cellular potential which has become separated from the *principle of the whole organism*."[60] In other words, the expression of genetic information and the procedures of cellular life both depend for their proper — which is to say, nonpathological — development on a structural and functional context set by the life of the organism considered as a whole. Elsewhere, Moss explicitly connects the intrinsic capacities of kinds of creatures to evolutionary processes:

> even if we are to focus exclusively on distinctively Darwinian mechanisms [to account for evolutionary change], the story is not that much different. . . . Variation that is random in the relevant sense can well be generated by an ostensibly purposeful system that acts to "roll its dice." The immune system's ability to generate variable regions of antibodies with binding capacities for antigens never seen before is a good example of this. The ability of organisms to both regulate the number of spontaneous mutations that "get through" proofreading and the ability to enhance mutability under stress are even more to the point. If the appearance of most or all variation is mediated by complex, highly structured enzyme systems, as generally appears to be the case, then Darwinian evolution can be seen to be built upon the ostensibly purposeful capacities of organisms as opposed to such.[61]

59. Moss, *What Genes Can't Do*, 95, emphasis in original. Similarly, Marjorie Grene argues that "Systems that convey messages . . . are necessarily hierarchical, in that the arrangement of their elements constrains, and thus controls, the behavior of those very elements as long as the system so constituted continues to exist." "Hierarchies in Biology," 506.

60. Moss, *What Genes Can't Do*, 125, emphasis in original. Moss is here summarizing the results of research by Johannes Müller, but clearly with approval.

61. Lenny Moss, "Representational Preformationism to the Epigenesis of Openness to the World? Reflections on a New Vision of the Organism," *Annals of the New York Academy of Sciences* 981 (entitled "From Epigenesis to Epigenetics") (December 2002): 21-230. Again, compare Grene, who observes that current debates over the mechanisms of evolution presuppose a context in which "not only genes and organisms, but species as well, are taken seriously as historical entities, and hence as possible causal forces." "Hierarchies in Biology," 508.

This takes us back to where we began, because it implies that the explanation of these processes must include some ineliminable reference to the kind of creature that is under consideration, in terms of which we can meaningfully speak of the "principle of the whole organism" — that is to say, its formal cause, understood in terms of the intelligible and goal-directed operations expressing its nature as a creature of a particular kind.

Let me emphasize, once more, that my point is not that the processes of evolution in particular, or biological processes more generally, require special divine intervention or other kinds of external causation. On the contrary, the analysis just developed is entirely consistent with a view according to which biological processes can be wholly and completely explained through natural causes. What I do want to challenge, however, is a widespread yet impoverished understanding of what counts as a natural cause.[62] The considerations discussed above are important because they all indicate that the development and evolution of living creatures cannot be explained in terms of the cumulative effects of random chance alone. They also require us to appeal at some points to considerations stemming from the kinds of creatures with which we are dealing. The famous finches on the Galapagos Islands have the capacity to develop rapidly in response to changing patterns of food supply because of the kinds of creatures they are; and for the same reason, they do not have the capacity to evolve directly into rhesus monkeys, or into mushrooms. We cannot fully understand the evolutionary history of any kind of creature without appealing to some considerations stemming from the kinds of creatures with which we are dealing. And that means that at some points we must appeal to formal causes, that is to say, explanations which irreducibly refer to the kind of creature that is in question.

Yet even granting the force of the preceding arguments, it might seem that we have done only part of what we set out to do in this section. That is to say, we have seen that formal causality, understood in an Aristotelian sense, is compatible with contemporary biological science. But what are we to say about the possibility of making teleological claims, based on our reflective observations of living creatures? Surely this is ruled out by contemporary biology?

62. As Stephen Clark points out in *Biology and Christian Ethics* (24-29), the denial of formal causality implies not only the correlative denial of final causality (see below), but of efficient causality as traditionally understood, that is to say, as an intelligible exercise of efficacy in accordance with a creature's proper mode of existence. On this view, "the dominant model of explanation came to be the Stoics' reworking of material cause: one thing causes some effect in another only by pushing or pulling in quantifiable ways. Only material, extended objects can be causes" (26).

As Moss remarks, the incompatibility between teleological claims and contemporary evolution is a shibboleth, so widely accepted that it has become difficult even to canvass the relevant issues.[63] Or at least, that would have been the case until recently. However, over the past few years two different strands of thought have converged to undermine this assumption. The first follows historical and philosophical reappraisals of Aristotle's understanding of teleology, and its afterlife in later scientific thought. The second draws on efforts by biologists themselves to make sense of the proper subject matter of their field. As Michael Ruse points out, "Design language reigns triumphant in evolutionary biology," and while no serious biologist interprets this language in terms of externally imposed design, it is clear that it does carry connotations of purpose and function.[64]

But whose purposes, and which functions? Here we come to the crux of the matter. In the early modern period, there was a widespread tendency, among both biologists and theologians, to interpret the design of living creatures in terms of externally imposed agencies and aims, mostly God's but also, secondarily, our own. Hence, living creatures were regarded as if they were God's artifacts, designed in such a way that each of the creature's organs and functions was set up to serve a specific and discernible purpose. Paley's argument from design neatly illustrates these assumptions. Moreover, living creatures were thought to serve purposes external to themselves, for which God had designed them — they were meant to serve human needs in various ways, and perhaps also reciprocally to serve the needs of other kinds of creatures.

63. In *What Genes Can't Do,* 4.

64. Ruse, *Philosophy of Biology,* 16; Ruse does not offer his own views on the relevant issues, however. It is generally acknowledged that living creatures give at least the appearance of design, but evolutionary biologists have typically tried to account for this by arguing that the relevant features of living creatures can be explained now, by appealing to the adaptive benefits that these features conferred in the past. The advantage of this kind of historical explanation is that it does not commit us to saying that the relevant features serve any purpose now — or so it is claimed. More recently, this line of argument has been attacked from a number of directions. In *Things That Happen Because They Should: A Teleological Approach to Action* (Oxford: Clarendon, 1996), 99-112, Rowland Stout summarizes the relevant arguments, arguing that explanations of biological functions and organs are properly focused on types of features. More recently, Paul Davies, in *Norms of Nature: Naturalism and the Nature of Functions* (Cambridge: MIT Press, 2001), has argued that the "historical" explanation of seeming design is inconsistent with a thoroughgoing naturalism, and that we must analyze the properties of living creatures in terms of their place in the overall functioning of the creature, without any reference to purpose, past or present; see especially 107-56. Although he denies that this line of analysis is teleological, it does show that the diverse features of living creatures can only be properly understood in relation to the overall, hierarchically structured functioning of the organism as a whole — which on the Aristotelian view is tantamount to the formal cause.

But this is not the only way to think of teleology in living creatures. As a number of scholars have recently observed, Aristotle's understanding of teleology differs in significant ways from the more familiar early modern view.[65] For Aristotle, the language of purpose and function is legitimate and indeed necessary in speaking of the organs, structures, and recurrent activities of living creatures, *within* a context set by the well-being of the creature itself. In other words, for him teleological language finds its appropriate context by reference to the kind of well-being characteristic of the creature itself, and correlatively, to the ordered activities through which the creature pursues its well-being; that is to say, to the creature's own goals, broadly construed. Thus understood, teleological language does not imply any reference to externally imposed purposes, whether ours, those of some demiurge or creator, or a generalized nature or evolutionary process. Rather, in this context the language of purpose functions in such a way as to render the different components of a living creature intelligible, in terms of their contributions to the life processes of the creature. As Lennox puts it, "the 'package' which constitutes a distinct bird form precisely adapts it to its way of life — specifying 'what it is to be a Spoonbill' is explaining how its differentiae are precisely those needed to live as it does."[66] Interpreted in this way, the observation that the eye is meant for seeing does not presuppose a story about the way the physical mechanism of the eye reflects the contrivance of an omnipotent designer (as it would do on the modern understanding of design). Rather, it presupposes a more straightforward account of the role the eye plays in promoting the overall well-being of the creature by means of providing an organ for sight, which will include a further account of what sight itself is good for, given an overall orientation toward life, growth, and reproduction shared (in some way) by all living creatures.

An Aristotelian approach to teleology may seem on this interpretation to be trivial — don't we all know that one sees through the eyes, and don't we all agree that sight is a good thing? And it is certainly true that this kind of explanation is not generally developed in such a way as to provide new information. However, what it does provide is an interpretation in terms of which the different components of living creatures — including both organs and activities — can be rendered intelligible in terms of their relation to an overall pattern of functions and activities, all directed toward the aims shared by all liv-

65. In addition to Lennox and Clark, cited above, see James Wallace, *Virtues and Vices* (Ithaca, N.Y.: Cornell University Press, 1978), 15-38, for a lucid explanation of what is distinctive in Aristotle's approach.

66. Lennox, *Aristotle's Philosophy of Biology*, 129.

ing creatures. While this kind of explanation may seem trivial when applied to familiar kinds of creatures, it is far from trivial when applied to less familiar kinds of creatures, or to puzzling aspects of the bodily structure and activities of familiar kinds. By the same token, teleological explanations provide biological science with fruitful agenda for research — not so much by supplying new information as by suggesting interpretations of data and generating hypotheses.[67]

It will be apparent that teleological explanation shares many of the same characteristics as the appeal to formal causality discussed above. And this is hardly surprising. For Aristotle himself and for those who follow his lead on these issues, formal causes and teleological explanation, or in other words, explanations in terms of final causes, are inextricably linked. The proper form of a given kind of living creature can only be adequately understood by reference to some idea of a paradigmatic instance of the form, that is to say, a healthy and mature individual of the kind in question. It is only by reference to this paradigm that we are able to identify immature, sick, or defective individuals of this kind as such, that is to say, as (less than perfect) representatives of the kind.[68] By the same token, appeals to formal and final causality provide a framework within which to develop and test hypotheses about the functions of the characteristic organs and operations of a given kind of creature, and to explain them in terms of their contributions to the functioning of the organism considered as a whole.

Teleology understood in this sense fits well with many of our attitudes and intuitions about the living things around us, and while this consideration

67. This point is made in a general way by Wallace, *Virtues and Vices,* 18-25. Michael Tkacz discusses Albert the Great's use of Aristotelian teleological analysis to explain the morphology of living creatures in "Neo-Darwinians, Aristotelians, and Optimal Design," *The Thomist* 62 (1998): 355-72, and Aquinas draws on teleological analysis to explain the distinction of the senses, as Pasnau points out; *Thomas Aquinas,* 172-80. To mention a more recent example, Lennox discusses the place of teleological hypotheses in Harvey's research on the circulation of the blood in *Aristotle's Philosophy of Biology,* 218-20. Similarly, it might be argued that contemporary cancer research has been undermined by a reluctance to take broadly teleological considerations seriously; that at least seems to be implied by Moss, *What Genes Can't Do,* 117-82.

68. Davies denies this point, and it is on this grounds that he denies that explanations in terms of functions are teleological in any sense; see *Norms of Nature,* 157-58. In my view, however, such a move would undercut any appeal to teleological explanations in identifying types of living creatures or setting forth the appropriate way of life for a creature of a given kind in a given environment — which would eliminate a good deal of biological research. See Wallace, *Virtues and Vices,* 18-25; Stout, *Things That Happen,* 99-112; and Pasnau, *Thomas Aquinas,* 21-22, for further development of this line of argument (not, of course, developed in reference to Davies specifically).

is not probative in itself, it does lend credence to the line of interpretation that I am developing. To begin with the most fundamental point of all, some distinction between living and nonliving creatures appears to be basic to human (and indeed, animal) functioning. This rough distinction, in turn, is invariably fleshed out through a set of ideas concerning what it means to be a healthy, functioning, flourishing creature of a certain kind. We can tell a scrawny puppy from a robust puppy, a sick horse from a healthy horse, a dying ficus from a happy ficus. These kinds of discriminations are fundamental to functioning in the world, even in our urban, postmodern society, and it would be absurd to consider them to be arbitrary or wholly the product of cultural construction.

Moreover, these distinctions serve as a basis for normative judgments in a variety of ways. Up to a point, these are judgments of a straightforward, nonmoral kind; for example, we judge that if someone wants a healthy ficus tree, she should water it. But our discriminations about the well-being of living creatures can be extended to normative judgments which arguably do carry moral connotations. This raises complicated issues, precisely because our sense of the moral status of animals is currently in flux. Yet as some have recently argued, the integral flourishing of nonrational animals (at least) does seem to place constraints which we ought to recognize in our dealings with them, even if we generally do not.[69] There is something not only sad but perverse in the spectacle of cattle bred to build up so much muscle mass that they cannot walk, chickens kept in confinement so that they cannot scratch for food, dogs that have been bred to be too nervous to live in close proximity with any other animals, human or otherwise. It would perhaps be imprecise to say that animals in conditions such as these have been wronged, but at least we can say that they have missed out on forms of happiness specific to them as the kinds of animals they are — and this is at least something to be regretted, perhaps even a wrong which should be corrected.

The Thomistic account of the natural law being developed here presupposes that we can make similar judgments about what would count as a flourishing human life, and what it means to respect and foster such a life. Of course, such judgments as applied to human beings will invariably be more complex, if only because human life is capable of assuming a far greater variety of forms than we find among any nonrational species. Yet these are not altogether unlimited. There are constraints on human flourishing, and perhaps

69. These arguments are summarized, without much sympathy, by Bernice Bovenkerk, Frans W. A. Brom, and Babs J. Van den Bergh in "Brave New Birds: The Use of 'Animal Integrity' in Animal Ethics," *Hastings Center Report*, January-February 2002, 16-22.

more importantly, there are recurring components of human existence which will form the basis for happiness and well-being for almost all persons.

At this point, it will be helpful to summarize our conclusions so far. Contemporary biological science, including but not limited to the theory of evolution, has widely been regarded as incompatible with the kinds of teleological claims presupposed by the scholastic approach to the natural law. But as we have seen, this need not be the case. Admittedly, some scientists and philosophers do claim that we cannot speak in terms of natural teleologies, but many others contest this claim. Moreover, they do so on grounds that have nothing to do with theological or moral concerns, but stem from fundamental commitments to a particular way of construing the subject matter and modes of research of biology as a science. These commitments represent a stance toward living creatures which is plausible on its own terms, and which provides us with a secure basis for defending a version of natural teleology. At the same time, it is important to be clear about the kind of teleological judgment that is in question — not one rooted in the purposes of functions or organs, but a judgment stemming from an assessment of a whole organism in terms of some ideal of flourishing. Understood in this way, a teleological assessment is inseparably related to a judgment regarding the kind of creature under consideration. We cannot form a concept of a kind of living creature without at the same time forming a judgment about the way of life proper to a mature and fully developed creature of that kind.

This brings us to a fundamental point. The Thomistic theory of the natural law being developed here presupposes that everything just said about living creatures more generally can also be applied to human beings. We too are a kind of living creature; it is possible to form a concept of the kind of creature that we are; and this concept is intrinsically teleological, in the way just indicated. As we will see more clearly in the next chapter, this teleological concept of human nature does not lead directly and perspicuously to moral conclusions. Nonetheless, it provides the necessary point of connection between the natural and as it were the animal life of the human creature and the properly moral norms stemming from human nature more comprehensively considered.

4. Toward a Concept of Human Nature

But are we really entitled to the assumption that we can form a teleological conception of the human person, in the same way we can form concepts of parakeets and ficus trees? Given the conclusions of the previous section, this question might seem straightforward, although practically difficult to answer. Just as we form concepts of other kinds of creatures, which are tested and refined through experience, scientific inquiry, and ongoing systematic reflection, so it should be possible to develop a concept of the natural kind, Homo sapiens. And that is in fact the view I will defend. But this conclusion may seem too quick. Even granting the validity of a broadly realist position along the lines sketched above, it might well appear that the human person is too complex or too distinctive to be captured in a concept of human nature, in just the same way as we form concepts of other kinds of living creatures.

This objection can be pressed from more than one direction. We are often reminded that we have no direct access to human nature, and our attempts to understand it are bound to be conditioned by our own cultural and even personal presuppositions, which are likely to determine our sense of what counts as natural. How can we free ourselves of these presuppositions in order to develop the requisite kind of concept of human nature? This objection raises doubts about whether we can get the necessary kind of access to human nature; other objections question whether the human person even has a nature, of a kind that can be understood by analogy to the natures of other kinds of living creatures. Since the early decades of the last century, a number of prominent theologians have argued that the human capacities for rational reflection, self-determination, and historical change place the human agent outside the constraints of nature more generally considered — if not completely, then at least to such an extent that the human person cannot be said to have a determinate natural end, as other kinds of living creatures do.[70] More recently, a number of philosophers and cultural critics have argued that the idea of a fixed human nature is suspect because it fails to take account of the socially constructed, radically contingent character of all communal practices and moral norms.[71] To put the claim in traditional terms, we cannot an-

70. This view can be traced to the influential work of Henri de Lubac; see *The Mystery of the Supernatural,* trans. Rosemary Sheed (New York: Herder and Herder, 1967), 131-53. For a lucid elaboration of this view, see Anton Pegis, "Nature and Spirit: Some Reflections on the Problem of the End of Man," *Proceedings of the American Catholic Philosophical Association* 23 (1949): 62-79; for a more recent defense, see Denis Bradley, *Aquinas on the Twofold Human Good* (Washington, D.C.: Catholic University of America Press, 1997). The contrary position is forcefully argued by Kevin Staley, "Happiness: The Natural End of Man?" *The Thomist* 53, no. 2 (1989): 215-34; Bonnie Kent, *Virtues of the Will: The Transformation of Ethics in the Late Thirteenth Century* (Washington, D.C.: Catholic University of America Press, 1995), 24-34; and Steven Long, "On the Possibility of a Purely Natural End for Man," *The Thomist* 64 (2000): 211-37.

71. There are probably few scholars who would claim that we cannot speak of a stable human nature in any sense at all. Nonetheless, skepticism about human nature has had a far-reaching impact on academic discourse as well as popular culture. Barbara Ehrenreich and Janet

alyze our social conventions in terms of their natural origins because there are no natural origins (or at least, we have no systematic access to any such origins) — so far as we are concerned, all we have are conventions, all the way down.

Even though the defenders of this general view would disagree profoundly among themselves on many issues, nonetheless they share a certain perspective on the distinctiveness of the human person and her relation to the natural world, more broadly understood. That is, they agree that the human person is so unique, in virtue of her capacities for reason or language, or her enmeshment in a historically particular culture, or her supernatural destiny, or any combination of these, that she cannot be understood in any meaningful way in terms of the regularities that apply to the nonhuman natural world. This romantic perspective is deeply rooted in the culture of postindustrial societies — as much so as the reverence for nature and the ideal of naturalness to which it is so often opposed. Hence, it is not surprising that our societies, which give such importance to our continuities with the natural world, should also reflect deep discomfort with these continuities, particularly among the intelligentsia — for example, in the academic popularity of deconstruction and critical theory, and in academic and popular forms of evangelical religion which mount radical critiques to any kind of scientific perspective on human life.

Recent attempts to analyze cultural practices, including morality and religion, in terms of their evolutionary origins reflect the other half of the dichotomy just described.[72] Considered as a research program, sociobiology or evolutionary psychology attempts to account for regularities in human practices in terms of the processes of evolutionary adaption. And so, for example, it might be argued that men tend to be promiscuous while women tend to be more choosy, because a man's chances of reproductive success increase with the number of his partners, whereas women have a greater stake in securing assistance with the ongoing processes of child rearing. Considered as a basis for a morality, evolutionary psychology usually serves as a more or less explicit argument for accepting the inevitability of certain social practices, for

---

McIntosh describe an encounter in which a lecturer tried to defend Victorian science, in a tentative way, by observing that it had led among other things to the discovery of DNA — to which a member of the audience replied, "You believe in DNA?" See "The New Creationism," *The Nation*, June 9, 1997, 1-16, for further details.

72. In fact, recent attempts of this kind have a long history, dating back to Darwin himself; see Paul Lawrence Farber, *The Temptations of Evolutionary Ethics* (Berkeley: University of California Press, 1998), for details. For a good summary of the most recent developments in this area, including Farber's own assessments (largely critical, as we might expect), see 148-75.

example, certain ways of structuring the relations between the sexes. In either case, evolutionary psychology derives its cultural force from its appearance of scientific rigor, in virtue of which it seems to show the inevitability of certain social arrangements. In this way, it represents a contemporary attempt to fulfill the aspiration of the early modern natural lawyers for a truly scientific theory of the natural law.

Some readers may be surprised that I have made so little use of evolutionary psychology in this project. For anyone interested in the natural roots of morality, this body of work offers much of interest. Moreover, as Stephen Pope has shown in some detail, a Thomistic moral theology can fruitfully draw on the best of this research, while at the same time providing a basis for critiquing some of its more troubling applications.[73] Nonetheless, I have been persuaded that this approach is scientifically dubious, at least in its more ambitious and comprehensive forms, because all too often it presupposes a simplistic account of adaption and its role in natural selection.[74] Used with caution, the more careful and limited arguments of the evolutionary psychologists do offer valuable insights into the regularities of human nature, but I am convinced that other avenues of research, especially anthropological studies and comparative studies of the other primates, can be of more value in this respect.

In any case, the dichotomy between two ideals of human nature, the romantic and the (strictly) scientific, is too deeply rooted and pervasive to be either resolved or ignored. Nonetheless, it is possible to keep a critical perspective on both ideals, if only because each offers persuasive correctives to the other. Certainly, recent attempts to account for every aspect of human behavior, including quite specific cultural practices, in terms of their evolutionary origins or genetic roots can be shown to be misguided on scientific terms, to say nothing of any philosophical or theological questions that they might raise. Moreover, on any plausible showing, the regularities of human nature

73. See Stephen Pope, *The Evolution of Altruism and the Ordering of Love* (Washington, D.C.: Georgetown University Press, 1994), and more recently, "The Evolutionary Roots of Morality in Theological Perspective," *Zygon* 33, no. 4 (December 1998): 545-56.

74. In addition to Farber, cited above, see Francisco J. Ayala, "The Biological Roots of Morality," *Biology and Philosophy* 2 (1987): 235-52, and the essays collected in Hilary Rose and Steven Rose, *Alas, Poor Darwin: Arguments against Evolutionary Psychology* (New York: Random House, 2000); Stephen Gould's essay, "More Things in Heaven and Earth," 101-26, is particularly noteworthy, as it offers a good summary of his influential critiques of sociobiology. Pope likewise cautions against accepting the conclusions of sociobiology uncritically in *The Evolution of Altruism*, 99-127. For the record, I used to be more enthusiastic about evolutionary psychology than I now am; see *Natural and Divine Law*, 100.

underdetermine the social practices in which they are expressed — that is one reason why we cannot move directly from a normative conception of human nature to a set of substantive norms. Nonetheless, it is difficult to make a plausible case that there is no sense in which we can be said to share in a common nature, or that this nature cannot in any way be understood in terms of its continuities with the natural world more generally understood. We know a great deal about what we might call the natural history of the human animal, the environmental conditions it needs to live and flourish, and its characteristic patterns of behavior and way of life. In his recent *The Blank Slate,* Steven Pinker lists over two hundred behavioral constants that ethnographers have identified in all societies, beginning with "anticipation in speech and thought," running through "sexuality as focus of interest," and ending with "white" and "world view" — or "toys," if one takes account of later additions.[75]

Yet even if we grant the accuracy of Pinker's list, we might still ask whether this kind of knowledge about human universals adds up to anything like a systematic concept of human nature. What we need, after all, is not simply a lot of information about human beings, even information about universally recurring characteristics of human beings. Rather, what we require — if the development of a natural law grounded in human nature is to get off the ground — is some kind of framework placing these bits of information into a coherent form, derived from our best assessment of the form of the humanity itself — of the kind of creature that we are, understood by reference to some account of mature and fully developed human functioning.

This brings us to a further concern. Even if we can develop and defend the requisite kind of conception of humanity, would it be desirable to do so? There is a widespread uneasiness about this kind of project which is not just scientific or philosophical — it also reflects a serious worry about the moral implications of such a move. After all, if we believe that we have identified the defining characteristics of a "real" human being, doesn't this imply that those who lack these characteristics, for example, the very young or the profoundly handicapped, would not count as human persons? And might this not imply that they would be denied the protections normally accorded to human persons, including most fundamentally the right to life? In this way, a discussion

75. This list — and what a list it is! — is actually taken from Donald E. Brown, *Human Universals* (1991). See Steven Pinker, *The Blank Slate: The Modern Denial of Human Nature* (New York: Viking Press, 2002), 435-39. Pinker has come in for considerable criticism for his somewhat unnuanced accounts of human nature, and I would not want to defend all of his conclusions; nonetheless, at the very least he offers a valuable compendium of current research on human capabilities and forms of functioning, as manifested in political interactions (283-305), propensities to violence (306-36), sex differences (337-71), and the care of children (372-79).

of theoretical questions having to do with the concept of human nature quickly intersects with painful and difficult debates over abortion, infanticide, and euthanasia. For just that reason, it might seem the better part of wisdom for the moral theologian to leave these questions to one side.

Nonetheless, we cannot avoid trying to sort through these theoretical questions, if we are to retrieve scholastic insights into the natural law. In this section I will argue that it makes sense to speak of a concept of human nature, even though we do not have, and should not expect to have, a fully developed and comprehensive such concept. I will also argue that such a claim does not in any way imply that immature or handicapped persons are not fully human persons — any more than an immature chick or a sick hen is not a bird. The parallel is significant, because as I will try to show, it is a fundamental misunderstanding to regard a general concept as if it provided necessary and sufficient conditions for inclusion within a category. On the contrary, the point of such a concept is precisely to enable us to recognize less than perfect examples of a kind — including, in the case of living creatures, individuals who are immature, ill or injured, or otherwise impeded from optimum functioning in an appropriate environment — and to analyze them in terms of the ideal set by the concept. Let us begin, then, by returning to the question of what it means to have a concept of any kind of living creature.

In the last section, I quoted Mayr as saying that beyond the most basic level of species, the higher taxa of creatures are defined in accordance with intrinsic characteristics: "Birds is the class of feathered vertebrates. Any and all species that satisfy the definition of 'feathered vertebrates' belong to the class of birds. An essentialist definition is satisfactory and sufficient at the level of the higher taxa." If this is so, it would seem that we have straightforwardly answered the question of whether we are able to form concepts of kinds of creatures, because here we have an example of such a concept. That is to say, if Mayr is correct, then we have a concept, expressed in a classical Aristotelian definition, of what it is to be a bird: a bird is a vertebrate (general kind) with feathers (specifying characteristic). And in fact, I would argue that Mayr's definition does provide us with some true knowledge of what it is to be a bird — and furthermore, that we can, and in fact do, have knowledge of an analogous kind concerning what it means to be a human being.

However, it would be a mistake to assume that Mayr's definition of "bird" should count as a complete definition, expressing a fully adequate concept of what it is to be a bird. Indeed, it is not clear that such a thing would be possible, given the current and foreseeable state of biological science. We need to examine this point a little further, because in order to understand the character and scope of the knowledge that we can genuinely have of biological kinds — including ourselves — we first of all need to be aware of the limitations of this kind of knowledge.

In the first section, I referred to MacIntyre's theory of rationality as tradition-based inquiry in order to make the point that realism is compatible with the view that all inquiry is shaped by the social context within which it emerges. In order to do so, it is necessary to explain how culturally bound processes of inquiry can yield genuine, nonarbitrary assessments and critiques of claims arising from within rival contexts. MacIntyre's own theory represents one such account, not the only one possible, but one I find persuasive. I return to MacIntyre's theory now, because it suggests an account of the way in which we can come close to attaining adequate concepts of kinds of living creatures, even though our access to these creatures will always be mediated through a framework of socially specific perceptions and beliefs. The main lines of that answer are suggested by his 1990 Marquette University Aquinas lecture, *First Principles, Final Ends, and Contemporary Philosophical Issues.*[76] In this lecture MacIntyre focuses on Aquinas's claim that all reasoning takes its starting points from first principles that need no justification, because they are *per se nota.* Given MacIntyre's own critique of Enlightenment foundationalism, we might expect him to reject this claim out of hand. On the contrary he defends it, arguing that even though Aquinas's *per se nota* principles are in some sense the starting points for all reflection, they nonetheless do not function as foundational first principles in an invidious sense.[77]

76. Alasdair MacIntyre, *First Principles, Final Ends, and Contemporary Philosophical Issues* (Milwaukee: Marquette University Press, 1990). Compare the much briefer but essentially similar analysis of deduction, dialectic, and the idea of a science according to Aristotle and Aquinas in *Whose Justice? Which Rationality?* 172-73. For further details on the Aristotelian ideal of science and its medieval reception, see Eileen Serene, "The Interpretation of Aristotle's *Physics* and the Science of Motion," in *The Cambridge History of Later Medieval Philosophy,* 521-36, especially 479-80. Coleman likewise emphasizes the Aristotelian underpinnings of Aquinas's metaphysical realism, and I suspect that she and MacIntyre are now closer on this point than would have appeared when she wrote; see "MacIntyre and Aquinas," passim. Finally, Lisska appropriates the work of Saul Kripke and Hilary Putnam to defend a similar realism about definitions; see *Aquinas's Theory,* 82-115. However, I am persuaded by David Charles that the Kripke/Putnam theory of reference is finally inconsistent with an Aristotelian — and, I would add, Thomistic — theory of meaning and scientific inquiry. See his *Aristotle on Meaning and Essence* (Oxford: Oxford University Press, 2000), 4-22, for a summary of the argument.

77. A principle is *per se nota* ("known through itself") if the predicate is in some way implied by the meaning of the subject; however, such principles are not necessarily self-evident to us, because the meaning of the relevant terms may only be apparent after extensive reflection. MacIntyre denies that we will always be able to discern the truth of these principles a priori, or correlatively, that a correct grasp of these principles provides the necessary starting point for inquiry into the relevant subject; see *First Principles,* 30-31.

The key to understanding Aquinas's account, he argues, is found in the Aristotelian conception of a perfect science, which Aquinas takes over and extends.[78] On this view, a perfected science would consist of a series of propositions perspicuously derived from first principles, which are primary in the sense that they cannot be justified in terms of the principles of the relevant science, although they may be justified in terms of some higher science.[79] So far, this would seem to be very different from, not to say antithetical to, MacIntyre's more familiar theory of rationality as tradition-guided inquiry. But he adds a critical qualification to this account — namely, the role which the first principles play in a completed science is logical or conceptual, but not epistemic. The claims of a true science do in fact follow from its first principles, but this may not be apparent until the science actually is completed, in such a way as to render the relationship between principles and conclusions perspicuous.[80] Matters are very different when we are dealing with a science that is still in the process of development, and this of course would apply to nearly every actual form of inquiry with which we have to deal.[81]

At this point, the incongruity between MacIntyre's interpretation of Aquinas's theory of knowledge and his own account of rationality as tradition-guided inquiry is dissipated. Even though he does not describe a developing science as a tradition in *First Principles*, his description of a science in the process of formation is similar in several key respects to his account of a developing tradition in *Whose Justice? Which Rationality?* It begins from contingent starting points; it develops through a process of self-

78. MacIntyre, *First Principles*, 25, 28-29.

79. MacIntyre, *First Principles*, 36-37.

80. On the logical as opposed to epistemic priority of first principles, see MacIntyre, *First Principles*, 10; cf. 34-35. MacIntyre also emphasizes this point in *Whose Justice? Which Rationality?* 172-73. MacIntyre goes on to say that the relation between the first principles and the claims of the science is a result, not a starting point for investigation, at *First Principles*, 30.

81. In my view, a plausible case can be made that physics is on the way to becoming a perfected science, and it is conceivable that some other physical sciences (astronomy, geology) and some branches of mathematics might similarly attain this status. However, given MacIntyre's very strong remarks on the inability of any intellect to know that it has attained final and definitive knowledge on some subject, he might well claim that no science can be considered to be perfected, even if we may reach a point at which we cannot imagine what a successful challenge to the science would look like. If I have understood him correctly, Lennox interprets Aristotle as developing a science of biology along the lines suggested by MacIntyre's analysis, although he does not refer specifically to MacIntyre; see *Aristotle's Philosophy of Biology*, 1-109. Similarly, Tkacz's analysis of Albert's biological writings in "Neo-Darwinians, Aristotelians, and Optimal Design" suggests that Albert too understood biology as a science in this sense. That being said, if it is indeed true that the processes of evolutionary development are irreducibly contingent, that would of course limit the extent to which biology ever could become, even in principle, a fully perfected science.

correction and expansion, until it reaches a level of complexity at which encounters with alternative explanations of the same set of phenomena can be fruitful; and it vindicates itself through an ongoing series of encounters with its rivals, showing how its explanations are more successful in terms which proponents of the rival views can themselves acknowledge.[82]

Consider, in this context, what MacIntyre has to say about the role of definitions in a perfected science:

> A perfected science is one which enables us to understand the phenomena of which it treats as necessarily being what they are, will be and have been, because of the variety of agencies which have brought it about that form of specific kinds has informed the relevant matter in such a way as to achieve some specific end state. *All understanding is thus in terms of the essential properties of specific kinds.* What those kinds are, how they are to be characterized, what the end state is to which those individuals which exemplify them move or are moved, those are matters about which — it seems plain from Aristotle's own scientific treatises as well as from modern scientific enquiry — there may well have been changes of view and even radical changes of view in the course of enquiry. The final definition of these matters in a perfected science may be the outcome of a number of reformulations and reclassifications which have come about in the course of enquiry.[83]

For those of us who find Aristotelian categories congenial, it is easy to assume that adequate definitions are a prerequisite of fruitful inquiry. But as MacIntyre shows, this assumption is at best overly simplistic. Certainly, in order to begin inquiry we need to be able to give at least rough definitions of some key concepts. But definitions which are adequate in this sense need not be adequate in the sense of fully representing "the essential properties of specific kinds." Indeed, we cannot expect to begin inquiry with these kinds of definitions, because successful definitions of this kind will be included in the outcome of a successful inquiry. We cannot define anything until we know what kind of thing it is, and we can only know this by locating it, in accordance with its specific kind, in relation to an array of other kinds of creatures. Moreover, the kinds of relations in question will be causal — they will be relations of derivation and generation grounded in first principles — and therefore they will also be hierarchical, pro-

82. See, respectively, MacIntyre, *First Principles* 31, 34-35, 37-38, and 32.

83. MacIntyre, *First Principles,* 27-28, emphasis added. MacIntyre's interpretation seems to me to be supported, at least in its outlines, by Charles's detailed analysis of the relevant Aristotelian texts; see *Meaning and Essence,* 274-304.

ceeding from fundamental and simple to remote and complex. Hence, on this account a fully adequate definition presupposes a fully developed causal theory, and can only be formulated in relation to that theory.

MacIntyre leaves it an open question whether any actual field of inquiry should count as a perfected science. It may well be that given the limitations of actual inquiry, the idea of a perfected science will always remain a regulative ideal, which actual fields of inquiry will more or less approximate, and which some kinds of inquiry may be incapable of attaining, even in principle. Even so, the idea of a perfected science offers a persuasive and useful regulative ideal, in terms of which the notion of adequacy of explanation can be analyzed, and our efforts of definition can be evaluated.[84]

Considered as such, that is to say, as a regulative ideal rather than an attainment, the ideal of a perfected science fits modern evolutionary biology very well. As the title of his best-known book indicates, Darwin himself regarded his explanation of the origin of species to be his definitive accomplishment: "I had two distinct goals in view," he once remarked, "firstly to show that species had not been separately created, and secondly, that natural selection had been the chief agent of change."[85] In other words, what Darwin claimed to provide is an analysis of what needs to be explained — the species of living things — in terms of a causal account of their origin and development from first principles — most prominently, natural selection. Seen from this perspective, what makes Darwin's explanation so persuasive and powerful is that it does place biology on the way toward becoming a perfected science, through which the basic terms of the science are related causally to first principles. Whether Darwin actually did provide such an explanation or not, whether some alternative explanation might be better, how comprehensive such an explanation can be — these are the issues which have informed evolutionary biology ever since, and appropriately so, since these are the kinds of questions that must be addressed if biology is to respect the regulative ideal set by the idea of a perfected science.

84. Even granting the "ideal" character of Aristotle's ideal of a science, however, this position implies a very strong realism indeed. In particular, it implies that at least some of the laws of nature formulated through (successful) scientific inquiry refer to logically necessary relations among kinds of things. This is a minority opinion among philosophers of science; it is well defended by Martin Tweedale in "Universals and Laws of Nature," *Philosophical Topics* 13 (1982): 25-44. This brings us back to the point of the first section; that is, there is no inconsistency between recognizing the contingent starting points of all inquiry (as MacIntyre does) and defending a very strong form of realism (as he also does).

85. Charles Darwin, *The Descent of Man*, 2nd ed. (London: Murray, 1889), p. 61; quoted by Stephen J. Gould, "Darwinism and the Expansion of Evolutionary Theory" (1982), in *Philosophy of Biology*, 100-117, here 100.

If a fully adequate definition of a biological kind presupposes that biology has already attained the status of a completed science, then needless to say, Mayr's definition of a bird is not a fully adequate definition. At the same time, neither is it false or even inadequate for most purposes. Not only does this definition distinguish "bird" from other taxa in accordance with a unique conjunction of distinguishing characteristics, it does so in terms of characteristics which can be related fairly straightforwardly to the fundamental principles of biological science. Certainly, Mayr's definition is too compressed to convey the necessary relations (which is one reason why it does not constitute a complete definition), but these could be spelled out in terms of the evolutionary advantages conferred by feathers, and the ways in which these are connected to a distinctive form of life within a particular environmental niche.

Assuming that we can develop Mayr's definition in the ways indicated, we do have (or potentially can have) some knowledge of the nature of a bird, which genuinely attains to what it is to be a bird, even though it is not comprehensive and complete. Yet this knowledge does not presuppose that we have direct access to the essence of avian existence. Rather, we attain it through a process of inquiry and reflection that is situated within a particular social context and never takes us outside the framework of some such context, although not necessarily the one with which we began.

Reflection on the natures of kinds of living creatures constitutes one of the oldest, best-developed, and culturally diverse traditions of inquiry, and we would expect to find that we know a great deal about these creatures. And so we do. Among other things, we know enough about a wide variety of creatures to recognize them, to relate them to other kinds of creatures, and to predict how they will behave and respond in a variety of circumstances. The beliefs in question are extensive and complex, and because they inform the background assumptions out of which we interact with other living creatures, they will almost always be at least partially implicit. Nonetheless, through reflection we can bring at least some of these beliefs to consciousness and formulate them in terms of modal statements describing the characteristic properties of kinds of things (for example, "all birds have feathers," "some mushrooms are poisonous," or "no cat reads Proust"). Once we have done so, we can assess them for truthfulness, and the odds are that many of them will indeed be true. (Otherwise, it is difficult to see how we could have survived long enough to carry out the exercise.)

These verified propositions, in turn, form the basis for causal and predictive theories about the origins, projected development, and possible modifications of both kinds of creatures and individuals within those kinds. To a significant degree, the relevant beliefs and theories concern patterns of behavior rather than morphological characteristics. They also include judgments about what counts as maturity and well-being for given kinds of creatures, and these in turn are largely couched in terms of the optimal way of life and patterns of behavior observed in creatures which are flourishing in accordance with their specific ideal of existence. Such beliefs, theories, and judgments do not lend themselves to formulation in a summary definition, and this provides a second reason — in addition to the incompleteness of biological science — why these definitions are incomplete. Nonetheless, they do serve as useful summary reminders of all that we do know about the natures of other kinds of living creatures, and so long as their limitations are kept in mind, they can generally be regarded as accurate expressions of those natures.

One other general point is in order. It is possible to offer an adequate definition of a natural kind in terms of the distinctive characteristics which mark it out from other kinds, without claiming that each and every member of the natural kind possesses all those distinctive characteristics. This may seem paradoxical, but if so, that is only because we assume that the characteristics identified by an adequate definition will necessarily be present in each and every member of the class identified by the definition. But we need not assume this. On the Aristotelian/Thomistic account adopted here, definitions are always in part (even if implicitly) relational — that is to say, they identify kinds of things by locating them within a framework of causal relationships, analyzed in light of the first principles of the science. This kind of causal analysis allows for the possibility that some members of a kind may actually lack some defining characteristic of that kind, in which case they would be considered incomplete, immature, or defective members of the kind. What this line of analysis does presuppose, however, is the possibility of telling some further causal story about the way in which the formal principles which define the kind in question have been partially engaged — otherwise, the individual in question would not be a member of the relevant kind at all — but not fully engaged — hence, the individual lacks some basic characteristic proper to the kind. Normally, such an account will be developed in one of two ways: through a narrative of proper development, in terms of which the individual is characterized as incomplete or immature; or through a narrative of lack, deficiency, or interference, in terms of which the individual is characterized as defective.

And at this point we see further confirmation for the conclusion of the last section. That is, on this account, any conception of a kind of creature that is even approximately adequate will necessarily be teleological. That is to say, it will necessarily incorporate some account of the complete, mature, or ideal state, in terms of which incomplete, immature, or defective individuals can be identified as such. Correlatively, an adequate conception will normally presuppose some causal account in terms of which incomplete development and deficiency can be explained in terms of the unfinished or thwarted expression of formal principles. Once again, we see that formal and final principles are mutually implicating, and both must be understood in such a way as to connect them to relevant forms of efficient causality — as we noted above.[86]

This brings me at last to the point of this section. We ourselves also constitute a kind of living creature, and it is therefore not surprising that we have the same kinds of beliefs, theories, and judgments about our own nature as we have for other kinds of living creatures. Pinker's list of cultural universals represents only a small fraction of what we know about ourselves. Indeed, there can be no doubt that we have an enormous fund of such beliefs, theories, and judgments — this is the stuff of folk wisdom, proverbs, the healing arts, sex manuals, educational practices, negotiating strategies, and the whole spectrum of psychological and social beliefs which form one part of the patrimony of the human race. Undoubtedly much of this — perhaps most of it — is inaccurate or limited in scope and relevance, but it is difficult to believe that there is nothing here which constitutes, or could even serve as a foundation for, genuine knowledge of human nature. When we take into account, in addition, the cumulative results of philosophical speculation and scientific research and theorizing, including the work of the social as well as the "hard" sciences, it appears that we can confidently claim to know a great deal about what it means to be human, and by implication, what a good life for the human person would look like.

In recent years, a few philosophers and not a few scientists have been prepared to say that we do indeed know something about the characteristic constitution of human nature, and by implication, we do know what it means to enjoy a distinctively human form of flourishing. There would perhaps have been more such voices if not for the prevalent assumption that unless our knowledge of human nature is comprehensive, complete, and subject to exhaustive formulation, we do not have any such knowledge — that is to say, our provisional, incomplete, and partially implicit knowledge about what it is to be human cannot count as knowledge of human nature. But as we have

86. This implies that explanations in biology will be teleological at two levels — in addition to the fundamental teleological component inherent in all forms of explanation, and particularly important with reference to living creatures, there is also a second distinctive level connected with the teleology inherent in adaptive explanations.

seen, our knowledge of the nature of every kind of living creature is necessarily provisional, incomplete, and partially implicit. There is no reason to expect our knowledge of ourselves to escape these limitations — and by the same token, there is no reason to deny that our beliefs about ourselves, partial and limited though they are, nonetheless offer at least the foundations for true knowledge of human nature.

At the beginning of this section, we noted that the claim that there is such a thing as a determinate human nature which reflects our continuities with a wider natural order has generated considerable unease. The scholastics would have been sympathetic to these worries — after all, as we will see further on, they also insisted on the discontinuity between the human person and the rest of creation, a discontinuity captured in the rich, pervasive motif of the Image of God. But for them, this discontinuity can only be understood in the context of the many continuities between the human person and the rest of creation. Indeed, the distinctive dignity of the human person owes a great deal to this interplay between the natural, broadly understood to include the human being's status as an animal and a created being, and the rational, which is itself the mark of a distinctive kind of nature, operating however in such a way as to go beyond the boundaries delimiting other kinds of natures.

For Aquinas, the distinctiveness-in-continuity of the human person is expressed in terms of the relation between the eternal law and the natural law.[87] The eternal law is nothing other than God's wisdom expressed in the providential sustenance of the created order, considered as a kind of law (*ST* I-II 91.1; 93.1); all creatures are said to be governed by the eternal law, insofar as they exist and operate in accordance with the intelligible principles proper to them as created natures of a given kind (93.4, 5). The human person participates in the eternal law in a distinctive way, insofar as she is capable of free judgment and self-direction through her own actions: "Hence, it is plain that the natural law is nothing other than a participation of the eternal law in the rational creature" (91.2). But it is no less apparent that the distinctive operations of the human person represent one form of a universal phenomenon, that is to say, the participation of all creatures in divine providence through their proper operations, stemming from their natural inclinations. That is why Aquinas can also say that "The natural inclination in those things devoid

87. Aquinas is one of only a few scholastics who appeal to Augustine's notion of the eternal law to explicate the natural law, and he does so in such a way as to emphasize the wisdom, rather than the authoritative character, of eternal law; see my *Natural and Divine Law,* 160-64, for further details.

of reason indicates the natural inclination belonging to the will of an intellectual nature" (I 60.5). This remark does not impugn the distinctiveness of human nature (or much less angelic nature, which he is discussing at this point), but it does remind us that human nature expresses, in its own distinctive way, to be sure, those general principles of intelligibility which are the marks of God's creative wisdom.[88]

Hence, the human person's distinctiveness does not preclude a knowledge of human nature, nor does it obviate the need to reflect on human well-being in naturalistic terms. After all, whatever we may say about the human person's self-transcending capacities and divine destiny, men and women are first of all and most obviously part of the natural order, animals among other animals, creatures among other creatures. There is no reason to deny that we know a great deal about ourselves under these rubrics, or to affirm the normative, and ultimately the moral significance of much of this knowledge.

Of course, our knowledge of ourselves will be more complex, and for that reason more subject to provisionality and error, than our knowledge of other kinds of creatures — because we are hardly disinterested observers of ourselves, and even more because we are considerably more complex than even the most advanced subrational animals. Our ideas about what counts as human flourishing, in particular, will be more complex than parallel views regarding other kinds of animals, if only because there appear to be a wide variety of ways in which human persons can flourish and no immediately obvious criteria by which to judge among them. To return to a point that has already been made, our shared nature underdetermines the particular set of moral ideals and practices in which it is expressed, for just the same reason that our nature underdetermines the particular social form in which it is expressed. Our knowledge of human nature will always be to some degree inferential. We do not have direct access to human nature apart from the mediation of some cultural form or other, and for this reason our knowledge of what it is to be human will necessarily be dependent, to a considerable degree although not entirely, on a process of comparative assessments of the diverse forms that human life can take, and correlatively, abstraction from particular social expressions. We will always need to be particularly careful not to gener-

88. As Bastit would remind us, this does not imply that there is any immediate link between rational and intellectual natures and the broad principles of intelligibility they express, along the lines of a Platonic hierarchy intermediate between God and creatures; rather, we can understand rational intellectual natures by analogy to nonrational natures, up to a point, because all these kinds of creatures stem from one cause, namely, God, and all express the principles of intelligibility proper to that cause — albeit in ways we cannot comprehend. Again, see "Le thomisme est-il un aristotélisme?" passim.

alize our own particular customs and preferences into general characteristics of humanity. But none of this should lead us to conclude that we have no knowledge of human nature at all, or that the knowledge we have is unimportant or morally irrelevant.

Yet the fact that we know a great deal about human beings does not, in itself, mean that we grasp the concept of "human being," even in the provisional and tentative way outlined in this section. As Janet Coleman reminds us, human nature refers to "what is essentially human according to a *definition* of human being," and even if we cannot arrive at a fully articulated and adequate such definition, we need something more than an account of recurring features of human existence.[89] We also need an account of the way different components of human existence fit together as a "unified set of goal-ordered capacities." In particular, we need some idea of the overall goal toward which the fundamental capacities or inclinations of the human person are oriented, and in terms of which they can be rendered intelligible — and as we have already noted, this goal will be nothing other than the full flourishing of the creature, in accordance with the proper specific ideal of human nature. Obviously, this idea will be of special interest to moral theorists, but more fundamentally, we cannot even begin to grasp what it means to be a human being unless we have some idea of what it means to do well as a human being. The formal cause, considered as the intelligible interrelationship of the different capacities of the creature, and the final cause, considered as the ideal for the full development and functioning of a specific kind of creature, are in reality one and the same, even though they differ with respect to the terms of our own understanding.[90] In this way, some consideration of the meaning of human flourishing turns out to be integral to our efforts to understand what it means to be human, and not simply a further, additional inquiry, obviously relevant to moralists but optional for everyone else.

Seen in this context, our pluriform knowledge of ourselves is an embarrassment of riches. How can we bring order and coherence to the range of things we know about ourselves? As we noted above, Aquinas suggests that we can arrive at some understanding of what it means to be human by an analysis of the inclinations of the human creature, interpreted by analogy with the characteristic inclinations of other kinds of creatures (I 60.5). Further on, in his much-cited analysis of the coherence of the natural law, he analyzes distinctively human inclinations in terms of an ordered progression, from the most general and universally instantiated inclinations, to those that are

89. Coleman, "MacIntyre and Aquinas," 71, emphasis in original.

90. As Pasnau remarks; see *Thomas Aquinas,* 8, and more generally, 88-95.

proper to living creatures and to animals, up to those which are distinctive to the rational creature (I-II 94.2). This analysis provides us with the outline of a conception of human nature, in terms of which the characteristic inclinations of human life can be traced to the orderly set of goal-oriented capacities proper to human nature.

Given the preceding discussion, the advantages of this framework for formulating a provisional concept of human nature should be clear. Aquinas explicitly locates diverse human inclinations within a framework set by an analysis of the levels of created existence, beginning with the most basic level of simple existence and proceeding through ever more comprehensive levels of engagement with one's environment and world, that is to say, life, sentience, and rationality. The human person incorporates all these levels and thus exhibits inclinations proper to each, albeit in a distinctively human way. In addition, the human person displays inclinations presupposing rationality, which are as such characteristic of human nature. Nonetheless, human existence and flourishing cannot be understood in terms of these characteristically human inclinations alone; an adequate concept will also take account of the way in which the inclinations we share with other kinds of creatures are integrated into a characteristically human way of life.

Within this framework we can at least indicate in a preliminary way how diverse aspects of human existence and functioning might fit together to make up the "ordered set of goal-directed capacities" proper to human existence as such. If we follow Aquinas's analysis of basic inclinations as set forth at I-II 94.2, the first and most fundamental thing to be said about the human person is that she exists, a creature among other kinds of creatures, and as such, naturally desires continued existence. This most basic inclination underlies and informs the orientation toward the good which, in Aquinas's view, represents the fundamental active dynamism of every creature. For the human person, as for every other kind of creature, this orientation takes the form of an orientation toward one's own specific form of goodness — hence, for the human person, it takes the form of an orientation to exist as a human being, and to enjoy the fullest and most complete form of human existence available to it. This orientation is expressed, most fundamentally, in a natural desire to stay alive, to remain healthy, and to enjoy unimpeded functioning in accordance with one's basic capacities for action. Correlatively, if these are indeed fundamental inclinations of human nature, we would expect to find them expressed in diverse but recognizable forms in all (or nearly all) human societies — as seems indeed to be the case.

At the same time, the natural orientation toward goodness cannot simply be equated with the desire to exist and to attain perfection in accordance with one's specific kind, even for nonrational creatures. Aquinas claims, on the contrary, that every creature naturally desires the perfection — that is to say, the full and integrally complete development — of the cosmos considered as a whole, more than it desires its own existence and perfection. And even if we bracket this metaphysical claim, it does seem evident that the proper inclinations of nonrational creatures must sometimes be interpreted in relation to the existence and well-being of a more comprehensive reality than the individual — for example, one's kin or descendants, one's herd, or even one's species considered as a whole. Otherwise, the inclination of the male black widow spider to mate would be unintelligible, as would be the inclination of the female bird to lure predators away from her nest by offering herself as prey.

For the human person, the natural orientation toward the good is potentially even more expansive because it is mediated through the rational intellect, which is capable of forming judgments about what counts as good, and directing action accordingly. This capacity creates a conceptual space for distinctively moral judgments and assessments, because it opens up the possibility of acting in pursuit of lesser, partial, or seeming goods, in spite of greater, more comprehensive, or genuine goods. Of course, this claim raises questions to which we will need to return. In this context, I simply want to make the point that the distinctively human capacity for rational reflection on the good also opens up the possibility of identifying oneself with more comprehensive or abstract goods, and orienting one's desire for existence accordingly. Indeed, our knowledge of the inevitability of death provides a standing invitation to all reflective men and women to identify themselves with some more comprehensive reality, since finally the only alternatives to doing so are heedlessness or despair. That is why men and women can intelligibly choose to identify themselves with communities, causes, and ideals, to which they can sacrifice themselves, and it is also why people care so intensely about their family, their community, their glory and reputation after death; to the rational creature these larger goods are tantamount to life itself, natural forms of immortality for the sake of which one's individual existence might well be sacrificed. Nor need such choices be perverse — although of course, they can be.

Turning to a second level of analysis, we see the human person is not only a creature but a creature of a particular kind — that is to say, a living creature, and more specifically an animal. This means that for the human creature, the inclination to exist and to develop in accordance with one's specific ideal of perfection is at the same time an inclination to stay alive — for the living creature, existence *is* life — and to do so in a way appropriate to an animal, that is to say, attaining sustenance and security through an active engagement with one's environment. Hence, for the human creature, the inclination to exist will normally be expressed through natural desires to eat, drink, stay warm, and the like, desires we share with the other animals, and to some extent with plants as well. In addition, we also share a further desire with the higher animals, which can be analyzed as a further expression of the fundamental desire to exist and to exercise one's distinctive forms of causality. This is of course the inclination to reproduce one's kind, which for us, as with many other animals, takes the form of a desire to mate and to reproduce sexually. Here again, we must keep in mind that for the human person, these inclinations are mediated through reason, and they can accordingly be expressed in forms more or less detached from their most literal and basic manifestations. This is particularly true of the inclination to reproduce, which can be interpreted and expressed in terms of one's contributions to a community or an ideal apart from actual physical procreation, in somewhat the same way the fundamental inclination to continue in existence can be formulated and expressed in terms of sacrificing one's individual life to a greater whole. Furthermore, even taken in its most literal sense, human reproduction goes beyond physical procreation to include the education and socialization of one's children — a point the scholastics recognized, as we noted above.

Aquinas adds a third level of analysis, namely, those inclinations which express our distinctive character as rational animals, including inclinations to live in society, to seek the truth, and to worship God. At this point, however, contemporary scientific reflection on human nature suggests an expansion and development of Aquinas's analysis. It is becoming apparent that the inclination to live in society is not so distinctively rational as Aquinas and his contemporaries would have assumed. On the contrary, many kinds of animals exhibit structured social lives, and in the other higher primates, these take forms similar in many respects to what seem to be commonalities in human social existence — for example, the formation of mating and parental bonds, the existence of more or less structured hierarchies, and the regulation of the social unit through boundaries enforced through rewards and sanctions.[91] I describe this as a modification of Aquinas's analysis because the rational mediation of the social inclinations does make a critical difference to the ways in which these inclinations are experienced and expressed. Yet in order fully to appreciate this difference, it is necessary to place it within the context of the more fun-

91. For an engaging and persuasive interpretation of recent research on the social primates, defending this general conclusion, see Frans de Waal, *Good Natured: The Origins of Right and Wrong in Humans and Other Animals* (Cambridge: Harvard University Press, 1996).

damental natural inclination it expresses, namely, an inclination to a characteristically social form of life which we share with other higher animals.

Aquinas's analysis of the fundamental inclinations of the human person in terms of their (admittedly partial) analogies with the inclinations of other kinds of creatures provides us with a framework within which diverse human functions and activities can be rendered intelligible. I emphasize functions and activities rather than (for example) needs, capacities, or recurring characteristics advisedly, in order to emphasize once again that any adequate concept of a kind of living creature will reflect a grasp of the kinds of activities proper to that creature, or in other words, the "ordered functions" which constitute its proper form. Morphology and recurrent physical characteristics will also be relevant in this context, but not fundamental, if only because these are intelligible only in terms of the role they play in the proper functioning of the creature.

This, incidentally, points to a further reason why concepts of living creatures are not tied to necessary and sufficient conditions for falling within a class. If what is at stake is a particular ordered way of life, in which diverse individuals are integrated in a variety of ways, then no one individual need display all the characteristics exhibited in this way of life, nor will we necessarily find that every individual shares some one characteristic. What we should expect to find, however, is that each individual shares some combination of distinctive characteristics, in terms of which it intelligibly participates in the ordered functions and way of life common to the kind as a whole.

In the case at hand, an adequate concept of the human person will be a concept of the way of life characteristic of the species. And while the distinctively human way of life can of course be expressed in an indefinite number of ways, we can identify broad, species-specific patterns of behavior proper to our existence as highly sophisticated social primates. We have already mentioned the main lines of this pattern: we form relatively long-lasting bonds with our mates, and sexual behavior is in some way regulated to respect these bonds; we care for our children over an extended period of time; we draw distinctions among the social roles proper to different sexes and ages, although the precise content of these distinctions is indefinitely variable; we organize our communities hierarchically, although again the exact form this takes, and the strength and permanence of the relevant relations, vary very widely; and we maintain social roles through a complex network of sanctions and rewards. So far, all these reflect patterns of behavior that we share with at least some other animals. As the last item on the above list would suggest, even morality can be understood — up to a point — in naturalistic terms as an expression of the distinctive form of functioning proper to us as a kind of creature.

We will turn in later chapters to a consideration of those inclinations and forms of activity that do seem to be distinctively human, beginning with the distinctively human way in which we carry out social activities. As we will see, human social life, and much more human morality, cannot be understood solely in terms of an analysis proper to other animals. At the same time, however, neither can we understand human social behavior, and even human morality, until we recognize that it is a distinctive expression of a more general phenomenon, namely, a way of life characteristic of all the higher primates. Once again, we are brought back to a scholastic insight; the distinctiveness of the human does not obviate our continuities with the rest of the created world.

These considerations give us a context within which to assess the familiar argument, long associated with David Hume and G. E. Moore, to the effect that we cannot draw moral conclusions from factual premises.[92] In its most powerful form, this argument turns on the observation — in itself hardly controversial — that the conclusions of a syllogism cannot include anything not contained in the premises; hence, we cannot deduce moral conclusions from factual premises. However, taken as a generalized argument against any kind of naturalistic ethic, this argument presupposes a strict distinction between factual and normative claims, a distinction that does not stand up to close scrutiny. As Philippa Foot argued over forty years ago, evaluative terms have an inextricable descriptive content, which cannot be separated from the attitudes they express without intolerable distortions of meaning.[93] (For example, it would be nonsensical to say that someone who spends his life in a state of perpetual, quivering anxiety is a brave man — or at least, such a claim

92. The relevant texts are David Hume, *A Treatise of Human Nature,* ed. L. A. Selby-Bigge (Oxford: Oxford University Press, 1888), 469, and G. E. Moore, *Principia Ethica* (Cambridge: Cambridge University Press, 1903; reprinted 1948), 46-58.

93. Specifically, in "Moral Arguments," first published in 1958, and "Moral Beliefs," published in 1958-59, reprinted in Philippa Foot, *Virtues and Vices and Other Essays in Moral Philosophy* (Berkeley: University of California Press, 1978), 96-109 and 110-31 respectively. Of course, Foot has returned to these issues many times since; she summarizes the later trajectory of her thought in the introduction to her *Moral Dilemmas and Other Topics in Moral Philosophy* (Oxford: Clarendon, 2002), 1-3. More recently, Hilary Putnam has argued that Hume's argument should not be understood as a claim about the validity of certain forms of inference, nor did Hume himself understand it in that way. Rather, it depends on Hume's wider thesis about the proper division between matters of fact and values, a thesis which depends on his overall metaphysics. This seems exactly right to me, although I do not share Putnam's further view (if I have understood him correctly) that we should dispense with metaphysics altogether. See Hilary Putnam, *The Collapse of the Fact/Value Dichotomy and Other Essays* (Cambridge: Harvard University Press, 2002), 7-45.

would call for a lot of explanation.) If we grant the legitimacy of a teleological conception of human nature, the same point can be made at a more basic level. That is, on this view statements about human nature need not be "merely" factual, in the sense presupposed by this objection. No doubt some will be, but many others will reflect the inextricable interconnection between descriptive and evaluative terms, as these are applied to living creatures.

This brings me to a more general observation. The arguments of Hume and Moore were developed within the context of Enlightenment foundationalism, and as such have been shaped by a presupposition well described by John McDowell: "Modern philosophy has taken itself to be called on to bridge dualistic gulfs, between subject and object, thought and world."[94] In the case at hand, appeals to a naturalistic fallacy presuppose a gulf between the factual and the normative, and insist that this gulf cannot be bridged, with the consequence that moral arguments must be in some way self-standing, based on sentiments (as Hume claims), or nonnatural properties attaching to states of affairs (according to Moore), or some other distinctive and nonfactual basis, which nonetheless mirrors the objectivity of the factual in some way. Throughout the past century, the very existence of such a gulf has been challenged on a number of grounds (not all of them consistent with the theory being advanced here), and the persuasiveness of "naturalistic fallacy" arguments has correspondingly been undermined.[95]

Yet arguments along these lines continue to be advanced, albeit not usually in the precise terms set forth by Hume and Moore. The persistence of these arguments suggests that there is, after all, something to them, at least in the sense that they reflect a widespread unease about the prospect of moving too quickly from supposed facts about human nature to moral conclusions. And we ought to take this unease seriously, because even if we conclude that "nature as nature" is morally significant, that does not mean that everything we know about ourselves carries a perspicuous moral significance, or much

94. McDowell, *Mind and World,* 93.

95. In addition to the authors cited above, see A. N. Prior, *Logic and the Basis of Ethics* (Oxford: Oxford University Press, 1949), and Julius Kovesi, *Moral Notions* (London: Routledge and Kegan Paul, 1967), especially 37-65. Foot was especially influenced by Prior, but as Charles Pigden points out, Prior actually defends Hume in his 1949 monograph, although he later came to change his mind; see "Logic and the Autonomy of Ethics," *Australian Journal of Philosophy* 67, no. 2 (1989): 127-51. He himself takes the line that the Hume/Moore argument is valid but limited in scope; see 127-28 in particular. He also provides a helpful summary of recent work on this question in his "Naturalism," in *A Companion to Ethics,* ed. Peter Singer (Oxford: Blackwell Press, 1993), 421-31. Finally, Lisska defends Aquinas against the charge of committing the naturalistic fallacy in *Aquinas's Theory,* 195-201.

less that we can or should regard our actual mores and social arrangements as the inevitable expressions of a morally charged nature. In the last chapter, we noted that the scholastics themselves rejected Aristotle's approach to natural law, according to which social norms are immediate and organic expressions of human nature, in favor of a Ciceronian approach that gives a central role to rational reflection and social construction. The defenders of a deterministic "evolutionary ethics" based on evolutionary psychology might be regarded as Aristotle's heirs in this respect (and only in this respect), whereas the theory of the natural law that I am proposing adopts, in this respect, a Ciceronian rather than an Aristotelian approach. On this approach, a teleological conception of human nature represents an essential first step in developing an account of the natural law, but further steps need to be taken. We turn now to a closer examination of this point.

5. Ethical Naturalism, Reason, and the Natural Law

If the teleological conception of the human person outlined above is persuasive, it might seem that we have said all that needs to be said about the basis for moral judgments, and our only remaining task is to fill in the details. Philippa Foot endorses this view when she says that "I believe that evaluations of human will and action share a conceptual structure with evaluations of characteristics and operations of other living things, and can only be understood in these terms. I want to show moral evil as 'a kind of natural defect.' *Life* will be at the centre of my discussion, and the fact that a human action or disposition is good of its kind will be taken to be simply a fact about a given feature of a certain kind of living thing."[96] In the next chapter, it will be apparent how much I owe to the ethical naturalism developed by Foot and others. Nonetheless, I believe she moves too quickly here.

I have argued elsewhere that the scholastic approach to the natural law presupposes a kind of ethical naturalism, and the theological approach being developed here certainly does so.[97] "Ethical naturalism" can be understood in more than one way; what I presuppose, more specifically, is that human morality in all its culturally diverse forms is an expression of the distinctive inclinations and activities proper to the human animal, especially (but not only)

96. Foot, *Natural Goodness*, 5, emphasis in original.

97. *Natural and Divine Law*, 98-120. "Naturalism" can be understood in more than one way of course, as Pasnau observes (*Thomas Aquinas*, 202), and needless to say, I do not mean to endorse any version of naturalism which would imply that God does not exist, or which would rule out the Aristotelian essentialism defended here.

the distinctive forms of human social behavior. As such, morality should be understood first of all as a natural phenomenon, "natural" in contrast to "transcendentally grounded" or "implicitly divine." At the same time, human morality in all its diverse forms reflects the goodness of the human creature, and as such it is an expression of God's will that creatures should exist and flourish — whatever we are to say more specifically about the substance of particular moralities.

But of course, most people expect more out of an account of morality, namely, some criterion or method by which to assess and correct (or reject) different moral claims and systems. This is the point at which we are brought up against the limits of a naturalistic approach to morality, taken by itself. For even granting that we can formulate a concept of what it is to be human, including centrally an account of the characteristic activities proper to us as a kind of living creature, nonetheless it is apparent that these characteristic activities can be expressed in indefinitely many ways. Appeals to human nature at this level will not help us decide among these alternatives, because what they have in common is precisely their status as expressions of our shared nature. Thus, as John Kekes argues, human nature underdetermines moral norms, at least at a level sufficiently concrete to be put into practice.[98] At best, we might be able to formulate general principles expressing these natural patterns of behavior, but if these are to be at all plausible as expressions of universal tendencies, they will necessarily be too broad to serve as moral principles, without further — necessarily particular and contentious — specification. This becomes apparent when we consider candidates for such principles: "Do not take human life without adequate reason," for example, or "Observe limits in pursuit of sexual relations." For this reason, any attempt to move from the naturalistic foundations of morality to a fully developed account of the natural law will call for further theoretical elaboration — and that will be the task of subsequent chapters.

At this point, however, some may want to pose an objection. That is to say, given that nature underdetermines morality in this way, why appeal to nature at all? The trajectory of Catholic moral theology since at least the middle of the twentieth century suggests an obvious alternative. Why not develop a natural law ethic based on the deliverances of practical reason alone? After all, reason is natural to the human person, arguably the proper and defining characteristic of humanity, so a morality of reason can justifiably be regarded as a kind of natural law morality.

Yet on closer examination, appeals to reason as a basis for morality run

98. John Kekes, "Human Nature and Moral Theories," *Inquiry* 28 (1985): 231-45, here 244.

into similar difficulties. "Reason" is a protean term, just as much as "nature," and it is by no means clear just what the deliverances or proper operations of reason are supposed to be. Even if we grant (as I would do) that there are certain fundamental laws of logic which must be observed if a given discourse is to count as reasoning, these principles by themselves notoriously cannot yield substantive conclusions. Similarly, even if we accept (as I do) Aquinas's claim that practical reason also starts from first principles, including most fundamentally the principle that the good is to be sought and done, and the bad avoided, these principles are too general to yield practical conclusions by themselves. Reason, like nature, underdetermines the moral conclusions that are supposed to flow from it.

Or does it? This latter claim is challenged by the "new theory of the natural law" developed over more than thirty years by Germain Grisez, John Finnis, and their associates. As we saw in the last chapter, this theory postulates basic goods which are self-evidently such, which provide the fundamental reasons for all actions, and which cannot rationally be rejected through direct actions. While no one can pursue all the basic goods and must perforce prefer some to others in practice, there is no objective basis for preferring one to another, such that we might be justified in sacrificing an instance of one good in order to secure or preserve some instance of another. Hence, in order for an action to count as fully reasonable, which is to say morally justified, it must reflect a stance of openness toward all the basic goods, insofar as it does not involve acting directly against any of them. It would take us too far afield to spell out exactly what it would mean to act against or directly to reject a basic good, but the general idea is simple enough; actions which involve destroying some instantiation of a basic good (e.g., killing someone), or directly forestalling the instantiation of such a good (e.g., the use of contraceptives), are paradigmatic examples of such acts.

The scholastic approach to the natural law is similar to this theory in one respect. That is, the scholastics would generally agree that human persons are naturally — implying, in this context, spontaneously, without reflection — oriented toward fundamental goods such as life and procreation. Our natural orientation toward such goods provides the starting points for human desire, practical reflection, and choice, and in that sense they can be described as basic goods. By the same token, we do not need extensive theoretical analysis in order to perceive these basic goods as desirable, nor do we necessarily need to reflect much in order to pursue them appropriately. Precisely because we are naturally oriented toward these goods, we spontaneously find them desirable and pursue them — at least until conflicts or circumstances force us to reflection.

But it is one thing to say that we are naturally oriented toward certain desiderata, and this orientation provides a natural starting point for practical reflection and moral action. It is something else again to say that we have a rational grasp of certain basic goods, elemental enough to be regarded plausibly as self-evident to all and yet provided with enough content to provide an immediate basis for practical reflection. This is a less plausible claim. According to Grisez and Finnis, there are eight basic goods, namely, life (including health and procreation), knowledge and aesthetic appreciation, skilled performances of all kinds, self-integration, authenticity or practical reasonableness, justice and friendship, marriage, and religion or holiness.[99] The claim that these goods are self-evidently manifest as such as soon as they are experienced is indeed plausible with respect to some of these, such as life or knowledge. Even with respect to such goods, however, Grisez and Finnis find it necessary to qualify what these goods comprise in order to show how certain moral conclusions flow from them; for example, life is expanded to include procreation, in order to justify the claim that the use of contraceptives involves "acting against" the good of life. While a case can be made that the inclination to procreate is indeed an expression of a more fundamental inclination to live and flourish, this conclusion can hardly be said to be self-evidently contained in the apprehension of the goodness of life itself. On the contrary, it requires a metaphysical argument along the lines sketched in the preceding section — precisely the kind of argument Grisez and Finnis reject as a basis for moral conclusions.

At any rate, with respect to most of the other basic goods, the claim that these are self-evidently recognized to be good and worthy of pursuit as soon as they are grasped is more dubious. Is it self-evident that personal integrity is a basic good? What about practical reasonableness? There do seem to be people who don't care about either of these goods, and while we may consider their attitude to be reprehensible, it is difficult to make out a case that it is somehow incoherent. What is more, it is difficult to say just what it would mean to *experience* such goods as integrity and practical reasonableness, or much less justice. After all, these terms refer to assessments of a person's character, or his choices and actions. The kinds of assessments in question can only be carried out through a framework of prior judgments, including moral and more broadly normative judgments, concerning the standards by

99. This list (with the exception of marriage) is taken from Germain Grisez, *The Way of the Lord Jesus 1: Christian Moral Principles* (Chicago: Franciscan Herald Press, 1983), 124. Marriage is a later addition; see *The Way of the Lord Jesus 2: Living a Christian Life* (Chicago: Franciscan Herald Press, 1993), 568.

which character and acts are to be evaluated. Since this is the case, it is difficult to see how these goods can count as basic in the requisite sense — certainly, they are not even experienced, much less incorporated into moral reflection, prior to the deployment of a range of normative commitments. Even more seemingly straightforward goods such as friendship seem to raise similar problems — after all, what counts as friendship, and how can we experience it apart from a normatively laden social context of interactions? Marriage offers a still more obvious example of a good that does not even exist, much less manifest itself to a rational apprehension, apart from social construction.

Even if Grisez and Finnis were able to make out a plausible case for self-evident basic goods in the requisite sense, they would still need to show that our grasp of these goods can yield specific moral conclusions without the need of appealing to anything beyond the deliverances of practical reason, taken together with facts providing the subject matter, as it were, of human action. This requires further specification of just what practical reason is supposed to deliver. The basic goods are said to be not only self-evidently desirable and productive of action, but also the *only* fully justifiable reasons for action; if any other kinds of reasons were admitted, this would mean that moral claims might depend on something other than the requirements of practical reasonableness alone. By the same token, these goods cannot be ranked or placed within the framework of some overarching aim or meaning of life, because any such criteria for ranking and contextualizing the goods would have to be derived, illegitimately, from scientific or metaphysical claims. Finally, in order to translate our intuitions of the basic goods into moral norms, it is necessary to appeal in addition to what Grisez describes as eight "modes of responsibility," similarly self-evident to any rational person, including most notably modes which rule out any kind of activity which impedes a basic good from coming about, or damages or destroys an instantiation of such a good.[100]

In order for their theory to work, Grisez and Finnis must not only show that these principles capture the way in which practical reason works, when it is functioning correctly; they must also show that these principles express the way practical reason necessarily must work when functioning in good order. And it is difficult to see how this case could be made, if only because we do not reason about practical matters in the way that Finnis and Grisez suggest we do. We desire and seek objects or states of affairs, and these are desirable to us because they fit into ongoing needs, desires, projects, and long-standing

100. See *The Way of the Lord Jesus 1*, 205-28; the eight modes are summarized at 225-26.

commitments, whether our own or those of people, communities, or ideals toward which we are committed. Even if these desiderata could be analyzed without remainder into a set of basic goods (and this is not apparent), we do not desire them simply *as* instantiations of basic goods; we desire them because they promote the overall well-being of people and other entities about which we have some concern, or avert harm from them. By the same token, we inevitably find ourselves weighing different desiderata against one another in the light of our overall concerns and commitments, and this process will on occasion lead us to "act against" some goods, precisely in order to preserve other weightier or more urgent desiderata. As Aquinas remarks, reason in its practical operations properly engages in the task of ordering diverse aims in accordance with one's overall end in acting: "this has right reason, that one should make use of those things which are for an end in accordance with a measure which is congruent to the end" (II-II 152.2). As he goes on to explain, this implies that exterior goods are ordered to the well-being of the body; bodily goods are oriented toward the well-being of the soul, and the goods which are proper to the active life are ordered to the goods of the contemplative life (152.2). Ordering, comparative judgments, and preferential choices are integral aspects of practical reasoning as we experience it.

Of course, Grisez and Finnis might reply that we are wrong, radically so, about what practical reason involves. But why should we accept such a claim? They justify it on the grounds that only on their analysis can practical reason avoid illegitimate inferences from states of affairs or metaphysical claims to moral judgments. As such, they offer a good illustration of McDowell's observation that "Ordinary modern philosophy addresses its derivative dualisms in a characteristic way. It takes its stand on one side of a gulf it aims to bridge, accepting without question the way its target dualism conceives the chosen side. Then it constructs something as close as possible to the conception of the other side that figured in the problems, out of materials that are unproblematically available where it has taken its stand. Of course there no longer seems to be a gulf, but the result is bound to look more or less revisionist."[101] But if we agree with McDowell that there is no such gulf, then there is no compelling theoretical justification for the radically new structure of practical reasoning that Grisez and Finnis have proposed.

It is impossible to prove a negative, but the difficulties raised by the

101. McDowell, *Mind and World,* 94. The revisionist character of the "new natural law" is most evidently manifested by the fact that its defenders have to resort to increasingly complex arguments about the implications of self-standing reason, in order to justify claims that were traditionally justified more straightforwardly by appeals to the moral significance of nature broadly considered.

Grisez/Finnis theory of the natural law at least suggest that "pure reason" is no more promising than "pure nature" as a basis for a theory of morality. If this is so, then whatever the promises and limits of a naturalistic ethic, we cannot claim that a moral theory grounded in reason provides us with a clear alternative. And there are, in addition, at least two positive reasons for taking a naturalistic ethic seriously as a starting point for developing a theological account of the natural law. The first is more general, and the second is more properly theological.

The first of these may be simply stated. Even though it is true that the natural origins of morality underdetermine its particular expressions, nonetheless these are not simply displaced by the specific moralities which express them. To put the same point positively, the social structures and patterns of interaction natural to us as a species seem to recur in some form in nearly all moral systems. A given morality can thus be understood as a culturally and historically specific way of expressing the general social structures natural to us as a species. Certainly, we have no direct access to these general structures, but we can infer quite a bit about them through cross-cultural comparisons, taken together with studies of the social structures displayed by the other higher primates. And our knowledge of these structures, inferential and incomplete though it will necessarily be, can nonetheless provide us with a framework within which particular moralities can be recognized for what they are — that is to say, specifications of general patterns of action — and compared accordingly. By itself, this framework will not provide us with a sufficient basis for comparative assessments, but it will provide needed starting points and framework for such assessments.

Moreover, the basic social structures natural to us as a species do provide some standards for evaluation, not so much for the moralities which instantiate them as for the second-order theories which attempt to rationalize these moralities. In other words, the natural social structures which inform morality provide criteria for plausibility and adequacy for theories of morality — whether explicitly or (usually) not. Moral theories which imply that fundamental aspects of human social existence are without value, or worse, positively wicked — for example, kin preferences — strike most theorists as prima facie implausible.[102] Sometimes this reaction is expressed in terms of the impossibility of putting certain kinds of theories into practice, and sometimes it takes the simpler form of frank unwillingness to accept the implications of a particular line of argument, but in either case (I would suggest) it

102. Pope offers a defense of kin preferences by appealing to a Thomistic natural law argument in *The Evolution of Altruism,* passim.

reflects a deeper sense that a moral theory has become detached from the fundamental realities that it was meant to interpret.

In the conclusion of his detailed and illuminating comparison of the accounts of virtue developed by Aquinas and the Chinese philosopher Mencius (fourth century B.C.E.), Lee Yearley observes that these accounts can usefully be understood as occupying a kind of middle space between two levels of theoretical speculation. Drawing on a distinction by the anthropologist Robin Horton, he observes that all cultures presuppose a body of observational knowledge and rough predictive theories about the natural world and human life. He refers to this as the primary level of theorizing, in contrast to a secondary level of theoretical reflection, which attempts to make sense of common experiences through specific philosophical, religious, and scientific theories. As we would expect, theories at the second level vary widely from one culture to another, even though there is considerable cross-cultural consensus at the primary level — indeed, if there were not, we would not be able to recognize the secondary theories as conflicting theories of the same set of realities.[103]

Moral theories, or as Yearley prefers, practical theories, occupy a middle space between these two levels, precisely because they represent attempts to interpret experiences of human life at the primary level in terms of theoretical constructs developed at the secondary level. As such, these theories reflect a broad cross-cultural consensus on the saliency of certain recurring situations, for example, the need to regulate violence or to provide for the care of children, the value of some recurrent traits such as courage or generosity, and the undesirability of others such as cowardice or selfishness. These broad areas of convergence help to explain why there is so much cross-cultural consensus on moral questions, particularly with respect to the fundamental virtues and vices. This wide consensus has led many to assume that there is in fact a substantive universal morality. But as Yearley cautions us, this consensus is broad, but it is also relatively thin — that is to say, it conceals deep disagreements about the substantive content and practical implications of widely shared commitments and ideals. Moreover, as he also notes, the further we move toward theoretical interpretation of moral practices and ideals, the greater the role that culturally specific secondary theories will play in one's overall practical theory, even though once again this can easily be overlooked in the face of the broad consensus on moral questions that is likely to present itself on a first

103. Lee Yearley, *Mencius and Aquinas: Theories of Virtue and Conceptions of Courage* (New York: SUNY Press, 1990), 175-82; the last point, however, I take from MacIntyre rather than from Yearley. Robin Horton's own position is set forth in "Tradition and Modernity Revisited," in Hollis and Lukes, *Rationality and Relativism*, 201-60.

examination. Yearley does not refer to ethical naturalism as such, but clearly his analysis is consistent with the view that culturally specific moralities, and by the same token, reflective moral theories, reflect the social patterns characteristic of us as a species. Correlatively, his analysis helps us explain why moral systems and theories reflect such an odd mixture of commonalities and divergences — that is, they reflect specifications and, secondarily, theoretical rationalizations of broadly common patterns of behavior.

As the reference to courage suggests, a naturalistic approach to ethics even provides substantive content, in addition to offering a framework within which to locate and compare diverse moralities. This content does not at this level take the form of precepts, such as are traditionally associated with a natural law morality, but rather the form of ideals of desirable or praiseworthy states of character — that is to say, ideals of virtue. As Yearley's analysis would suggest, these ideals occupy a middle position between a primary level of general knowledge about recurrent human patterns of behavior and a secondary level of reflective theories. It does appear to be the case that certain key virtues are identified and admired in nearly every society, including not only courage but self-restraint, justice or fairness, and practical judgment. We can formulate these and similar traits of character at a level general enough to identify them cross-culturally, while still retaining substantive content, because they take their context and point from what we might call the recurring challenges of human life — we must all learn to deal with fears and with conflicting and inappropriate desires, to live together on a basis of shared expectations, and to act in puzzling or unfamiliar situations. These ideals are too indeterminate, taken by themselves, to generate a full-fledged universal morality, but they nonetheless play a central role in the development of a theological ethic of the natural law.

The status of the virtues as a kind of bridge between the naturalistic roots of morality and its culturally and theoretically specific formulations helps to explain what might otherwise seem puzzling. That is, outside of theological circles, the most enthusiastic defenders of ethical naturalism tend to be advocates of virtue ethics rather than defenders of natural law, including Philippa Foot, James Wallace, and more recently, Rosalind Hursthouse.[104] As Hursthouse shows, the virtues can be analyzed and commended in terms of the contributions they make to overall well-being, whether of the individual or of the group. This need not lead us to a narrowly instrumental theory of the virtues, which Hursthouse rejects; rather, it helps us to understand the

104. In addition to Foot and Wallace, cited above, see Rosalind Hursthouse, *On Virtue Ethics* (Oxford: Oxford University Press, 1999).

virtues in terms of their contributions to the overall human good, which is tantamount to saying that her analysis helps us to see the natural value of these traits of character.[105]

All the same, we will only endorse the value of these traits of character if we recognize the value of the distinctively human form of social existence from which they stem. And it is worth underscoring that there is no universally valid, logically compelling reason for doing so. Here again we find a grain of truth in "naturalistic fallacy" arguments — while teleological evaluations are implicit in our concept of humanity (as in our concepts of other kinds of living creatures), these evaluations do not, in themselves, compel us to endorse a distinctively human way of life as something to be valued and promoted. This does not mean that it is *irrational* to value a distinctively human way of life, and to act accordingly — we do not need a special justification for acting in accordance with our natural inclinations for action, any more than we need a special justification for forming beliefs based on the deliverances of our senses. Nonetheless, there is no logically compelling argument against a radical rejection of a natural morality, any more than there can be a logically compelling argument against radical skepticism.

I noted above that a naturalistic approach to morality helps to explain why radical theories of morality — those theories, namely, which claim that some pervasive feature of human social life is unjustified — are generally regarded as implausible. However, this observation should not be taken to imply that radical theories of this kind are necessarily wrong. Such a conclusion would only follow on the basis of a further judgment to the effect that the social patterns natural to us as a species are in some way good or desirable in themselves, such that any attempt to alter or eliminate them in some fundamental way would be ruled out. And so far as I can see, nothing compels such a judgment — that is to say, if someone wishes to argue for the overriding authority of some principle or ideal which would contradict fundamental aspects of human social interactions, nothing logically would prevent her from doing so. As I suggested above, that is what Grisez and Finnis have done, although they would not construe their project in that way. This is also the approach taken, more self-consciously, by a number of radical theorists, most notably Peter Singer, who attempt to carry the principles of a strict consequentialism to their logical conclusions. We will return to a fuller consideration of their views in a later chapter. At this point, we should simply note that while no universal principles of logic or reason rule out such an approach, neither are there any such principles which require it.

105. In particular, see *On Virtue Ethics*, 163-91 and 217-38.

This brings us to the second reason mentioned above for taking a naturalistic account of ethics as the starting point for developing a theological account of the natural law. This reason, unlike the first, is distinctively theological. That is, we have distinctively theological reasons for valuing the human person, considered simply as such — and this implies that we have theological reasons for valuing those distinctive forms of social life proper to us as a species, even prior to considering how these are to be specified in accordance with our overall theological beliefs and commitments. These reasons are fundamental and simple: we believe that God created the world, and correlatively, that the world is an intelligible and good reflection of God's wisdom and loving will; that each kind of creature, including ourselves, manifests divine wisdom and love in the mode of orderly and purposeful existence proper to it; and in addition, human beings are images of God in a more distinctive sense, sharing in some way in divine capacities for self-determination and providential care.

If it is indeed the case that we need no special justification for living, and valuing, in accordance with the specific forms of social activity proper to us as human beings, then by the same token it might appear that a theological justification for endorsing the value of human existence is not needed. Seen from one perspective, this is indeed true — that is, it is no part of my argument that modern societies will collapse into nihilism or radical utilitarianism unless they adopt this theological perspective. Yet given the pervasiveness of radical challenges to our ordinary assumptions about morality, it is not out of place to reflect on one set of reasons for endorsing morality as we commonly experience it — even granting that these reasons are not logically compelling. More importantly, those of us who come to the task of moral reflection from a Christian standpoint have a stake in reflecting on our distinctive reasons for endorsing morality, even at the level of a naturalistic ethic. Only in this way can we locate moral theology within a more comprehensive theological project. Moreover, we can only see *how* we are to affirm the basic patterns of human social existence — that is to say, we can only begin to arrive at judgments about the specific morality that we, as Christians, are committed to endorsing — once we have considered *why* it is that morality matters to us specifically as Christians.

It is far from obvious why this should be the case — there are formidable theological arguments to be made that morality as such does not matter, that the Christian should live her life on the basis of God's direction or commands. Of course, these arguments turn on what is packed into the phrase "morality as such." In their most persuasive forms, they are directed against attempts to elevate morality to the level of transcendence, or to defend its universal and overriding authority over against every other sort of claim. Theologians have rightly protested against these and similar attempts to divinize morality, seeing in them evidences of our perennial temptation to divinize ourselves. But once we recognize that human morality, in all its forms, is good precisely insofar as it stems from and reflects the wisdom and goodness of our Creator, we will take a different perspective on morality, valuing it as no more, but also no less, than an expression of God's will that we live and flourish.

Let me approach this point from another direction. One of the defining claims of the natural law tradition, at least in its Christian formulations, is the contention that nature, understood in some comprehensive way, reflects God's will for humanity. This claim does not commit its advocates (of whom I am one) to the view that nature provides us with sole, comprehensive, or sufficient such indications; that is to say, it is compatible with a view that the deliverances of nature, however these are to be understood, must be supplemented, completed, or reformulated in light of other sources for moral knowledge. Furthermore, it leaves room for considerable uncertainty and debate over just what should count as nature, and more specifically, it leaves open the possibility that seemingly natural practices are actually particular to a given culture or historical period, or even worse, fatally distorted by sinfulness. Nonetheless, whatever qualifications might be added, the natural law tradition is fundamentally committed to the goodness, and therefore the moral significance, of nature, however more exactly that is to be spelled out.

This helps to account for what is otherwise a surprising aspect of scholastic natural law reasoning. That is to say, to a remarkable degree the natural law functions for the scholastics in a fundamentally permissive and constructive way.[106] Starting from the assumption that nature reflects the wisdom and benevolence of its Creator, the scholastics regard the naturalness of a tendency or practice as prima facie evidence for its moral legitimacy. This line of argument is limited, precisely because the scholastics also realize that prerational nature does not generate specific social practices in any straightforward or specific way. For this reason, a natural law justification at this level cannot be pressed much beyond an assessment of human practices considered in general terms.

Yet even this kind of large-scale analysis can have significant moral and theological implications. Most fundamentally, it reminds us that nothing that stems from human nature can be considered to be sinful without remainder, whatever temptations to sin it might provide. This might seem to be obvious,

106. For further details, see my *Natural and Divine Law,* 76-85.

but in fact it is not. The deep tendencies toward asceticism and perfectionism within the Christian tradition continually pull us in the opposite direction, toward a rejection of mundane human existence with its this-worldly and self-referential concerns. Without these tendencies, Christianity would lose the edge of radical self-sacrifice and indifference to the world which is an integral part of discipleship as the New Testament portrays it. Nonetheless, unless these tendencies are balanced in some way, Christianity can all too easily develop into some form of dualism, according to which fundamental aspects of human existence are not merely distorted by sin, not even tragic, but radically evil. The difficulty with this, in turn, is that it implies a denial of the fundamental doctrine that God is the Creator of the world, with its corollary that God's wisdom and goodness are in some way continuous with the goodness and intelligibility of the world as we experience it.

Of course, this still leaves open the question of just what it is in nature that is considered to be morally normative. And at this point, we must be particularly careful not to conflate the scholastic approach to the natural law with later Catholic versions. Modern Catholic theories of the natural law, at least before the advent of Grisez's and Finnis's "new theory," reflected the assumptions of the natural theology that emerged in the seventeenth century and dominated scientific as well as religious thought for the next two hundred years. On this view the world, and more particularly living creatures, reflect God's intelligent design, in just the same way as the design of an artifact reflects the design of the craftsman.[107] On first glance, this might seem to be nothing more than a variant of the scholastic view that creatures reflect an intelligibility and goodness in virtue of their essential forms. But on the modern view, the intelligibility of creatures is understood by reference to an inferred design which is external to the creature itself. What this meant, practically, was that design was analyzed in terms of the manifest functions of organs and physical processes, which were taken to be their purposes without any necessary reference to the overall well-being of the organism. The eye is meant for seeing because that is what eyes do, and the intelligent design of the eye is therefore manifested in the physical constitution of the organ, in terms of which it can function as it does.

Given this context, we can readily appreciate why modern natural law thinkers tended to assume that God's will is expressed through the functions

107. Livingstone offers a helpful analysis of the relevant issues in "The Idea of Design"; in addition, see Ron Amundson, "Typology Reconsidered: Two Doctrines on the History of Evolutionary Biology," *Biology and Philosophy* 13 (1998): 153-77, and Gregory Peterson, "Whose Evolution? Which Theology?" *Zygon* 35 (2000): 221-32.

of human organs and processes, without any necessary reference to the overall well-being of the human person — a view well expressed by the theologian Hürth, quoted above. We can also see why this view came to be condemned as a kind of "biologism" or "physicalism," which safeguards the integrity of "mere" nature at the expense of legitimate human interests, and why it was widely supplanted in the twentieth century by some version of personalism, according to which the integral well-being of the human person is considered to be the fundamental touchstone for moral evaluation.[108]

In fact, however, the scholastic approach to the natural law is closer to personalism, at least in this respect, than to the modern approach to the natural law exemplified by Hürth. The reason has to do with the scholastic approach to nature described above. On this view, the goodness of a creature is inextricably bound up with its intelligible form, that is to say, with the ordered functioning proper to the kind of creature it is. Organs and functions are interpreted teleologically in light of their contributions to the overall life and flourishing of the creature, or the well-being of its family, social group, or kind. Hence, on this kind of analysis the focus is not on the design of particular organs or functions, but rather on the way they can be rendered intelligible in light of a whole way of life.

Seen within this context, God's will as expressed through human nature cannot be analyzed in terms of the functions of specific organs or faculties — it must be understood in terms of the overall functioning and well-being of

108. Thus McCormick says in "Human Sexuality" that "I use this term [personalist] in a specific sense and in a quite restrictive context. The context is the determination of the morally right and morally wrong of human actions. The specific sense is that it is the human person in all facets and dimensions who is the criterion of the moral rightfulness and wrongfulness. That formulation is meant to contrast with an approach that employs an isolated dimension of the human person as criterion" (191). He goes on to specify that by the latter approach he is thinking in particular of the interpretation of the natural law represented by Hürth, which he describes, following John Courtney Murray, as "biologist," an approach which confuses the natural with the primordial. (The reference to Murray is taken from *We Hold These Truths* [New York: Sheed and Ward, 1960], 296). At the same time, however, it is also possible to develop a personalist defense of traditional Catholic sexual ethics, arguing that the norms in question represent the only way in which a fully authentic and personal sexual love can be expressed. See, for example, German Martinez, "An Anthropological Vision of Christian Marriage," *The Thomist* 56, no. 3 (July 1992): 451-72. More generally, Janet E. Smith argues that the Pope's interpretation of the natural law in *Veritatis Splendor* should be seen as a personalist approach, because it interprets the norms of the natural law as expressions of the demands of an authentic interiority; see "Natural Law and Personalism in *Veritatis Splendor*," in *Veritatis Splendor: American Responses*, ed. Michael E. Allsopp and John J. O'Keefe (Kansas City: Sheed and Ward, 1995), 194-207. Finally, see the helpful discussion and critique of personalism developed by Stephen Pope in *The Evolution of Altruism*, 19-26.

the human creature and humankind, considered in the first instance as expressions of God's will that the creature live and flourish. And if this is so, then a theological account of the natural law must proceed by way of reflection on the meaning of human flourishing. As I have argued elsewhere, the scholastics generally did follow this approach, more or less explicitly, but it is developed most explicitly and fully in the theology of Aquinas. In the next chapter, I will attempt to develop an account of human well-being and happiness, taking Aquinas's account as my starting point and frame of discussion.

CHAPTER THREE

Virtue and the Happy Life

It is not difficult to set forth a cogent concept of human nature, so long as we do not hold ourselves to the unattainable standard of a complete, fully articulated and nonrevisable concept. We cannot hope to reach this ideal until the biological and human sciences attain a level of development proper to a perfected science in the Aristotelian sense, and they are very far from that point, if indeed they could attain it at all. Nonetheless, even now we can attain — indeed, we actually have — a concept which is to some degree implicit and certainly provisional, but adequate for most purposes. This concept is relational, locating "human being" within a framework of progressively more specific descriptions — a human being is a living creature, an animal, a mammal, a primate — and further specifying the kind by reference to the illuminating similarities and distinctive differences among human beings and other kinds of animals. Correlatively, an adequate definition of "human being" would acknowledge that humans are one kind of higher primate, characterized by a particular pattern of social interactions, and distinguished by rationality, a complex capacity which includes distinctive abilities for action as well as thought. Moreover, the concept of "human being" reflected by such a definition is normative precisely insofar as it is descriptively adequate, because it will reflect a grasp of an ideal of human existence, in terms of which individual human beings can be recognized as such. So far, we have simply summarized the conclusions of the last chapter.

If this approach to understanding human nature is justified, it might seem that we have said all we need to say in order to lay the foundations for a natural law ethic. After all, if the concept of human nature is intrinsically normative, in the same way and for the same reasons as other concepts of kinds of living creatures are normative, then norms for human life are built into the concept itself. As we noted in the last chapter, a number of philosophers have argued for just this approach.[1] But as we also noted, normative judgments at this level underdetermine distinctively moral norms, at least any norms specific enough to be put into practice as a socially embedded morality. If the concept of a human being sketched above is generally correct, then we are justified in saying that human flourishing includes not only such things as health and physical security, but also participation in some kind of social life. But of course, the relevant qualifier here is "some kind" — there are as many kinds of social life as there are human cultures, each of them expressing characteristically human patterns of social interaction and providing a means by which individuals can enjoy a distinctively social existence. Yet there are considerable differences among these cultures, so much so that it strains credibility to suggest that there are no moral differences among them.

It is clear, therefore, that the ideal of flourishing implicit in an adequate concept of human nature cannot serve as the basis for a natural law account of morality without the introduction of further principles to provide specification. At the same time, if the considerations advanced in the last chapter are persuasive, we will be suspicious of any attempt to "specify" the concept of human flourishing in such a way as, in effect, to render morally irrelevant our shared nature as living creatures of a specific kind. The task at hand, therefore, is to specify the general idea of human flourishing in such a way as to give it moral content, while still holding on to the main lines of the idea in some recognizable way.

As a preliminary to this task, a terminological clarification is in order. In what follows I will refer to the condition indicated by a general normative ideal of human flourishing as well-being, and I will refer to the distinctively moral ideal specifying and qualifying it as happiness.[2] Well-being will thus be

1. Particularly noteworthy from the standpoint of this project are those philosophers who have attempted to defend a naturalistic ethic of the virtues, including most notably Philippa Foot, whose program is set forth most recently in *Natural Goodness* (Oxford: Oxford University Press, 2001), and Rosalind Hursthouse, *On Virtue Ethics* (Oxford: Oxford University Press, 1999). Similarly, Alasdair MacIntyre begins a recent book on the virtues by observing that "I now judge that I was in error in supposing an ethics independent of biology to be possible," and goes on to develop an Aristotelian/Thomistic account of the virtues that reckons "not only with our animal condition, but also with the need to acknowledge our consequent vulnerability and dependence." See *Dependent Rational Animals: Why Human Beings Need the Virtues* (Peru, Ill.: Carus/Open Court, 1999), x-xi. What follows is also indebted to James Wallace's unjustly neglected *Virtues and Vices* (Ithaca, N.Y.: Cornell University Press, 1978).

2. It will be clear in what follows that the immediate context for my reflections is set by the classical and Thomistic conception of happiness conceived as the objective perfection of the individual. As George Weiland observes, this general conception of happiness was widely shared

understood in terms analogous to the normative ideal of flourishing proper to any other kind of creature, and as such, it will include all the components of a humanly desirable life, including life itself, health, security, and participation in a network of family and social relations. Happiness will be understood to qualify this basic ideal by specifying the best or most appropriate way in which men and women can attain and enjoy the activities constitutive of well-being. Of course, this is an ancient approach to moral reflection, and it raises a host of classical difficulties — much of this chapter will be taken up with addressing these difficulties. Thus, the task of this chapter might be described as moving from an account of well-being to an account of happiness, in such a way as to retain a substantive connection between the two.

The concept of happiness plays a central role in Aquinas's systematic accounts of the moral life.[3] By implication, his concept of happiness offers a basis on which to draw out the eudaemonistic logic of the scholastic concept of the natural law, along lines which extend Aquinas's own teleological account of the natural law, although they go beyond what he says at some points. Or so I will argue in this chapter. The concept of happiness is central to a Thomistic theory of the natural law because it provides a framework within which to integrate two dimensions of human existence, namely, human nature comprehensively understood and the distinctively human character of natural existence, that is to say, human reason. At the same time, this concept

---

by Aquinas's immediate predecessors and contemporaries; see "Happiness: The Perfection of Man," in *The Cambridge History of Later Medieval Philosophy from the Rediscovery of Aristotle to the Disintegration of Scholasticism, 1100-1600,* ed. Norman Kretzman, Anthony Kenny, and Jan Pinborg (Cambridge: Cambridge University Press, 1982), 675-86, here 673. I owe the language of well-being to Bernard Williams, *Ethics and the Limits of Philosophy* (Cambridge: Harvard University Press, 1985), 30-53, although as I note below, the term "well-being" has somewhat different meanings in other contexts. It will be apparent that I do not share Williams's negative appraisal of the Aristotelian theory of morality; briefly, I believe that he does not take due note of the distinction between basic well-being and happiness, and concludes, falsely, that the relation between well-being and happiness can only be instrumental. As I will argue below, this is a misapprehension.

3. This is so, not only in the *prima secundae* of the *Summa theologiae,* which begins with an analysis of the ultimate end of human life (I-II 1) and goes on to specify that end as happiness (*beatitudo,* I-II 2), but also in the *Summa contra gentiles* III; see especially III 25, 37. Among contemporary moral theologians, Servais Pinckaers is almost alone in insisting on the significance of the concept of happiness for Aquinas's moral thought; see *Les sources de la morale chrétienne: Sa méthode, son contenu, son histoire* (Fribourg: Editions Universitaires Fribourg, 1985), 28-33, and more recently, *L'Evangile et la morale* (Fribourg: Editions Universitaires Fribourg, 1990), 103-16. While I am in agreement with much of what he says, we differ insofar as I place greater weight on a conception of terrestrial happiness conceived as the practice of the virtues; see *L'Evangile et la morale,* 108-9.

also offers a way to bring together two approaches to moral reflection which we often take to be distinct and indeed antithetical, namely, an ethic of virtue and an ethic of law.

Yet Aquinas's concept of happiness resists straightforward analysis. Matters are not helped by the fact that in his most extended discussion of human happiness he focuses on the supernatural end of human life, and his remarks on the form of happiness connatural to the human person are terse and undeveloped. Moreover, even apart from the difficulties incidental to Aquinas's discussion, the concept of happiness is a deceptively simple idea calling for careful unpacking. We have already noted that happiness, considered as a moral ideal, cannot be equated with well-being. What is more, on some views true happiness is not only distinct from but wholly independent of well-being, in such a way that it makes sense to say of someone that she is happy even though she is sick, isolated, and deprived of capacities or opportunities for effective action. Indeed, there is a classical and Christian tradition of reflection on happiness which is more or less independent of the tradition of reflection on the natural law, and it is not evident that Aquinas's attempt to synthesize them can be successful.

As might be anticipated, I do believe this attempt is successful, even though it remains underdeveloped in some respects. In this chapter I will offer a development and defense of Aquinas's concept of happiness, seen in relation to the natural law. This approach will bring us to the natural law by means of what may seem at first a detour, namely, through an analysis of the virtues and their place in a naturalistic ethic. But as I hope to show, this approach is not so indirect as it may at first seem. Aquinas's account of the virtues provides him with a starting point for analyzing moral norms in such a way as to account for their dual character as norms of nature and expressions of a natural and divine law. In order to carry out this task, we will need to be clear on the complexities involved in the concept of happiness itself, and we will also need to explore the relationship between this concept and the account of natural human well-being developed in the previous chapter. These will be the tasks of this chapter.

In the course of reviewing recent work on the biological roots of morality, Stephen Pope contrasts divine command approaches to ethics to the revised natural law theory currently being developed by some contemporary Catholic moral theologians, including himself, observing that this latter approach "understands the authority of moral claims to be warranted not by divine dictates but by their contribution to human flourishing."[4] The Thomistic

4. Stephen Pope, "The Evolutionary Roots of Morality in Theological Perspective," *Zygon*

theory of the natural law to be developed here shares in this fundamental approach, insofar as it takes happiness to be the aim of, and correlatively the ultimate criterion for, moral behavior. But the concept of "happiness," as classically understood and as appropriated by Aquinas, is more specific and morally rich than the idea of "flourishing," which is usually equated with what I am calling well-being. As such, the concept of happiness provides resources for developing an account of morality which gives a central place to the intelligibilities structuring human life — a natural law theory of morality, in other words.

As we will see, Aquinas identifies terrestrial happiness — that is to say, the kind of happiness that can be achieved either naturally or through grace in this life — with the practice of the virtues. In doing so, he appropriates and develops one well-established option in the classical debates over happiness, an option he takes from Aristotle. I suspect that this claim will strike contemporary readers as puzzling or unpersuasive, but I will attempt to defend it throughout the chapter. The arguments of this chapter will take us beyond what Aquinas explicitly says, although I do not believe I will contradict him at any point. At any rate, while I believe that the following analysis represents what is implicit in Aquinas's views, I will not attempt to defend the arguments of this chapter as interpretations of Aquinas — my aim, rather, is to take Aquinas's analysis as a starting point for thinking about the relationships among happiness, virtue, and natural law.

1. Natural Well-Being and the Concept of Happiness

We have already noted that it is not difficult to come up with a persuasive account of human well-being, constructed on analogy with our best accounts of well-being as applied to other kinds of animals. Admittedly, this account will be general and tentative, but even so, it provides a substantive and plausible account of what it means to be a human being. It expresses in summary form what we take to be the "ordered functional capabilities" which are essential to human existence, and correlatively, it expresses our best judgments

---

33, no. 4 (December 1998): 545-56, here 554. Pope's own work in this area is best exemplified by his book *The Evolution of Altruism and the Ordering of Love* (Washington, D.C.: Georgetown University Press, 1994). Similarly, Christine Traina argues that properly understood, a Thomistic theory of the natural law offers an important resource to feminism, precisely because it provides a basis for explicating and defending women's claims to full human flourishing, in *Feminist Ethics and Natural Law: The End of the Anathemas* (Washington, D.C.: Georgetown University Press, 1999).

about the meaning of "human being" as a biological kind. As such, it provides a summary statement of the kinds of judgments that are presupposed or implied when we discriminate between mature and immature human beings, or identify various types of incapacities as forms of illness or disability. It also serves to call attention to the basic criteria by which we are able to identify others, whose appearance and behavior may be strange and disconcerting, as being fundamentally human like ourselves — no longer a real issue today, but as we noted in the last chapter, a genuine problem in the past.

Almost no one would deny that human well-being, so understood, is relevant to moral reflection in a number of ways. In the first place, the pervasive potentialities and limitations of human existence provide the conditions within which morality is meaningful, and secondly, they provide a necessary context for formulating substantive norms of nonmaleficence and beneficence. If we were not capable of acting in certain kinds of ways, responding to reasons or motivations of particular kinds, morality would not be possible, and if we were perfectly altruistic, or invulnerable to harm, or free from any kind of scarcity, morality would be pointless. By the same token, the kinds of harms to which we are typically vulnerable, and the kinds of needs and desires we typically experience, provide the matter, as it were, for the prohibitions against harm and injunctions to do good that are the main substance of most moral systems. An account of well-being of this kind will also provide some guidance, although admittedly not complete guidance, for determining when persons are mature enough and healthy enough to assume moral responsibility and to begin to participate in the relations of mutual accountability which structure all human societies.

These and similar considerations indicate that the basic conception of human well-being is relevant to moral reflection. However, it is also clear that we can allow for the relevance of well-being in these terms without granting it independent moral significance. On this view, basic facts about human needs and desires, together with the pervasive regularities informing our lives, provide the raw materials, as it were, out of which nearly any moral system can be constructed. Nonetheless, on this view we can formulate moral principles without any necessary reference to these regularities, or to the natural intelligibilities structuring human existence that they represent. Need we say anything more about the moral significance of human well-being? To put the question in another way, do we need to move from a concept of well-being to a concept of happiness in the classical sense?

At any rate, to those familiar with the classical tradition of reflection on happiness as a moral ideal, it will be apparent that well-being understood along these lines cannot just be equated with a morally significant conception of happiness. Indeed, it is not clear that the same concerns always inform ancient reflections on happiness and contemporary reflection on well-being. The account of human well-being just sketched finds its immediate context in a broadly scientific inquiry about what it is to be human. Even though it has moral relevance, it is not clear that it is a moral concept in any interesting sense. The idea of human happiness, in contrast, was classically regarded as a moral concept, indeed *the* moral concept par excellence; as Julia Annas puts it, "The question 'In what does my happiness consist?' is the most important and central question in ancient ethics."[5] This remark follows immediately after the observation that the general concept of happiness in ancient ethics was "an extremely weak and unspecific" concept, equivalent to whatever the individual might consider to be his final good. Seen in this light, the "weak and unspecific" character of the ancient concept of happiness was thus not a defect, but an accurate reflection of the complexity and inconsistency of popular and philosophical ideals of happiness.

Is it necessary to work through these complexities, in order to appropriate the core insight that human well-being is morally significant? For those impressed by the moral salience of basic human well-being, there might seem to be attractive reasons for avoiding a further appeal to a concept of happiness. A morally significant concept of happiness might seem to be a thought too much for the purposes of moral reflection — difficult to work out, and problematic insofar as it imposes contentious and possibly coercive ideals onto the indefinite diversity of human desires. Why not focus directly on the moral claims placed on us by the activities characteristic of human well-being, and the needs and desires stemming from these?

Taken in one way, this describes the basic utilitarian program in both its classical and radical forms; taken in another way, it describes recent attempts to defend human rights on the basis of universal human functions or capabilities. These two programs have generated an extensive literature on the concept of well-being itself, in which basic notions of need and desire are analyzed in terms of their relationships to concepts of satisfaction, on the one hand, and characteristic or proper human activities on the other.[6] If nothing else, this lit-

5. Julia Annas, *The Morality of Happiness* (Oxford: Oxford University Press, 1993), 46.

6. For a thorough and illuminating discussion of the idea of well-being as developed in these contexts, see James Griffin, *Well-Being: Its Meaning, Measurement, and Moral Importance* (Oxford: Clarendon, 1986), especially 7-74. It seems to me that in his own preferred construal of the concept, Griffin comes very close to endorsing something like the classical ideal of happiness as perfection, even though he is not prepared to endorse classical perfectionism without qualification; see 56-72 for further details. I do not attempt in this project to sort through related debates over the meaning of "welfare" in current ethical and economic theory. Ronald

erature shows that we do indeed have the resources for a rich and detailed concept of human nature in terms that could fill in the sketch proposed at the end of the last chapter. Nonetheless, it is not clear that appeals to well-being, in either utilitarian or rights-based forms, can generate moral conclusions while still avoiding the difficulties inherent in a morally significant concept of happiness. I will say more in the next chapter about utilitarianism, but at this point, some comment on the capabilities approach is in order.

The appeal to functions or capabilities as a basis for international human rights was initially proposed by the economist and philosopher Amartya Sen, and it was subsequently appropriated by the United Nations Development Programme as the basis for its *Human Development Reports*.[7] In what follows, however, I will focus on the influential version of this theory developed by Martha Nussbaum as the basis for a universally persuasive defense of human rights, especially as these apply to women. Nussbaum's theory is particularly relevant to this project, because it takes its starting point from Aristotle's ideas about human functioning, together with Karl Marx's appropriation of these ideas. Nussbaum's theory can thus be regarded as a contemporary appropriation of Aristotelian teleology, which as we have seen focuses on the ordered functional capabilities proper to a given kind of organism. She similarly focuses on capabilities and functions — that is to say, potencies for action and activities themselves — rather than needs, desires, or experiences of satisfaction in developing her account of human well-being. As she explains:

> The intuitive idea behind the approach is twofold: first, that certain functions are particularly central in human life, in the sense that their presence or absence is typically understood to be a mark of the presence or absence of human life; and second — this is what Marx found in Aristotle — that there is something that it is to do these functions in a truly human way, not a merely animal way. . . . The core idea is that of the human being

Dworkin offers a helpful summary of the main positions in *Sovereign Virtue: The Theory and Practice of Equality* (Cambridge: Harvard University Press, 2000), 11-64; I should note that I share Dworkin's reservations about the idea of welfare as currently understood.

7. Sen has developed his own version of the capabilities approach through a series of books and articles; for a good recent statement, see *Development as Freedom* (New York: Random House, 1999), especially 54-86. My comments on the subsequent reception of the theory are taken from Martha C. Nussbaum, *Women and Human Development: The Capabilities Approach* (Cambridge: Cambridge University Press, 2000), 70. She lays out the main lines of her own, slightly different version of the capabilities approach in 34-110. Griffin's preferred concept of well-being, similarly, focuses on identifying prudential values which are worth pursuing whatever else one desires in life, an approach I believe Nussbaum would endorse; see *Well-Being*, 64-68.

> as a dignified free being who shapes his or her own life in cooperation and reciprocity with others, rather than being passively shaped or pushed around by the world in the manner of a "flock" or "herd" animal. A life that is really human is one that is shaped throughout by these human powers of practical reason and sociability.[8]

As we will see, Nussbaum's "intuitive idea" is likewise central to the Thomistic theory of the natural law that I am developing, since for Aquinas (as for Aristotle, and the classical world more generally) happiness on any plausible construal must consist in an activity, which is in some way characteristic of the human person as such.[9] Reading on, however, we find that Nussbaum departs from Aristotle (and from Aquinas as well) in one critical respect. That is, Aristotle offers what he regards as a morally significant analysis of the distinctively human activity constituting happiness, which he identifies with contemplation and the practice of the civic virtues.[10] In the terminology proposed above, Aristotle does not simply equate "well-being" with "happiness"; rather, he develops a moral theory of happiness on the basis of a particular construal of the components of human well-being, understood in a more fundamental sense. Nussbaum, in contrast, resists making any such move. Rather, she regards the basic functions and capabilities as given by experience and observation, confirmed in a number of different societies; their moral significance depends on a "freestanding moral idea," which Nussbaum expects to be widely persuasive:

> The basic intuition from which the capability approach begins, in the political arena, is that certain human abilities exert a moral claim that they should be developed. Once again, this must be understood as a *freestanding moral idea,* not one that relies on a particular metaphysical or teleological view. Not all actual human abilities exert a moral claim, only the ones that have been evaluated as valuable from an ethical viewpoint. (The capacity for cruelty, for example, does not figure on the list.) Thus the argument begins from ethical premises and derives ethical conclusions from these alone, not from any further metaphysical premises.[11]

Nussbaum's insistence that her moral conclusions are "freestanding" and in need of no metaphysical grounding is reminiscent of the claims of

8. Nussbaum, *Women and Human Development,* 71-72.

9. As Annas points out; see *The Morality of Happiness,* 36-38.

10. Annas's analysis of the distinction (not always explicitly recognized) between "nature" and "mere nature" in Aristotle is particularly helpful here; see *The Morality of Happiness,* 142-58.

11. Nussbaum, *Women and Human Development,* 83, emphasis in original.

Grisez and Finnis to derive moral conclusions on the basis of self-evident intuitions of value, without any need to appeal to empirical or metaphysical claims. I suspect that she and Grisez and Finnis share at least one part of the motivation for this move; that is to say, they hope to develop moral theories that will be universally persuasive, and for that reason they attempt to keep their metaphysical and other commitments to a minimum. Be that as it may, Nussbaum's distinction, between the capabilities themselves and the moral significance they bear, would seem to imply that we can arrive at a morally neutral account of what the capabilities are. Once we have done so, then the "freestanding idea" that these capabilities demand respect enters in to do the moral work. There is no need on this account to propose a contentious concept of happiness; we need only apply fundamental moral intuitions to what we know about the conditions for, and the constituents of, human well-being. In our terms, she attempts to derive her moral conclusions from a neutral account of well-being, interpreted in the light of fundamental intuitions about the claims attaching to considerations of well-being.

By the same token, Nussbaum's approach raises a difficulty similar to that raised by the Grisez/Finnis theory of natural law. That is, it is not clear that Nussbaum's appeal to a "freestanding moral idea" can do the work she wants, even with respect to the most basic capabilities, let alone those which might be more contentious. Capabilities are not developed and exercised in isolation; rather, they are exercised in an orderly and reciprocally conditioned way, in and through the pursuit of a way of life which will always necessarily be to some extent culturally specific. Our moral intuitions about the claims attached to these capabilities will always be conditioned, to a greater or lesser degree, by our moral judgments regarding an overall way of life. That does not mean that we cannot move beyond our first judgments to arrive at a more generally applicable account of human well-being and happiness — that is, after all, one of the aims of this chapter — but it does mean that we cannot *begin* with our own intuitions about the moral significance of basic human capabilities, as if these were rationally compelling, without further argument, to all well-disposed people.[12] What is more, these arguments will require

12. Nussbaum attempts to forestall the objection that her account of the basic capabilities is culturally conditioned by developing that account in conversation with women in India over the course of two visits carried out as part of the research for her project (for details, see *Women and Human Development*, xvi-xviii). But it is hard to know what to make of the agreements on basic values that she reports. Nussbaum's contacts in India seem to have consisted mostly of women involved in development projects sponsored by Western development and relief agencies, and while these would include important segments of Indian society, it is not so clear that they would be representative of Indian society taken as a whole. It is worth noting

what Nussbaum hopes to avoid, namely, contentious theoretical accounts of what it means to flourish in a properly human way.

This conclusion is strengthened when we note that Nussbaum's list of basic capabilities has been shaped by her prior moral convictions — indeed, we have just seen that she omits some pervasive capabilities because they are morally problematic. Her list of basic functions and capabilities includes items that clearly reflect moral judgments, for example, "having opportunities for sexual satisfaction and for choice in matters of reproduction"; being educated in such a way as to attain "literacy and basic mathematical and scientific training"; and to enjoy guarantees "of freedom of expression with respect to both political and artistic speech, and freedom of religious exercise."[13] I would agree with Nussbaum about the desirability of these things, and yet it is not evident that they are so integrally tied to human well-being that someone deprived of them would be appropriately regarded as sick, suffering, or deformed. Nussbaum would seem to anticipate this objection when she observes that what matters, morally, is that individuals have the freedom to exercise and develop the basic capabilities if they so choose.[14] But this reflects a moral judgment about the overriding value of autonomy that is itself, at least arguably, culturally specific — and as we will see, theologically specific as well. In contrast, neither Nussbaum, nor to my knowledge almost anyone else, defends moral claims stemming from the human capabilities for aggression, dominance, and the like.[15] Yet these are also pervasive human capabili-

---

that anthropologists and cultural psychologists working in India have documented strikingly different moral commitments among some Indian women — these studies are not necessarily representative either (nor is any such claim made), but they do suggest that the situation is more complex than Nussbaum seems to suggest. For a good discussion of the relevant research and its implications for cross-cultural moral dialogue, see Richard Shweder, *Why Do Men Barbecue? Recipes for Cultural Psychology* (Cambridge: Harvard University Press, 2003); for particulars on the author's research on cultural attitudes among Indian women, see in particular "The Return of the 'White Man's Burden' and the Domestic Life of Hindu Women," with Usha Menon, 217-75.

13. Nussbaum, *Women and Human Development,* 78-79.

14. Nussbaum, *Women and Human Development,* 87-88.

15. Presumably, Nussbaum would include these among the morally problematic capabilities that do not exert a moral claim, but why should she do so? Cruelty offers an easy case, since it is morally bad by definition, but the same cannot be said about aggression as such. John Casey comes as close as anyone I know to defending the positive value of aggression in his subtle exploration of the way a proper self-respect presupposes capacities for both anger and the ability to make demands on others; see *Pagan Virtue: An Essay in Ethics* (Oxford: Clarendon, 1990), 10-28. Similarly, he suggests at 67-83 that at least some forms of courage and nobility may require capacities for aggressive action that not everyone possesses — although I am not clear how far he wants to push this line of argument.

ties — why, then, are they not considered to generate demands for fulfillment? I cannot see any obvious answer to this question that would be couched in terms of well-being alone — after all, capabilities for aggression and dominance are not only pervasive, they would appear to serve essential functions in sustaining individual and social life. It is difficult to avoid concluding that some human capabilities — or needs or desires, depending on the particular theory in question — are considered to be more properly human than others.

Once we begin to make these kinds of judgments, we have moved from assessments of well-being to the development of a concept of happiness in the traditional, morally freighted sense. And this brings me back to the point that was made above. The notion of well-being seems initially to offer an attractive alternative to more substantive and contentious accounts of the ideal or proper form of human existence, that is to say, happiness. But it would appear that notions of well-being and happiness cannot be so neatly separated after all. In the process of moving from an account of well-being to moral theory, it seems that we will inevitably find ourselves making the kinds of value judgments about the proper form of human life that we were hoping to avoid. By the same token, an explicit and fully developed conception of happiness will require us to articulate and defend judgments about the proper shape of human life. If we are going to inevitably find ourselves making such judgments in any case, it is surely preferable to do so explicitly, in terms we are committed to defending, rather than doing so implicitly and without argument.

Nonetheless, it is still true that happiness understood as a moral ideal stands in an uncertain and paradoxical relation to well-being, on almost any construal of these two notions. Indeed, the relation between them is central to the moral debate over the meaning and significance of happiness. As Annas notes,

> Because happiness does have this suggestion of satisfaction with and positive attitude towards one's life, it tends to be associated, before we have reflected much, with the things that make most people satisfied with their lives — wealth, honour, and in general the results of success. We shall see that theories that divorce happiness from this kind of worldly success pay a price. But we have seen already that happiness is vague enough to serve as merely a thin specification of the final goods and we shall find that there are good reasons to develop the ideas that happiness applies to the agent's life as a whole, that it requires activity and that it is different in kind from the other goods that we aim at — even when these develop-

ments threaten the positive suggestions that the word happiness tends to have.[16]

We need not pursue the specifics of the classical discussion of happiness as Annas recounts them in order to see why we might want to resist the straightforward identification of well-being with happiness in the moral sense. First, and most fundamentally, if happiness is a moral concept, then it would seem that we should praise and admire people for being happy in the requisite sense, as well as simply congratulating them, and by the same token, it would seem that a failure to be truly happy must somehow carry implications of blame or reproof. It may be difficult to say exactly what that connotation should be, whether, for example, it presupposes responsibility on the part of the individual who fails in the relevant way. We tend to assume that moral evaluations are strictly limited to acts and states for which an individual is directly or indirectly responsible, but this is not obvious. It is not clearly absurd to admire someone for her courage, and to feel disdain or disapproval for her cowardly sister, even if we know that these character traits stem from inborn dispositions which the girls could not have controlled. Of course, this example raises its own questions which we cannot pursue. My point is that *even if* we allow for the possibility that nonvoluntary traits might legitimately provoke moral responses, these would still be traits of character, tendencies and capacities which are expressed directly through characteristic kinds of actions. Even on this assumption, it seems absurd to attach moral responses to bodily excellences or deficiencies such as physical strength, beauty, or (conversely) blindness. Yet if we are to place human well-being, as described above, on a parallel with other forms of well-being, then clearly bodily excellences do contribute to an individual's well-being, and bodily deficiencies detract from or undermine it. Thus, whatever we consider human happiness in the moral sense to be, it cannot be equated with well-being as understood above.

I just noted that it would be absurd to attach a moral connotation to a bodily defect such as blindness. But in fact, "absurd" may seem too weak — many would find such a suggestion offensive, and for similar reasons, even the suggestion that such a person lacks something essential to full human flourishing will strike many as deeply problematic. After all, we may want to say, a blind man need not lack anything that is essential to being a *person*, even if he suffers from a deficiency that impairs his functioning at a practical level. He may well be as good a person as his sighted wife; indeed, he may well

16. Annas, *The Morality of Happiness*, 46.

be a better person, we may admire and envy him, we may even conclude that his personal excellence has developed (in part) through his response to his blindness, and shows forth through it. In this spirit, we may want to say that his blindness has been his good fortune, since it has given him the opportunity to develop genuine human excellence — although if we are wise, we will leave it to him to say this if he chooses.

These responses reflect a set of intuitions which we can trace to ancient reflections on the nature of true happiness. That is, on this view, true happiness or (we might say) authentic human existence is not a matter of animal well-being at all; rather, it is a matter of character, through which the individual expresses her distinctive identity as a moral being. Correlatively, on this view what it means to be human *is* just to be a moral being, capable of a unique kind of excellence. On this view, bodily existence and a minimal degree of health are necessary if one is to attain and exercise moral excellence, but once this minimum has been attained, the deficiencies and misfortunes one suffers as a physical and animal being have nothing to do with one's true excellence. Indeed, since moral excellence can be regarded as a more or less permanent attainment, or alternatively as something supremely valuable although perishable, even those injuries which impede or destroy one's continuing capacity to exercise moral excellence should not be regarded as true harms, once the individual has attained moral excellence. Even death need not be considered a harm for the truly good man or woman. Indeed, death in a good cause may well be regarded as the supreme achievement of virtue, a masterstroke of good fortune.

Those familiar with ancient reflections on moral excellence and happiness will recognize the emerging picture — namely, the image of the morally good man or woman who cannot be harmed by any external agency, because no outside force can cause a good person to surrender the only thing worth having, that is, moral virtue. It is this picture which lies behind the paradoxical claims about happiness that we find in some ancient literature — the good man who loses family, friends, health, and homeland and is nonetheless happy, who is happy on the rack, who is happy even posthumously (and not just because he has escaped so many misfortunes). These claims have frequently been dismissed as absurd excesses of moral zeal, but we can see why they would have seemed compelling, given certain assumptions. That is, if we do define true human existence, and by implication human happiness, in terms of one's existence and excellences as a moral agent, then it would seem to follow that the various ills to which the flesh is heir are simply irrelevant to one's true existence and happiness. And of course, this ideal resonates through the modern period, in Kant's claim that a morally good will is the only unconditional good, for example, or in Iris Murdoch's powerful defense of the unconditional value of virtue.[17]

Yet this is a paradoxical conclusion, and it was felt to be such in antiquity; as Aristotle remarks, perhaps in exasperation, no one can seriously say that a life of the greatest sufferings and misfortunes is happy.[18] This remark reflects another set of intuitions, summarized by Annas's remark that "Because happiness does have this suggestion of satisfaction with and positive attitude towards one's life, it tends to be associated, before we have reflected much, with the things that make most people satisfied with their lives" — if not wealth and honor, at least the fundamental satisfactions of a healthy, fulfilled animal existence. If we are to take the classical association between happiness and satisfaction seriously, then by the same token we should not be so quick to dismiss the relevance of basic well-being to an adequate moral ideal of happiness. Even though we cannot simply equate happiness with well-being, we may still want to argue for some positive relationship between the two. Of course, the difficulty which emerges at this point is, what kind of relationship might that be? And how can we develop an account which does justice both to the considerations for separating well-being and happiness, and to those urging their connection? In order to begin to answer these questions, we turn now to Aquinas's interpretation of the classical concept of happiness.

In the introduction to the first question of the *prima secundae,* Aquinas sets out his immediate plan, indicating that he will begin by considering the final end of human life, turning then to a consideration of the way that end is to be attained. "And because the final end of human life is said to be happiness," he adds, "it is necessary first to consider the ultimate end generally understood, and then to consider happiness" (I-II 1 intro.). He goes on in I-II 1 and 2 to develop this program. After establishing that it is proper to the human person to act for an end and drawing out some of the implications of that claim (I-II 1.1-3), he goes on to argue that human life has an ultimate end, at least in a minimal sense that would rule out an indefinite series or a plural-

17. Thus, Kant says that "The only thing that is good without qualification or restriction is a good will. That is to say, a good will alone is good *in all circumstances* and in that sense is an absolute or unconditioned good. We may also describe it as the only thing that is good *in itself,* good independently of its relation to other things" (*Groundwork of the Metaphysics of Morals,* trans. H. J. Paton [1948; reprint, New York: Harper, 1964; 3rd ed. 1956], 17, emphasis in original). Iris Murdoch similarly defends the unconditional value of virtue in *The Sovereignty of Good* (London/New York: Routledge and Kegan Paul/Methuen, 1970), 77-104; in particular, note her comment that the good person sees "the pointlessness of virtue and its unique value and the endless extent of its demand" (104).

18. Specifically, *Nicomachean Ethics* I.4, 1095b35-1096a1.

ity of ends (1.4). Clearly, this claim is only plausible if the end is formulated in general terms, and so it is not surprising to read further that each person has one ultimate end, namely, perfection understood as the fullest possible development and exercise of one's active powers (1.5); what is more, each person desires and does everything on account of this last end (1.6). All human beings share in this same last end, insofar as each person naturally desires his or her perfection (1.7); indeed, in a sense we share this last end with all other creatures, since every creature is naturally oriented toward pursuing and maintaining its existence in accordance with a full and perfect development of its specific form (1.8). At the same time, however, the human person desires and pursues perfection in a distinctive way, through deliberate actions carried out with an aim toward securing or maintaining that end (1.8).

At this point, Aquinas joins the classical tradition of reflection on happiness. As he has already explained in another context, happiness is equivalent to the perfection proper to a rational or intellectual creature: "by the name of happiness is understood the ultimate perfection of a rational or intellectual nature; and hence it is something that is naturally desired, since everything naturally desires its own ultimate perfection" (I 62.1). He thus moves directly from his analysis of the end of human life, generally considered, to a more focused analysis of the concept of happiness (I-II 2-5). He sets out, first of all, to give a substantive meaning to the formal concept of happiness, considered as perfection, and after rejecting various alternatives (I-II 2.1-7), he concludes that the final end of human life can only be God, attained through contemplation — an answer which might also have been given in antiquity, except for the further qualification that the mode of attainment in question utterly transcends the natural capacities of the human (or any other kind of) creature (I-II 2.8; cf. I 12.4; I-II 5.5).[19]

Aquinas goes on to argue that the beatific vision meets the criteria for happiness which emerged in the classical discussion, and does so better than any of the traditional alternatives (I-II 3.8). It is completely satisfying, because it reflects the fullest possible development, that is to say, perfection, of our capacities for knowing and desiring; it is comprehensive and complete; and it can be enjoyed with perfect security, since it endures eternally and can in no way be lost (3.8; 5.3, 4; cf. 2.4; 3.2 *ad* 4).[20] It is thus apparent that the happiness

19. These points are developed more fully in the *Summa contra gentiles,* in which Aquinas first establishes that the ultimate end of human life can only be the direct contemplation of God in the beatific vision (III 37), and then goes on to argue that the kinds of contemplation of God accessible to us in this life do not constitute ultimate happiness (III 38-40).

20. Again, the relevant arguments are set forth more fully in the *SCG;* see in particular III 63.

of the beatific vision fulfills Aquinas's own formal definition of happiness offered in the *prima pars,* insofar as it constitutes the ultimate perfection of a rational nature. By this standard, every putative candidate for happiness falls short, so much so that only the beatific vision can be said without qualification to be happiness (I-II 3.8).

Aquinas's remarks on this last score are so emphatic that some commentators have concluded that he denies (or at least does not advert to) the possibility of a form of happiness which is connatural to the human being considered as a specific kind of creature.[21] Yet elsewhere he explicitly refers to a kind of happiness that is connatural to the human person and is as such proportionate to those virtues we can attain through our own natural powers, unaided by grace (I-II 5.5, 7; 62.1; 63.3). What is more, these alternatives do not exhaust the possibilities for Aquinas. He also refers to a kind of happiness that is not connatural to us, because it presupposes grace, but which falls short of ultimate and complete happiness (5.3 *ad* 1, and more clearly 69.1, 2), and he also describes the fulfillment of one's will as a kind of happiness (5.8). Drawing on a distinction going back to William of Auxerre, he identifies terrestrial happiness in both its natural and supernatural forms as a kind of imperfect happiness, in contrast to the perfect happiness of the beatific vision (see, for example, 4.6-8 and 5.3-5).[22]

Aquinas's account of happiness is thus complex. Not only does he distinguish between perfect and imperfect happiness, he also identifies more than one kind of imperfect happiness, and correlatively, he understands "imperfect" in this context in more than one way. The happiness of those who have grace is an imperfect anticipation of happiness in the unqualified sense, and yet it has the potential to develop into full happiness (I-II 69.1, 2); the kind of happiness that is properly connatural to us, in contrast, is not just relatively limited and incomplete, but qualitatively different from perfect happiness (62.1; 63.3). As for the fourth kind of happiness, equated with the fulfillment of one's will, Aquinas only mentions this in passing. However, it appears from the context that this kind of happiness, unlike the others, can include not only limited and imperfect but downright false kinds of happiness, since men and women do in fact seek happiness in all kinds of distorted ways (I-II 5.8; cf. II-II 23.7).

It would thus be a mistake to assume that Aquinas recognizes only one

21. The alternatives are clearly set out in Anton Pegis, "Nature and Spirit: Some Reflections on the Problem of the End of Man," *Proceedings of the American Catholic Philosophical Association* 23 (1949): 62-79, and Kevin Staley, "Happiness: The Natural End of Man?" *The Thomist* 53, no. 2 (1989): 215-34; for further references, see chap. 2, n. 70.

22. As Weiland points out; see Weiland, "Happiness," 679.

kind of happiness, namely, the supreme happiness of the beatific vision; but we would be equally mistaken to conclude that he envisions a plurality of forms of happiness, having no intrinsic relation to one another. We have already noted that he argues, near the beginning of the *prima secundae,* that there can be only one ultimate end of human life (I-II 1.4). As Kevin Staley puts it, "Thomas does not argue that man has two ends, the one natural and the other supernatural. Rather, he speaks of a single end which is twofold, which is realized at both a natural and a supernatural level, and which he describes in the *Summa Theologiae* as imperfect and perfect beatitude respectively."[23] Aquinas advisedly begins with a consideration of the last end of human life understood in a general and formal sense, because this provides him with a framework within which to analyze and relate the diverse senses of happiness, seen as different ways within which the human person might be said to attain the ultimate end.

This ultimate end, we should recall, is identified by Aquinas as perfection, that is to say, the fullest possible development of one's potentialities in accordance with one's specific form. This implies that different senses of happiness are to be understood in terms of diverse levels or modalities of perfection. Admittedly, his distinction between perfect and imperfect forms of happiness would seem to imply that we ought to think, paradoxically, in terms of perfect and imperfect kinds of perfection. We can make sense of this line of analysis, however, if we formulate it in terms of different stages or levels of perfection. Thus, the imperfect happiness that we enjoy through grace would be regarded as imperfect in the sense of incomplete, undeveloped but potentially capable of being perfected in the full sense. The kind of happiness that is connatural to us as creatures of a specific kind, in contrast, is imperfect by contrast to the greater possibility revealed to us, yet considered on its own level it represents (at least ideally) the complete perfection of the human creature in accordance with its natural principles of operation.[24]

23. Staley, "Happiness," 227; Weiland makes a similar point in Weiland, "Happiness," 678-80. I would add, however, that Aquinas does in fact recognize the existence of a kind of natural happiness which could be experienced and enjoyed as a limited but distinctive kind of happiness even if we had not been called to any further end; on this point, I agree with Steven Long, "On the Possibility of a Purely Natural End for Man," *The Thomist* 64 (2000): 211-37.

24. Of course, this kind of happiness would be transitory and limited at best, and we would be aware of those limitations — yet, as Long suggests, this does not necessarily imply that we would not find natural fulfillment to be satisfying, or that we would be tormented by unfulfilled longings, if we had not in fact been called to the higher happiness of direct union with God. See "On the Possibility," 226-29. I should add that in my view, the natural desire for happiness should not be equated straightforwardly with a natural desire to see God; however, it would take us too far afield to pursue this complex and much-debated topic.

Finally, the derivative kind of happiness to which Aquinas refers in I-II 5.8, consisting in the fulfillment of one's will, need not amount to the attainment of genuine perfection in any sense at all. It can only be regarded as a kind of happiness because the human creature, unlike nonrational kinds of creatures, can only attain happiness through a knowing pursuit of a final end, which opens up distinctive possibilities for going wrong. In particular, it opens up the possibility of sin — and as we read elsewhere, the sinner desires his own good, but does so wrongly, in accordance with a false conception of what he truly is (II-II 25.7). Yet every human person necessarily desires his or her perfection, whether truly or falsely understood, and this is tantamount to happiness — and thus whatever anyone desires as a supremely fulfilling good can be regarded as a kind of happiness, albeit in a derivative sense (Aquinas does not explicitly argue in these terms, but cf. II-II 23.7).

When Aquinas turns explicitly to the question, "What is happiness?" (I-II 3), he introduces a further distinction. That is, he begins his consideration of this question by noting that happiness can be described (as we might say) either objectively or subjectively, that is to say, in terms of whatever is pursued as a supremely fulfilling good or in terms of one's actual attainment and enjoyment of that good (3.1). This suggests a sharp division between perfect happiness and the different forms of imperfect happiness that we can attain in this life, because as Aquinas has just said, no finite good can fulfill the human desire for happiness; only God can do so. Yet reading on, we find that taken in another sense, this line of analysis opens up a further way of interrelating the different proper senses of happiness. That is to say, considered from the perspective of a human state or attainment, happiness in every sense is something created (3.1), and more specifically, it is a certain kind of operation: "insofar as the happiness of the human person is something created existing in the person, it is necessary to say that human happiness is an operation. For happiness is the ultimate perfection of the human person. Now anything is so far perfect, to the extent that it is in act; for a potency without act is imperfect. Hence it is necessary that happiness should consist in the ultimate act of the human person" (3.2).

In order to see what Aquinas is getting at here, we need to recall that on his view, every kind of creature is naturally oriented toward the fullest possible development of the ordered mode of functioning natural to its kind. Perfection is understood, correlatively, as the fullest possible development and expression of the creature's dispositions and capacities, in accordance with the inclinations proper to the specific kind of thing it is. For living creatures, including ourselves, perfection is expressed in a particular way of life developed through the exercise of the "ordered functional capacities" constituting the creature's form — that is to say, perfection consists in operations. What is more, actuality is the fundamental characteristic of any kind of existence — every actually existing thing is in act, and can be said to be perfect insofar as it is fully in act.[25] Thus, happiness as perfection is correlated with the more general idea of actuality as perfection — the happiness of the rational creature is nothing other than its way of being in act, of being perfect in accordance with its specific kind. The complexity of the human creature implies that unlike other animals, we can attain perfection in diverse ways and at disparate levels, including some which go beyond our natural capacities. But no matter how perfection is understood, it will necessarily involve some degree of proper development and exercise of the capacities distinctive to us as creatures of a specific kind — that is just what perfection is.

This line of analysis opens up a way of making sense of the otherwise paradoxical notion of imperfect degrees of perfection, because as Aquinas's comments suggest, one's active powers can be engaged and developed at different levels. The beatific vision represents the greatest possible exercise and development of distinctively human capabilities for knowledge and rationally informed love, and overflows into the other faculties as well (I-II 3.3-5). No finite object can engage human capabilities in a similarly complete and fulfilling way. Yet our distinctively human capabilities for knowledge and love are of course engaged and operative in this life — and while the finite objects of our knowledge and love cannot be said objectively to constitute happiness, the operations themselves can be said to constitute a kind of happiness, insofar as they are genuinely good, and as such genuinely perfective of the agent. Indeed, given the connection between happiness and perfection on which Aquinas insists, he could hardly say anything else.

This brings us to what we might describe as the substantive content of the different forms of terrestrial happiness. At I-II 3.5, Aquinas remarks that imperfect happiness consists primarily in the operations of the speculative intellect, and secondarily in the operations of the practical intellect. This might seem to suggest that he has simply taken over Aristotle's assertion that the contemplative life offers the only true form of happiness, even bracketing the possibility of a supernatural fulfillment. In some of his earlier writings, he does indeed seem to say as much, but by this point he has clearly qualified and revised this view.[26] As Weiland points out, the logic of his analysis of hap-

25. For further details, see Robert Pasnau's illuminating discussion of the metaphysics of actuality in *Thomas Aquinas on Human Nature: A Philosophical Study of "Summa theologiae" Ia 75-89* (Cambridge: Cambridge University Press, 2002), 143-51.

26. See, for example, *De veritate* 27.2.

piness as perfection implies that happiness must be a perfection of the whole human being, not just one's speculative intellect; what is more, his commitment to the unity of human nature rules out an Aristotelian view according to which there are two substantively different kinds of happiness, represented by the contemplative and active life respectively.[27] These two ways of life must rather be regarded as emblematic of two aspects of an overall human good, which must as such be brought into some integral connection.

Reading further, we find that he identifies the kinds of happiness attainable in this life with the operations of the intellect, whether speculative or practical (I-II 4.5) — which is to say, with the operations of the virtues, through which (as we later read) the capacities of the human person are developed in such a way as to operate properly (4.6; 55.4). Thus, he goes on to say that connatural human happiness, of a sort that can be attained through the appropriate development of our natural powers, consists in the operations of the virtues (5.5; cf. 62.1; 109.2). Similarly, the happiness we enjoy in this life through grace consists in the practice of the infused virtues and the accompanying gifts of the Holy Spirit (69.1). As such, it is given substantive content by the Beatitudes, which represent both conditions for and enjoyments proper to the kind of terrestrial happiness proper to the life of grace (69.1-2).[28] Certainly, the life of virtue cannot be the ultimate end of human life. Nonetheless, Aquinas identifies both forms of genuine terrestrial happiness, which admittedly fall short of ultimate happiness, with the practice of the virtues, whether acquired or infused.[29]

At this point, it might seem that we have lost sight of well-being and its relation to happiness. Aquinas does not in fact include anything resembling a nonmoral form of well-being among the different senses of happiness that he identifies, and this fact is significant. But it does not imply that well-being as understood here has no importance for him. On the contrary, virtue presupposes well-being, both conceptually and practically — that is to say, the inclinations and satisfactions proper to a life of basic well-being provide the starting points, and as it were, the material for the development, practice, and reflective understanding of the virtues. Indeed, properly human well-being *is*

27. See Weiland, "Happiness," 678-80. I am bracketing the difficult question of whether this was in fact Aristotle's view.

28. The Beatitudes have received little attention in theological ethics. The work of Servais Pinckaers represents a noteworthy exception, however; see, for example, *L'Evangile et la morale*, 56-64.

29. Thus, in the *SCG* III 34-35 Aquinas says *ultimate* happiness does not consist in the practice of the moral virtues or prudence; but in contrast, other putative candidates for happiness are said without qualification not to count as happiness.

more or less equivalent to the life of virtue — more or less, because some aspects of well-being can be attained without virtue, and conversely, it is possible to attain and practice acquired virtue (and even more, infused virtue) under conditions which rule out the full enjoyment of natural well-being. As we will see, the ideal of virtue is not only more comprehensive than the ideal of well-being, it can take forms which seem, at least prima facie, to renounce aspects of the more basic ideal — the obvious example being the monastic ideal of poverty, celibacy, and obedience, explicitly defended by Aquinas and his contemporaries as a life of praiseworthy renunciation of fundamental human goods. Nonetheless, we will see that human well-being stands to the life of virtue not only as condition or ground, but also as a touchstone for the paradigmatic instantiation of what turns out to be a wider and more complex ideal.

We are accustomed to regard natural law and virtue as two distinct and even opposed approaches to moral reasoning, although in recent years there have been some important attempts to bring them together.[30] For Aquinas's own interlocutors, the line of analysis proposed here, according to which the natural law takes its norms from the virtues, would not have seemed especially surprising or original. Other scholastic theologians note that the precepts of the natural law are the first principles of the civic or political virtues, and both William of Auxerre and Albert develop their natural law theories in the context of a wider discussion of the virtues. What is distinctive about Aquinas's account is rather the way he identifies terrestrial forms of happiness with the practice of the virtues. In what follows I take this connection as a starting point for developing a Thomistic account of the natural law.

More specifically, I will argue that happiness is the proximate origin for the norms of the natural law. The kind of happiness in question is terrestrial happiness, understood in both its natural and graced forms as equivalent to the practice of the virtues. The virtues, in turn, are dispositions perfecting our capacities for knowledge and love, as these are exercised throughout the whole range of activities necessary to sustaining human life. Thus, considered

30. These would include, among philosophers, Hursthouse, *On Virtue Ethics,* especially 25-42, and among theologians, Servais Pinckaers, *Ce qu'on ne peut jamais faire: La question des actes intrinsèquement mauvais, Histoire et discussion* (Fribourg: Editions Universitaires Fribourg, 1986), 131-36; Pamela Hall, *Narrative and the Natural Law: An Interpretation of Thomistic Ethics* (Notre Dame: University of Notre Dame Press, 1994); and Martin Rhonheimer, *Natural Law and Practical Reason: A Thomist View of Moral Autonomy,* trans. Gerald Malsbary (New York: Fordham University Press, 2000). Pinckaers's remarks on this subject are illuminating but somewhat sketchy; I discuss Rhonheimer and Hall in more detail below. Annas sets out the main lines of classical reflection on this question in *The Morality of Happiness,* 84-108.

as normative ideals, they stem from and are ineliminably shaped by the natural inclinations and needs of the human organism. Hence, our paradigms for virtuous behavior, together with the reflective ideals grounded in those paradigms, represent the point of connection between well-being and the norms of the natural law — between nature as nature, in Albert's words, and nature as reason. Admittedly, this argument goes beyond anything Aquinas explicitly says. He does say, however, that precepts stem from the virtues, and not conversely, which at least suggests that a line of argument proceeding from exigencies of virtuous behavior to norms of natural law is not foreign to his overall intent (*De malo* 2.6). At any rate, as I hope to show in more detail in what follows, this line of analysis draws on and develops his remarks on the virtues and their relation to human well-being on the one hand, and ideals of human perfection on the other.

2. Well-Being, Happiness, and the Practice of the Virtues

In the *ST,* Aquinas develops an account of virtue out of the analysis of a more general notion of a *habitus.* This, he explains, is a stable disposition of a human capacity for knowledge or desire, through which the capacity is given sufficient determination to be exercised through some action (I-II 49.3, 4). More specifically, the moral virtues are *habitūs,* or stable dispositions, of the distinctively human capacities for intellectual activity, judgment, and desire, through which the human person is disposed to act in good and appropriate ways, and to avoid vicious kinds of actions (55.1).[31] This implies that the virtues are operative habits, oriented toward producing identifiable kinds of actions (55.2); what is more, in order to count as a virtue, a disposition must be oriented toward a good kind of action, since "virtue" implies a kind of perfection, which is always as such good (55.3). Aquinas goes on to say that the definition of virtue set forth by Peter Lombard in the *Sentences* is the best of the traditional definitions available: "Virtue is a good quality of the mind, by which we live righteously, of which no one can make bad use, which God brings about in us, without us" (55.4). Of course, he has to tweak this defini-

31. "Somewhat the same way," because without the habit of virtue a person can act out of desire — she just cannot act well. It may be that Aquinas would make the stronger claim that without some stable inclination to act in one way rather than another (i.e., a virtue or a vice), an individual is not capable of acting out of desire in sense proper to human action, that is to say, out of a reasoned idea (legitimate or faulty) of the object of the desire as an appropriate and attainable good. But in any case, the weaker claim will do for the purposes of the theory being developed.

tion in order to bring it into line with his overall analysis. He interprets "a good quality of the mind" in such a way as to render it equivalent to his more technical notion of a *habitus*. Even more importantly, he notes that the last clause of the definition applies only to the infused virtues, which God bestows on us without action on our part. Thus, he introduces a distinction between infused virtues, which have union with God as their direct or indirect aim, and acquired virtues, which are directed toward the attainment of the human good as discerned by reason and can be attained by human action (as the name suggests).

In subsequent questions, we find that Aquinas identifies the acquired virtues with the traditional cardinal virtues, that is to say, temperance, fortitude, justice, and prudence (I-II 61.1). These can be understood either as general qualities of moral goodness or as specific virtues with their own characteristic forms of expression (61.2-4). The acquired virtues are distinguished from the traditional theological virtues, faith, hope, and charity, which cannot be acquired but must be bestowed on us directly by God (62.1, 2). However, he goes on to say that the infusion of charity brings with it infused cardinal virtues, which are specifically different from their acquired counterparts because they are directed toward a different end (63.3).

I have reviewed the main lines of Aquinas's theory of virtue in order to provide a context within which to return in a more focused way to the question raised above. What (if anything) do the virtues, so understood, have to do with the attainment of happiness? We might assume that the virtues provide a means to the attainment of happiness — either in the sense that we earn eternal happiness through a virtuous life, or through serving as instrumental means to the attainment of happiness here and now. Aquinas makes it clear that we can be said to merit eternal life only in an extended and carefully qualified sense, because he is at pains to insist on the complete gratuity of the grace from which the infused virtues stem.[32] Moreover, there is no indication that he regards earthly happiness as a divinely apportioned reward for virtuous living. This leaves other possibilities for relating the virtues to happiness in this life, however. One obvious possibility is that the virtues are instrumental means to the attainment of well-being or happiness, or at least to some of the goods necessary to well-being. This general view has been defended by a number of moral philosophers, most notably Rosalind Hursthouse, and in

32. Joseph Wawrykow offers a comprehensive and insightful analysis of the relevant texts in *God's Grace and Human Action: Merit in the Theology of Thomas Aquinas* (Notre Dame: University of Notre Dame Press, 1995); he discusses Aquinas's mature teaching, including especially the *Summa theologiae*, at 147-259.

his recent *Contingency and Fortune in Aquinas' Ethic*, John Bowlin has argued that this is Aquinas's view as well.[33]

In Bowlin's view, the virtues as Aquinas understands them can only be understood in relation to "goods of fortune" — health, material possessions, friendship, and the like — which are contingent in the sense that they may or may not be acquired or retained. Bowlin does not regard these "goods of fortune" as constituting an overall state of flourishing or happiness, but he does attempt to locate Aquinas's virtue ethic within the framework of classical concerns about the permanence or contingency of human flourishing, insofar as it is dependent, or not, on such goods. For that reason, his analysis provides us with a useful starting point for considering the relation between virtue and more basic forms of well-being in Aquinas's thought.

As Bowlin interprets it, Aquinas's theory of virtue attempts to hold together two disparate approaches to the virtues: an Aristotelian perspective according to which the virtues are directed toward attaining happiness in a world governed by fortune, and a Stoic perspective, which Aquinas inherits from Augustine, according to which the virtuous person is invulnerable to harm.[34] Bowlin goes on to argue that the Aristotelian view predominates in Aquinas's virtue ethic, since he agrees with Aristotle that the virtues have the functional aim of securing an uncertain and difficult human good. Yet Aquinas also wants to claim that the exercise of the virtues, and their efficacy in securing the human good, is more or less invulnerable to the vagaries of fortune. For this reason, he is attracted to the Stoic view according to which the exercise of the virtues is good in itself. In the last analysis, Bowlin claims, Aquinas does not accept this view, but he does attempt to show through a series of complex arguments that the human good secured by virtue is nonetheless relatively stable and secure. Hence, on Bowlin's view Aquinas understands the virtues to be instrumental, at least so far as this-worldly goods are concerned.

This line of interpretation has much to commend it. Most importantly, Bowlin reminds us that for Aquinas the virtues are normally exercised in and through the pursuit of discrete goods, and therefore they cannot be under-

33. Hursthouse argues for this view in *On Virtue Ethics*, 170-74. However, she goes on to claim that we should not expect to convince the wicked of the desirability of virtue, and this would seem to imply, at the very least, that virtue is not simply instrumental to the attainment of morally neutral desiderata; see 178-87. Bowlin's views are set forth in *Contingency and Fortune in Aquinas' Ethic* (Cambridge: Cambridge University Press, 1999).

34. For a summary of the main lines of the argument, see *Contingency and Fortune*, 12-18; Bowlin argues for what he describes as the "functional character" of the moral virtues (138) at 138-66.

stood without some reference to these goods. As we will see, the relation between the virtues and happiness cannot be understood unless this fundamental point is kept in mind. Yet that does not mean that the virtues serve as instrumental means, even for the attainment of happiness insofar as we can achieve it in this life — on the contrary, as we have seen, Aquinas identifies terrestrial happiness with the practice of the virtues. If the practice of the virtues is constitutive of terrestrial happiness, then it hardly makes sense to say that these virtues are also instrumental means for attaining the discrete goods associated with well-being in a more basic sense. If there is a link between the virtues and these kinds of goods, it would seem to go in the other direction — that is, we might suspect that these goods are means toward the practice of the virtues, as Aquinas seems at some points to suggest (see, for example, I-II 2.4; 4.5-8).

At this point we should recall that for Aquinas, genuine happiness on every level is understood in terms of perfection, which is further interpreted in terms of actuality expressed through operations.[35] The corollary, which Aquinas explicitly states, is that happiness cannot be identified with the possession of any finite good (I-II 2.8), even though created goods (especially the body itself) are necessary conditions for the operations which comprise happiness, at least in this life (for example, see 4.6, 7). The only good that can be associated with happiness, objectively understood, is God (2.8), and even this infinite good is attained through an operation of the blessed. Given Aquinas's equation of happiness with perfection and therefore with the practice of the virtues, it would seem that even connatural happiness as Aquinas understands it cannot be identified, even in part, with the attainment of discrete goods. At most, the attainment of these goods might be equated with happiness in the fourth and weakest sense identified above — that is to say, for the individual who does consider these goods to be constitutive of her happiness, and who pursues them accordingly, the attainment of these goods might be

35. Bowlin claims that the connections that Aquinas draws among "virtue, perfection, nature and goodness" are "largely metalinguistic. They specify the grammatical rules that govern our talk about perfections, human and other. They circumscribe the logical space where talk of this sort takes place" (*Contingency and Fortune,* 144). Of course, any theory will serve, inter alia, to identify the proper domain for a relevant kind of discourse. Kant's theory of morality implies that the domain of moral discourse applies to God, angels, and human persons, but not to rabbits (except perhaps as objects of moral duties); the theory of evolution by natural selection implies that the discourse of the development of species has no direct application to data about acquired characteristics. But that does not mean that such theories are "metalinguistic," in the sense of being theories about the use of language rather than theories about the realities discussed in the relevant language. As for Bowlin's further claim that Aquinas's concept of perfection does no moral work (144), I hope to show in what follows that this is not the case.

equated with happiness under the rubric of satisfying her will. But as we have already seen, Aquinas considers the fulfillment of one's will, whatever it may be concretely, to be happiness in an attenuated sense; seen from the perspective of true and complete happiness, or the incomplete but genuine forms of happiness possible to us in this life, the kind of happiness sought in the attainment of specific goods would be regarded as a mistaken form of happiness.

Of course, Aquinas also acknowledges that in this life we need certain discrete goods in order to exercise the virtues, because we need a minimum of the necessities of life in order to act at all, and also because our pursuit and use of these goods constitute the fields of operation for the virtues (at least in part; again, see I-II 4.5-8). Nonetheless, happiness as such cannot consist in the enjoyment of goods at this level, if only because they can be used badly or well. As Aquinas remarks, explaining why happiness cannot consist in power, "power stands in relation towards good and towards evil. Happiness, however, is the proper and perfect good of the human person. Hence some happiness could rather consist in the good use of power, which comes about through virtue, than in power itself" (2.4).

It would seem, then, that even terrestrial forms of happiness cannot be identified with the enjoyment of the discrete goods proper to human well-being. Aquinas thus would seem to agree with those classical philosophers who insisted that the good person cannot be harmed, because she or he cannot lose the only thing in which genuine happiness consists — namely, virtue itself. By the same token, basic human well-being would likewise seem to have no intrinsic relationship to happiness in any genuinely positive sense. If this is so, it would have implications for Aquinas's account of natural law, as well as his account of virtue. If the basic forms of well-being that we share with the other animals, and the correlative kinds of harms to which we are invulnerable, are matters of indifference to the virtuous person, then it is difficult to see how considerations stemming from well-being at this level could find any direct place in his moral theory. We might draw support for this interpretation from his frequently repeated remark that virtue, at least in its connatural forms, is grounded in reason. This might well suggest that for Aquinas the natural law stems from the exigencies of reason alone, without any direct indebtedness to the intelligibilities intrinsic to human nature more comprehensively considered. Hence, there would be no place in his moral theory for the idea of "nature as nature," as understood by his contemporaries.

Yet this cannot be right, either. In the first place, Aquinas clearly does believe that the premoral components of human nature do have moral significance. Even though he does not use the language of "nature as nature" in his later works, he does share wider scholastic assumptions about the intelligibility of prerational nature and its moral significance. Indeed, we find more examples of appeals to nature in this sense in Aquinas than we do in many of his contemporaries.[36] This fact would suggest that the relation between virtue and the pursuit and attainment of discrete goods as Aquinas understands it might be more complex than we have so far acknowledged. By the same token, it gives us reason to suspect that for him there is a closer connection between well-being and happiness than we have so far recognized.

There is one further consideration that should lead us to proceed carefully at this point. That is, we have already noted that those ancient philosophers who equated virtue with happiness concluded that the good person cannot be harmed. And yet, as Bowlin rightly insists, Aquinas does say more than once that someone who loses one of the discrete goods, for example, life or honor, suffers harm (see, for example, I-II 100.5, and still more clearly, II-II 123.4; 124.3, 4). Given what we have said so far, we might expect him to explain these claims by arguing that someone who loses (for example) life, thereby loses any further chance to exercise virtue. And that is part of the story for him, but not the whole story. More fundamentally, he identifies certain harms as such by reference to the kinds of goods which are connatural to the human person — for example, life is the most fundamental human good because it reflects the still more fundamental good of simple existence, which every creature strives to maintain (see, for example, II-II 123.8). If this is so, then it would seem that an implicit idea of human well-being does play a role in Aquinas's moral thought, if only a negative role — that is, it is presupposed in his remarks about what counts as a harm.

Does this conclusion imply that after all, happiness should be equated, at least in part, with well-being? This conclusion would be too quick, for as we have seen, Aquinas also says happiness consists in the practice of the virtues and not in the enjoyment of particular goods. But at the very least, Aquinas's remarks about harm suggest that for him the concepts of happiness and harm are not strictly correlative.[37] That is to say, he apparently holds that someone can be genuinely harmed through the loss or deprivation of some particular good, even if that loss cannot undermine the individual's happiness. Admittedly, this sounds paradoxical. The sense of paradox is decreased, however, when we recall that for Aquinas happiness in almost every sense is

36. I marshal the relevant texts in *Natural and Divine Law: Reclaiming the Tradition for Christian Ethics* (Ottawa: Novalis; Grand Rapids: Eerdmans, 1999), 94-95.

37. Hursthouse makes a similar point, although not in reference to Aquinas; see *On Virtue Ethics*, 185-86.

equated with perfection, that is to say, with the full development and expression of one's tendencies and capacities in accordance with one's specific kind.

We have already observed that the idea of perfection, like the idea of happiness, is complex, particularly as applied to a rational creature. It can be realized in diverse ways and on different levels. Furthermore, these levels stand in a complex realization to one another — it is possible to realize perfection on one level, or in some respects, while suffering imperfections at another level. It is possible to attain some aspects or forms of well-being without developing more than a rudimentary degree of virtue, and conversely, it is possible to live a life of outstanding virtue while still suffering significant deprivations at the level of fundamental well-being. Moreover, a level of well-being necessary to attain virtue may not be necessary in order to retain it — we might even regard it as an act of supreme virtue to surrender those goods, up to and including life itself, which originally made it possible to acquire and practice one's virtues. For all these reasons, there can be forms of harm which genuinely undermine one's well-being while still leaving one's perfection qua moral agent untouched — and since Aquinas equates happiness in its most proper senses with this kind of perfection, he can consistently say that such harms, while really such, nonetheless do not take away one's happiness (I-II 5.4).

Nonetheless, Aquinas does recognize that even a virtuous person is genuinely harmed by injury or loss, and at the very least this would suggest that virtuous dispositions need not imply a stance of indifference to basic well-being and the goods constituting it. The virtuous person can reasonably and legitimately attempt to avoid harms at the level of well-being, and this at least suggests that he can legitimately pursue goods at this level. We can take this line of thought one step further. Recall that for Aquinas the life of happiness, at every level but the most basic, is a life of perfection, that is to say, a life of full development and appropriate use of one's active powers. This is why happiness (except in the most rudimentary sense) consists in the practice of the virtues — the virtues are themselves perfections of the active powers of the human creature. Correlatively, each of the distinctively human faculties of the soul has its corresponding virtue, or virtues. The intellect itself is perfected through virtues which (with the exception of prudence) are morally neutral, and for this very reason Aquinas hesitates to describe them as virtues without qualification (I-II 57.1). The appetitive capacities of will and passions, in contrast, are perfected through the moral virtues, which are such in the full sense of the term (58.1). More specifically, prudence or practical wisdom, strictly speaking a virtue of the practical intellect but considered together with the moral virtues properly so called, enables the agent to apply her knowledge of the moral good to specific acts; justice orients the will toward fairness and the common good; courage or fortitude shapes the irascible passions in such a way as to resist obstacles to attaining what is truly good; and temperance shapes the passions of desire in such a way that the agent desires what is truly in accordance with her overall good (I-II 61).

The salient point is that these capacities — the intellect in its practical functions, the will, and the passions, divided by Aquinas into the two broad categories of irascible and desiring — can be analyzed teleologically in terms of the nonmoral functions they play in human life. Indeed, each of these capacities is essential to human life, at anything beyond the level of bare subsistence proper to a very young child. As such, they are shaped by their orientation toward the necessary functions of human life, even prior to their qualification by virtues or vices. For that very reason they are oriented toward some aspect of well-being, even prior to their orientation toward happiness through virtue. Indeed, it is this general orientation which provides the field of operation for the capacity, which is presupposed by the determination of the *habitus* of virtue or vice. Correlatively, the perfection of the capacity brought about by the attainment of virtue must be recognizably a perfection of a capacity which is oriented toward the agent's well-being — otherwise, it would not count as a perfection, that is to say a development and completion, of this particular capacity. In that case, as Aquinas frequently remarks, it would imply the destruction, rather than the perfection, of nature.

If this conclusion is valid, then it suggests that the relationship between well-being and happiness as Aquinas understands it may after all be closer than we might think, given Aquinas's insistence that terrestrial happiness consists in the practice of the virtues. I want to argue that this is in fact the case. This relationship goes in both directions, so to speak. On the one hand, the pursuit and attainment of well-being requires, by its own intrinsic exigencies, at least the rudiments or similitudes of moral virtue; on the other hand, happiness in the proper sense will always be expressed through what is recognizably a form of well-being, albeit what may sometimes appear from some perspectives to be a deficient form. It begins to appear that those forms of happiness comprised of the operations of virtue in this life are integrally related to the pursuit and exercise of human well-being in some form. It is important to keep the qualification "some form" in mind, because the reflective practice of the virtues can itself have the effect of transforming the individual's conception of what well-being looks like. Nonetheless, if the virtues are to be genuinely perfections of the active powers of the human creature, they must be oriented in some way toward some form of well-being. If this is so, then it would appear that the ideal of well-being, which stems from reflection on the intelligibility of nature even in its premoral components, is after all relevant to the life of virtue. And this, as I will argue in more detail in the next section, is indeed the case.

It will be clear by now that we need to qualify the earlier claim that happiness cannot consist in the attainment of particular goods. Nothing that has been said up to this point implies that happiness can be secured through the attainment of particular goods, in the sense that the possession and enjoyment of concrete goods themselves, without regard to the ways they are attained, constitutes happiness. And yet, if earthly happiness consists in the practice of the virtues, and if these virtues operate in and through the pursuit of the goods proper to human life, then there *is* a sense in which happiness is intrinsically connected with the pursuit and enjoyment of more basic forms of well-being. Thus, Bowlin is right to say that Aquinas draws an integral connection between the practice of the virtues and the enjoyment of the proper conditions for, and concomitants of, human well-being. The connection is not instrumental, however, but conceptual — the virtues are nothing other than ordered ways of pursuing, preserving, and enjoying the functional capacities proper to the human creature, and as such they cannot be acquired and exercised except in and through the pursuit and use of discrete goods.

Consider, first of all, the simple case of someone whose virtues are acquired or developed in the context of a life of well-being of a straightforward and easily recognizable kind. By hypothesis, this individual's activities will be shaped by and carried out in the context of a life lived within the parameters which structure most people's lives in every society — marriage, the bearing and education of children, participation in the life of one's family and the wider society, some pursuit of artistic and sporting activities, religious observances, and the like. The point to note is that this individual will exercise his virtues in and through the pursuit, enjoyment, and safeguarding of the many goods which are constitutive of well-being in its most straightforward sense. He will exercise temperance in and through an appropriately moderated enjoyment of enough food and drink to sustain him in his necessary and appropriate activities, and he will exercise sexual chastity in and through the faithful enjoyment of sexual relations with his spouse. He will exercise courage in and through his defense of his family and homeland, patience in educating his children, and perseverance through enduring the difficulties inherent in pursuing his occupation. The same kind of point could be made with respect to every other virtue — in the case we are imagining, we will find that the virtuous person will practice the virtues in and through living a life of well-being of a more fundamental sort.

Does this mean that terrestrial happiness does, after all, depend on the attainment of particular goods? No. It is not the goods themselves, or even their attainment as such, which renders the individual happy. Rather, happiness consists in the practice of the virtues, which itself consists (in part, at least) in the pursuit, attainment, and protection of the basic components of human well-being *in a specified way.* The "specified way," that is to say, a way informed by the ideals of virtue, is constitutive of terrestrial happiness; thus, it is not the enjoyment of the goods as such which counts as happiness, but the exercise of one's virtuous dispositions in and through this enjoyment. That is why Aquinas denies that happiness consists in the attainment of particular goods, even though these are included in the necessary conditions for the practice of virtues. Nonetheless, the qualification of a necessary condition implies a closer relationship than we might have assumed. Normally, the exercise of virtue will be closely bound up with the pursuit and maintenance of human well-being, so much so that the happiness proper to the virtues can be identified on one level, with the qualification just noted, with well-being as it is attained by the virtuous man or woman. And since Aquinas includes enjoyment and delight among the range of virtuous responses, this means that for him the virtuous life will normally be an enjoyable life, satisfying through its participation in the kinds of things that most people, in most times and places, do regard as desirable and fulfilling — marriage, children, a secure place in society, and the like.

As Annas's observations would suggest, Aquinas's claim that happiness consists in the practice of the virtues will only be plausible if it appears that the life of virtue is normally an enjoyable life, which most people would spontaneously find pleasant and desirable. It is therefore significant that Aquinas (following Aristotle) holds that one of the signs of genuine, unimpeded temperance and fortitude is the ability to lead an enjoyable life, enjoyable in terms of full appreciation of the good things we naturally find pleasant. This is not so apparent with respect to fortitude, which after all finds its field of operation in contexts of danger or struggle, but Aquinas insists that even in such situations the individual of true virtue will find some enjoyment in the exercise of his virtue (II-II 123.8). With respect to temperance, the connection between virtue and enjoyment is clear. The truly temperate individual does not have to struggle against desires which are contrary to her own true good, because she does not have such desires, except perhaps fleetingly. To put it another way, it is the mark of true temperance that the individual's desires and enjoyments are in accord with her overall best interest, comprehensively understood (65.3 *ad* 3; 155.1). Furthermore, not only is the temperate individual free from conflicts over inappropriate desires, she spontaneously desires and really enjoys those satisfactions which are consistent with her overall good. By the same token, Aquinas regards insensibility, indifference to pleasure or the inability to enjoy it, as a defect of character (II-II 142.1). Aquinas does not equate happiness at any level, even the most defective, with enjoyment in the sense of emotional satisfaction (I-II 4.1). But recall Annas's reminder that happiness, however understood, connotes some measure of satisfaction with one's life. Seen from this perspective, it should count in favor of Aquinas's overall conception of happiness that for him the life of happiness is, normally and properly, also an enjoyable life. And it is at least suggestive that the joys and pleasures of the happy life are intimately bound up with enjoyment of those goods which are proper to the life of well-being.[38]

The enjoyable character of a life of virtue becomes still more apparent when we turn our attention to those virtues which characteristically operate within the sphere of human relationships. Hursthouse makes this point in the context of explaining how the virtues can be said to be good for their possessor. She imagines someone explaining why honesty is a desirable character trait. At first, her imaginary interlocutor offers reasons referring to goods which could also be secured by other means: "It's so much easier than being dishonest; you don't have to keep a constant guard on your tongue and worry about the details of what you should say."[39] But the interlocutor then goes on to say, "It's such an essential part of good relationships that there should be trust between you; as Bacon says, 'A principal fruit of friendship is the ease and discharge of the heart. . . . No receipt openeth the heart but a true friend, to whom you may impart whatsoever lieth upon the heart to oppress it.' And who would want to be loved and respected for a facade one presents rather than what one is?"[40] In other words, the virtue of honesty is an integral constituent of certain kinds of human relationships, such as open and intimate friendship. It is not a means to the attainment of this kind of friendship, as if it were possible (but just, perhaps, a bit harder) to attain the kind of friendship Bacon describes by deceitful means as well as by mutual honesty; rather, the enjoyment of this kind of friendship *is* in part the practice of the virtue of honesty. We can readily think of other virtues which are similarly constitutive of certain kinds of human relationships; one obvious example would be fidelity, seen in relation to a mutually satisfying marriage, and we could also mention compassion and tenderness in the context of a parent-child relation, mutual respect in the context of public relations, and the like. As Candace Vogler

38. Again, Hursthouse makes a similar point in *On Virtue Ethics,* 185-86.

39. Hursthouse, *On Virtue Ethics,* 168.

40. Hursthouse, *On Virtue Ethics,* 168, ellipsis in original.

puts it, "some modes of intercourse with our fellows are only possible if we side with the ethical, and some joys are not available to the wicked."[41]

At the same time, the practice of virtue, and correlatively happiness, does not depend on the attainment or the secure possession of any one of the goods associated with well-being, or even necessarily a sufficiency of them. This is why it is possible on Aquinas's terms to say that someone can attain and sustain virtue, even in the face of deprivations and losses which undermine basic well-being understood in any plausible way. The criteria for perfection which inform the virtues are taken, in part, from the exigencies of well-being, but if well-being cannot be achieved or sustained for some reason other than the individual's own wrongdoing, she can still attain virtue in and through pursuing the ideals of virtue to the extent possible to her. By the same token, someone who is deprived of important elements of well-being need not lose the capacity to exercise virtue, unless he is so unfortunate as to lose all ability to act as a responsible agent. Finally, as we will see, the exigencies of reflection on the virtues themselves open up the possibility that the happiness proper to virtue may be consistent with ways of living which involve the deliberate renunciation of some aspects of well-being.

Hence, the attainment of well-being is neither necessary nor sufficient for the attainment of happiness. Nonetheless, a life of well-being, pursued and lived in a certain way, provides the paradigmatic instance of a virtuous life — paradigmatic, because this reflects the form that the life of virtue will actually take for most people, and paradigmatic in the more basic sense that the exigencies of human well-being will inform the criteria for the ideals of the virtues. Hence, even though the practice of the virtues, and therefore happiness, does not depend on the attainment of well-being for Aquinas, the idea of well-being does have a normative function in his overall account of moral virtue. Virtues are dispositions of human capacities oriented toward well-being, and as such they take their norms, in key part if not entirely, from the exigencies of basic well-being (see, for example, II-II 141.6). And since the idea of well-being forms the link between nature in the more comprehensive sense and the norms of the natural law — between nature as nature and nature as reason — this suggests that for Aquinas the idea of human well-being yields natural law precepts through the mediation of ideals of virtue, which are themselves developed from general paradigms to reflective ideals through a process of reflection on what it means to live a complete, fulfilled — in a word, perfect — human life.

41. Candace Vogler, *Reasonably Vicious* (Cambridge: Harvard University Press, 2002), 203.

At this point, we need to guard against two misunderstandings. The close connection between virtue and law in Aquinas's thought has sometimes been invoked to support an interpretation according to which the natural law has no, or at most very minimal, moral content.[42] But this way of reading Aquinas again makes the mistake of interpreting his moral thought in light of our own presuppositions about the virtues. Aquinas makes it clear that ideals of virtues do have normative content, expressed (among other ways) through their correlation with specific precepts of divine (that is to say, revealed) law. Yet we would fall into a contrary error if we concluded that the virtues consist in nothing more than dispositions to follow determinate, independently formulated rules of conduct.[43] Both lines of interpretation distort Aquinas — and render him less interesting than he really is — by failing to take account of the way he understands virtues and precepts of law as mutually conditioning one another, both at the level of the acquisition and attainment of moral knowledge and at the level of theoretical formulation.

When we examine what Aquinas has to say about the virtues, the natural law, and the fundamental principles underlying both, it is apparent that he presupposes a richer and more persuasive account of their relationship than either of these alternatives offers. In the first chapter, we observed that for Aquinas the natural law represents the rational creature's distinctive mode of participating in God's providence. This implies that the natural law is intrinsically oriented (in some way) toward the attainment of the agent's final end, since God's providence is precisely that aspect of God's activity through which all creatures are directed in orderly ways toward their final end — their individual perfection, first of all, and secondly the perfection of the cosmos taken as a whole. Moreover, as we noted in the last chapter, God's providential care is expressed in and through the operation of the inclinations proper to each kind of creature. As Aquinas explains in his commentary on pseudo-Dionysius's *The Divine Names,* God is said to govern the universe through "voluntary laws":

> It may happen, however, that some prince, who may be desirable in his own person, will nonetheless give onerous laws to his subjects, which he himself does not keep, and therefore his subjects are not effectively sub-

42. This is Bowlin's view; see *Contingency and Fortune,* 93-137. For a further, highly influential statement of this position, see Daniel Mark Nelson, *The Priority of Prudence: Virtue and Natural Law in Aquinas and Its Implications for Modern Ethics* (University Park: Pennsylvania State University Press, 1992).

43. This seems to be the view adopted, for example, by John Finnis in *Aquinas: Moral, Political, and Legal Theory* (Oxford: Oxford University Press, 1998), 167-70.

> jected to him. But since this is excluded from God, [Dionysius] adds that he sets *voluntary laws* over *all;* for the law of God is the proper natural inclination placed in every creature to do that which is appropriate to it, in accordance with nature. And therefore, since all things are held by divine desire, so all are held by his law. (*De divinis nominibus* X, 1.1, 857)

This general observation would apply to us, as well as to every other kind of creature. That is why, as Aquinas elsewhere explains, the precepts of the natural law pertain to the natural inclinations of the human person, and stand in an ordering to one another determined by those inclinations (*ST* I-II 94.2). At the same time, however, the inclinations of the human person are indeterminate in a way that the inclinations of nonrational creatures are not. They can be expressed in ways that undermine the agent's attainment of her good, as well as in ways that promote it. If the inclinations are to function in such a way as to promote the agent's true good, they must be directed by appropriate dispositions toward action — and that is precisely what the virtues are. Hence, as Aquinas remarks, each natural inclination corresponds to a particular virtue, disposing it to operate in an appropriate way (II-II 108.2). This implies what Aquinas elsewhere says explicitly, namely, that the virtues are internal principles of action, dispositions of the agent from which his acts stem. At the same time, however, the precepts of the natural law constitute a set of complementary external principles of action — external, in the sense of reflecting the objective norms by which acts are to be evaluated (see the introduction to I-II 49). Each virtue is thus correlated with one or more precepts, as an examination of the discussions of particular virtues in the *summa secundae* will confirm. Yet these precepts themselves are not imposed "from without," so to speak; rather, as we will see, they emerge out of natural and rational exigencies emerging from the operation of the virtues themselves. That is why Aquinas can say at different points that both the precepts of the natural law and the virtues stem from the first principles of practical reason (I-II 94.2; II-II 47.6).

This brings us to a central point. In Aquinas's view, the substantive content inherent in ideals of virtue cannot be understood apart from some consideration of the virtues as perfections of the agent. Hence, ideals of virtue cannot be formulated unless we take account of the intrinsic connection between happiness and the practice of the virtues. This does not mean that Aquinas derives norms of virtue from a general idea of well-being or happiness. To a very considerable degree, he takes the normative ideals associated with particular virtues from his sources, classical as well as Christian, and to the extent that he relies on these sources he does not derive norms of virtue from any general principle.[44] At the same time, however, he interprets these sources in light of his overall conception of happiness, in such a way as to present ideals of particular virtues as exemplifications of a general ideal of perfection. Moreover, while it is certainly possible to question his reading of this or that particular author, on the whole, this approach works — it enables him to integrate the diverse perspectives of a wide range of sources into a coherent account of the virtues, while still offering credible interpretations of his particular sources. The success of his approach, in turn, lends credence to his overall claim that this-worldly happiness consists in the practice of the virtues.

Of course, Aquinas's approach would be broadly congenial to most of the authors on whom he draws, because as we have seen, his connection between virtue and happiness has well-established classical antecedents. This fact might suggest that Aquinas's approach is successful because he is participating in a self-referential tradition of reflection on the virtues, the assumptions of which he broadly shares. But it is also possible that the persistence and apparent success of this approach tells us something about the virtues and their place in human life — more specifically, that it reflects the fact that the life of virtue is credibly a happy life, and that traditional ideals of virtue have been shaped through an extended process of reflection on happiness and its relation to more basic forms of well-being. That, at least, is the possibility that we will explore in the next section.

3. Ideals of Virtue and Norms of Nature

Happiness, at least in its terrestrial forms, consists in the life of virtue. Correlatively, the ideals of particular virtues which have emerged over time, through common experience and reflection as well as theoretical speculation, provide us with a rich, albeit rough and unsystematic, fund of moral norms stemming from a teleological ideal of human nature. Thus, by indicating how diverse elements of well-being ought to be pursued and enjoyed, the virtues provide mediating principles between a basic teleological conception of hu-

44. By "particular virtues" *(speciales virtutes)*, Aquinas means habitual dispositions of particular faculties (the will or passions, for example), which incline the agent to act in identifiable ways within some delimited sphere of human life — in contrast to "general" virtues, that is to say, the virtues considered as general dispositions which operate across the whole range of human actions. He acknowledges the legitimacy of both ways of speaking, but prefers the former. The basic distinction is set forth in I-II 61.3; he indicates his preference for the former way of speaking at I-II 61.4.

man nature and the properly moral norms of the natural law. To put the point in another way, they provide us with a point of connection between an account of human nature, considered as intelligible and good — "nature as nature" — and natural law precepts considered as expressions of human rationality — "nature as reason." These, at least, are the conclusions suggested at the end of the last section.

In this section I will defend and expand upon these conclusions, in order to show how Aquinas's account of the virtues and happiness points the way toward developing a conception of natural happiness which is manifestly grounded in a more basic idea of well-being, but which also has substantive moral content. The key to this line of argument lies in the claim that the paradigmatic ideals of the virtues emerge out of fundamental exigencies of human life and reflect plausible conditions for the exercise of the basic capabilities of the human creature. As we saw in the last section, this does not mean that the virtues should be regarded as instrumental means to the attainment of well-being, or to the various goods enjoyed in a life of well-being. Terrestrial happiness comprises operations and activities — the practice of the virtues — through which the goods of life are sought and enjoyed in specific ways, rather than the possession of the goods in itself. By the same token, it would be a mistake to think of a life of basic well-being as something that could be envisioned and pursued — much less, actually enjoyed — apart from some specification through a set of ideals of virtue or the good life. To return to the point made above, the life of virtue *is* the life of well-being in its fullest and most proper form, and for that very reason the practice of the virtues cannot be regarded as an instrumental means to the attainment of well-being.

By the same token, however, our conceptions of the virtues reflect the conceptual link between these ideals and more basic notions of well-being. The virtues are dispositions perfecting capacities for knowledge and reasoned desire (including the passions, insofar as these are shaped by reason, as well as the properly rational appetite, the will), which are themselves naturally oriented in diverse ways to the well-being and perpetuation of the individual and the species. For this reason, dispositions perfecting these capacities will inter alia shape them in such a way as to incline them to pursue individual and communal well-being in an effective and reliable way — otherwise, they would not be perfections of the capacities in question. Correlatively, our general conceptions of the virtues will be shaped by their integral connection to the pursuit of well-being. The virtues are not instrumental means to an end for the agent who possesses them, but they are dispositions of a kind which takes part of its point from an orientation to the human good, and which can thus be expected to promote individual or communal well-being. For this reason, our general paradigms for virtuous behavior — our images of what it means to be an honest person, to behave reliably, and the like — reflect a general sense that these kinds of behavior are useful as well as admirable. And this, as we will see, provides a starting point for the reflective generation and appropriation of ideals of virtue.

At the beginning of this chapter, I noted that it is easy to arrive at a basic idea of human well-being, developed by analogy to the forms of well-being proper to other kinds of higher primates. A well-developed and mature human being will be appropriately nourished, sheltered and physically healthy, and will be involved in a range of social activities of broadly recognizable kinds, for example, participation in family life as well as the life of a wider community. Taken by itself, this account of human well-being is not specific enough to generate concrete norms, of a kind which would enable us, for example, to choose among diverse forms of family and social life. And yet, it does appear to provide us with a basis for identifying traits of character which would seem to be desirable, or even necessary, for the pursuit of well-being in almost any form. Or at least, it suggests a way of interpreting widely admired traits of character in terms of their contributions to individual and communal well-being — it provides us, in other words, with a starting point for a naturalistic analysis of the virtues, along lines similar to those proposed by Foot, Hursthouse, and others.

We have already seen some indications of how such an analysis might proceed in virtues of moderation with respect to food and drink, which are traditionally associated with the more comprehensive virtue of temperance. The fundamental necessities for food and drink give rise to certain basic desires, which can readily be seen to be natural in view of the important functions they play in human life. They are also experienced by nearly everyone, but that is not why they are regarded as natural; rather, we regard them as natural because they admit of a teleological explanation in terms of overall human well-being. (In fact, these desires do not seem to be experienced by absolutely everyone; otherwise, there would be no such thing as a vice of insensibility; see II-II 153.3 *ad* 3.) At the same time, these desires, and likewise our spontaneous aversions, are by no means infallible guides to what is actually good for us. I have a wicked sweet tooth, but because of a family history of diabetes I should avoid sweets; my husband dislikes any kind of health food, even though nothing would be better for him. Even apart from such idiosyncrasies, nearly everyone experiences some inclinations to eat and drink more than is good for her on some occasions. These almost universal experiences provide the field of operation for virtues of moderation and appropriate abstinence with respect to food and drink. Because our inclinations regarding food and drink are so vital to our life and well-being, and yet are so unreliable as guides toward our overall interest, we need dispositions of restraint with respect to them — or better still, we need to discipline and shape them in such a way that they serve as more reliable guides to what is truly good for us. By the same token, we only need a little experience and reflection to see that these qualities of temperance are desirable for ourselves and admirable in others.

Similar kinds of arguments can readily be developed for other kinds of virtues. The virtues of temperance with respect to sexual pleasure — chastity, fidelity to a spouse or partner, and the like — are more difficult to explain in terms of the agent's own well-being. Sometimes sexual restraint will be in one's own self-interest, but very often the demands of chastity will at least seem to impose limitations which have little or nothing to do with one's own well-being. But as Hursthouse points out, we can consider traits of character to be virtues when they benefit a community, or even the species as a whole, and not only when they benefit the agent himself. And the ubiquitous presence of boundaries for proper sexual relationships suggests that some kinds of restraint in sexual matters are indeed necessary, or at least expedient for human life. By the same token, the universally admired character trait of courage may lead the individual to risk or even to sacrifice her well-being, and yet human society could not function without the presence of courageous people. The virtue of justice is notoriously complex, and yet it can plausibly be said to draw on attitudes and traits of character — a sense of fairness, empathy and concern for others, a respect for communal norms and agreements — which are widespread and clearly necessary to any kind of social life. Indeed, the social dispositions which give rise to justice in human societies are apparently shared by other higher primates.[45] This does not mean that other primates observe norms of justice in the sense that we do, but it does provide us with a point of comparison in terms of which we can better understand the point of the social dispositions. As we might expect, the relevant research suggests that these dispositions serve to maintain the unity and cohesiveness of social groupings, just as they seem to do in human societies. Finally, because individual and corporate activities call for the continual exercise of foresight, discretion, and good judgment, practical wisdom in some form is universally admired.

45. In general, see Frans de Waal, *Good Natured: The Origins of Right and Wrong in Humans and Other Animals* (Cambridge: Harvard University Press, 1996). Marc Bekoff argues that the play behavior of social animals can best be construed in terms of a process by which norms of fairness and social conduct more generally are internalized; see "Social Play Behaviour: Cooperation, Fairness, Trust, and the Evolution of Morality," *Journal of Consciousness Studies* 8 (2001): 81-90.

Anyone even slightly familiar with virtue ethics will recognize that I have just sketched a naturalistic framework for interpreting and defending the four cardinal virtues. Of course, other virtues could be interpreted and defended in a similar way.[46] Nonetheless, the cardinal virtues seem to be widely recognized as cardinal, or primary or fundamental, for a good reason. These represent traits of character which contribute in straightforward and fundamentally important ways to human well-being, whether at the individual or collective level, or (usually) both. Moreover, they seem to be almost universally recognized and admired in some form, and this is of course not unrelated to the fact that they contribute to human well-being in such basic ways. Almost everyone can see that restraint, courage, fairness, and good judgment have some point, given the exigencies and common aspirations which structure human life, and it is this grasp of the point, the telos of these qualities, which makes it possible to recognize them, even when they take unfamiliar forms. The language of the virtues provides the closest thing we have to a universal moral language.

For this very reason, our conceptions of the virtues repay closer analysis. I want to argue that these conceptions are grounded in the notions of paradigmatic kinds of actions which we associate with particular virtues — either exemplifying them or representing contrary vices. Whatever we may conclude about particular virtues as a result of systematic analysis, we normally think and speak of them by reference to the kinds of actions that we take to exemplify them. When we think of temperance with respect to food and drink, we think of someone choosing moderate amounts of each, avoiding excess while at the same time taking enough to meet his needs. We can readily recognize or envision these kinds of actions because the range of human needs and desires with respect to food and drink is relatively stable, and we all know, more or less, what it is. Certainly, there are exceptional situations in which moderation would take unexpected forms, but the point of a paradigmatic case is precisely that it reflects a touchstone for recognizing and evaluating exceptional cases. Moreover, these virtues are widely correlated with specific vices, and for these we can identify paradigmatic acts of vice which would seem to be vicious under almost any circumstances. It is impossible to regard gorging oneself until vomiting, or alternatively starving oneself to death or drinking to insensibility, as temperate acts. We may well regard actions of this kind as (normally, typically) nonvoluntary and therefore not morally vicious, and there may even be exceptional circumstances in

46. See, for example, James Keenan, "Proposing Cardinal Virtues," *Theological Studies* 56 (1995): 709-29.

which we would regard an act of this kind as justified. But there is no plausible way to construe these kinds of actions as acts of the virtue of temperance, because they so clearly involve acting contrary to the fundamental requirements of human well-being with respect to nourishment.

Aquinas also acknowledges that our understanding of particular virtues is closely tied to concrete ideals of virtuous behavior. Indeed, not only does he acknowledge this point, it is central to his analysis of a virtue as a *habitus,* that is to say, a disposition inhering in a capacity of intellect or desire which is oriented toward action. As such, a virtue disposes the capacity in which it inheres toward acting in a specified way, and correlatively, it is defined in terms of the kind of action it characteristically produces (I-II 54.2). Hence, every particular virtue is conceptually linked to a specific kind of action, which represents a paradigmatic instance of acting out of the virtue in question (see, for example, II-II 23.4). Aquinas refers to the kind of action associated with a virtue as the object of the virtue, or more precisely, the object of an act stemming from the virtue. As such, the object lends itself to formulation in abstract terms, but formulation at this level presupposes that we are familiar with concrete kinds of actions that provide the paradigms for actions expressing the virtue in question.[47]

To avoid misunderstanding, I should add that when I refer to paradigmatic kinds of actions, I am referring to our images of the kinds of actions which are typical of, or appropriate to, a given disposition toward action (whether a virtue, a vice, or a tendency to apply a specific rule of conduct). As such, these paradigms are not equivalent to the object of an act as Aquinas understands it, since as we will see in the next chapter, the object represents a proper exercise of the agent's causal powers in some specified way. Nonetheless, the paradigmatic kinds of actions associated with a disposition are connected to the object of an act stemming from that disposition, insofar as they represent typical or noteworthy instances of kinds of actions exemplifying the proper object of the disposition. In other words, our paradigms for kinds of actions offer concrete examples and images, in terms of which we are able to formulate reflective concepts of the object of a kind of action stemming from a given disposition.

Aquinas typically argues that the ideals informing particular virtues are exemplified in a particularly clear and normatively significant way in situations of special difficulty or importance; thus, the ideal of fortitude is especially evident in the face of the dangers of death, and similarly, the general

47. I follow Julius Kovesi on this point; see *Moral Notions* (London: Routledge and Kegan Paul, 1967), 37-65.

ideal of temperance is especially evident with respect to the intense pleasures connected to the processes sustaining human life (II-II 123.2 *ad* 2; 123.4; 141.4). This line of analysis enables him to identify the central qualities of the virtues, and by the same token it provides him with a way to harmonize the diverse and seemingly incompatible judgments on particular virtues mediated to him by his sources.

We find a good example of this approach in Aquinas's analysis of fortitude. This virtue presents a special problem, because it tends to be associated by classical authors with one paradigmatic kind of action, namely, bravery on the battlefield, and to be linked by Christian authors with a very different paradigm, namely, martyrdom (II-II 123.5; 124.1, 2). Yet as Aquinas observes, these paradigms do share at least one common feature, as both reflect a willingness to endure death for the sake of some greater good. This observation suggests that we might take this willingness to be definitive of fortitude as such. Yet people can show courage in other contexts, through risking significant goods that fall short of life itself — or so it would seem. Aquinas accordingly asks whether fortitude can be exercised only with regard to the dangers of death. He replies that

> it pertains to the virtue of fortitude to guard the will of the human person lest it draw back from the good of reason on account of the fear of some bodily evil. Now it is necessary to hold firmly to the good of reason over against any evil whatever, for no bodily good can be equated with the good of reason. And therefore we must say that fortitude of the soul is that which securely holds the will of the person to the good of reason over against the greatest evils, because he who stands firm against great things, can consequently stand firm over against lesser things, but not conversely. Also, this belongs to the concept of a virtue, that it is determined by its utmost expression. Now the most terrible among all bodily evils is death, which does away with all bodily goods. . . . And therefore, the virtue of fortitude concerns fears arising out of the danger of death. (II-II 123.4)

It is important to note that Aquinas does not say that fortitude is only displayed through a willingness to risk death for the sake of some greater good. Rather, his point seems to be that these kinds of actions represent paradigmatic instances of fortitude.[48] This willingness reflects the fullest possible exemplification of what fortitude means, and correlatively, we can only fully un-

48. This point is emphasized by Lee Yearley, to whose subtle analysis of Aquinas's conception of courage I am very much indebted; see his *Mencius and Aquinas: Theories of Virtue and Conceptions of Courage* (New York: SUNY Press, 1990), 129-35.

derstand what it means to be truly courageous by reflecting on the example of the person who is willing to die for the sake of the good. In that sense, only such an individual can be said to possess fortitude simply as such: "fortitude is appropriately expressed in bearing with all adverse things. However, a person is not considered to be brave without qualification from bearing any adverse things whatever, but only from this, that he well endures even the greatest evils. From bearing other things, however, someone is said to be brave in some respect" (II-II 123.4 *ad* 1). As the latter comment implies, however, those willing to risk lesser goods can legitimately be said to be brave in a qualified sense — thus, we can account for the widespread sense that someone who risks, say, a large sum of money for the sake of a cause is genuinely courageous, although perhaps not so fully courageous as a soldier or a martyr.

Aquinas goes on to explain that the ideal of fortitude is exemplified particularly well in the context of wartime, because "the danger of death which comes from sickness, or from a storm at sea, or from the incursions of robbers, or from other things of this sort, does not seem to threaten a person directly as a result of pursuing some good. But the danger of death in war does threaten a person directly as a result of pursuing some good, insofar, that is, as he is defending the common good through a just war" (II-II 123.5). Clearly, military valor functions here as a paradigm of virtue, because it expresses the distinctive features of a virtue in a particularly clear way. Yet as Aquinas goes on to explain, this does not mean that fortitude is expressed only in wartime contexts; it is also expressed in other contexts in which persons risk death for the sake of some good. Indeed, among the characteristic acts of fortitude it is martyrdom, rather than any act of military heroism, which holds pride of place as an act of exemplary Christian virtue (at least in some sense; see II-II 124.2, 3).

As this example suggests, the connection between virtues and paradigmatic kinds of actions offers us a promising way to move from general knowledge about the kinds of actions conducive to human well-being to substantive moral ideals. Yet as soon as we attempt to develop this program in detail, we find ourselves confronting formidable difficulties. In the first place, the paradigmatic kinds of actions we associate with particular virtues cannot always be identified so clearly and concretely as our examples so far might suggest. It is relatively easy to envision paradigmatic acts of courage in the face of commonly recurring dangers, or moderation with respect to food or drink, because the parameters within which these virtues operate are set by ubiquitous human needs and experiences. But not every virtue can be correlated with readily identifiable paradigmatic acts in the same way. In particular, the virtue of justice would seem to presuppose a recognized system of relationships and expectations in order to be exercised at all. Moreover, this seems to be the case to some extent even for more fundamental social dispositions, for example, fairness, respect, and compassion. Admittedly, we can probably recognize an act of compassion when we see it, although even then it is not so easy to capture what we are seeing in a generally recognizable description, such as we could offer for an act of moderation or courage. But for a disposition such as fairness or respect, it is hard to see how we could even identify the relevant acts without some knowledge of culturally specific expectations. We will return to this issue below.

Prudence or practical wisdom presents a different problem. It is difficult to imagine any kind of particular act which would exemplify this virtue, because the point of practical wisdom is to direct choices in every aspect of human life. We might well say, as Aquinas does, that every act which is genuinely an act of a particular virtue is at the same time also an act of prudence (I-II 58.2 *ad* 4; II-II 33.1 *ad* 2). But as the adverb "genuinely" suggests, this line of approach raises a further question. That is, it is not always the case that an act which seems to exemplify a particular virtue really represents the best or most appropriate course of action, all things considered. In general, courage in the face of danger is praiseworthy, but sometimes what looks like courage might appear on reflection to be foolhardiness — for example, playing chicken on a country road in order to impress one's girlfriend. Moreover, what look like paradigmatic acts of virtue are sometimes carried out by vicious people in pursuit of manifestly wicked ends — the courage of the devoted Nazi soldier is the parade example. It seems odd to say that these are acts of practical wisdom, with its connotation of praiseworthy discernment.

This brings us to a fundamental problem. That is, the language of the virtues, formulated in terms of their paradigmatic kinds of actions, would appear to be ambiguous.[49] An action that seems to exemplify some virtue, for example the display of courage on the battlefield, may turn out on closer inspection to be a vicious act, for example, courage in defense of a thoroughly bad cause. If the virtues are morally good qualities, then it seems odd, to say the least, to find a virtue being exercised in pursuit of an immoral end — yet it seems just as odd to say that the wicked soldier is not really brave, just because he is wicked.

Aquinas formulated this problem in terms of a distinction between the virtues and their similitudes (see, for example, the introduction to II-II 53). Virtues properly so called stem from an overall commitment to the true good,

49. This problem has long been acknowledged; for an illuminating discussion of the relevant issues, see Hursthouse, *On Virtue Ethics*, 25-42.

and are exercised accordingly; their similitudes lead to what seem to be similar kinds of actions, but carried out in pursuit of bad ends. Hence, the distinction between true virtues and their similitudes is grounded in the claim that the virtues are connected, in such a way that anyone who truly has one virtue must necessarily have all the fundamental virtues.[50] There has been considerable debate over whether this thesis is persuasive. But even if it is (as I would argue), we still have a problem. That is, if the paradigmatic acts of the virtues are morally ambiguous in this way, then it would seem that we cannot, after all, derive moral norms from a consideration of these acts. And if this is so, then it would appear that we cannot derive stable moral norms from the general parameters of human well-being, from which our ideas of these paradigmatic acts emerge.

These and related difficulties have discouraged many philosophers from attempting to develop a systematic virtue ethic grounded in the particular kinds of actions associated with the virtues. There is a second way of approaching the virtues, however, which is almost equally ancient and would seem to have the advantage of providing analytic simplicity and clarity. On this approach, the kinds of actions typically linked to the virtues are at best useful for illustrative purposes — indeed, on this approach there is little need to speak of particular virtues at all, except provisionally. This approach to the virtues proceeds by identifying what it is about virtuous behavior in any form that we find praiseworthy, usually conformity to a general ideal of nobility, reasonableness, or charity. We find examples of this latter approach among both classical and Christian authors. According to the Stoics, virtue is nothing other than a disposition to act in accordance with reason; Augustine reformulated this claim by substituting love for reason, while retaining the formal simplicity of the Stoic view.[51] Similarly, Hursthouse argues that a naturalistic ethic is tantamount to an ethic of reason:

> there is a standard claim to the effect that there *is* something characteristic of human beings, that we *do* have a characteristic way of going on, but not in the way that is true of the other animals. . . . Our way of going on is just one, which remains the same across all areas of our life. Our characteristic

50. For further details on the considerations motivating the thesis of the unity of the virtues, see Annas, *The Morality of Happiness*, 73-84. Hursthouse defends what she describes as a weak version of this thesis in *On Virtue Ethics*, 153-57.

51. I am here following John Rist, *Augustine: Ancient Thought Baptized* (Cambridge: Cambridge University Press, 1994), 148-202, both with respect to the Stoics' views and Augustine's appropriation of them. As Annas points out, the Stoics identified the emotions with judgments, and thus for them right judgment, appropriate feeling, and a disposition toward right action would be closely linked; see *The Morality of Happiness*, 61-66.

way of going on, which distinguishes us from all the other species of animals, is a rational way. A "rational way" is any way that we can rightly see as good, as something that we have reason to do. Correspondingly, our characteristic enjoyments are any enjoyments we can rightly see as our good, as something we in fact enjoy *and* that reason can rightly endorse.[52]

There is a case to be made that Aquinas likewise identifies virtuous behavior with rational behavior, understood in terms of "something that we have reason to do." At a number of points, he seems to adopt the Stoic position, albeit supplemented with an Augustinian sense of the transformative power of charity. As he repeatedly reminds us, the virtues are dispositions to act in accordance with reason (see, for example, I-II 57.5; 58.4; 65.1). That is in fact precisely why they can be said to be perfections of human capacities — they dispose the capacities and desires of the agent in such a way as to bring them into accord with reason, which is the distinctive human capacity and as such is the touchstone for ideals of human flourishing (for example, see II-II 47.6; 123.12; 141.6). Hence, we might think that Aquinas cuts through the complexity of traditional ideals of virtues by reducing them all to injunctions to act reasonably.

The difficulty with this line of interpretation, however, is that it does not specify what the norms of reasonableness are. It is tempting to agree with Hursthouse that "A 'rational way' is any way that we can rightly see as good, as something that we have reason to do," but unless we are prepared to pack a great deal into "rightly," this is fairly clearly not what Aquinas means. However, in his *Natural Law and Practical Reason,* Martin Rhonheimer offers a more sophisticated and plausible interpretation of this same approach, in the process developing an account of the natural law focusing on its interconnection with the virtues.[53]

52. Hursthouse, *On Virtue Ethics,* 222, emphases in original. Similarly, Wallace says, "I propose to characterize the human *ergon* [roughly, function] as a social life informed by convention, rather than activity in accordance with *logos* [reason]"; *Virtues and Vices,* 37. This, it seems to me, is not so much of a break with Aristotle as Wallace supposes. Aristotle regarded the practice of civic virtue as activity in accordance with reason, and therefore as tantamount to a secondary kind of happiness, and so Wallace's program might better be described (in a way analogous to my own) as the development and extension of one strand of Aristotelian ethics. But in any case, Wallace's emphasis on observance of social conventions as *the* touchstone for the human good leads him to a position similar to Hursthouse's equation of the human good with rationality tout court.

53. So far as I can determine, Rhonheimer develops and refines but does not essentially alter his views in *Praktische Vernunft und Vernünftigkeit der Praxis: Handlungstheorie bei Thomas von Aquin in ihrer Entstehung aus dem Promelmkontext der aristotelischen Ethik* (Berlin: Akademie Verlag, 1994); see especially 124-34. In addition, the main lines of his approach are

He begins by identifying what he sees as two widespread yet mistaken ways of interpreting Aquinas's theory of the natural law.[54] On the one hand, he rejects the view that for Aquinas the natural law is somehow grounded in an order of nature, comprehensively understood to include prerational aspects of human nature as well as the natural world more generally. On the other hand, he also rejects a more recent interpretation according to which Aquinas's understanding of the natural law is equivalent to a theory of "autonomous morality." On this view the natural law is understood, in terms reminiscent of Hursthouse's naturalism, as an imperative to act reasonably and responsibly. And since this imperative is best understood in terms of some balancing of premoral goods and evils, Aquinas's moral theory would be at least consistent with some version of consequentialism on this reading. Rhonheimer rejects this (rightly, as I believe), both as an interpretation of Aquinas and as a cogent theory of morality. Yet how is it possible to reject this interpretation without falling into the opposite error, as Rhonheimer conceives it, of arguing that Aquinas derives moral norms from prerational nature?

Rhonheimer attempts to answer this question by analyzing what he describes as the fundamentally personal structure of practical reason. On his view, defenders of the "autonomous morality" approach are right to insist that for Aquinas the natural law is grounded in the functioning of the practical reason, not in the intelligibilities of prerational nature. (Rhonheimer too affirms the autonomous rationality of morals, understood in that sense.)[55] However, they are wrong to conclude that practical reason functions without any constraints whatever, beyond very general requirements to act reasonably and responsibly. Rather, Rhonheimer argues that the practical reason generates its own norms through the exigencies of its own personal structure:

> The human intellect reflects on these natural judgements of practical reason, thereby discovering this moral order and this "human nature" as an

helpfully summarized in "The Cognitive Structure of Natural Law and the Truth of Subjectivity," *The Thomist* 67, no. 1 (January 2003): 1-44. Finally, he responds to my earlier review of *Natural Law* in "The Moral Significance of Pre-Rational Nature in Aquinas: A Reply to Jean Porter (and Stanley Hauerwas)," *American Journal of Jurisprudence* 48 (2003): 253-80. Unfortunately, I did not see this article in time to incorporate it into the following discussion. However, it does not seem to contradict what I say regarding Rhonheimer's defense of a unitary ideal of virtue (cf. 269). At any rate, the difference between us seems, briefly, to be this: Rhonheimer denies, and I assert, the priority of speculative knowledge to practical knowledge, both in Aquinas and in fact.

54. Rhonheimer, *Natural Law,* 3-22; for further discussion and critique of the "autonomous morality" position (not to be confused with the Kantian conception of autonomy, seen in contrast to heteronomy), see further 181-92.

55. As he says in *Natural Law,* 181.

object of the speculative intellect, as an anthropological reality full of normative reason. But great care should be employed here: this normativeness is not deduced from or read in a nature that is "in front of" knowing man — on the contrary, it is the original normativeness of practical reason itself which, due to its location within the dynamics of the natural inclinations, explains itself through natural judgements on the human good. These last form an original, irreducible, and fundamental experience. It is an experience in which simultaneously the human being (the anthropological identity of the subject) and the normative aspect of this human identity manifest themselves.[56]

Thus, the norms of the natural law stem from human nature, but not in such a way that we can draw moral conclusions from the intelligibilities of nature as these are apprehended through speculative reason; rather, Rhonheimer holds that the relevant knowledge of human nature depends on prior acts of the practical reason. Elsewhere he claims that practical reason constitutes the order of the virtues, and correlatively, the order of the natural law.[57] Thus, when Aquinas ties the natural law to fundamental inclinations of human nature at I-II 94.2, we should not take this to imply that the inclinations are morally significant in virtue of their orientation toward prerational natural ends, which the human person is bound to respect.[58] Rather, they flow from our existence as an integrated bodily-spiritual reality, and are apprehended as such by the practical reason, which perceives them as intelligible human goods which deserve respect as aspects of human existence. More specifically, practical reason apprehends these goods in their distinctively human and personal meaning, and it is this grasp of the goods as personal goods which gives rise to the norms of morality. Thus, for example, Rhonheimer argues that human sexuality, as a practical good, is nothing other than married love, and "sexual acts that stand outside this context are in contradiction to it — that is, they are 'immoral' in the objective sense — not because they are 'unnatural,' but rather because they contradict the (practical) *truth* of the natural, as it appears on the horizon of apprehension and regulation by the reason."[59]

56. Rhonheimer, "Cognitive Structure," 31; this view is elaborated in *Natural Law*, 316-22.

57. Rhonheimer, *Natural Law*, 1-58; on the equivalence of virtue and natural law, see further 80-87; similarly, in *Praktische Vernunft und Vernünftigkeit der Praxis*, 117, he claims that reason constitutes its object as a practical good.

58. Rhonheimer, *Natural Law*, 70-80; similarly, in *Praktische Vernunft und Vernünftigkeit der Praxis* he argues that reason is the proper good of the human person, although he adds that it is expressed in and through the operations of the other faculties; see 124-25.

59. Rhonheimer, *Natural Law*, 569-70, emphasis in original; similarly, see *Praktische Vernunft und Vernünftigkeit der Praxis*, 127-28.

Rhonheimer also reminds us of Aquinas's remark that the inclinations are regulated by the virtues; this, he argues, is equivalent to acting with due regard for the human/personal orientation of these inclinations. He thus provides us with one important exception to the generalization that our contemporaries hold virtue and law apart; on the contrary, he insists that "the natural law is recognized to be nothing other than the preceptive activity of the practical reason, as it constitutes the order of the virtues *(ordo virtutum)* and as it constitutes the content of this order — itself an *ordo rationis*."[60] He develops this point at some length in a discussion of contraceptive use, seen in contrast to natural family planning. The latter is a legitimate expression of responsible parenthood (given right intention, of course), because it depends upon the regulation and disciplining of the sexual impulse itself. The former is morally illegitimate in part, at least, because it dispenses with the necessity for the exercise of virtue, or at least for the exercise of specifically sexual virtue; it enables persons to achieve the effect of sexual abstinence, that is to say, the avoidance of conception, without actually having to discipline and control the sexual impulse itself.[61]

Rhonheimer offers a powerful and attractive interpretation of Aquinas's theory of the natural law, according to which basic human goods — components of human well-being, in my terms — are interpreted in terms of their human, that is to say, their personal, meaning. On this view, the virtues and the natural law precepts stemming from them are all expressions of one fundamental norm or ideal, that is to say, rationality understood in terms of a reasoned integration and expression of basic human impulses. Even when Rhonheimer refers to a specifically sexual virtue of abstinence, it is clear that the norm of the virtue stems from a general ideal of rational discipline and self-control, and not from the exigencies of sexuality as such. Read in this way, Aquinas's account of the virtues and the natural law would be very close indeed to the Stoic ideal of action in accordance with reason, qualified and tempered by an Augustinian sense of the overarching ideal of charity.

Yet there is at least one consideration that counts against this view, considered both as a reading of Aquinas and as a substantive view. That is, this approach to the virtues would appear to be at odds, if not incompatible, with the focus on paradigmatic kinds of actions described above. If we understand the virtues in terms of an ideal of reasonableness (however interpreted), why do we need to associate particular virtues with specific kinds of actions, such

60. Rhonheimer, *Natural Law,* 59.

61. Rhonheimer's overall appraisal of contraceptive use is more complex than this summary indicates, however; see *Natural Law,* 109-38, for further details.

as abstaining from sexual activity or risking death on the battlefield? Not only would this kind of specificity seem to be unnecessary, it even seems inappropriate. After all, we can readily imagine circumstances in which a given action, which we normally would regard as a paradigmatic act of a virtue, would be unreasonable or vicious in the particular situation at hand. And yet, Aquinas does identify particular virtues with paradigmatic kinds of actions, and this fact at least suggests that he does not regard the virtues as so many expressions of one univocal ideal of reasonableness (or charity). Admittedly, we might see this as a concession to his sources, and to the demands of preaching and the practices of the confessional. But such a conclusion would be too quick. Aquinas explicitly says that while the cardinal virtues can all be understood as expressions of one general quality of reasonableness, they are better understood as specifically distinct dispositions, each informed by its own normative ideal of appropriateness as displayed in a particular sphere of life (I-II 61.4; a similar distinction informs the earlier articles of the question). This implies that even at the level of theoretical analysis, a particular virtue cannot be understood simply in terms of the general ideal of virtue; it must also be understood in terms of specific kinds of actions with which it is correlated. What is more, Aquinas has theoretical reasons for holding together general and specific aspects of the virtues in this way.

Recall once again that for Aquinas a virtue is conceptually tied to the paradigmatic kind of action toward which it disposes the agent. Hence, the logic of his analysis of the virtues demands that he analyze them in terms of the kinds of actions they produce. But how are these actions to be characterized? It is not enough to describe them as acts of reason, or (in the case of infused virtues) of charity. Precisely because these descriptions apply to every (relevant) act of virtue, they cannot serve to discriminate among the particular virtues.[62] Moreover, Aquinas's account of the virtues as perfections of the agent implies that any adequate account of a particular virtue will include some account of the way that virtue is indeed a perfection of the faculty which is its subject. And Aquinas does indeed insist on this point. The particular virtues are good and desirable as such, even apart from whatever the agent accomplished through them, because they are perfections of the faculties of the agent (I-II 55.3; 56.1). Correlatively, the virtues disposing the passions — that is, fortitude and temperance and their associated virtues — are dispositions *of*

62. As we will see further on, every act of virtue is ipso facto an act of reason, insofar as every act of virtue is informed by prudence, whether acquired or infused, but not every act of virtue is an act of charity. Strictly speaking, it is not the case that every act of an infused *habitus* is an act of charity, since the infused *habitūs* of faith and hope can exist without charity; however, they cannot strictly speaking function as virtues without charity (I-II 65.4).

the passions, inclining the agent to feel and respond in certain ways, and not simply dispositions to act in accordance with reason in the face of contrary passions (I-II 56.4). If this were not so, the agent's acts would fall short of the standard of full and integral goodness (56.4); what is more, if the virtues were sheerly dispositions to act in accordance with reason, they would render the passions otiose (60.5). By the same token, distinct forms of the cardinal virtues are infused together with charity — otherwise, grace would be less perfect in its operations than would nature, since it would operate without fully perfecting the capacities of the agent by directing them to her ultimate end (65.3).

So Aquinas has good reason to try to hold together the formal and the concrete poles in the language of virtue, in such a way as to render them mutually illuminating rather than allowing them to collapse into one another, or to separate into mutual incoherence. He attempts to do so through appropriating and expanding Aristotle's doctrine of the mean of virtue, which he appropriates in order to specify what it means to act in accordance with reason with regard to different aspects of human life. "The mean" does not refer to moderation in feeling and action, as if the ideal life were a life of muted feelings and modest actions; rather, Aquinas, following Aristotle, understands the mean of a virtue in terms of a norm of appropriateness, which can imply intense emotion and violent action in some circumstances.[63] Even so, this norm would still be overly abstract, if it were not further qualified through an analysis of the way in which the mean is to be understood for particular virtues. As Aquinas explains, all virtues are governed by a rational mean — which is to say, they are governed by a general standard of reasonableness which can be formulated in different ways, depending on context. In addition, justice and its associated virtues are also governed by a real mean, which turns out to be comprised of interpersonal norms of fairness and equity (I-II 64.2; II-II 58.10). To put the same point another way, acts of justice are rational in virtue of their correspondence with interpersonal norms of fairness, as these have developed in various areas of human life, in contrast to the other moral virtues.

Temperance and fortitude and their associated virtues, in contrast, are governed by the rational mean alone, since in these cases the mean is determined relative to the agent's own needs, circumstances, and disposition. Our capacities for desire and resistance to harm, which are informed by the virtues of temperance and fortitude respectively, are naturally oriented toward whatever is perceived to be desirable or undesirable through the senses, the

63. As J. O. Urmson points out in "Aristotle's Doctrine of the Mean," in *Essays in Aristotle's Ethics*, ed. Amélie Rorty (Berkeley: University of California Press, 1980), 157-70, here 160-61.

passions, and the imaginative capacity (in general, see I-II 60.2, and more specifically I-II 56.6 *ad* 3; II-II 59.12). In order for these capacities to function appropriately, in a way that promotes the individual's overall good, they must be shaped in such a way that the person spontaneously desires and is averse to what is genuinely good or harmful. Hence, the mean for these virtues is agent-relative, as the mean of justice is not (again, see II-II 58.10). Furthermore, the mean of these virtues is agent-relative in the further sense of being determined by reference to the individual's needs and disposition, for reasons noted above.

The agent-relative character of the mean for temperance and fortitude should not obscure the fact that the standards for reasonableness for these virtues are not just formal, in such a way that they could be interpreted in terms of any criteria for reasonableness whatever. The mean of these latter virtues also observes an objective standard, namely, the overall good of the agent who is exercising them. Aquinas claims that when we are speaking of the exercise of reason in a moral context, "this pertains to right reason, that one should make use of those things which lead to an end in accordance with the measure which is appropriate to the end" (II-II 152.2). Here we see what he means by that claim. Reason operating within the field of temperance and fortitude brings order to human desires and aversions, in such a way as to direct them toward the agent's overall good; thus, the norms governing temperance are set by the necessities of human life (141.6). Correlatively, the mean with respect to these virtues does have substantive content — it reflects whatever configuration of desires and aversions best reflects the agent's overall good, taking account of the proper place the objects of desire and fear have in relation to her life as a whole.[64]

Nonetheless, even granting that temperance and fortitude observe objective standards, it is difficult to see how they could be correlated with the kinds of paradigmatic act descriptions that Aquinas seems to have in mind when he refers to the proper acts of particular virtues. Given the agent-relative character of these virtues, how is it possible to correlate them with general paradigms, which presumably apply to a wide range of people? This would seem to be possible only if we describe the relevant paradigms in very general terms indeed — identifying temperance about the pleasures of the table with "appropriate moderation in food and drink," for example. This ap-

64. Moreover, practical reason relates the individual's good to wider contexts: as directed by justice, to the good of others and the community of the whole; as directed by hope and charity, to the supreme good of union with God, which extends to fellowship with other actual or potential participants in that good. Justice and charity are thus architectonic virtues, insofar as they direct the acts of the other virtues to more comprehensive ends (II-II 23.8; 58.6).

proach would return us once again to a level of formality that would seem to be inconsistent with the requirements of Aquinas's overall analysis of the virtues. At any rate, as we have seen, Aquinas does analyze particular virtues by reference to the paradigmatic kinds of actions instantiating them. The problem here is thus internal to Aquinas's analysis of the virtues. At the same time, it is centrally related to the overall project of this chapter.

It will be helpful at this point to review what is at stake. At the beginning of this section, it was suggested that reflection on the virtues can provide a bridge between a basic conception of human well-being and a morally significant account of happiness. But in order to develop this connection, we must find a way to hold together two diverse and seemingly incompatible approaches to the virtues. Seen from one perspective, the virtues, particularly those associated with temperance and fortitude, are understood in terms of concrete kinds of actions which reflect restraint, courage, and the like in the context of ubiquitous human needs, desires, and circumstances. So understood, the virtues certainly reflect exigencies of human well-being, but they are not clearly moral qualities, at least insofar as they can be exercised in the service of bad ends. Alternatively, we might understand the virtues in more formal terms as expressions of some one overarching ideal, for example, reasonableness or charity. Understood in this way, acts of virtue are by stipulation moral acts, but they would seem to have little or no intrinsic connection to concrete paradigms for virtuous behavior. And since it is these paradigms which reflect the exigencies of well-being, it would seem that the virtues understood in the latter sense have no intrinsic connection to human well-being, either.

So if we are to make good on the suggestion that the virtues provide a link between well-being and happiness properly so called, we must show that there is an intrinsic connection between paradigms of particular virtues and the ideal of reasonableness governing all the virtues. To put the question in Aquinas's terms, we must work out the relation between the mean, as determined with respect to the self-referential virtues of temperance and fortitude, and the paradigmatic kinds of actions with which these are correlated. (Justice raises distinctive problems, and will be considered separately in the next section, and further in the next chapter.) I will address this question by way of considering a prior question, which Aquinas does not discuss (except in passing) but which can be addressed starting from what he does say. That is, what is the process by which the virtues are acquired and developed (or in the case of the infused cardinal virtues, simply developed)? This line of inquiry may seem to take us away from the issue at hand, but I hope that its relevance will soon become clear. Keep in mind that we are focusing at this point on temperance and fortitude.

In the context of analyzing the process through which the will is moved toward a specific good, Aquinas observes that the human will is naturally oriented toward certain fundamental desiderata, which provide the starting points for all subsequent deliberation (I-II 10.1). These correspond more or less to the inclinations outlined in I-II 94.2, including the most fundamental components of well-being such as life itself and the goods which support life. Hence, the natural orientation of the will toward these goods represents the distinctively human form of the general inclinations to maintain and extend one's existence found in all creatures.[65] Aquinas does not say that these goods are necessarily desired in every situation in which they might be pursued (10.2). His discussion suggests, rather, that these are starting points in the straightforward sense that they are among the first things the human creature desires, and that these basic desires set in motion the development of the child's capacities for deliberation and choice.

Experience would seem to confirm this basic picture. From the day of birth, the infant expresses desires and aversions, usually in unmistakable ways — for food and warmth, against being cold or wet or physically insecure.[66] These basic desires, and the child's capacities to express them, expand and develop as the child matures, even though the child's desires will be focused at first on the most basic natural goods. Even at a very young age, however, we begin to see these fundamental desires transformed through deliberation. The child begins to show evidence of thinking about how best to attain its desires, and it begins to rank them, developing preferences and expressing willingness to forgo some pleasures in order to pursue others. Of course, these

65. Correlatively, the will is a natural capacity with a determinate structure, and can be analyzed accordingly, a point emphasized by both Pinckaers and Pasnau; see respectively *Ce qu'on ne peut jamais faire,* 125-26, and *Thomas Aquinas,* 200-209.

66. My understanding of childhood development has been deeply influenced by George Herbert Mead, *Mind, Self, and Society from the Standpoint of a Social Behaviorist* (Chicago: University of Chicago Press, 1934), although I do not follow him in every particular. At any rate, I believe that the main lines of the following general account would not be controversial. In addition to Mead, in what follows I draw on Martin Hollis, *Models of Man: Philosophical Thoughts on Social Action* (Cambridge: Cambridge University Press, 1977), 87-142; Drew Westin, *Self and Society: Narcissism, Collectivism, and the Development of Morals* (Cambridge: Cambridge University Press, 1985); Barbara Rogoff, *Apprenticeship in Thinking: Cognitive Development in Social Context* (Oxford: Oxford University Press, 1990); MacIntyre, *Dependent Rational Animals,* especially 81-118; and Richard Shweder, "Culture and Mental Development in Our Poststructural Age," in *Why Do Men Barbecue?* 276-90. I am also very much indebted to two recent efforts to draw out the implications of an Aristotelian theory of virtue for an account of moral formation, namely, M. F. Burnyeat, "Aristotle on Learning to Be Good," in *Essays in Aristotle's Ethics,* 69-92, and Diana Cates, *Choosing to Feel: Virtue, Friendship, and Compassion for Friends* (Notre Dame: University of Notre Dame Press, 1997), 154-207.

basic desires are mediated through what are clearly sensual attractions — toward the sweet, the bright, the warm, the fuzzy — which may or may not reflect what genuinely promotes the child's well-being. But this is just what developmental theory — or for that matter, Aquinas's analysis of the passions — would lead us to expect.

Of course, this process does not unfold without a certain amount of direction from the child's parents and caretakers. Again, this direction begins almost immediately, through an endless series of choices about when and how to feed the infant, when to change it, whether to allow it to cry, how to urge it to sleep, and so forth. To some degree, at least, the caretakers' choices in these regards will be prompted by theories and judgments regarding the child's own best interests, together with some sense of what is appropriate or desirable from a social or moral viewpoint. As the child matures, her caretakers will increasingly respond to her expressions of desire out of wider judgments of these kinds. The child will not be allowed to have ice cream before dinner because that would spoil her appetite; she will be forced to bathe, even though she hates it, because society frowns on smelly girls. And as she matures, the reasons for these strictures will be explained to her in more detail.

Very early in this process, the child's caretakers will begin to convey their own ideals and expectations to her as they move from fundamental kinds of training to a process of education in a fully human sense. In this way, the child's training and education will be at one and the same time practical, in the broader sense of the term, and specifically moral. In many instances the ideals and justifications presented to the child will be simplified versions of paradigms of the virtues, or sometimes their correlative vices, presented in such a way as to convey that if the child patterns her behavior on these paradigms she will be praiseworthy or admirable, or correlatively naughty, deserving of censure — as well as healthy, comfortable, safe, or alternatively, sick, uneasy, or threatened. And so, for example, a child who wants an ice-cream cone before dinner may be urged to behave like a grown-up girl who can wait for her pleasures, while at the same time she is warned that she will get sick if she eats so many sweets. In this way, a very basic ideal of temperance is inculcated, together with the practical counsel not to overeat. And appropriately so — because the ideal of temperance *is,* constitutively if not exclusively, a capacity to judge and desire with respect to food, in accordance with one's needs and overall well-being.

At some point, if all goes well, the child will begin to internalize these paradigms of restraint and courage, and to govern his own behavior accordingly. And just as these ideals combine broadly practical considerations with moral ones, so the child who internalizes them will come to regard certain kinds of behavior as both practically wise and admirable. He will realize that if he behaves like a pig, he will get sick; if he runs away from bullies, he will spend his life cowering in corners; and if he behaves like a bully himself, he will have no friends. At the same time, however, he will find self-restraint, bravery, and friendliness to be admirable qualities, and he will want to be the kind of boy who exhibits them. Of course, most children (and for that matter, most adults) will not separate the practical and moral aspects of these qualities that carefully. Given that the virtues in question are oriented toward the rational pursuit of well-being, there is no reason why they should do so, at least in normal circumstances. On the contrary, the close interconnection between these two aspects of these virtues provides a basis for further moral reflection, of a kind which the growing child must undertake at some point in order to move to the next stage of maturation.

Even before adolescence, most children will be capable of reflecting to some extent on their behavior, seen in the light of the ideals which are presented to them. As they do so, they will come to realize that these ideals are desirable, not only because they are beginning to find them admirable, but also because they form the necessary presuppositions for the pursuit of any other kinds of aims. Without some rudimentary capacity for self-restraint, courage, and the associated virtues, it is impossible to do more than respond to one's immediate environment, and without more than rudimentary capacities for such virtues, it is impossible to act independently or pursue long-term goals in the light of immediate temptations or difficulties. Not for nothing did Aquinas, following Aristotle, describe intemperance as a childish vice, and no child wants to be childish (II-II 142.2). This insight, in turn, forms a necessary basis for moving to the next stage of reflection.

One of the central tasks of adolescence is the development of some ability to come to terms with the ideals of one's society, to adopt them as one's own and to shape one's actions accordingly. (Or not — but a life of principled opposition to the ideals of one's society will likewise presuppose a process of maturation.) This process cannot get off the ground unless the adolescent has internalized these ideals to some degree — as Aristotle says, moral education proper cannot begin unless the youth has been brought up in such a way as to admire and try to emulate virtuous behavior. Furthermore, we are assuming that the young adolescent has grasped, at least in an inchoate way, that the virtues of temperance and fortitude in particular are essential to whatever other ideals or goals she may have set for herself. Once again, the practical and moral elements of the virtues are intertwined, but the connection between these two elements is tied specifically to the young person's sense of herself as a rational agent, someone capable of directing her own actions in the light of her best rational judgments. At this point, she begins to see these virtues as perfections in Aquinas's sense (although not necessarily in these explicit terms) — that is to say, as capacities which express and foster her development and unimpeded functioning precisely in terms of what she most truly and fundamentally is, namely, a rational agent. Correlatively, the maturing child is now in a position to move beyond simply internalizing ideals of temperance and fortitude, modifying them so as to better fit her own needs and situation.

At this point, we return to the question concerning the relation between concrete ideals and formal norms of reasonableness raised above. Once again: the rational ideals of temperance and fortitude are agent-specific, insofar as they reflect standards for self-restraint and courage which are grounded in the individual's own character and circumstances. Yet in the process of developing these virtues in the child, his caretakers will inevitably draw on a social stock of paradigms of these virtues and their associated vices. Only a greedy little boy would eat three Big Macs in one sitting; a brave little girl will not allow herself to be pushed around by the class harridan; and so forth. How can these stereotypical paradigms serve to develop the kind of individualized ideals which Aquinas associates with these virtues?

By now, however, we can see that the difficulty is not so formidable as it initially seemed to be. Clichés of temperance, bravery, and the like are clichés for a good reason — they convey patterns of behavior which would exemplify the virtues for most persons under most circumstances, because they reflect needs and situations common to us all. Just as no individual can function without developing some capacities for self-restraint, endurance, and courage, no society can function without developing a stock of ideals of these qualities through which its members can learn to discipline and control themselves, at least much of the time. By the same token, these ideals will necessarily be somewhat general and pluriform, in order to allow for their application and adaption in a variety of circumstances.

In order to internalize these paradigms as ideals for himself, the young person will need at some point to understand why these kinds of behavior reflect valued and admirable qualities of restraint and courage, given the needs and conditions common to most of human life. In other words, he will need to grasp the point of these paradigms, seen precisely as paradigms of virtuous behavior.[67] Grasping the point in this instance will imply some recognition that these kinds of behavior are instantiations of reasonable behavior, which

67. The claim that moral judgment, and correlatively moral development, depend critically on grasping the point of moral concepts is developed at length by Kovesi in *Moral Notions;* see 1-36 for a summary of the overall argument.

are as such admirable and worthy of imitation. But at the same time, someone who grasps the point of these concrete paradigms will see them as reasonable expressions of desire, aversion, pugnacity, and the like — will see them, that is, not as expressions of reasonableness in the abstract, but precisely as reasonable expressions of basic human passions, as these are expressed in the context of ubiquitous human situations.

We now begin to see how the more concrete and the more formal components of the ideal of virtue fit together, at least in the case of temperance and fortitude. The paradigmatic kinds of actions associated with these and similar virtues reflect collective judgments about the kinds of reactions and behavior that would be broadly reasonable for most persons in most circumstances. It should be noted that the norms in question are not simply abstract norms of rationality, but norms of reasonable desire, reasonable aversion, reasonable resistance to harm, and the like. In other words, these paradigmatic acts convey ideals of reasonable passions, as these are evoked and expressed in the recurring situations that are characteristic of a distinctly human way of life. As such, they cannot be analyzed reductively in terms of purely formal ideals of reasonableness, to be applied in an ad hoc and seriatim fashion to each and every instance of choice. What count as reasonable desires, aversions, and the like are to some extent determined — not exhaustively, to be sure, but substantively — by basic human needs and desires, on the one hand, and by the exigencies of human agency on the other. For this reason, ideals of temperance and fortitude provide the link we have been seeking between basic well-being on the one hand and happiness understood in Aquinas's terms as a life of virtue on the other.

Of course, these paradigms must be adapted and applied to an individual's own situation if they are to serve as norms for temperance and fortitude for that individual. But someone who has grasped the point of these paradigms will be able to make the necessary adaptions, precisely because she has grasped why acts of restraint, courage, and the like are generally desirable and admirable. The maturing person who grasps the point of an ideal of, say, temperance with respect to food will be able to apply it with greater discrimination than someone who simply avoids eating very much for fear that he will appear greedy. By the same token, she will be able to adapt the ideal to her own needs and circumstances, transforming it while still retaining what Aquinas would describe as the essential formal character of the virtue.

At the same time, in and through this process of reflective appropriation the individual will also develop the virtue of practical wisdom, which is nothing other than a developed capacity to judge in accordance with one's overall aims, and to choose a particular course of action accordingly. It might appear from what has been said so far that the capacities for judgment emerging through the process described above would constitute practical wisdom with respect to temperance and fortitude. This intuition reflects an important truth; practical wisdom is typically exercised in and through the acts of the other cardinal virtues, and every genuine act of the other virtues is necessarily also an act of practical wisdom. But if this were all we could say, we might well ask how practical wisdom can be distinguished from the other virtues. In fact, however, the process of reflective appropriation which forms the seedbed of practical wisdom will necessarily go beyond reflection on any one virtue. In order to see why, we need to return once again to some consideration of what it means to grasp the point of a virtue.

At the most basic level, even a fairly young child can grasp the point of a virtue like temperance with respect to food — that is, she can grasp that it is good to restrain and redirect her desires for food in order to avoid getting sick. What she grasps, in other words, is a fundamental connection between well-being and the ideal of the virtue. But this connection will only take her so far, so long as she stays focused on the dynamics of hunger and satiety. In order to further develop her grasp of temperance, she will need to broaden the scope of her reflection by considering the point of physical well-being as sustained through food and drink. As the saying goes, we should eat to live, not live to eat; the consumption of food should be placed at the service of one's overall well-being, and not oriented immediately and exclusively toward the satisfaction of immediate appetites. This principle might be described as the basic and foundational mean of temperance with respect to food and drink. But if it is true that we should eat to live, what does it mean to live well, and how does that affect one's sense of what it means to eat well (in every sense of the expression)? Should one's consumption of food be oriented toward ideals of health and longevity, or physical strength, or expansive amplitude? Each of these reflects an ideal currently in force within our society, and they cannot all be pursued at the same time — and we have not even begun to consider the ways in which Christian ideals might transform even this very basic ideal of virtue.

The virtues of temperance with respect to food and drink are relatively straightforward, because they have an immediate connection to the physical needs of the body. When we turn to those virtues associated with temperance and fortitude which pertain to other forms of human desire and aversion, including sexual desire, anger, and the closely related impulses of fear and aggression, we see that these ideals are more complex, and call for more sophisticated reflection about the place of our basic desires and aversions in an overall life. Firstly, the practice of the relevant virtues will necessarily draw us into interactions with other people, whose needs and claims must somehow be incorporated into ideals of sexual temperance, courage, and the associated virtues. Furthermore, the dynamics of sexual desire, fear, and aggression naturally invite reflection on the overall development of one's sexuality, the natural progression and decline of human strength and the corresponding encroachment of vulnerability. The relevant virtues must take these dynamics into account, in such a way as to prepare the individual to deal appropriately with the natural development and decline of basic human capacities. At the same time, these capacities must be seen in their interconnection, if the individual is to reflect on the overall shape of her life, to decide which desiderata are to be given priority, which risks are worth taking, which renunciations and deprivations are to be endured.

The point I want to emphasize is that reflections along these lines will inevitably draw the individual into some consideration of one's life as a whole, the proper place for discrete goods within such a life, and the kinds of sacrifices and risks that make sense in light of one's overall aims and commitments. I say "some consideration" advisedly, because the degree of consideration in question will naturally vary with the extent to which individuals can make real choices about the shape of their lives. For those societies in which individuals' lives are more or less prescribed in accordance with fixed roles, there may be relatively little scope or need for this kind of reflection at the individual level.[68] However, in societies such as our own, which present a relatively wide range of choices to individuals and place a high positive value on autonomy and self-determination, some consideration of the overall point and shape of one's life will be practically inescapable for most persons.

In any case, reflection on one's life as a whole can take many forms, depending on the individual's needs and circumstances. But for anyone who is engaged in this process in a thoroughgoing way, it will be necessary to reflect at some point on what it means to attain a satisfying and complete life — to attain some kind of terrestrial happiness, in other words. The process of consideration itself will elicit such reflections both from below, so to speak, and from above. From below, because one's reflections on the overall shape of life will be informed to a considerable degree by one's reflective experience in practicing the virtues of temperance and fortitude, which are grounded in the most basic desires and needs of the human animal. From above, because in reflecting on the overall shape of a human life, it will be

68. At the same time, even those societies which place a higher premium on communal solidarity than our own also leave scope for individual reflection and self-determination, as Richard Shweder points out; see "The Return," 272-75.

necessary at some point to try to place the satisfaction of these basic desires and needs into the context of one's overall sense of a desirable or ideal human life.

Moreover, for most people the governing ideal of human life will give a central place to the fulfillment of these basic needs and desires, in a way that is unsurprising and wholly appropriate. This brings us back to the conclusions of the last section. That is to say, the happiness which consists in the practice of the virtues cannot be separated from the more basic forms of flourishing and satisfaction which constitute a more basic form of well-being. The connection is conceptual — that is, the paradigms of action which give meaning to ideals of particular virtues will be drawn, to a considerable extent at least, from communal ideals of appropriate action with respect to fundamental human needs and desires. To a greater or lesser extent, the connection will be practical as well. Each of us must make some provision for meeting the most basic needs of human life if we want to have a life at all — neglect or failure in this regard is a sign of incapacity or insanity, not virtue. In the process of doing so, it is practically inevitable (at least) that each individual will appropriate communal ideals of restraint and courage to some degree. Furthermore, for most of us our deepest and most enduring satisfactions will be integrally tied up with the pursuit and fulfillment of the fundamental inclinations to bring forth and raise children and to live in a community of our fellows. Nor should this strike us as humanly or theologically problematic. If human existence is a good, the processes by which it is produced and sustained, both at the biological level and at the social level, are also good, worthy of our attention and best efforts.

The virtue of practical wisdom emerges out of this process of reflection on the overall shape of one's life, and correlatively, the exercise of this virtue will be governed by one's best judgments on this matter. This brings us to another point that we touched on earlier. That is, practical reason, when it is well disposed through the virtue of practical wisdom, functions in such a way as to bring order to diverse aims and considerations, even those which may have no predetermined standard of comparison. Again, we are reminded that according to Aquinas, right practical reason operates by placing diverse desiderata into an appropriate relationship to the overarching aim governing the agent's actions (II-II 152.2). As he goes on to explain, this implies that exterior goods are ordered to the well-being of the body; bodily goods are oriented toward the well-being of the soul, and the goods which are proper to the active life are ordered to the goods of the contemplative life (152.2). Some theorists have resisted this claim, because they feared it would allow for inappropriate kinds of harms to oneself or others, in pursuit of supposedly higher goods.[69] This is not the case for Aquinas, and it need not be the case for us, but in order to see why not, we will need to look more closely at a virtue we have so far bracketed, the virtue of justice.

4. Self-Love, Neighbor Love, and the Norms of Justice

Although he recognizes that according to one common usage justice is simply equivalent to moral uprightness, Aquinas prefers to speak of justice as a particular virtue (II-II 58.5-7). As such, it is grounded in a particular human capacity and functions within a delimited sphere of operations, just as the other virtues do. This suggests that if we are to complete our account of happiness considered as the practice of the virtues, we will need to give more attention to justice regarded precisely as such. By doing so, we will also prepare the way for the discussion of the precepts of the natural law in the next chapter.

Let us begin, then, with a closer look at what it means to regard justice as a virtue. As we noted above, Aquinas follows a long-standing tradition in regarding justice as one of four cardinal virtues. More specifically, he endorses the classical jurists' definition of justice preserved in Justinian's *Digest* as "the constant and perpetual will to render to each one that which is his due" (II-II 58.1). This definition serves to identify the primary distinguishing marks of the particular virtue of justice. It is a virtue of the will, in contrast to temperance and fortitude, which are virtues of the passions, and prudence, which properly speaking is an intellectual virtue (56.6; 58.4). Its proper object is *jus,* that is to say, the due or right, whatever is owing to another through nature or through human conventions (57.1).

Correlatively, the distinctive field of operation proper to justice regards external actions, through which we maintain (or violate) right relations with other persons (I-II 60.2, 3; II-II 58.8). This is a puzzling claim, since Aquinas also holds that every virtue, and not justice alone, is conceptually tied to the paradigmatic kinds of actions it produces (I-II 60.2). As he goes on to explain, for temperance and fortitude and their associated virtues external actions are significant insofar as they exemplify and express proper dispositions of the passions; nonetheless, the point of these virtues lies in disposing the passions in accordance with the agent's rational grasp of the good. In contrast, justice is not only expressed through external acts, but its point is pre-

69. Thus, Bowlin argues that this line of interpretation necessarily leads to a consequentialist reading of Aquinas, which he rightly believes Aquinas would reject; see *Contingency and Fortune,* 107-15.

cisely to rectify external actions, considered as the medium through which we maintain relationships with others. Justice is thus at one and the same time the distinctive virtue of the will (together with its associated virtues, it is the only virtue of the will that can be acquired without grace) and the virtue which rectifies our interactions with others. We will see that these two aspects of justice are in fact closely related.

Aquinas's claim that justice is a virtue of the will tends to be overlooked, or at least passed over with little comment. Part of our difficulty with this claim, I suspect, lies in the fact that we tend to regard the virtues as dispositions or modalities of feeling and responsiveness. As we have just seen, this assumption is borne out with respect to temperance and fortitude. However, as Aquinas insists, the particular virtue of justice is not primarily expressed in and through the passions, and by the same token, it cannot be contrasted straightforwardly with vices of the passions such as greed or vengefulness. If we think of the virtue of justice as a settled commitment, on a par with a commitment to a marriage, for example, it is easier to see Aquinas's point. In most postindustrial societies, it is generally expected that two people marry out of love for each other. Yet the commitment an individual makes to his marriage, even though it may be motivated by feelings of love for his spouse, cannot simply be equated with a feeling or passion of love. It implies a settled policy to act in such a way as to promote the marriage relationship and to avoid actions which would tend to undermine that relationship. Included in this policy is a commitment to nurturing and fostering those feelings which originally motivated the marriage. Yet a commitment to a marriage is compatible with a whole range of other feelings toward one's spouse, and it may persist after the original feelings of love have faded away. These facts do not imply that one's commitment to a marriage is or should be passionless; they only underscore the point that such a commitment can be compatible with, and expressed in terms of, a wide range of passions. In the same way, justice as a commitment of the will can exist together with the whole range of human passions, which will be integrated into the acts of the just person in appropriate and praiseworthy ways. Indeed, as Aquinas notes, this commitment will itself give rise to passions under the right circumstances, for example, anger or sorrow in the face of manifest social injustice (my example, not his). Yet precisely because justice is a virtue of the will, it cannot be identified with any one of these passions, nor does it require any particular set of feelings in order to be exercised. Justice as a virtue of the will need not be, and probably will not be, exercised without any passion at all, but precisely because it is compatible with a range of passions, it cannot be identified with any one of them.

It is critically important to realize that justice involves a disposition of rationally informed commitments to maintaining certain kinds of relationships with others, rather than a disposition to feel and respond in a particular way, because unless we take account of this contrast we will miss the implication of the claim that justice is a virtue of the will. The point I want to underscore is that justice stands in a relation to temperance and fortitude analogous to the relation of the will to the passions. And we must understand this relation in order to see how it is that justice perfects the agent, and therefore how it plays an indispensable role in happiness, considered as the practice of the virtues.

As we saw above, the virtues of the passions dispose the agent to feel and respond in accordance with reason, that is to say, in accordance with the agent's best judgments about whatever corresponds to his overall well-being and happiness within a given sphere of operation. These virtues are necessary because even though the passions are spontaneously oriented toward goods connatural to the human person as these are perceived through the senses, these spontaneous desires and aversions do not reliably reflect the agent's genuine good. For that very reason, they need to be informed by some rational grasp of the agent's overall good through the virtues of temperance and fortitude. Correlatively, the fundamental norm for both temperance and fortitude is set by the agent's own good, although for fortitude this basic criterion is qualified by the close link between fortitude and justice.

In contrast, the will does not need to be informed by a particular disposition in this way, because it is already spontaneously oriented toward the agent's overall good, in accordance with her best understanding of what that is. Moreover, in itself this orientation is entirely natural and proper. Aquinas's analysis of the will is at this point clearly correlated with his fundamental claim that every person necessarily seeks happiness. Not only is self-love in this sense regarded as a distinctively human expression of a metaphysical necessity, right self-love is also regarded as a moral duty (see, for example, II-II 64.5; it should be noted that what is in question here, as also in the case of charity, is love considered as a stance of the will, not the passion of love). This appears most clearly and explicitly in Aquinas's analysis of the order of charity, where he says that charity obliges the individual to love himself or herself more than any other creature (II-II 26.4). Hence, love of self comes second only to love for God in Aquinas's analysis of charity. Of course, the love of charity is not a natural love, nor does it express the development of our capacities for love through our own connatural powers; it is an expression of the supernatural dynamisms of grace. Nonetheless, Aquinas makes it clear that the love of charity follows the natural ordering of human love in all of its forms; otherwise, as he says in another context, charity would be the perversion rather than the perfection of nature (I 60.5; cf. I-II 109.3).

These claims are likely to shock us, because we are accustomed to think of self-love as the essence of sin, and to regard self-abnegation as the height of Christian virtue. Aquinas is aware of these objections, and in the course of addressing them he introduces an important qualification to his claims about self-love. At II-II 25.7 he addresses the question of whether sinners love themselves. Unsurprisingly, his response depends on a distinction. Sinners do love themselves, insofar as they desire and pursue whatever they think will make them truly happy. But they are in some way mistaken about this: they have made the fatal mistake, signaled as a possibility in I-II 1.7, of locating their happiness falsely in some kind of temporal well-being.[70] Hence, there is a sense in which they do not love themselves — they do not love themselves as they truly are, that is to say, they do not desire and pursue those aims in which genuine happiness consists. And as we have already seen, the life of genuine happiness, understood on every proper level, consists in the practice of the virtues. Hence, someone who understands her nature will realize that her happiness, that is to say, her perfection as a certain kind of creature, consists in the life of virtue, and she will act accordingly. There is thus no conflict between genuine self-love and moral rectitude, because — again — the life of virtue *is* the genuinely happy life.

Yet this cannot be the whole story. In order to aim at true happiness, the human person must grasp what he truly is, and this, as already noted, presupposes correct judgments of the speculative intellect (II-II 25.7).[71] But in addition, the truly virtuous person is characterized by a distinctive disposition *of*

70. The mistake in question, which Aquinas identifies with the sin of definite malice, is not a simple misapprehension; rather, it stems from a knowing preference for lesser, as opposed to greater, goods. This is possible, on Aquinas's view, because while the will can only incline toward something presented to it by the intellect as a good, there is no logical necessity compelling it to choose a greater over a lesser good. In her generally excellent analysis of Aquinas's theory of practical reason, Candace Vogler claims that Aquinas's theological presuppositions function in such a way as to foreclose what otherwise follows from his theory, namely, that there is nothing in the exigencies of reason as such to rule out immoral choices (see *Reasonably Vicious,* 39-41). But Aquinas does not hold that vicious choices are, strictly speaking, irrational, even for someone who is aware of the real possibility of salvation — indeed, the sin of definite malice consists precisely in the choice of lesser, temporal goods, in preference to the greater good of eternal salvation (I-II 78.1; Aquinas explains how this is, and is not, a sin of ignorance at I-II 78.1 *ad* 1). Of course, this kind of viciousness is contrary to reason in the sense that it is inconsistent with the human person's true good, but the same may be said about every sinful choice.

71. I follow Ralph McInerny on this point; see *Aquinas on Human Action: A Theory of Practice* (Washington, D.C.: Catholic University of America Press, 1992), 184-206.

the will. Of course, this disposition presupposes intellectual judgments, in this case regarding one's proper relations to others and to the wider community. Nonetheless, justice is distinctively and characteristically a virtue of the will, because it disposes the agent to have standing commitments of respect and regard for other persons. Hence, justice is necessary precisely in order to reorient the will away from its spontaneous orientation toward the agent's own good, so as to create a standing disposition to regard and pursue the good of others. And given our analysis so far, this raises fundamental questions. Can justice understood in this way be regarded as a perfection of the agent, as part of her happiness understood as the practice of the virtues? Indeed, is justice compatible with Aquinas's strong affirmations of a proper self-love? We might seem at this point to have uncovered an inconsistency in Aquinas's thought. I don't think this is the case, but in order to see why not, we will need to go beyond his explicit remarks on justice and self-love.

In order to sort out the relation between self-love and justice, we should first of all note that both are natural to the human person, but not in the same way. In one sense, self-love is a natural necessity — that is to say, the human person, like every other creature, necessarily loves its own existence in the sense of seeking to maintain it. By the same token, every functionally normal person necessarily desires happiness, which is tantamount to saying that every person capable of rational reflection seeks to live and flourish in accordance with his best understanding of what he most truly is. At the same time, however, right self-love, love of oneself in accordance with what one truly is, is natural in the sense of stemming from and perfecting human nature, but that does not mean that the human person will spontaneously love himself in this sense. Nonrational creatures move toward perfection in accordance with their specific kinds through the spontaneous operation of their natural inclinations, which are naturally determined toward the kinds of actions consistent with that orientation. But precisely because human inclinations are not determined in this way, the human person is capable of going astray in pursuing her own perfection — not in the sense that she can fail to seek her perfection, but in the sense that she might pursue it wrongly.

Aquinas says more than once that it is natural to both human beings and angels, and indeed to every kind of creature, to love God more than oneself (again, see I 60.5; I-II 109.3). This somewhat startling claim must be understood in the context of Aquinas's usage, according to which even the inclinations of inanimate creatures can be called a kind of love or desire, without however implying any consciousness on their part (again, see I-II 109.3).[72]

72. This connection is spelled out still more clearly in the *SCG* III, 16-17.

Even so, we will miss Aquinas's point unless we recall that this natural love is tantamount to the creature's love, inclination, or ordered tendency to seek the universal good, even in preference to its own individual good. In the case of the rational creature, this inclination or tendency will be expressed through some concept of a form of goodness transcending the individual. As such, this tendency might be expressed through a natural love for God as an object for philosophical contemplation; as transformed through grace, it would be expressed through charity. Although Aquinas does not explicitly say so, it seems plausible that the orientation of the will toward a universal good can also be expressed through a love of other kinds of comprehensive goods, including the political community (perhaps in its ideal form), or a moral or aesthetic idea. Aquinas does say that we are naturally inclined to love the common good of the political community more than ourselves; if it were not for the effect of sin, he observes, we would naturally and spontaneously sacrifice ourselves for the common good, just as we spontaneously sacrifice a limb of our bodies in order to preserve the body taken as a whole (I 60.5; II-II 26.4 *ad* 3).

But of course, we do not act in this way spontaneously — only someone who has attained a high degree of justice and courage could even approach this ideal. The love of God, and by implication love of a universal good, more than oneself is natural, insofar as it is an appropriate and fitting expression of what we naturally are, but given the actual state of human nature wounded by sin, such an attitude does not "come naturally" to us (as Aquinas observes at I-II 109.3). If human nature had not been wounded by sin, the individual would spontaneously sacrifice himself for the greater good — but given our condition as it actually is, this kind of self-sacrifice is only possible through great struggle, and even lesser sacrifices only come at some cost. That is why justice can be regarded both as necessary — because in one sense we are not oriented to act in accordance with its imperatives — and natural — because it stems from and perfects the natural capacities of the agent, as do all the virtues.

But how can justice so understood be regarded as a perfection of the agent, when Aquinas also says each person necessarily seeks his own happiness? Here is a plausible answer. We might say with Aquinas that each person naturally and necessarily seeks his own happiness, while adding that one's happiness is not all that the agent seeks. After all, on Aquinas's view the will is oriented toward the good as such, not toward this or that particular good, and for that very reason it can only operate on the basis of intellectual judgments that this or that object or state of affairs is good. We are certainly capable of conceiving of good things or situations which are greater than ourselves. So it would seem that nothing prohibits us from loving and pursuing these greater goods, in addition to or even to the detriment of our own individual good.

Seen in this way, justice would add something to the natural orientation of the will which not only develops and completes it, but supersedes it.

The difficulty with this line of interpretation, at least considered as an extension of Aquinas's thought, is that he not only says that the human person necessarily pursues her own happiness, he adds that all of her actions are in some way ordered to this fundamental end (I-II 1.6; 10.2). The claim that every person necessarily directs all of her actions toward a final end may seem implausible at first, but on Aquinas's view, this claim is a necessary implication of the view that the human person acts voluntarily, that is to say, in pursuit of some end. If the agent did not have a final end in view, her pursuit of intermediate ends would have no rationale or point — which is tantamount to saying that her behavior would not be sufficiently rational to count as action at all. This does not necessarily mean that the agent always acts in pursuit of whatever she regards, in accordance with her settled, reflective judgment, as constituting her true happiness.[73] But if we recall that Aquinas recognized that happiness can be understood in a variety of ways, including the most primitive sense of simply getting one's way, we can more readily see the force of the claim that everyone always acts for the sake of happiness. The point is that the human person always acts in pursuit of aims which can ultimately be traced to some conception of his ultimate good, however transitory or debased that conception might be.[74]

If this is so, then we cannot resolve the tension between self-love and justice by regarding these as two discrete ends, which can be pursued independently of each other and may even sometimes conflict. There is another way of resolving this tension, however, which seems to me closer to Aquinas's own meaning, and which offers a more fruitful way of developing the overall ideal of happiness as the practice of the virtues. That is, it might be that there is no conflict between self-love and justice, because in order for the agent to

73. Scott MacDonald makes this point clear in his "Aquinas' Ultimate Ends: A Reply to Grisez," *American Journal of Jurisprudence* 46 (2001): 37-50. It is possible to get a good overview of the relevant issues by consulting this article together with the essay to which it responds, Germain Grisez, "Natural Law, God, Religion, and Human Fulfillment," 3-36, in the same issue.

74. In particular, Aquinas's conception of the ultimate end does not rule out the possibility of acts performed "for their own sake," as Vogler suggests (*Reasonably Vicious,* 134). Human happiness, at least in its terrestrial forms, can only be attained over time; no particular choice or action will fully express the overall goodness of a happy life, but by the same token, every particular choice or act made in accordance with a virtuous disposition will represent a component part, and thus a partial fulfillment, of happiness tout court. This applies even to acts chosen "for their own sake," for fun or relaxation, let us say — if these are chosen at all, they reflect some belief that an act of the relevant kind is suitable and appropriate here and now, and in this way consistent with the agent's overall happiness (I-II 1.6 *ad* 1, 2).

attain her true good she must stand in a right relation to other persons and to her community — and ideals of right relation are precisely the defining ideals of justice as a virtue. Aquinas himself suggests this line of argument (see, for example, I-II 92.1 *ad* 3; II-II 47.10), but without further development it could easily lead us into a stipulative resolution of our problem. There is a more substantive and interesting way of accounting for the congruence between self-love and justice, as I will attempt to show in what follows.

As Aquinas observes, a right self-love can only stem from a correct appraisal of one's nature (II-II 25.7). With respect to the issue at hand, this will include recognizing the fact that we are naturally social animals, and our characteristic way of life involves participating, from birth to death, in a complex network of social relationships. As Aristotle long ago remarked, we are social animals, and today we are frequently reminded of the relational character of human existence. While this claim has been interpreted in dubious ways, there is a sense in which it is certainly true — the sense, that is to say, in which it points to a fundamental feature of our distinctive way of life as animals of a certain kind, namely, highly social primates. Hence, reflection on our relational character will bring us, once again, to look at the way in which "nature as nature," stemming from prerational aspects of our nature, informs "nature as reason," that is to say, the moral exigencies of a distinctively human natural law.

This may strike some readers as implausible, because we are accustomed to think of justice as a quintessentially human virtue, which reflects distinctively human capacities for reason and deliberation if any aspect of human life does so. Yet the close study of several generations of other social animals, including the other advanced primates, dogs, elephants, and dolphins, has made it clear that our own ways of interrelating in structured social units are not unique; rather, our own forms of social life fit into a larger pattern which we find replicated in many different kinds of large-brained animals. To some extent these continuities even extend to aspects of the moral life. In the words of the primatologist Frans de Waal, "The question of whether animals have morality is a bit like the question of whether they have culture, politics, or language. If we take the full-blown human phenomenon as a yardstick, they most definitely do not. On the other hand, if we break the relevant human abilities into their component parts, some are recognizable in other animals."[75] He goes on to enumerate these, including attachment; empathy; ad-

75. De Waal, *Good Natured,* 210. However, not everyone would go as far as de Waal. Compare Marc D. Hauser, *Wild Minds: What Animals Really Think* (New York: Henry Holt, 2000): "I suggest that although animals have the mental tools to distinguish between living and nonliving things, to use object motion to generate expectations about behavior, and to have emotional experiences about their interactions with the physical and psychological world, my hunch is that

justment to and special care for the disabled; internalization of "prescriptive social rules"; concepts of giving, trading, and revenge; tendencies toward peacemaking and social maintenance; and the practice of negotiation.[76]

The scholastics were not unaware of these continuities; on the contrary, as we noted in the last chapter, they emphasized the similarities between human action and the behavior of other kinds of animals to a striking degree. Nonetheless, we undoubtedly have a clearer and better-informed sense of the ways in which our own social behavior exemplifies a way of life that is common to many other kinds of creatures besides ourselves. To this extent, human social interactions cannot be placed neatly on one side of a line separating those inclinations we share with other animals from those inclinations which presuppose a distinctively human rationality.

But what lessons should we draw from this observation? It is sometimes suggested that once we recognize the prerational components of human social behavior, we will be compelled — practically or morally, or both — to accept various features of our societies as they actually exist as natural, in the very specific sense of unalterable. But this conclusion does not follow simply from the naturalness of social behavior, and considered on its own merits it is not plausible. Once again, we must remind ourselves that however we construe it, human nature underdetermines its various forms of expression. The bewildering variety of forms of human social existence should suffice to make the point in this context. It probably is the case that some broad features of our social existence are natural in the sense of being practically unalterable, including hierarchical structure and some kinds of distinctions between the sexes and the generations. But these broad features allow for an indefinite variety of actual expressions, including those which emphasize equality and individualism rather than hierarchy and role distinctions. We certainly can, and very often should, find different ways of arranging our so-

---

they lack the moral emotions or moral senses. They lack the capacity for empathy, sympathy, shame, guilt and loyalty. The reason for this emotional hole in their lives, I believe, is that they lack a fundamental mental tool — self-awareness" (224). As he goes on to explain, what he means by this is specifically awareness of one's own beliefs and desires, seen in distinction from those of others — hence, they cannot experience empathy in the necessary sense, because they have no clear sense of their inner states as distinctively theirs. This being said, I think there is no necessary contradiction between de Waal and Hauser. The debate turns on how high one sets the bar for calling something a moral feeling or instinct. If these simply refer to an emotionally charged sense of one's place in a social network, including a sense of what counts as transgressing same, then it seems clear that the social mammals do have social emotions — even though they lack empathy, and therefore the capacity for a fully developed moral sense. Hauser seems to me open to conceding this much.

76. De Waal, *Good Natured*, 210.

cial lives, including reconfiguring the relationships between the sexes and the generations, reducing or eliminating the growing gap between the richest and the poorest members of our society, and the like. There is nothing in our nature as social animals that would rule out these kinds of social reforms.

The lesson we should draw from comparisons with other kinds of social animals, rather, is suggested by Aquinas's comment that the inclinations of rational creatures are to be interpreted by analogy to the inclinations found in prerational creatures (I 60.5). By reflecting on the social lives of other kinds of animals, we can arrive at a better sense of the point of our own social inclinations, that is to say, their purpose seen in the overall context of our species-specific way of life. Indeed, as we reflect on our own social behavior as seen in the context of other social animals, it is apparent that patterned social interaction *is* our species-specific way of life. We pursue, attain, and enjoy the basic components of animal well-being — food and drink, shelter, security, mating and reproduction, protection while ill or infirm — in and through structured interactions with our fellows. It is possible to image someone surviving in complete isolation from her fellows, but only under very unusual circumstances. And it is almost impossible to regard such a life as a life of well-being, any more than we could regard someone who was ill or deprived of basic necessities of life as enjoying well-being.

We are at this point focusing on the ways the social dimension of our existence is intertwined with other aspects of basic well-being. But we should not lose sight of the fact that for the human person, even basic well-being presupposes the development and expression of distinctively rational capacities, and these likewise presuppose social forms of existence. Most fundamentally, language almost certainly requires some kind of communal context, and the exigencies of social existence appear to inform language in the sense of providing it with a context of structures of meaning.[77] By the same token, most other distinctively human activities, such as the practice of the arts and religion,

77. There have been many theories about the origins of language and the conditions necessary for its existence and functioning, but I cannot imagine any plausible account according to which language could emerge as a full-fledged system of communication apart from some process of social interaction. It should also be noted that other animals do communicate. However, they do not seem to employ symbols tethered to abstract ideas, which can be detached from an immediate referential context and expressed in the form of modal propositions — in other words, their communication lacks what Hauser describes as "referential flexibility" (*Wild Minds*, 175-210). Moreover, even when animals do seem to learn language in our sense, they must be taught through a process which incorporates them, to some extent, into our own species-specific way of life — that is to say, language use is not a spontaneous part of their species-specific ways of living (201-8). In McDowell's terms, they are not capable of spontaneity; see *Mind and World*, 108-26, for further discussion.

would also seem to require some kind of social context, if only because they are unimaginable as sustained practices apart from the use of language.[78]

Both of these aspects of human social existence must be kept in mind if we are to appreciate the ways in which life in society is good for the individual, as well as the society. On the most fundamental level, no one could come into existence and develop into a flourishing maturity without the care and guidance of others, and not just one's immediate family, either.[79] In innumerable ways throughout our lives we rely on others for basic sustenance, security, and protection and support in times of need. Moreover, apart from some communal context we would not be able to exist and to flourish in accordance with our most distinctive capacities for rationality as expressed in speech and deliberation. By the same token, most or all of the activities, commitments, and goals which give meaning and structure to our lives presuppose some kind of communal practice.

What is more, each of us takes the basic components of his or her personal identity — as son or daughter, as a member of an extended family or community, as a spouse, as a practitioner of some profession, art, or religion, and the like — from our place in a family and a network of wider communities. Once again, I am speaking of personal identity in an extended sense, along the lines that MacIntyre suggests when he speaks of one's identity as constituted by the narrative unity of one's life.[80] Even in this sense, one's identity is not wholly subsumed by one's social roles and relations to others — but these do provide the starting points and much of the substance of the distinctive individual identities that we shape through our experiences and choices throughout our lives. I am not just a daughter, a wife, a teacher, and a friend, and I can imagine a life that would be recognizably mine in which I never married, for example, or entered a different profession. But at some point, I would have to say that a life constituted by a different set of relationships to others would no longer be imaginable as *my* life in any recognizable or meaningful sense.

78. Of course, individuals can be brought into the practices of art or religion even though they are incapable of language use — otherwise, it would be impossible to initiate small children into these practices. What we have in these cases, I would suggest, is some kind of guided insertion into a practice which is by its nature self-reflective and self-correcting, and therefore can be fully developed and expressed only through discourse. Shweder makes a similar point in "Culture and Mental Development," 283-90.

79. MacIntyre places special emphasis on this point; see *Dependent Rational Animals*, 63-80.

80. See *After Virtue: A Study in Moral Theory*, 2nd ed. (Notre Dame: University of Notre Dame Press, 1984), 217-18.

So far, we have been identifying some of the ways in which the well-being of the individual depends on participation in a social network. Yet we might still question whether the virtue of justice is essential to, or even always compatible with, the individual's well-being and happiness. The issues here are ancient and familiar. It is all too possible to take advantage of the benefits and protections of society without even trying to observe any recognizable norms of justice. Whether one does so by exploiting the weaknesses of one's social structures as they present themselves, or by overturning social strictures through sheer brute force, it is certainly possible to attain many of the advantages of society for oneself without being just. And by the same token, a commitment to justice might well lead the individual to sacrifice her basic well-being in all sorts of ways, all the way from dying for her country, to accepting the inconveniences of paying taxes, to fulfilling her contractual obligations and the like.

In response, I would claim that the relation between happiness and well-being should be understood in the same way for justice as for the other virtues. In the last section, we concluded that the virtues, and the happiness they constitute, are paradigmatically connected to more basic forms of well-being. That is, the virtues are conceptually linked to pursuing and enjoying well-being in a particular way, even though it is possible to pursue and enjoy a virtuous life while forgoing many of the components of well-being. The same may be said of justice. This virtue takes its field of operation from the complex interactions proper to the social life of the human animal, and the kinds of actions paradigmatic of this virtue express a characteristic stance toward one's community and toward other individuals with whom one is interacting. As we might expect, the relationship between the virtue of justice and its characteristic kinds of actions is complex. Nonetheless, as is the case with the other virtues, acts of justice can be recognized as such once we grasp their point — that is, once we see them as expressions of a particular stance toward the social context of a human life.

But what stance is that? It is particularly important to address this question for the same reason that it is difficult to do so. That is, justice as a virtue is more complex than temperance or fortitude, particularly understood in the expansive way in which Aquinas interprets it. It takes in the whole sphere of human interactions, which are shaped by a wide range of moral considerations, some of them clearly relevant to justice, others not. Moreover, it is dependent on conventions to a greater extent than the other virtues, even granting that temperance and fortitude are also shaped by conventions, probably to a greater degree than Aquinas or the other scholastics would have recognized. If we are to identify justice with paradigmatic kinds of actions, therefore, we need to have some sense of what these kinds of actions have in common. To rephrase the question above, can we give a plausible account of what it would look like, concretely, for someone to possess and exercise "a constant and perpetual will to render to each individual his or her due"?

In order to answer this question, it will be helpful to proceed once again by reflecting briefly on the processes by which the virtue of justice is acquired in the developing child. De Waal's remarks suggest how this process gets started. That is, even very young children share in what he describes as the distinctively social emotions — shame or guilt when violating a transgression, anger when one's own desires are violated, and pride when one perceives oneself to be well regarded by others. These, as we have seen, are common ground between us and the other higher primates. In addition, the human child has capacities to grasp the idea of itself as an object of other people's attitudes, and to draw appropriate connections between these social emotions and the judgments of others. These capacities, in turn, make it possible for the child to empathize with the feelings of others — that is to say, the child can grasp how someone else is feeling, while at the same time realizing that these are the feelings of another, (perhaps) directed at oneself, and not one's own feelings. He thus has the potential, in Mead's terms, to regard himself as "me," the object of others' feelings and evaluations, and to internalize the appropriate responses, all the while retaining a sense of himself as "I," a self-determining agent.[81]

Of course, the capacity to see oneself as the object of others' perceptions takes time to develop. In the young child, the whole process of experiencing the social emotions and responding accordingly will remain mostly at the level of the passions — that is to say, what we see here are affective responses to immediate perceptions of oneself and others' reactions to oneself. Like all affective responses, they involve a response to what is immediately perceived as desirable or harmful, in this case the warm and affirming, or negative and rejecting, responses of others to oneself. This is so even when these responses are mediated through remembered or anticipated reactions of others; in cases such as these, the child must rely on imagined rather than actual encounters with others, but these would still be examples of affective responses to an immediately perceived good or evil. As such, these responses reflect "nature as nature" — they are informed by the intelligible structures of basic human interrelationships — but they do not reflect a mature rationality. That is, they do not depend on general concepts of right relations, which the child could express in some terms (even inadequately) and generalize across a range of

81. This distinction is summarized in Mead, *Mind, Self, and Society,* 173-75.

situations. So far, the child's passions are engaged, but not yet his considered judgments or his will.

Yet even at this level, rationality begins to inform the child's reactions and incipient deliberations. The passions of even a young child are human passions, presupposing some level of judgment about the situations she faces.[82] Moreover, these situations themselves are shaped by a system of human relationships which are structured (imperfectly, no doubt, but genuinely) in accordance with ideals of justice. Hence, even at a very early stage, the child's passions will be shaped by, and will themselves reflect, a communally shared sense of justice and right relations. Moreover, the child's caretakers build upon, develop, and foster this incipient sense by mirroring back to the child, in tones of approval or disapproval, how she is being perceived within this framework. A child who is selfish, demanding, bullying, or unkind, who cheats at games, lies to her parents, and pushes away her siblings, will be presented to herself under these descriptions in decidedly negative terms; when she manages to correct her behavior, to be unselfish, kind, helpful, honest, and fair, she will be presented to herself as a pleasant and, more importantly, admirable child.

Just as for the other virtues, these paradigms must be internalized if the child's process of development is to continue. This will involve, first of all, coming to regard the positive images of oneself as unselfish, kind, honest, and the like as desirable for oneself, and their contraries as undesirable. But in addition, it will also require the maturing child to grasp some sense of the point unifying these paradigms. Unless she is able to achieve some sense of why it is admirable to be honest, for example, she will not be able to generalize an ideal of honesty outside her immediate circle to include relations with strangers, whose reactions may not matter so much as the reactions of her family and friends. Moreover, she will not be able to apply these paradigms to unfamiliar situations — to realize, for example, that presenting the words of others as one's own is a form of dishonesty, just as cheating at a card game is.[83]

So far, we are moving along familiar lines. But in order to grasp the point of the paradigms related to justice, seen in contrast to temperance and fortitude, the child must make one further move. She must integrate a very diverse range of typical actions and reactions by bringing them together under the rubric of one ideal, that is to say, an ideal of justice, or if one prefers, an ideal of fairness or uprightness. She must grasp the point that a very wide

82. For further details on the passions and their relation to reason, see Pasnau, *Thomas Aquinas*, 257-64.

83. I have read that editors of children's magazines have to watch out for this — small children generally do not grasp the concept of plagiarism.

range of ideals, involving a spectrum of different kinds of passions as well as dispositions to observe various kinds of rules, are all to be understood with reference to an overarching abstract ideal, which as such cannot be neatly correlated with any one set of affective responses or their contraries. She must do so because these diverse ideals are likely to come into conflict, in such a way as to force her to adjudicate among them. Is it better to be kind to one's importunate classmate by allowing her to copy one's exam, or is this ruled out as a kind of dishonesty? Is it more important to follow one's religious vocation by entering a monastery, or to stay home to care for one's aging mother? Does a right relation to one's country demand support for the government in a time of crisis, or an ongoing commitment to critical self-appraisal? We could multiply such examples indefinitely; the point is, they all require the individual to go beyond an assessment of particular affective responses, or indeed of the demands of particular rules considered seriatim, to consider what is due to others and to one's community, all things considered.

And so we find ourselves returning to the classic definition of justice as a constant and perpetual will to render to each his or her due. This definition has been criticized for its generality, and by itself it certainly does not give us much guidance in determining what counts as someone's due. Nonetheless, this definition does capture the essential quality of justice regarded as a virtue, that is to say, as a distinctively human perfection. In the first place, it locates justice in a broad standing commitment to respect the claims of others, without any necessary reference to one's particular desires or aversions. This is one implication of the claim that justice is a virtue of the will; the commitment to render what is due to others does not depend on any one set of emotional responses, and can be effectively exercised even contrary to one's desires and aversions. (This is not at all the same thing as saying that the ideal of the just person implies emotional detachment, but only that this ideal is not tied paradigmatically to any particular set of emotional responses.) Secondly, by tying the relevant stance of the will to the abstract idea of "the due," this definition indicates the way in which justice is a distinctively human perfection. That is, it depends on some reflective sense of what it means to live in a community, what one's place in that community is, and what kinds of claims others can make on oneself. This sense need not be elaborate or theoretically developed, but it does need to stem from some level of abstraction from one's own immediate circumstances and surroundings, to take account of one's place in a wider social context. And finally, justice presupposes that this reflective sense of one's place in a wider community will inform one's sense of self-identity, in such a way that one views one's individual life in the context of a communally sustained way of life. That is why, seen from the perspective of someone who is genuinely just, any conflict between one's individual happiness and the demands of justice turns out to be illusory — because the good of the individual is constituted, in part at least, by the right relations with others and with her community, such as the virtue of justice disposes her to seek and maintain.

At this point, someone may object that this all sounds very good in theory, but in fact there are lots of people who enjoy the benefits and protections of society while exploiting others at every turn. We can now see that even though this objection is true, as far as it goes, still it misses the point. The distinctive forms of perfection and happiness associated with the virtue of justice do not consist simply in attaining those elements of well-being which involve existence in society. Rather, they consist in attaining and enjoying these elements in a particular way, out of an intelligent appreciation of the many forms of human goodness which can only be enjoyed and sustained in relationship with others and an informed regard for them, seen as genuinely one's fellows and potential friends. My point is that this kind of disinterested regard for communal values and for the individual lives of others is itself a good, as well as being a necessary condition for the attainment of other goods such as genuine friendship. And this good cannot be attained apart from justice because in a sense, it *is* justice — more exactly, the kind of attitude in question is a necessary component of justice, regarded as the constant will to render to each his or her due.

The just person is such — that is to say, just, and not merely disposed for self-interested reasons to observe the norms of justice — because she is genuinely committed to an ideal of a just society, which she grasps intellectually and loves for its own sake. By the same token, she sees herself, at least regarded from a terrestrial perspective, as primarily and essentially one person in an actually or ideally just community of persons. Recall that each person seeks happiness in accordance with what she considers herself to be; the just person considers herself to be a participant in a just community — even if that community exists only as an ideal in her own mind. Hence, for her there can be no conflict between justice and happiness, because she would undermine and destroy her own identity, in MacIntyre's sense of personal coherence and self-consistency, by acting in an unjust way for immediate gain.

Perhaps this sounds too idealistic. Yet seen from a purely terrestrial perspective, this ideal of happiness is attractive and persuasive — indeed, it has seemed for centuries to be compelling, and I believe it is the ideal structuring many people's lives today. A life lived in accordance with an ideal of justice is plausible as a candidate for the happy life, even understood on Annas's terms as a life which is satisfying and attractive as well as objectively perfective, in light of the same circumstances which make justice in some form a necessary human virtue. That is to say, we are all vulnerable in innumerable ways to losing whatever we most enjoy or value in our personal lives, and even the most fortunate of us will someday die. Furthermore, nearly every adult knows all this — it is a mark of maturity and sanity to do so. That is why it is natural, in the sense of reason as nature, to identify ourselves with communally embodied values or ideals which are not similarly vulnerable and which we can hope to outlive us. As Holmes Rolston puts it, "Almost everything that the self cares about has to be cared about in concert with others, and all these others have their myriad connections in turn. The cultural self comes to transcend, even to replace in part, the biological self. What one wishes to survive is one's ideas, one's values, or more accurately, those ideas and values into which one comes to be educated and in which one meaningfully participates."[84] Perhaps this "cultural self" will be identified with a particular community, but even then, devotion to a community is inextricably tied up with some sense of what that community ideally is or should be. By the same token, a reflective commitment to communal devotion opens up a more general ideal of justice, which can itself become a focus for an individual's devotion and self-identification. But in any case, it is far from absurd to suggest that seen from the perspective of terrestrial happiness, such as we can achieve through our own powers, the happy life most properly understood is a life which has been rendered meaningful through devotion to ideals of justice.

Seen in this context, devotion to an ideal of justice is not inconsistent with self-love, even when it requires some form of self-sacrifice. On the contrary, devotion to justice, and to the communities and relationships through which it is sustained, is an appropriate expression of the individual's natural desire to live and to extend his life through the exercise of his causal powers — one of the highest such expressions possible to us through our own connatural powers. Aquinas observes that because the human person's desire to sustain its existence is mediated through judgments of the intellect, we are capable of grasping the possibility of an unlimited existence. And since we naturally desire our own existence, the desire for an unlimited life necessarily follows. There has been considerable debate over just what this means, and whether it implies a natural desire for immortality or for union with God. It is not necessary for our purposes to resolve these debates.[85] In any case, it

84. Holmes Rolston III, *Genes, Genesis, and God: Values and Their Origins in Natural and Human History* (Cambridge: Cambridge University Press, 1999), 281.

85. That being said, I agree with Steven Long on this point — this desire need not necessarily express itself in anything like the Christian desire for union with God, although that is *one* expression of a general human phenomenon; see Long, "On the Possibility," 221-26.

seems to me that this claim is most plausible if we construe it in terms of a natural desire for an unlimited life, a life that transcends one's individual limitations. So understood, this desire need not express itself through a desire for personal immortality; it can also express itself through identification with, and devotion to, an ideal or a cause greater than oneself. Understood in this way, devotion to an ideal of justice may require self-sacrifice in the sense of giving up some aspect of one's well-being, even life itself; and yet, because the just individual identifies herself with the wider community and its governing ideal, she can cogently regard such sacrifices as expressions of love for herself, considered as someone whose life has been expansively joined to something beyond herself. Even at the level of mundane affairs, someone who hopes to save her life must be prepared to lose it.

Of course, much more would need to be said in order to develop an adequate account of justice, particularly considered as a socially embodied set of right relations. We should note, in particular, that the link between individual happiness and allegiance to a communal ideal does not necessarily imply that communal interests should supersede the well-being of the individual in every instance. Devotion to an ideal of justice can all too easily be perverted into fascism, but such a development is a perversion, not an appropriate expression of the ideal itself. Nearly every plausible ideal of justice protects some space for individual interests and freedom, although this is one of the central points at which different ideals of justice diverge.

We should also keep in mind that from a Christian standpoint, the ideal of justice is ambiguous. The city of God and the city of this world are two separate realms, and the Christian will have to choose at some point where her final allegiance will lie. The scholastics, including Aquinas, tended to affirm the goodness and value of the earthly city and its constitutive ideal of justice, even while they relativized its claims. In any case, the demands of the earthly and heavenly cities came together at many points, particularly with respect to the basic norms of nonmaleficence set forth in the Decalogue. These were regarded, by Aquinas and his contemporaries, as a summary statement of the practical demands of the natural law, and as such they were seen as being at one and the same time imperatives of divine law and demands of reason. As such, they provided the paradigmatic framework for explaining what it means to say, with Huguccio, that reason is a law. We will return to this point in the next chapter.

5. The Happy Life, Revisited

We have been examining the way in which the virtues provide a link between a basic idea of human well-being and a morally significant conception of happiness, interpreted by Aquinas as the kind of perfection proper to a rational or intellectual nature. In the process of doing so, the larger contours of the conception of happiness construed as the practice of the virtues may have receded. At this point, therefore, it will be helpful to look once again at the substantive conception of happiness implied by this claim. Of course, the most that can be done within the scope of this project is to sketch out the main lines of this conception, because it allows for a wide variety of actual instantiations. Moreover, the account of happiness as the practice of the virtues will not be complete until we have looked more closely at justice and prudence, seen in relation to the precepts of the natural law. Nonetheless, hopefully even the incomplete sketch that follows will be sufficiently detailed to indicate that this conception of happiness does have substantive content, even though it is not possible (or desirable) to offer a fully determinate account of the (one and only one) happy way of life.

Aquinas's claim that earthly happiness consists in the practice of the virtues has ancient and well-established antecedents, and moreover he interprets this claim in such a way that it follows from his overall metaphysics and philosophy of nature. Even so, the equation of happiness with the life of virtue is likely to strike the contemporary reader as quaint, at best. Yet as the arguments of this chapter have shown, this claim is not so far-fetched as we might at first assume. The practice of virtue is paradigmatically linked with a way of life that most people do in fact find desirable and attractive — a life lived in pursuit of the basic satisfactions of human existence, including material sufficiency, security, and especially the foundation of a family and the upbringing of children. Of course, these are desiderata on almost any account of human well-being. As we have seen, however, the life of virtue is paradigmatically linked to pursuing and enjoying these goods in a particular way, which is itself enjoyable and satisfying. In other words, the practice of the virtues is an intrinsic part of the satisfactions enjoyed in the happy life, not a means to the attainment of goods which could also be attained — perhaps, not so reliably — in some other way. It is of course possible to attain superficially similar goods by other means, but the enjoyments proper to a life of virtue consist in the enjoyment of human goods in a particular way, that is to say, in and through the practice of the virtues themselves.

Even the fundamental virtues of restraint and courage bring pleasure, which is inextricably connected to enjoying basic human goods in a particular way. The virtues which inform family life are still more clearly linked to happiness. A life of mutual love between husband and wife is intrinsically satisfying to most persons, as is the delicate combination of love and pride which informs relations between parents and children. Yet none of these desiderata is possible without some measure of fidelity, trust, gratitude, and a host of other interpersonal virtues. We have also noted that human well-being even at the most basic level presupposes integration into some larger community, sustained through relationships with one's fellows. What is more, most of us value a life structured by mutual exchange, friendly relationships, trust, and a sense of participating in something beyond ourselves. Just as the satisfactions of a loving and mutually respectful family life presuppose some level of interpersonal virtues, so the rewards of mutual respect and shared values proper to life in community presuppose some level of justice and associated virtues. This means that the life of virtue will include not only such virtues as temperance, courage, and the like, but also more properly civic virtues, namely, justice and its associated virtues. Of course, the more individually oriented virtues also have relevance for the well-being of the commonwealth, and justice has a role to play in the life of the family. My point is simply that when we focus our attention on more properly civic virtues, we see that these too have their own proper enjoyments and satisfactions — the joy of participating as a respected member in communal deliberations, satisfaction in orderly civic interactions, civic pride. Even the maintenance of justice in human relations, however imperfect and ambiguous at the best of times, brings its own distinctive joy to those who take part in it.

By now a paradigmatic life of virtue is beginning to look attractive, including as it does much that men and women generally do desire and seek — a distinctive way of enjoying basic human goods, the satisfactions of marriage and family life, and the complementary satisfactions of participation in one's community and civic affairs. Of course, the practice of the virtues is not equated with happiness because it is satisfying and enjoyable — rather, the practice of the virtues represents the greatest possible terrestrial perfection of the human creature, in accordance with its specific form. By the same token, the claim that this way of life is normally enjoyable and satisfying need not commit us to the view that everyone will find it desirable. As Hursthouse notes, it is unrealistic to expect that a defense of virtue along these lines would convince someone who is not in some way already inclined to find this way of life attractive.[86] Human desires are naturally open and pluriform, and for this very reason the human person is quite capable of desiring and seeking

86. Hursthouse, *On Virtue Ethics*, 178-91.

objects and states of affairs which will not in fact promote her genuine well-being, as Aquinas points out. Nor does it count against this picture of happiness that it is in various ways incomplete and insecure, as we have already seen.

But at this point another question may arise. That is, even granting the attractiveness of the paradigmatic picture of the happy life sketched above, and even granting that terrestrial happiness in any proper form consists in the practice of the virtues, it still seems implausible to claim that this is the only form that a happy life can take. After all, Aquinas himself, together with nearly every other scholastic, believed that there are alternative, indeed superior ways of practicing the virtues, for example in a life structured around vows of community allegiance and celibacy. It is not difficult to think of still other examples of kinds of virtuous lives in which the typical goods of marriage, family life, and even communal participation do not play a central role — a life of dedication to a profession or to artistic achievement, for example.

In response, we should recall that what is at stake here is a paradigmatic conception of the happy life, which is not to be equated with the only possible form happiness can take. The paradigm of the happy life stands in the same relation to happiness as the paradigms of particular virtues have to the rational ideals of these same virtues — unsurprisingly, since the paradigm of the happy life, which consists in the practice of the virtues, emerges out of the paradigmatic acts of particular virtues, envisioned as taking place in an orderly way over the course of a whole life. That is, the relation between the paradigm of a happy life and its rational ideal is conceptual, but this does not imply that a life of virtue can only be lived in accordance with the specifics of the paradigmatic ideal. Rather, the paradigm represents what the happy life will normally or typically look like, and it is through reflection on this paradigm that we grasp some sense of the overall aims and the point of this way of life. Once we have done so, we will be able to recognize other, less typical forms of happiness for what they are, and to explain why these should also count as ways of practicing the virtues over the course of a lifetime.

It would be a mistake to assume that reflection on the paradigm of a happy life will yield a comprehensive formula or theory, in terms of which nonstandard candidates can be completely and infallibly evaluated. The most we can hope to develop in this regard, once again, is a kind of practical wisdom, which enables us to judge more or less reliably in these matters. But the judgments in question will be rational judgments, and we will therefore be able to back them up by appealing to supporting considerations, even though these will normally not be conclusive. What kinds of considerations might these be?

Without claiming that judgments about virtue and happiness will necessarily always take the following form, I suggest one way of approaching these issues would go as follows. Every human life will necessarily involve some comparative choices about the kinds of goods and satisfactions that are to be pursued and the kinds to be passed by or even sacrificed, in order to enjoy the preferred aims more completely or securely, or sometimes to enjoy them at all. This is so even in the case of the paradigmatically happy life sketched above — a life devoted to marriage and family will involve a range of choices, including (in many societies, at any rate) choices about whom to marry, where to live, which ways of life and civic associations to pursue, and the like. This observation, in turn, suggests the possibility that central components of this paradigmatically happy life might themselves be subject to a similar kind of comparative assessment. It is notoriously difficult to combine marriage and family with a wholehearted devotion to certain kinds of professions or artistic pursuits, and of course these are inconsistent with some attractive ways of life, such as vowed celibacy. And yet the life of a vowed religious, or of someone who devotes herself to a demanding art, can be a virtuous and happy life — or so experience suggests. What we would need to do, in order to make a case for this conclusion, is to show that such a life would allow a comparably wide scope for the development of human inclinations through the practice of the virtues, within a framework of respect for one's own needs and the legitimate claims of others. This is not all that could be said, or would need to be said, in defense of a nonstandard alternative, but it would at least serve to focus a real comparative evaluation of what such a life would look like.

We can see the point of this line of inquiry more clearly if we consider a different kind of example — a proposed paradigm of happiness which might plausibly be said to fail. Consider, for example, the life of someone who devotes himself single-mindedly to accumulating wealth, for example, Dickens's Ebenezer Scrooge.[87] In his supernaturally prompted recollection of his life, Scrooge comes to see how early losses prompted him to seek his security in business and the accumulation of wealth, with the result that he ultimately sacrificed every human and familial tie — his relationship with his fiancée, his ties with his nephew and his family, any kind of human relationship with his employees or others in his community. And the consequence of this way of life is brought home to him at last — a lonely life and a forlorn death, his only friend a ghost, his only future an afterlife of impotent isolation. It is amply clear that Dickens regards this kind of life as anything but genuinely happy, and we may well be disposed to agree with him. But why do we do so?

87. Charles Dickens, *A Christmas Carol* (1843), available in many editions today.

I would suggest that this case illustrates one normative standard which emerges from reflection on paradigms of happiness and their proposed alternatives — not the only one, to be sure, but one which focuses the relevant issues in a perspicuous way. That is, correlated to the ideal of the virtuous life we can identify at least one natural vice, the vice of perversity, which might be described as the vice of sacrificing one's human capacities and inclinations for unworthy or inappropriately limited aims. I describe this as a natural vice, under the rubric of "reason as nature," because any kind of reflection on the overall shape of one's life will naturally give rise to an idea of perversity (not necessarily under that name) as something to be foresworn, if one is to attain a desirable or defensible way of life. The point is that every human life involves some sacrifices of capacities and goods — but at least we can avoid inappropriate sacrifices, or sacrifices which are contrary to the ideals of virtue themselves.

But which kinds of sacrifices are these? To put the question in another way, what standards of appropriateness will govern our reflections here? This is a still more fundamental question, and it turns out to be more difficult to answer. Indeed, I want to suggest that it is impossible to answer so long as we stay within the terms set by the ideal of happiness understood as the practice of the virtues. We must appeal in addition to further considerations, drawn from our convictions about what for lack of a better term we can call the wider significance of human life. Without some such appeal, we have no good basis for distinguishing legitimate variations among ideals of happiness from perversions. Aquinas regarded a life of vowed celibacy not only as potentially happy, but as a way of life especially well adapted to the attainment of human perfection (II-II 186.4). Hume, in contrast, had nothing but scorn for celibacy and the other "monkish virtues," which he regarded as pointless and probably disingenuous expressions of a misguided denigration of this-worldly joys.[88] Which is right? How can we say, unless we are prepared in some way to take sides with one or the other in their profound disagreements about the ultimate significance of human life?

Something similar may be said about the ideals of the other-regarding virtues, including such traits as compassion and mercy, as well as justice itself. These virtues too seem to be correlated with natural vices, including callousness and cruelty, the vices of indifference to the suffering of others, or worse, a delight in their suffering. The callous person does not care whether she

88. See David Hume, *An Enquiry Concerning the Principle of Morals* (1751), ed. Thomas Beauchamp (Oxford: Clarendon, 1998), 9.1. I am grateful to my colleagure Jennifer Herdt for locating this reference.

harms others, and so makes no efforts to avoid or minimize whatever suffering her (perhaps otherwise justified) actions may bring about. The cruel person likes the idea of hurting others, a sensation he may describe to himself as righteous zeal, and so he seeks out putative justifications for inflicting harm. In contrast, the genuinely just person accepts the necessity of sometimes harming others for the sake of the community as a whole, or to protect the interests of third parties. But like Augustine's good judge, she continually hopes to be delivered from her necessities, and takes care to minimize harm as far as she can, in accordance with the demands of neighbor-love more comprehensively understood.[89] At the same time, in order to spell out what this means practically, we must be prepared to say just what kinds of considerations of neighbor-love can justify inflicting specified kinds of harms. Just as perversity can only be understood by reference to some assessment of the kinds of desiderata which can and should be sacrificed for other kinds of goods, so callousness and cruelty can only be understood by contrast to some account of the kinds of harms that are justified or exigent in given situations.

These may appear to be surprising concessions. If the happy life consists of the practice of the virtues, then why can't we arrive at a sufficiently substantive account of happiness by way of reflection on the substantive ideals of particular virtues? The difficulty here is that the ideals of particular virtues are themselves indeterminate, and stand in need of further specification in order to be appropriated and applied. This does not mean that our ideals of virtue are simply "formal," if by this we mean "empty of all content." The paradigms for virtuous action associated with particular virtues provide these ideals with a rich and extended, if unsystematic, meaning, and as such they provide starting points and touchstones for more reflective formulations. Moreover, if the analysis of the preceding sections is on track, we should expect to find considerable overlap among ideals of virtue from one society to another, since our paradigms for virtuous behavior stem from the inclinations of our nature.

Nonetheless, our ideals of the virtues will inevitably be open-ended and indeterminate, to such an extent that in the very processes of developing and exercising them we will find it necessary to specify what they concretely mean.[90] What is more, we cannot resolve this problem simply by appealing to the mean of the virtues, because on closer examination the determination of the mean turns out to require resolving this very problem. As we noted above,

89. See *De Civitate Dei* 19.6, in *City of God,* trans. W. C. Greene (Cambridge, MA: Loeb Classical Library, 1969), vol. 6, 142-46.

90. In addition to the authors cited below, I am especially indebted in what follows to Richard Sorabji, "Aristotle on the Role of Intellect in Virtue," in *Essays in Aristotle's Ethics,* 201-19, and Michael Stocker, *Plural and Conflicting Values* (Oxford: Clarendon, 1990), 129-207.

we can only discern the rational mean of a virtue through some reflection on the point of the disposition manifested through the paradigms of the virtue in question. But this reflection will itself be incomplete, unless we expand its scope to include some consideration of the overall point of the virtue seen within the wider context of human life. At some point, we will inevitably find that reflection on particular virtues draws us into some consideration of the proper interrelationship of the virtues, in such a way that we cannot adequately specify ideals of particular virtues without beginning to develop an account of what it means to live virtuously — which is to say, happily.

To put the point in another way, it is almost certainly true that temperance and fortitude, at least, reflect human needs and circumstances to such an extent that at least some paradigms for these virtues can be recognized — and moreover, admired — in nearly all human societies. Nonetheless, when we begin to ask questions along the lines of "What counts as *true* restraint, true moderation, true courage?" — questions which, as we have seen, the logic of virtue language prompts us to ask — we find ourselves sooner or later driven to appeal to considerations stemming from specific beliefs, commitments, and practices.

This is least apparent for temperance in food and drink, since these virtues take their norms — their mean — from relatively invariant human needs and desires. Even in these cases, however, the virtues in question are shaped by wider cultural ideals; for example, social ideals favoring delicacy and refinement will produce one set of paradigms for restraint in eating, ideals favoring hearty enjoyment will produce another. Norms of temperance about sex, in contrast, can scarcely even be formulated without some reference to norms for sexual behavior in some particular society. Courage also offers good examples of the plasticity of the virtues. The kinds of displays of physical prowess that would seem deeply admirable in a society structured around the ideals of the warrior will seem pointless or silly, or worse still, rash, in a society structured around technical expertise and the exchange of information.

Even within the parameters of one society, it is easy to imagine real, substantive debates over what counts as true courage. Imagine the situation of someone who spends much of his adult life as a professional soldier, with much experience of battle and many occasions for displaying physical courage. Now suppose that this man undergoes a kind of moral or religious conversion, which leads him to adopt a strict pacifism. This conversion will lead him to renounce much of what he previously prized and did under the rubric of courageous behavior — aggressively attacking the enemy, withstanding hostile fire on the battlefield, and the like. Yet he may well find himself called upon to exercise other forms of courage, perhaps as difficult in their way —

patience in the face of ignominy, willing submission to arrest and detention (supposing, say, he refuses to follow orders to fight), even submission to death (supposing he is court-martialed and shot). These qualities of patience, forbearance, and the willing submission to death are defensibly forms of courage, or closely allied to it — they find their field of operation in situations of risk and potential or actual loss, and they are characterized by a willingness to risk or forgo lesser goods for more important goods. Yet these are not just examples of turning the same quality of aggressive physical courage to different ends, as if the soldier were to switch sides in the middle of a war; they represent distinctive ways of acting and comporting oneself in response to the actions of others, informed by very different views about the overall value of physical aggressiveness, and therefore its appropriateness, or not, as an expression of courage.

What has just been said about specific virtues applies as well to the practice of the virtues which comprises the happy life. It is probably the case that every society promotes something recognizably like the paradigmatic image of happiness sketched above, in which the satisfactions of marriage and family life play a central role. Even within the boundaries of this basic paradigm, there is room for considerable cultural diversity, since the details will depend to a very considerable degree on ideals and practices with respect to marriage, the proper relation between the sexes and the generations, the relation between the extended and the nuclear family, and the like. Moreover, nearly every society also cherishes more specific ideals of human perfection which are not only distinct, but in some cases radically at odds with one another. As Lee Yearley observes, "To think we can pick and choose among ideals of human flourishing as we pick and choose among food, wines, or clothes is to be deeply mistaken." He goes on to say:

> The most revealing examples of this inability to shop occur in those painfully illuminating moments when you deeply appreciate something you know is an unacceptable option for you and will not, you hope, become an option for those you love most. Examples are many, especially if one studies either other cultures or Western history. Some strike especially close to home: Mencius's refusal to greet a bereaved person in order to honor ritual *(li);* Aquinas's defenses of virginity; Chuang Tzu's powerful notion of compassion, which leads him to overlook evident wrongdoing. Others are more distant and yet they still bite: Confucius's validation of the heroism evident in a gamekeeper's refusal, at risk of death, to answer an improper summons so that proper rank and relations may be protected; the way that Indian villagers, responding to their sense of social

> and even cosmic harmony, find more objectionable a widow who eats fish three times a week than a doctor who refuses to treat a sick patient because that patient is poor. With these latter, more distant options we enter that vexing territory where, especially in cross-cultural contexts, conflicts among justifiable goods shade into conflicts between justifiable and unjustifiable goods.[91]

Elsewhere he observes that there does seem to be considerable agreement across cultural boundaries on the value of central virtues (his own example, and the focus of his more extended study, is courage).[92] It seems likely that the same thing can be said about the paradigmatic life of happiness, as I have sketched it here — that is to say, a life in which central virtues are practiced in the context of an ordinary family and community life. Yet even granting this point, the fact remains that this broad agreement (if it does indeed exist) does not rule out the emergence of diverse and apparently incompatible ideals of spiritual perfection, as Yearley's comments illustrate. Moreover, these ideals will inevitably be developed in such a way as to shape the paradigm of an ordinary good life to which they are related. For that matter, the terms of this relation, and the framework of practices within which both ideals are formulated and pursued, will themselves vary considerably.

When we begin to take these factors into account, it becomes apparent that the broad consensus on the virtues and the paradigmatic form of practicing the virtues cannot be regarded as a fully universal ethic. It seems safe to say that this broad consensus does exist, and it does have substantive content. The exigencies of human life which give rise to the virtues, and which give family and communal life in some form a central place in all societies, also provide sufficient content to ideals of virtue to enable them to be recognized across a broad range of cultural expressions. Even though the relevant commonalities probably cannot be formulated except in general terms, our capacities for recognizing the virtues reflect genuine, substantive understanding. Nonetheless, at best this understanding is incomplete, and reflection on the virtues tends by its own dynamics to push us toward questions that cannot be answered without some reference to specific commitments and values. That is why any virtue ethic will call for some specification in terms that paradigmatic ideals of the virtues cannot supply, and by the same token, that is why even the most basic paradigmatic idea of the happy life, seen as the prac-

91. Both quotes are taken from Yearley, "Conflicts among Ideals of Human Flourishing," in *Prospects for a Common Morality*, ed. Gene Outka and John P. Reeder, Jr. (Princeton: Princeton University Press, 1993), 233-53, here 246.

92. But this is carefully qualified; see Yearley, *Mencius and Aquinas*, 1-23.

tice of the virtues, can only be developed within the framework of wider convictions about the meaning and purpose of human life.

For the Christian, these wider convictions will be drawn from Scripture, and from the tradition of reflection and practice it has generated. For Aquinas and the other scholastics, ideals of human existence and action are focused more specifically on the claim that the human person is made in the Image of God, a claim they interpreted to mean most fundamentally that the human person is capable of rational knowledge and self-direction. At the same time, the motif of the Image of God was explicitly linked to the natural law by way of its connection with conscience, considered (together with synderesis) as the source or even the core meaning of the natural law, and more generally by way of the motif of "reason as nature" mentioned above.

This motif suggests a way to complete our sketch of the ideal of happiness, understood in Thomistic terms as the practice of the virtues. If the human person is to be understood as the Image of God, that is to say, as a creature capable of knowledge and self-direction, then perfection and happiness for such a creature will give a central place to the exercise of intellectual capacities and rational autonomy. But in order to spell out what this means, we will first of all need to look more closely at the way rationality itself should be understood in this context, remembering that Aquinas and his interlocutors would not have separated human reason from the natural intelligibilities from which it stems, and which give it structure and point. Once again, we will need to take account of the way in which the ideals of the virtues inform rational deliberation, in such a way as to inform it through ideals of reasonableness proper to the diverse needs and capacities of the human animal.

At the same time, the scholastic conception of reason also carried an implication of law — the scholastics held that reason legislates, albeit in a non-Kantian sense. The laws of reason were at the same time held to be more or less isomorphic with the fundamental tenets of divine, that is to say, revealed law, although of course the "more or less" will call for careful unpacking. Much of what we think of as the lawlike, or precept-governed, character of the natural law stems from this aspect of moral reasoning; this is also the aspect of the natural law which focuses most directly on the duties of beneficence and nonmaleficence. We now turn to a closer examination of these issues.

CHAPTER FOUR

Nature As Reason: Act and Precept in the Natural Law

The assumptions and beliefs about prerational nature summed up in the expression "nature as nature" mark a clear boundary between the scholastics and us. This boundary can be crossed, as I hope the last two chapters have shown. Yet the effort required to do so serves as a salutary reminder that the scholastic approach is not our own, and for that very reason has something distinctive to offer to contemporary theological reflection. In contrast, when we begin to consider the scholastics' approach to "nature as reason," we seem to be on more familiar ground. This expression refers in a summary way to the view that reason discerns or generates moral norms, or functions in some way as a moral norm itself. The scholastic consensus on this point is well summarized by Huguccio, in a passage that is already familiar to us:

> the natural law is said to be reason, insofar as it is a natural power of the soul by which the human person distinguishes between good and evil, choosing good and rejecting evil. And reason is said to be a law [*jus*], because it commands [*jubet*]; also, it is said to be law [*lex*] because it binds [*ligat*] or because it compels one to act rightly [*legitime*]; it is said to be natural, because reason is one of the natural goods, or because it agrees supremely with nature, and does not dissent from it. Concerning this natural law, the Apostle says, "I see another law in my members, which opposes the law of the mind," that is to say, the reason, which is called law, just as has been said. (Lottin, 109)

These words will sound familiar to those who have studied recent natural law theories, since as we have seen, most contemporary versions of the natural law agree in equating it with the deliverances of practical or moral reason. Yet it is necessary to proceed cautiously at this point. The similarities between the scholastics' formulations and our own can have the effect of obscuring more fundamental differences, unless we keep in mind that the scholastics' understanding of "reason" may not be identical to ours. As we will see, some of the scholastics do offer accounts of practical reason which resemble contemporary versions in some respects. Yet the very fact that they consistently connect "nature as nature" with "nature as reason" suggests that they do not understand reason in precisely the same way we do. While they distinguish between the rational and the natural more comprehensively understood, they also insist on the continuities between reason and the intelligibilities inherent in prerational nature. Reason stems from these intelligibilities, even as it determines the appropriate forms for their expression. By the same token, however, reason never operates in isolation from the intelligibilities informing prerational nature, nor can the normative force of reason be understood apart from its grounding in wider forms of intelligibility.

Out of many possible examples, it will be instructive to return to Huguccio to illustrate this point. In the course of a general discussion of the meaning of marriage, Huguccio remarks that in his view Saint Paul's statement that each man should have his own wife pertains to the bodily union of marriage (in contrast to the spiritual union brought about by the consent of the partners). He goes on to say,

> And this latter union is derived both from that natural law which is said to be an instinct of nature, and from that which is said to be reason. For a man is moved by a certain appetite of the natural sensuality, that he should be joined in the flesh to a woman, and immediately reason follows, directing him that he should not be joined with anyone except a wife, and in a legitimate way, that is, for the sake of children, or to pay his debt; for any other union, whether with the wife or with another woman is not derived from any natural law, but is contrary to it. (Lottin, 110-11)

In other words, the natural law which stems from prerational nature, our "natural sensuality," provides a fundamental impetus toward sexual union, which the natural law stemming from reason specifies and completes. The basic drive toward sexual union does not suffice by itself to generate moral precepts pertaining to marriage, but it does provide a directed inclination toward action without which rational reflection on marriage would have no meaning or point. Marriage lends itself to this general approach for obvious reasons, but the scholastics applied a similar analysis to other kinds of specific precepts, including the basic norms of the Golden Rule (which at least one author associates with the prerational components of our nature), prohibitions against killing, and inheritance.[1] In each case, the injunction or prohibition is correlated with an inclination stemming from our prerational nature, which is in turn represented as being appropriately expressed or completed in some way through judgments of reason.

Clearly, this approach needs to be qualified and developed in order to be persuasive and usable as a starting point for moral reflection. As we might expect, the scholastic theologians have more to say about reason and its practical operations than do the canonists, and moreover the theologians differ among themselves on this point. In this chapter I will continue to rely on Aquinas to provide the starting points and much of the substance for my own constructive theory. Aquinas's conception of practical reason is of interest precisely because he represents a distinctive option among the scholastics, and does not fit neatly into leading contemporary alternatives either. But in order to make this clear, it will be necessary to place him within a twofold context, set by contemporary debates over practical reason on the one side, and the scholastic approach to "nature as reason" on the other. That will be the task of the first two sections of this chapter. In this way I hope to highlight what is distinctive and fruitful about Aquinas's conception of reason, and to set a framework for its constructive development.

This development, in turn, will return us to issues raised in the last chapter, and it will also move us forward to a more focused consideration of "nature as reason" as a kind of law. At the end of the last chapter, we noted that an adequate account of happiness, understood in Thomistic terms, can only be developed by reference to a normative account of the meaning and purpose of human life. Aquinas shares a widespread consensus that rationality is the defining mark of the human person, but without clarifying what he understands by reason, it is difficult to assess the implications that this view has for his overall account of morality. This analysis, in turn, will bring us to the insight suggested by the first of Huguccio's remarks quoted above, namely, that reason is a *law,* which yields authoritative precepts binding us to compliance. In order to do justice to the lawlike character of the natural law, it will be necessary to turn in the third section to a closer examination of the way reason can be said to command or prohibit kinds of actions, which are understood in terms of their complex yet comprehensible relations to the natural patterns of action characteristic of the human species. By doing so, we will expand the account of justice begun in the last chapter, and lay the foundation for a closer look at the

1. For further details and examples, see my *Natural and Divine Law: Reclaiming the Tradition for Christian Ethics* (Ottawa: Novalis; Grand Rapids: Eerdmans, 1999), 76-85.

virtue of prudence — thus completing the sketch of the virtues seen as components of the happy life begun in the last chapter.

1. Contemporary and Medieval Approaches to Practical Reason

I just remarked that we tend to assume that when the scholastics refer to reason in a practical or moral context, they understand reason in the same way we do. This observation needs to be qualified, however, because the characteristics and especially the moral significance of practical reason are among the most widely debated issues in contemporary Anglophone philosophy. The assumptions governing contemporary interpretations of the scholastics are thus themselves shaped by the interpreters' views on matters of present-day controversy. More particularly, interpretations of Aquinas's theory of the natural law tend to place him on one side or the other of a contemporary debate over practical reason.[2] In order to get a clearer sense of the distinctive contours of the scholastic approach to reason, therefore, it will be helpful to begin by examining a current debate over practical reason, and seeing whether we can locate the scholastics within these parameters.

Broadly speaking, this debate is framed by two contrasting approaches to accounting for the role of reason as it functions in moral or practical contexts. The first of these might be characterized as the Kantian approach, with the understanding that most contemporary moral philosophers are Kantian in an extended sense only. The second is often described as instrumentalist, since it takes reason to be an instrument of something else; depending on the account of what that "something else" might be, this approach is typically developed through some version of consequentialism, Humean sentimentalism, or some combination of the two approaches. There are other options in con-

2. Or so it has seemed to many involved in recent debates over Aquinas's analysis of the moral act. I agree with Servais Pinckaers that any interpretation of Aquinas according to which the object of the act is elided with its other components (i.e., its circumstances and the agent's intention) at least implies that he is a consequentialist; see *Ce qu'on ne peut jamais faire: La question des actes intrinsèquement mauvais, Histoire et discussion* (Fribourg: Editions Universitaires Fribourg, 1986), 41-42; Martin Rhonheimer expresses a similar worry in *Natural Law and Practical Reason: A Thomist View of Moral Autonomy,* trans. Gerald Malsbary (New York: Fordham University Press, 2000), 351-81. They are reacting against a widespread line of interpretation stemming from Peter Knauer's highly influential article, "La détermination du bien et du mal par le principe du double effect," *Nouvelle Revue Théologique* 87 (1965): 356-76. But in fairness, there are very few interpreters of Aquinas who would explicitly identify his theory as a version of consequentialism.

temporary moral philosophy, of course, including pragmatic accounts of morality and various forms of virtue ethics. Nonetheless, these options set the parameters for much of the contemporary debate over the character and scope of practical reason. Even more importantly for our purposes, they represent two important alternatives for interpreting Aquinas's conception of reason among those who regard him as a starting point for reflection on the natural law.

The broadly Kantian approach to moral reason is characterized by a fundamental commitment, however expressed, to what Kant himself refers to as the autonomy of morality. That is to say, those who defend this approach believe that moral norms are grounded in the deliverances of practical reason itself, without any necessary appeal to what the scholastics would have regarded as the province of speculative reason, including metaphysical or theological truths as well as facts about the natural world, except perhaps as these set the conditions and contexts for the application of moral norms.[3] By the same token, practical reason is said to function independently of the agent's emotions and desires, even though it might be regarded as giving rise to a distinctive desire or motive to observe the requirements of moral law. Hence, to continue with Kant's language, moral norms are categorical, which is to say that they are obligatory for every rational agent, whatever her particular desires or circumstances may be. As such, they are contrasted with hypothetical norms which presuppose some nonmoral desire or goal, for example, a prudential norm stating that *if* you want to be healthy (and perhaps you do not), *then* you will avoid smoking cigarettes (but if you don't care, why, light up!). It might be said that categorical norms reflect a distinct and overriding aim, that is to say, the aim of being rational or respecting rationality, or alternatively categorical norms might be regarded as bearing an obligatory force apart from any purpose at all. The categorical force of moral norms is generally associated with what are taken to be their distinguishing marks, that is to say, their universality, their absoluteness, and their overriding force vis-à-vis other kinds of practical considerations.

How does practical reason generate these distinctive kinds of norms? For Kant himself, it was especially important to account for moral reasoning in such a way as to separate it from the interconnected and necessitating

3. This needs to be qualified, because many Kantians would admit that very general facts about human life, or alternatively facts about a specific case, may provide a necessary context within which moral norms become relevant, or else provide the framework within which to apply a norm in a given situation; for example, we would not need norms of nonmaleficence if we were not vulnerable to harm. The point is that the basic principles of duty are not derived from these kinds of considerations, even so.

forces of natural causality. He did so by arguing that practical reason generates moral norms through a self-reflective and discursive unfolding of its own exigencies. To some extent, he seems to have understood this process in terms of the unfolding of requirements of rational self-consistency; hence, the first two formulations of the categorical imperative require the agent to act in the same way as she would will every other agent to act, that is to say, to act consistently with the requirements of universal law.[4] At the same time, self-consistency by itself does not seem to have captured everything that Kant understood by the exigencies of practical reason. The third formulation of the categorical imperative requires that one act in such a way as to respect rationality itself, whether in one's own person or that of another, respect being understood in terms of the well-known formula that a rational agent is to be treated as an end in itself, and never as a means to another end. While some theorists do analyze this formula in such a way as to express it in terms of self-consistency, others develop it through a discursive account of what it means to treat another (or in some contexts, oneself) as an end and not a means, usually developed in terms of respect for another's rational autonomy.

The most influential contemporary theories of the natural law fall within the parameters of a Kantian account, broadly construed. As we noted in the second chapter, the "new natural law" developed by Grisez and Finnis and their followers analyzes moral norms in terms of the exigencies for the rational pursuit of basic goods, which provide the self-evident starting points for all practical deliberation.[5] This might seem at first glance to be a desire-based, and therefore instrumentalist account of morality, but Grisez and Finnis are careful to point out that the starting points for rational reflection are not provided by our desires in themselves.[6] Rather, these desires provide

4. The three formulations are, first, "Act only on that maxim through which you can at the same time will that it should become a universal law" (Kant, *The Groundwork of the Metaphysics of Morals,* trans. H. J. Paton [New York: Harper and Row, 1956], 88); secondly, "Act as if the maxim of your action were to become through your will a universal law of nature" (89); and finally, to observe a law according to which one treats oneself and others "never merely as a means, but always at the same time an end in himself" — which turns out to be equivalent to legislating for a kingdom of ends (101). It is worth noting that Kant says clearly that these are three versions of one and the same principle — see 88, 103.

5. Although their theories differ from the "new natural law" in many respects, the influential interpretations of the natural law developed by Martin Rhonheimer and Wolfgang Kluxen similarly attempt to ground the natural law in the deliverances of practical reason, seen in Kantian terms as an autonomous source for moral norms. See Rhonheimer, *Natural Law,* 58-178; Kluxen, *Lex naturalis bei Thomas von Aquin* (Wiesbaden: Westdeutscher, 2001), 29-38.

6. Robert George is especially helpful on this point; see *In Defense of Natural Law* (Oxford: Oxford University Press, 1999), 17-30.

the necessary occasions for the rational apprehension of certain desiderata as basic goods, and it is these rational apprehensions, rather than the desires occasioning them, which serve as the starting points for practical deliberation. Indeed, according to Finnis, "allowing one's emotions sway over one's reasons for action is indeed the paradigmatic way of going, and doing, wrong."[7] As Alan Donagan points out, this account of morality, according to which moral norms are grounded in respect for the basic goods instantiated in persons' lives, is very similar to the Kantian view that moral norms are grounded in respect for rational agents tout court.[8]

Of course, contemporary natural lawyers are not the only ones defending a broadly Kantian approach to moral philosophy.[9] Over forty years ago, John Rawls complained that contemporary moral philosophy had been taken over by the consequentialists, and he set out to provide an alternative through a contractarian development of the Kantian imperative of respect for rational agency.[10] The resulting book, *A Theory of Justice*, will almost certainly be remembered as one of the most important philosophical works of the twentieth century. Since its publication, broadly Kantian approaches to moral philosophy have proliferated, so much so that much Anglophone moral philosophy over the past forty years can be traced more or less directly to the influence of Kant. Examples would include the work of Donagan, who develops what he described as "the theory of morality" out of a syllogistic reformulation of common morality grounded in the principle of respect for persons; the rights theory of Alan Gewirth, grounded in what he takes to be the requirements of self-consistency reflecting on the necessities for rational action; and Onora

7. John Finnis, *Aquinas: Moral, Political, and Legal Theory* (Oxford: Oxford University Press, 1998), 73.

8. Alan Donagan, *The Theory of Morality* (Chicago: University of Chicago Press, 1977), 60-66. But as will appear below, he was wrong to associate this view with Aquinas himself. Daniel Westberg likewise identifies the Kantian strain in the Grisez/Finnis theory, but correctly disassociates this approach from Aquinas's conception of prudence; see *Right Practical Reason: Aristotle, Action, and Prudence in Aquinas* (Oxford: Clarendon, 1994), 10-11.

9. See John Rawls, *A Theory of Justice,* 2nd ed. (Oxford: Oxford University Press, 1999; 1st ed., Cambridge: Harvard University Press, 1971); Donagan, *The Theory of Morality;* Alan Gewirth, *Reason and Morality* (Chicago: University of Chicago Press, 1978); and Onora O'Neill, *Towards Justice and Virtue: A Constructive Account of Practical Reasoning* (Cambridge: Cambridge University Press, 1996). Among Continental scholars, Jürgen Habermas is probably the most influential advocate of a Kantian constructivism; see *Moral Consciousness and Communicative Action,* trans. Christian Lenhardt and Shierry Weber Nicholsen (Cambridge: MIT Press, 1990), which together with the fine introductory essay by Thomas McCarthy (1-20) provides an accessible introduction to his work.

10. Rawls, *A Theory of Justice* (2nd ed.), xvii.

O'Neill's influential attempt to develop a Kantian theory of practical reason in conversation with virtue-oriented approaches. The Kantian approach is also well represented on the Continent, Jürgen Habermas offering the most noteworthy and influential example in his theory of the rational exigencies of communicative action. As these examples illustrate, Kantian approaches to ethics have taken many forms which represent, in some ways at least, striking departures from Kant's own views. Nonetheless, these approaches share a commitment to analyzing moral norms in terms of the proper functioning of practical reason, seen as operating independently of any kind of speculative considerations. Typically, defenders of these views argue that moral reason functions in such a way as to generate moral norms through the canons of logical consistency, developed with some reference to the agent's own sense of what she or he requires in order to function as a rational agent, or more generally with reference to basic norms of respect for rational agency.

Hilary Putnam has recently observed that even though there are a few distinguished exceptions, "most moral philosophers today find Kant's moral philosophy overly dependent on the rest of Kant's metaphysics, which few if any philosophers are able any longer to accept."[11] I suspect that Putnam overstates the extent to which contemporary moral philosophers have turned away from a Kantian approach, but it does seem that Kant's theory of morality is grounded in his overall philosophy, which would indeed find few defenders today. In order to defend a Kantian approach to morality without the Kantian apparatus, it is necessary to argue that morality as he understands it reflects the exigencies of reason functioning practically — and that, as we would by now expect, is just the approach taken by many modern Kantians.[12]

11. Hilary Putnam, *The Collapse of the Fact/Value Dichotomy and Other Essays* (Cambridge: Harvard University Press, 2002), 17.

12. Alan Gewirth offers what is perhaps the most thoroughgoing attempt to derive moral conclusions from the canons of rational consistency. His argument turns on the logical implications of regarding oneself as an agent. He notes that he will construct the argument through using the canons of deductive and inductive logic alone, since these "achieve logical necessity and reflect what is empirically ineluctable, [and therefore] deduction and induction are the only sure ways of avoiding arbitrariness and attaining objectivity" (*Reason and Morality,* 22). On this basis, he hopes to establish a fundamental moral principle through sheer rational analysis: "Now such an answer is obtainable if a supreme moral principle can be shown to be logically necessary so that its denial is self-contradictory" (23). He proceeds by reflecting on the logical presuppositions of action itself: "it has not hitherto been noted that the nature of action enters into the very content and justification of the supreme principle of morality" (26). Specifically, he argues that any agent, considered as a rational agent who acts for purposes, is logically committed to regarding himself as the bearer of certain rights to the necessary conditions for same; and consistency demands that he accord these rights to others as well (48-103). Gewirth's ap-

But as many other philosophers have argued (and I would agree), no one has yet shown how norms of self-consistency, taken by themselves, can yield practical principles specific enough actually to guide conduct.[13] What appear to be the exigencies of practical reason turn out, on closer inspection, to be expressions of commitments for which we can account in other terms, usually through a closer inspection of the values implicit in the philosopher's social setting — or so, at least, the arguments go.

But what, then, is the alternative? If practical reason does not generate its own aims (or functions without reference to any aims at all), the obvious alternative would be to say that it takes its starting points from somewhere else — from the agent's own desires, or from the commitments and values shared by a given society. In other words, if practical reason is not autonomous, then it would appear to be instrumental to aims generated outside it.[14] This alternative can be conveniently divided further, in accordance with two approaches represented by two of its best-known defenders, David Hume and Jeremy Bentham.[15]

Understood in Humean terms, reason is instrumental to desires, but

proach has been widely criticized, but his general approach to establishing ethical norms out of canons of self-consistency is still persuasive to many. O'Neill offers a recent example: "The more guarded constructivism that I shall outline follows Rawls in that it does not look for the vindication of ethical principles in metaphysical argument, or in discoveries about the world . . . it assumes only an abstract, hence non-idealizing and banal, account of agents and of conditions of action. Secondly, it aims to articulate and to vindicate a conception of practical reason without appeal either to unvindicated ideals or to unvindicated particulars" (*Towards Justice and Virtue,* 48). As O'Neill's remarks suggest, Rawls's attempts to establish a metaphysically neutral account of practical reason through a program of constructive reconstruction has had a very far-reaching influence.

13. For a recent and (I believe) persuasive development of this line of criticism, see Simon Blackburn, *Ruling Passions: A Theory of Practical Reason* (Oxford: Clarendon, 1998), 214-24; Candace Vogler develops a similar argument in *Reasonably Vicious* (Cambridge: Harvard University Press, 2002), 223-29.

14. As Putnam observes, the collapse of the credibility of Kant's project led the logical positivists, who dominated Anglophone philosophy at the beginning of the last century, "to go back to a vastly inflated version of Hume's idea that ethical judgements are not statements of fact but either expressions of sentiment or disguised imperatives" (*The Fact/Value Dichotomy,* 17). Current sentimentalist accounts of practical reason may be seen as the heirs of the logical positivists in this respect. The other strand of instrumentalism, that is to say, versions of utilitarianism and consequentialism, did not need to be revived because it never went away; thus, Rawls could say in 1971 that "During much of modern moral philosophy the predominant systematic theory has been some form of utilitarianism" (*A Theory of Justice,* vii).

15. The relevant texts include David Hume, *A Treatise of Human Nature,* ed. L. A. Selby-Bigge (Oxford: Oxford University Press, 1888), and Jeremy Bentham, *An Introduction to the Principles of Morals and Legislation* (New York: Macmillan, 1948; originally 1789).

these desires themselves include sentiments of approval which are patterned (in most people) in morally significant ways. These sentiments, when expressed in a communal context, yield the familiar virtues, including both natural virtues such as gratitude and amiability and artificial virtues such as justice. Let us call this the sentimentalist approach to morality.[16] Understood in Benthamite terms, reason serves to fulfill desires which can be analyzed in such a way as to be reduced to a common denominator, whether a desire for pleasure (as Bentham himself held), or for desire maximization or the avoidance of pain. In the case of an isolated individual, reason would thus function in such a way as to yield a kind of rational egotism, but seen in the context of the community, reason promotes courses of action yielding the greatest possible fulfillment of desires for the greatest number of people. Bentham himself referred to his theory as utilitarianism, but his general approach might better be described as consequentialism.[17]

16. In addition to Blackburn, the most influential advocates of a broadly sentimentalist approach today would include Annette Baier, *Postures of the Mind: Essays on Mind and Morals* (Minneapolis: University of Minnesota Press, 1985) and *Moral Prejudices: Essays on Ethics* (Cambridge: Harvard University Press, 1994), and Alan Gibbard, *Wise Choices, Apt Feelings: A Theory of Normative Judgment* (Cambridge: Harvard University Press, 1990). Baier has suggested, and I would agree, that Judith Shklar also falls within this camp, although this is less clear; see Judith Shklar, *Ordinary Vices* (Cambridge: Harvard University Press, Belknap Press, 1984).

17. Recent and current defenders of utilitarianism or some version of consequentialism would include J. J. C. Smart, "An Outline of a System of Utilitarian Ethics," in Smart and Bernard Williams, *Utilitarianism For and Against* (Cambridge: Cambridge University Press, 1973), 3-76; R. M. Hare, *Moral Thinking: Its Levels, Method, and Point* (Oxford: Clarendon, 1981); James Griffin, *Well-Being: Its Meaning, Measurement, and Moral Importance* (Oxford: Clarendon, 1986); Richard Brandt, *Morality, Utilitarianism, and Rights* (Cambridge: Cambridge University Press, 1992); and Robert Goodin, *Utilitarianism as a Public Philosophy* (Cambridge: Cambridge University Press, 1995). In addition to these more moderate versions of consequentialism, recently a number of philosophers have called for a radical critique or reconstruction of common morality through a program of strict consequentialist analysis. The locus classicus for this approach is Peter Singer's essay "Famine, Affluence, and Morality," *Philosophy and Public Affairs* 1 (1972): 229-43; for more recent statements of his views, see *Rethinking Life and Death: The Collapse of Our Traditional Ethics* (New York: St. Martin's Press, 1994). Other influential examples include Derek Parfit, *Reasons and Persons* (Oxford: Oxford University Press, 1984), and Shelly Kagan, *The Limits of Morality* (Oxford: Oxford University Press, 1989). Peter Unger proposes a similar critique, but not on strictly consequentialist grounds, in his *Living High and Letting Die: Our Illusion of Innocence* (Oxford: Oxford University Press, 1996). Finally, over the past forty years there has been considerable debate among Catholic moral theologians over whether the approach to moral analysis and/or decision making known as proportionalism should be regarded as consequentialism. Many different variants of this approach have been developed, but it seems to me that most of them are indeed versions of consequentialism. For a recent defense of this approach, which rests explicitly on what he calls the principle of value maximization, see

Even though sentimentalists and consequentialists would agree in rejecting the Kantian claim that reason by itself is morally significant and authoritative, they do not necessarily agree on related questions concerning the foundation and logical status of moral norms. The relevant debates complicate the dichotomy between Kantian and instrumentalist approaches to practical reason, because the lines of division over the status of moral norms do not track the Kantian/instrumentalist divide in any neat way. And as we might expect, the relevant options themselves represent families of subtle and diverse views, rather than clear and sharply defined alternatives. Nonetheless, we can identify and map out the relevant alternatives regarding the status of moral norms in terms of the familiar distinction between cognitivism and noncognitivism — by now a rough distinction, but adequate to our present purposes.

Proponents of the two main versions of instrumentalism tend to divide over just this question, that is, the cognitive status of moral propositions. Most consequentialists are cognitivists — that is to say, they regard moral statements (at least in some forms) as meaningful propositions which are either true or false. Some early defenders of this approach, notably John Stuart Mill, went so far as to define moral terms by reference to optimum attainments of nonmoral goods or values, an approach which prompted Moore's charge that these theories render moral claims as such otiose.[18] Later consequentialists have not attempted to define moral terms by reference to nonmoral states of affairs, but they do remain committed to the view that moral claims depend for their truth or falsity on empirical states of affairs, open in principle to empirical investigation. This is of course very different from the Kantian approach, and yet the consequentialists and the Kantians share a basic commitment to the view that moral statements are meaningful propositions which can be judged to be either true or false on the basis of objective criteria.

In this respect, Kantians and most consequentialists stand together over

---

Garth L. Hallet, *Greater Good: The Case for Proportionalism* (Washington, D.C.: Georgetown University Press, 1995): "Within a prospective, objective focus, and in the sense thus specified, an action is right if and only if it promises to maximize value as fully, or nearly as fully, as any alternative action, with no restriction on the kind of value concerned, whether human or nonhuman, consequential or nonconsequential" (2, emphasis omitted). He goes on to note (2) that this is a criterion for rightness, not a procedure for judgment, which seems to bring his views fairly close to rule-utilitarianism. In contrast, Josef Fuchs explicitly denies that proportionalism should be equated with consequentialism, on the grounds that moral judgment cannot be systematized at all; see Josef Fuchs, "Natural Law or Naturalistic Fallacy?" in *Moral Demands and Personal Obligations* (Washington, D.C.: Georgetown University Press, 1993; originally 1988), 30-51, here 42-43.

18. G. E. Moore, *Principia Ethica* (Cambridge: Cambridge University Press, 1903), 46-58.

against the sentimentalists, who claim that moral norms are expressions of sentiment, attitudes, or commitments. In general, contemporary sentimentalists would agree with Moore's critique of consequentialist theories — not surprisingly, since it is reminiscent of Hume's claim that certain kinds of moral theories involve a fallacious inference from "is" to "ought." By the same token, they are typically committed to noncognitivism, a view according to which moral statements should not be construed as propositions bearing a truth value, spelled out in terms of some kind of "fit" with some objective state of affairs.[19] In the early twentieth century, Ayer and Stevenson proposed a theory, emotivism, according to which moral claims are simply expressions of the feelings of the speaker. This theory was widely regarded as insufficient, however, because it cannot account for what appear to be logical relations among moral claims. It was accordingly supplanted by the prescriptivism of R. M. Hare, according to which moral statements reflect a complex combination of empirical judgments and universalizable attitudes. More recently still, we have seen a revival of a broadly Humean theory of moral sentiments, according to which basic, nonanalyzable feelings of approval and disapproval provide a foundation for all moral judgments.

We should flag one other broad contrast between consequentialist and sentimentalist approaches. Recently, consequentialist approaches to ethics have been dominated by self-professed radical theories of morality — radical, because they attempt to work out the implications of the claim that moral judgments are grounded solely in a principle of maximization of benefits (or minimization of harms). Certainly, consequentialism relativizes what would traditionally be regarded as moral absolutes, for example, the prohibition against murder. Nonetheless, many consequentialists have held that the differences between traditional moral views and consequentialism are not, in practice, all that sharp, arguing that the traditional moral rules can themselves be justified on consequentialist grounds, or limiting the scope of a consequentialist analysis. But as we will see further on, defenders of more radical versions of consequentialism will have none of this. They argue, on

19. Blackburn would agree with the cognitivists that moral statements may be said to be true — but only on a very accommodating coherentist account of truth (see *Ruling Passions,* 48-83). The other authors mentioned are A. J. Ayer, *Language, Truth, and Logic* (New York: Dover Books, 1952; originally 1946); Charles Stevenson, *Ethics and Language* (New Haven: Yale University Press, 1944); and R. M. Hare, *The Language of Morals* (Oxford: Oxford University Press, 1952/1964) and *Freedom and Reason* (Oxford: Oxford University Press, 1963/1965). As the above reference indicates, Hare went on to develop a broadly consequentialist account of morality in *Moral Thinking,* but without rejecting the main lines of his earlier prescriptivist analysis; he is thus one of the few to defend a noncognitivist version of consequentialism.

the contrary, that a really thoroughgoing and consistent consequentialism undermines much or all of traditional morality, including the claims of special relationships and obligations, the moral significance of motivation and intention, and the distinction between acting and allowing something to happen. Our assessments of moral obligations would look very different indeed if we were to deny the moral significance of these kinds of considerations. Indeed, this approach implies that none of us lives up to the demands of morality, and if we want to even approximate those demands we should be prepared to make radical changes in our way of life.

The sentimentalists, in contrast, are more conservative in their assessments of common morality. For them, the moral attitudes and sentiments that people actually have and express are foundational, at least taken globally within a particular community. This does not mean that particular judgments cannot be challenged or revised, or even that collective judgments cannot develop and change over time, but it does mean that the sentimentalists cannot readily allow for the possibility that our moral attitudes and reactions might be radically and comprehensively wrongheaded. "Conservative" should not be taken as pejorative in this context, because as we might expect, a Thomistic theory of the natural law is also conservative in this respect, as are most Kantian theories. Indeed, the radical implications of a consistent consequentialism, which some of its defenders embrace, are held up by many critics as a fatal flaw. For these critics, the implications of radical consequentialism are so profoundly counterintuitive that they rule it out of court.[20] After all, if a theory of morality undermines most of what we regard as the substance of morality, what standards are left for assessing and defending the theory itself? Yet the radical consequentialists do appeal to some moral intuitions, generally those having to do with consistency; in this respect, radical consequentialism resembles a kind of radically purified Kantianism.

As this brief summary indicates, the division between Kantian and instrumentalist theories of ethics, while broadly right, also needs to be qualified in light of the differing lines of affinity among the variants of these approaches. Most Kantian theories attempt to conserve as much of common morality as possible, and in this respect they tend to resemble sentimentalist theories, at least in their broad conclusions. However, if one emphasizes the

20. This line of criticism is especially indebted to Bernard Williams, although he himself directs it against consequentialism generally considered; see "Persons, Character and Morality," in *Moral Luck: Philosopical Papers, 1973-1980* (Cambridge: Cambridge University Press, 1981) and *Ethics and the Limits of Philosophy* (Cambridge: Harvard University Press, 1985), 71-119. As we will see below, even some of those who are basically sympathetic to the radical utilitarians' fundamental claims find their conclusions difficult to accept.

formal requirements of a purified moral reasoning, the more thoroughgoing versions of Kantianism and radical consequentialism can be seen to converge. Both approaches emphasize the formal requirements of reason, apart from and even in spite of a range of other considerations which we usually regard as practically significant. Radical consequentialist theories generally go further than do versions of Kantianism in defending counterintuitive commitments, but these are implied by some versions of Kantianism as well. It is significant in this light that the Grisez/Finnis interpretation of the natural law insists on the incommensurability of the basic goods precisely in order to block consequentialism; without some such stipulation, the logic of their views would lead them in the same direction as Kagan and Singer.[21]

These comparisons suggest an uncomfortable thought. That is, it appears that two of the contending theories of practical reason on the contemporary scene, Kantianism and consequentialism, are unstable — each tends to collapse into its contrary, absent some stipulation about the proper objects and scope of practical reason itself. If so, we must ask how much work the idea of practical reason itself is really doing in these theories. To put the point another way, can practical reason by itself decide between respect for persons or basic human goods, on the one hand, or some version of maximization on the other, as starting points for moral reflection? Or must this issue be decided on other grounds, for example, by arguments about the metaphysical status of the human person, or an analysis of human actions — in short, by appeals to speculative considerations?

It begins to look as if practical reason alone is after all not sufficient to generate a moral theory. Thoroughgoing Kantians could not accept such a conclusion, of course, but it would appear that consequentialists need not reject it out of hand — indeed, my examples of possible speculative arguments are taken from consequentialist authors, Derek Parfit in the first instance, Shelly Kagan and Peter Singer in the second.[22] However, consequentialism is

21. The significance of the "incommensurability thesis" as a kind of fire wall against consequentialism is clearly brought out by Robert George in "Does the 'Incommensurability Thesis' Imperil Common Sense Moral Judgments?" in *In Defense of Natural Law,* 92-101; however, I do not want to presume that George would agree with me that without this stipulation the Grisez/Finnis account of basic goods would imply radical consequentialism.

22. Parfit grounds his moral theory in an analysis of personal identity which essentially denies that the boundaries between persons, or even the relations among earlier and later states of persons, are morally significant: "On this Reductionist View, persons do exist. But they exist only in the way in which nations exist. Persons are not, as we mistakenly believe, *fundamental*" (*Reasons and Persons,* 445, emphasis in original). For Singer's analysis of action and responsibility, see "Famine, Affluence, and Morality"; Kagan's similar views are set out in *The Limits of Morality,* 83-127.

vulnerable to a further line of criticism, first developed (to my knowledge) by Henry Sidgwick, who attempted in his classic *The Methods of Ethics* to develop a defense of consequentialism on purely rational grounds.[23] It may seem odd that this should yield a critique. What Sidgwick concludes, however, is that consequentialism represents one of two possible options for developing and deploying one's practical reason; the other is ethical egoism, the consistent pursuit and maximization of one's own benefit. Thus, even if we take practical reason to consist in some form of value maximization, the agent must still decide whether to maximize values tout court or relative to oneself; impartiality is itself a moral stance which is not rationally compelling. And this would seem to be the case no matter what one's views on the metaphysics of personal identity, the proper analysis of human actions, or the like — on any showing, there is no rationally compelling reason why someone committed to value maximization must interpret this principle in a general or impartial way, as opposed to a self-referential way. It might be possible to mount such an argument on the grounds of fairness or respect for persons as independent moral principles, but these are just the kinds of independent foundational — indeed, Kantian — principles that a thoroughgoing consequentialism rules out of court. If Sidgwick's argument is persuasive (as I believe it to be), then clearly we cannot defend consequentialism as the necessary implication of practical rationality.

At this point, we may seem to have strayed some distance from the aim of this section, which was to place Aquinas's understanding of reason in its contemporary and scholastic contexts. Surely, whatever our assessments of contemporary versions of consequentialism may be, it is clear the scholastics would have had no time for such an approach. Yet this is not so obvious as one might assume. As Ewart Lewis pointed out over sixty years ago, medieval natural law thinking is governed by considerations of expediency to a far greater extent than has usually been recognized.[24] And the scholastics do

23. In general, see Henry Sidgwick, *The Methods of Ethics,* 7th ed. (New York: Macmillan, 1907), republished with a new introduction by John Rawls (Indianapolis: Hackett, 1981). Throughout this book, Sidgwick builds up a defense of a rule-utilitarian approach to ethics through an analysis of what he takes to be the central ideas of a commonsense morality. Yet at the end, he admits that reason alone cannot decide the issue between egoistic hedonism and utilitarianism: "But in the rarer cases of a recognized conflict between self-interest and duty, practical reason, being divided against itself, would cease to be a motive on either side; the conflict would have to be decided by the comparative preponderance of one or other of two groups of non-rational impulses" (508).

24. Ewart Lewis, "Natural Law and Expediency in Medieval Political Theory," *Ethics* 50 (1940): 144-63.

sometimes speak in such a way as to lend credence to this line of interpretation. Consider, for example, Albert's explanation of the third sense of the natural law, in which nature is considered equally as nature and as reason:

> In the third sense, natural reason is equally reason and nature, and accordingly, that which is provided from right reason for the convenience and the usefulness of the human person pertains to the natural law (always in general principles, in accordance with the universal seeds of law, and not in accordance with a case or a particular determination), as does, for example, to provide for a household, to regulate a family, to choose prelates to punish wrongdoers and to praise the good, to care for what is one's own, and other things of this sort. (*De bono* V 1.2)

Nonetheless, the suggestion that the scholastics were consequentialists has generally been treated with suspicion, and rightly so. The scholastics reflected on moral reasoning within the parameters of the texts within which they operated. And these texts, Scripture above all, clearly indicate that morality is to be understood in terms of a law with binding and authoritative force. The scholastics understood law primarily as an ordering principle, but in this context it was also regarded as a source of specific norms; after all, their paradigms for law included both the different formulations of the Golden Rule, which is a very general norm, and the precepts of the Decalogue, which are fairly specific. This latter paradigm, in particular, disposed them to think of moral reasoning in such a way as to underscore its relation to specific norms, regarded as more or less nonnegotiable in their force. Albert once again illustrates the point, in a passage immediately preceding the text just quoted. He is explaining the meaning of the phrase "nature as reason":

> If however [nature] is understood more as reason, it concerns those things which pertain to religion and justice and human decency, in oneself and in relation to others, in such a way, however, that it should have something from nature, and that it not be [taken] entirely from reason. But then nature is understood as being in good order through the seedbeds of good as it pertains to life. Those seedbeds are the natural law, and thus, the commandments of each table [of the Decalogue], as they are generally and indeterminately understood, are of the natural law. And more briefly, whatever is decent after its fashion is of the natural law. (*De bono* V 1.2)

Although the specifics of the analysis would vary from author to author, Albert expresses the general scholastic consensus that the precepts of the

Decalogue are considered to be in some sense touchstones for moral reasoning. And if this is so, then a purely consequentialist account of moral reasoning would be ruled out.

But what, positively, does this imply about the scholastic conception of practical reasoning? Albert's comments suggest an alternative which has not yet been considered. That is, it might appear that the scholastics don't have much of a conception of practical reasoning, nor do they need one. Rather (it might be said), they adopt a strong version of a divine command approach, according to which moral norms depend for both their substance and their authority on God's commands as mediated through Scripture. But this would be a mistake. The scholastics are clear that the basic norms of Scripture reflect deliverances of reason, however that is to be understood. It is true that scriptural norms also serve to correct and extend rational deliverances, and given the constraining effects of sin, they are to some extent necessary if we are to arrive at anything like an adequate moral knowledge. Nonetheless, the scholastics believe that reason and the moral norms of Scripture are fundamentally in harmony, and they develop their accounts of moral reasoning with the aim of showing how this is so.

Of course, we find more than one such account, developed with varying degrees of detail and sophistication.[25] Albert himself argued that basic moral terms associated with the precepts of the Decalogue, such as "murder" and "theft," are included among the "common conceptions" of the soul. Hence, these are immediately understood without prior instruction to refer to wrongful kinds of actions, although we do need to learn from instruction and observation what counts as murder, theft, and the like. Albert appears to have been influenced by a traditional view according to which the natural law is innate and therefore cannot be taught. As a result, his theory has some affinities with the Kantian conception of the natural law developed by Grisez and Finnis, although for Albert it is basic moral terms, rather than basic goods, which provide the starting points for practical deliberation. At any rate, however, Albert's approach was not universally accepted. As one anonymous theologian put it,

> The law of Moses or Aeschylus does not concern the common conceptions of the soul. For it is not the case that as soon as someone hears, "do not steal," he understands that he is not to steal, and so with respect to the other commandments. Thus, many doubt whether fornication is a mortal sin. But the natural law is concerned with the common conceptions of the

25. For further particulars, see my *Natural and Divine Law,* 85-98.

> soul, as for example, "do not do to another what you do not wish to have done to yourself;" hence, it is by means of the natural law that we understand and are conscious, that is, as soon as we apprehend something, we understand that so it must be done; for "to know with" [*conscire*] is conscience. (Lottin, 125)[26]

This author represents what seems to have been the more usual scholastic position, according to which reason generates very general first principles of nonmaleficence, which are then given content through empathetic reflection on the agent's own aversions and desires. Again, the similarity to a broadly Kantian account of practical reason is evident. We find still other approaches to moral reasoning among the scholastics; for example, the secular theologian William of Auxerre claimed that we intuit the substance of the precepts of the Decalogue through an innate perception of God seen as the fount of justice, which William believes to be innate to every person.[27] This kind of thoroughgoing Neoplatonism does not seem to have been common, however.

2. Practical Reason, Will, and First Principles

Where does Aquinas fall within this spectrum of options? He clearly does not adopt William's Neoplatonic approach, since he holds that we are not capable of perceiving the divine essence naturally, or perceiving it at all in this life. He does seem to hold that moral terms such as "murder" include a moral judgment in their very meaning, but he does not follow Albert in claiming that these are therefore included among the common conceptions of the soul and thus does not treat them as starting points for moral knowledge (*ST* I-II 100.8 *ad* 3). Nor, somewhat surprisingly, does he refer to the Golden Rule as a self-evident first principle, at least in the *Summa theologiae.* Significantly, he says the precepts of the Decalogue can only be known through some reflection, albeit of a minimal sort that is well within the reach of all persons (100.1, 3). He does say that the precepts of love of God and neighbor are self-evident, but he does not spell out the link between these precepts and those of the Decalogue

26. The reference to Aeschylus *(eschylii),* the Greek tragedian (d. ca. 456 B.C.E.), is somewhat puzzling, but Cicero does mention him, and the scholastics may therefore have been aware that his plays deal with the universal demands of justice. I am grateful to my colleague Brian Daley for identifying the reference and suggesting what its rationale may have been.

27. See the *Summa aurea* III 18.4; further discussion may be found in my *Natural and Divine Law,* 89.

by appealing to formal self-consistency (100.3 *ad* 3). Rather, the bridge between the precepts of love and the more specific norms of the Decalogue seems to be provided by general norms of nonmaleficence and special obligations to others (100.5); we will return in the next section to a closer examination of what this might mean for him.

Even more strikingly, Aquinas denies that reason operating by itself leads to action. On the contrary, he holds that practical reflection and action always take their starting points from some desire (I-II 9.1, especially *ad* 2; II-II 47.4). It is true that reason functioning practically takes its starting points from first principles, including those mentioned above and, even more comprehensively, the often-cited principle that "good is to be sought and done, and evil is to be avoided" (I-II 94.2). But these principles by themselves do not lead to action, much less generate norms for action, until they are engaged by desires prompting practical reflection and action. As Daniel Westberg observes, this rules out any interpretation of right practical reason understood in Kantian terms as self-legislating reason: "Movement towards perfection or completion of a being's nature is described by Thomas as attraction to the good. Moral goodness is established in judgement about actions, but the motivation is attraction, not a sense of duty. Thus the term prudence signals a rejection of a Kantian view of morality based on duty and opposed to inclination."[28]

Correlatively, the operations of practical reason are to be analyzed and evaluated in terms of the desires they serve. (I refer to "practical reason" for simplicity's sake, but Aquinas does not regard practical reason as a distinctive capacity. Rather, he holds that there is one and the same potency, the intellect, which functions speculatively or practically; see I 79.11.) That is why the intellectual virtue of prudence, which is the virtue rectifying the operations of practical reason, cannot operate apart from the moral virtues properly so called — the latter rectify the desires which provide practical deliberation with its starting points and aims (I-II 58.2, 5; II-II 47.6; note that prudence is said to be numbered with the moral virtues, although it is strictly speaking an intellectual virtue, II-II 47.4). By the same token, a person is said to be morally good, or not, in accordance with the dispositions of her desires; this is equivalent to saying that a person's character is to be evaluated in accordance with her possession of the moral virtues properly so called, which are dispositions of desire rather than intellect (I-II 56.3).

All this implies that whatever Aquinas understands practical reason to be, he does not regard it as an autonomous principle of moral norms. This suspicion is confirmed when we look more closely at what he says about the

28. Westberg, *Right Practical Reason*, 4.

field of operation proper to the virtue of prudence. He limits the operation of prudence to directing choice at the level of particular acts (II-II 47.1-3). And this limitation is significant, because particular acts are chosen with reference to some further end that the agent has in view — whether as a means to an end, or as one component of a more complex good, or as a way of expressing or enjoying one's end in a particular act (47.1 *ad* 2). As Candace Vogler puts it in her illuminating analysis, Aquinas understands practical reason to be calculative; it takes the form of identifying a particular course of action representing a sound or appropriate way to attain, safeguard, or enjoy some further end.[29] Correlatively, prudence does not determine the ends of the virtues (47.6). Rather, it determines what counts as a consistent or appropriate expression of the virtues in particular choices — which is to say, in terms of the Aristotelian analysis he appropriates, that prudence determines what counts, concretely, as attaining the mean of the virtues in particular instances of choice (47.7). Thus prudence does not yield moral norms, at least not directly.[30]

Given Aquinas's analysis of prudence, we might conclude that if we are to align him with one of the main contemporary alternatives for understanding practical reason, he would be closest to the sentimentalist position. After all, he holds that our actions stem from desires, in such a way that both persons and their acts take their moral character from the desires they hold, or express (I-II 56.3; II-II 47.4; cf. I 82.4). Moreover, as we have just noted, he limits the scope of practical reason to attaining the means to the ends set by desire, understanding "means" in the comprehensive sense indicated above. His analysis of practical reason is thus strikingly reminiscent of Hume's, although it is hard to imagine him proclaiming that reason is the slave of the passions.[31] It would seem that there is a case to be made for interpreting Aquinas as a kind of precursor to Hume, at least with respect to his moral theory. This line of interpretation would not be foreclosed by his commitment to the Decalogue as the

29. Vogler, *Reasonably Vicious,* passim. The reference to some "further end" represents my modification, however; see below. Westberg develops a similar line of argument in *Right Practical Reason,* 26-39; in addition, at 119-83 he offers a detailed and illuminating analysis of the processes of deliberation and action, showing how rational judgment and desire reciprocally condition and inform these processes throughout.

30. As will appear below, I agree with Pamela Hall that Aquinas's account of prudence implies that prudential reflection contributes indirectly to the formulation of moral norms; see *Narrative and the Natural Law: An Interpretation of Thomistic Ethics* (Notre Dame: University of Notre Dame Press, 1994). Nonetheless, any such claim goes beyond what Aquinas explicitly says regarding the functioning of prudence.

31. John Bowlin likewise calls attention to the similarity between Aquinas and Hume, although on somewhat different grounds; see *Contingency and Fortune in Aquinas' Ethic* (Cambridge: Cambridge University Press, 1999), 17-18.

expression of God's law, because as Simon Blackburn has shown, a sentimentalist moral theory is compatible with a commitment to moral rules — it is just not compatible with cognitivist interpretation of such rules.[32] Indeed, Hume himself argues that the virtue of justice depends on the observance of a complex system of rules, built up through reflection on natural moral sentiments as these are shaped by the exigencies of life in society.[33]

It is also true that Aquinas says that the ends of the virtues are themselves set by reason (II-II 47.6). But reason in this context refers to the understanding, rather than to practical reason in its discursive operations — that is to say, it refers to the faculty through which we grasp the first principles necessary for any exercise of reason, whether speculative or practical (I-II 58.4). Hence, when Aquinas says that the ends of the virtues are set by reason, he is referring specifically to the first principles of practical reason, which are regarded as the first principles of both natural law and virtue. These do not operate apart from some engagement through desire, through which they are, so to speak, activated by being applied to action (cf. I-II 9.1, 4). Moreover, as we saw in the last chapter, these first principles take on normative force in and through reflection on what counts as rational desires of various kinds. Thus, however we are to understand the normative force of the first principles, it is clear that they cannot be understood as generating autonomous norms in a Kantian sense. Rather, these principles are engaged through the operations of various forms of desire, and they are only given normative specification in and through the formation of rational modalities of desire and action.

Yet if this account of the first principles of practical reason does not fit with Kantian ideas about the autonomy of moral reason, neither does it sound particularly Humean. What kind of sense could we make, on Hume's terms, of passions informed, shaped, or governed by reason? It begins to look as if Aquinas is not a sentimentalist after all. This suspicion is reinforced when we read further on that the proper function of practical reason is to place diverse aims and considerations in some kind of proper ordering (II-II 152.2). Admittedly, it is not immediately clear how this claim is consistent with the claim that practical reason functions in such a way as to determine appropriate ways of attaining one's ends. We will return to this issue below. At any rate, it is at least clear that Aquinas's claims about the ordering function of practical reason do not fit well with a sentimentalist interpretation of his

32. The main lines of the argument are set out in Blackburn, *Ruling Passions*, 48-83.

33. See David Hume, *A Treatise of Human Nature* (1739-40), ed. L. A. Selby-Bigge (Oxford: Clarendon, 1888; repr. 1973), 484-513. Again, I am grateful to Jennifer Herdt for locating this reference.

moral theory. Reference to a proper ordering implies that there is some criterion according to which desires can be evaluated apart from the concatenation of desires that we just happen to have, even understood comprehensively to take into account the relative strength of desires, their compatibility, and the like. Clearly, this is indeed Aquinas's view. He claims that reason orders our diverse aims in accordance with some consideration of what counts as our true good, comprehensively considered. From a Kantian perspective, this looks suspiciously like hypothetical reasoning, yet at the same time, no thoroughgoing Humean could accept a view according to which the objects of desire can be ordered either properly or improperly, in accordance with some criterion not derived from these desires themselves.

In fact, Aquinas cannot be regarded as either a Kantian or a sentimentalist; rather, he offers a distinct alternative to both accounts of practical reason. In order to appreciate the real difference between Aquinas's understanding of reason and these contemporary alternatives, we need to look more closely at the notions of desire correlated with these accounts of reasoning.

In his *Ruling Passions,* Simon Blackburn illustrates the difference between his Humean model of deliberation and the Kantian model in terms of a Platonic image of a person as a ship: "For Hume or Smith, the ship is worked by a crew, each representing a passion or inclination or sentiment, and where the ship goes is determined by the resolution of conflicting pressures among the crew. After one voice has prevailed, various things may happen to the losers: they may be thrown overboard and lost altogether, or they may remain sullen and mutinous, or they may continue to have at least some effect on the ship's course."[34] For Kant, in contrast,

> there is indeed the Humean crew. But standing above them, on the quarter-deck, there is another voice — a voice with ultimate authority and ultimate power. This is the Captain, the will, yourself as an embodiment of pure practical reason, detached from all desire. The Captain himself is free. But he always stands ready to stop things going wrong with the crew's handling of the boat. Sometimes, it seems, the happiest ships will have no crew at all, but only a Captain, for, making surprising contact with Stoic and Buddhist thought, Kant holds that it is only with complete independence from inclinations and desires that bliss is possible.[35]

Hence, Blackburn presents two alternatives: we envision the self either as a set of desires controlled by reason, or — Blackburn's own preferred option

34. Blackburn, *Ruling Passions,* 245-46.
35. Blackburn, *Ruling Passions,* 246.

— as a set of desires which come together spontaneously into a more or less stable harmony. The point of contrast that he emphasizes is thus the role reason plays in the two models. But this disagreement is tethered to a significant, albeit tacit, point of agreement. That is, both models presuppose essentially the same conception of desire as a kind of undifferentiated tendency or inclination urging the person toward action. While desires differ in strength and scope, they are all fundamentally the same in kind, and they operate, so to speak, on the same level. Hence, they must either be controlled by something other than desire (on the Kantian model) or brought together through a contingent process of interaction leading to equilibrium (on the Humean model).

Anyone familiar with Aquinas's psychology will recognize that his model of the person does not fit either of these alternatives. Certainly, he does not believe that human action (much less human identity tout court) can be explained in terms of the contingent equilibrium of heterogeneous desires. But neither would he accept a view according to which the human person is governed by the will, understood as "pure practical reason, detached from all desire." We have already observed that Aquinas gives a certain priority to desire in the processes of action, insofar as he claims that reason in practical matters discerns how to attain the ends set by desire. More to the point, Aquinas unequivocally says that the will *is* a kind of desire, or in his terms, a kind of appetite. The will is the form of appetite proper to a rational creature, insofar as it depends on judgments of reason to specify its particular objects. As such, it is distinguished from other kinds of desires, that is to say, the passions, which are common to the rational person and other kinds of animals. Yet it shares important elements in common with these, and also with the more general forms of appetite found in all creatures. Correlatively, the passions as they exist in rational creatures have a cognitive component. For both these reasons, desires cannot be considered simply as heterogeneous forces for Aquinas; they are differentiated, and operate and interact with one another, in accordance with their distinctive intelligible structures. Hence, if we are to understand what is distinctive about Aquinas's approach to practical reason, we will first need to take account of what is distinctive in his account of desire.[36]

The main lines of Aquinas's analysis of the will and the passions are well known, and for our purposes a brief sketch of that analysis will suffice.[37] Ac-

36. I am grateful to Elizabeth Agnew for helping me to see the significance of this point.

37. The main lines of this account are set forth in Robert Pasnau, *Thomas Aquinas on Human Nature: A Philosophical Study of "Summa theologiae" Ia 75-89* (Cambridge: Cambridge University Press, 2002), 209-64. In addition, Westberg offers a lucid analysis of what he calls the "metaphysics of agency," including the significance of the will's orientation toward the good, in *Right Practical Reason*, 43-61, and he goes on to analyze the reciprocal relation between will and

cording to Aquinas, the will and the passions are both forms of appetite, and as such, each is oriented toward some perceived good. The difference between them lies in the way in which each apprehends the good. The will is directed toward the good as apprehended by reason; that is to say, it takes its objects from a rational judgment according to which this or that is in some way good, and therefore a fitting object for pursuit or enjoyment (I-II 8.1; 9.1, 2). The passions, in contrast, are oriented toward what Aquinas describes as desirable or noxious objects, as mediated by the apprehension of the senses and imagination (I-II 22.2, 3). At the same time, human passions also have a cognitive component, insofar as their objects are presented to them, in part at least, through a rational construal of circumstances and events. This is more apparent for some kinds of passions than others. Aquinas seems to think that at least some sensual desires have minimal or no rational components, while at the other extreme there are passions such as anger which can only arise as a result of some kind of rational judgment.[38] At any rate, the cognitive component of the passions gives them a certain independence vis-à-vis the rational judgments of the will; to change metaphors, they can be governed, but only in a way appropriate to the rule of those who have an independent voice in their own affairs, politically rather than despotically (I-II 58.2).

As a number of commentators have noted, this way of analyzing will and desire gives reason a certain kind of primacy in determining the overall orien-

---

intellect at 61-115. Bonnie Kent offers a helpful analysis of Aquinas's theory of will and intellect seen in the context of medieval appropriations of Aristotle in *Virtues of the Will: The Transformation of Ethics in the Late Thirteenth Century* (Washington, D.C.: Catholic University of America Press, 1995), 94-149.

38. Aquinas says at II-II 156.4 that the movement of the desiring faculty is wholly in accordance with sensuality, and in no way in accordance with reason, in contrast to the passion of anger, which is partially determined by rational judgment. But this does not seem to reflect his overall view, since he says elsewhere that the passions, explicitly including those stemming from the desiring faculty of the soul (concupiscence) as well as those stemming from the irascible faculty, have their own proper movements in virtue of which they can be shaped and directed by reason; that is why reason is said to govern the passions politically, not despotically (I-II 56.4; on the last point, see 56.4 *ad* 3). Subsequently, he argues that the virtues not only coexist with the passions, but in some cases cannot exist without them, since (some of, not all of) the virtues have the passions as their proper matter (I-II 59.5). What is more, Aquinas seems to regard sensation itself as having a cognitive component; see Pasnau, *Thomas Aquinas*, 277, and more generally 267-68. At any rate, I would argue that Aquinas should recognize that even our most basic perceptions and passions have a cognitive component, even if he does not; otherwise, as John McDowell has shown (not in reference to Aquinas specifically), he cannot maintain the strongly realist accounts of perception, judgment, and language to which he is clearly committed. See McDowell, *Mind and World* (Cambridge: Harvard University Press, 1994), 3-45, for the main lines of the argument.

tation of one's life and character.[39] Since the will depends on the judgments of reason to specify its acts, its overall orientation will only be as sound as the judgments of the intellect presenting it with its objects (I-II 8.1). That is why it is so important for someone to have a correct appraisal of that in which her happiness truly consists, because otherwise she will not direct her will toward her genuine perfection, much less orient her actions accordingly (II-II 4.7; cf. I-II 5.8; II-II 25.7). That is also why Aquinas holds that the foundational theological virtue is faith, which for him is necessarily linked to (although not subsumed in) right belief regarding matters of revelation (I-II 62.4; II-II 2.5, 6). Even so, the primacy of reason in this sense cannot be equated with the primacy of practical reason in the contemporary sense. Faith is a virtue of the speculative intellect for Aquinas, since it is a disposition toward right beliefs which, as such, has no necessary connection toward action (II-II 4.2 *ad* 3). By the same token, natural happiness presupposes correct knowledge about the mode of perfection proper to human life. Yet as Ralph McInerny argues in some detail, the relevant knowledge in itself is speculative rather than practical.[40] It is formulated at the level of our general conception of the human person, and by itself does not yield judgments regarding particular actions. Moreover, apart from the impetus provided by the natural desire for happiness, it would have no necessary connection to action.[41]

But there is another aspect of the will and the passions which is more often overlooked, and is equally important for understanding Aquinas's ac-

39. The relevant issues are clearly and helpfully set forth by both Westberg and Pasnau; see Westberg, *Right Practical Reason,* 95-115, and Pasnau, *Thomas Aquinas,* 234-41.

40. Ralph McInerny, *Aquinas on Human Action: A Theory of Practice* (Washington, D.C.: Catholic University of America Press, 1992), 184-206.

41. In Kluxen's view, there is a sharp distinction between practical and speculative reason, in that the former is directed toward whatever can be done, whereas the latter is directed toward knowledge of the world existing apart from action; this is why practical reason is autonomous vis-à-vis speculative reason, as he explains in *Lex naturalis bei Thomas von Aquin,* 29-32. But this is not quite the distinction that Aquinas draws; these two functions of the intellect differ on the aims toward which reflection is directed, not on the object of reflection. As he explains in *De veritate* 3.3, the intellect is said to function practically when its operations are oriented toward action (immediately or remotely). It functions speculatively when it considers something apart from any orientation toward action, even if the object of its reflection is some practical science. Thus, someone who studies medicine with an aim to practicing it, immediately or at some point in the future, is engaged in practical reflection; however, someone who studies medicine for fun, with no intention of ever putting her knowledge into practice, is engaged in speculative reason. Similarly, he says in I 79.11 that "the speculative intellect is that which apprehends, directed not to some deed but only to the consideration of truth; whereas the practical intellect is said to be that which apprehends, directed to some deed" — and since this is an *accidental* difference, it cannot be said to divide the intellect into two distinct potencies.

count of practical reason. That is, both the will and the passions are forms of natural appetite.[42] This implies that both will and passions are naturally oriented toward the good in accordance with their own distinctive modes of operation, because for Aquinas an appetite is nothing other than any sort of ordered inclination toward some end, which is by definition a (perceived or actual) good (I-II 8.1). More specifically, an appetite is an inclination toward some end which is exigent, or at least appropriate to the existence and flourishing of a specific kind of creature. Every creature, whether sentient or not, is said to desire existence and perfection, that is to say, the fullest possible development in accordance with its specific kind; this does not imply that inanimate objects enjoy a kind of dim consciousness, but only that all creatures sustain their existence in and through operations which are given order and direction by the creature's specific form. The appetites of sentient creatures are thus expressions, proper to their distinctive modes of existence, of a more general metaphysical phenomenon, and as such, they must be understood in terms of the parameters set by that general phenomenon.[43]

And what are these parameters? In the first place, as we have already noted, both the passions and the will are necessarily oriented toward the good, each in accordance with its characteristic way of apprehending its proper object (I 81.2; I-II 23.1, 2; I-II 8.1). Secondly, both the passions and the will stem from the specific nature of the human person. Aquinas does distinguish between voluntary desires and the natural desires of nonrational creatures. As he explains, however, this distinction depends on the fact that the natural desires of nonrational creatures are necessarily determined to a particular kind of object, whereas the will is indeterminate with respect to particular kinds of objects (I-II 8.1). This distinction does not imply that the will can be understood apart from some consideration of human nature, because as Aquinas goes on to explain, the will can itself be said to be a natural appetite, insofar as it is the kind of desire natural to and characteristic of a creature of our kind, that is to say, a rational desire or appetite (I-II 10.1). This aspect of Aquinas's theory is not so commonly noted, and yet it is central to his overall account of practical reason and its relation to the will.

The point I want to underscore is this. Because the will is a natural appetite, in the sense just indicated, it stems from a specific nature and takes its orientation and ordering from the mode of existence proper to that nature.

42. This point is insisted upon by both Westberg and Pasnau; see Westberg, *Right Practical Reason,* 54, and Pasnau, *Thomas Aquinas,* 200-209. Similarly, Pinckaers analyzes the freedom of the will in terms of its natural structures in *Ce qu'on ne peut jamais faire,* 117-37.

43. Again, this is set out most clearly in the *SCG;* see in particular III 3; III 25 n. 3.

Aquinas's remarks about the indeterminacy of the will must be understood in this context. The will is oriented toward the good as perceived by reason, but that does not mean reason can coherently present anything whatever to the will as an object of desire and enjoyment. Aquinas would not have agreed with R. M. Hare that we can logically desire a saucer of mud (without some stipulations rendering such a desire appropriate).[44] Rather, he clearly states that the will is oriented toward goodness as it is in some way natural and appropriate to the human creature (I-II 10.1, 2). By the same token, the first principle of practical reason, "Good is to be sought and done, and evil is to be avoided," finds its proper field of operation in the pursuit and safeguarding of distinctively human forms of goodness and perfection.

By the same token, the indeterminacy of the will as Aquinas understands it is consistent with the claim, which he also asserts, that the will is naturally moved toward some objects (again, see I-II 10.1, 2). As Pasnau remarks, the human will is, so to speak, the unifying and individuating appetite of a human individual, that is to say, her overarching desire to exist and to flourish in accordance with her proper form of perfection.[45] As such, it is naturally oriented toward her perfect flourishing — just as every appetite of every creature is oriented toward some kind of perfection, of the creature itself or of some aspect of its existence (10.1). In the case of a human individual, this is tantamount to saying that the will is naturally oriented toward happiness, which is nothing other than the perfection of a rational or intellectual creature. This orientation is not only natural but necessary, in the sense that the will is necessarily directed toward whatever the person understands happiness to be, if she is actually considering it (10.2). In addition, since the will moves all the other faculties of the human person to act, it is also naturally oriented toward the diverse objects of these faculties, including knowledge, life itself, and other similar desiderata (10.1; 10.2 *ad* 3). If these are apprehended as necessary conditions for, or concomitants to, the attainment of happiness, they will likewise be necessarily desired in the same sense as happiness itself is necessarily desired. In any case, Aquinas clearly holds that the will is naturally and spontaneously oriented toward what were described in the last chapter as components of well-being, including life itself, health, reproduction, and the like.

This claim, that the will is naturally and (under some conditions) necessarily oriented toward certain objects, provides a critical link between "nature as nature" and "nature as reason" understood in a Thomistic sense. But

44. I have been unable to locate the reference for this remark.

45. Pasnau, *Thomas Aquinas*, 240.

in order to be clear about this connection, we need first to say something more about the sense in which the will is necessitated, and correlatively, the sense in which it is free. Aquinas insists on the freedom of the will, but it will be apparent that he does not understand it in quite the way many of our contemporaries do.[46] For him, the freedom of the will is analyzed by contrast to the natural necessity informing other kinds of appetites. These latter are oriented toward their objects as a concomitant of the dynamic expression of the proper form which structures the existence of the creature (or it may be, some component of a complex creature). A salt crystal has a natural desire to be a salt crystal because that is the specific intelligible character proper to its existence — that is what it is, and therefore that is what it necessarily desires to be. (Of course, "desire" in this context carries no implication of consciousness, but only of a directed operation toward an end.) The more complex forms proper to living creatures and animals can sometimes admit of more than one particular object, but they are nonetheless determined to a specific category of object, in accordance with the kind of existence and operation in question. For example, the eye of an animal is directed toward seeing (that is what an eye is), and as such, the objects toward which it is properly oriented all fall within one determinate category, namely, "the visible," even though there are of course an indefinite plurality of visible objects.

When Aquinas contrasts the freedom of the will with natural necessity, what he means is that the will is not in this way necessarily determined to particular objects or even to determinate categories of objects. Rather, the will is oriented toward the good as such, meaning the good apprehended by reason, which comprises anything that reason can intelligibly regard as good, given the natural orientation of the will as just described. In other words, the objects of the will are always mediated to it through rational judgments to the effect that this or that overall state of affairs, or this or that particular object, is good and therefore merits pursuit. The mediating function of reason guarantees the freedom of the will in a twofold way. First of all, it leaves the will free with respect to its exercise, because the will cannot be oriented toward any object, even happiness, unless it is actively being considered (I-II 10.2). Secondly, even when it is actively considering some particular object which the intellect presents to it as good, the will is not compelled, because no finite object will be good in every respect, and can therefore be regarded by the reason as being in some way noxious, or at least deficient (10.2). This is true even with respect to the natural objects of the will mentioned above. While some

46. In what follows, I rely especially on Westberg, *Right Practical Reason*, 81-115, and Pasnau, *Thomas Aquinas*, 214-33.

of these are generically necessary for the attainment of happiness (in particular, life itself), the will can intelligibly turn from or even set itself against such objects in specific instances of choice. The natural goal of staying alive may be regarded as futile by someone in an extremity of pain, or it might be superseded by the agent's commitment to some other good, such as the well-being of his community. The relevant choices may or may not be immoral — Aquinas holds that suicide is always a vicious choice, but self-sacrifice may be an act of virtue — but the point is that they are not foreclosed by the natural orientation of the will toward those goods generically necessary for well-being and happiness (II-II 64.5, especially *ad* 5).

This account of the will seems problematic to some commentators because it seems to place the will under the control of reason.[47] There is a sense in which this is true; Aquinas certainly holds that the will never operates except on the basis of some rational judgment or other. What we must keep in mind, however, is that will and reason do not operate in isolation from one another.[48] Just as the will depends on reason to present it with its objects, so reason (together with every other human power) is only activated through the will, which moves the other powers to action. What this means, practically, is that reason and will are always in a process of dynamic interaction. As reason presents the will with possible objects for pursuit, and suggests courses of action directed toward these goods, so the will prompts reason to consider this or that alternative, to deliberate on the best way to attain this or that end, and the like. In this sense, as Aquinas says, the will moves itself, because by willing something as an end it engages a process of deliberation on proper means, and so actively brings itself to will the means toward that end, or to will some specific action as a component or expression of a more comprehensive end (I-II 10.3).[49]

Moreover, mutual interactions of reason and will cannot be understood apart from the wider context set by the personal disposition and history of the acting person. Reason and will operate together in a more or less unified

47. For a forceful and influential defense of this view, see James Keenan, *Goodness and Rightness in Thomas Aquinas's "Summa Theologiae"* (Washington, D.C.: Georgetown University Press, 1992); for a response (in my view, convincing), see Westberg, "Did Aquinas Change His Mind about the Will?" *The Thomist* 58 (1994): 41-60.

48. As Stephen Brock points out, the will has at least some power over its own formation; see *Action and Conduct: Thomas Aquinas and the Theory of Action* (Edinburgh: T. & T. Clark, 1998), 186-89. A similar point is made by both Westberg, *Right Practical Reason,* 50-60, and Pasnau, *Thomas Aquinas,* 221-53.

49. Westberg offers a most helpful and detailed analysis of the relationship between will and deliberation in *Right Practical Reason,* 119-83.

fashion, which is given shape and direction by the agent's overall beliefs about what constitutes the good, in general and especially for himself, and by the overall disposition of his will. These overarching orientations are further conditioned by the dispositions of his passions, which affect the reason, and thereby the will, by influencing the way in which he perceives what is desirable or noxious in a particular situation (I-II 9.2). The agent's persistent dispositions of intellect, will, and passions — his virtues, in other words, or perhaps his vices — together with his overall beliefs, desires, and commitments as shaped by his particular history and circumstances, all come together to inform the exercise of will and reason at any given point in time.

There is indeed a sense in which we might say, to borrow a phrase from Blackburn, that the will is oneself — although not in the Kantian sense of identifying the will with pure practical reason, and not in any sense that would directly correspond to Aquinas's usage either. For Aquinas, the human individual is individuated by the form, which is identical with the substantial soul, as soon as it comes into existence; indeed, individuation by a human soul is what it means to come into existence as a human individual for Aquinas.[50] This seems right to me. Nonetheless, it seems legitimate to speak in a secondary sense of someone's identity as constituted by, and identified with, her overall disposition and character. This, I take it, is what Alasdair MacIntyre has in mind when he speaks of the narrative unity of a life:

> . . . I am what I may justifiably be taken by others to be in the course of living out a story that runs from my birth to my death; I am the *subject* of a history that is my own and no one else's, that has its own peculiar meaning. . . . To be the subject of a narrative that runs from one's birth to one's death is, I remarked earlier, to be accountable for the actions and experiences which compose a narratable life. It is, that is, to be open to being asked to give a certain kind of account of what one did or what happened to one or what one witnessed at any earlier point in one's life than the time at which the question is posed.[51]

In Aquinas's terms, we are accountable because our actions are voluntary, that is to say, they stem from the will (I-II 6.1, 2). At the same time, the will provides the ultimate unifying principle of our actions through its orien-

50. That is why the human person as such does not come into being at the "moment of conception," but only at a point at which the fetus is sufficiently developed to sustain the operations of a distinctively human soul; see Pasnau, *Thomas Aquinas,* 100-130, for further details.

51. Alasdair MacIntyre, *After Virtue: A Study in Moral Theory,* 2nd ed. (Notre Dame: University of Notre Dame Press, 1984), 217-18, emphasis in original.

tation toward happiness, understood in terms of whatever the agent takes to constitute a complete and fulfilling — that is to say, perfect — life. Moreover, to the extent that an individual's actions are fully rational, they will in some way be oriented toward the ultimate end of happiness as the agent understands it, whether pursuing or safeguarding it, or simply enjoying whatever aspects of happiness are available to the individual at a particular point. In this way, the will is not only the principle of freedom and accountability for particular acts; it is also the unifying principle holding an agent's ongoing history of actions together, by reference to the overarching desire for happiness giving shape and purpose to every aspect of the individual's life. Of course, this desire is informed by a particular conception of the good, which is the product of deliberation — but the process of deliberation is itself commanded by the will when the maturing child recognizes the need to reflect on the overall course of his life, a point Aquinas believes to come quite early in childhood (I-II 89.6).

At this point we may seem to be approaching the giddy vistas of an infinite regress. The will brings unity to one's life, but only on the basis of previous reflection; this reflection, in turn, is commanded by the will, on the basis of an apprehension to the effect that one needs to get clear on the overall direction of one's life; but this apprehension can only stem from some kind of rational reflection commanded by the will, as is every exercise of the intellect; this further presupposes some apprehension that it would be good to command the relevant kind of reflection . . . and so on. Clearly, this cannot be quite right. These processes must have a starting point, and in the nature of the case, the starting point cannot be an act of the will or the intellect, since each presupposes the other.

This difficulty is more apparent than real, however. As Aquinas notes, this process of desire and reflection is naturally and normally initiated through the will's spontaneous orientation toward the basic components of well-being, including both the necessities of life and the proper objects of one's specific powers (I-II 9.4). In the very young child, these kinds of desires will reflect passions rather than the will; but when the child begins to be able to conceptualize these desiderata as goods, and to direct his actions accordingly, it is legitimate to speak of these as stemming from the will, albeit in an immature and imperfectly developed state. As we saw in the last chapter, the ongoing processes of desire and aversion gradually take on coherence in the developing child, first through the discipline of her caretakers and then through her own reflection. This process, in turn, leads by its own dynamics to reflection on the relative importance of the diverse desires, ideals, and other considerations, as they come together to give shape to the individual's own life. At a certain point, the child will attain the use of reason, at which point the first object of her rational reflection will be some consideration of herself, the overall purpose and direction of her life, and correlatively the end toward which her actions should be directed (I-II 89.6). This is the first object of consideration, I would add, because it is only at this point that the human person can be said without qualification to act rationally and therefore fully to exercise the will.

Will and practical reason thus emerge together out of a process of action and reflection which is perhaps purely instinctual at first (and thus cannot really be regarded as action), and which remains for a considerable period at the level Aquinas would describe as the imperfectly voluntary, insofar as this process does not yet reflect a full rational grasp of one's own good. Nonetheless, even the voluntary acts of a very young child are informed by reason in a sense, because they stem from her natural inclinations toward connatural goods. And these inclinations are themselves informed by a kind of reason — that is to say, they reflect the intelligibility proper to the specific form of the creature whose inclinations they are. Once again, we see that "nature as nature" informs and directs "nature as reason." Reason takes its starting points from inclinations which are not simply blind surges of desire, but intelligibly structured orientations toward goods connatural to the human creature, and it is informed through a process of ongoing reflection on those intelligibilities. In this way, the natural law as Aquinas understands it stems from and respects the intelligible order of nature — not (primarily) by tracking a natural or moral order to be found in relations or states of affairs outside the creature, but by respecting and bringing coherence to the intelligible order of the human creature itself.

Aquinas holds that the moral virtues strictly so called require only two intellectual virtues, namely, understanding of first principles and prudence (I-II 58.4). We are now in a position to better understand the force of this claim, and by the same token, to begin to spell out a distinctively Thomistic account of practical reason. I will conclude this section by looking more closely at the force of claiming that there are first principles of practical reason. Later in this chapter, we will take a closer look at prudence.

As Aquinas frequently notes, the first principles of practical reason stand in the same relation to reflection on action as the first principles of speculative reason stand to demonstration and to speculative knowledge generally (I-II 94.2). That is, they provide the necessary starting points for all practical reasoning, and as such, they cannot themselves be justified. Nor do they need justification, for they fall within the category of principles *per se nota* — anyone who truly grasps the subject of the proposition will recognize that what is affirmed of the subject is contained within its *ratio,* its intelligible character. The most frequently cited such first principle is "good is to be sought and done, and evil is to be avoided," and Aquinas almost certainly regards this as the most comprehensive of the first principles of practical reason. But he also mentions other first principles, which are more restricted in scope but equally foundational within their sphere of operation, including "Do no harm" and "Observe one's particular obligations." In addition, he refers to the twofold imperative of love of God and neighbor as *per se nota* (I-II 100.3, especially *ad* 1; II-II 122.1).

It is tempting to interpret these claims in Kantian terms, as if Aquinas were saying that reason generates these norms through its own autonomous operations, presumably through canons of self-consistency. If this were what he meant, we would be forced to conclude that his claims are at best dubious. It is not evident that "to be pursued" is analytically included within the meaning of "good," and much less is it evident that the imperatives to love God and neighbor, to avoid harm, and to fulfill one's obligations are analytically necessary, given some abstract meaning of "God," "neighbor," and the like. But this is not what Aquinas says; the first principles are not said to be self-evident, in the sense of analytic, but "known through themselves" in the sense that anyone who grasps the meaning of the subject will grasp the predicate. For this reason, knowledge of these principles presupposes an informed grasp of the *ratio* of their relevant subjects — and this may well require reflective deliberation, such as can only be expected of "the wise." That is why Aquinas remarks, to our ears paradoxically, that a principle can be *per se nota* in itself, but not necessarily to us — the meanings of its terms need not be apparent, and may in fact never be apparent to us (I-II 94.2).

This distinction may not seem to be practically important, but it is critical if we are to appreciate the difference between Aquinas's account of practical reason and a Kantian account. On the latter view, the autonomy of practical reason implies that moral reasoning takes its starting point from principles which do not in any way depend on factual or metaphysical truths. For Aquinas, in contrast, the first principles of practical reason are nothing other than the rational creature's grasp of the intelligibilities inherent in created existence, tout court or as expressed in some specific form of created being.[52] It is not accurate to say that the first principles of practical reason are

52. In "MacIntyre and Aquinas," in *After MacIntyre: Critical Perspectives on the Work of Alasdair MacIntyre,* ed. John Horton and Susan Mendes (Notre Dame: University of Notre Dame Press, 1994), 65-90, Janet Coleman observes that "For Aquinas there is a notion of actual existence that is more basic than logical existence. . . . For both Aristotle and Aquinas actual ex-

derived from metaphysical and natural principles, only because these first principles *are* metaphysical and natural principles of motion as grasped by the rational creature. They need not be formulated in order to be grasped; on the contrary, at least the most basic of these, "good is to be sought and done . . . ," is grasped by everyone. However, some level of philosophical or theological understanding is needed to formulate these principles, and more would be needed to place them within the proper context of a metaphysically informed conception of human nature.

When we place Aquinas's own formulations of the first principles of practical reason in the context of his metaphysics and philosophy of nature, we find that these first principles are indeed expressions of more general metaphysical principles of motion, and Aquinas interprets them as such. The most fundamental of these principles, "Good is to be sought and done, and evil is to be avoided," is nothing other than the reflection in the human intellect of a universal tendency to seek the good in accordance with the creature's own specific form of perfection, a tendency which in the case of the human creature is expressed through the universal desire for happiness (I-II 93.5, 6). Similarly, the injunction to love God, which Aquinas also describes as *per se nota,* reflects the universal tendency, which Aquinas explicitly describes as natural to every created existence, to love God more than oneself, in the sense of in some way desiring the universal good more than one's own good (I-II 109.3). The precepts to love the neighbor, and to avoid harm and to respect one's particular obligations (which are specifications of the general imperative to love), do not appear to reflect general metaphysical tendencies in the same way (although the imperative to love oneself does). However, I believe we can take a cue from the comments of some of Aquinas's predecessors, and

---

istence is intuited as a first principle that is indemonstrable" (69). Something similar should be said about the first principles of practical reason; that is, they reflect exigencies of operation stemming from the human person's character as a creature, an animal, and an animal of a specific kind. In other words, they stem from and reflect our rational awareness of the human form as the immediate impetus and structuring principle of all our activities. Contrast John Finnis's interpretation of the first principles: "They are not inferred from speculative principles. They are not inferred from facts. They are not inferred from metaphysical propositions about human nature, or about the nature of good and evil, or about the 'function of a human being,' nor are they inferred from a teleological conception of nature or any other conception of nature. They are not inferred or derived from anything" (*Natural Law and Natural Rights* [Oxford: Clarendon, 1980], 33-34). I would agree with this if the weight of the claim rested only on "inferred or derived," but the overall development of Finnis's theory indicates that he wants to claim that the first principles are altogether independent of the intelligibilities of human nature, which can also be grasped through metaphysics and natural philosophy. If this is so, then the claim is not tenable.

interpret these as expressions of our nature as animals, and more specifically as social animals.[53]

At this point we can see why Aquinas's account of practical reason is distinctive from both Kantian and sentimentalist accounts, although it offers points of contact with both. His account of practical reason is correlated with a distinctive account of desires, according to which the desires of the human person stem from and reflect the proper form of humanity. As such, they are not just blind surges of affect; they reflect the intelligible structures of human existence and thus can be evaluated in terms of their contributions, or otherwise, to the overall perfection of the agent. This orientation is built into human desires themselves, including the passions as well as the will; that is why even the former, as Aquinas puts it, participate somewhat in reason and are governed constitutionally, as befits quasi-independent members of a commonwealth (I-II 58.2). The passions and (much more) the will are thus appropriately subject to rational evaluation on account of their own intrinsic structures and their integral place in the overall framework of human life, and that is why Aquinas is not a Humean. By the same token, however, reason cannot operate autonomously in the Kantian sense. In its practical functioning, it takes its starting points and structures from human desires, and what is more, its first principles represent a rational grasp of the metaphysical and vital structures of human existence. Practical reason is not independent of the metaphysical structures of the agent; it is on the contrary an immediate and direct expression of those structures, as they are expressed in action.

This way of interpreting practical reason brings us back to Aquinas's preferred account of the natural law with which we ended the first chapter. As we saw, Aquinas regards the natural law as the participation of the rational creature in God's providence, a participation which consists in being provident for oneself and others. As he explains, God's providence operates in all creatures in and through the natural inclinations which God has implanted in them, through which they pursue their proper ends:

> It may happen, however, that some prince, who may be desirable in his own person, will nonetheless give onerous laws to his subjects, which he himself does not keep, and therefore his subjects are not effectively subjected to him. But since this is excluded from God, [Dionysius] adds that he sets *voluntary laws* over *all;* for the law of God is the proper natural inclination placed in every creature to do that which is appropriate to it, in

53. For further particulars, see my *Natural and Divine Law,* 76-85.

> accordance with nature. And therefore, since all things are held by divine desire, so all are held by his law. (*De divinis nomnibus* X, 1.1, 857)

The inclinations of the human person similarly provide the intelligible principles in terms of which she attains her perfection, thus attaining union with God in the way connatural to her as a specific kind of creature. Yet precisely because she is the kind of creature that she is, not only the likeness but the very Image of God, she pursues and attains this end in a distinctive way, through rationally grasping and acting upon the principles structuring her proper inclinations (cf. I 93.1, 2).

However, we would be mistaken to conclude that social conventions and moral norms stem directly from these natural inclinations, apart from some process of rational reflection. Aristotle apparently thought that the structures of family and civic association stem directly from the natural tendencies of the human person. As Cary Nederman has shown, the scholastics, in contrast, adopt Cicero's approach, according to which our natural tendencies and inclinations can only be translated into practical norms by way of a process of communal reflection.[54] This approach is strikingly illustrated by Rufin, one of the earliest commentators on Gratian's compendium of canon law (writing between 1157 and 1159):

> Since, therefore, the natural power within the human person had not been entirely extinguished, undoubtedly he began to strive that he should be distinct from the beasts by his law of life, just as he is distinct from them by the prerogative of knowledge. And while the human person resolved to live with his neighbor, the traces of justice, that is, the precepts of modesty and shame emerged, which taught him to turn the rustic and wild ways of humankind into decorous and honorable ways of living, and to subject himself to agreements of concord and to enter into certain pacts. These indeed are called the law of nations, insofar as practically all nations observe them, as for example the laws of selling, of leasing and the exchange of goods, and other similar laws. But indeed, since our weakness would scarcely be able through this means to restore the full measure of good, the merciful God, helping us, set forth the law of life, which he had inscribed in the human heart at the beginning of time, in writing, comprising ten mandates. (Weigand, nos. 238-40)

54. See Cary Nederman, "Nature, Sin and the Origins of Society: The Ciceronian Tradition in Medieval Political Thought," *Journal of the History of Ideas* 49 (1988): 3-26, and "Aristotelianism and the Origins of 'Political Science' in the Twelfth Century," *Journal of the History of Ideas* 52 (1991): 179-94.

Up until the last sentence, this passage is a close paraphrase of Cicero's *De inventione,* and as such it reflects Rufin's appropriation of a particular way of understanding the normative force of the natural law.[55] That is, the basic principles of intelligibility constituting the natural law must be translated into social norms through a process of communal reflection, in order to be practically effective. This approach gives considerable weight to the mores, practices, and laws of human societies, but not in quite the same way as Aristotle's approach did. That is, on the Ciceronian view reflected here, social practices represent one possible expression of the natural law, but at the same time they are also regarded as conventional expressions, mediated through rational reflection in a particular society. This implies that the specific norms expressing the natural law in particular societies are to some degree contingent to that society, and that is why they cannot be identified with the natural law in its most proper sense. At the same time, the scholastics by and large are remarkably optimistic about the validity and soundness of the customs and laws of most human societies. The diversity of practices in human societies need not be construed as perversions (although sometimes they are), precisely because the natural law in its primary sense allows for a diversity of expressions. In any case, the practices and laws of any society can be analyzed in terms of the diverse aspects of the natural law which they reflect, and this reflection, in turn, provides a basis for normative critique, both positive and negative.

But as Rufin's last remark reminds us, scholastic optimism on this point only goes so far. Human social life has been distorted by human weakness and original sin, and for that reason our attempts to formulate the natural law stand in need of correction and completion. This is provided by God's divine law as revealed in Scripture, above all through the "ten mandates" of the Decalogue, which summarize God's will for human social existence. Rufin's remarks remind us that for the scholastics, the precepts of the Decalogue are at once divine — that is to say, revealed — and natural law, insofar as they reflect fundamental deliverances of moral reasoning. As such, they provide paradigms for correct moral reasoning, in much the same way as appeals to common morality function for many moral philosophers today. Thus for the scholastics, Aquinas included, any adequate account of moral reasoning must in some way display the reasonableness of the Ten Commandments, or at the very least, must not force the conclusion that they are unreasonable.

This commitment undoubtedly reinforced and focused the scholastics' view, already suggested by the natural law tradition itself, that moral reason-

55. See *De inventione* I.I-II, 2.

ing in some way constitutes a law, which can be analyzed, at least up to a point, by analogy to positive law. In the next two sections, I want to defend this view as a generally plausible account of moral reasoning. The lawlike character of morality turns out to be one implication of the distinctive features of the virtue of justice. As such, it both expresses and safeguards the distinctively human form of happiness constituted by the practice of the virtues — or that, at least, will be my argument in what follows.

3. Natural and Divine Law: The Decalogue as Moral Law

Rufin represents a long-standing theological consensus when he says the precepts of the Decalogue were revealed in order to supplement and correct moral reflection. The scholastics might have interpreted this consensus as some later theologians did, emphasizing the divinely revealed status of these precepts, and arguing on this basis that morality itself is fundamentally a matter of obedience to God's commands. But as we have already noted, this is not the line they took. While they did not deny God's supreme authority, they placed more weight on God's wisdom, and correlatively they were committed to showing the reasonableness of God's revealed moral law. For this very reason, the Decalogue was as much a problem for them as a solution to problems — or perhaps it would be better to say that reflection on the Decalogue forced them to confront problems intrinsic to moral reasoning itself.

These problems were brought into sharp focus through considerations of the conundrums raised by the seemingly sinful acts of the saints of ancient Israel as recorded in Scripture, for example, the polygamy of the patriarchs and Abraham's attempted sacrifice of Isaac.[56] These and similar actions seemed on their face to be violations of the natural law as the scholastics understood it, and yet the ancient Israelites were not condemned for them — on the contrary, in some cases at least they acted directly in response to God's express commands. Precisely because the scholastics did not accept a divine command model of ethics, which would have rendered God's decrees rationally opaque, these passages posed a serious theological problem. The God who promulgates the Ten Commandments apparently also sometimes commands their violation. This seems to imply that God is inconsistent, or worse yet, wicked or perverse; but clearly, these are intolerable conclusions.

Typically, the scholastics resolved this problem by arguing that God, as the author of the natural law and the Decalogue, can dispense from its pre-

56. For further particulars, see my *Natural and Divine Law,* 146-64.

cepts. This line of argument does not amount to an appeal to God's sheer authority as legislator because the scholastics also identified conditions and constraints for divine dispensation, generally limiting it in scope to include only particular expressions of the natural law, not its fundamental principles. For Aquinas, however, the authority of the Decalogue does not admit of dispensation, even by God:

> The precepts of the Decalogue contain the very intention of the legislator, that is, God. For the precepts of the first tablet, which ordain to God, contain the very order to a common and final good, whereas the precepts of the second tablet contain the very ordering of justice to be observed among human persons, that is to say, that nothing should be done to another without due cause, and to each should be rendered his due; for it is in accordance with this rationale that the precepts of the Decalogue are to be understood. And therefore the precepts of the Decalogue do not in any way admit of dispensation. (I-II 100.8)

Yet for Aquinas too, appeals to the norms of the Decalogue cannot resolve all the questions generated by moral reflection. In response to the objection that even human persons can give dispensations from some of the norms of the Decalogue, he goes on to explain that

> killing a person is prohibited in the Decalogue insofar as it has the character of something unjustified; for the precept contains the very rationale of justice. And human law cannot grant this, that a person might licitly be killed without justification. But the killing of malefactors or enemies of the republic is not unjustified. Hence, this is not contrary to a precept of the Decalogue, nor is such a killing a murder, which the Decalogue prohibits. . . . And similarly, if something is taken from another, which was his own, if he is obliged to lose it, this is not theft or robbery, which are prohibited by a precept of the Decalogue. . . .
>
> So therefore, these precepts of the Decalogue, with respect to the rational character of justice which they contain, are unchangeable. But with respect to some determination through application to individual acts, whether for example this or that is murder, theft or adultery, or not, this indeed is changeable; sometimes only by the divine authority, namely in those things which are instituted by God alone, as for example marriage and other things of this sort; and sometimes by human authority, with respect to those things which are committed to human jurisdiction. For with respect to those things, human persons act as the vicar of God, not however with respect to all things. (I-II 100.8 *ad* 3)

Aquinas's insistence that even God cannot dispense from the precepts of the natural law as expressed through the Decalogue might appear to underscore their supremely authoritative status and absolute character. But as these comments indicate, that is not his point. Rather, Aquinas emphasizes the rational character of these precepts, and correlatively, rejects the appeal to dispensations as inconsistent with God's wisdom as lawgiver. By the same token, Aquinas's analysis helps us to see more clearly just why these precepts, considered as a formulation of a rational moral law, posed a problem for Aquinas and his interlocutors. That is, these precepts are presented in Scripture, and regarded by the scholastics, as apodictic laws applying in every imaginable situation and allowing of no exceptions. Yet the scriptural context itself, to say nothing of the complexities of life in the scholastics' own time, confronted them with many instances of seemingly justifiable exceptions to these laws. How should these be understood?

Aquinas responds to this difficulty by arguing that when we are faced with a seeming exception to a moral rule, we should look for an explanation along these lines: this act is not an exception to the precept in question, because when we analyze the precept in the light of its underlying rationale, it is apparent that the act in question falls outside its scope. (If we cannot arrive at a persuasive explanation along these lines, then the dubious act will turn out after all to be a violation of the relevant rule.) Hence, when confronted by seeming exceptions to a moral rule, we should not look for grounds for dispensation or excuse; rather, we should reflect more carefully on our understanding of the rule itself, in terms of which it is to be interpreted and applied. This seems to me the right way to approach the problem at hand. Nonetheless, so far Aquinas has only suggested a starting point for an analysis of moral rules. A strategy of interpretative application can only work insofar as it is spelled out in terms of persuasive criteria for interpretation and application. Otherwise, what is to prevent us from justifying anything whatever on the grounds that the proposed course of action falls outside the scope or rationale of the relevant precepts? This is a central problem for a Thomistic theory of the natural law; indeed, I would argue that any adequate account of practical reason and moral judgment can only be developed in and through a process of working through this problem.[57]

In order to see how Aquinas addresses this problem, note first that the norms of the Decalogue are not only immediate expressions of the natural

57. I defend this claim in more detail in *Moral Action and Christian Ethics* (Cambridge: Cambridge University Press, 1995), 8-40; however, anyone familiar with that book will see that I have changed my mind on some points.

law for him, but also the precepts of a particular virtue, namely, justice (I-II 100.1; II-II 122.1). It is important not to be misled here by a supposed contrast between the ideals associated with the other virtues and the precepts associated with justice. We have already observed that the kinds of actions associated with the other virtues are in fact correlated with precepts, and by the same token, the precepts of the Decalogue likewise identify kinds of actions which are characteristic of justice as a virtue, directly or by contrast.[58] We have also seen that he analyzes every virtue in terms of its overall point or rationale as manifested by the paradigmatic kinds of actions associated with it. When Aquinas refers to the rationale of justice underlying the precepts of the Decalogue, he is invoking just this kind of analysis. In this case, the relevant paradigms are mostly negative rather than positive, and thus they represent a moral ideal negatively, as it were, by contrast with the paradigms of immoral behavior they present. Nonetheless, the same interpretative strategy that applies to the paradigms of the other virtues can also be applied to the paradigms of just and unjust behavior identified by the precepts of the Decalogue. Seen in this way, Aquinas's analysis of the precepts of the Decalogue would represent an attempt to clarify and extend the fundamental ideal of justice, namely, to render to each his or her due, through a more finely grained analysis of what we owe to one another in the way of mutual aid and forbearance (II-II 122.1).

This line of interpretation gains support when we examine passages in which Aquinas sets out explicitly what he takes the principles underlying the Decalogue to be. There we find that he takes the twofold injunction to love God and neighbor to be the epitome of justice, spelled out through all the precepts of the Decalogue (I-II 100.3, especially *ad* 1). He identifies this injunction as one of the *per se nota* principles of practical reason from which the norms of the Decalogue can be derived with minimal reflection (100.3, 5). With respect to the neighbor-regarding precepts, the rationale of justice is summarized by the injunctions to do no harm, and to respect one's special obligations (100.5, especially *ad* 4). Since the failure to respect one's particular obligations can itself be regarded as a kind of harm, we are justified in concluding that all the neighbor-regarding precepts can be regarded as expressions of a fundamental injunction to do no harm. And as we saw above, not only does Aquinas regard this injunction as basic, he also includes it among the *per se nota* principles of practical reason.

58. This line of analysis presupposes that there is no fundamental logical difference between moral rules, commonly so called, and the normative ideals associated with virtues such as temperance; I argue for this conclusion in more detail in my *Moral Action*, 125-66.

Given our usual understanding of self-evident principles, the injunctions to love God and neighbor, together with the norms of nonmaleficence and observance of particular obligations specifying the latter, may strike us as unlikely candidates for foundational practical principles. We may well agree that these are general norms, without agreeing that someone who denies them is guilty of self-contradiction or some other form of evident inconsistency. However, if we interpret them along the lines indicated in the previous section, as general metaphysical or natural principles as expressed in a rational creature, we can more readily see how Aquinas can regard them as *per se nota.* We already noted that for him the love of God is an expression of a universal tendency to love God in the sense of tending toward one's own perfection and toward the good of the cosmos considered as a whole. Similarly, love of neighbor, and its specifications in terms of particular obligations and nonmaleficence, should be understood as expressions of our specific nature as social animals. Among the inclinations informing our lives as creatures of a specific kind, we experience inclinations to live together with others of our kind in accordance with a structured way of life — and this implies not only seeking the company of our conspecifics, but doing so in such a way as to respect the structures which make a common life possible. Expressed in terms of fundamental practical principles, these would be equivalent to the injunctions Aquinas mentions as *per se nota* starting points for moral reflection pertaining to our life with others.

Whether the preceding captures Aquinas's intention or not, it seems to me the right way to understand the force of particular obligations and nonmaleficence as starting points for moral reflection. That is, these norms spontaneously present themselves to us as reasonable because they reflect basic aspects of our nature more broadly considered, and by the same token, the patterns of our individual and social lives are structured by these norms before it ever occurs to us to reflect on them.[59] Understood in this way, the precepts to love the neighbor and to fulfill one's particular obligations are plausible expressions of our nature as animals of a certain kind, that is to say, naturally social animals.

However, the prohibition against harming others raises a further difficulty. That is, if Aquinas, together with nearly every other scholastic in this period, regards "Do no harm" as a foundational principle for moral reasoning, then we would expect him to say that it is never morally permissible to

59. It is worth recalling that at least some of the scholastics in this period regarded love of neighbor and nonmaleficence as expressions of that nature we share with other animals; see my *Natural and Divine Law,* 81-82, for details.

inflict harm on another. Yet that does not seem to be his view. Aquinas and his fellow scholastics clearly believe it is sometimes legitimate to act in such a way as to inflict suffering, damage, and loss on another person. What is more, given the social nature of the human animal, it is difficult to see how they could fail to do so. In order to maintain a structured way of life among individuals who are less than perfectly cooperative, kindly, and just, and in circumstances which are usually not ideal, it would seem that some use of force, involving actual or implied threat of harm, would be an unfortunate necessity. Hence, the same aspects of our nature which give rise to imperatives of neighbor-love and its associated norms would also seem to generate an imperative that we violate one of these norms, namely, the norm of nonmaleficence itself.

This might suggest that for Aquinas and his interlocutors, the injunction to do no harm should be understood as a touchstone for evaluating action, but not necessarily as an absolute prohibition against harm which can never under any circumstances be violated. This line of argument gains in plausibility when we recall that "Do no harm" is presented as one specification of a more general injunction to love the neighbor.[60] To a considerable degree, our interpretation of nonmaleficence will turn on the way we relate it to this more general obligation. If we take the norm of nonmaleficence to be the sole or overriding criterion for applying the norm of neighbor-love, it would indeed seem to imply that we are never justified in inflicting harm for any reason whatever. But given the requirements of social life, and also given Aquinas's own suggestion that love of neighbor comprises respect for special obligations as well as nonmaleficence, we appear to be justified in interpreting the obligation of neighbor-love as the more comprehensive obligation, which can sometimes justify harming someone if broader or more exigent demands of neighbor-love require it.

On its face, this is an attractive reading. It offers a way of holding together seemingly inconsistent claims in Aquinas and the other scholastics. Even more importantly, it suggests a way of interpreting the substantive principle of nonmaleficence which takes it seriously while still acknowledging that the principle itself may require inflicting harm in some situations (for example, in defense of innocents). Nonetheless, a more comprehensive examination of Aquinas's specific moral views raises questions about this line of analysis, regarded as an interpretation of his views. By the time he analyzes

60. James Childress makes this point in the specific context of reflection on the legitimacy of war from a Christian standpoint in "Moral Discourse about War in the Early Church," *Journal of Religious Ethics* 12, no. 1 (1984): 2-18, specifically at 4-11.

the Decalogue, Aquinas has already defined "harm" as a *sinful* infliction of damage or loss.[61] This need not rule out the possibility that he is using the term in a more comprehensive way in I-II 100, but it does suggest that for him the idea of a legitimate harm is at least paradoxical. What is more, Aquinas unequivocally rules out some courses of actions that might conceivably be justified by a criterion of balancing and weighing harms; for example, he insists that killing the innocent can never be morally justified, even for the sake of the common good (II-II 64.6).

It might still be said that Aquinas allows for the infliction of harm in pursuit of more compelling duties of neighbor-love — *if* we understand "harm" in a general and nonmoral sense, and *if* the relevant criteria are not spelled out in a consequentialist way. However, we can arrive at a more precise formulation of Aquinas's own views, which will in turn point us toward a more satisfactory way of interpreting and specifying the basic moral precepts of the Decalogue. The key to understanding Aquinas's views, I want to suggest, lies in the fact that for him the virtue of justice is properly and characteristically directed toward rectifying the human person's actions *ad extra*, because these are the media through which the individual enters into and sustains, or violates and disrupts, right relations with others and with the community as a whole (I-II 60.2, 3; II-II 58.7, 8).[62] This observation, in turn, suggests that the norms of justice can only be analyzed and interpreted within a context set by his theory of human action. The remainder of this section will be devoted to developing this line of interpretation; in the process, I also hope to show that this way of analyzing moral norms is persuasive on its own terms.

In I-II 18, "On the goodness and evil of human actions, generally considered," Aquinas appropriates a set of traditional distinctions, which were subsequently to form the standard vocabulary for Catholic moral theology. In that question, he identifies four components of the human act, the traditional

61. As Brock observes in *Action and Conduct*, 55. The reference in question is I-II 73.8 *ad* 1, and it is worth noting that Aquinas uses the same word for "harm," *nocumentum*, both here and in the formulation of the principle "that no harm is to be done . . ." in I-II 100.5.

62. Acts *ad extra* should be distinguished from exterior acts, which are actions brought about immediately (that is to say, elicited) by some faculty other than the will, although under the command of the will — they are thus "exterior" to the principle in virtue of which they are human actions, that is to say, the will itself. Acts *ad extra*, in contrast, comprise what we usually think of as actions, that is to say, performances carried out through bodily movement, with (actual or intended) effects on the outside world. All acts *ad extra* will also be exterior acts, but the converse is not true; for example, a purely mental act of deliberation would be an exterior act because it would be elicited by the intellect, although under the command of the will. For further details, see Brock, *Action and Conduct*, 173.

"four fonts" in terms of which human acts are to be evaluated.[63] The first of these, the goodness of the act considered simply as such, does not enter in as a variable in moral analysis, since every action is necessarily good, considered in its most basic terms as an actually existing event. Nonetheless, this point serves as a valuable reminder that human action is intelligible as such, and therefore subject to moral evaluation, precisely insofar as it is a definite something, an event, stemming from the causal powers of some creature. The other three components of human acts do yield criteria for distinguishing between morally good and morally evil actions. That is, an act must be evaluated in terms of its object (I-II 18.2), the circumstances in which the act is done (18.3), and the agent's aim in acting (18.4). In order for an act to be morally justifiable, it must be good in every respect, that is, good or at least neutral in its object, with due consideration of circumstances, and directed toward a good, or at least an innocent aim (18.4 *ad* 3). Thus, an action which is bad with respect to its object cannot be redeemed by a good aim, and yet an act which is generically good will be corrupted by a bad aim, or by the agent's failure to do what she should in the circumstances in which she acts.

The object of an act, as Aquinas understands it, is expressed in terms of that description which indicates its species, or as we would say, indicates the kind of act it is, considered from a moral point of view (I-II 18.2). For example, we might describe a particular action as an act of murder, theft, or adultery, or alternatively, an act of capital punishment, reclaiming one's own property, or marital intercourse. Neither the agent's end in acting nor the circumstances of the act can be collapsed into the object. Thus, to take his own example, someone who steals in order to commit adultery is guilty of a twofold transgression in one act; that is, the object of his act of theft cannot be elided into his purpose in acting, namely, to have the means to commit adultery (18.7). Similarly, the circumstances in which the agent acts do not change its object, unless they have some intrinsic relation to it. Hence, for example, the place from which something is stolen is normally circumstantial, rather than defining the kind of act in question — an example that is relevant to a further point, as we will see (18.10, 11).

It might appear that on Aquinas's own terms, the aim for which an agent acts would always be a positive factor in the evaluation of the act, since as we know, every agent necessarily acts in pursuit of an actual or perceived

63. The history and context of Aquinas's analysis are usefully summarized by Pinckaers, *Ce qu'on ne peut jamais faire,* 20-33; for a more detailed account, see Odon Lottin, "Le problème de la moralité intrinsèque d'Abélard à saint Thomas d'Aquin," in *Psychologie et morale aux XIIe et XIIIe siècles,* vol. 2 (Louvain: Abbaye du Mont César, 1948), 421-65.

good. However, it is also the case, according to Aquinas, that the aim of the agent is determined by what the agent knowingly does, and if what she does is wrong in itself, her aim is ipso facto bad (I-II 19.1, especially *ad* 1). Thus, for example, someone who aims to sleep with a woman he knows to be someone else's wife has the intention of committing adultery, even though what he wants is not the act of adultery per se, but the pleasure he anticipates from the act. Thus, a morally bad intention cannot be redeemed simply by the fact that the agent acts with a view to securing some good. On first glance, it seems that Aquinas's analysis of actions in terms of the traditional "four fonts" provides us with a straightforward system for moral analysis. On this view, once we have established the object of the act, taken account of the agent's aim in acting, and determined whether the act is appropriate to its circumstances, we can readily decide whether it is morally justified or not, simply by applying the formula that a morally good act must be good in every respect. But matters are more complex than that. In order to apply Aquinas's analysis in the way just indicated, we must first of all be able to arrive at a correct description of the object of the act, seen from a moral point of view, and this will not always be an easy matter. This becomes apparent when we look more closely at the distinction between object and circumstance:

> . . . the process of reason is not determined to any one thing, but when anything is given, it can proceed further. And therefore, that which is considered in one act as a circumstance added onto the object, which determines the species of the act, can be considered a second time by ordaining reason as a principal condition of the object that determines the species of the act. And so, to take what is another's has its species from the formal notion of "another" [*ratione alieni*], and by this fact the act is constituted in the species of theft; and if the notion of place or time should be considered beyond this, it would fall under the formal description of a circumstance. But since reason can ordain also with respect to place or time, and other things of this sort, it happens that the condition of place is considered with respect to the object, as contrary to the order of reason; as for example, that reason ordains that no damage should be done to a sacred place. (I-II 18.10)

As these examples suggest, the object of an action is not simply given perspicuously in the description of an act. It certainly cannot be equated with "what is done," described in a supposedly neutral and straightforward way. Any action allows for indefinitely many possible true descriptions of "what is done," and for that reason, any description which focuses on certain aspects of the action as definitive of *the* object will necessarily be the *outcome* of an evaluative process, not its starting point.[64] But what kind of evaluation is required? At one point I was persuaded that the kind of evaluation in question can only be a moral judgment; that is to say, we must first arrive at a correct description of an act from a moral point of view, in order to determine the object of the action and to distinguish it from the aim and circumstances.[65] The difficulty with this line of interpretation, as I have now come to see, is that it cannot do justice to what Aquinas says about the object of the act as a distinctive and irreducible component of analysis. To put the point in another way, if the object of a particular act could only be established through a moral assessment of the act, then it would be dependent on an overall assessment of what is done (or proposed) in a particular situation, taking into account the agent's intentions and the circumstances in which she acts. This would imply that the determination of the object of the act — deciding whether a specific action should count, for example, as an act of murder, or of justified killing — would be dependent on a global assessment of intention and circumstances in a way that Aquinas explicitly rules out.[66]

The problem just described may seem to be a theoretical quibble of little practical interest. In order to appreciate what is really at stake here, we should

64. This is a very familiar point in the philosophy of action. Brock offers a helpful analysis of the relevant issues in *Action and Conduct,* 55-61. The main lines of contemporary discussion of these issues were set by Elizabeth Anscombe and Donald Davidson; see in particular Anscombe, *Intention,* 2nd ed. (Ithaca, N.Y.: Cornell University Press, 1963), 34-47, and "Under a Description" (1979), reprinted in *The Collected Philosophical Papers of G. E. M. Anscombe,* vol. 2 (Oxford: Basil Blackwell, 1981), 208-19; and Davidson, "Actions, Reasons, and Causes" (1963) and "The Individuation of Events" (1969), published in *Essays on Actions and Events,* 2nd ed. (Oxford: Clarendon, 2001), 3-20 and 163-80 respectively.

65. Specifically in my "The Moral Act in *Veritatis Splendor* and in Aquinas's *Summa theologiae:* A Comparative Analysis," in *Veritatis Splendor: American Responses,* ed. Michael E. Allsopp and John J. O'Keefe (Kansas City: Sheed and Ward, 1995), 278-95. To do myself justice, however, I do say even here that moral judgment involves an irreducible appeal to the object of the act, understood in a quasi-juridical way.

66. It is thus not surprising that John Bowlin accuses me of making Aquinas out to be a consequentialist in *Contingency and Fortune,* 107-14, and Charles Pinches warns me that "we must stop short of attributing to Aquinas' analysis such a fluidity that almost anything can be the object of the act, and therefore the source of its identifying species" (*Theology and Action: After Theory in Christian Ethics* [Grand Rapids: Eerdmans, 2002], 130-31). (As we noted above, similar worries are expressed, not about my own work, by both Pinckaers and Rhonheimer.) I do not believe that my earlier interpretations of Aquinas necessarily imply that he is a consequentialist, but Bowlin would be right to claim that I need to say more than I have done in order to forestall such an interpretation. Pinches's worry seems to me well placed — that is indeed just the problem that needs to be addressed.

keep in mind that the object of the act, as Aquinas interprets it, is equivalent to what we might describe as the moral concept under which the act is properly described. In other words, the object of the act identifies the kind of act in question, for example, an act of murder, theft, or sacrilege, or more positively, an act of almsgiving, chastity, or courage. As these examples indicate, the object is thus correlated with a moral precept forbidding or commending a particular kind of action, or with an ideal of virtue. (As we saw in the last chapter, the virtues are conceptualized in terms of their relation to kinds of actions; hence, every virtue corresponds to one or more objects of acts.) We thus come back to the problem with which we began this section. Do moral rules, understood in the usual way as precepts forbidding or commending certain kinds of actions, have an irreducible status in moral reasoning, or should they be interpreted as being without remainder expressions of some more fundamental moral principle or ideal? On the latter view, we might construe the traditional rules of morality as "rules of thumb," indicating courses of action that generally do not correspond to what our reasonable judgment overall would indicate as the correct course of action. As such, they would be provisional, and always finally dependent on some overall assessment of a particular act, seen in the context of its circumstances and intentions.

In the last chapter, we noted that the language of the virtues is ambiguous, because the paradigmatic kinds of actions associated with particular virtues may be inappropriate in a particular situation, or may be performed in service of vicious ends. As we saw, this ambiguity has led many to argue that virtue should be interpreted in terms of some one unitary principle or ideal, rather than being tied too closely to paradigms of particular virtues. It is now apparent that the same problem arises with respect to the kinds of actions correlated with traditional moral rules. These concepts function for us as paradigms for immoral or morally praiseworthy conduct (as the case may be). Yet it is easy to imagine situations in which a kind of action traditionally condemned might appear to be praiseworthy or even required — for example, confronted with a patient in extreme, intractable pain, a doctor may feel justified, or even morally compelled, to carry out an act of euthanasia. The force of examples such as these, and the debates they have generated, have led many moral theorists to argue that moral duty or rectitude should be analyzed without remainder in terms of some one ideal or principle. In Charles Pinches's felicitous phrase, they defend some version of "principle monism," according to which all moral judgments can be analyzed as derived from, or exemplifying, one supreme norm.[67]

67. Pinches, *Theology and Action,* 40-41; in what follows, I am indebted to his develop-

Usually, this unitary moral norm is identified with rationality, and rationality in turn tends to be interpreted along one of the two lines identified in the first section of this chapter. (Although those persuaded by a sentimentalist account of morality tend to emphasize the particularity and heterogeneity of moral discourse, and therefore typically do not take part in this particular exercise.) Many theorists argue that a moral act should be evaluated in terms of its overall circumstances, including especially its consequences, thus evaluating it in terms of the overall balance of good versus bad outcomes that it produces — however specifically these are to be understood and assessed. This approach yields some form of consequentialism, either utilitarianism in its moderate or radical forms or some version of proportionalism as defended by many Catholic moral theologians since Vatican II. Others analyze morality by reference to the agent's intention, understood in terms of his stance toward some rationally apprehended ideal, principle, or intelligible good. This approach would yield some version of Kantianism, or a theory akin to the "new natural law" defended by Grisez and Finnis. Both approaches focus on the evaluation of particular acts, and they develop that evaluation by reference to some single rational criterion in terms of which every other putative moral criterion must be either interpreted or disregarded. Hence, on neither view is there any place for an independent appeal to the kind of action in question. This is apparent with respect to consequentialist approaches, but it may not be so evident with respect to Kantian approaches. However, as Grisez and his collaborators have recently argued, on their view the proper moral description of an action is exhaustively determined by the agent's intention, understood in terms of the stance of his will toward intelligible goods, and not by the kinds of objective features traditionally identified as constituting the object of the act — an approach which again leaves no place for the object of the act, considered as an independent component of moral evaluation.[68]

In both its consequentialist and Kantian forms, this line of analysis identifies morality *tout court* with an ideal of practical rationality, however more precisely that ideal is to be understood. Thus, on this view our concepts of morally problematic kinds of actions, which provide us with paradigms for moral wrongdoing, are at best approximations (by contrast) of an ideal of ra-

---

ment of a similar critique at 34-58, although I do not want to presume that he would agree with what I say here. I also draw on Steven Long's critique of Grisez and Finnis developed in "A Brief Disquisition regarding the Nature of the Object of the Moral Act according to St. Thomas Aquinas," *The Thomist* 67 (January 2003): 45-71. The same demurral of course applies.

68. See John Finnis, Germain Grisez, and Joseph Boyle, "'Direct' and 'Indirect': A Reply to Critics of Our Action Theory," *The Thomist* 65 (2001): 1-44; Long's article cited above is a response to this article.

tionality, which as such are dispensable once we have adequately formulated the ideal itself. To put the same point in Aquinas's terms, on this view the object of the act has no independent weight in the overall moral assessment of the act, but is elided into either the circumstances or the intention, one or the other of which would be regarded as morally determinative. Framed in these terms, it is apparent that this is not Aquinas's view.

Moreover, considered on its own merits, this line of analysis is not plausible. In the first place, it cannot account for the moral concepts we actually have, in terms of which we develop our best understandings of what it means to live a morally good life or to act wrongly. In effect, this approach counsels us to dispense with the basic concepts in terms of which we reflect morally, terms which are necessarily presupposed in the formulation of the problems at hand. We cannot rule out this possibility in advance. But this is clearly a counsel of desperation, and we have every reason to avoid it if we can. Secondly and more fundamentally, this line of analysis runs into the same difficulty we encountered with respect to the parallel way of analyzing the virtues generally. That is, it cannot provide norms of reasonableness as embodied in a particular inclination, and for that reason it leaves us with no way to account for Aquinas's insistence that morality is a perfection of the agent, implying the full and appropriate development of his diverse capacities. Similar considerations led us to conclude in the last chapter that for Aquinas, reasonableness as a norm of virtue is not formulated with respect to general ideals of consistency or expediency, but is drawn in the first instance from the intelligible structure of the capacity for action disposed by the virtue in question. The same line of analysis applies to justice, considered as a virtue of the will and the preeminent virtue disposing us to right action — or so I hope to show in what follows.

At this point it will be helpful to return to the Thomistic formulation of the problem at hand. That is, Aquinas holds that the moral evaluation of an action must take account of its object, aim, and circumstances. It would seem that we cannot determine the object of the act without evaluating it in some way, and yet this evaluation cannot be a moral evaluation. What, then, are the terms in which the object of the act is to be evaluated? Aquinas answers this question in terms suggesting that he is after all prepared to analyze moral norms in terms of a unitary ideal of reason; that is, he claims that the object of the act is determined by reason (I-II 18.5). In the last chapter, we noted that he makes a similar claim about the virtues, claiming that they take their norm from conformity to reason. And here, once again, we need to ask just what Aquinas means by this claim.

In order to begin to answer this question, it is helpful to turn to the *secunda secundae*, where we find Aquinas's discussion of the specific details of the moral life. It is here that he repeatedly raises and addresses questions of the form, "What kind of act is this?" or in other words, what is the moral species of this or that kind of action? And since the object of the act determines its species (I-II 18.5), it follows that the generic descriptions which give the species of actions will also describe their objects. When we turn to an examination of the relevant texts (especially, but not exclusively, found in the treatise on justice, II-II 57-122), we confirm that the generic concepts in terms of which Aquinas identifies the objects of acts are generally correlated with traditional moral rules: for example, murder (II-II 64), injury (65), theft and robbery (66), fraud (77), usury (78), and lying (110). In most cases these kinds of actions also involve some kind of harm to another, or to the agent herself (I-II 100.5; II-II 72.1).

But this is not the whole story. When we look more closely at these generic concepts, it becomes apparent that they are also typically associated with particular natural kinds, or species, of actions (cf. I-II 1.3 *ad* 3). In very many cases, the moral concepts can be analyzed in terms of natural kinds, plus some qualification. Murder is a kind of killing, but there are also legitimate forms of killing; fornication and adultery are forms of sexual intercourse, but there is also a legitimate type of sexual intercourse; and so forth. Not every morally significant kind of action fits this pattern so clearly; on the one hand, some are not linked in any obvious way with a natural action kind (for example, fraud), and on the other hand, there are a few which seem to be identified without remainder with a natural action kind (in particular, the unnatural sexual sins).[69] Nonetheless, the analysis of such concepts as "murder" suggests what is at least a general approach for Aquinas — we identify a natural kind of action ("killing"), which is then qualified through reason into two or more moral action kinds ("murder," "capital punishment").

We will turn in a moment to a closer examination of the kinds of qualifications that Aquinas has in mind. At this point I want to focus on the other element of this analysis, namely, the distinction between the natural and the moral species or object of an action. As Aquinas observes, almost in passing, two actions may fall within the same natural species while falling within two distinct moral species (I-II 1.3 *ad* 3). Taken by itself, this observation would seem to be so straightforward as to be almost banal. But on reflection, it invites

69. Nonetheless, I believe that every moral action kind could in fact be analyzed in terms of a distinction between a natural kind of action and the act as qualified morally; I return to this point below. At this point in the argument, however, it is only necessary to show that such an analysis applies to many moral concepts, including many of central importance to us.

interesting questions. That is to say, how do we determine the natural species of the act — how do we determine that this particular act should count as an act of killing, or an act of sexual intercourse, or an act of giving succor, or an act of self-protection or self-defense? It may seem that the answers to these kinds of questions would be obvious, and in many instances they will be — it is very difficult to mistake a standard act of sexual intercourse for anything other than what it is. But in other cases the answer will not be so obvious — there are many ways to kill, to defend oneself, to give aid, and so forth. If this is so, then it would seem that in some cases, at least, we will find it just as difficult to determine the natural object of an action as to determine its moral object.

Once again, we are back to our initial problem — that is to say, we cannot describe an act in the correct way without some kind of evaluation. But at this point, we begin to see more clearly what kind of evaluation is required. That is, in order to determine the natural object of an act, we need to evaluate it from the perspective of the way of life characteristic of the human person, considered as one kind of living creature among others. And there is nothing especially puzzling or problematic about this kind of evaluation. We have all the resources we need to carry it out from our working concept of human nature, developed along the lines set forth in the last two chapters. Recall that our concept of human nature is centrally a concept of the way of life proper to us as a specific kind of creature, in terms of which we can develop a (tentative) definition through an account of the "ordered functional capacities" that constitute the human form of existence. This kind of account, in turn, will imply — will, indeed, largely consist in — an account of the kinds of actions through which a distinctively human life is characteristically or typically expressed. The kinds of actions will be identified not in terms of their material descriptions, whatever exactly those would be, but by reference to functional capabilities to do the kinds of things that are necessary for the individual or social flourishing of the kind of creature we are — capabilities to sustain one's life through eating and drinking, to care for one's young through giving succor, to defend oneself aggressively, and the like. Hence, evaluations at this level will be normative, but not in a moral sense; rather, they will be normative in the broader teleological sense determined by reference to the well-being, understood as the proper and normal functioning, of the human animal.

Once again, we can helpfully follow Aquinas's advice to compare human inclinations with those of nonrational animals, in order to arrive at a clearer understanding of the former. As we saw in chapter 2, our concept of any kind of living creature will consist centrally in having some grasp of the way of life characteristic of that kind of creature. And clearly, this implies that we have a good idea of the kinds of operations that a given kind of creature typically performs. A black widow spider typically spins a web, and has her mate as a postcoital snack; these are typical kinds of operations for this species of spider, but not for every species of spider. For an animal this simple, we will often be able to identify and describe typical kinds of operations in terms of the relevant observable behaviors, and for this reason the fundamentally teleological character of these assessments may not be apparent. But when we turn our attention to only slightly more complex kinds of animals, we see more clearly that we cannot reliably identify the kinds of operations an animal is performing without some sense of the way these kinds of operations contribute to the well-being at an individual, social, or species-wide level. There is more than one way even to build a nest, and many ways to stalk one's prey or to forage for food, to engage in mating and dominance rituals, and to give sustenance and care to one's young. The more complex the kind of animal, the wider the range of behaviors that can count under these kinds of descriptions, and the more we will need to be able to grasp the point of a given item of behavior in order to determine what kind of operation it represents.

The greater complexity of the human person makes it still more difficult to identify particular acts in terms of their natural objects. Nonetheless, we too are naturally inclined to certain kinds of actions which are proper to the patterns of activity characteristic of us as a species. And since we are a kind of living creature, these kinds of actions can be identified and described in terms of their contribution to individual or communal well-being. As a kind of animal, we are inclined to some kinds of actions which sustain, express, and extend our existence in straightforward ways, either directly by taking in means of sustenance and reproducing our kind (eating, sexual intercourse), or indirectly by warding off threats through acts of defensiveness or aggression (flight, attack, killing). These kinds of actions are not just random patterns of response and activity — they stem from, and are informed by, the intelligibilities proper to our nature. Furthermore, because we are rational animals, we are capable of understanding and experiencing these kinds of actions in terms of these natural intelligibilities — we spontaneously think of eating, sexual intercourse, and the like as positive and desirable, whereas we typically regard killing as fearful and to be avoided. These natural intelligibilities do not themselves exhaust moral judgment, but our moral judgments build on them and qualify them in various ways. Moreover, they set constraints of plausibility (not logical necessity) on those judgments. Finally, because these kinds of actions are natural to all of us, they have a special saliency, both for our experience of ourselves as rational agents and our assignations of responsibility to others. As Eric D'Arcy observes, there seem to be some kinds of actions — killing is again the parade example — that are always morally significant, even if not always in a clear or decisive way.[70] In other words, some natural kinds of actions are always morally relevant in the sense of prompting a moral evaluation, even though they do not force a negative (or positive) evaluation.

Aquinas's distinction between the natural and the moral object of an act thus indicates how we might determine the object of an act through an evaluation that does not depend on a moral assessment of a particular action, globally considered. This evaluation will proceed in two stages. In the first stage, we identify the natural object of an action through an analysis framed in terms of human well-being. Analysis at this level involves a normative assessment of the act, insofar as it relates the act to the overall aim of human flourishing broadly considered. Yet this will not be a moral analysis, since as we have seen, the ideal of well-being taken by itself does not yield moral norms. Hence, at this level we identify the natural object of the act through a judgment which is evaluative but not yet moral, and which therefore does not presuppose a moral assessment of the act taken as a whole.

At the same time, Aquinas clearly holds that we can sometimes determine the moral object of a particular action prior to forming an overall moral assessment of it. This implies that our evaluation of the object of an act must move to a second stage, in which we identify the moral object of the act in terms that are in some way tethered to our assessment of the natural object — since even at this level we need to develop an evaluation of the object in terms that do not depend on an overall assessment of the particular act. That is to say, we need to identify rational considerations enabling us to distinguish between morally permissible and prohibited forms of (for example) killing, apart from some consideration of the overall circumstances of the act and the agent's aim in acting. However — and this is the critical point — not just any kinds of rational considerations will do. Rather, these considerations must be intelligibly connected in some way to the place that the natural kind of act in question holds in the way of life characteristic of human beings. That, at least, is the conclusion suggested by the way in which Aquinas distinguishes, and then connects, the natural and moral species of the act.

In the last chapter, we saw that Aquinas interprets the norm of reasonableness in terms of reasonable expressions of desire, anger, and the like. In a similar fashion, he interprets reasonableness with respect to human interactions in terms of what counts as a reasonable expression of aggression, self-

70. See his *Human Acts: An Essay in Their Moral Evaluation* (Oxford: Clarendon, 1963), 18-39.

defense, aid and succor, and the like. Although he does not say so explicitly, this line of interpretation further implies that these norms of reasonableness are drawn from the exigencies of social existence, of a kind typical of the social animal we are. Just as the other virtues consist in dispositions to act in accordance with the fullest possible development of our faculties for desire and aggression, understood with reference to the criterion of the well-being of the agent, so the virtue of justice consists in a disposition to act in accordance with the fullest possible development of our capacities as social animals, with reference to criteria set by the well-being of others, and the community taken as a whole.

Understood in this way, Aquinas's analysis of actions in terms of their object, circumstances, and aim presupposes and incorporates the general scholastic approach to natural law analysis, according to which actions are analyzed in terms of the natural inclinations they represent, together with the rational judgments which shape and direct them. Indeed, this form of analysis is almost ubiquitous. We have already seen one example in Huguccio's analysis of marriage. For another example, which will bring us still closer to Aquinas, consider the way Philip the Chancellor analyzes the prohibition against murder:

> Since therefore it belongs to nature as nature to preserve the individual, to kill a person is said to be contrary to the natural law in this respect, insofar as nature as nature directs this. Nature as reason directs us not to kill an innocent person. However, since it is often the case that a person is evil and a malefactor, nature as reason directs concerning such a person that he should be killed. And so a judge kills a malefactor, insofar as the law is consonant with nature considered as reason, and in this case, to kill a person would not be contrary to the natural law understood in this way. However, to kill an innocent person knowingly would be contrary to the natural law, because it is contrary to that which nature, as reason, directs. (Lottin, 114)

When we compare Philip's remarks to Aquinas's own analysis of the distinctions between legitimate and illegitimate kinds of killing, it is apparent that Aquinas presupposes the kind of analysis exemplified in Philip's longer text. As Philip observes, and as Aquinas would agree, we have traditionally identified certain kinds of killing as defensible — killing in self-defense, in pursuit of a justified war, or as a state-sanctioned form of punishment. Other kinds are regarded by default as murder — a line of interpretation summed up (and oversimplified) by the slogan, "No direct killing of the innocent."

But is there anything more to be said about the distinctions between justified and unjustified forms of killing (to continue with this example), than the sheer fact that these are the distinctions we make? Philip's remarks remind us that for the scholastics, appeals to a natural law are fundamentally permissive in force — that is, if anything can be considered a genuine expression of human nature, it is regarded as good, and therefore as morally justified. But what counts as a genuine expression of human nature? Aquinas's account of the inclinations, regarded as expressions of human nature, provides us with the key to developing such an account. We have already remarked on his claim that the human inclinations are correlated with some virtue (or presumably, virtues) through which they can be appropriately expressed. Correlatively, any kind of action which can reasonably be construed as an appropriate expression of a human inclination is regarded as morally justified, with the norms of appropriateness being formulated in the light of exigencies of individual well-being (in the case of acts of temperance or fortitude) or the demands of others or the common good (in the case of acts of justice).

This does not mean that individual or communal well-being, taken by itself, determines what counts as an act of justice, any more than the other virtues can be formulated at the level of well-being taken by itself. We will return to this point in the next section. At this stage, however, I simply want to observe that justified kinds of actions are regarded as justified because they can be construed as reasonable expressions of natural inclinations. The object of an act of communal defense is defined in terms of its orientation toward the common good, and as such, it is a legitimate expression of one's aggressive inclinations, given the exigencies of social existence (II-II 64.2; a particular act of communal defense may of course be immoral, even though this kind of act is legitimate). Similarly, as Aquinas famously notes, an act of self-defense is properly defined in terms of the agent's intention to preserve her own life (II-II 64.7). Because self-preservation reflects a genuine inclination of human nature, and because no one is required to prefer the life of another to her own, therefore even a lethal act of self-defense should be regarded as an act of self-preservation, which is good in kind, and not an act of murder, which would of course be bad in kind.

At the beginning of this section, we noted that it is difficult to see how Aquinas can identify "Do no harm" as one of the *per se nota* principles of practical reason, in light of the fact that he seems to allow for justified acts of harming others. We can now see more exactly how he interprets this claim. Any kind of action which can legitimately be construed as a reasonable expression of a natural human inclination toward some good is regarded in the light of the natural good at which it aims; in other words, the generically positive character of the act is morally decisive in such an instance, and any damage or loss incurred by the act is regarded as lying outside the agent's proper intention. In other words, on this view a given kind of act only counts as a legitimate expression of a natural human inclination if it can be construed as a necessary or appropriate way of securing individual or collective well-being. The norms for necessity and appropriateness are not themselves given by this analysis alone; rather, they must be developed through further reflection on the exigencies of well-being and virtue, as these are pursued individually and communally. Nonetheless, this kind of reflection can be carried out prior to assessment of particular acts; indeed, it almost certainly will be, through communal processes of reflection on the proper shape of human life, the scope and limits of our shared responsibilities, and the like.

At the same time, however, it would be a mistake to conclude that the relevant norms can be formulated with reference to general considerations of individual and communal well-being alone. We noted above that on Aquinas's analysis, each virtue is informed by an ideal of reasonableness grounded in the capacity disposed by the virtue — and so, for example, the proximate norm for the virtue of temperance is set by the exigencies of reasonable desire, determined through reflection on the proper relation between desire and well-being. Can we develop the same kind of analysis here, showing how the kinds of actions proper to the virtue of justice stem from an ideal of reasonableness grounded in the will?

In order to appreciate the force of this question, it will be helpful to recapitulate the main lines of Aquinas's analysis of justice. On his view, every human act is elicited or commanded by the will. Nonetheless, Aquinas regards justice as the distinctive and characteristic moral virtue of the will, because it pertains to justice to rectify the will seen in relation to others and to the good of the community as a whole. That is to say, just as temperance and fortitude dispose the passions in such a way as to correspond to the agent's overall good, so justice disposes the will (which is naturally disposed toward the agent's overall good) to desire and pursue the interests of others, and of the community as a whole. That is why Aquinas also regards justice as the characteristic virtue of our acts *ad extra;* it is through such acts that the individual expresses and maintains relationships with others and with the community.

We are therefore looking for an analysis of the precepts of justice which accounts for these in terms of the exigencies of rational action, regarded both as stemming from the will and as properly ordered with respect to others' well-being and the common good. In the next section, I will develop such an analysis. I will do so by returning to a question flagged earlier in this section — that is to say, is it possible to defend the irreducible character of our basic moral concepts against the different versions of principle monism represented by Kantian and consequentialist alternatives? As we noted, such a defense requires us to show that we can plausibly distinguish between what we do and what we allow to happen; moreover, it requires some account of why this distinction matters morally in the way that common morality presupposes that it does. This task, in turn, will call for further analysis of the structure of human acts, considered both as expressions of human agency and as a medium of human interrelationships. And that, of course, is just the kind of analysis we need in order to show how the precepts of justice stem from the intelligible structures of the characteristic appetite of the human creature — that is to say, the will.

4. Moral Norms as Law and Boundary

At this point it will be helpful to summarize our conclusions thus far. Aquinas, together with his interlocutors, regards reason as a law, insofar as reasoned reflection on basic human needs and inclinations gives rise to definite, binding rules for action. The precepts of the Decalogue are regarded as a canonical summary of these rules, and the Decalogue thus comprises a set of paradigms by which correct moral reasoning is evaluated. At the same time, Aquinas also regards these as the paradigmatic precepts associated with justice as a virtue. This suggests that these precepts can be analyzed in basically the same way as we would analyze the paradigmatic ideals associated with the other virtues, even though these precepts are mostly negative, and undoubtedly point to a more complex ideal than we find associated with temperance or fortitude. Seen in this light, the precepts of the Decalogue reflect an ideal of justice, or as we might prefer to say, an ideal of personal and social right relations, which is intelligible and defensible as one component of the life of virtue. Thus, this ideal finds its meaning and point in the context of an ideal of happiness, which presupposes but cannot be reduced to an account of human well-being. Hence, the ideal of right relations being developed here is tantamount to an ideal of the good life as enjoyed by individuals in their relations to one another and to their wider communities. As such, it implies that the precepts informing the ideal of justice are integrally connected to aspects of human well-being, even though justice, like the other virtues, cannot be equated without qualification to well-being.

For better or for worse, this line of analysis suggests a picture of morality that fits with many of the most basic assumptions underlying common morality. On this view, moral reflection and judgment are properly focused in the first instance on what the agent does, and more specifically on the kinds of actions he performs or fails to perform. Of course, moral reflection also focuses on attributions of responsibility, judgments of character, and the like — on assessments of agents rather than their acts — but these kinds of judgments are conceptually dependent on our judgments about the kinds of actions the agent performs, through which she merits praise or blame, or reveals her character. As Alan Donagan puts it, judgments about acts are first-order judgments, whereas judgments about agents are second-order judgments.[71] Moreover, on this view our reflections on acts are informed at critical points by our concepts of kinds of actions which carry some moral value in themselves, even apart from any consideration of the agent's intention or the circumstances in which he acts. While some of these are regarded as positive in themselves, many others are morally bad in themselves, for example, murder, theft, and fraud. These latter kinds of actions cannot be morally justified, even in those situations in which we could achieve an important good or prevent a serious evil by performing an act of the relevant kind. To put the point in another way, at least some moral precepts forbidding certain kinds of actions are either absolute — they cannot be overridden under any circumstances — or very nearly absolute, if we hold open the possibility that they might be overridden in exceptional situations. "Absolute" carries unfortunate connotations, since it can suggest that the relevant norms are not only exceptionless, but stand in need of neither interpretation nor application in order to be carried out — a view that is not credible, as Aquinas certainly recognized. For that reason, we will do better to follow contemporary usage by referring to this as a deontological view of moral norms, with the understanding that this term should not be understood here in a Kantian sense.

I noted that a Thomistic theory of the natural law fits with common moral assumptions for better or for worse. I would say "for better," because we would expect a theory of the natural law to offer an account of widespread and pervasive features of morality, which have at least some claim to be regarded as expressions of a characteristically human way of life. The fit between the theory and one of the most basic assumptions of common morality thus counts in its favor, because it suggests that this theory does indeed capture aspects of our shared nature as reflected in the basic structures of morality. But many others would say "for worse," on the grounds that moral absolutism, even in its weaker versions, cannot be defended.[72] On the one hand, there is a widespread sense that this view is too stringent — it commits us to

71. The distinction between first- and second-order precepts is taken from Donagan, *The Theory of Morality,* 52-56.

72. Kagan lays out these alternatives in *The Limits of Morality,* 3-4.

courses of action that are manifestly worse for all concerned than would otherwise be the case, for no clear and defensible reason. On the other hand, it might be argued that this view is not stringent enough. It allows us to evade responsibility for loss and suffering that we could have prevented, on the grounds — specious, on this view — that we did not inflict these damages through our actions, nor did we have a particular obligation to prevent them. Actually, a number of critics hold both views, arguing that moral absolutism is too stringent in some respects and not stringent enough in others.

The convergence of these two lines of criticism suggests that they have something in common, and on closer inspection this turns out to be the case. That is, both depend — not exclusively, but to a very considerable extent — on challenging the distinction between acting and allowing necessarily presupposed by any consistent version of a deontologial morality. For critics of such views, the relevant distinction either cannot be drawn or cannot be made to bear the moral weight their defenders place on it. And as these critics rightly point out, unless we can draw such a distinction, a deontological position is logically incoherent. For on the latter view, we are sometimes obliged to avoid doing an action of a certain kind, even though as a consequence, something (arguably) much worse will come about. If there is no moral difference between doing and allowing, then it would seem that we are just as responsible for the bad outcome we permit as we would be for the bad act, were we to perform it. In such a case, we would be faced with a conflict of duties that could not be resolved, even in principle, and such a conclusion would put paid to a defense of the reasonableness of morality. Those who deny this distinction are faced with no such dilemma; on their view, we should simply choose whichever course of action will produce the best results overall (however precisely that is to be spelled out).

This approach has the merit of logical simplicity, but in contrast to a Thomistic theory of natural law, it runs deeply counter to widespread moral intuitions. Taken to its logical conclusion, it would seem to imply that there is no moral difference between actively harming someone and failing to come to her aid; and since we are always confronted, more or less directly, with people in severe distress, this seems to imply that we are continually engaged in courses of action that are tantamount to the infliction of severe injury, loss, and death. Some philosophers and a few theologians have not hesitated to draw this conclusion.[73] Many others find themselves in the uncomfortable

73. Among philosophers, the most noteworthy defenders of this position would include Singer, Kagan, and Unger; see n. 17 above for citations. In addition, the theologian Garth Hallet defends a similar view in *Priorities and Christian Ethics* (Cambridge: Cambridge University

position of Jonathan Bennett, who argues at some length that the making/allowing distinction does not stand up to close analysis, but then goes on to say that he cannot accept the moral consequences of his own arguments: "For me, then, the proposed morality is too demanding (not to be *plausible,* but) to be *acceptable:* I am unwilling to hold myself to such a standard."[74] Hence, he is left with two alternatives, neither of which is satisfactory: "either to accord fundamental weight to the making/allowing distinction [which on his own analysis is not tenable], or to accept the tremendously exigent morality's condemnation of our conduct, as some have done and I will not."[75] (I prefer the formulation "doing/allowing" on sheer stylistic grounds.)

Bennett goes on to admit that this is an awkward conclusion. "Awkward" hardly seems to do justice to the case; if he is right, then we may well have to conclude that, properly understood, the demands of morality are so impossibly burdensome that we are not only unable to attain them, but cannot even regard them as a desirable or attractive ideal for living. In contrast, I would agree with Philippa Foot that "one criterion for a good moral system is that it should be possible to demand reciprocity from every individual because of the good the system renders to him. But I am sure that this is not the only condition for a good moral system. It has also, for instance, to be such that *anyone* can conform to it and still live well in the ordinary, non-moral, sense. This condition may well be what limits the demands of altruistic action, and a whole new non-utilitarian enquiry should open up here."[76]

As Foot's comments suggest, the point at issue is connected to the questions posed at the end of the last section. In that section I argued that an ac-

---

Press, 1998). It should be added that neither Unger nor Hallet advocates strict consequentialism, at least in the relevant projects. Unger recognizes the legitimacy of some claims arising out of particular relationships and believes these place constraints on acceptable courses of action; see *Living High,* 12-13. As for Hallet, he elsewhere defends a principle of value maximization (as we noted above), but insists that his arguments in *Priorities* do not depend on that principle. Rather, he argues on the basis of what he describes as the Christian obligation to give absolute priority to the claims of the poor — to prefer the neediest to the nearest, as he puts it. The main lines of the argument are set out at 1-38. It is not clear to me that such a commitment would be consistent with a principle of value maximization.

74. Jonathan Bennett, *The Act Itself* (Oxford: Clarendon, 1995), 162, emphasis in original.

75. Bennett, *The Act Itself,* 163; the chapter as a whole, 143-63, offers an excellent summary and analysis of the relevant issues.

76. Philippa Foot, "Morality, Action, and Outcome," in *Moral Dilemmas and Other Topics in Moral Philosophy* (Oxford: Clarendon, 2002), 88-104, here 104, emphasis in original. Similarly, Leo Katz argues that the act-omission distinction is central to law because it draws on "some very powerful and deep-seated intuitions" (*Ill-Gotten Gains: Evasion, Blackmail, Fraud, and Kindred Puzzles of the Law* [Chicago: University of Chicago Press, 1996], 46; see more generally 1-132).

tion which represents an appropriate pursuit of a natural inclination should be regarded as a legitimate expression of human nature, and therefore as good in kind, even if it also involves inflicting damage or loss on another. Clearly, if this line of analysis is going to have real moral force, we need a credible account of the relevant criteria for appropriateness. These criteria will be drawn from the ideals proper to the virtue of justice, which for Aquinas and his interlocutors includes norms for right relations among others as well as proper norms for social institutions. As the following analysis will indicate, the ideals of justice comprehensively understood are in fact integrally connected with the boundaries sustained through human action, as these inform common morality. These ideals cannot be analyzed without remainder in these terms, but they presuppose them and incorporate them — just as the ideals of the other virtues presuppose and formulate the goods and exigencies proper to other forms of human well-being.

The issues raised in debates over the scope and limits of moral responsibility are inextricably connected with the theory of action, and these topics taken together constitute one of the most complex and widely debated sets of topics among both moral philosophers and (in somewhat different terms) theologians. It would go well beyond the scope of a book devoted to another topic to attempt to address these issues in any detail. My aim in this section is more modest. I hope to show that a Thomistic account of the natural law has the resources necessary to defend a credible distinction between acting and allowing, and to draw out the moral implications of that distinction as seen within the context of this theory of the natural law. I will not attempt to assess and respond to all the relevant arguments in the contemporary debates, and for that reason the conclusions of this section will necessarily be tentative. Nonetheless, I do at least hope to show that a Thomistic theory of the natural law can provide a cogent and persuasive account of what Bennett describes as "the act itself," and moreover, that this account is integrally connected to an ideal of justice consistent with a way of life that (as Foot would say) anyone can adopt, while living well — both in the ordinary, nonmoral sense and in the sense of enjoying a life of happiness constituted by the practice of the virtues.

Let us begin, therefore, by examining the case that there is no morally relevant distinction between bringing something about and allowing a similar outcome to occur through adopting an alternative course of action. In order to see what is at stake, it will be helpful to return to the example of killing.[77] To a

77. Debates over the morality of killing have generated an enormous literature. For a most helpful and comprehensive guide, see John Reeder, Jr., *Killing and Saving: Abortion, Hunger, and War* (University Park: Pennsylvania State University Press, 1996).

very considerable extent, debates over the doing/allowing distinction take their starting points from our distinctions between killing someone and allowing him to die, whether in a medical context or in the context of giving or withholding lifesaving aid. Suppose, for example, the case of a dying man in extreme and intractable pain. His doctor sincerely wants to relieve his suffering, and moreover she knows that whatever she does she cannot cure him or save his life. As it happens, she has two courses of action open to her — she can refrain from giving some further life-sustaining treatment, thus allowing her patient to die, or she can simply kill him, (let us say) through the administration of a fast-acting painless poison. Is there a moral difference between these two courses of action?

Until recently, almost no one would have denied that the latter act, killing the patient by poison, is a morally impermissible act of murder, even though many would be hesitant to judge too harshly in such painful circumstances. Yet no such onus was attached to the former course of action. There is no obligation to give or undergo medical treatment, especially when such treatment will forseeably yield little or no long-term benefits. Hence, the doctor who chooses not to prolong the life of a terminally ill patient in great pain would be regarded as acting in a wise and compassionate way, not as someone guilty of murder. Yet in either case the outcome is the same — that is to say, the patient is dead. What is more, in each case the patient's death comes about through a choice to act in a way that will forseeably have just this outcome. What, then, is the basis for the moral distinction between the two cases? It might appear that there is no such distinction — that is, we might claim that an individual is responsible for whatever forseeably comes about as a result of her choices, whether these result directly and immediately from what she does or come about as a result of her inaction. This line of argument can cut either way; some have argued that the doctor in the former case is *just as* guilty of the death of her patient as she would be if she killed him outright, but others have argued that the doctor is *no more* guilty of murder in the latter case than in the former case.

We may feel intuitively that even when two courses of activity bring about the same results, nonetheless it matters morally how these results come about. Nonetheless, it has proven to be difficult to spell out just why the specific causal chain leading to some final outcome should matter so much, or even to say with precision just what the relevant causal chains are. These difficulties have led naturally to the conclusion that either there is no credible general distinction to be made between doing and allowing, or at the least, that this distinction cannot bear the moral weight it has traditionally been given. Hence, critics of the deontological position mount what is essentially a negative argument, but it is a powerful argument nonetheless. If we cannot offer a convincing analysis of a supposedly fundamental distinction, then it is indeed reasonable to suspect that our initial intuitions are muddled and in need of correction.

This line of attack is sometimes augmented through an analysis of what it might mean to say that someone causes a given result, or more generally speaking, brings something about through acting in some way. No one to my knowledge has developed this line of analysis more carefully, or to more telling effect, than Bennett. The key to Bennett's analysis is reflected in the ironic title of his book, *The Act Itself* — ironic, because Bennett believes it is a mistake to regard actions (or events) as somehow individuated in themselves. He does not deny the reality of activity, events, and causation, but on his view these are better understood as forming an ongoing process rather than a series of distinct bits forming numerable individuals: "There is no trouble in the concept of *what is done.* The clumsy awkwardness of the act concept comes from its way of cutting up what is done into things that are done, that is, comes from its nature as a count concept. Behaviour or action is of the same ontological kind as acts, differing from it only as mass from count — as grass differs from blades, footwear from shoes, money from coins. So although I refuse to work with the act concept, I have no qualms in quantifying over items or portions or stretches of behaviour."[78] Bennett's examples are somewhat misleading, since particular blades of grass, shoes, and coins really are individuals. Nonetheless, his point is clear — even though there is no actually existing individual corresponding to "the act itself," we can identify a particular act by isolating the segment of behavior that interests us. Nonetheless, we impose these distinctions in view of our purposes and interests, including our moral interests — and as such, they cannot at the same time serve as a foundation for a moral judgment.

How would the example just given look in these terms? I believe Bennett's analysis would go something like this: Between T (a moment in time) and T + 1 (whatever interval we choose), we can trace a stream of causal interactions involving the doctor, her patient, and much else besides, including both unusual or noteworthy sequences — the multitude of events within the patient's body, constituting his illness — and sequences that we normally take for granted — the presence of oxygen in the room, its chemical interactions in the blood of both doctor and patient, and the like. Within this interval, let us suppose, we move from a state of affairs in which the patient is still alive, to one in which he is dead. Now we are invited to consider two alterna-

78. Bennett, *The Act Itself,* 35, emphasis in original.

tives. In the first, the doctor contributes to the outcome by means of activities representing positive interventions into the process — she measures the poison into a syringe and injects her patient with it. In the second, she simply refrains from activities that she might otherwise perform, in order to save the patient — she does not fill a syringe with antibiotics, does not inject the patient, and so forth. But it would be a mistake to say she does nothing, because throughout this sequence she is performing other actions she has chosen in the knowledge that one consequence of doing these, rather than actively intervening in the patient's process of dying, will be the death of her patient.[79] In Bennett's terms, her agency with respect to the outcome is exercised in a positive way in the first alternative and in a negative way in the second — but on either alternative she is exercising her agency in such a way as to contribute knowingly to a sequence of causal interactions resulting in the agent's death. Bennett's point, finally, is that we cannot credibly reformulate the distinction between positive and negative agency into a morally freighted distinction between doing and allowing.[80]

How might we respond to this from within the framework of a Thomistic theory of the natural law? As we saw in the preceding section, Aquinas would not accept Bennett's initial assumption that we cannot identify individual acts, much less distinguish among different components of an action. On the contrary, Aquinas believes that human actions have a natural structure, and this implies that they are discrete individuals, in reality and not merely as a result of social convention (cf. I-II 1.3 *ad* 3). Moreover, he clearly regards the structure of the act as morally significant — in other words, he offers just what the critics of deontological morality demand, namely, a credible basis for a distinction between doing and allowing, which can serve as a basis for moral judgments. However, in order to defend these distinctions, it will be necessary to go further into Aquinas's theory of action. We will need to go where Bennett will not, into an examination of the metaphysics of human action. Fortunately, there has recently been some fine work on Aquinas's theory of action, seen in the twofold context of his own metaphysics and theology, and contemporary Anglophone work on the philosophy of action. In what

79. At this point, a Thomistic analysis of acts would actually strengthen Bennett's point. Even if the doctor in this case does nothing other than stand by the window while her patient is dying, she is still engaged in some action, even if only the interior act of the will consisting of her choice not to intervene in the process. This line of analysis presupposes, of course, that the doctor knows (or reasonably believes) that her nonintervention will result in the patient's death.

80. I am here summarizing a complex series of arguments; see *The Act Itself,* 62-73 ("Making/Allowing") and 85-104 ("Positive/Negative") for further details.

follows, I rely in particular on Stephen Brock's *Action and Conduct,* although I do not follow him in every detail and do not want to imply that he would agree with the moral arguments with which this section closes.[81]

Seen in its most basic terms, human action is a kind of operation, that is to say, an exercise of causal power by the human person, as agent, on some terminus, whether this be some aspect of the agent herself (I teach myself how to cook) or something external to the agent (I cook dinner). As such, human action reflects the same structure as we find displayed in the operations of creatures more generally. It stems from the distinctive form of the human person in some way or other — unsurprisingly, since as we have seen, a creature's form is nothing other than the principle for its proper operations. It is characterized, moreover, by efficacy and finality. Efficacy, as a human action, like any other operation, represents an exercise of the creature's proper causal powers, through which some change is brought about in the terminus of the act. The change in question should not be understood as if it amounted to nothing more than triggering a process of motion. Rather, in some way or other it represents a communication of the agent's proper form, in whole or in some aspect, to a terminus that is in some way apt to be informed in the relevant way. Correlatively, the human act, like every other operation, is directed toward an end, namely, the communication of the form of the agent to an appropriately receptive terminus.

This brings us to the second hallmark of action, namely, its finality. We have already observed that every creature acts for an end, through which its operations are rendered intelligible. This is nothing other than the final cause, which stems from the creature's form and is to be construed in terms of a communication of that form in some sense or other. The act of reproduction is the parade example of an operation that communicates the form of a living creature in a comprehensive and integral way. But other operations can also be regarded as stemming from the form of the creature, and communicating or preserving some aspect of that form — for example, taking in nutrition or warding off dangers. Human action too is to be analyzed in its most basic terms as an operation of a creature's causal powers, which is as such intelligible in terms of the end, that is, the final cause, toward which it is directed. In

81. See Brock, *Action and Conduct,* cited above. I do not attempt to follow Brock on terminological usage; for example, he refers to human action as "conduct," whereas I simply use "action," relying on the context to make it clear whether this refers to creatures' operations in general, or specifically human action. Moreover, it will be apparent that what follows is a drastically condensed summary of a long and complex monograph, and it may well be that in the process of summarizing Brock's arguments, I have interpreted them in a way he might not accept.

our case, too, natural kinds of actions represent a communication or preservation of some aspect of the human form, in terms of which the action can be regarded as an intelligible object of intention. This is so even in the case of a kind of action that is naturally repugnant in itself, for example, the act of killing, which considered as a natural object would typically be an act of self-defense oriented toward the preservation or security of the agent.[82] I am inclined to think that every human action can be analyzed in these terms. In saying this, I do not mean to imply that human acts can be analyzed *without remainder* in terms of a natural object, constituted by the communication or preservation of the human form — after all, as rational creatures, our distinctive way of life includes contemplating, enjoying, and communicating ideas, the natures of things, intelligible beauty, and the whole panoply of culture. Nonetheless, it does seem to me that every human action will represent some natural object of action, whatever other aims it represents. At any rate, even if it is not the case that every human action includes a natural object in this sense, such acts constitute a very extensive part of all that we do, including many of our most morally significant acts.

Of course, the proper operations of a human agent — her human actions, in the full sense — represent a distinct form of operation, in accordance with the characteristic way of acting pertaining to her as a human being. More specifically, human action stems from the agent's knowing and deliberately chosen exercise of her causal powers, in pursuit of some aim that she rationally judges to be both good, and attainable through the chosen action. (Remember: Aquinas believes every particular action is chosen because it represents a means to, or component of, some wider end.) Hence, Aquinas would agree with most contemporary philosophers in giving a special place to the reasons or intentions for which an agent acts. However, these reasons

82. This line of analysis thus explains an otherwise puzzling feature of Aquinas's account. He argues that the object of the action is always regarded as in some way good — yet at least some kinds of actions, killing for example, have as their object something destructive and in itself repugnant (I-II 100.5 *ad* 5). It will not do to say that in such cases the object of the act is determined by whatever the agent hopes to achieve through (for example) killing, since that would be tantamount to collapsing the object of the act into the agent's aim in acting. However, the problem dissolves once we recognize that certain kinds of actions, repugnant in themselves, are nonetheless natural to the human person in the sense that they represent typical and normal expressions of human capacities, intelligible in terms of their overall contribution to human well-being. To continue with the example of killing, this is an extreme expression of a capacity for aggression, which as such does have a natural place in human life as one expression of a more general capacity for warding off dangers. Thus, killing as a natural action kind is an intelligible object of desire insofar as it represents an expression of a human capacity, exercised in pursuit of the natural aims of safety and security.

are not themselves causes of action in the modern sense; rather, the action is itself an exercise of causal efficacy *by* the agent, *through* her own proper powers, *in order to* attain some end constituting the reason for which she acts.[83] Correlatively, an act is linked back to its agent through some reference to her reasons for acting. Aquinas would agree with the current consensus that an agent can be said to intend an action, or to act voluntarily, only insofar as she knowingly aims at bringing about some result. When Oedipus killed an old man on the way to his kingdom, he did not intentionally kill his father, even though the man he killed was in fact, but unknown to him, his father.

Understood in this way, a human action is an event constituting a particular kind of relationship, namely, that obtaining between an agent and the terminus of its active power.[84] As such, a particular action can be individuated from the web of causal interactions within which it is necessarily embedded. It takes place over time, originating with the first moment at which the agent begins to exercise his powers and terminating when the effect of those powers has been communicated to the terminus of the action. So understood, any action *ad extra* will necessarily involve some kind of bodily movement, since that is the only way in which embodied creatures can exercise their causal powers. However, the act will not be conceptually identical to any predetermined set of bodily movements; rather, it is properly analyzed in terms of the exercise of causal power taking place in and through those movements.[85] Correlatively, the agent can only intend what he can reasonably expect to bring about through his specific causal powers.[86] We may wish for things that we know we

83. I agree with Vogler, over against Davidson, on this point. Davidson's argument that reasons are causes is developed throughout the essays collected in *Essays on Actions and Events;* for Vogler's response, see *Reasonably Vicious,* 213-22. I would add that reasons are *final* causes, but that does not seem to be what Davidson means.

84. On the individuation of actions thus understood, see Brock, *Action and Conduct,* 49-93; cf. Vogler's observation in *Reasonably Vicious,* 58-59, that even though "intentional action" is not a sortal, our concepts of kinds of actions are sortals (that is, we cannot count "intentional acts" over some stretch of time without further specifying what we are counting, but we can count acts of killing, taking property, and the like).

85. Thus, every action will take place in and through what Davidson describes as a primitive action — a configuration of bodily movements, generously construed to include such activities as standing fast, cogitating, and the like — but the object of the act will not (normally) be conceptually tied to any one such primitive action. Rather, it will be tied to the causal efficacy of the act, seen in the context of an appropriately human way of life. There are many ways to kill — with a knife, a gun, strangling, and so forth — but the act of killing is not conceptually tied to any of these primitive actions; rather, it is defined by reference to an exercise of lethal aggression. For further details on primitive actions, see Davidson, "Agency," in *Essays on Actions and Events,* 43-62.

86. As Brock points out in *Action and Conduct,* 139-41. If I understand them correctly,

cannot bring about, but such wishes are just that, not voluntary choices directed toward specific acts. By the same token, the agent's choice cannot be meaningfully described, apart from some reference to the particular way in which he chooses to exercise his causal powers. Hence, it is impossible to characterize someone's will in terms of a general orientation toward goodness, or for that matter evil, apart from some account displaying the goodness or badness of what he actually does. We cannot even speak meaningfully in terms of the stance of the agent's will toward some specified human good, apart from some account of what he brings about with reference to that good.

Set out in bare outline, Aquinas's theory of action may appear to be too abstract to be of much practical significance. But Aquinas himself clearly believes that a general theoretical analysis of action has moral consequences, as we see from his analysis of the goodness and evil of human actions beginning at *ST* I-II 18 and continuing through the following three questions. While it is true that Aquinas is at this point adapting a traditional set of distinctions, it is also the case that he interprets them in accordance with the general theory of action sketched above. A human act represents an exercise of causal efficacy; the proper description of that event, formulated in terms of the immediate and proper effect of the agent's active powers, provides us with the object of the act.[87] (Hence, the object, properly so called, should not be identified with some person or thing on which the agent acts; rather, "the object" refers to the act itself under a description along the lines indicated.) At the same time, a particular action is chosen in view of some further good, toward which it serves as a means, a component, or an expression. If the object is intrinsically related to the aim, we may elide them in describing and evaluating the overall action; otherwise, they represent two distinct components of one action, each of which carries an independent moral significance. (Aquinas offers Aristotle's example of the man who steals in order to have the means whereby to commit adultery; see I-II 18.7.) Finally, because an action is individuated in terms of the exercise of causal efficacy that it represents, we can distinguish it from the ongoing stream of conditions and consequences within which every event is embedded. These are the circum-

---

Grisez and Finnis hold that the agent's intention can be specified without any necessary reference at all to the specific form of the causal efficacy comprising the intended act; see most recently Finnis, Grisez, and Boyle, "'Direct' and 'Indirect.'" I agree with Long, "A Brief Disquisition regarding the Nature of the Object of the Moral Act according to St. Thomas Aquinas," that this is tantamount to collapsing the object of the act into the agent's intention. More generally, I am persuaded by Brock that it is not conceptually possible to specify intention without some reference to the agent's proper exercise of causality.

87. Again, I owe this point to Brock, *Action and Conduct,* 89.

stances, and while they too are morally significant, nonetheless they are to be distinguished from the act itself.

Thus, Aquinas's analysis provides us with a plausible way to identify particular human acts, separating them off from the stream of causes and effects in which they are naturally embedded. It is important, however, to proceed carefully here. Aquinas's analysis of acts presupposes a particular conception of causality, according to which the exercise of efficient causality will always proceed in some intelligible way from the agent's form, and will be correlatively directed toward some good which represents the communication or preservation of the form. It is this structure of intelligibility which enables us to identify discrete human acts in terms of their natural objects. The object of the act is constituted by the causal relation set up between the agent and whatever is the terminus of her efficacious activity. (Or more exactly, it is given by what the relationship would be, assuming the act is successful.) As such, the object of the act cannot be analyzed apart from a consideration of the actual exercise of causal efficacy it represents. We are able to identify the relevant causal relation, in turn, through our grasp of the kinds of activities characteristic of a distinctively human way of life. We can identify an act of giving aid, or communicating, or killing, because we grasp the point of these kinds of activities in terms of our species-specific way of life, and correlatively, we know how to recognize their characteristic effects seen in those terms.

This last point needs to be underscored. It would be a mistake to assume that we could analyze the relevant causal relation by tracing causal sequences, distinguishing those that flow from the agent from contributing causes, background conditions, and the like, prior to making a judgment about the causal relation constituting the object of the act. This is essentially what Bennett advises us to do. Bennett's approach only works, however, if we presuppose that causes are simply undifferentiated exercises of power, bearing no essential or theoretically interesting relations to their agents. On this view, there is indeed no objectively apparent way to individuate particular sequences of cause and effect, and it does make more sense to think of activity as being something like a stream or a mud puddle — something we can quantify for our own purposes, but which does not naturally break apart into individual bits. Aquinas, in contrast, brings a very different conception of causality to his analysis of human actions. On his view, the exercise of efficient causation is inherently intelligible in terms of its relation to formal and final causality. This is just what makes it possible to identify individual events and actions, and to distinguish the cause and effect constituting a particular act from enabling conditions, remote consequences, and the like.

This last point is relevant to another set of issues, distinct from yet related to the status of the doing/allowing distinction. That is to say, what is the moral significance, if any, of the distinction between means and end? It is widely held that some choices are ruled out because they employ a bad means in order to bring about a good end, thus violating the injunction not to do evil so that good may come about. This intuition has classically been formulated in terms of the doctrine of double effect. According to this doctrine, really a schema for evaluating ambiguous acts, a particular act is morally permissible if it is good or neutral according to its object; if the bad effect is not the causal means to the good effect; the agent's intention is sincerely good; and the bad effect is not disproportionate to the good that is sought.[88] The objection to this line of analysis, once again, asks why we should place so much weight on the causal structure of the act, in this instance the relation of means to end. This question is sharpened by the fact that some morally legitimate kinds of actions clearly do involve securing a good end through the infliction of damage or loss — killing in wartime, for example, or even more clearly, the execution of a wrongdoer. Why is it immoral to bring about some kinds of good effects through destructive means, when in these kinds of actions, it is not immoral to do so?

Within the scope of this chapter, I can offer only the briefest comments on these complex issues. I would agree with defenders of the doctrine of double effect that the causal structure of human actions does matter. This structure matters, however, because it is one of the determinants of the *natural* object of the act, even prior to its role in determining the moral structure of the act. Natural kinds of actions have a typical structure, in terms of which a given aspect of human well-being is pursued, enjoyed, protected, or communicated in a given way; thus, if we want to determine the kind of act in a particular instance, we need to look first of all at the causal relation between what the agent does and the human good that is thereby attained. This line of analysis will of course be especially relevant with respect to actions involving some kind of damage or sacrifice in pursuit of some good. Admittedly, this point would need to be developed with some care. The general thought is straightforward enough, however: if a given act requires the infliction of damage or loss as a necessary or causally immediate way of bringing about some end, then the object of the act is determined by that end. Steven Long makes this point by analyzing Aquinas's argument that fornication is not a legitimate means of self-defense, since this kind of act can be a defensive act only accidentally. In the case of lethal defense, in contrast,

88. Reeder once again offers a comprehensive and illuminating guide to the relevant literature; see *Killing and Saving*, 106-53.

> lethal defense has a *natural* relation to the stopping of unjust endangering assault. Homicide "sometimes" follows because it is accidental to defense as such that it requires homicide: but it is not accidental to *this* defense that it be such as actually to require it. Granted that there are cases wherein killing is only a consequence of a defense, there are other cases where lethal means need be deliberately employed to defend the innocent, and where they are employed within the generic *ratio* of defense, solely because this is the only proportionate means which can effectuate defense. Hence there is — as St. Thomas says — one species for such an act from which homicide at times follows, namely, the species of a defensive act. While the means chosen is deliberately lethal, what is *intended* in the slaying is defense, and the slaying is an essential determination of this act of defense.[89]

I would add that lethal defense has a natural relation to the act of defense because killing one's assailant is one evident manifestation of a general human capability to ward off attack through aggressive means. As such, killing in self-defense is a recognizable kind of action that is natural to the human person as such. Sexual activity, in contrast, has no natural orientation toward self-defense, and that is why an act of sex cannot be regarded as a natural act of self-defense. This does not mean that someone who consents to a sexual act under threat of death should be regarded as guilty of a sexual sin, any more than we would regard someone who hands over someone else's property under a similar threat to be guilty of theft. Rather, those who act in these ways should be considered to act under coercion.[90] But in neither case is the act in question naturally an act of self-defense, even though in each case the act is done from defensive motives.

At any rate, Long's remarks help us to see the difficulty with the doctrine of double effect as traditionally formulated. That is, this schema presupposes that we begin with a clear sense of what constitutes the natural object of the act, whereas in most relevant situations that is precisely what we need to establish by means of a causal analysis of the immediate structure of the act. I would further suggest that the doctrine of double effect can most helpfully be

89. Long, "A Brief Disquisition," 61, emphasis in original. Brock argues along similar lines; see *Action and Conduct*, 197-208.

90. Christine Traina argues that consenting to sexual intercourse under threat of death should be regarded as a form of material cooperation; see "Oh Susanna: The New Absolutism and Natural Law," *Journal of the American Academy of Religion* 65, no. 2 (summer 1997): 371-401, but in my view it is more in accordance with our overall judgments to regard this as a coerced action. Needless to say, this is itself a moral judgment and would need to be defended as such; I will not undertake to do so at this point, however.

reformulated as a schema for analysis to be used when we are in doubt about the *natural* object of the act — when we are unclear, to refer to another traditional example, whether a given act should count as the administration of a medicine with lethal side effects or as an act of killing. In these cases, a close analysis of the causal structure of the act may be necessary in order to establish the kind of causal efficacy that the act represents. In many cases (admittedly, not all), once we have established the natural object of the act, its moral object will likewise become apparent — or at least we will have grounds to conclude that the act should not be categorized in a particular way. Once we realize that a particular medical intervention is immediately palliative in its effect, and only indirectly lethal, we can safely conclude that the act is not an act of killing — and therefore, it cannot be an act of murder.

Let us return at this point to the wider issues at hand. I am arguing that Aquinas offers a credible way of distinguishing between doing and allowing in the form of a more fundamental analysis of the structure of human action, in terms of which we can (nonironically) speak of "the act itself" and distinguish it both from its consequences and from the agent's overall intention. In terms of this same analysis, we can also distinguish between what the agent intends — most immediately, the object of the act — and those effects which may be regarded as outside the agent's intention. To return to the example with which we began, a doctor who refrains from treating a moribund patient cannot be said to kill him, even though she allows him to die. On no plausible construal can the acts she does perform in this situation be regarded as constituting an exercise of her defensive and aggressive capacities in a lethal way — hence, they cannot be construed as exemplifying a natural act of killing. In contrast, if she administers poison to him, such an act can only be regarded as an act of killing, because in this case she does exercise her natural capacities for defensive aggression (even though her motive is not defense or aggression), and the natural and immediate effect of her agency is precisely the patient's death. In this kind of situation I would hesitate to say that the doctor murders her patient, but I cannot see how such an act could be morally justified. (But even if this were considered an instance of justified killing, it would still be an act of killing, and not some other kind of action.) In a third kind of case, suppose the doctor administers a drug that has an immediately beneficial effect, for example, relieving pain, but which in this instance will also have a lethal further effect, perhaps because the required dose is so large. In this case, the act is defined in terms of its immediate palliative effect, and as such falls within the object of an act of healing rather than killing — and to that extent, at least, it is morally justifiable. (The particular act may still be rendered immoral in view of other considerations, of course.)

So far, I have sketched the case to be made within a Thomistic theory of the natural law for drawing a distinction between a particular act and its consequences, on the one hand, and the agent's overall intention, on the other. At this point, let me turn briefly to the other task of this section. Even granting that it is possible to distinguish in a clear and consistent way between an act and its consequences, in the way required by a deontological ethic, why should we give moral weight to this distinction? In general terms, the answer goes as follows: the relevant distinctions, and correlatively the deontological structure of morality itself, are so deeply embedded in a distinctively human way of life that any plausible ideal for human well-being will necessarily respect them. (This is not to say, however, that the specific moral judgments in terms of which the relevant distinctions are formulated will likewise be a part of any such ideal, as opposed to constituting the ideal as embodied in a specific way of life.) And since the ideal of the life of virtue must be such that it can plausibly be regarded as a perfection and not perversion of human well-being, it follows that however we are to construe our obligations to one another, they must in some way respect the boundaries and the limits of obligation marked out by human actions.

As a number of moral theorists have pointed out, an unlimited obligation to relieve suffering and to avert loss, strictly observed, would be inconsistent with giving any special priority to the needs and demands of those closest to the agent. Similarly, it would be incompatible with the pursuit of any individual projects or commitments.[91] Hence, if we were to give absolute priority to relieving suffering, we would be unable to sustain a network of family ties, friendships, and communal associations, nor would we be able to devote resources to serious scholarly study or artistic pursuits — to say nothing of the multitude of less weighty interests and pursuits that are a part of a normal life. Life lived on these terms would scarcely be recognizable as a human life, much less as a life characteristic of human well-being. I am persuaded that this fact in itself is enough to rule out radical consequentialism as a plausible ideal of justice. At this point, however, I want to focus on a different issue.

Near the beginning of his discussion of the sins opposed to justice, Aquinas remarks that the kinds of actions prohibited by the Decalogue share the common feature that they deprive another of the kind of honor which is

91. For a good example among philosophers, see the influential essay by Bernard Williams, "A Critique of Utilitarianism," in *Utilitarianism For and Against,* 77-150; Gilbert Meilaender develops a theological critique along similar lines in "*Eritis Sicut Deus:* Moral Theory and the Sin of Pride," *Faith and Philosophy* 3 (1986): 397-415.

his due (II-II 72.1). The language of honor may suggest that what Aquinas has in mind are violations of the distinctive claims attaching to positions of preeminence, and indeed he does regard the violation of these kinds of claims as one sort of harm. But in this instance, Aquinas is referring to a characteristic violated by general norms of nonmaleficence, which apply without qualification to all persons. Hence, he is thinking here of the respect and forbearance duc to each human individual, simply as such. Seen in this light, the norms of nonmaleficence express a collective sense of what it is to be human. As such, they qualify and extend the general ideal of justice, to render to each his or her due, by setting forth in a mostly negative way just what is due to human individuals considered as such, prior to the claims of preeminence, special relations, and the like. Correlatively, by observing these prohibitions, an individual takes his or her place as an accountable member of the moral community, and by so doing affirms that he or she also merits respect and forbearance as one in a community of peers. In this way, these prohibitions both express and make possible a whole way of life, within which the idea of human persons as individuals, capable of responsible action and worthy of respect, finds its social embodiment.

A number of our own contemporaries have expressed a similar idea. As Charles Fried says, "[T]he very *form* of categorical norms (norms of right and wrong) expresses the same conception of human personality as do the *contents* of the norms."[92] He continues,

> To be sure, morality is concerned in some way or another with all the consequences to which we might contribute or which we might avoid. The categorical norms, however, designate what it would be wrong to *do* . . . but their absolute force attaches only to what we intend, and not to the whole range of things which come about as a result of what we do intentionally. The link of intentionality between a moral agent and what he accomplishes . . . is simply another aspect, the procedural aspect, of the substantive contents of the norms. Both aspects express an underlying moral conception of the person. It is respect for persons as the ultimate moral particulars which is expressed by the contents of categorical norms. The mode of application, the procedural aspect, expresses this same certainty of the individual's personal efficacy as a moral agent.[93]

In my view, the distinction between doing and allowing rests ultimately on the metaphysics of human action, and not on our "moral conception of

92. Charles Fried, *Right and Wrong* (Cambridge: Harvard University Press, 1978), 14.
93. Fried, *Right and Wrong*, 20-21.

the person." Nonetheless, in these comments Fried offers a clear and succinct summary of the normative implications of this distinction, and in so doing he helps us to see how and why it is morally salient. At the level of basic well-being, norms of mutual forbearance form boundaries marking out fellow members of one's community from other kinds of objects — to borrow a phrase from Kant, they serve to distinguish things, which can be used or enjoyed at will, from persons, who cannot just be reduced to the means of one's own ends. These components of human well-being are further specified through an ideal of justice and right relations, through which the boundaries of forbearance and respect are spelled out in terms of a community's overall commitments, practices, and institutional structures.

We have already noted that the distinction between doing and allowing is presupposed by a deontological morality, and this would lead us to suspect that the moral salience of this distinction is similarly grounded in the exigencies of well-being for creatures of our kind. The fundamental human experience of oneself as an agent capable of bringing about change in the world requires a sense of one's own actions, and correlatively the actions of others, as paradigmatic expressions of personal agency. And if this is so, then we would expect omissions and refusals to act to be regarded as normally less blameworthy, or blameworthy only in some contexts or in a qualified way — which does indeed seem to be the case.

Moreover, this line of analysis suggests why the distinction between doing and allowing has particular relevance in just the kinds of cases we have been considering, namely, those which involve matters of life and death. That is, this general distinction appears to be closely connected to a primitive sense that persons ought to be immune from attack, understood in terms of an assault on the physical integrity of another.[94] I describe this as a primitive sense, because it appears to be rooted in the child's earliest experiences of sometimes acting as a causal force in the world, and sometimes being the object of the acts of others.[95]

94. Thus, I would generally agree with Foot, Reeder, and Warren Quinn that the moral weight that we give to the distinction between doing and allowing rests on a sense that the claims of forbearance are more exigent than claims to receive aid. Foot has developed this argument throughout her career; for recent statements, see "Killing and Letting Die" and "Morality, Action, and Outcome" (both originally 1985), in *Moral Dilemmas and Other Topics in Moral Philosophy,* 78-87 and 88-104; Quinn's view is set forth in "Actions, Intentions, and Consequences: The Doctrine of Doing and Allowing," *Philosophical Review* 48, no. 3 (July 1989): 287-312; Reeder's view is summarized in *Killing and Saving,* 172-75. However, I would resist the implication that this distinction is itself the basis for the doing/allowing distinction.

95. H. L. A. Hart and Tony Honoré make a similar point in *Causation and the Law,* 2nd ed. (Oxford: Clarendon, 1985), albeit generally and not with reference to children in particular; see 28-32. Although I would not want to overstate the similarities, it is instructive to compare

These experiences mediate the child's first relationships to those around her, and it is through them that she learns what it means to be treated as a person rather than an object, and to respond to others in the same way. She learns that people (and other sentient creatures) should not be struck, scratched, or bit, while at the same time she experiences the hurt and humiliation that come from being struck, scratched, and bit herself. (I am not presupposing that her parents have odd ideas of discipline, but only that she is interacting with other children and animals during this period.) If all goes well, these experiences generate a capacity for empathy in her, a sense that when she strikes out against others, they suffer in ways comparable to what she herself has experienced. And this sense of empathy, I believe, is one necessary condition for understanding what it means to respect another person as oneself. Our idea of what it means to regard others as persons has a concrete meaning from the very beginning, and central to this meaning is the idea that a person is not an appropriate object for physical attack. That is why the importance of bodily integrity is so central to our moral and legal intuitions in a wide variety of cases, and it is also why certain kinds of wrongdoing which outrage bodily integrity in particularly egregious ways, rape and torture, for example, are especially horrifying to us.

A failure to avert harm from another, in contrast, does not express a disregard for the humanity of that person in the same immediate way. If I allow someone to die, my action or inaction might be cowardly, regrettable, callous, even tantamount to murder, depending on the overall situation, but at least I do not insult the dignity of the other through a direct assault on her bodily life. This is the context in which to understand the duty to rescue. A wrongful killing involves an assault on the fundamental dignity of another, whereas a failure to save another from death need not express similar disregard for his humanity. Yet such a failure might express culpable disregard for the humanity of another, similar to the disregard expressed by murdering him; in particular, we consider this to be so if someone is able to rescue another person from imminent death at little or no risk to herself, and yet does not do so.

Doesn't this imply that the distinction between acting and allowing breaks down after all? Not at all: it simply shows that our assessments of responsibility and guilt in life-and-death cases reflect other considerations in addition to the fundamental distinction between doing and allowing. More

---

their analysis of the concept of causality presupposed in law with the account being developed here; see 9-61 for the main lines of that analysis. Diana Cates approaches the same issue in a somewhat different way through her insightful analysis of what it means to develop compassion for another in *Choosing to Feel: Virtue, Friendship, and Compassion for Friends* (Notre Dame: University of Notre Dame Press, 1997), especially 131-53.

specifically, the obligation to rescue someone who is in imminent danger of death reflects a sense that in this case, the sufferer and his potential savior are brought into relationship with one another by the exigencies of the situation itself. Someone who is confronted with another human being in mortal distress and turns his back, literally or figuratively, expresses his sense that this is a life not worth saving by his withdrawal from the situation. That does not mean that what he does is logically equivalent to killing; it simply means that in such a case, we consider ourselves to have a responsibility which is roughly equivalent to our responsibility not to attack another.

Two further comments are in order before concluding this section. In the previous section, I remarked that the norms of well-being informing the ideal of justice are fundamentally social norms, reflecting a sense of the collective way of life proper to a kind of animal that is both social and rational. This might seem to imply that the claims of the individual are secondary to, or even subordinated to, the claims of the community. But as we have just seen, this is not so even at the level of basic well-being. We are social animals, and our way of life is characteristically communal. Yet the kind of community in question is structured by norms of forbearance within which each member of the community enjoys a protected place. This much seems to be true of all social animals; in addition, we as rational animals have the capacity to conceptualize ourselves as belonging to a kind of creature deserving of respect and forbearance. In order to attain the fully developed form of well-being constituted by the practice of the virtues, it is necessary to translate this basic concept into respect for the claims of others — that is to say, it is necessary to adopt and live by an ideal of justice.

Notice that I speak in this context of *an* ideal of justice, rather than *the* ideal of justice. Human well-being requires a communal life in which the individual enjoys a protected place. But this requirement, taken by itself, does not determine the specific boundaries through which respect for human persons as such is expressed. It does not even presuppose that all persons within a community will be respected equally, or enjoy the same claims on forbearance — it simply presupposes that (at least) all functional adults within a community will be regarded as enjoying some kinds of claims of forbearance. The ideal of equal regard, according to which each human person is owed the same basic kinds of respect, is one ideal of justice. What is more, I would argue that it is the right ideal of justice, but this claim can only be justified on theological grounds — it is not a necessary expression of the exigencies of human well-being, nor is it logically necessitated by one's sense of oneself as an agent, or by the requirements of communication. We will return to these issues in the next chapter.

5. Prudence and the Limits of Moral Knowledge

The investigations of the preceding chapter and this one might suggest that practical reason and its characteristic virtue, prudence, play only an ancillary role in moral reflection and action. And certainly, compared with the centrality given to practical reason or prudence by many other contemporary formulations of a Thomistic ethic, prudence does play a more limited role in the Thomistic theory of the natural law proposed here. As we have seen, some of our contemporaries hold that practical reason generates moral norms through the exigencies of its own functioning, prior to the operations of speculative reason. For others, the operations of prudence render moral rules unnecessary, although they may still play a secondary role as summaries of the past judgments of the wise, helpful as general guidelines but not in any way foundational to moral judgment.[96]

As the preceding discussion would suggest, I do not believe that the former position can be sustained, considered either as a reading of Aquinas or on its own merits. As we have already observed, for Aquinas practical reason always functions at the level of choice, that is to say, it always serves to identify particular actions which serve as a means to, or a component or instantiation of, some further end. This does not mean that practical reason is restricted to the narrowly instrumental function of determining means toward clearly specified ends, but it does imply that practical wisdom as such does not set the ends governing our actions. Aquinas makes this clear at II-II 47.6, where he denies that prudence sets the ends for the operation of the moral virtues. These are set by the first principles of practical reason as habitually known through synderesis. These first principles, in turn, can only function practically insofar as they are informed by the natural inclinations of the human creature and given concrete meaning through the agent's speculative beliefs about, and overall orientation toward, whatever he regards as his final good. Practical reason is dependent for its functioning on speculative judgments, and by the same token the virtue of prudence presupposes

96. Rhonheimer offers what is probably the most influential current version of the first position. The Grisez/Finnis theory resembles this view insofar as the precepts of the natural law do not depend on speculative knowledge, but as George observes, it is not accurate to say that they consider reason to generate norms through the exigencies of its proper functioning; see George, *Defense of Natural Law,* 89. In recent years, the latter view has been defended as a reading of Aquinas by several authors, including most notably Daniel Mark Nelson, *The Priority of Prudence: Virtue and Natural Law in Thomas Aquinas and the Implications for Modern Ethics* (University Park: Pennsylvania State University Press, 1992), and Bowlin, *Contingency and Fortune,* 93-137.

— it does not directly generate — right judgments about the agent's appropriate aims.

We have not yet had occasion to address the second reading, and the scope of this project does not permit an extended discussion. But as a number of scholars have recently argued, it cannot be sustained either as a reading of Aquinas or as an account of moral reflection generally.[97] We will return below to the theoretical questions raised by this position, considered as an account of moral judgment. Considered as a reading of Aquinas, it does not seem to me borne out by the relevant texts. It is certainly true that Aquinas also gives a far more prominent and fundamental role to the virtues than many commentators have recognized, identifying them as among the internal principles from which human action stems. But virtue, so understood, is coordinated with law and grace, which comprise the external principles of human action, equally necessary to its explanation, albeit in a different way (I-II 49, introduction). More specifically, he says "God instructs us by law" (I-II 90, introduction), which at least suggests that the law in question has some substantive content. Moreover, in the *secunda secundae* Aquinas devotes 124 questions to the moral norms associated with the cardinal virtues alone, including precepts of temperance and fortitude as well as justice. While many of these norms do seem to be general ideals, many others clearly correspond to moral rules as currently understood, and in many cases Aquinas elaborates these through a painstaking moral casuistry. Once again, see that Aquinas regards the operations of practical reason to be dependent on norms that it does not generate.

At the same time, the operations of practical reason, including the exercise of prudential judgment, cannot be understood as if they were exactly parallel to those of speculative reason.[98] In particular, moral reasoning can-

97. In my view, Pamela Hall offers a decisive response to this line of interpretation in *Narrative and the Natural Law*, to be considered in more detail below. Westberg likewise criticizes it in *Right Practical Reason*, 216-60; more generally, his discussion there helpfully sets out the main lines of Aquinas's discussion of prudence as a virtue. For my own responses to the above, see *Moral Action*, 125-66, and "What the Wise Person Knows: Natural Law and Virtue in Aquinas's *Summa theologiae*," *Studies in Christian Ethics* 12 (1999): 57-69.

98. I agree with Pinckaers and Kevin Flannery that Aquinas's analysis of the moral act (Pinckaers) and the intrinsic order of natural law precepts (Flannery) provide a basis for a genuine, systematic moral knowledge, but I am more hesitant than they are to say that this constitutes a science; see Pinckaers, *Ce qu'on ne peut jamais faire*, 36, and Flannery, *Acts Amid Precepts: The Aristotelian Logical Structure of Thomas Aquinas's Moral Theory* (Washington, D.C.: Catholic University of America Press, 2001), xv. Similarly, Eileen Serene remarks that Aquinas holds that the natural and moral sciences, broadly so called, can approximate the ideals of a true science, even though they cannot attain it completely; see Eileen Serene, "The Interpretation of Aristotle's

not by its nature enjoy the same level of certainty as some (not all) forms of speculative reasoning, because moral reasoning always deals with individual objects, which do not admit of perfect scientific understanding. In Aquinas's view, science properly so called is the knowledge of universal and necessary principles and their conclusions, and correlatively, we cannot attain scientific knowledge of singular and contingent objects as such. This implies that practical reason, which is directed toward human actions which are of course singular and contingent, cannot attain scientific certainty in its operations. Yet this does not mean that there are no criteria by which the exercise of practical reason can be evaluated, nor does it rule out the development of facility and skill in its exercise.

On the contrary, the distinctive functions and limitations of practical reason provide the rationale and the field of operation for a distinctive virtue, namely, the virtue of practical wisdom or prudence. At the same time, since this virtue also perfects a specific human capacity, one without which diverse aspects of well-being and happiness could not be achieved, it is itself an integral component of happiness considered as the life of virtue (cf. I-II 57.5). And as we will see, the limitations of practical reason provide a greater scope for creativity in the operations of prudential judgment than we might suspect, given its dependence on speculative judgment. Even though prudence does not generate moral norms directly, it does contribute in indirect but important ways to the formulation of these norms — as we will see. Let us turn, therefore, to a closer examination of the fourth of the cardinal virtues, taking Aquinas's account as our starting point.[99]

At the beginning of Aquinas's account of prudence in the *secunda secundae,* we read that prudence is an intellectual virtue (II-II 47.1), and more specifically a virtue of the practical intellect (47.2), which has as its distinctive matter the application of general principles to particular actions (47.5) with an aim to the overall perfection of the agent's life (in contrast to the arts; I-II 57.4). Prudence is thus necessarily concerned with contingent singulars, and

---

Physics and the Science of Motion," in *The Cambridge History of Later Medieval Philosophy from the Rediscovery of Aristotle to the Disintegration of Scholasticism, 1100-1600,* ed. Norman Kretzman, Anthony Kenny, and Jan Pinborg (Cambridge: Cambridge University Press, 1982), 506-7. Nonetheless, Aquinas insists that we cannot attain true scientific knowledge of contingent singulars, and since this includes actions, practical reason cannot attain certainty in its operations; for a particularly clear statement of these points, see the *Sententia libri Ethicorum* (the commentary on the *Nicomachean Ethics*), VI 1.3, para. 1145 and II 1.2, para. 258-59 respectively.

99. In addition to the authors cited below, I am especially indebted in what follows to Richard Sorabji, "Aristotle on the Role of Intellect in Virtue," in *Essays in Aristotle's Ethics,* ed. Amélie Rorty (Berkeley: University of California Press, 1980), 201-19.

that is why, as we have seen, its deliberations at best lack scientific certainty (II-II 47.3). Its central actions are to inquire with respect to what is to be done in a given situation, to form a judgment based on that inquiry, and to command the action or actions so determined (II-II 47.8). Moreover, the moral virtues properly so called (that is, temperance, fortitude, and justice) cannot exist without prudence (I-II 58.4), nor can prudence in its turn exist without the moral virtues (I-II 58.5).

As we have already remarked, prudence operates at the level of choice, and as such, it does not determine the ends for which the agent acts. Yet this does not mean that prudence is nothing other than the ability to discern effective and appropriate means by which to attain specified and determinate ends. Rather, as Aquinas goes on to explain, it pertains to prudence to determine the mean of the moral virtues (II-II 47.7). The mean, he goes on to explain, is nothing other than conformity with reason with respect to that area of life that is the matter of the virtue in question. In other words (as Aquinas has just explained), the mean of a virtue is nothing other than the end of this virtue as set by synderesis, that is to say, the habitual grasp of the first principles of practical reason. Yet as we have seen, conformity with reason has different, although analogous, meanings for the different virtues. What is more, what concretely counts as conformity to reason in a given situation is not predetermined through synderesis, but must be determined by prudential judgment (II-II 47.7, especially *ad* 3; cf. I-II 66.3 *ad* 3).

The critical point is this. Any interpretation of the inseparable connection between prudence and the moral virtues properly so called must take account of the intimate dialectical interrelationship that obtains between them in practice. On the one hand, the virtues of the passions and will are not just desires to do good deeds, which are independently prescribed by prudence. Rather, they find expression in the individual's desires for the good, both in general terms and in terms of her admiration and desire for the fitting, the noble, the decent, the praiseworthy, as these ideals have been inculcated in her by her formation in the ideals of the virtues, and by her desire to live a life that is virtuous and happy overall. These desires, in turn, set the orientation of the whole person, her mind as well as her passions and her will. Precisely because she desires the good, in general and in a variety of specific ways, the virtuous person notices certain features of a situation and does not see, or discounts, other features. Some aspects of a state of affairs have a saliency for her that they would not have for someone not generally concerned about goodness.[100]

100. I take this point from Ronald de Sousa, who argues that the passions set patterns of salience in such a way as to determine both perception and choice in one way rather than an-

Thus, the desires of the virtuous person inform her judgments, in such a way as partially to determine the descriptions under which she views situations and thinks about her prospective actions.

At the same time, prudence consists in something more than the capacity to figure out how to attain the ends set by virtue. Indeed, a little consideration makes it clear that this is not a realistic way to think of virtuous activity anyway. While there may be circumstances in which the virtuous individual knows clearly what he needs to do in a given situation, and is puzzled about the means by which to carry out his good aim, normally the uncertainties of the well-meaning, virtuous person will not be like that. Compare, for example, the uncertainties of the individual who feels moved to give something to a charity but cannot decide which charity is most effective, to the uncertainties of the father who wants to be generous to his son but is worried that a large present of money would really be ungenerous, because it would encourage dependency and passivity on the boy's part. In the latter case, unlike the former case, what is uncertain is precisely what would count as a generous act, all things considered. What prudence provides in the latter sort of case, in other words, is a determination of what would count as a virtuous action in a specific situation; that is what it means to say that prudence determines the concrete content of the mean of the virtue, in specific instances of choice.

What this implies will vary from virtue to virtue and from case to case. With respect to fortitude and temperance and their associated virtues, the deliverances of prudence will have an ineluctable relation to the agent himself, because as we have seen, the mean of these virtues is determined with reference to the agent's own individual good (I-II 60.2; 64.2; II-II 57.1; 141.6). Thus, while the prudent person will be guided in his deliberations by the paradigms for sobriety or patience or whatever, his determinations of what counts as sober behavior (for example) will necessarily involve some reference to the balance of indulgence and abstinence that is most in accordance with his overall good. On the other hand, the mean of the virtue of justice is determined with respect to objective criteria of fairness and equity between persons (I-II 60.2; II-II 57.1). As such, the objective requirements of justice can be discerned and carried out, at least in some cases, by those who are not particularly virtuous or prudent; so much is implied, at any rate, by Aquinas's

other; see his *The Rationality of Emotion* (Cambridge: MIT Press, 1987), 171-204. He does not apply this point specifically to the virtues, but on Aquinas's account, the virtues of the passions *are* materially equivalent to the passions themselves, as qualified by the *habitus* of the virtue to bring one set of saliences rather than another to the individual's perceptions and desires. For a detailed and illuminating analysis of what this might mean practically with respect to one particular set of passions and virtues, see Cates, *Choosing to Feel*, 131-53.

remarks at I-II 100.1, to the effect that the norms of the Decalogue are readily apparent to most persons (and Aquinas does not have high expectations for the majority of persons; see I 49.3 *ad* 5; I 63.9; cf. I-II 109.2). At the same time, it would be a mistake to conclude that the demands of justice are secondary or external to the life of virtue.[101] Justice, after all, is itself a virtue, and therefore, like temperance and fortitude, it is a perfection of the capacities for action of the individual who possesses it (I-II 56.6; 60.3). Specifically, it directs the individual to the common good, which for Aquinas is necessary for the full perfection of the individual himself (I-II 56.6; II-II 47.10; 58.12); at the same time, it qualifies both temperance and fortitude, providing norms by which true temperance and fortitude can be distinguished from incomplete or counterfeit forms of these virtues (II-II 58.5, 6).

As the investigations of the last chapter and this one have already indicated, moral reasoning as Aquinas understands it is integrally connected to this process of discerning the mean. Yet it would be a mistake to equate the operation of prudence with this process *tout court,* as if practical judgment could always be analyzed in terms of discerning the mean of one virtue, operating in splendid isolation from the other virtues. Normally, the choices we face in everyday life will raise considerations relative to more than one virtue and will engage more than one virtue in their exercise. Hence, practical reason requires balancing diverse considerations, in order to arrive at a choice which is not only virtuous in this or that respect, but virtuous without qualification. The hallmark of the prudent person will therefore be this ability to balance diverse considerations in order to arrive at a settled judgment concerning the best course of action, all things considered. This brings us back to an earlier observation — that is, one of the hallmarks of moral reasonableness is the ability to place diverse considerations in a proper ordering. That is why Aquinas holds that the virtues are connected, in the sense that no one can fully possess or truly exercise one virtue without possessing and exercising them all (I-II 65.1).

This would be misleading, however, if we assumed that ordering meant arranging the diverse considerations of human life in accordance with a single, unitary scale, perhaps ranking these in accordance with higher versus lower ends, or analyzing every consideration in terms of a single standard (for example, value maximization). It has sometimes been argued that choice would not be possible unless we were able to place every desideratum on a

101. As Giuseppe Abbà claims in the conclusion of his generally excellent *Lex et Virtus: Studi sull'evoluzione della dottrina morale di san Tommaso d'Aquino* (Rome: Libreria Ateneo Salesiano, 1983), 265-71.

single scale in this way. As Michael Stocker argues, however, if this were true we would almost never be able to make practical judgments: "Practical situations, thus, often call for a balancing of various virtues and thus of various distinct emotions and their distinct proper objects. If such balancing is to be understood in terms of reaching a mean on a continuum with a homogeneous scale, these situations precipitate endless conflicts within the Aristotelian good person. Alternatively, if these situations do admit of a correct resolution, such resolutions cannot require a homogeneous continuum."[102]

As he goes on to argue, the Aristotelian good person can make practical judgments in the requisite way, because she is able to place them within an overarching framework, what Stocker calls a "higher-level synthesizing category."[103] This higher-level category may be as simple as my idea of a good day, on the basis of which I decide between shopping and cleaning house (my examples, not Stocker's), or as comprehensive as my conception of happiness or the life of virtue. At any rate, a higher-level category provides a framework within which to assess the significance and relative value of different considerations, and as such, it enables me to make a choice informed by reasons, brought together in some kind of comprehensible order — in other words, a nonarbitrary, rational choice. It is important to note that even so, this framework will not typically require one and only one choice, because there will usually not be one and only one way of assessing diverse considerations which makes sense, even within the frame of a particular synthesizing category. But this need not surprise us, since as we have already noted, practical reason leads us to conclusions which are reasoned, but not certain and compelling.

Stocker's analysis of practical reasoning takes Aristotle's doctrine of the mean as its starting point, but what he says would be consistent with Aquinas's analysis of prudence as well. On a Thomistic analysis, the proper synthesizing category for the judgments of practical reason is provided by happiness, understood as the practice of the virtues. Correlatively, if we are to adjudicate among diverse moral considerations and to resolve moral conflicts, we will need to appeal to, or develop, an account of the proper interrelationships of the virtues. This implies that there is indeed *one* sense in which diverse considerations are ranked on a scale of lower to higher — that is to say, the claims of the higher virtues, and particularly justice and (where applicable) charity, shape and direct the exercise of the lower virtues (as Aquinas

102. Michael Stocker, *Plural and Conflicting Values* (Oxford: Clarendon, 1990), 133; more generally, see 129-207.

103. Stocker, *Plural and Conflicting Values*, 172.

says; see II-II 23.8; 58.12). But this does not mean that our desires for higher goods, such as intellectual activity or religious worship, should always supersede our desires for lower or more basic goods. On the contrary, the demands of justice may well require us to forgo higher goods in some instances in order to respond to the just claims of others on us. Moreover, Aquinas holds that there are limits to what can be done to the individual, even in pursuit of genuine common goods (I-II 96.4; II-II 68.3). Charity and justice are architectonic virtues, but that does not mean that conflicts of virtue can be resolved by a simple ranking of goods in accordance with a scale of higher and lower, or greater and lesser. Apart from any other consideration, the special claims of others, and our general obligations of fairness and nonmaleficence, place constraints on behavior, and these must be taken into account in our attempts to assess the overall demands of virtue in particular cases.

The kind of reflection that is needed is illustrated at II-II 101.4, where Aquinas asks whether religious observances (particularly entry into religious life) should be forgone on account of one's duties to one's parents. He replies by observing that what is at stake here is a seeming conflict between two virtues, religion and piety (which is the proper disposition toward one's parents), and he goes on to argue that there can be no such conflict in reality:

> No virtue is opposed to or inconsistent with another virtue, because according to the Philosopher . . . good is not opposed to good. Hence, it is not possible that piety and religion should mutually impede one another, so that the act of one is excluded on account of the act of another. For the act of each virtue, as is plain from what was said above, is limited by due circumstances, which, if these be lacking, the act will not be an act of virtue, but of vice. Hence it pertains to piety to carry out one's duty, and to show due reverence to one's parents, in the requisite way. But it is not requisite that one should intend to show reverence to one's parents, more than to show reverence to God.

And as we would expect, he concludes from this that one's obligations to God should generally take priority over one's obligations to one's parents. Someone who gave greater weight to the latter would be acting viciously, rather than virtuously, and his act would therefore not be an act of true piety at all. Hence, there can be no conflict because in such a case, the higher obligation does indeed trump the lower.

But supposing that one's parents depend on her, in such a way that they cannot secure the necessities of life without her assistance. In that case, Aquinas says, the relative weight to be given to the demands of religion and piety is altered: "And so if our observances are necessary to our parents in the flesh, in such a way that they cannot be sustained without it, then neither do they lead us to something contrary to God, and we ought not to leave them in order to enter religious life. If however we are unable without sin to be free to fulfill our observances towards them without sin, or if they can sustain themselves without our aid, it is licit to leave off our observances towards them, in order that we might more readily be free for religious life" (II-II 101.4 *ad* 3).

We can here discern a complex family situation, calling for difficult personal choice, and beyond that, a complex social world which places inescapable demands on individuals. We may well suspect that Aquinas speaks out of hard personal experience here. At any rate, it is clear that the competing demands of the individual and his most intimate associates, God and the family, family and wider community, cannot be adjudicated and resolved prior to a contextual consideration and assessment of the differing claims and their relative priority or weight. Sometimes this assessment can be resolved by appeal to what seem straightforwardly to be higher considerations, but this will not always be the case. In particular, the demands of justice, and more especially the basic norms of special obligation and nonmaleficence, will set boundaries around what can count as permissible choices, even though these may force us to disregard what would otherwise be weighty considerations.

Or so it seems. Yet these boundaries themselves may sometimes be difficult to locate, or their application to the case at hand may be unclear. This brings us back to the question of the relation of prudential judgment to the traditional moral rules raised at the beginning of this section. It is impossible to devote sustained attention to moral norms without getting some sense of the complexities and ambiguities involved in actual moral decision making. This is not to say that moral decision making will be intellectually difficult and ambiguous in every instance. Aquinas's analysis of moral norms in terms of the structure of human acts provides us with powerful resources for sorting through a wide range of difficulties. Moreover, even apart from some such theoretical framework, most responsible adults can usually determine the right course of action in the many choices, large or small, which confront us in our daily lives. Yet we cannot altogether eliminate the possibility that we will encounter another kind of difficulty, that is, a properly intellectual difficulty arising from the ambiguities of our moral concepts themselves. We might find that we are genuinely perplexed about whether a given moral norm applies in the situation we face; if we are clear that it does, we may still be unclear about how to apply it.

Why should this be the case? Because — as is widely acknowledged —

moral concepts are always necessarily indeterminate to some degree.[104] That is, they do not perspicuously determine their own application in each and every case, nor can we always be certain that a given concept is the only or best way of approaching a particular situation. Nor, finally, is it possible to formulate a set of rules for applying a moral concept, of sufficient comprehensiveness to remove this indeterminacy altogether, since these rules themselves would need to be applied, and we would in some cases need rules to apply the rules, and so on to infinity. . . . At some points it will be necessary simply to decide that we will apply a given moral concept in one way rather than another. This decision is not arbitrary — on the contrary, it is a paradigmatic example of rule-governed behavior, since a concept is a rule, and to apply it is to engage in following a rule. By the same token, the process of applying moral concepts is not opaque — we will normally be able to justify our specific judgments in terms of salient reasons, which can be recognized as such by ourselves and our interlocutors. What we cannot do, however, is to provide reasons which would compel any and every rational person to agree that our application of the concept is uniquely correct.

Hence, the application of moral rules itself requires some exercise of judgment. Once this is recognized, we can see that dichotomy between prudence and rule-governed behavior is not persuasive. The prudent person applies moral rules through a process of judgment rather than employing a decision procedure similar to that of a mathematician, because there is no other way to apply rules formulated in the terms of natural languages. Is there any advantage, then, to being virtuous and prudent? What can the practically wise individual do, that the rest of us cannot? To answer this question, let us look again at the claim that for the wise person moral rules function as maxims. There is a grain of truth in this claim, insofar as moral rules cannot be grasped apart from some knowledge of the cases that exemplify them. However, the language of summarizing, the insistence on seeing rules as maxims or rules of thumb, suggests that rules are nothing more than condensed accounts of cases, which provide a shorthand reminder of past decisions but add no new element to what we could (and indeed, ideally would) learn from a seriatim study of the cases themselves.

Yet this is hardly a realistic picture even of an ordinary summary, much less of the traditional moral rules. No summary is simply a collection of items. Every summary is guided by a rationale, and unless that rationale is

104. In what follows, I summarize arguments that I developed at length in *Moral Action and Christian Ethics*. In addition to Kovesi, cited above, I also relied especially on J. M. Brennan, *The Open-Texture of Moral Concepts* (New York: Barnes and Noble, 1977).

understood, neither can the summary itself be understood *as* a summary. The same can be said about any sort of classification whatever.[105] In order to understand the biologist's system for the classification of animals, it is not enough to be able to say what sorts of creatures have been fitted into what categories. One must be able to explain the *point* of the classifications that have been made, and to make use of those classifications by applying them intelligently to new sorts of creatures.

Similarly, what distinguishes the prudent person is not her freedom from moral rules per se, but her capacity to apply the correlative moral concepts in an intelligent and humane way, in accordance with an intelligent grasp of the point of these concepts. For the person who is not so prudent, on the other hand, the moral rules will most likely function as summaries or reminders of lists of cases, composed seriatim. Because he has little or no intelligent grasp of the point of the rule, he will be reduced to the desperate expedient of attempting to imitate the moral paragons of the past without understanding. This deficiency may result in moral flightiness, or else it may lead to rigidity and a veneration for rules for their own sake. Yet in either case, what distinguishes the prudent from the imprudent person is not the fact that one does not need moral rules whereas the other does; what distinguishes them, rather, is that the prudent person is capable of an intelligent grasp and application of the moral rules whereas the imprudent person lacks this capacity.

More generally, prudence is the virtue which enables an individual to discern and to choose in particular situations in accordance with her best ideals of a happy life. It is itself a virtue, hence a perfection of the agent possessing it, and it is necessary to the exercise of all the other virtues. As such, it is necessary to happiness, understood as a life of virtue. At the same time, we cannot understand Aquinas's account of moral reasoning unless we understand prudence and its place in the moral life, because the exercise of prudence *is* practical reason, when it is well disposed and functioning in good order.

I remarked above that the exercise of prudence allows greater scope for creativity than we might at first expect. I hope that by this point it is apparent why this should be so. In order to exercise prudent judgment, it is necessary to discern which out of an indefinite range of acts would count as a genuine act of virtue, both with reference to particular virtues and with respect to the virtues seen in their necessary interconnections. While the relevant judgments will often be obvious, this will by no means always be the case — that is

105. Kovesi is particularly helpful here; see his *Moral Notions* (London: Routledge and Kegan Paul, 1967), 92-143.

why moral discernment calls for the virtue of prudence, rather than the mastery of an algorithm or technique for applying rules to cases.

By the same token, the processes of prudential judgment inform our grasp of the ideals and precepts informing the other virtues, and in this way they contribute indirectly to the formation of moral norms. We cannot understand moral rules, or (what comes to the same thing) general concepts of kinds of actions, without some grasp of the ways in which these apply to, and are instantiated in, concrete cases, which comprise paradigmatic instances of the relevant virtues (and vices). Correlatively, as we accumulate experience of applying these concepts through prudential judgment, our sense of the paradigms becomes more extensive, subtle, and sophisticated — which is to say that we grasp the relevant ideals and precepts more securely and can formulate them more adequately than we previously could have done. As Pamela Hall explains,

> Prudence on this view functions, even in imperfect exercise, within our discovery of the natural law and the goods to which it directs us. Just so, it helps to generate the very rules (of the natural law) that it will then work to apply and extend. For no rule, let alone those of the natural law, can be applied or constituted without an accompanying understanding of the rule's point as understood by prudence. This is so because to know how to apply a rule or even to know which rule to apply requires the exercise of practical judgement; such judgement would have to pick out of the situation at hand the relevant particulars in order to know which rule is appropriate for it. . . . One cannot intelligently select and apply a rule without some (prudential) grasp of the good that the rule is seeking to secure or protect.[106]

At the same time, it would be a mistake to assume that these processes of prudential discernment are limited to the individual level. On the contrary, we as individuals presuppose a fund of collective prudential judgment, on which we draw and to which we contribute in turn. By the same token, the community cannot arrive at an adequate grasp of basic moral precepts except through collective processes of experience, debate, and reflection — all of which must be informed by the prudential discernment of individuals if they are to go well.[107] This is the level at which the creative scope of prudence will be most apparent, as each community develops its own specification of the natural law within the context of its own circumstances and his-

106. Hall, *Narrative and Natural Law,* 40.

107. As Hall goes on to argue; see *Narrative and Natural Law,* 23-44.

tory. By the same token, the communal processes through which moral norms are formulated will operate within the same constraints of uncertainty and ineliminable contingency that we find operative within prudential judgment at the individual level. Thus, we would expect to find considerable room for variability in the natural law as it is specified in particular societies. This is precisely what Aquinas says. At I-II 94.4 he raises the question whether the natural law is the same for all, and he replies:

> . . . as was said above, those things pertain to the law of nature, to which the human person is naturally inclined; among which, it is proper to the human person that he is inclined to act according to reason. However, it pertains to reason to proceed from what is general to what is specific. . . . The speculative reason is constituted in one way with respect to this procedure, however, and the practical reason, in another way. Since the speculative reason deals chiefly with necessary things, concerning which it is impossible that it should proceed otherwise than it does, the truth is found without any defect in specific conclusions, as also it is found in general principles. But practical reason deals with contingent things, among which are human operations, and therefore, even though there is some necessity in its general principles, the more one descends to specifics, the more defect is found. . . . With respect to things that are done, there is not the same truth or practical rectitude for all people with respect to specifics, but only with respect to general principles; and with respect to those things about which there is the same rectitude in specifics for all, it is not equally known to all.

In the next chapter, we will examine the implications of these remarks in more detail.

In the first chapter, I indicated that the aim of this book is to develop a contemporary theological account of the natural law, taking my starting point from Aquinas's comment that the natural law represents the rational creature's distinctive way of participating in the eternal law (I-II 91.2). The main lines of that account have now been set out, and it will be helpful at this point to take stock of what has been accomplished so far.

By locating the natural law within the more general context of the eternal law, Aquinas underscores both the distinctiveness of the natural law and its continuity with components of created reality more generally considered. More specifically, as he explains here and elsewhere, the natural law represents the rational creature's way of attaining the final end that is proportionate to its nature — which is also to say, union with God, considered as the first principle and final end of all created existence. The distinctiveness of the natural law stems from the distinctive character of the human person, which implies that she can only attain her proper end through a process of rational choices, informed by some grasp of what that end might be. At the same time, however, this process is grounded in inclinations which stem from our created nature and reflect the intelligibilities structuring that nature, even in its prerational components. Seen from this perspective, the natural law reflects one expression of the more general tendency of all creatures to seek their final end, and in that sense to seek God, in and through activities structured by their natural inclinations.

In order to defend this approach to the natural law, therefore, it is first of all necessary to defend the broad claims that human beings as such have an intelligible nature and some conception, albeit imperfect, of that nature. That was the aim of the second chapter. As I attempted to show, the scholastic concept of human nature, together with the broader approach to nature which it reflects, is credible and persuasive, even seen within the context of contemporary biological science. More specifically, within this context we can develop a Thomistic conception of human nature taking our starting points from an account of the teleological structure of basic human inclinations. At the same time, it would be a mistake to move too quickly from such an account to moral conclusions. Aquinas's theory of the natural law reflects a synthesis of the scholastic natural law tradition with Aristotelian eudaemonism, and on this view the natural law reflects the teleological orientation of the creature considered as a whole, rather than the teleological orientation of particular inclinations, much less particular organs and functions. Hence, the cornerstone of a Thomistic theory of the natural law will be an account of happiness, understood as the final end and ultimate perfection of the human creature.

The claim that the human person has a final end, and even more, the claim that moral norms stem from this end, are likely to sound strange to most of our contemporaries. By arguing that the terrestrial last end of the human person consists in the practice of the virtues, Aquinas undoubtedly closes the gap between morality and an ideal of flourishing, but at the risk of offering a stipulative account of the relation between them. However, as I attempted to show in the third chapter, this relation does not depend on a simple equation of happiness with the practice of the virtues. Rather, it presupposes a rich and persuasive account of the various ways in which basic human inclinations, initially oriented toward ordinary nonmoral goods, are directed by their own intrinsic dynamics toward the pursuit and enjoyment of these goods in a particular, that is to say, a virtuous way. Hence, the intelligible structures of the basic human inclinations themselves give rise to certain ideals of virtue and render them naturally desirable and admirable. Correlatively, the life of virtue is seen to have a paradigmatic connection to a more basic form of well-being, which renders it plausible as a candidate for a satisfying and enjoyable kind of life.

Understood in this way, a Thomistic theory of the natural law is not at odds with a virtue-oriented approach to morality; indeed, this theory of the natural law *is* a theory of virtue. At the same time, Aquinas and the other scholastics also interpret the natural law within a context of more general assumptions and beliefs about the reasonable and lawlike character of morality. As we saw in this chapter, this context reflects genuine aspects of moral judgment. That is to say, morality is indeed lawlike or deontological, in the sense that the moral reasoning operates through determinate concepts of kinds of actions, which serve to set boundaries around permissible kinds of behavior. The deontological character of basic moral norms reflects basic structures of human action, which are morally salient because they structure the interactions constituting human communities. This is why fundamental moral norms, such as we find in the Decalogue, must be understood as overriding rules for action and not merely as disposable maxims, and it is also why we naturally frame moral reflection within a framework of distinctions among different kinds and degrees of agency and responsibility.

What this theory provides, in short, is an interpretation of human morality which locates it within the correlative doctrines of creation and providence. Seen within this context, human morality reflects the intelligibility and goodness of human existence, and as such, it expresses God's creative decree bringing a given kind of creature into existence. Correlatively, the ideals and practices constituting human morality in all its complexity and variety represent the proper and fundamental way in which the human creature participates in God's providence, "being provident for itself and others." Clearly, this theory as developed incorporates philosophical presuppositions and arguments, including much of the metaphysics and philosophy of nature informing Aquinas's own theory, and contemporary work in the philosophy of biology and moral naturalism. But these components should not detract from the fundamentally theological character of the theory. Given the strong emphasis which both the scholastics and the current theory place on the intelligibility of creation, seen as an expression of God's creative wisdom and love, we would expect to find much of theological importance in philosophical reflections on nature and morality.

In the first chapter, I noted that the scholastic concept of the natural law appears paradoxical from our perspective, insofar as the scholastics develop a scriptural and theological account of what they themselves regard as a universal natural law. By now, it will be apparent that the Thomistic theory of the natural law developed in this book is likewise paradoxical, although not in precisely the same way. Scholastic distinctions between reason and revelation, nature and grace, have been transformed over the centuries into distinctions among diverse cultures and ways of life, and it has become a matter of great urgency for us to bridge those distinctions. For this reason (among others), our own contemporaries have focused a great deal of attention on the relation between particular and universal in moral reflection. Among theologians, debates over the distinctiveness of Christian theology and especially the Christian way of life have set a large part of the agenda for Christian ethics for several decades now. The Thomistic theory of the natural law is paradoxical because it straddles these divisions, affirming both that the natural law reflects universal aspects of human existence and that it can only be fully understood in theological terms. Yet as I hope to show in what follows, the paradoxical character of this theory does not render it incoherent. In order to make this case, it will be necessary to sort through the particular and universal elements of the natural law in more detail. That will be the task of the last chapter.

CHAPTER FIVE

Theological Ethics and the Natural Law

In the first chapter, I remarked that until recently, work on the natural law among Christian theologians has tended to divide along broadly denominational lines, insofar as Protestant scholars have generally focused on the theological significance of the natural, widely construed, while Catholic scholars have given more emphasis to the rational character and normative content of the natural law. It will be apparent by now that the Thomistic theory of the natural law developed in this book combines elements of both the Catholic and the Protestant approaches, understood along these general lines. With the Catholic approach, it shares a confidence in our capacity to arrive at genuine moral knowledge, even though our limitations as creatures and as sinful men and women set constraints on our capacities for moral discernment. In one respect it also reflects a point of continuity with the modern Catholic approach (at least up until the early part of the twentieth century), namely, in its affirmation of the moral significance of prerational nature. With the Protestant approach, it shares a commitment to locating the natural law within a specifically theological and scriptural context and drawing on it as a basis for a distinctively Christian theological ethic.

Of course, it is always tempting to split the difference in current academic debates in hopes of preserving the best insights of the various positions while incurring none of their liabilities. That being so, it is worth emphasizing that the Thomistic theory of the natural law offered here does not do everything that contemporary defenders of natural law ethics would want. In particular, as we have more than once observed, it does not offer a comprehensive and substantive set of moral rules which are universally valid and can be recognized as such. Yet the point of this theory is not to provide a set of moral rules. Rather, it is meant first of all as a theologically informed interpretation of human morality, considered as a natural phenomenon and therefore as an expression of the distinctively human form of created goodness, and secondly as a theology of the moral life that locates and contextualizes it in relation to other central scriptural and doctrinal concerns.

At the end of the last chapter, I observed that the Thomistic theory of the natural law developed in this book may appear to be paradoxical, given contemporary debates over the distinctiveness or universality of Christian ethics. Yet this paradoxical character does not reflect incoherence — rather, it reflects the fact that this theory of the natural law construes the relation between the universal and particular elements of the natural law in a different way than do most of our contemporaries. In this respect I follow the scholastics, Aquinas included, who affirmed traditional views on the universality and supreme authority of the natural law, and yet saw no inconsistency in developing a theological perspective on the natural law. In this chapter, I want to say something more about the natural law seen from this twofold perspective as a universal human phenomenon and as a topic for theological reflection.

As I will try to show, a scriptural and theological perspective on the natural law is not inconsistent with affirming its universality — properly understood. Admittedly, such a perspective is inconsistent with a view according to which the natural law comprises a universally accessible set of determinate moral rules. Yet this does not imply that the natural law can be reduced to a purely formal norm. It does have substantive moral implications, including some that are generally available to human reason, although many others only become apparent from the perspective of revelation. That, at least, will be the argument of the first section of this chapter. I will then attempt to develop this argument over the next two sections by looking more closely at one particular issue, the doctrine of natural or human rights, seen from the perspective of a Thomistic account of the natural law.

Hence, this chapter will provide an occasion to examine an issue of immediate practical interest, and not only to Christians. Like the early modern natural law theorists discussed in the first chapter, we are facing a situation in which questions of moral universalism and pluralism have become urgently relevant. It is hardly surprising that within this context, secular as well as religious thinkers would turn once again to the natural law tradition, and even more to its successor, the human rights tradition, to provide a framework for adjudicating moral claims in a cross-cultural and international context. These attempts, in turn, will provide us with a starting point for working through some of the practical implications of a Thomistic theory of the natural law. By now, we will not expect this theory to provide an account of determinate rights which is compelling to all rational persons. And yet, it offers us more substantive moral guidance in this matter than we might initially expect, given the fundamentally theological character of the theory. It provides an interpretation of the idea of rights which displays the distinctively theological origins of this idea, while also accounting for its widespread diffusion in a wide variety of contexts; it provides a theological basis for discerning whether, and in what ways, we as Christians have a stake in supporting current human rights movements; and it offers reasons to hope that the language of rights will continue to provide a framework for moral dialogue in a pluralistic and conflictual world.

At the same time, the point of this theory of the natural law is to provide a way of thinking about the theological significance of human nature and the moralities stemming from that nature. So far, I have emphasized the connection between the doctrines of creation and providence and the natural law. In the final section of this chapter, I will attempt to draw out the implications of placing the natural law in a further doctrinal context, provided this time by the doctrine of grace.

1. The Natural Law as a Basis for a Christian Ethic

In *De republica* (as we noted in the first chapter), Cicero famously said of the natural law that "There will not be one law for Rome and another for Athens, nor will there be one law now and another one in the future, but one everlasting and immutable law will govern all peoples at all times."[1] This ideal of a universal and unchanging natural law, often expressed in Cicero's very words, runs through patristic and medieval authors, in both Christian and philosophical formulations, up to our own day. Yet as we have seen, Cicero's remarks need not be read as if they referred to a determinate set of moral rules, accessible to all persons of good will in all times and places. For the scholastics, the "one everlasting and immutable law" is nothing other than the law to which Paul refers in Romans 2:14, which is written on the hearts of the men and women of the nations, through which they judge what is good and evil, and in terms of which they will themselves be judged on the last day. The existence of the natural law is thus confirmed by revelation. Of course, this need not imply that our knowledge of the natural law depends on revelation. Rather, the scholastics recognized that, in common with many other fundamental elements of the faith, including the existence of God, the existence of

1. *De republica* III.XXII, 33. The translation is mine, but checked with the Loeb edition's translation.

the natural law could also be established through human reason apart from revelation. Indeed, the scholastics had ample evidence, including Cicero's remarks, among much else, that the existence of the natural law had in fact been recognized apart from revelation.

At the same time, however, it would be a mistake to conclude that Scripture simply confirms our best independently established theoretical formulations of the natural law. Here again, a comparison with rational and revealed knowledge of God is instructive. The existence of God can also be established through rational reflection — or that, at least, is a long-standing and officially sanctioned view among Catholic theologians, and one which I share. But this does not mean that God's self-revelation through Scripture adds nothing to our knowledge of God's existence, apart from providing welcome confirmation for our prior theories in this regard. Scripture reveals God's existence in and through revealing God's identity, God's stance and character in relation to us. It depicts God as one who is turned toward creation in providential care, and who is turned toward us in a loving offer of friendship. All this amounts to something more than a confirmation of what we already know about God, even with some supplemental knowledge thrown in. Rather, it provides definite content for what would otherwise be a series of placeholders for whatever we take to be ultimate in given categories of explanation — in Aquinas's lapidary words, whatever it is "that all call God" (*ST* I 2.3). As such, revelation not only confirms and supplements what we knew or thought we knew about God, it also indicates the proper significance of God's existence for us, in the process transforming even those elements that could be independently established.

It will be apparent by now that I believe the scholastics were right to hold that the existence of the natural law is confirmed by Scripture, which is not to say that we need accept all the details of medieval exegesis with respect to this doctrine.[2] At the same time, however, we should understand this confirmation along the same lines as we understand the scriptural revelation of God's existence. That is, revelation does not just confirm our independently established theories about natural law; rather, it reveals the existence of a natural law in and through indicating its significance within a more comprehensive theological framework. Seen in this context, the natural law is first of all a distinctively human manifestation of the intelligibility and goodness which

2. In what follows, I summarize arguments developed at more length in my *Natural and Divine Law: Reclaiming the Tradition for Christian Ethics* (Ottawa: Novalis; Grand Rapids: Eerdmans, 1999), 121-86, and "Natural Law as a Scriptural Concept: Theological Reflections on a Medieval Theme," *Theology Today* 59, no. 2 (July 2002): 226-41.

comprise the marks of creation. Correlatively, it represents God's providential care for creation. It provides the means by which men and women themselves participate in God's providence in their own affairs and in their relationships with one another and the rest of creation. What is more, as Paul's remarks suggest, the natural law plays a providential role in a more specific way, providing a basis for God's engagement with humanity through a revealed divine law and through the redemption made available in Christ. As such, it provides a necessary context for human reception of God's revelation, if only by providing a touchstone for our recognition of ourselves as sinful and of God's law and grace as holy and redeeming.

This brings me to a further point. In chapter 2, I observed that for the scholastics the doctrine of creation does not just establish that the world was caused by God. It further implies that the world is not opaque to God, but reflects, however imperfectly and obscurely, something of God's own goodness and intelligibility. I would argue that the same is true of the natural law, seen as a distinctively human expression of creation's reflection of the Creator. I do not mean to suggest that God's holiness and goodness should be understood in moral terms, as if God were just like a very good human being, only more so. Yet properly human forms of moral goodness, including our best ideals as well as our intermittent attainments, are reflections of the divine goodness in which we have been created, and as such are not wholly alien to God's goodness. This point is significant, it seems to me, because it gives us a basis to hope that there is some congruence between our moral ideals and aspirations on the one hand, and God's providential will for us on the other.[3] Indeed, this seems to me the most important implication of Aquinas's claim that the natural law reflects God's providential care. On this basis, we can have confidence that God's call and judgment of us will not be wholly at odds with our best ideals for ourselves — which is not to say that we judge God by human standards, but rather that we acknowledge that our own standards are themselves reflections (however fragmentary and distorted) of God's creative wisdom. We can be confident that God's call will be healing and liberating, not perverting and annihilating, of who and what we are — God's works may be terrible, but they are never strange.

Yet this theological construal of the natural law only works if we understand the law as Aquinas and the other scholastics did, that is to say, primarily in terms of our capacity for moral judgment and the general principles

3. Oliver O'Donovan brings out this point especially well — albeit with reference to a theology of the created order, rather than natural law as such — in his *Resurrection and Moral Order: An Outline for Evangelical Ethics* (Grand Rapids: Eerdmans, 1986); in particular, see 31-52.

through which that capacity operates. Otherwise, if we connect the natural law in its primary sense too closely with determinate rules, we will find ourselves in just the position that critics of the natural law have warned against — we will begin to project our moral standards onto God, in the process losing the sense of the absolute qualitative distance between God's goodness and our own. To put the point in another way, our created congruity with, and yet distance from, God's goodness is reflected, albeit imperfectly, by the congruence and yet distinction between the first principles of the natural law and the specific norms and social practices through which those first principles are expressed. This need not imply that the natural law has no normative implications. So long as we hold on to traditional and scholastic flexibility, our theology can accommodate secondary yet legitimate senses in which the natural law is comprised of determinate precepts, whether revealed or rationally discerned or both at once.

Clearly, this approach will have implications for any attempt to appropriate the natural law as a basis for a theological ethic. If the natural law in its primary sense is understood in terms of a basic capacity operating through first principles, and if we add, as we must, that these underdetermine the specific norms in terms of which they are expressed, then clearly we cannot speak of *the* natural law ethic, seen as foundational to, or indeed as a contrast to, *the* distinctively Christian way of life. Earlier I remarked that any socially embodied morality can be regarded as a natural law ethic, and the same can be said of the moralities that have emerged through the practice and reflection of the church in its many embodiments. (Of course, to a very considerable degree Christian and secular moralities will overlap in any society in which Christianity is influential.) For this reason, I would suggest that we should extend scholastic flexibility by speaking of natural law moralities in the plural, including some which predominate among "the nations," and others which are distinctively Christian.[4]

The implications of this approach may be clearer if we place it in the context of recent debates over the significance of the natural law for Christian

4. As I noted in the first chapter, David Novak has developed a Jewish interpretation of the natural law which is similar in key respects to the Thomistic theory of the natural law developed here, particularly in its emphasis on the doctrine of creation and the correlative emphasis on God's wisdom, rather than on God's power; see *Natural Law in Judaism* (Cambridge: Cambridge University Press, 1998). If he and I are both right, then it would make sense to speak of distinctively Jewish and Christian, or even Judeo-Christian, moralities of the natural law. However, as Novak himself points out, many Jewish scholars would deny that natural law is a meaningful or helpful category within Jewish thought (just as many Christian theologians deny the legitimacy of speaking of a Christian natural law; see *Natural Law,* 62-91, for further discussion).

ethics. At the beginning of this chapter, I noted that one of the ongoing theological debates over the natural law has to do with the proper attitude of the Christian as such toward what might be described in broad terms as the common values and aspirations of the human race. Traditionally, this debate has developed along denominational lines, according to which Catholics are more inclined to endorse the values of the wider society, while Protestants are more likely to challenge the values of one's culture, or of human morality more generally.[5] We see a good example of this traditional divide in Stanley Hauerwas's widely influential book *The Peaceable Kingdom.*[6] In a section titled "Church and World: The Ethics of a Critical Community," Hauerwas begins by quoting the Catholic moral theologian Richard McCormick's claim that "Love and loyalty to Jesus Christ, the perfect man, sensitizes us to the meaning of persons. . . . In this sense, the Christian tradition only illumines the human values, supports them, provides a context for their reading at given points in history."[7]

Hauerwas, for his part, regards this approach to the Christian moral tradition as wrongheaded, because "this assumption presumes that Chris-

5. The disjunction is deliberate, because it would be misleading to suggest that most mainstream Protestants challenge social mores in just the same way that Hauerwas does. My point is that Catholics tend both to affirm human morality as such and to be relatively positive to the mores of the societies in which they live, whereas Protestants have traditionally taken more oppositional stances to one or the other.

6. Hauerwas, *The Peaceable Kingdom: A Primer in Christian Ethics* (Notre Dame: University of Notre Dame Press, 1983). Of course, Hauerwas has written a great deal since this book came out, but I do not believe he has changed his views substantially on the matters discussed in what follows. I refer to this, rather than to his later works, because it has been widely influential over the past twenty years, and also because it sets out the relevant issues in an especially clear and illuminating way.

7. Richard McCormick, "Does Faith Add to Ethical Perception?" in *Readings in Moral Theology No. 2: The Distinctiveness of Christian Ethics,* ed. Richard McCormick and Charles Curran (New York: Paulist, 1980), 156-73, here 169; quoted in Hauerwas, *The Peaceable Kingdom,* 59. I believe Hauerwas is right to take McCormick's remarks to be representative of mainstream Catholic moral theology during most of the last century. Most of the essays collected in *The Distintiveness of Christian Ethics* bear this out; in addition to McCormick's essay just cited, originally published in 1979, see especially Joseph Fuchs, "Is There a Specifically Christian Morality?" (originally 1970), 3-19. More recent examples will be offered below. However, special note should be made of the work of the Jesuit theologian Norbert Rigali, who has long insisted on the distinctiveness of Christian ethics and the importance of taking its cultural and historical context into account: see Norbert Rigali, "Christ and Morality" (1978), reprinted in *The Distinctiveness of Christian Ethics,* 111-20; "Moral Pluralism and Christian Ethics," *Louvain Studies* 13 (1988): 305-21; "The Uniqueness and Distinctiveness of Christian Morality and Ethics," in *Moral Theology: Challenges for the Future,* ed. Charles E. Curran (New York: Paulist, 1990), 74-93; and "Christian Morality and Universal Morality: The One and the Many," *Louvain Studies* 19 (1994): 18-33.

tians will never be radically anti-world — that is, aligned against the prevailing values of their cultures." He rightly traces this assumption back to the long-standing Catholic commitment to an idea of natural law, which leads him to add that "too often natural law assumptions function as an ideology for sustaining some Christians' presuppositions that their societies — particularly societies of Western democracies — are intrinsic to God's purposes." He goes on to add that while there are commonalities between Christian ethics and other moralities, these "are not sufficient to provide a basis for a 'universal' ethic grounded in human nature *per se.* Attempts to secure such an ethic inevitably result in a minimalistic ethic and often one which gives support to forms of cultural imperialism."[8]

Certainly, Hauerwas and McCormick disagree sharply about the extent to which Christian ethics might be compatible with a secular morality. Yet their disagreement is framed in terms of a more fundamental presupposition that Scripture and natural law represent two distinct sources for Christian ethics, which ideally complement one another but may also come into conflict. Yet from the standpoint of a Thomistic theory of the natural law, this assumption is mistaken — the natural law cannot rightly be understood apart from Scripture, which itself establishes a central place for the natural law in Christian ethical reflection. If this conclusion is sound, it calls into question other dichotomies that have traditionally been mapped onto the distinction between Scripture and natural law, including especially the dichotomies presupposed by both McCormick and Hauerwas, between the ideal of the truly human and the ideal of the uniquely Christian, and correlatively between an ethic centered on the church community versus an ethic that is open to a pluralistic world.

First and most fundamentally, this approach to the natural law has the effect of locating Christian ethical reflection squarely within the world — that is to say, within the socially and historically specific locations within which actual Christians find themselves. Where else should Christian ethical reflection take place? We are not angels, and in the church triumphant there is no need for moral judgment. Indeed, the dichotomy between the church and the world, cast in these terms, is misleading. The church, whether considered as a congeries of institutions or as individuals sharing a common faith, is always necessarily located within a particular society. As such, it will be continuous with that society in some respects, both physically — even the desert fathers and mothers relied on the wider community for material support — and culturally — even the most radical rejection of dominant values will in-

8. These quotes are all taken from Hauerwas, *The Peaceable Kingdom,* 59, 60-61.

corporate those values, if only as a way of giving meaning to their rejection. The boundaries between the church and the world will always be permeable, and for this reason the task of Christian ethics will always necessarily involve appraisal and selective affirmation, as well as critique and rejection, of the alternatives presented to it by its complex history and social location.

By the same token, however, Hauerwas is right to challenge the idea that Christian ethics can be founded on, or much less, equated with, an ideal of the "truly human," for the simple reason that there can be no one, determinate such ideal. Because we are complex creatures, there can be a variety of adequate expressions of our nature — as the scholastics knew — and correlatively, these expressions will inevitably take the form of social conventions developed through some form of communal reflection — as they also knew. There is thus ample room for cultural and historical variation in socially particular expressions of the natural law, and this is why we can legitimately speak in terms of natural moralities, rather than in terms of one determinate set of natural law precepts.

If this is the case, then it is at best misleading to say, as McCormick does, that our allegiance to Jesus Christ, regarded as the exemplar of human perfection, calls us to endorse human values tout court. The question raised at this point by a Thomistic theory of the natural law is: Which values, and which expressions of those values? Hauerwas quotes other remarks by Catholic theologians which focus the issue still more sharply; for example, Timothy O'Connell's remark that "the fundamental ethical command imposed on the Christian is precisely to be what he or she is. 'Be human.' That is what God asks of us, no more and no less."[9] The difficulty with this injunction is that it presupposes that there is one and only one way of being human, perhaps exemplified by Jesus' humanity (exactly how is not explained). If the Thomistic theory of the natural law developed here is valid, however, this is exactly what we cannot presuppose. There are many ways of being human, including a plurality of defensible and legitimate expressions of the basic inclinations of human nature.

This conclusion may seem to be at odds with the naturalism and realism of a Thomistic theory of natural law. If the arguments of the past three chapters are sound, then we do have a concept of human nature, incomplete and imperfect, to be sure, but developed enough to justify us in claiming that we have a real and substantive grasp of our own humanity. Moreover, this concept

9. Quoted in Hauerwas, *The Peaceable Kingdom,* 56. More recently, Hans Küng has similarly argued that a morality of "basic humanity" should serve as one basis for interreligious dialogue, a proposal subsequently endorsed by Jacques Dupuis; see Hans Küng, *Global Responsibility: In Search of a New World Ethic* (New York: Continuum, 1996), 55-64, and Jacques Dupuis, *Towards a Christian Theology of Religious Pluralism* (Maryknoll, N.Y.: Orbis, 1997), 321-26.

of human nature can account for much of the substance of morality, including the emergence and centrality of ideals of virtue, the lawlike character of morality, and the scope and limits of moral responsibility. These components of morality may not comprise everything that we think of as common morality, but they are not purely formal, either; they include both substantive ideals of some of the virtues, and general norms of nonmaleficence, fairness, and accountability which have clear practical implications.

From this point we might seem to have all we need to develop a full-blown substantive set of moral norms which are grounded in human nature and can therefore be justified without reference to any particular theological, philosophical, or cultural tradition. But on reflection, that is not so obvious. Difficulties begin to emerge when we attempt to move from the substantive commonalities mentioned above to moral specifics. Let's grant, for example, that the virtue of courage is given conceptual shape by broad exigencies of human life, which also render it admirable and valuable for all persons. This would seem to be a prime example of a universally valid moral norm. Yet it is far from obvious that this level of consensus could yield agreement on substantive moral claims. As Lee Yearley pointed out in his exhaustive comparison of ideals of courage in Aquinas and the Chinese philosopher Mencius, agreements on the virtues tend to be broad but shallow, whereas relevant differences tend to be more focused but deep.[10] Yet these deep differences concern substantive issues which must be resolved if individuals and societies are to function. Courage offers a particularly good example of this point, precisely because it seems to represent a universally shared ideal for human life. Nearly everyone would agree that true courage is admirable — but what counts as true courage, seen in contrast not only to cowardice but to similitudes of courage? Once we begin to explore these questions, culturally specific ideals and commitments quickly come into play. One society's heroic martyrs are another society's murderous and perverse suicide bombers.

Similar observations could be made even about the basic norms of nonmaleficence summarized in the Decalogue. In a widely influential passage in his *The Concept of Law*, H. L. A. Hart argues for what he describes as "the core of good sense" in the traditional doctrine of natural law, understood as comprised of these basic norms.[11] His argument is simple: There are some re-

10. I take this point from Lee Yearley; see *Mencius and Aquinas: Theories of Virtue and Conceptions of Courage* (New York: SUNY Press, 1990), 169-203.

11. H. L. A. Hart, *The Concept of Law*, 2nd ed. (Oxford: Clarendon, 1994; 1st ed. 1961), 199. He sets out what he describes as the minimum content for any viable morality at 193-99; more generally, see 185-212. The overall point is commonly made; in a theological context, see Hans Schwarz, *Creation* (Grand Rapids: Eerdmans, 2002), 202-3.

curring tasks and difficulties within human life which every society must address, in the context of human capabilities and limitations which do not fundamentally change. Men and women must find some way to live together amicably, or at least with mutual forbearance, to cooperate to procure the necessities of life, and to secure the existence and stability of the next generation, all in the context set by approximate equality, mutual vulnerability, limited altruism, and the natural scarcity of needed resources. These "truisms" provide, as he says, "reasons" why any moral code must include certain kinds of content. Yet as he goes on to observe, this does not mean that all moral codes must address these matters in the same way. On the contrary, it is apparent that they do not. It is probably true, as Hart observes, that almost every society places some limits on the taking of human life. But what follows from that fact? Can we draw any definite conclusions that would not be a repetition of the basic observation itself? It certainly does not follow that every society agrees with us that persons should only be killed if they are attacking someone, or else have already done so. What is more, in some societies killing is regulated through a system of restorative fines; this is indeed a way of placing limits on killing, but it is nonetheless strikingly different from contemporary Western systems of prohibiting killing through stringent retributive penalties.[12]

It is very tempting, when faced with these and similar conundrums, to make short work of them by moving back to a level of generality at which agreement can be secured. The temptation should be resisted. If we formulate our claims at a sufficiently high level of abstraction, we will almost certainly be able to come up with some normative claims that everyone could accept. The difficulty is that once we have moved to that level, we will find ourselves at the level of very general statements along the lines of "Courage is good" or "Killing should be avoided, outside carefully defined parameters." These kinds of generalities are not simply empty or formal; they do have some substance, and as I argue below, they can be made to do normative work. Nonetheless, by themselves they fall short of the kinds of determinate, substantive norms that are needed to provide actual practical guidance in specific situations of choice. No individual or society can live at the level of general ideals of virtue and unspecified admonitions to place constraints on certain kinds of actions.

12. For a good example of the legal and practical differences between our system of retributive justice and a system based on a principle of restoration (not limited to the differing treatments of killing), see Diana Jeater's discussion of British efforts to impose their legal system on the indigenous peoples of (then) Southern Rhodesia, "'Their Idea of Justice Is So Peculiar': Southern Rhodesia 1890-1910," in *The Moral World of the Law*, ed. Peter Coss (Cambridge: Cambridge University Press, 2000), 178-95.

In the last chapter, we observed that the paradigmatic moral concepts associated with nonmaleficence are typically associated with natural kinds of actions, specified by the relevant moral concepts as illegitimate or unjustified forms of killing, appropriation of goods, and the like. Hart's point can usefully be reformulated in these terms. There is a distinctively human way of life, comprised of characteristic patterns of activity carried out in the context of recurring human capabilities and needs. These patterns of activity comprise natural kinds of actions, which as we have seen are always morally salient — because, as Hart implies, every society must find a way to both provide for some legitimate pursuit of these kinds of activities while at the same time placing boundaries around them. Correlatively, the boundaries in question will be fundamentally social norms, rather than abstract rules which are then put into practice. That is to say, the relevant norms will necessarily emerge out of processes of practice and prudential reflection carried out communally, as Pamela Hall has shown; by the same token, these norms will be manifested and maintained through social expectations and sanctions.[13] Theoretical reflection on moral (or indeed legal) norms will always be subsequent to, and to some degree informed by, these processes of communal formulation.

These processes, in turn, will always incorporate contingent elements, such as we find informing the moral traditions of particular societies — again, a Thomistic analysis of the limitations of prudence implies as much, as we saw in the preceding chapter. That is why it would be impossible, even in principle, to specify how the norms of a particular society would develop under ideal conditions, through the reflection of perfectly reasonable and impartial agents. Hilliard Aronovitch makes a convincing case for this point through a defense of a tradition-based model of moral reasoning, developed as an alternative to John Rawls's (superficially similar) idea of a wide reflective equilibrium among our moral intuitions and analytic arguments. Aronovitch says the alternative approach he is defending rests on the familiar but controversial claim that,

> as distinct from both deductive reasoning which traces out conceptual implications, and from inductive reasoning which constructs generalizations based on an appropriate sample of instances, there is an additional type of reasoning which proceeds from case to case, from particular to particular, ascribing a property to a novel case or a particular based on its likeness to a known one or limited cluster of known ones. I might argue,

13. Pamela Hall, *Narrative and the Natural Law: An Interpretation of Thomistic Ethics* (Notre Dame: University of Notre Dame Press, 1994), passim.

> for example, that since racquetball is like squash, in set-up, equipment, object, etc., your being good at the former game makes it likely that you will be good at the latter; or that since marijuana is like alcohol, in being an inebriant that is not necessarily dangerous or addictive, it should be legalized just as alcohol is; or that, as the US Supreme Court held, since burning the flag is like a form of dissenting speech it should be lawful and tolerated. Though each of these arguments may be debated, it is the form of the argument that is of interest to us. And as a type, reasoning by analogy is well known in the history of philosophy, and has even been thought by some to be pre-eminent; it is in any case a type for which criteria of assessment have been articulated; and a type widely and confidently applied in a host of everyday and theoretical contexts, nonnormative and normative, including very notably (common) law.[14]

The dominance of analogical or casuistical forms of reasoning in moral and legal contexts has been widely defended on grounds that I take to be persuasive, so long as deductive and inductive forms of moral reasoning are not altogether ruled out.[15] What this implies, as Aronovitch goes on to note, is that moral conclusions will not generally carry the same certainty as we expect to find in other domains: "Unlike deductive arguments which are either valid or invalid, analogical arguments are more or less persuasive; that is, their conclusions are probable or reliable to one degree or another, though sometimes definitively so for all practical purposes."[16] Hence, an element of contingency is introduced into moral reasoning by the dominant form it takes:

> . . . WRE [wide reflective equilibrium] construes the relation between principles and particulars as deductive or conceptual. In fact, it should be seen as analogical; that is, principles, more general notions, arise out of the preceding particulars and are constituted by them; and being thus constituted, the principles are limited in scope and import (and are also not to be confused with inductive generalizations). This is also to say, therefore, that it would be a mistake to think the earlier elements in the sequence

14. Hilliard Aronovitch, "Reflective Equilibrium or Evolving Tradition?" *Inquiry* 39 (1996): 399-419, at 402. Aronovitch speaks in terms of the specificity of traditions, whereas I speak in terms of the specificity of moralities or of moral systems, because I prefer to reserve "tradition" for self-consciously reflective, "academic" trajectories of study and debate, for example, the tradition of reflection on the natural law.

15. For a good introduction to recent discussions of casuistry and its contemporary implications, see James Keenan and Thomas Shannon, introduction to *The Context of Casuistry,* ed. Keenan and Shannon (Washington, D.C.: Georgetown University Press, 1995), xv-xxiii.

16. Aronovitch, "Reflective Equilibrium," 402.

> somehow imply or entail the later ones, that the link at those points [is] deductive or conceptual. That mistake is a version of what can be called the deductivist fallacy, which falsely supposes that because B follows A and is somehow logically connected to it, the link is deductive when actually it is analogical or, as we may say, interpretative and associative.[17]

I have quoted Aronovitch at some length because he offers a particularly clear and cogent account of the processes and limitations of practical reasoning on a social level. At the end of the last chapter, we noted that moral concepts are always necessarily indeterminate to some degree, and this indeterminacy places limits on the degree of certainty that we can attain in particular instances of choice. What is more, this indeterminacy of particular choices inevitably introduces elements of contingency at the social level, where moralities emerge and develop out of the intelligibilities informing human nature. This does not mean that the development of particular moralities is an arational process, any more than moral judgment at the individual level is arational. Nonetheless, the kind of rationality in question cannot be analyzed in such a way as to imply that the social processes of moral discernment can or should (even "in principle") yield a rationally compelling set of moral norms purged of all contingent elements.

This brings us to a critical point. The intelligibilities of human nature inform social norms, and for that reason we can analyze and evaluate particular moralities in terms of their natural origins. In that sense, the Thomistic theory of the natural law is a realistic theory, and implies a version of moral cognitivism.[18] Yet the intelligibilities of human nature underdetermine their forms of expression, and that is why this theory does not yield a comprehensive set of determinate moral norms, compelling to all rational persons. In order to move from our best accounts of human nature to moral judgments, we must first of all take account of the diverse social forms through which our shared nature is expressed, and secondly, we must appraise these in terms of criteria that will inevitably be contingent to some degree. It is here, in the process of moving from a reflection on human nature to moral judgments, that

17. Aronovitch, "Reflective Equilibrium," 408. In my view, the link between general moral norms and particulars is conceptual (not deductive), but not in such a way as to affect Aronovitch's point.

18. "A version of . . ." because on this view, the formulation and specification of moral propositions will always be relative to some particular socially embodied morality. I agree on this point (at least in general terms) with Bernard Williams and John Searle; see respectively *Ethics and the Limits of Philosophy* (Cambridge: Harvard University Press, 1985) and *The Construction of Social Reality* (New York: Free Press, 1985).

theological judgments will have their most immediately apparent practical impact. The historically specific determinants of Christian ethics — Scripture, traditions of moral reflection, the teachings and practices of particular churches, the experiences and struggles of individuals — have all informed our sense of what it means to live as God would have us live. And while it would be a mistake to be overly confident on this score, we have reason to hope that in and through these determinants God has begun to reveal to us which out of many different configurations of human nature are to be preferred, or at least, which are most congruent with the life of the church. This does not mean that other ways of living are necessarily wicked or perverse, but it does mean that an appeal to human nature alone is not sufficient to determine God's will in moral matters. Human nature offers a set of starting points for action and reflection, and these are not simply obviated by theological considerations. Nonetheless, they must be given direction and shape by theological reflection in order to be translated into an adequate Christian ethic.

Thus, because it leaves room for recognizing a plurality of natural moralities, a Thomistic theory of the natural law provides a starting point for developing a theologically informed natural law ethic. Because it takes its starting points from the natural givens of human life, a theological ethic will not be wholly discontinuous or unintelligible, seen from the standpoint of other moralities. At the same time, however, insofar as this ethic necessarily presupposes a theologically informed construal of human nature, set in the framework of a particular understanding of the meaning of human life, it will not simply be equivalent to an ethic of the "fully human." There are many ways of being human, and what we must do, in order to develop a theologically adequate account of the natural law, is to develop an account — by no means the only one possible, but our best account here and now — of what it means to be human in a Christian way.

At the same time, the construction of a Christian ethic is not the only task for Christian moral reflection. We are also called upon to participate in the ongoing processes of formation, critique, and re-formation of moral norms in the societies in which we live. Does the minimal moral realism of a Thomistic theory of the natural law provide sufficient resources for this task? In the remainder of this section, I want to suggest that it does. Admittedly, this theory recognizes the plurality of possible expressions of human nature at the level of social morality. For this reason, we cannot speak of *the* natural law at the level of determinate norms, but must rather speak in terms of natural moralities in the plural. At the same time, however, it stretches credulity to claim that all of these moralities are equally sound or desirable — from a Christian's viewpoint or anyone else's. A rational grasp of the exigencies of our nature does offer criteria for distinguishing between better and worse social arrangements. Correlatively, some arrangements will be more satisfactory from the standpoint of Christian convictions than others, even though this need not imply that the alternatives are necessarily unnatural, corrupt, wicked, or illegitimate. What is more, we have some reason to be hopeful about the prospects for persuading others, whose fundamental convictions may be very different from ours, to share our moral judgments, even as we open ourselves to persuasion and correction by them.

After all, the Thomistic theory of the natural law does identify morally significant constants in human nature, considered as such. We cannot establish a determinate yet universally compelling moral code on the basis of these constants, but that does not rule out the possibility of arguing for their moral significance with a reasonable expectation that others will find our arguments persuasive. This possibility does not presuppose that we can step outside the parameters of our own socially situated moralities, or our traditions of reflection on those moralities. We can arrive at moral judgments from within our own particular contexts of beliefs and practices, while hoping that these might prove persuasive to others in quite different cultural contexts. The fact remains that we cannot arrive at judgments which *must* be rationally compelling to all persons of good will, or even judgments that all persons would endorse under ideal circumstances. Nonetheless, this fact does not at all rule out the possibility that we might actually persuade others, here and now.

It is worth underscoring the point that practical reflection, at the social as well as the individual level, focuses on choice — that is to say, it focuses on what is to be done in the light of specific aims and circumstances, rather than attempting to ascertain some independently existing state of affairs. This implies that dialogue across cultural boundaries cannot rely on shared observations to provide touchstones for adequacy and correctness, but by the same token, it also implies that a given practical dilemma will have more than one defensible answer. While this plurality of options undoubtedly undercuts efforts to defend the moral necessity of specific social arrangements, for better or worse, it also lowers the bar for arriving at defensible answers to practical dilemmas here and now. We need not show that a given set of norms or social arrangements is necessary, or inevitable, or the best solution possible, in order to defend it as a rational expression of our shared human nature. Nor do we need to show that this arrangement was implicit in the moralities of the various participants in the dialogue, or that it could have been justified in advance in the relevant cultural contexts, if anyone had thought to do so. All we need to show is that a given arrangement is defensible here and now, in terms that all parties can accept as reasonable, all things considered. We have no guarantees that even this level of agreement will be possible in every instance, but if the Thomistic theory of the natural law is correct, we have good reason to hope that it will be possible in many, perhaps most instances.

This brings us back to considerations raised at the beginning of this section. That is, the Thomistic theory of the natural law does imply that we can identify morally significant components of human nature. And even though these components underdetermine the moral concepts expressing them, we can say something about their practical implications. We may not be able to decide among competing versions of courage, for example, but at least we can confidently predict that daring or perseverance in the face of danger will be universally admired; by the same token, it counts in favor of a practice or way of life that it fosters bravery, and a way of life that encouraged pervasive and continual fear would seem on its face to be vicious. A different yet related criterion is suggested by what I described in earlier chapters as natural vices, or more exactly, conceptions of broad kinds of vices which emerge as correlates to the ideals of the cardinal virtues. These, it will be remembered, include perversity with respect to individual well-being, and cruelty and callousness in one's relations with others. Again, these "vicious ideals" do not specify their substantive applications — one person's ideals of purity and self-denial will be another person's monkish virtues, which are virtues in name only. Nonetheless, these paradigms of viciousness do provide points of reference in terms of which particular arrangements can be challenged, and perhaps justified, by reference to considerations that will be generally understood and acknowledged as valid and relevant. For example, an ideal of family life which requires women to sacrifice most or all opportunities for education, development of intellectual pursuits, or autonomy of judgment might be defended on the grounds that this kind of differential sacrifice is necessary in order to ensure some higher ideal. Nonetheless, the onus is against it, on the grounds of both perversity (it requires women themselves to sacrifice inclinations which are central to their identity precisely as human beings) and callousness or cruelty (on the part of those, both men and women, who blithely take these sacrifices for granted).

From the standpoint of a Thomist theory of the natural law, these kinds of considerations have saliency and force because a Christian is committed on theological grounds to respecting and promoting human well-being and happiness in whatever ways she can. As we will see more fully below, the Thomist account of happiness and its relation to the virtues provides a rationale for taking these considerations seriously, and the theological virtue of charity makes it imperative to do so. But does this mean that others, who need not share these theoretical and practical commitments, cannot appreciate the force of these kinds of arguments? By no means. Ideals of virtue and the paradigms of vice corresponding to them, together with a range of other considerations, are natural to the human person, and so we would expect to find that these kinds of arguments are raised in a variety of circumstances, and felt to be relevant even where their exact justification and application remain uncertain.

And this, I want to suggest, is just what we do find. In some form or other, admiration for the cardinal virtues is nearly universal, and by the same token, individuals or social arrangements seen as undermining these virtues are deplored. Perversity, cruelty, and callousness are likewise almost always condemned, even though what counts as perverse, callous, or cruel behavior in specific instances may remain under dispute. On this theory of the natural law, these kinds of judgments are explained as reflections of the intelligible structures of human nature, as these spontaneously express themselves in human judgments. But it is by no means necessary to share that theoretical perspective in order to share in the judgments — as long-standing human experience confirms.

If this line of argument is sound, then the prospects for moral dialogue and reasoned consensus are not so grim as we might have feared. Moral reasoning is constrained by inherent limits, with the result that at the level of substantive norms the natural law is not the same for all, nor is it known to all (cf. I-II 94.4). Nonetheless, this does not mean that reasoned moral dialogue and even consensus are impossible or available only within the parameters of preestablished moral agreements. In our pluralistic and increasingly fragmented world society, we may not be able to agree on everything, but we may yet find that we can agree as rational interlocutors on some things. At least, the hope that we might be able to do so is not an irrational hope.

In the next two sections, I will attempt to develop and defend these claims through a closer examination of the idea of natural or human rights. This idea, I want to suggest, offers a parade example of a moral concept which emerged out of a theologically specific construal of what is natural to the human person, and then caught on as a framework for moral judgment and discourse in a wide range of disparate contexts. As such, it offers an illustrative — and practically very significant — example of a moral concept which emerges within one socially specific moral context, and then proves to be persuasive to a wide range of others, operating in different contexts.

2. From Natural Law to Human Rights

Over the past half-century, the idea of natural or human rights has been transformed from a rhetorical flourish to a central focus for scholarly concern among philosophers, social theorists, and theologians. In this way, it resembles the idea of natural law itself — and this is hardly surprising, since there are clear affinities between a natural law ethic and a view according to which we enjoy basic rights stemming from shared characteristics of our human nature. Indeed, to a considerable extent the contemporary revival of interest in the natural law stems from growing scholarly interest in the idea of human rights.[19]

Yet it would be a mistake to assume that we can move directly from the scholastic period to our own, by way of a supposedly shared doctrine of natural or human rights. In the first place, until recently the historiography of human rights insisted on a break between the medieval and modern periods, precisely on this issue. On this view, the doctrine of human rights is a distinctively modern view, which may draw on the language and inspiration of earlier natural law theories but reflects a decisive new emphasis on the claims of the individual. Recently, this view has been challenged by the medievalist Brian Tierney, who shows that the language and substance of the (supposedly) modern doctrine of natural rights can be found as early as the thirteenth century.[20] Even if this is the case, however, the relation between natural law and natural rights raises further questions. Most fundamentally, it forces us to confront basic questions concerning the universal validity — or otherwise — of rights claims, and by implication, concerning their independence from, or indebtedness to, a distinctively Christian view of the human person.

Most recent theories of natural or human rights have argued that rights claims are not only universally valid but universally defensible, in terms of arguments persuasive to any rational and well-disposed person. Yet whatever the theoretical force of these arguments, the history of the doctrine of natural rights tells against it. As Paul Hyams observes,

> We increasingly experience confrontations between western nations and those of the so-called Third World over notions of human rights, corruption, etc., which we in the West see as self-evident but which they sometimes characterize as western impositions unsuited to the conditions of their states. These misunderstandings are firmly rooted in formulations

19. For two very different examples, see John Finnis, *Natural Law and Natural Rights* (Oxford: Clarendon, 1980), and Martha Nussbaum, *Women and Human Development: The Capabilities Approach* (Cambridge: Cambridge University Press, 2000) — although admittedly Nussbaum does not develop her theory in terms of natural law as such.

20. Brian Tierney, *The Idea of Natural Rights: Studies on Natural Rights, Natural Law, and Church Law, 1150-1625* (Atlanta: Scholars Press, 1997); the earlier arguments are summarized at 13-42, and Tierney's own response is developed at 42-77.

> of the issues inherited from Roman Law. Not just the specific content of these rights but their whole orientation is very largely owed to legal ideas expounded by the classical jurists of the first centuries of our era, codified under Justinian in the sixth century, then taken up and developed in European law schools from the eleventh century onwards. They are now so deeply engrained into our culture that I for one frequently espouse the illusion of their indisputable rightness as passionately as anyone else and experience angry frustration at the inability of outsiders to see the truth. So hard is it to see them for what they are, as context-dependent as any other aspect of our culture.[21]

Hyams's reference to the Roman jurists may suggest that the doctrine of natural rights, while culturally specific to Western societies, is not theologically specific. Yet as he goes on to observe, even though this doctrine incorporates elements from the earliest beginnings of the Western legal tradition, the doctrine itself only emerged relatively late, even granting, with Tierney, that it is medieval rather than modern in origin. Referring to Tierney's conclusions, Hyams states:

> He notes that the notion of subjective rights inherent in human beings *qua* human beings is "a distinctively western invention." The Greeks had nothing like it. Nobody could realistically suggest that the Ten Commandments conferred or recognized any such rights. Roman law, it is true, accepted the existence of an "objective natural law," but never took the short step from treating dominion as a right to the recognition of "a doctrine of subjective natural rights." That most of the characteristic arguments of modern natural rights language can already be found in the middle ages is due almost entirely to canon lawyers. The process nicely demonstrates, indeed, the way that canon law functioned as a learned law that dealt with the real world, and so adapted civilian doctrine to the real-life situations that faced them in court and confessional.[22]

If it is indeed true (as I believe) that we owe the first explicit claims for the existence of subjective natural rights to medieval canon lawyers, this implies that theological convictions played a decisive role in the processes out of which these claims emerged. If this further conclusion is justified, it lends credence to

21. Paul Hyams, "Due Process versus the Maintenance of Order in European Law: The Contribution of the *Jus Commune*," in *The Moral World of the Law*, 62-90, here 62.

22. Hyams, "Due Process," 67. The "civilians" to whom Hyams refers are the early scholastic commentators on Justinian's *Institutes*.

the view that the idea of subjective natural rights has been decisively shaped by theological perspectives on the human person and the moral order. In this section, I will attempt to show that this is indeed the case. More specifically, I will argue that the early assertions of natural rights emerged as a reasonable, albeit not a necessary, development of the scholastic concept of the natural law, and correlatively, central elements of later natural rights theories can be shown to stem from the theological commitments informing this context.

Anyone familiar with Tierney's groundbreaking work on the medieval origins of natural rights doctrines will quickly see that I rely on it for much of what follows. However, I want to approach the issues from a different direction, one which will require us first to do a bit of backtracking. That is, I want to approach the issue of the universal scope of human rights by way of returning to the more general issue of the universality of the natural law, focusing now on the way the scholastics themselves dealt with this issue.

As we observed above, the natural law tradition as the scholastics received it was, on its face at least, strongly committed to the universal reasonableness and force of the natural law. But as the scholastics also recognized, this commitment was in tension, to say the least, with other aspects of the natural law tradition: "However, there still remains an objection; for according to the natural law, all would enjoy liberty, and all things would be possessed in common; these however are changed through the law of nations" (Lottin 106). This remark, taken from the anonymous canonical treatise known as the *Cologne Summa,* is repeated in almost the same words throughout canonical reflections on the natural law, and the problem it signals is taken up by the theologians as well.[23] If the natural law cannot be changed, then how can we account for so many widespread social conventions which seem to be inconsistent with what were traditionally regarded as the mores of primitive or uncorrupted nature?

For better or for worse, neither the scholastics nor their Roman forebears were prepared to answer this question by saying, in effect, "so much the worse for social conventions." However, it appears that the Roman jurists, together with the scholastic scholars of secular law known as the civilians, were inclined to adopt the contrary answer, in effect saying, "so much the worse for the natural law."[24] On this view, the natural law is equated with prerational inclinations which we share with the other animals. Hence, in their discus-

23. For further particulars on the scholastics' ways of addressing tensions between universal and particular at the level of social institutions, see my *Natural and Divine Law,* 247-59.

24. As Michael Crowe observes, with respect to the civilians at least, in *The Changing Profile of the Natural Law* (The Hague: Martinus Nijhoff, 1977), 110; also see my *Natural and Divine Law,* 47.

sions of the natural law the civilians gave priority to the definition of the Roman jurist Ulpian, as found in Justinian's *Institutes:* "The law of nature is that which nature teaches all animals. For that law is not proper to the human race, but it is common to all animals which are born on the earth and in the sea, and to the birds also."[25] Understood in this way, the natural law is present and operative only in vestigial forms in human society. Correlatively, for the secular jurists ideals of equity or reasonableness rather than natural law provide normative touchstones for evaluating actual laws.

In contrast, scholastic canon lawyers and theologians were not prepared to relegate the natural law to the prolegomena of morality in so sweeping a fashion. Initially, the question of natural law was put on the agenda of theologically informed scholasticism by the canonist Gratian, whose analytic concordance of church law commonly known as the *Decretum* begins as follows: "The human race is ruled by a twofold rule, namely, natural law and custom. The natural law is that which is contained in the law and the Gospel, by which each person is commanded to do to others what he would wish to be done to himself, and forbidden to render to others that which he would not have done to himself. Hence, Christ says in the Gospel, 'All things whatever that you would wish other people to do to you, do the same also to them. For this is the law and the prophets'" (D.1, introduction).[26] These words have baffled most contemporary commentators. Yet Gratian's point becomes clearer once we realize that Justinian's *Institutes* similarly begins, or very nearly so, with Ulpian's definition of the natural law cited above. Gratian, in contrast, begins his own compendium of church law with a scriptural definition taken almost verbatim from the theologian Hugh of St. Victor, who himself had been arguing against a one-sided philosophical view of nature and the natural law. In this way, Gratian indicates that whatever the sources of law may be, they must all be understood and interpreted in terms of the most fundamental law of all, namely, that law of nature which is attested in Scripture — and which, by implication, is to be understood by reference to that attestation.

Approached from this perspective, the natural law becomes important on both theological and broadly juridical grounds, which are developed in tandem. The twelfth and thirteenth centuries constituted a period of ex-

25. The *Digest* I 1.1.3; the parallel in Justinian's *Institutes* is I 1.2.

26. All translations of Gratian are my own. However, I checked my translations against Augustine Thompson's; see *Gratian: The Treatise on Laws (Decretum DD. 1-20), with the Ordinary Gloss,* trans. of Gratian by Augustine Thompson, trans. of the Gloss by James Gordley, with an introduction by Katherine Christensen (Washington, D.C.: Catholic University of America Press, 1993). I defend the interpretation of Gratian presented here at more length in *Natural and Divine Law,* 129-33.

traordinarily far-reaching institutional reform, and the scholastics were deeply involved in these processes.[27] In particular, the natural law provided canon lawyers and theologians with a basis for institutional critique, reform, and innovation which does not depend (at least, not in any obvious way) on existing customs and laws, and thus can be set over against local and civil authorities as a higher source of authority. The theological significance of the natural law guaranteed that natural law arguments would have saliency and force in the scholastics' society. Correlatively, the account of the natural law took on theoretical texture and depth through the scholastics' efforts to apply it to the practical questions of their day. At the same time, beginning in the thirteenth century scholastic theologians began to appropriate the emerging concept of the natural law to work through a range of theoretical problems, including conundrums of scriptural interpretation as well as questions of moral theology.

Because they were committed to holding on to a strong account of natural law, the canonists and theologians could not simply evade the tensions running through the natural law tradition as they received it; they were committed to offering an account of the natural law which displays both its universal and unalterable status, and its expression in diverse and seemingly inconsistent forms. As we have seen, they approached this challenge through drawing distinctions among different natural laws, or (more commonly among the theologians) different levels or forms of expression of one natural law. This approach allowed them to bring together seemingly incompatible perspectives on the natural law by correlating them with these different forms or levels of expression, in such a way as to claim that the natural law in some basic or foundational sense is universal and immutable, whereas its derivative or particular expressions are not.

This brings us to a critical point. The scholastics' development of the natural law tradition was of course informed by the wide range of perspectives mediated through that tradition, including classical and Jewish as well as Christian approaches. For this very reason, their own conception of the natural law cannot be understood in terms of any one of these perspectives, even the scriptural perspectives they took to be supremely authoritative, or much less as a summary of all of them. In order to appreciate the distinctiveness and theological character of the scholastic concept of the natural law, we need in addition to take account of the processes of selective interpretation and synthesis through which they drew together the diverse elements of the earlier natural tradition. There is no one element in the scholastic concept of the

27. Again, further details are provided in my *Natural and Divine Law,* 34-41 and 259-67.

natural law which is uniquely scriptural or Christian in provenance. Yet these elements are interpreted and synthesized in accordance with the exigencies of a developing Christian theology in a new and distinctive way. These exigencies were not only, or even primarily, generated by specific doctrines (which were themselves contested and in flux); rather, they arose in the first instance from the commitment to preserve the internal coherence of Scripture and its congruence with other authoritative texts which, as we have already noted, was foundational to scholasticism in all its forms.

This commitment led the scholastics to formulate a concept of the natural law which regards an interior power or capacity for moral discernment as natural law in the primary and paradigmatic sense, in terms of which other kinds of appeals to the natural law are to be understood. As Tierney observes, this approach was anticipated by the Stoics' claim that there is a natural law within the human person; yet "a decisive shift of meaning and emphasis occurred in the twelfth century. For some of the Stoics and for Cicero there was a force in man through which he could discern *jus naturale,* the objective natural law that pervaded the whole universe; but for the canonists *jus naturale* itself could be defined as a subjective force or faculty or power or ability inherent in human persons."[28] On the one hand, this approach provided the scholastics with a way of harmonizing diverse perspectives on the natural law and, just as importantly, of resolving prima facie inconsistencies among (seeming) scriptural references to the natural law. On the other hand, and more immediately relevant to the emergence of a doctrine of natural rights, it provided them with a way to justify and safeguard claims to autonomy and self-direction that were being lodged by men and women in defense of spiritual and emotional, as well as more immediately practical, interests.[29] As Tierney goes on to argue, this way of approaching reflection on the natural law does not necessarily imply a doctrine of natural rights, but it can readily serve as a foundation for developing such a doctrine, and by the early thirteenth century some of the scholastic canon lawyers had begun to do so.

In order to appreciate the force of Tierney's point, we must anticipate a point to be developed in the next section. That is, the language of rights admits of a wide range of interpretations.[30] Very often, "rights" are regarded as

28. Tierney, *Idea of Natural Rights,* 65.

29. With reference to the former point, see my *Natural and Divine Law,* 129-56, 247-59. With respect to the latter point, Giles Constable provides an indispensable sense of the religious and broadly spiritual impetus behind the desire for freedom so pervasive in this period; see *The Reformation of the Twelfth Century* (Cambridge: Cambridge University Press, 1996), 257-93.

30. Richard Tuck provides a concise and helpful discussion of the distinction between objective and subjective rights and its relevance to the early history of natural rights theories in

simply one way of expressing whatever counts as fairness, equity, or moral probity in any given situation. Theorists sometimes speak of rights in this sense as objective rights, the point being that they are regarded as claims arising out of an objective moral order. Understood in this way, the language of rights represents one way of expressing moral claims which could also be expressed in other terms, not so effectively perhaps but with no loss of meaning. There is no doubt that the scholastic concept of the natural law implies a doctrine of objective rights, so understood — but the same can be said of any other version of moral realism.

However, Tierney goes on to argue that at least some of the scholastics affirmed the existence of natural rights in a stronger sense, according to which rights claims imply something more than a set of mutual obligations arising within an objective moral order. On such a view, a natural right properly so called attaches to a person as, so to speak, one of the individual's moral properties. In contemporary language, such a right would be regarded as a subjective rather than (only) an objective right. As such, it is a power of the person which she can choose to exercise, or not, and which if exercised gives rise to a distinctive moral claim over against some other person or the community as a whole. Hence, on this view natural rights exist prior to particular social arrangements, even though their effective exercise may require the existence of specific institutions, such as law courts.

In his analysis of the medieval origins of this stronger doctrine of rights, Tierney observes that

> If we are to find an earlier origin for natural rights theories we need to look for patterns of language in which *jus naturale* meant not only natural law or cosmic harmony, but also a faculty or ability or power of individual persons, associated with reason and moral discernment, defining an area of liberty where the individual was free to act as he pleased, leading on to specific claims and powers of humans qua humans. I want finally to argue that this whole complex of associated ideas, this lattice work of language, first grew into existence in the works of the medieval Decretists.[31]

I would add that the "decisive shift" that Tierney identifies was not just a reflection of the social conditions of the twelfth and thirteenth centuries, although it was indeed partly that. (Nor does Tierney himself make such a

---

Natural Rights Theories: Their Origin and Development (Cambridge: Cambridge University Press, 1979), 6.

31. Tierney, *Idea of Natural Rights,* 54.

claim.) It also reflected the exigencies set by scriptural interpretation and the development of a coherent theology, as the scholastics understood these tasks. The force of these considerations becomes apparent when we consider the centrality of reason to the scholastics' concept of the natural law. Tierney rightly emphasizes the influence of the canonist Huguccio's claims that the natural law in its primary sense is to be identified with reason, and only in a secondary or even improper sense is it to be identified with precepts, including scriptural precepts.[32] As he goes on to observe, this meant that Huguccio regards even Gratian's preferred definition of the natural law as a secondary meaning. This might seem to suggest that Huguccio is moving away from Gratian's scriptural perspective. Yet as we saw in the first chapter, the identification of the natural law with reason, identified in this context with a power of moral discernment, was itself a scriptural claim — or so at least it would have been understood at this time, thanks to the authority of the Ordinary Gloss on Romans 2:14.[33] What is more, this line of interpretation was not only authorized by Scripture, it was practically necessary if the scholastics were to hold together the traditional conception of the natural law as universal, with their distinctively theological approaches to that universal law. The capacity for moral judgment, together with the principles by which it operates, may credibly be regarded as universal and unchangeable, precisely because it functions at such a general level. At the same time, the natural law so understood leaves considerable room for variation at the level of interpretation, formulation, and application.

As Tierney goes on to observe, it was only a short step from Huguccio's preferred definition of the natural law in terms of reason, to the scholastic identification of the natural law with a force, capacity, or power of the individual person; and from there it is a further short step to an idea of a right as a subjective power of the individual.[34] Here again, we see that scholastic thought was informed and directed by scriptural and theological considerations. This becomes apparent when we turn to the passage from the Gloss on which Huguccio and other scholastics based their interpretation of the natural law as a capacity for moral discernment. We see that this capacity is said to represent the Image of God in which the human person is created, and which therefore cannot be extirpated even, as we are frequently reminded, in Cain himself. It is found in every human person, man, woman, and child, includ-

32. Tierney, *Idea of Natural Rights*, 64-65.

33. What is more, Huguccio himself surely would have understood his claim in this way, since he cites the Gloss in support of the equation of the natural law with reason, as we saw in chapter 1.

34. Tierney, *Idea of Natural Rights*, 58-69.

ing sinners as well as the righteous, and even the damned.[35] What is more, the Image is not just identified with reason generically understood; it is interpreted more specifically in terms of the human capacity for autonomous self-direction, mastery over one's own choices and acts, which is central to a conception of a subjective natural right. This emphasis on rational autonomy comes through very clearly in a remark of the Eastern theologian John of Damascus, as quoted by Aquinas at the beginning of the second part of the *ST:* "Because, as the Damascene says, the human person is said to be made to the Image of God insofar as through the Image is signified 'understanding and free judgement and power over oneself,' thus, after having spoken of the exemplar, that is to say God, and of those things which proceed from the divine power in accordance with God's will, it remains to us to consider God's image, that is to say, the human person, insofar as he is himself the principle of his works, as it were possessing free judgement and power over his works."

As these remarks illustrate, for scholastics the human capacity for self-direction is not simply one human power among others, but the definitively human way in which a creature of this kind reflects God's wisdom and goodness; what is more, it is a distinctive reflection of that wisdom and goodness because it mirrors the distinctive notes of divine activity itself. As such, this capacity deserves not only appreciation as a likeness of God, but reverence as the very Image of God. Here again, we are not far from a doctrine of natural rights, seen now as commending reverence for the image of divinity reflected in rational freedom and self-direction.

The scholastic concept of the natural law thus includes at least one tenet of modern natural rights theories, namely, the affirmation that the human person possesses capacities for moral discernment and free judgment which are properly expressed through free self-direction. Yet this affirmation of the "faculty or ability or power" of the human person, important though it was to the development of a doctrine of subjective natural rights, did not by itself imply an assertion of subjective natural rights. Only some of the scholastics developed their concept of the natural law in this direction, and it is probably not surprising that those who did were canon lawyers, not theologians. This does not mean that the assertion of natural rights was an improper or unjustified application of the broader concept of natural law. The idea of natural rights represented a practical application of a broader moral

35. For further details, see my *Natural and Divine Law,* 266-67. James Barr argues that this interpretation is at least congruent with the meaning of the scriptural references to the human person as Image of God; see his *Biblical Faith and Natural Theology* (Oxford: Clarendon, 1993), 156-73. For a contemporary theological defense of a similar view, see Kieran Cronin, *Rights and Christian Ethics* (Cambridge: Cambridge University Press, 1992), 233-66.

concept, and as we noted in the previous section, practical applications of this kind are not necessitated by the concepts from which they stem. Nonetheless, this idea can readily be understood as a cogent application and development of the broader scholastic concept of the natural law, even if not the only one possible.

This raises a further point, mentioned in passing but now calling for closer attention. That is, the idea of a subjective right emerged from the scholastic concept of the natural law as that concept was developed and applied in a specific context, set by the circumstances and needs of thirteenth-century society. Thus, we cannot understand the emergence of the idea of natural rights apart from its social context; but neither can we distinguish sharply between theological and social influences in the development of this idea, much less place them at odds with one another. To a very considerable extent, the social context of the twelfth and thirteenth centuries was itself shaped by theological beliefs and commitments.[36] The scholastic concept of the natural law, in turn, served as one basis for justifying and guiding these social developments, and was itself transformed in the process into an idea with considerable critical and juridical force. Let me offer two examples of this process.

The first of these has to do with the reforms of marriage which began in the late eleventh century and continued throughout the period we are considering.[37] Initially, these reforms appear to have been motivated by a growing conviction that marriage is a true sacrament, which ought to be under the control of the church. Probably they were also given impetus by the desire of church leaders to secure their independence from the extended families which dominated much of European society at that time. Predictably, these reforms were resisted, yet they were remarkably successful, so much so that by the end of the period we are considering, marriage was almost entirely governed by ecclesiastical law.

In order to defend and implement these reforms, scholastic canon lawyers developed an analysis of marriage through which legally valid marriages can be distinguished from invalid unions and conflicts among spouses and other interested parties can be adjudicated. Perhaps the most important aspect of this analysis is its appropriation of the Roman doctrine that consent makes marriage, which was generally interpreted, at least in the later twelfth and thirteenth centuries, to mean that the consent of the parties was suffi-

36. Again, see Constable, *The Reformation*, 257-93, on this point; further details and references may be found in my *Natural and Divine Law*, 34-41.

37. Further details on the reform of marriage and subsequent theological debates may be found in my *Natural and Divine Law*, 206-12.

cient by itself to establish a marriage, with all the legal consequences following from that state. This doctrine emerged out of complex theological considerations, but it had clear affinities with the scholastics' more general emphasis on the central importance of human capacities for free judgment and self-direction. By the same token, once this interpretation of consent gained wide acceptance, it was incorporated into the developing scholastic account of the natural law, in such a way as both to reinforce and to interpret the appeal to general capacities and principles central to that account. In particular, this way of understanding consent underscored the egalitarian implications of the scholastic account of the natural law. The doctrine that the mutual consent of a couple is sufficient to establish a valid marriage functioned as a powerful safeguard for the right to marry; as such, it opened up a space in which people could act freely in a matter of fundamental importance, whatever their place in a social hierarchy.

This implication, in turn, was made explicit by direct assertions of the rights of those in a state of servitude to marry, as we find in Gratian's *Decretum* (C. 29, q. 2). Although this view was contested, it was subsequently incorporated into church law in 1155 by a decree of Pope Hadrian IV, *Dignum est,* which unequivocally affirmed the right of unfree persons to marry without the approval of their masters.[38] Near the end of the period we are considering, Aquinas explicitly grounds the right to marry in an appeal to natural equality. Because all persons are equal with respect to the possession and exercise of sexual capacities, he explains, these capacities comprise a natural constraint on the obligations of obedience which one person can place on another. For this reason, no one can be forced either to marry or to forswear marriage (*ST* II-II 104.5).

Appeals to the natural law and to ideals of naturalness were important in a second context, namely, the reforms and innovations of organized religious life which went on throughout the period under consideration. As is well known, Saint Francis's vision for the community which grew up around him included an ideal of absolute poverty, which carried connotations of humility and surrender of power as well as asceticism. Of course, this did not mean that the Franciscans renounced all use of material goods, since to do so would have been suicidal. Nonetheless, they claimed that their use of material goods was consistent with a life of radical poverty, and as this commitment

38. On this and subsequent church legislation on the marriage of unfree persons, see Antonia Bocarius Sahaydachcy, "The Marriage of Unfree Persons: Twelfth Century Decretals and Letters," in *De Jure Canonico Medii: Festschrift für Rudolf Weigand, Studia Gratiana,* XXVII (1996), 483-506. As Sahaydachcy goes on to show, *Dignum est* was subsequently challenged, but the popes consistently upheld the validity of the marriages of unfree persons.

came increasingly under attack, they appealed to the now-familiar distinction between possession and ownership to claim that they could take possession of external things, in the sense of making use of them, while leaving ownership in the hands of others, usually a patron or the church itself.

At first glance, this may seem to be a parochial argument of little general interest. However, it had far-reaching implications, because the Franciscan defense of the ideal of radical poverty had the effect, whether intentional or not, of reinforcing the egalitarian implications of the scholastic account of the natural law. The Franciscans defend their position (in part) by claiming that they are simply recapturing the way of life appropriate to the natural human being, at least to the extent of renouncing ownership. Understood in this way, the Franciscan ideal of radical poverty can be construed as an effort to live in accordance with the primeval natural law. This line of thought is very evident in Bonaventure: "Nature itself, whether as originally constituted or as lapsed, provides this way [the counsel of poverty] in a distinctive fashion. For the human person was made naked, and if he had remained in that state [that is, unfallen], he would not have appropriated anything at all to himself; and indeed, the human person as fallen is born naked, and dies naked. And therefore this is the most upright way, that, not turning away from the limit to which nature is able to endure, one goes about poor and naked" (*De perfectione evangelium* 2.1).

On a first reading, Bonaventure's claim here is likely to strike us as a piece of naive naturalism. But seen in context of the debate in which he is engaged, his remarks take on a different cast. What we have here, I believe, is a deliberate, theologically informed construal of the natural which serves to highlight the conventional status of possessions, rank, and power, and in short, all the accouterments of culture which keep some in a position of subordination to others. Bonaventure does not intend by this to deny the legitimacy of culture, as his remarks elsewhere in this treatise indicate; he is simply clearing a space, as it were, for asserting the legitimacy of an alternative way of life. But in the process of doing so, he underscores the conventional status and therefore the contingency of relations of social inequality.

In this way, Bonaventure's remarks highlight a feature of natural law thinking which runs through both of these examples. That is, these are examples of a moral critique which is developed within the framework of a particular, socially embodied set of beliefs and practices, but which nonetheless provides an efficacious basis for critique and reform of those beliefs and practices. Bonaventure's interpretation of poverty, like the doctrine of consent in marriage, draws on elements of received traditions of reflection, and moreover it presupposes a set of specific social arrangements for its saliency and point. In both cases, distinctions between the natural and the conventional, and judgments about the moral weight to be given to those distinctions, are developed within the framework of the very conventions being critiqued. Yet in both cases, familiar elements are combined to mount a critique of existing practices or to envision significantly different alternatives. In these cases, clearly, moral critique does not presuppose an ability to move outside one's intellectual and moral traditions.

These examples point to a further significant feature of natural law thinking in this period. That is, in both these cases, the natural law is regarded as not only lawlike in its operations, but as a source for actual positive law, whether civil or ecclesiastical (or both). Of course, the scholastics realize that the natural law must be formulated and put into effect through positive legislation of some kind; there is no question here of regarding the natural law as itself an enactment with direct and immediate legal force. Nonetheless, they do believe that the natural law has juridical force, in the sense that it provides not only a source for laws, but more strongly, a criterion against which existing laws and institutions can be tested. In this way, the natural law can be regarded as yielding juridical claims which a just community must respect, creating new legal and judicial institutions to do so if necessary.

We are at this point very close to a doctrine of subjective natural rights. Certainly, any such doctrine presupposes a belief in the subjective moral authority of the individual, but such a belief by itself would not yield a doctrine of natural rights in any strong sense apart from a context within which the moral authority of the individual can be given moral and legal force. I want to suggest that the two features of scholastic reflection on the natural law just mentioned — its ability to generate internal critiques and its (potential) juridical force — provide the necessary context for the assertion of natural rights claims. The point of asserting a natural right is precisely to defend someone's claim, apart from, often in opposition to, the recognized claims of an existing social order. Moreover, in order for this claim to be effective it must have legal force; and given their correlative function as a basis for social critique, this implies that rights claims must be regarded, at least in some circumstances, as a source for new law, rather than as claims depending for their validity on already existing features of a legal system. Seen within this context, the assertion of a natural or human right carries at least three implications: the human person properly enjoys freedom of action in some sphere of life; this freedom can properly be asserted, and should be safeguarded, even over against competing claims; and finally, this claim has legal force, and if no mechanisms for defending it exist, they should be created.

These, I want to suggest, constitute the core of a Thomistic doctrine of natural rights. That is to say, I would defend these as justifiable practical implications of the Thomistic theory of the natural law, which, given our own social circumstances and immediate history, are practically exigent if we are to provide what Michael Ignatieff describes as "firewalls against barbarism."[39] Needless to say, such a doctrine would call for considerable elaboration. In particular, I do not mean to imply that every moral claim can or should be articulated in terms of a defense of rights — for example, it is not clear to me that this is the best framework within which to defend basic norms of nonmaleficence — nor will I attempt to comment here on the difficult questions of positive and collective rights. My aim is simply to point to a practical implication of the Thomistic theory of the natural law, without attempting to develop it in detail.

It is generally agreed that Aquinas himself did not advance a doctrine of natural rights in this strong sense, although he did speak in terms of "the right," understood as that objectively just state of affairs which constitutes the object of the virtue of justice. Nonetheless, such a doctrine represents a reasonable development of those elements of the scholastic concept of the natural law which he shared, and as such, it does not strain plausibility to incorporate it into a Thomistic theory of the natural law. And in fact, Aquinas himself comes closer at some points to defending a doctrine of natural rights than is commonly recognized, although admittedly he does not assert the existence of subjective natural rights.

The most striking such example occurs in his discussion of the obligations of obedience, which for him include every sort of obligation of a subordinate to a superior, in both civil and ecclesiastical contexts (II-II 104.5). Aquinas defends the general legitimacy of these kinds of relationships, as we would expect, but he also places strict limits on the extent of this obedience. In the first place, the requirements of obedience are limited by the point of the relationship (104.5 *ad* 2). Moreover, there are limits on the kinds of obedience that can be exacted of anybody, under any circumstances. These limits are set by the fundamental inclinations of human life, which all persons share, and with respect to which all are equal: "However, one person is held to obey another with respect to those things which are to be done externally through the body. Nevertheless, in matters arising from those things which pertain to the nature of the body, one person is not held to obey another, but only God, since all persons are equal in nature" (104.5; cf. I 96.4). Thus, he goes on to explain, no one can command another either

39. Michael Ignatieff, *Human Rights as Politics and Idolatry* (Princeton: Princeton University Press, 2001), 5.

to marry or not to marry, for example, because marriage stems from an aspect of human nature shared by all persons.

In this passage, Aquinas does not explicitly say individuals have a right to freedom, which can be asserted over against others and defended as such in a court of law. However, he comes close; that is, he defends human freedom in terms of an immunity from the interference of others with respect to the pursuit of certain basic human goals. Similarly, Aquinas holds that the rich have a general obligation to share their surplus wealth with the poor through alms, but he does not say that any one poor individual has a right to receive alms (II-II 66.7). Yet he does say that someone in extreme need who takes from another what is necessary to sustain life is not guilty of robbery or theft. In other words, someone in this situation is free to take from another, in the sense of enjoying immunity from guilt or punishment for the act in question. This is not equivalent to saying the poor person has a right which could be claimed against the rich person and defended at law, but it does imply that the rich individual cannot lodge a claim against the poor individual for the return of what the latter has taken. Hence, the poor individual cannot defend a claim against the rich, but neither can the rich individual defend an accusation of robbery or theft against the poor person in such a case. This is at least a subjective immunity, if not a full-fledged subjective right.

This latter example is particularly significant, because it reflects the context within which thirteenth-century canon lawyers did assert the existence of natural rights. Together with Aquinas and other scholastic theologians, these canonists held that the rich have an obligation to share their goods with the poor, at least under some circumstances. As we have just seen, Aquinas takes this obligation to imply that someone may take what is necessary to sustain life from another without sin, but he does not directly say that the poor individual has a right to the superfluous goods of the wealthy. However, other thirteenth-century scholastics do say just this. Tierney quotes the canonist Laurentius, who says that when the poor person takes from another under press of necessity, it is "as if he used his own right and his own thing."[40]

Even more significantly, as Tierney goes on to show, this right came to be regarded as a claim having juridical effect, insofar as it could be asserted and secured through a public process of adjudication. Of course, this does not mean that it could successfully be vindicated apart from some actual legal structure. Nonetheless the claim in question is not a positive right, in the sense of depending on positive law for its force; rather, it is one of the

40. Tierney, *Idea of Natural Rights*, 73; the translation is Tierney's. For the more extended argument, see 69-77.

benchmarks of a just society that it provide some kind of forum in which claims of this sort can be asserted and enforced. That is why the scholastics attempted to devise mechanisms through which the right to surplus wealth could be publicly defended and enforced:

> Alongside the formal judicial procedures inherited from Roman law the canonists had developed an alternative, more simple, equitable process known as "evangelical denunciation." By virtue of the authority inhering in his office as judge, a bishop could hear any complaint involving an alleged sin and could provide a remedy without the plaintiff bringing a formal action. From about 1200 onward several canonists argued that this procedure was available to the poor person in extreme need. He could assert a rightful claim by an "appeal to the office of the judge." The bishop could then compel an intransigent rich man to give alms from his superfluities, by excommunication if necessary. The argument gained general currency when it was assimilated into the *Ordinary Gloss* to the *Decretum.*[41]

Certainly, the position described here falls short of a comprehensive theory of natural subjective rights, and it is not clear how close the scholastics in this period came to articulating such a theory. Nonetheless, it would be captious to deny that the authors Tierney cites do assert the existence of a subjective right, explicitly referred to as a *jus,* which is grounded in the natural law rather than in specific social conventions.

3. The Paradoxical Status of Natural Rights

If the arguments of the preceding section are sound, the subsequent transition from natural law to fully developed doctrines of human rights should be understood not as a break, but as a development and transformation of tendencies already present in the thirteenth century, if not earlier.[42] But this claim would not necessarily be welcome to many contemporary defenders of the doctrine of natural rights. The reason for their uneasiness should also be apparent from the preceding section. For as Tierney shows in some detail, the scholastics' affirmation of natural rights emerged out of a widespread and in-

41. Tierney, *Idea of Natural Rights,* 74.

42. Nor should this trajectory be limited to the development of secular theories of human rights; as David Hollenbach argues, we can also trace the development of a distinctively Catholic doctrine of human rights in its social teachings. See *Claims in Conflict: Retrieving and Renewing the Catholic Human Rights Tradition* (New York: Paulist, 1979), 107-37, for details.

fluential account of the human person as a free and self-determining agent, and moreover, as an entity enjoying certain powers on the basis of his or her capacities for choice and self-direction. This account, in turn, was framed and defended in explicitly theological terms, taken ultimately from a reading of Scripture informed by patristic commentary — human freedom is understood to be the defining characteristic in virtue of which men and women are said to be in the Image of God.

Thus, the scholastic defense of natural rights emerged within a context of explicitly Christian theological claims about human existence, and the resultant idea reflects its theological origins. And this is of course a problematic conclusion, seen from the standpoint of most contemporary defenders of natural rights. After all, this doctrine is attractive precisely because it seems to offer a universally acceptable framework for adjudicating moral and legal claims, internationally as well as nationally. How can this universality be preserved, if the theological foundations of the doctrine are given too much emphasis?

Thus we return to the issues of universality and particularism discussed above. Most of those who defend human rights do so in the conviction that they are defending moral claims that ought to be acknowledged by all rational persons, even though the limitations imposed by local traditions, deficiencies of education, bad will, and the like may well prevent such an acknowledgment for the indefinite future. Contemporary rights discourse thus offers one of the most recent and powerful examples of the Enlightenment ideal of a universal moral reason, which has been embodied and promulgated by the nations of the West but is potentially an ideal for all peoples.

Correlatively, debates over universal human rights offer a particularly striking illustration of the attractiveness, and also the pitfalls, inherent in defending a set of practical claims in terms that will be persuasive to all. In order to make a plausible case for the universality of rights claims, it is necessary to couch those claims in very general terms. As Annette Baier remarks, "Lists of universal rights, if they are both to cohere and to receive anything like general assent, must be so vague as to be virtually empty."[43] The more we specify what we mean by rights, the more difficult it becomes to offer convincing arguments that these claims ought to compel acceptance by any rational person, whatever his or her beliefs and moral convictions. Or to be more precise, the more we specify what we mean by a right, the more difficult it becomes to of-

43. Annette Baier, "Claims, Rights, Responsibilities," in *Prospects for a Common Morality*, ed. Gene Outka and John Reeder, Jr. (Princeton: Princeton University Press, 1993), 149-69, here 152.

fer convincing answers to someone who finds the relevant rights claim to be unpersuasive or morally unjustified. It is hard to imagine anyone quarreling with the claim that everyone has a right to human dignity, for example, but when human dignity is spelled out in terms of the right of a religious dissident (or heretic) to express his views openly, or the right of a woman to go about with her face uncovered, we are on more contentious ground.

Defenders of human rights are of course aware of these problems, and they offer a number of strategies for addressing them. The most straightforward of these is to argue that those who deny the legitimacy of rights are simply wrong — understandably wrong, nonculpably wrong perhaps, but wrong just the same. It would take us well beyond the scope of this section to examine in detail all the arguments offered in defense of this view, but generally speaking they fall under one of two categories. Either they depend on some variant of Kant's idea that practical reason generates norms through canons of self-consistency, or else they rely on formulating the relevant rights claims at such a general level that they seem empirically to obtain in all cultures. Neither line of argument seems to me successful, for reasons detailed in previous chapters and the first section of this chapter.[44]

Yet it might still be claimed that even though we cannot come up with a universally convincing argument for the existence of natural rights, nonetheless, we do agree, at least in rough and general terms, on a core of rights which ought to be respected and safeguarded. And it is certainly the case that an impressive international consensus over the doctrine of human rights has

44. The most influential defenders of a Kantian theory of human rights would include Alan Gewirth and Jürgen Habermas. The main lines of Gewirth's theory are set out in *Reason and Morality* (Chicago: University of Chicago Press, 1978); for his more recent defense of the universality of rights claims with specific reference to cultural pluralism, see "Common Morality and the Community of Rights," in *Prospects for a Common Morality,* 29-52. For a recent, very helpful summary of Habermas's approach, which is grounded in a transcendental analysis of communicative acton, see his *Moral Consciousness and Communicative Action,* trans. Christian Lenhardt and Shierry Weber Nicholsen (Cambridge: MIT Press, 1990). For a good example of a similar approach developed in an explicitly theological context, see William O'Neill, "Babel's Children: Reconstructing the Common Good," *Annual of the Society of Christian Ethics,* 1998, 161-76, and "Ethics and Inculturation: The Scope and Limits of Rights Discourse," *Annual of the Society of Christian Ethics,* 1993, 73-92. The Declaration of the Parliament of the World's Religions offers a good example of the "generalization" strategy in its explanation of what it means to say that all persons should be treated humanely: "Commitment to a culture of non-violence and respect for life; commitment to a culture of solidarity and a just economic order; commitment to a culture of tolerance and a life of truthfulness; commitment to a culture of equal rights and partnership between men and women." For particulars, see *A Global Ethic: The Declaration of the Parliament of the World's Religions,* with commentaries by Hans Küng and Karl-Josef Kuschel (New York: Continuum, 1998), 24-34.

emerged since the end of the Second World War — as reflected in (for example) the United Nations declarations on human rights, the progressive embodiment of human rights language in international law, and more generally, the broad consensus endorsing certain basic rights that we find in nearly all democratic nations.[45] But what, exactly, is this consensus about, and what does its existence indicate about the grounds for, and the force of, rights claims?

In order to assess the significance of this consensus, we must first acknowledge that it is not quite a universal consensus. Considerable numbers of persons do not accept it — and these would include not only isolated dissidents, but important sectors of major religious and ethnic communities.[46] No doubt some of these dissents are motivated by self-interest, but we cannot dismiss all of them in these terms — they do have arguments for their rejection of the very idea of rights, arguments grounded in long-standing moral traditions. It is also the case that many of those who would defend human rights in theory — including, most notably, the United States government — are reluctant to endorse and participate in the international mechanisms which give this commitment practical force. Again, these ambiguities reflect a mixture of bad and good motivations and concerns.[47]

Mention of the United States' ambivalence toward human rights doctrines raises a further set of issues. The United States is not the only nation displaying ambivalence, or worse, toward the doctrine of human rights — many other nations, including the former Soviet Union, have enshrined the language of human rights in their constitutional documents even while they

45. For a powerful statement of this argument, including a good review of the relevant history, see Ignatieff, *Human Rights,* 3-52.

46. Karl-Josef Kuschel observes that some participants raised questions about the Declaration of the Parliament of the World's Religions concerning "the equal place given to men and women, the question of non-violence, and the character of the document as a whole, which was thought to be 'too Western'"; see "The Parliament of the World's Religions, 1893-1993," in *A Global Ethic,* 96. Even when governments do agree to affirmations of human rights, these agreements are not always free of more or less subtle coercion, as Xiaoqun Xu points out in "Human Rights and the Discourse on Universality: A Chinese Historical Perspective," in *Negotiating Culture and Human Rights,* ed. L. Bell et al. (New York: Columbia University Press, 2001), 217-41.

47. The recent practice of the United States in this regard has not been admirable. Nonetheless, even with the best will in the world, it will inevitably be difficult for nation-states to pursue a consistent policy of respect for human rights in their foreign policy — if only because of the complexity of the competing claims that would need to be adjudicated in order to do so. For illuminating discussions of the relevant issues, see Stanley Hoffmann, *Duties beyond Borders: On the Limits and Possibilities of Ethical International Politics* (Syracuse: Syracuse University Press, 1981), 95-140; Theodor Meron, *Human Rights and Humanitarian Norms as Customary Law* (Oxford: Clarendon, 1989), 3-78; and Ignatieff, *Human Rights,* 3-52.

pursue domestic and foreign policies which appear to be profoundly inimical to human rights on any construal. (And to avoid misunderstanding, I should add that the United States' ambivalence toward human rights in foreign policy is not reflected in the same way in its domestic policies, which generally have reflected a serious commitment to a tradition of civil rights — in spite of past egregious failures to live up to its national ideals in this regard, and recent attacks on traditional civil liberties in the name of national security.) Furthermore, even those nations and other agencies who are sincerely committed to an ideal of human rights would find it difficult to follow the letter of the relevant documents — the rights commended there are too various, and taken together, they would call for insanely ambitious and even self-contradictory social programs. This lends credence to the suspicion that the language of rights is an empty rhetorical flourish, commonly used to be sure, but devoid of much practical significance.

Nonetheless, the fact remains that a far-reaching consensus has developed around the idea of human rights over the last half-century. Even if this were solely a rhetorical consensus, we would still need to account for the fact that so many diverse individuals and groups of people find it appropriate or advantageous to use this particular rhetoric in so many different contexts. To some extent, this consensus does express dynamics of power — but it also appears to be the case that individuals and groups representing a wide range of cultures do find this language congenial, even when they must defend it over against powerful voices within their own societies. And in reality, the consensus about rights is not just a rhetorical consensus; it is also embedded in international law and custom in a variety of ways, and it appears to have had at least some practical effects.

This brings us to a critical point. The very fact that the idea of human rights has been embedded in law has prevented it from becoming a purely empty ideal; its concrete meaning has been specified through practice, and this practice has begun to have a cumulative effect.[48] It is true that the language of rights, considered as a legal language, means very different things in different contexts. But this plurality and heterogeneity of meaning is not

48. Although now somewhat dated, Meron's examination of the current state of legal theory and practice with respect to international human rights agreements clearly illustrates the complexity, but also the normative force, of human rights law as currently interpreted; see especially Meron, *Human Rights,* 79-135. Geoffrey Robertson provides a more popular but also more recent and generally excellent treatment of the same issues in *Crimes against Humanity: The Struggle for Global Justice,* 2nd ed. (London: Penguin Books, 2000); in particular, see 85-130. In addition, David Forsythe sets out the main lines of the international law of human rights in *Human Rights in International Relations* (Cambridge: Cambridge University Press, 2000), 53-83.

equivalent to semantic emptiness. Even if we cannot identify a coherent concept of rights, we can offer a range of meanings for the language of rights, and when we do we may perhaps find some common threads connecting these diverse meanings.

On one view, the consensus over human rights can be explained through an appeal to what might be called, in Rawls's term, an "overlapping consensus" — although this argument, as applied to rights claims, may be found in a wide range of authors who have no commitment to Rawls's overall program.[49] On this view, we find a consensus about rights, even among peoples whose overall moral and religious views are very diverse, because those diverse worldviews all have some elements which would support a rights commitment. On one level this is a very attractive argument, but there is no denying that it is also a very strange argument. What are we to make of a moral idea which can be supported by very different, and even contradictory, sets of considerations? One suspects that any such idea cannot have any particularly strong content, or else that it is not really supported by the considerations in terms of which it is defended.

Yet seen within the context of a Thomistic theory of natural law, this kind of convergence can be identified and explained in a way that does not render it nugatory, so long as we realize that the relation between theoretical and moral discourse does not all go in one direction. Even though we cannot provide a convincing foundationalist justification for a universal morality, which would be specific enough to be practically useful and yet would be rationally compelling to all persons of good will, we can nonetheless identify certain recurring aspects of moral practices which do seem to cut across cultural and historical lines. As we have seen, these reflect species-specific patterns of behavior, which provide an indispensable basis for morality and as such provide one touchstone for evaluating moral theories.

One upshot of this is that moral norms and practices are not simply derived from the beliefs and commitments of a particular community, even though these do play an indispensable role in shaping morality. Local mores are expressed, so to speak, within a framework set by the broad patterns of behavior characteristic of us as a species, taken together with the practical exigencies which characterize human life in almost all circumstances. Within that framework, there is very considerable room for variation, but not un-

49. The appeal to an overlapping consensus can be found in John Rawls, *A Theory of Justice* (Cambridge: Harvard University Press, 1971; 2nd ed., Oxford: Oxford University Press, 1999), 340; more generally, see 335-43. Nussbaum appeals explicitly to this idea, as does Ignatieff; see Nussbaum, *Women and Human Development*, 73-77, and Ignatieff, *Human Rights*, 54-55.

bounded room; and by the same token, particular traditions will converge on certain basic moral claims, simply because otherwise they would lose all credibility considered precisely as moral traditions.

But even if this is so, it might be objected that this general phenomenon does not apply in the case of the doctrine of natural rights. For in contrast to those broad general features that we find in nearly all moral systems, such as reciprocity and hierarchical organization, rights claims are clearly localized and grounded in particular traditions. Even if we take the widespread consensus on this subject as evidence that rights language has become a universal feature of morality (and as we noted, this is by no means obvious), this is a relatively recent development — even if we date the emergence of rights doctrines to the thirteenth century, that is still late in human history, and the consensus in question developed even later.

Of course this is true, and it prevents us from identifying rights straightforwardly with those fundamental patterns of behavior which are natural to us as a species. Yet the fact remains that once a doctrine of rights emerged, it took root and spread over a relatively short span of time. And that fact, in turn, suggests that while this language does not reflect a universally recurring feature of human nature, neither is it simply an expression of a local tradition, which for some odd or suspect reason has spread itself throughout the world. The relation between a substantive doctrine of rights and human nature is more complex than that. What we have here (I would suggest) is a doctrine which can be used in a variety of ways to express basic aspects of human nature, in such a way as to respond effectively to recurrent needs. In other words, what we have here is a kind of moral language which does not immediately stem from the inclinations and needs of human nature, but which is close enough to that nature, and at the same time supple and flexible enough, to become entrenched in a wide variety of contexts.

In their analytic taxonomies of forms of natural law, the scholastics sometimes included the Roman category of the law of nations, which they understood to include such things as the provisions governing the formation of treaties, generally accepted laws of war, and the like.[50] They were well aware that these norms are social conventions, and for that very reason, they did not consider them to be a kind of natural law properly so called; and yet, in virtue of the generality and universality of these norms, and their role in expressing the exigencies of reason in a perspicuous way, the scholastics were prepared to consider them as natural law in an extended sense. At this point, the idea of natural rights can be considered as natural law in this sense — that is, it has

50. See my *Natural and Divine Law,* 78, for details.

become enshrined in international rhetoric, customs, and law, to such an extent that it has begun to function as one of the broad features of our shared institutional and ideological context, out of which more specific norms and practices emerge and develop.

The language of rights could not have attained this level of general acceptance if it were tied to a very specific moral doctrine. But by the same token, neither would this language have been generally useful if it had no meaning at all. Appeals to rights are useful, particularly in the international sphere, because they convey certain things, and what they convey is not unconnected to the meaning of rights claims as they first took shape in the thirteenth century. To be sure, the meaning of rights claims today is far more complex, and also strategically vague and inconsistent, than the early development of the idea would lead us to suspect. Yet we can account for the general saliency of this idea, to a considerable degree at least, in terms of recurring features of rights claims, features which can in turn be traced to the emergence of rights claims in the medieval period.

The first and most basic of these general features might be described as the absoluteness of rights claims. In the words of the eminent philosopher of law Ronald Dworkin, rights are trumps — that is to say, they are generally regarded as a kind of claim that supersedes most or all competing claims, however serious these may be.[51] More specifically, as Dworkin argues, rights claims are particularly salient in situations in which the claims of the individual conflict with the general well-being of the community, or the needs and interests of the majority, or of powerful persons within the community. By the same token, they are often invoked as a way of defending the interests or freedoms of the individual over against the demands of traditional mores, and in this way they tend to have a modernizing effect. Of course, the absoluteness of rights claims is interpreted and qualified in a variety of ways by those who defend some version of a theory of rights, and indeed, not all of these would insist on the absoluteness of rights claims. At any rate, my aim here is not to defend a specific version of the absoluteness of rights; rather, I want to indicate the kinds of situations in which rights claims are typically made. That is, rights claims typically emerge in situations in which the freedoms or claims of indi-

51. Ronald Dworkin, *Taking Rights Seriously* (Cambridge: Harvard University Press, 1977/1978), xi-xii; he sets forth the main lines of his argument at xi-xv. In what follows, I am indebted to Dworkin's analysis. It should be noted, however, that Dworkin grounds rights most fundamentally in an ideal of equality, rather than liberty; see *Taking Rights Seriously*, 272-78, and most recently *Sovereign Virtue: The Theory and Practice of Equality* (Cambridge: Harvard University Press, 2000), 120-83, for the main lines of the argument. For a more general review of recent debates over the proper point and force of rights claims, see Cronin, *Rights and Christian Ethics*, 26-56.

viduals are challenged on behalf of communal interests, needs, or ideals, situations in which there would be strong moral, and not merely self-interested, reasons for overriding the individual's claims, if not for some kind of overriding moral consideration which can stand over against those reasons. However the absoluteness of rights may be spelled out, rights claims are regarded as more or less absolute because they are meant precisely to provide the needed safeguard for the individual in such a situation.

This brings us to a second feature in which rights claims are typically invoked. That is, rights language is particularly important in those situations in which positive law is for some reason inadequate as a defense for individual claims. Of course, on almost any account of rights it will also be the case that at least some natural rights are embodied (more or less adequately) in positive law, and these rights can be pursued and granted through straightforward legal procedures. Nonetheless, rights claims are particularly important in those situations in which either there is no adequate positive law — in a situation of widespread institutional breakdown, or where an individual is deprived of the protection of any government — or the government itself, together with its legal systems, turns on its own citizens, as happened most notably in the Holocaust. In these cases, rights claims become particularly important because they serve to make law in situations in which no adequate framework of positive law exists. They make law, more specifically, in the sense that they serve to interpret and justify judicial acts — for example, punishing those who perpetrated rights violations, compensating victims — and also in the more fundamental sense of calling for legal mechanisms through which they can be vindicated. As Dworkin notes, this aspect of rights claims is a corollary of the first — that is, insofar as rights claims are seen to be overriding, they also imply the existence of juridical standards that override positive law, not only from a moral standpoint but even considered *as* law.[52] And this, of course, further implies (as Dworkin goes on to argue) the rejection of Anglo-Saxon legal positivism, according to which all true law is essentially positive law. Hence, the assertion of natural rights implies that there are preconventional yet juridically significant principles in terms of which laws can and must be assessed.

Until relatively recently, the prelegal yet juridical basis of rights would have been a controversial notion.[53] It is a sign of the distance we have traveled on these matters that today the legal as well as the moral force of rights claims

52. Dworkin, *Taking Rights Seriously,* 184-205.

53. For a good illustration of this point, see Margaret MacDonald, "Natural Rights," *Proceedings of the Aristotelian Society,* 1947-1948, 40-60.

is commonly invoked, not only in theoretical analysis, but also in the actions of international tribunals. There is a third aspect of rights claims which would still be controversial, and yet I would contend that it is essential to a full account of the development of the consensus on rights. That is, rights claims are paradigmatically lodged by or on behalf of individuals, sometimes over against other individuals, but very often over against the community itself, understood in terms of its overall interests, or its prevalent traditions, or as represented by governmental agencies or large-scale institutions.[54] As such, rights claims are widely perceived, with some justice, to be subversive of social solidarity — although, as Jon Gunnemann points out, they can also function as one mechanism through which the values of a community can be expressed and safeguarded.[55] It is this third aspect of rights language, its individualism, which some contemporary critics find most objectionable.[56] And yet, if rights language were not fundamentally focused on the needs and claims of the individual in this way, it could not serve what has always been one of its primary functions — namely, the defense of individuals over against what would otherwise be compelling reasons to constrain or harm some persons for the sake of the community as a whole.

Recently, we have begun to pay more attention to rights claims lodged on behalf of transpersonal entities — the right to preserve a particular language or a traditional way of life, to participate collectively in economic development, or most importantly, to enter the community of nations through the formation of a nation-state of one's own. As we might expect, there is considerable controversy over the grounds, the scope, and even the legitimacy of these kinds of claims. For many defenders of human rights doctrines, rights of these kinds can only be understood as the collective expression of individual rights claims, which, it is said, can only be pursued and safeguarded through collective entities. It is not so clear to me that all of the collective claims expressed in these terms can be understood in this way as the corporate expression of individual rights claims. As we noted in the previous chapter, there are some forms of human goodness which can only be attained

54. I follow Hoffmann on this point; see *Duties beyond Borders,* 109-10. Similarly, Simon Ilesanmi has recently argued that the seeming conflict between civil rights and socioeconomic rights depends on a false dichotomy, at least in an African context, in "Civil Political Rights or Social-Economic Rights for Africa? A Comparative Ethical Critique of a False Dichotomy," *Annual of the Society of Christian Ethics* (1997): 191-212.

55. For a very helpful discussion of this point, see Jon Gunnemann, "Human Rights and Modernity," *Journal of Religious Ethics* 16 (1988): 160-89.

56. For a good summary of this line of criticism, see Cronin, *Rights and Christian Ethics,* 82-93; Cronin goes on to respond to these arguments at 109-14.

corporately, and which nonetheless deserve respect and protection — although it is not apparent that the language of rights offers the best way to express these claims, nor should we assume that these would always supersede the rights of individuals. In any case, even if there are legitimate and nonreducible collective rights claims, this would not belie the fundamentally individual character of the concept of rights. It is still the case that these kinds of claims are paradigmatically lodged by, or on behalf of, individuals, with the aim of safeguarding individual autonomy or well-being. The application of rights language to collectives reflects an extended usage, which may well be legitimate but should nonetheless be regarded as derivative.

When we compare these aspects of rights language with the scholastic accounts of natural law and natural rights, the substantive continuity between the medieval and contemporary approaches becomes apparent. As Tierney points out, when the scholastics began to reflect on the status of individuals within the complex social structures of the time, they were able to draw on a concept of the human person that emphasized the individual's power and authority over a realm of personal choice.[57] Moreover, this concept of the human person was explicitly linked to their most fundamental theological commitments — to the claim that the human person is created in the Image of God, and therefore enjoys, in a limited and created mode to be sure, something of the autonomy of her or his creator. Aquinas adds another element to this general concept by drawing an explicit link between equality and the fundamental needs of the body, in such a way as to identify the "zone of personal freedom" specifically with those inclinations and activities with respect to which all persons share in one common nature. The connection of rights claims to theologically significant aspects of the human person, in turn, led the scholastics to affirm both the absoluteness and the juridical character of rights claims. These claims deserve respect not only on general moral grounds, but also because they reflect aspects of individual authority which demand respect — even when the individual makes use of them in inappropriate or immoral ways. And by the same token, these rights call for juridical recognition, because they express one aspect of God's will for the ordering of human relationships and society as a whole.

It would take us well beyond the scope of this chapter to develop a full Christian theory of rights. Yet even without doing so, we can identify central elements of human rights claims as they are typically developed and defended, which historically stem from Christian commitments and which a Christian has a theological stake in defending. That, at least, is implied by the

57. Tierney, *Idea of Natural Rights*, 62-69.

arguments of this section so far. These components would include, first of all, a commitment to the freedom and self-determination of the individual, seen as the fundamental expression of the Image of God within which each person is created; secondly, the recognition that the human capacity for self-determination exercises moral and juridical force, which every society is bound to acknowledge; and thirdly, the further acknowledgment that the relevant claims have force, even over against community and tradition. These claims cannot be interpreted in such a way as to render them absolute — otherwise there would be no way to adjudicate among competing claims, to say nothing of any other questions — but they must be given substantive force, including at least a high level of individual control over bodily integrity and the expression of the most basic natural needs and inclinations. Oliver O'Donovan suggests other components of a Christian commitment to natural right, as embodied in post-Christian societies today:

> Under this heading [natural right] three elements may be singled out: first there is a *natural equality,* by which each human being may encounter any other as a partner in humanity, neither slave nor lord. Secondly, there are structures of *affinity* by which homely communities are built; the intimate affinity of the family, the wider affinity of the local community, and the wider affinities still which create our national and cultural homes, affinities of language, tradition, culture and law. Thirdly, there is the *reciprocity* between homes and homelands which permits each community in its own integrity to interact in fellowship with other human beings, thus establishing the communication of a universal humanity, not as an integrated super-home but as a network of meetings and mutual acknowledgments.[58]

Admittedly, O'Donovan is more skeptical about the Christian origins of subjective rights claims than I am, and so he would probably resist the suggestion that these represent components of a Christian doctrine of natural rights.[59] Nonetheless, it seems to me that he has identified key elements which would need to be incorporated into any such doctrine, either as rights claims or as the necessary contexts for such claims; and by the same token, to

58. Oliver O'Donovan, *The Desire of the Nations: Rediscovering the Roots of Political Theology* (Cambridge: Cambridge University Press, 1996), 262, emphasis in original.

59. See O'Donovan, *Desire of the Nations,* 247-48. At the end of the day, I am persuaded by Tierney's history rather than O'Donovan's on this point, even though I agree with O'Donovan's broad characterization of the Christian commitments continuing to structure contemporary liberal societies; see in general 243-88.

the extent that these elements are incorporated into the rights claims of secular society, the Christian as such has a stake in supporting them.

This brings us back to the issues of status and justification of rights claims raised at the beginning of this section. As we have already noted, most defenders of a doctrine of human or natural rights want to claim that this doctrine does not depend in any fundamental way on theological grounds, or on any other culturally specific norms and practices. Many of them are prepared to grant that this doctrine developed historically out of theological claims, along the lines just indicated. But that does not settle the issue, because it is not evident that this historical connection reflects a necessary condition for the emergence of the doctrine. It might be the case that a doctrine of natural rights could be generated and defended on other grounds — either in terms of some other set of religious commitments or through some purely secular starting points.

It is hard to know exactly how to formulate this alternative. Just what would it mean to develop the "same" doctrine of rights out of different starting points? And correlatively, how similar does the resultant doctrine need to be to render plausible the claim that we have substantively the same moral doctrine, developed however on different grounds? Once again, we must be wary of saving the universality of a doctrine of human rights by framing it in terms so general that no one could plausibly reject it. At any rate, the fact is that doctrines of natural rights explicitly so called developed in western Europe, and they did so on the basis of what were clearly theological claims. These doctrines were then progressively abstracted from their theological roots, in order to present them as secular and therefore universally valid and accessible to modern pluralistic societies. Yet once this process got under way, the general idea of human rights has indeed proven to be persuasive to men and women within a wide range of social contexts. A set of moral ideas which emerged within a specific theological context has been appropriated and fruitfully developed in a wide range of other contexts, in the process developing into something approximating a universal moral law.

This development is not so paradoxical as it might at first seem to be. The doctrine of rights emerged within the context of the scholastic approach to the natural law, which depended critically on a distinction between natural and conventional. Certainly, this distinction was developed within the context of a particular set of social conventions, and yet, as we have seen, it provided a basis for effective critique and innovation within that context. The doctrine of natural rights represents a further step in that same process — that is, this doctrine stems out of a further development of a theologically informed construal of the natural, which serves as a basis for critiquing conventional ideals and practices. Subsequently, this doctrine was adapted by European theologians and political philosophers to provide one basis for international law, and to provide some guidance in what we would now call cross-cultural contexts. Later still, it was taken up by men and women in other cultural contexts as a basis for critiquing their own societies, or making claims in an international context. In this way, the doctrine of human rights offers a striking example of a moral claim which emerges within the context of a particular social morality, develops into a basis for social critique first within and then outside that context, and finally is appropriated by men and women in other societies.

Is the doctrine of human rights a theological argument? The answer to this question depends on the perspective from which it is being asked. Is it theological in its origins? The history traced in the last section indicates that it is. Does it depend on theological claims for its validity? I have yet to see a persuasive philosophical argument, developed on grounds that would be compelling to all, for a doctrine of human rights, and this inclines me to the view that a theoretical defense of human rights must ultimately rest on theological grounds. Yet the widespread persuasiveness of this doctrine, and its appropriation in so many contexts, suggests that it also expresses basic human inclinations in a way that is attractive and persuasive to people who do not share its presuppositions. As such, it provides a basis for critique and reform in contexts of belief and practice different from those in which it first emerged — and appropriation and development of this kind needs no additional justification, either theological or philosophical, any more than the appropriation of the language of the virtues or the ideas of duty and obligation would do. The language of rights has become part of the shared patrimony of the race.

If this is so, then what follows concerning what we might describe, in general terms, as our standing policies toward human rights? I speak here specifically from the perspective of Christians, for whom the theological origins of rights doctrines need not be problematic. Let me begin to answer this question by making a somewhat obvious point. The national governments of Europe and its former colonies have long incorporated rights talk into their constitutions and public life, and intellectuals within these societies have followed suit by offering a wide range of secular and philosophical rights theories. We need not attempt to persuade them that they are mistaken to do so, except insofar as the exigencies of specific discussions draw us into closer examinations of particular institutions or theories. After all, it would be strange indeed if Christians, on theological grounds, were to attempt to dissuade our fellow citizens from making use of what we regard as fundamentally Christian concepts! Moreover, we have no theological stake in the validity of these arguments. Our own commitment to promoting human rights does not depend on their validity, but by the same token, we Christians, as such, have no stake in claiming that a commitment to rights can *only* be defended theologically (even though many of us may be persuaded on philosophical grounds that this is in fact so).

The question remains, what stance should we as Christians take toward the development and promotion of rights claims? Certainly, we should respect the rights of others and do our best to safeguard them; so much would seem to be required by charity, which calls on us to respect the demands of justice, in accordance with our best conceptions of what justice is. Within many political communities, this will mean respect for those political institutions safeguarding rights, and efforts to reform or rebuild those institutions when they do not do so. More difficult questions arise in those situations in which the idea of individual rights is itself contested — in international law, or in the case of conflicts between an individual and a community that does not acknowledge the force of rights claims. If we acknowledge that rights claims are theological in origin, and therefore cannot be regarded as universally valid and necessarily persuasive to all persons, are we therefore obliged to stay out of conflicts over rights in those communities and contexts in which rights talk is not already in place? To put it another way, would a Christian defense of rights in non-Christian contexts amount to a kind of cultural or religious imperialism?

Not necessarily. Suppose we take universal human rights as a practical project rather than as a theoretical *demonstrandum* — that is to say, let us consider universal human rights as a goal to be pursued, both at the international level and in the domestic policies of particular nations. In that case, our long-term aim would be to shape the law of nations as it is emerging in an increasingly interconnected world society, in such a way as to place respect for human rights at its core. Let us grant, moreover, that this outcome is not inevitable — that there is nothing in human nature, or the structures of practical reason or discourse, that would dictate such a result, and correlatively, no universally valid arguments through which such an outcome could be defended to all persons in advance of its attainment. In that case, it seems that we are confronted with two questions. Are we morally justified in working for this goal, even if we could not justify it *in advance* of its attainment in terms that all our interlocutors would be bound to accept? And even if we are justified in pursuing such a goal under these conditions, do we have good grounds for hoping that we can attain it?

In the first place, it seems apparent that we as Christians have ample motivation to pursue our own ethical agenda. After all, if we believe that God has in some sense or other revealed God's will for human life, then we have the best possible reasons for observing the relevant standards and trying to persuade others to do so as well. Yet this still leaves the question of whether our attempts at persuasion are justified and legitimate — do they amount to a form of cultural imperialism, or worse still, to an unjustified form of coercion? These are difficult questions, which cannot be answered in any definitive way outside the context of particular situations. But it seems to me that at the very least, we are no less entitled than anyone else to enter into the conversations and practical interactions through which the ideals and practices of society are continually formed and re-formed. This is so on an international as well as a national basis. Refusal to do so at all would seem to amount to a kind of condescension or even callousness toward our potential interlocutors. As David Hollenbach says,

> A religiously pluralistic community, by definition, does not already share a common vision of the good life. Moving toward such a shared vision, even in outline, will take intellectual work. This common pursuit of a shared vision of the good life can be called intellectual solidarity. It is an intellectual endeavor, for it calls for serious thinking by citizens about what their distinctive understandings of the good imply for the life of a society made up of people with many different traditions. It is a form of solidarity, because it can only occur in an active dialogue of mutual listening and speaking across the boundaries of religion and culture. Indeed, dialogue that seeks to understand those with different visions of the good life is already a form of solidarity even when disagreement continues to exist.[60]

The second question, regarding prospects for success in such a project, is complex. After all, exactly what does it mean to pursue the goal of incorporating respect for rights in the law of nations? The analysis of the preceding section would suggest that at the international level, as well as domestically, rights claims emerge in a range of contexts, with a corresponding range of wide or narrow meanings. It seems safe to say that the more general and basic the rights claims in question, the more we can hope to achieve a broad consensus around them — although even at this level, consensus, and still more the practical maintenance of consensus, would not be trivial achievements. The more specific the rights claims in question, the less confident we can be about attaining widespread international consensus — but even at this level, we have reason to believe that our persuasive efforts will not be in vain.

60. David Hollenbach, *The Common Good and Christian Ethics* (Cambridge: Cambridge University Press, 2002), 137-38.

Consider the most general and fundamental kinds of rights claims: those lodged by, or on behalf of, the victims (or potential victims) of the most egregious kinds of aggression and destruction, including genocide, ethnic cleansing, rape, and torture.[61] We are all too aware that each of these kinds of actions has been regarded as justifiable, even necessary, by some significant sectors of the world community at some point in the recent past. Nonetheless, there does seem to be an emergent consensus that these and similar kinds of actions are never justifiable, whatever their motivation may be. If we have any doubts about speaking of rights violations in this context, it would only be that this language is too weak — what we have here might better be described as atrocities or crimes against humanity. Yet rights language is not out of place in this context, precisely because a rights claim carries the connotation of an absolute claim, which can in no way be violated. And if there is any context in which we want to defend an absolute claim, generating a correspondingly absolute prohibition, this surely is it.

By the same token, if there are any plausible candidates for a universal moral consensus supported by overlapping warrants drawn from a diversity of traditions, the norms prohibiting genocide, torture, and the like are surely among them. We do not need to appeal to a theory of the natural law in order to justify these prohibitions. Yet this account of the natural law can provide another kind of contribution by illuminating why these prohibitions are widely accepted. Seen from the perspective of a naturalistic account of morality, it is apparent that these norms stem from and are reinforced by our natural capacities for empathy and compassion. By the same token, violations of these norms can persuasively be presented as paradigms of cruelty. Of course it does not follow that natural compassion by itself is sufficient to prevent their violation; yet given our natural dispositions, we need particular conditions, or some kind of special justification, to find the prohibited kinds of actions bearable, much less praiseworthy.

In addition, these norms also reflect a particularly clear application of the fundamental moral norm, "Do no harm." Not only do the acts which they prohibit represent particularly egregious kinds of harm, they also represent gratuitous kinds of harm. There are few or no plausible policy interests or personal goals which could realistically be attained by acts of this kind, and their very enormity makes them very implausible candidates for justified forms of punishment (to say nothing of the fact that they so often victimize

61. Robertson outlines the current state of international law regarding the most serious crimes against life and personal safety in *Crimes against Humanity,* 102-9; for a review of the most recent attempts to create an international tribunal to enforce these laws, see 346-92.

those who cannot be guilty of crimes, such as children). Of course, this does not imply that those kinds of harm (such as garden-variety murders) which normally do offer benefits to the perpetrator are thereby justified, nor much less that an act of genocide (for example) might be justifiable if in some extraordinary situation it were to confer tangible benefits on the perpetrators. My point is simply that the gratuitous character of these kinds of harm makes it relatively easy to arrive at a widespread consensus prohibiting them. There are few or no competing reasons, in any imaginable tradition, that might serve to justify these kinds of actions, and by the same token no one has a real stake in defending their legitimacy.

If these kinds of harm are so clearly recognized as gratuitous, and therefore unjustifiable, why has so much energy been invested in developing an international structure of rights in terms of which they can be prohibited? And correlatively, why is this task so often pursued through a language of rights, as opposed to some other, perhaps stronger language, such as atrocities or crimes against humanity? The answer to the first question is clear enough: Even though these kinds of actions are unjustifiable on almost any account, they continue to occur with shocking regularity. For this reason, we have a continuing stake in condemning them in such a way as to keep their heinous character firmly in our collective consciousness. Moreover, we have a powerful stake in translating moral condemnation into a framework for accusation, retribution, and redress — in other words, a legal system. And that brings us to the second question. We have attempted to develop condemnations of these atrocities in terms of a language of rights, I would suggest, because this language connotes a claim that has, or should have, legal force as well as moral significance. Hence, the relevance of a second aspect of the scholastic concept of rights — that is to say, rights are understood on these terms as claims which have juridical force, and which therefore create law, in the sense of being principles for the generation of moral norms. That is why this concept is particularly useful in those situations in which the normal protections that stable communities offer individuals have broken down — in international law, and also in situations in which the community has disintegrated, or has turned against some of its members for whatever reasons.

The Christian, as such, clearly has the strongest possible motives for supporting international efforts to translate our revulsion against atrocities into a legal structure of rights, recognized and enforced as international law. Needless to say, it is a duty of justice and charity to refrain from these kinds of actions, and to do whatever one can to prevent them from occurring. Moreover, the language of rights offers a theologically satisfying way to pursue the latter aim, since it carries with it the recognition of the irreducible value and inviolability of each person, regarded as the Image of God, together with the further acknowledgment that each person enjoys the individual authority, as an Image of God, to claim recognition of his or her value and inviolability.

But of course, there are many other contexts, international and domestic, legal and extralegal, in which rights claims are invoked, and by the same token, many different kinds of rights are claimed, not all of them as weighty or as compelling as the claims just considered. To the extent that these claims reflect central components of a Christian conception of natural rights as sketched above, the Christian has a stake in recognizing and safeguarding them, no matter by whom or on what grounds they are defended. Nonetheless, we cannot assume that all enlightened persons will eventually agree with us on these matters, or even that they should in principle agree with us. The more specific the rights claims in question, the more likely it will be that others will have good grounds, stemming from their own concrete conceptions of the human good, for questioning or rejecting them. How should we conduct ourselves in such situations?

It should be apparent, first of all, that we would not be justified in attempting to promote the ideal and practices of human rights through force and coercion. Is there not something intolerably paradoxical about the proposal that we should force others to be free? There may be circumstances in which national or international agencies are justified in using force to protect others from human rights violations, although in order to be justified in any meaningful sense such actions would presuppose some international consensus on the character and scope of human rights, or at the very least, a broad and relatively disinterested consensus about the justice of particular claims. Under the best of circumstances, we need to guard against a pervasive tendency to confuse imposing our way of life with liberating others, and for this reason the burden of justification should rest with those who advocate the use of force to safeguard and promote human rights.

Yet we can offer those ideals to others, and we can do so with the intent of making them as attractive as possible, with the aim of spreading them through persuasion and negotiation as far as we can. (I am still speaking of what we as Christians can do, but of course the following observations would apply more broadly as well.) We have already noted that moral suasion and negotiation play a necessary part in the development of any moral tradition, and if we cannot legitimately try to bring this process to premature closure, neither are we bound to refrain from participating in it as vigorously as we can. Moreover, in this context we know from experience that we will find many men and women from any and every cultural tradition who are open, even eager, to appropriate our ideals of rights and make them their own. It does not follow that the language of rights reflects what is most authentic or valuable in those traditions, or much less, that those who reject an ideal of rights from their own perspectives are necessarily unjustified in doing so. Nonetheless, the ideal of rights does reflect aspects of human nature that are genuinely there, and what is more, it taps into ideals and aspirations that are bound to be attractive to a wide range of persons, whatever their backgrounds. We have every reason to make common cause with them in promoting social ideals and legal structures reflecting our central commitments to the freedom and dignity of the individual, even as we acknowledge, in all humility, that there are other ways of construing the human good besides those embodied in our central theological and moral commitments.

And we should not be too quick to assume that moral pluralism represents a problem to be overcome through establishing a universal consensus, even over matters of the deepest concern to us. To put the same point in another way, it may be that the continuing existence of diverse moralities, differing conceptions of the human good and of proper human relationships, may itself be part of God's plan for humanity. This possibility is at least suggested by Jacques Dupuis's profound and persuasive theology of world religions, as set out in *Towards a Christian Theology of Religious Pluralism.* In that book, Dupuis clearly affirms that Jesus Christ is God's ultimate revelation and the means toward salvation; nonetheless, he argues, we can recognize God's trinitarian activity at work in other religious traditions, which appear from this perspective as manifestations of the Spirit and mediations of God's saving covenants with humanity. As such, these traditions have a positive role to play in the salvation of their adherents; what is more, they play a providential role in complementing and completing the ultimate saving revelation offered in Christ. Dupuis asks, "is there, in the divine plan, a mutual interaction between distinct elements which, while not representing the reality in the same way, belong nevertheless inseparably together?" And he goes on to answer:

> Where the dimensions of salvation history are concerned, the Trinitarian model will make it possible to lay stress on the universal presence and activity of the Word of God and of the Spirit of God throughout human history as the mediums of God's personal dealings with human beings independently of their concrete situation in history. . . . The Trinitarian Christological model will likewise throw light on the meaning of the various covenants which according to the Christian tradition God has struck

with humankind at various times; these need to be viewed as distinct but — equally importantly — as interrelated and inseparable.[62]

What Dupuis says about the providential function of the diversity of religions may well be applied to the diversity of moral traditions as well — all the more so, since to a very considerable extent diverse moralities will themselves be embedded in and reflect the diverse religions to which Dupuis refers. Just as the world religions reflect different aspects of God's Spirit at work in human history, which preserve something essential in their very diversity, so — perhaps — the diversity of moral traditions reflect a providential way of preserving distinctive forms of human goodness, which could not be captured in any one overarching moral system, however admirable and just. In the light of this possibility, we cannot claim without qualification that the Christian way of life represents God's unique will for humanity, even if we could be confident that we had grasped what "the Christian way of life" really implies.[63] Yet we can only live out of our best understandings of God's will here and now, and for us Christians that means affirming Christian moral commitments in whatever ways seem appropriate, including, I have argued, defending the rights of others and encouraging their recognition.

4. Nature, Grace, and the Natural Law

If the arguments of the preceding sections are sound, the idea of a theological natural law ethic is not so paradoxical as it may seem at first to be. While a Thomistic theory of the natural law cannot provide a basis for articulating a moral system that is both universally compelling and specific enough to have practical force, neither can it be reduced to a set of general ideals or purely formal norms. It does have practical implications which are immediately relevant for Christian ethics, and which offer a promising basis for moral dialogue with those whose fundamental convictions may be very different from our own.

62. Dupuis, *Towards a Christian Theology,* 211-12; the main lines of the argument are summarized at 203-10.

63. Dupuis himself does not raise this possibility, because he is too quick (I believe) to assume that the world's religions agree on a universal morality; see above, n. 9. The possibility that moral diversity has a providential role to play also makes me hesitant to affirm the ideal of a universal common good recently defended by Lisa Cahill in "Toward Global Ethics," *Theological Studies* 63 (2002): 324-44.

Nonetheless, the Thomistic theory of the natural law offered in this book is intended primarily as a framework for theological reflection on the moral life, rather than as a basis for moral arguments. In this section, I will turn back to the theological issues raised by this theory, and in particular, I will consider a question we have so far only noted in passing. That is, what is the relation between the natural law, understood in Thomistic terms, and the grace through which we are transformed into friends of God and participants in God's triune life?

In chapter 3, we saw that Aquinas's development of the concept of happiness allows us to use the term "happiness" in diverse ways, each of which represents the key idea of happiness as perfection more or less fully. We focused there on terrestrial forms of happiness, which Aquinas equates with the practice of the virtues. At the same time, we also noted that Aquinas holds that happiness in the most proper sense cannot be attained in this life at all; rather, he identifies happiness in this sense with the attainment of the Vision of God, which he regards as providing the fullest possible satisfaction of the human creature's capacities for knowledge and love. We have already observed that a number of Aquinas's interpreters have concluded that for him there is no such thing as a purely natural form of happiness. On this view, the spiritual nature of the human person can only be completed through a supernatural fulfillment, that is to say, the direct Vision of God. Correlatively, on this view the human person, alone among all creatures, has no proper form of natural perfection and flourishing. Thus, if we are to make sense of Aquinas's references to imperfect or terrestrial happiness, we must construe these as anticipations of the perfect happiness which we experience even in this life through divine grace.

In chapter 3, I argued that for Aquinas happiness, understood as the terrestrial perfection of the rational creature attained and instantiated through the practice of the virtues, provides the benchmark for the teleological analysis presupposed by the scholastic approach to the natural law. Of course, it might still be the case that the only kind of terrestrial happiness open to us is the terrestrial anticipation of beatitude conferred through grace. But if Aquinas does indeed connect the virtues with the natural law in the way suggested, then it would seem that he must also recognize a kind of happiness that is connatural to the human person. It would be odd, at best, to speak in terms of a *natural* law oriented immediately and directly toward supernatural fulfillment.[64] As he remarks in a different context, "For it is plain that nature is

64. It is thus not surprising that Henri de Lubac, who denies that we need speak of a natural end of human life, also denies that there is any relation between natural law and beatitude;

compared to happiness as what is primary to what follows afterwards, because happiness is added onto nature. Now it is always necessary to preserve what is primary in what comes after it. Hence it is necessary that nature be preserved in happiness; and likewise, it is necessary that the acts of nature are preserved in the acts of happiness" (I 62.7).

Of course, I might be misreading Aquinas, and the connection between the final form of happiness and its terrestrial anticipations is complex on any showing. But in any case, as we saw in chapter 3, Aquinas refers explicitly to a kind of natural happiness proportioned to and attainable through the natural powers of the human creature. Moreover, he appears to regard the attainment of natural happiness as a real possibility, albeit a possibility that has rarely been achieved — or at least, he regards the attainment of the acquired virtues, the practice of which constitutes natural happiness, as a real possibility (I-II 65.2; cf. 4.5; 62.1; 63.3). And given the overall parameters of Aquinas's metaphysics and philosophy of nature, it is difficult to see how he could say anything else. If human beings (and angels) had no proper form of natural happiness, we would be the only kinds of creatures who lack their proper form of perfection (cf. I-II 109.1). This would not be a relative or conditional kind of deprivation, along the lines of the human being's weakness and lack of natural defenses compared to other kinds of animals. As we saw in chapter 2, a creature is whatever kind of thing it is in virtue of some specific form, which is only intelligible in light of the ideal of perfection that it approximates and represents. To say that we have no proper form of natural perfection would be tantamount to saying that we are not a part of nature at all.

In effect, this is the line taken by those who claim either that the human person has no natural form of perfection or that it is not meaningful to speak in these terms. On this view, the spiritual faculties of intellect and will transcend nature, insofar as we have infinite capacities for knowledge and desire for the good. There is a grain of truth in this claim, but it must be carefully qualified if we are not to blur distinctions that Aquinas himself is at pains to maintain — between negative and positive senses of "infinite," between our conditionally unlimited capabilities and God's absolutely unconditioned Being, and between the created powers proper to us as beings with a determinate nature and the qualitatively different kinds of capacities required if we are to

see *The Mystery of the Supernatural,* trans. Rosemary Sheed (New York: Herder and Herder, 1967), 41-43. Similarly, Charles Curran questions the usefulness of traditional natural law approaches to morality on the grounds, among others, that the natural as such represents an abstraction that has never existed in history; see *The Catholic Moral Tradition Today: A Synthesis* (Washington, D.C.: Georgetown University Press, 1999), 42.

attain our final end of union with God.[65] In short, this line of interpretation blurs the distinction between the characteristic and distinguishing capacities of the human creature, considered as one kind of creature among others, and the altogether unique and unconditioned way of being that God is.

This distinction is apparent, first of all, in Aquinas's analysis of the Beatific Vision seen in relation to other kinds of knowledge, of God and in general, that we might attain. The knowledge of God that we will enjoy in the Beatific Vision is a direct perception of God's essential being, in its full personal and trinitarian reality (I 12.1, 13; I-II 3.8; 5.5). Because God is supremely intelligible and good, and the source of every other kind of intelligibility and goodness, the Vision represents the fullest possible satisfaction of the intellect and will (I-II 2.8; 3.8). Aquinas states unequivocally that this kind of knowledge of God goes beyond the natural powers of any creature, not only our own powers but those of the highest angelic intellect (I 12.12; I-II 5.5). It is simply different in kind from anything that could be natural to a creature, because it is a kind of perfection that is connatural to God alone. Hence, it cannot be attained except through a transformative act through which God bestows new principles of knowledge and love into the created intellect and will (in addition to the references above, see I-II 109.1; II-II 2.3). Even then, no creature is capable of comprehending the full essence of God, and that is why the Vision admits of degrees — some see God more fully than others, although each one of those enjoying the Vision enjoys thereby the fullest degree of perfection, that is to say, happiness, possible to him or her as an individual (I 12.6; I-II 5.2). In contrast, the highest form of the knowledge of God proper to us as creatures is knowledge through the effects of God's creative and providential acts, philosophical knowledge, in other words (I 12.11). Aquinas does not even seem to regard this kind of knowledge, taken by itself, as a form of happiness — certainly, it would not perfect all the powers of the creature, unless it were accompanied by the moral virtues.[66] At any rate, this kind of knowledge falls infinitely short of the knowledge we are called to enjoy.

Correlatively, Aquinas also distinguishes among different senses in which the human creature can be said to love God. The love of God stemming from the direct knowledge of God comprising the Vision is spontane-

65. These distinctions run throughout Aquinas's work, but they come out most clearly, at least in this context, in his systematic distinctions between the kinds of divine activity and assistance necessary to sustain the existence and operation of any created nature and the properly supernatural activities of grace; see in particular I-II 109.1-4. For an illuminating analysis of these distinctions as developed throughout the *ST*, see Jean-Pierre Torrell, "Nature et grâce chez Thomas d'Aquin," *Revue Thomiste* 101 (2001): 167-202.

66. Aquinas makes this point most clearly in the *SCG* III 38-40.

ous and all-encompassing (I-II 5.4; 10.2). Just as God is the supremely intelligible reality which satisfies the created intellect, so God is the supremely lovable desideratum which fulfills every desire — indeed, in a sense God is supremely lovable because supremely intelligible.[67] For this reason, the beatified individual loves God out of necessity, in a way that no other substantive object of the will can be loved (again, see I-II 10.2). In contrast, to the extent that we can attain a love of God through purely philosophical knowledge, it is bound to be a cool and abstract love, amounting to little more than the recognition that God, as the ultimate cause of all that exists, is likewise the proper object of the love by which all creatures are drawn to their final end (and even this goes beyond what Aquinas says; but he suggests the possibility at I-II 109.3).[68] As such, this kind of love of God might be said to represent the distinctively human form of the natural love for God, tantamount to the desire — say, ordered set of tendencies — to sustain and express its own existence in accordance with its specific kind that we find in every creature.

Aquinas thus postulates two different kinds of knowledge of God, namely, the kind of knowledge available through reason, which is necessarily limited and, so to speak, external to God's personal reality, and the supreme knowledge of God as a personal, trinitarian reality attained through the Beatific Vision. Similarly, he suggests two kinds of love of God, the rational love of God as ultimate cause and the completely fulfilling love of God that necessarily follows on the Vision. These imply a third distinction, which will bring us closer to the heart of his own moral theology and to the Thomistic theory of the natural law being developed here. That is, these distinctive forms of knowledge and love require two different kinds of operative principles. Given the main lines of Aquinas's metaphysics, this follows necessarily from the distinction between two disparate forms of intellectual and volitional fulfillment. The forms of knowledge and love which are connatural to the human person can of course be attained through the capacities and powers proper to the human creature as such — capacities and powers which stem immediately from her essence, from that which makes her the kind of creature she is. In contrast, because the Beatific Vision surpasses the proper capacities of any kind of creature, it can only be attained through operative principles of action bestowed directly by God,

67. In the sense, namely, that intelligibility and goodness are mutually implicated — whatever exists is both intelligible and good insofar as it exists and attains the perfection proper to it, in accordance with the exigencies of its specific form.

68. More specifically, as an examination of the article will show, he holds that this kind of natural love of God would be spontaneous if we had not suffered the effects of sin; but in human existence as it now is, we find it difficult, at best, to attain even the kind of love of God toward which we are naturally oriented.

culminating, in the blessed, with the bestowal of a distinctive capacity for knowledge — as a result of which, Aquinas says, we are made "deiform" (I 12.5). Yet this process of transformation begins in this life with the bestowal of a distinctive principle of operation, giving rise to habitual powers of knowledge, desire, and action leading toward the attainment of union with God. This operative principle is grace, and the habitual powers stemming from it are the theological virtues, together with the infused cardinal virtues and the gifts:

> the virtue of each thing is spoken of in relation to some preexisting nature; since indeed, each thing is so disposed, in accordance with that which is appropriate to its nature. Now it is plain that the virtues acquired through human actions, of which we have spoken above, are dispositions through which the human person is appropriately disposed in relation to that nature through which he is a human person. The infused virtues, in contrast, dispose the human person in a higher way, and to a higher end, and hence it is necessary that they be related to another, higher nature. That is, they are related to participated divine nature, in accordance with what is said in II Peter 1.4: "He has given us the greatest and most precious promises, that through these things we might be made to share in the divine nature." And insofar as we partake of this nature, we are said to be regenerated into the children of God. (I-I 110.3; cf. I-II 62.1; 63.3; 68)

For some time now there has been a tendency among both theologians and interpreters of Aquinas to downplay the distinction between nature and grace.[69] Very few theologians are prepared to deny that there is any such dis-

69. This view can be traced back to the deeply influential work of Henri de Lubac and Karl Rahner on the relation between nature and grace; in addition to de Lubac's work cited above, see Karl Rahner, "On the Relationship between Nature and Grace," in *Theological Investigations* (New York: Crossroad, 1961, 1965), 1:297-318, and *Foundations of the Christian Faith: An Introduction to the Idea of Christianity* (New York: Crossroad, 1985), 116-37, for good summaries of Rahner's view. For a general history of this distinction, see John Mahoney, *The Making of Moral Theology: A Study of the Roman Catholic Tradition* (Oxford: Clarendon, 1987), 72-115. Stephen Duffy sets out the immediate context for the de Lubac/Rahner reformulation of the doctrine of grace in *The Graced Horizon: Nature and Grace in Modern Catholic Thought* (Collegeville, Minn.: Liturgical Press, 1992), 50-65. This book also provides a helpful synopsis and analysis of the subsequent Catholic theology of grace, summarized at 196-234. For a different perspective on the legacy of de Lubac's work, see Gilbert Narcisse, "Le surnaturel dans la théologie contemporaire," *Revue Thomiste* 101, no. 1-2 (January/June 2001): 312-18. While (as I note) there are few Catholic theologians who would deny the legitimacy of speaking of grace in some sense or other, a few have come close; see, for example, George Vandervelde, "The Grammar of Grace: Karl Rahner as a Watershed in Contemporary Theology," *Theological Studies* 49 (1988): 445-59, who remarks, approvingly, that a radical appropriation of Rahner's thought may

tinction (for Catholics, this view would be problematic on doctrinal grounds, if no other), but many do argue that the distinction is purely abstract or doctrinal. On this view, all of creation is graced, insofar as God's offer of grace extends to every person, and all reality is viewed through the prism of this offer (whether recognized as such or not). Correlatively, there is no such thing as a state of pure nature actually in existence, and all of our supposedly natural capacities and powers can be regarded as reflecting the operations of grace, even if we cannot say precisely how grace is operative at any given point.

Whatever we may think of this approach to the question of nature and grace, considered on its merits, it is clear that it is not Aquinas's view. On the contrary, in Aquinas's writings the distinction between nature and grace is clearly drawn, consistent, and central to his overall theology.[70] This does not mean he presupposes or (much less) asserts the real existence of a state of "pure nature," as understood in early modern Catholic theology.[71] On his view, the first human persons were created in a state of grace, and human nature subsequently has been weakened and distorted through the effects of original and actual sin (I 95.1; 97; I-II 82). Nonetheless, the distinction between nature and grace is rendered meaningful in Aquinas's theology through a painstaking analysis of the different aims and operations of two fundamental principles of action, developed within a context of a well-articulated philosophy of nature and a philosophical theology. What is more, this distinction does a considerable amount of theological work for him — not only does it enable him to distinguish between two forms of happiness and their corresponding virtues, it also enables him to make sense of theological traditions about the way of life enjoyed by our first parents before sin, and to distinguish the supernatural gifts enjoyed in that state from both natural and graced capacities as we enjoy them now. In addition, this distinction enables him to identify pervasive human tendencies — most importantly, the orientation of the will toward a narrow self-love — as sinful, seen

---

lead us to "the abandonment of the entire framework of nature and grace as it has been handed down to us through the ages" (459).

70. In addition to Torrell's article cited above, see Joseph Wawrykow, *God's Grace and Human Action: Merit in the Theology of Thomas Aquinas* (Notre Dame: University of Notre Dame Press, 1995), 60-259; however, I do not want to imply that Wawrykow would agree with my arguments in what follows.

71. Even those scholastics (the majority) who believed that the human person was not created in grace did not assert the existence of "pure nature" in the early modern sense, as Torrell observes in "Nature et grâce chez Thomas d'Aquin," 181; more generally, my analysis of Aquinas's development of the nature/grace distinction is indebted to Torrell, and further references may be found in this article.

in comparison to what is proper to our nature as such (as we saw above; see I 60.5; I-II 109.3).[72]

The nature/grace distinction is seen in this light to be an immediate implication of the distinction between two forms of knowledge, love, and perfection, namely, a form that is connatural to the human creature and another that transcends the created capacities of any creature whatever. Nature provides the necessary principles of operation for those forms of knowledge and love connatural to us — that is just what it means to say they are connatural. The attainment of the Vision, in contrast, calls for distinctively new principles of operation, which are not natural to us except in the sense that our natural capacities are a necessary condition for their reception.

The distinction between nature and grace is likewise fundamental to the Thomistic theory of the natural law being developed here. This theory does not presuppose that we have access to a state of pure nature. Even apart from theological considerations, the idea of "pure nature" is not tenable, as we have seen, because human nature always exists in some culturally specific form; correlatively our knowledge of human nature is mediated through conventions and depends on analysis and argument, rather than direct observation. Nonetheless, just as we can distinguish, albeit imperfectly, between what is natural to the human person as such and what reflects particular social/cultural expressions, so we can distinguish between what is natural to us and what stems from grace. And it is important to do so, because the distinction between nature and grace serves to safeguard the integrity of nature, seen as a principle of action. Moreover, as we will see more clearly in what follows, we need to be able to distinguish between the operative principles of nature and of grace — that is to say, the acquired and infused virtues — if we are to have meaningful conceptions of the latter, con-

72. I believe it is also clear on textual grounds that Aquinas does not believe that grace is ubiquitous, in the sense of being offered to all persons at every time and place. He holds that grace is necessarily expressed through infused virtues, including both properly theological and infused cardinal virtues, which constitute its operative principles (I-II 62.1; 63.3; 110.3). Faith is the foundational theological virtue, necessary to all the rest (I-II 62.3, 4; II-II 4.7); and this virtue necessarily comprises some explicit beliefs, including since the coming of Christ some explicitly Christian beliefs that are not universally shared (II-II 2.5-8). Some interpreters have argued that Aquinas nonetheless holds out a possibility of implicit faith even now; see, for example, Thomas O'Meara, "The Presence of Grace outside Evangelization, Baptism and Church in Thomas Aquinas' Theology," in *That Others May Know and Love* (St. Bonaventure, N.Y.: St. Bonaventure University, 1997), 91-131. However, I am not persuaded by the case for attributing such a view to Aquinas himself — although I would agree that he suggests possibilities for developing a doctrine of implicit faith which could be regarded as Thomistic in a broader sense. Dupuis reaches a similar conclusion; see *Towards a Christian Theology*, 114-20.

sidered as substantive normative ideals. These conceptions, in turn, are central to a Christian natural law ethic, because the ideal of terrestrial happiness informing that account will be taken from our conceptions of the infused, rather than the acquired, virtues. At the same time, the infused cardinal virtues cannot be understood except in relation to their acquired counterparts, and both kinds of virtue can be understood only in relation to natural principles: "grace and virtue imitate the order of nature, which is set up in accordance with divine wisdom" (II-II 31.3).

In the context of explaining the key assumptions behind early modern natural theology, Ernan McMullin remarks that theological reflection in this period came to be dominated by what he describes as a voluntarist approach, according to which everything is to be explained by reference to God's unlimited power and sovereign will. On this view, it makes no sense to speak in terms of supernatural interventions in the created order, because "every temporal occurrence is equally the creation of [God's] will. There are no 'natures' to be overruled or intruded upon by some kind of special action."[73] Of course, contemporary theology (both Catholic and Protestant) differs from early modern natural theology in significant ways. Nonetheless, McMullin's remark identifies one point at which modern and contemporary approaches are both similar to and discontinuous with the approach represented by Aquinas. That is, in both perspectives there is little room to speak of nature as a distinctive principle of operations, which is intelligible in its own terms and therefore theologically significant as a reflection of divine goodness and wisdom. In this way, McMullin helps to clarify what is at stake in maintaining the nature/grace distinction in the way Aquinas does.

In contemporary Catholic theology, the distinction between nature and grace, while generally acknowledged to be doctrinally important, tends to play little or no interpretative or explanatory role. According to this widespread view, everything is permeated by grace, and at any rate all creation is itself a gratuitous gift of God. Thus, the distinction between nature and grace cannot be regarded as deep or theologically informative, because nothing in our experience serves to give concrete meaning to either nature or grace.[74] If there is no

73. Ernan McMullin, "Evolution and Creation," in *Evolution and Creation,* ed. Ernan McMullin (Notre Dame: University of Notre Dame Press, 1985), 1-58, here 31.

74. I believe this approach can be traced back to de Lubac's refusal to analyze human nature in any terms other than those immediately given to experience: "Yet ultimately, all that interests us is what exists in fact, the reality of our nature as it is, acting at this moment, in God's creation as it is" (*Mystery of the Supernatural,* 45). This stance makes sense in light of the highly artificial and implausible construal of the supernatural order against which he reacts (see 25-47), but as a result, there is no room in his theology for a consideration of human nature in

ascertainable distinction between different kinds of divine activity, including both "normal" acts of creation and providential sustenance, and "extraordinary" acts, including both the bestowal of grace and miraculous interventions, then *every* act of God becomes, in effect, miraculous — which is to say, an expression of God's omnipotent power. Correlatively, every act of God is equally mysterious and incomprehensible. The intelligibilities of nature are at best provisional and may well be regarded as human constructs; at any rate, they do not tell us anything about God, beyond pointing to God's sheer power. On this view, it makes sense to say that all of creation is graced — everything is a gift of God, and no one of God's gifts really tells us anything about the giver.[75]

In contrast, for Aquinas, together with most of his interlocutors, nature broadly considered is intelligible on its own terms, and as such it has independent theological significance as a reflection of the wisdom of God. As Jean-Pierre Torrell has shown, Aquinas's overall theological orientation implies a commitment to the distinctiveness of grace, not as a way of denigrating nature but precisely as a way of safeguarding its integrity and its value as an independent witness to divine wisdom.[76] More precisely, what is at stake for him is the intelligibility of natures, that is to say, the specific kinds of existence represented by the diverse kinds of creatures constituting the created order. These are intelligible precisely as finite and comprehensible forms of being, which represent so many ways of participating in infinite Being. God as infinite cannot be grasped by any finite intellect, and so we can only attain

---

terms of an intelligible form of created existence, which has its own structure and integrity and for that very reason can be considered in abstraction from a distinctive operative principle of grace. Similarly, Duffy, who accepts and develops de Lubac's approach, remarks in *The Graced Horizon* that "The 'natural' is patient of no easy circumspection and is best considered as a conceptual and theological residual. Grace, on the other hand, is experienced in all the love and labor, all the joy and misery that characterize the human condition. Nature and grace may be thematically distinct, but in lived experience lines of demarcation are not easily drawn" (198).

75. We see a good illustration of this approach in John Haught, whose process theology implies a rejection of the traditional doctrine of God as omnipotent Creator: "The doctrine of grace claims that God loves the world and all of its various elements fully and unconditionally. . . . Along with its nurturing and compassionate attributes, love brings with it a longing for the independence of that which is loved" (*God after Darwin: A Theology of Evolution* [Boulder, Colo.: Westview Press, 2000], 39). This is tantamount to equating creation and grace, or rather, substituting a kind of naturalized grace for creation. By the same token, on this view the order and intelligibility of the visible world is a result of immanent processes with no further theological significance. God functions as lure and goal — somewhat after the fashion of Aristotle's Unmoved Mover — but appears not to be involved in natural processes in any other way.

76. Torrell, "Nature et grâce chez Thomas d'Aquin"; see especially 198-201. Michel Bastit makes a similar point; see "Le thomisme est-il un aristotélisme?" *Revue Thomiste* 101 (2001): 101-16, 115-16.

conceptual knowledge of God through reflection on these created similitudes of God's unconditioned existence.[77] Yet nature considered in this light does provide genuine, albeit limited, insight into God's own proper mode of existence, considered as the supremely intelligible and good source of all that is intelligible and good in the world around us.

The intelligibility of nature, in turn, provides a context within which we can develop a genuine, albeit limited, account of what it means to speak of grace and its operations in human lives. The difficulty and importance of developing such an account should not be underestimated. Without some such account, the language of grace readily becomes a kind of in-house jargon, meaningful only within the context of a self-referential system of doctrinal terms. When this happens, the concept of grace loses its power to illuminate our experiences, to guide our choices, or to locate individual discernment within a wider context of theological commitments. Yet it is not so easy to develop a substantive conception of grace. Because it is oriented toward participation in God's inner life, grace itself is mysterious in somewhat the same way that God is mysterious — that is to say, it shares in the incomprehensibility of God, in a way that natural acts of creation do not.

The distinction between nature and grace provides us with a lever for developing a genuinely informative account of grace, without of course eliminating its ultimate incomprehensibility. Because the actions and effects of grace are located within a context of naturally grounded knowledge of God, they can be rendered intelligible in a sense, that is to say, relative to the context of our natural knowledge of God's goodness. Moreover, because we believe that grace is a further gift of a God whom we already know to be good in ways that we can recognize and affirm, we have reason to expect that God's grace will be continuous with, or at least not a perversion of, God's creative goodness. At the very least, this provides a principle of discrimination through which we can, so to speak, recognize the proper effects of grace and distinguish them from other phenomena — a principle for distinguishing the Spirit from the spirits, in other words. Collective experience, informed and bounded by ecclesial reflection and discernment, does much of the rest of the work here, but my point is that our reflection could not get a purchase on experience without the benchmark provided by a real distinction between nature and grace.

This basic distinction gives rise to further distinctions among the vir-

77. Even the blessed, who see God in God's essence, do not comprehend God in that vision (I 12.7). Our knowledge of God in this life is necessarily conceptual, and therefore falls short of attaining the reality of its object directly, even when it is transformed through the theological virtue of faith (I 12.13, especially *ad* 3).

tues. We have more than once observed that Aquinas understands the acquired virtues to be operative principles through which we attain a connatural form of happiness, which consists in the practice of these very virtues. The theological virtues of faith, hope, and charity, in contrast, are regarded as operative principles stemming from grace (much as the acquired virtues stem from human nature), through which we act in ways directed toward attaining our final end of direct union with God. In addition, Aquinas holds that the transforming effects of grace go all the way down, so to speak, transforming each of the operative capacities and powers of the human person through infused analogues of the acquired cardinal virtues. Hence, someone who has charity also possesses distinctive forms of prudence, justice, temperance, and fortitude and their associated virtues, each of which orients an intellectual or appetitive faculty toward union with God, and each of which is correlatively specifically different from its acquired counterpart (I-II 63.3, 4).

We now begin to see the implications of Aquinas's doctrine of grace for his moral theology. The distinctions between nature and grace, and between acquired and infused virtues, provide him with a framework within which the distinctively theological virtues, together with the infused cardinal virtues, can be rendered intelligible as moral ideals. More specifically, the acquired virtues, considered as ideals stemming from human nature, provide both a point of contrast and a set of parameters in terms of which the ideals of the infused virtues can be articulated. As Aquinas frequently remarks, grace perfects nature, it does not pervert it (see, for example, I 60.5). He also remarks, in the context of a discussion of the obligations of charity, that the operations of grace are not less reasonable than the operations of nature (II-II 26.2; cf. 31.3). We can now better appreciate the significance of these remarks. They imply that the inclinations and exigencies informing the acquired virtues are not simply washed out, as it were, through the infusion of their infused counterparts. "Nature as reason" informs the infused as well as the acquired virtues, even though the two kinds of virtues are specifically different, insofar as they are directed toward distinct ends (I-II 63.4). This point of connection, in turn, implies that our concepts of the acquired virtues can provide a basis for grasping what it means to possess and to act out of the infused cardinal virtues, and the theological virtues as well.

At this point, I have gone beyond what Aquinas explicitly says. Nonetheless, if we are to hold on to his principle that grace perfects nature, rather than destroying it or rendering it otiose, then it would seem to follow that the practical imperatives of grace are informed by, and to some extent constituted by, the imperatives stemming from nature. In this way, the natural law informs the infused virtues, providing them with much of their concrete normative content. And in fact, Aquinas offers examples illustrating how this might work. He claims that infused and acquired temperance both take their immediate orientation from the bodily needs of the human person, which set parameters around what may be done in pursuit of more comprehensive ends (II-II 141.6, especially *ad* 1). This claim is cashed out a few questions later, at which point Aquinas argues that it would be perverse and sinful to fast to the point of damaging one's health, even for the most exalted spiritual reasons (147.1 *ad* 2). The body can and should be disciplined and even chastised, but not harmed, in pursuit of spiritual aims.

This example presupposes a connection as well as a contrast between two forms of a cardinal virtue, but we also find a similar point developed in relation to the theological virtues, which have no acquired counterparts. Most notably, Aquinas argues that the obligations of justice expressed in our relations to family members and other close associates inform the obligations of charity (II-II 26.6-13). As he explains, "The affection of charity, which is an inclination of grace, is no less well ordered than natural appetite, which is an inclination of nature, for each inclination proceeds from divine wisdom" (26.6). He then goes on to develop a complex account of the ordering, the extent, and the relative priority of the obligations of love and beneficence proper to charity, in which consanguinity, civic and personal affinity, and graced sanctity are all taken into account.

The precepts of justice are regarded by Aquinas as paradigmatic imperatives of the natural law; at the same time, they also seem to have an especially close link to charity, since they represent specific and centrally important ways of expressing love of the neighbor (II-II 59.4). Since this is so, the interrelationships between justice and charity offer a particularly fruitful set of starting points for developing an account of the way in which moral reflection informed by grace might actually work. This account, in turn, will suggest a way in which distinctively Christian ideals and beliefs can be said to inform the development of a natural law ethic in a Christian context, in such a way as to give rise to a substantive natural law ethic which is at one and the same time a distinctively Christian ethic. We have just observed that for Aquinas the demands of justice inform the normative ideals of charity in well-defined ways. What I want to argue is that the relation between justice and charity is reciprocal. That is, not only do the demands of justice inform charity; charity also gives rise to normative ideals which inform and transform our conception of justice, and correlatively, our sense of the substantive content of the natural law. That, at least, is the basic claim; let's see how it might be spelled out.

Aquinas regards charity as a particular virtue, and this means it is associated with its own proper kinds of actions, in terms of which it is conceptualized as a virtue. The paradigmatic act of charity, unsurprisingly, is love, more specifically the love of God and of ourselves and others for God's sake (II-II 27.1; II-I 25.1). This might seem to imply that charity stands in relation to justice and the other moral virtues as motive to precepts; that is to say, someone who acts out of charity will do so out of distinctive motivations, insofar as she loves the neighbor for God's sake, but she will not do anything differently from her neighbor who acts out of a (mere?) commitment to justice as an ideal. Of course, charity does bring distinctive motivations to action, and it will sometimes be the case that the acts of the charitable person will overlap with those of someone who observes the demands of justice for other reasons. But this cannot be the whole story. As Aquinas goes on to explain, charity is also associated with distinctive kinds of exterior actions, which constitute the characteristic (although of course, not the only) ways in which the fundamental act of love, seen in relation to other people, is expressed. Most fundamentally, the exterior action of beneficence is an act of charity because it shares in its formal object: "For the formal rational character of the object of charity and of beneficence is the same; for each regards to the general rational character of good, as is plain from what was said above [II-II 31.1]. Hence, beneficence is not a virtue different from charity, but designates a certain act of charity" (II-II 31.4; cf. 31.1). Similarly, we read that almsgiving "is properly an act of mercy . . . and because mercy is an effect of charity, as was shown above [30.2], in consequence to give alms is an act of charity, mediated through mercy" (32.1). Fraternal correction, which Aquinas understands as a form of discipline directed toward the good of the sinner himself or herself, is a further way of showing love for one's neighbor through external actions (33.1).

It is sometimes said that these kinds of actions should not be regarded as acts of charity, but rather as acts of the moral virtues from which they stem.[78] But as the above remarks make clear, for Aquinas these kinds of actions do stem directly and immediately from charity, or from the dispositions generated by charity. In this way, they are distinguished from the characteristic acts of the other virtues performed by the charitable person; these are said to be commanded by charity, which directs them to its proper end, whereas the proper acts of charity are elicited by the virtue of charity itself (II-II 23.8). At the same time, however, there is an important grain of truth in the claim that the proper acts of charity are acts of other virtues. Aquinas's commit-

78. See, for example, James Keenan, "The Problem with Thomas Aquinas's Concept of Sin," *Heythrop Journal* 35 (1994): 401-20.

ment to the thesis of the connection of the virtues implies that most (perhaps all) virtuous acts will be acts of more than one virtue. As we have already noted, every truly virtuous act will be an act of prudence as well as the virtue immediately eliciting it, and for the person possessing grace, every virtuous act will likewise be an act of charity. More specifically, it might be said that the other-regarding acts of charity are also acts of justice. Admittedly, Aquinas distinguishes between the exterior acts proper to charity and those proper to justice, arguing that acts of justice properly so called reflect specific obligations of some kind (II-II 31.1 *ad* 3). Yet he also holds that justice is the primary virtue concerned with other-regarding acts as such, and correlatively, he regards dispositions toward acts that are not strictly due, for example, friendliness, as virtues associated with justice, even though they fall short of the formal character of justice properly so called (II-II 80; note that this does not mean that they are lesser virtues, in the sense of being less praiseworthy or less central to human life). It does not seem inconsistent with his overall approach, therefore, to regard the exterior acts of charity as being also acts of justice in a similarly extended sense.

This brings us to a critical point. Even if we grant that the other-regarding acts of charity can also be regarded as acts of justice, this does not mean that we could arrive at the relevant precepts by reflection on the demands of justice, apart from the new perspective conferred by charity itself. Nothing in Aquinas's analysis rules out the possibility that our considered judgments about the substantive demands of charity might rest, in part at least, on grounds that would be inaccessible to us apart from revelation and our experiences of trying to live by its demands. This, I want to suggest, is in fact the case. That is, our judgments about the requirements of charity stem from an extended process of communal discernment regarding what it means concretely to love the neighbor *for the sake of* God, and also, to the extent possible and appropriate, to love the neighbor *as* God loves the neighbor. This process will involve wide-ranging reflection on distinctively theological claims about who God is, what it means to say that God loves men and women, what the possibilities and limitations of imitating this love might be, and who the neighbor is, seen as an object of God's love and as a potential or actual companion in grace. Clearly, reflection along these lines will take us well beyond an analysis of what it means to be fully human, unless this is simply equated with reflection on what it means to be human, seen from the perspective of faith.

In this way, reflection on the demands of charity will not only draw on a sense of the demands of justice, it will also and correlatively shape the conception of justice itself. It is important to note that this process amounts to transforming, and not merely supplementing, justice as we would otherwise understand it. In the first place, the precepts implied by the exterior acts of charity might turn out to be inconsistent with what we might otherwise regard as demands of justice. For example, if we believe that forgiveness is one of the exterior acts required by charity, we may find ourselves committed in principle to forgo certain forms of retributive punishment that would otherwise seem to be permitted, perhaps even required, by the demands of justice. Secondly, on almost any showing the other-regarding obligations of charity are universal in scope, and they imply the equal value of each person, at least in some respects (cf. II-II 26.5, 6). If this is so, then it implies that we must specify the domain of justice in such a way as to include all persons, and to regard them all as equally valuable in some fundamental respects — judgments we would not otherwise be compelled to make, rationally or on broader natural considerations.

Finally and most fundamentally, the normative ideal of charity implies a particular way of regarding the human person. If other-directed charity stems from the love of God, and regards others as most fundamentally actual or potential companions in that love, then this gives a particular saliency to certain aspects of human nature. The bestowal of grace presupposes capacities (not necessarily operative) for rational judgments and self-direction based on such judgments. The human person has an unbounded capacity for knowledge and rationally informed desire, and while these capacities do not give rise to knowledge and love of God through their natural operations, even on the implicit level, they do form the necessary conditions for that knowledge and love. It is not even thinkable that God could bestow charity or the Beatific Vision on a cat.

These and similar considerations, I want to suggest, led the scholastics to identify the natural law in its most fundamental sense with the Image of God, understood to include those human capacities which render us capable of charity, and intelligibly objects of the charity of others. This line of interpretation, in turn, was reinforced by their reading of Scripture and reciprocally shaped that reading. The Ordinary Gloss on Romans 2:14 quoted in chapter 1 offers a good illustration of this process. There, it will be recalled, we read that all people have "the natural law, by which one understands and is inwardly conscious of what is good and what is evil, what is vice insofar as it is contrary to nature, which in any case grace heals. . . . For that is not altogether removed which was impressed there through the Image of God when the human person was created."

How does this way of construing human nature shape our account of the natural law, considered as a substantive theological ethic? It would take us beyond the scope of this book to answer this question in any detail, but we can point to illustrative examples, many of which have already been mentioned. As we saw in the preceding section, the scholastic construal of human nature gave rise to an incipient notion of natural rights. Correlatively, this construal implies that all persons are naturally equal in certain key respects. The doctrine of natural equality, in turn, leads to an expansive construal of the scope of justice, and it also implies limits on the scope of authority and obedience.[79] In the last section, we briefly mentioned the emergence of a doctrine of marriage according to which the consent of the two parties is the essential ingredient; this doctrine would have made no sense except on the supposition that both parties, woman as well as man, possess the necessary capacities for free judgment and self-disposal, and it served to give a critical institutional expression to that supposition. To return to more immediate examples, the idea that fraternal correction is a fundamental moral duty, to be distinguished from deterrent or retributive punishment, expresses a sense of the value of even erring or destructive individuals which is very far from being obvious, apart from the perspective of charity.

So far, I have been defending the claim that reflection on human nature informed by the theological virtues and contextualized by Scripture and doctrine does give rise to a distinctively theological ethic of the natural law. Indeed, it might seem that we have gone so far in this direction that nature has finally dropped out of the natural law. If the demands of charity shape and transform our conception of justice, and by implication our account of the substantive precepts of the natural law, then have we really left nature any substantive role to play in our ethic? Is there a real difference between a theologically informed construal of nature and a projection onto nature?

In order to address these questions, I return to a point that was made earlier. That is, for Aquinas the exigencies and inclinations of human nature, generally considered, are not simply obviated by grace or subsumed under its imperatives. They continue to exercise independent normative force, even over against what might otherwise be regarded as spiritual aims. This point is sometimes obscured by the language of higher and lower aims and inclinations; the hierarchical ordering of human inclinations does not imply that the needs stemming from more basic inclinations should always give way to the demands stemming from more distinctively human inclinations. On the contrary, very often the most basic needs are the most urgent, and exercise the most exigent demands; as Aquinas puts it, we cannot enjoy or pursue any

79. As I have elsewhere argued in more detail; see "Natural Equality: Freedom, Authority, and Obedience in Two Medieval Thinkers," *Annual of the Society of Christian Ethics* 21 (2001): 275-304.

other aims unless we manage to stay alive (II-II 124.4). At any rate, it is the human person considered as a whole, in all her complex interrelated needs and inclinations, who exercises moral demands on herself and others. These demands inform the virtues in complex ways that cannot be reduced to simple rules of priority and precedence among the inclinations.

The conception of human nature informing a Thomistic account of the natural law is finally a theological conception, insofar as it considers what it means to be human in the light of theological perspectives epitomized by the motif of the Image of God. But that does not mean this concept does not enable us to recognize salient aspects of our commonly shared human nature and to give them their due moral weight. We return here to a problem considered at the beginning of chapter 2; that is, our concept of what it is to be human, like our concepts of other kinds of creatures, will inevitably emerge within some particular set of beliefs and culture-bound assumptions, and will correlatively be limited and provisional. That does not mean it is bound to be incorrect, nor does it rule out very considerable convergence among different conceptions of human nature. Moreover, both Aquinas and the other scholastics, and we ourselves, have developed our conceptions of human nature in conversation with others who do not share our specific theological convictions, including for the scholastics classical, Jewish, and Muslim perspectives, and for us a very wide range of religious and secular voices. This diversity of views helps to ensure that we can develop an adequate sense, albeit never a perfect sense, of what the commonalities of our shared human nature are, and to take due account of these in our moral reflections.

These considerations are particularly relevant with respect to justice, which once again provides a focal point for the substantive demands of the natural law. Justice is the quintessential virtue of personal and social interactions, governed by norms which are publicly known and acknowledged as such; if this were not the case, the ideal of justice could not serve its primary function of providing a framework within which people can interact against a background of shared standards of fairness and equity. Even in Aquinas's time, and much more in our own, a conception of justice governed purely by Christian ideals and commitments could not have played this role. Admittedly, Aquinas does not address this issue in these general terms. Nonetheless, he attempts to deal with similar concerns through appeals to an idea of natural justice. The obligations or charity or religion do not supersede the demands of natural justice (II-II 104.6). As such, natural justice provides a framework within which Christians and non-Christians can live together, and Christians are bound by natural justice in their dealings with non-Christians (II-II 10.10, 12). Seen from our perspective, the idea of natural justice itself appears as a theological construct, but it is a construct enabling us to take account of the claims which stem from our shared humanity, in the context of pluralistic societies.

At this point, let me attempt to summarize the overall conclusion of this section. In the third chapter, I argued that a Thomistic theory of the natural law takes its teleological focus from an account of happiness, understood as the practice of the virtues. This section clarifies and develops that claim by showing that the relevant conception of happiness is to be identified with the practice of the infused virtues, including faith, hope, and charity as well as the infused cardinal virtues. Thus, the theory of the natural law being presented is tethered to an ideal of terrestrial happiness, but the terrestrial happiness in question is directly oriented toward a still more complete form of happiness, which it anticipates in ways we cannot now grasp.

This line of argument raises a further question which cannot fully be addressed at this point, but which should at least be flagged. That is, what are the implications of this approach for the status of those who do not share Christian beliefs? This question takes on particular force within the context of a set of doctrinal commitments shared by Catholic theology and many other Christian communions. That is, there is a long-standing doctrinal commitment to the view that one's standing before God, and one's ultimate salvation, depend on the grace of God and not on one's individual attainments or moral excellences. Taken by itself, this claim is not necessarily troubling, but it has usually been linked to an account of grace which ties it to specific Christian beliefs and practices. We have noted that Aquinas himself takes this approach, as do the other theologians of his time. If this is so, however, then it would seem to follow that non-Christians cannot attain salvation, no matter how exemplary their lives may otherwise be. And this has proven to be a hard conclusion to accept. Admitting that God's ways are not our ways, are we prepared to say that God's dealings with us are quite so arbitrary? Or — dare we say it? — unfair?

The bishops of the Second Vatican Council attempted to close off this line of thought, affirming that the Holy Spirit, in ways known only to God, offers salvation to all who sincerely try to follow the guidance of their own consciences.[80] This clearly implies that grace is somehow available to all men and women, whatever their historical or cultural location, and apart from any distinctively Christian beliefs or practices. Is this perspective on grace consistent with the view developed in this section, according to which grace is tied to the practice of virtues which are understood in explicitly Christian terms?

80. *Gaudium et Spes*, no. 22.

At the end of the last section, I referred to Dupuis's recent work on religious pluralism, in which he argues that diverse religious perspectives can be regarded as expressions of the activity of God's Spirit, which as such have Christ as their ultimate point of reference but also have an independent and irreducible value within God's providential plan for the salvation of all persons. This seems to me to offer a most promising way through the complex difficulties raised by the teaching of Vatican II on the salvation of non-Christians. (Lest there be any doubt on this point, I should add that I fully accept and endorse this teaching.) I would suggest that the account of grace and the virtues developed in this section might offer a way to complement and extend this line of interpretation. While I cannot develop this suggestion in detail here, let me at least sketch out how such an argument might proceed.[81]

On the view developed here, the infused virtues are paradigmatically expressed in kinds of actions which presuppose distinctively Christian beliefs and practices — which are embedded, in other words, in the way of life specific to the church. But as we noted in chapters 3 and 4, the relationship between virtues and their paradigmatic kinds of acts is conceptual; it does not imply either a necessary or a sufficient connection between the possession of the virtues and the display of the paradigmatic kinds of acts. That is to say, it is possible to claim that someone possesses a virtue even though he does not perform the kinds of actions we initially regard as paradigmatic for that virtue. In order to cash this out, we would need to give an account of the way a given set of actions resemble what we regard as the paradigmatic acts of the kind of virtue in question. But there need be nothing difficult or mysterious about this. This is the kind of process through which, for example, we might come to regard the principled refusal of the conscientious objector to be as much an expression of courage as the valor of the soldier. This judgment would imply a change (although not a radical break) in our earlier conception of courage, but surely we want an account of the virtues which allows our understanding of them to develop in this way.

My point is that nothing prevents us from making similar kinds of judgments with respect to the infused virtues. That is, we conceive of these virtues in terms of distinctively Christian beliefs and practices — and properly so, since apart from this context the distinction between infused and ac-

81. I do not want to claim that Dupuis would agree with what follows; I suspect he might not, since he is more sympathetic to a Rahnerian analysis of grace than I am. I would suggest, however, that this approach might actually be more in accord with Dupuis's deepest insights, since it builds upon his insistence that we must build our accounts of religious pluralism out of an engagement with diverse religions as they concretely exist. But that is an argument for another day.

quired virtues would have no point. But this is a conceptual link, not an assertion of a set of necessary and sufficient conditions. Nothing prevents us from acknowledging that these same virtues might appear, in different but recognizably analogous forms, in other contexts. This implies, of course, that grace is operative in those contexts — even though, as the Council so carefully puts it, the exact mechanisms of grace are known only to God. Indeed, I would suggest that at least a part of the impetus for the current interest in interreligious dialogue stems from just this sort of experience. We see men and women of every religious belief, and none, displaying what we can only regard as exemplary moral goodness, and even charity. How can we deny that the Spirit of God is present when we see its fruits? We can affirm this much, while leaving further theological difficulties for another day.

It is perhaps appropriate to conclude this account of the natural law on a note of tentativeness and uncertainty. On the Thomistic account of the natural law that I have attempted to develop, there is nothing particularly mysterious about the phenomenon of human morality itself. On the contrary, morality on this account is an expression of the natural life of the human creature. As such, it is an expression of the creative wisdom of God, a reflection of the divine Image borne by each human being, and an expression of the distinctively human mode of participation in God's eternal providence; for all these reasons, it deserves our respect, even our reverence. But as Aquinas and his contemporaries remind us, whatever is distinctive in human morality can only be rendered meaningful within a broader context of continuities with the modes of functioning proper to other kinds of creatures. In the last analysis, human morality as such deserves reverence and admiration because it reflects God's wisdom as Creator — but so do the ways of life or existence proper to other kinds of creatures. By the same token, we ourselves are creatures, and our capacities for moral judgment and action reflect a distinctive and limited way of life. They are not themselves divine or transcendent qualities, through which we are somehow taken out of the natural order of existence.

Although this generalization would need to be qualified in many ways, it seems safe to say that Catholic theologians have historically been inclined to overemphasize the absolute quality, the goodness and what we might call the intrinsic divinity of human morality. Protestant theologians, in contrast, have focused on the pervasiveness of sin and corruption, concluding that our moral qualities are limited at best and certainly not a point of contact with divinity. Neither perspective seems to me quite right. Certainly, the traditional Protestant approach is right to emphasize the limitations of human morality and to insist that in itself it is not salvific. Yet the fact that human morality cannot save us does not by itself imply that we are incapable of a kind of genuine goodness, or that everything that is not clearly graced must therefore be a kind of sin. In this respect, the traditional Catholic approach seems more adequate, insofar as it insists on the human capacity for genuine goodness, and holds out the hope that human morality can be transformed through grace without losing its character as a recognizable form of human goodness.

But what would it mean for morality to be transformed by grace? This is the question to which we must return in every generation, as the collective experience of the church teaches us to recognize our own limitations, on the one hand, and to see the presence of the Spirit in unexpected ways among others, on the other hand. At this point we do come up against the limitations of transcendence and mystery, because grace is nothing other than a mode of participation in the inner life of God, who remains incomprehensible even to the blessed. Yet as Aquinas teaches us, we can in some ways approach the mystery of grace through reflection on the moral life — which is not to say that grace can be identified with, much less reduced to, the operations of morality.

Nature and grace are held together, on this view, through the operations of the virtue of charity, which transforms the imperatives of morality in any form even as it is informed by them. Through charity, we love others and ourselves for God's sake, and we love and reverence God in and through a proper reverence for God's creation. How can we do so — how can we even grasp what this might mean — without some sense of what it means to respect and benefit, or denigrate and harm, ourselves and others? At this point, the obligations to ourselves and others stemming from the natural law do take on an absolute force, because they are subsumed in the unconditional demand to love God, and to love the neighbor as oneself. At the same time, the dynamics of charity, informed as it is by faith and hope (in some form or other), function in such a way as to transform our sense of the imperatives stemming from our nature, as I have tried to suggest in this chapter.

In the first letter to the Corinthians, Paul remarks that "it is a very small thing that I should be judged by you or by any human court. I do not even judge myself" (1 Cor. 4:3). In one sense, of course, we cannot escape the necessity of judging ourselves and each other — we are social animals, as we have often remarked, and this means, among other things, that we cannot evade the fundamental necessity of setting norms for our behavior, and enforcing them through rewards and sanctions. Yet these norms have a provisional character at best, and we can never say with certainty whether in a particular case they are informed by grace, reflective of the unconditional will of God — not even with respect to ourselves, much less with respect to others. We can only hope that God will inspire and guide our efforts to live in charity, and look with mercy on our failures. The doctrine of final judgment promises us that God will at least not relegate our efforts to meaninglessness, or look upon them with indifference — they will be assessed in the light of God's own wisdom and love, and whatever is good in them will be preserved. At the end of the day, we must hope for this judgment for others and for ourselves, remembering that in God justice and mercy are one.

Bibliography

1. Ancient and Medieval Sources

Throughout this book, I make use of texts excerpted in Lottin (1931) and Weigand (1967). References to these sources are given in the body of the text by name and page number in the case of Lottin, or name and paragraph number in the case of Weigand. All translations from both collections are my own, as are all other translations except where otherwise indicated.

Albert the Great. *De Bono.* Vol. 28 in *Alberti Magni Opera Omnia ad fidem codicum manuscriptorum.* Münster: Aschendorff, 1951.

Aristotle. *Nicomachean Ethics.* Translated by Terence Irwin. Indianapolis: Hackett, 1985.

Augustine. *De Civitate Dei,* book 19. Translated by W. C. Greene. In *City of God,* vol. 6. Cambridge, Mass.: Loeb Classical Library, 1969.

Bonaventure. *Collationes de decem praeceptis.* Vol. 5 in *Opera Omnia.* Florence: College of St. Bonaventure, 1891.

———. *Quaestiones disputatae de perfectione evangelium.* Vol. 5 in *Opera Omnia.* Florence: College of St. Bonaventure, 1891.

Cicero. *De Inventione, De Optimo Genere Oratorum, Topica.* Translated by H. M. Hubbell. Cambridge, Mass.: Loeb Classical Library, 1949.

———. *De Republica, De Legibus.* Translated by Clinton Walker Keyes. Cambridge, Mass.: Loeb Classical Library, 1928.

Glossa Ordinaria. Biblia Latina cum Glossa Ordinaria. Vol. 4. Brepolis: Turnhout, 1992.

———. *Patrologiae Cursus Completus.* Vol. 114. 1852.

Gratian of Bologna. *Decretum Gratiani Emendum et Notationibus Illustratum una cum Glossis.* Rome: in aedibus Populi Romani, 1582.

———. *Gratian: The Treatise on Laws (Decretum DD. 1-20), with the Ordinary Gloss.*

Gloss translated by Augustine Thompson and James Gordley. Washington, D.C.: Catholic University of America Press, 1993.

Justinian. *The Digest of Justinian.* Philadelphia: University of Philadelphia Press, 1985.

———. *The Institutes of Justinian.* London: Longman's Green and Company, 1888.

Thomas Aquinas. *Quaestiones disputatae de malo.* Vol. 23 in *Opera Omnia iussa edita Leonis XIII P.M.* Rome/Paris: Commissio Leonina/J. Vrin, 1982.

———. *De Veritate.* Vol. 22 in *Opera Omnia iussa edita Leonis XIII P.M.* Rome: Ex Typographia Polyglotta S.C. de Propaganda Fide, 1970-76.

———. *De virtutibus, q.1, Quaestiones disputatae, t.2: quaestiones disputatae de virtutibus in communi,* 707-51. Rome: Marietti, 1965.

———. *Sententia libri Ethicorum.* Vol. 49 in *Opera Omnia iussa edita Leonis XIII P.M.* Rome: Ex Typographia Polyglotta S.C. de Propaganda Fide, 1969.

———. *Summa contra gentiles.* Vols. 13-15 in *Opera Omnia iussa edita Leonis XIII P.M.* Rome: Ex Typographia Polyglotta S.C. de Propaganda Fide, 1918-30. Abbreviated *SCG* in the text and notes.

———. *Summa theologica.* Vols. 4-12 in *Opera Omnia iussa edita Leonis XIII P.M.* Rome: Ex Typographia Polyglotta S.C. de Propaganda Fide, 1888-1906. Abbreviated *ST* in the text and notes.

———. *Super Librum Dionysii De divinis nominibus.* Vol. 29 in *Opera Omnia.* Parisiis apud Ludovicum Vives, 1871-80.

William of Auxerre. *Summa Aurea, Liber Quartus.* Paris: Centre National de la Recherche Scientifique, 1985.

2. Modern and Contemporary Sources

Abbà, Giuseppe. *Lex et Virtus: Studi sull'evoluzione della dottrina morale di san Tommaso d'Aquino.* Rome: Libreria Ateneo Salesiano, 1983.

Adams, Marilyn McCord. "Universals in the Early Fourteenth Century." In *The Cambridge History of Later Medieval Philosophy from the Rediscovery of Aristotle to the Disintegration of Scholasticism, 1100-1600,* edited by Norman Kretzman, Anthony Kenny, and Jan Pinborg, 411-39. Cambridge: Cambridge University Press, 1982.

Amundson, Ron. "Typology Reconsidered: Two Doctrines on the History of Evolutionary Biology." *Biology and Philosophy* 13 (1998): 153-77.

Annas, Julia. *The Morality of Happiness.* Oxford: Oxford University Press, 1993.

Anscombe, Elizabeth. *Intention.* 2nd ed. Ithaca, N.Y.: Cornell University Press, 1963.

———. "Under a Description." 1979. Reprinted in *The Collected Philosophical Papers of G. E. M. Anscombe,* vol. 2, 208-19. Oxford: Basil Blackwell, 1981.

Arnhart, Larry. *Darwinian Natural Right: The Biological Ethics of Human Nature.* New York: State University of New York Press, 1998.

Aronovitch, Hilliard. "Reflective Equilibrium or Evolving Tradition?" *Inquiry* 39 (1996): 399-419.

Bibliography

Ayala, Francisco J. "The Biological Roots of Morality." *Biology and Philosophy* 2 (1987): 235-52.

Ayer, A. J. *Language, Truth, and Logic.* New York: Dover Books, 1952; originally 1946.

Baier, Annette. "Claims, Rights, Responsibilities." In *Prospects for a Common Morality,* edited by Gene Outka and John Reeder, Jr., 149-69. Princeton: Princeton University Press, 1993.

———. *Moral Prejudices: Essays on Ethics.* Cambridge: Harvard University Press, 1994.

———. *Postures of the Mind: Essays on Mind and Morals.* Minneapolis: University of Minnesota Press, 1985.

Barr, James. *Biblical Faith and Natural Theology.* Oxford: Clarendon, 1993.

Barth, Karl. *Church Dogmatics* II/2. Translated by G. W. Bromiley et al. Edinburgh: T. & T. Clark, 1957.

Bastit, Michel. "Le thomisme est-il un aristotélisme?" *Revue Thomiste* 101 (2001): 101-16.

Bekoff, Marc. "Social Play Behaviour: Cooperation, Fairness, Trust, and the Evolution of Morality." *Journal of Consciousness Studies* 8 (2001): 81-90.

Bennett, Jonathan. *The Act Itself.* Oxford: Clarendon, 1995.

Bentham, Jeremy. *An Introduction to the Principles of Morals and Legislation.* New York: Macmillan, 1948; originally 1789.

Biggar, Nigel. Conclusion to *The Revival of Natural Law: Philosophical, Theological, and Ethical Responses to the Finnis-Grisez School,* edited by Nigel Biggar and Rufus Black, 283-94. Aldershot: Ashgate Press, 2000.

———. *The Hastening That Waits: Karl Barth's Ethics.* Paperback edition with new conclusion. Oxford: Clarendon, 1995.

Black, Rufus. "The New Natural Law Theory." In *The Revival of Natural Law: Philosophical, Theological, and Ethical Responses to the Finnis-Grisez School,* edited by Nigel Biggar and Rufus Black, 1-28. Aldershot: Ashgate Press, 2000.

Blackburn, Simon. *Ruling Passions: A Theory of Practical Reason.* Oxford: Clarendon, 1998.

Bovenkerk, Bernice, Frans W. A. Brom, and Babs J. Van den Berg. "Brave New Birds: The Use of 'Animal Integrity' in Animal Ethics." *Hastings Center Report,* January-February 2002, 16-22.

Bowlin, John. *Contingency and Fortune in Aquinas' Ethic.* Cambridge: Cambridge University Press, 1999.

Boyle, Joseph, John Finnis, and Germain Grisez. "'Direct' and 'Indirect': A Reply to Critics of Our Action Theory." *The Thomist* 65 (2001): 1-44.

———. "Practical Principles, Moral Truth, and Ultimate Ends." *American Journal of Jurisprudence* 32 (1987): 99-151.

Bradley, Denis. *Aquinas on the Twofold Human Good.* Washington, D.C.: Catholic University of America Press, 1997.

Brandt, Richard. *Morality, Utilitarianism, and Rights.* Cambridge: Cambridge University Press, 1992.

Brennan, J. M. *The Open-Texture of Moral Concepts.* New York: Barnes and Noble, 1977.

Bresnahan, James F. "An Ethics of Faith." In *A World of Grace: An Introduction to the Themes and Foundations of Karl Rahner's Theology,* edited by Leo J. O'Donovan, 169-84. New York: Crossroad, 1981.

Brock, Stephen. *Action and Conduct: Thomas Aquinas and the Theory of Action.* Edinburgh: T. & T. Clark, 1998.

Burnyeat, M. F. "Aristotle on Learning to Be Good." In *Essays in Aristotle's Ethics,* edited by Amélie Rorty, 69-92. Berkeley: University of California Press, 1980.

Cahill, Lisa. "Toward Global Ethics." *Theological Studies* 63 (2002): 324-44.

———. *Sex, Gender, and Christian Ethics.* Cambridge: Cambridge University Press, 1996.

Casey, John. *Pagan Virtue: An Essay in Ethics.* Oxford: Clarendon, 1990.

Cates, Diana. *Choosing to Feel: Virtue, Friendship, and Compassion for Friends.* Notre Dame: University of Notre Dame Press, 1997.

Charles, David. *Aristotle on Meaning and Essence.* Oxford: Oxford University Press, 2000.

Childress, James. "Moral Discourse about War in the Early Church." *Journal of Religious Ethics* 12, no. 1 (1984).

Clark, Stephen. *Biology and Christian Ethics.* Cambridge: Cambridge University Press, 2000.

Coleman, Janet. "MacIntyre and Aquinas." In *After MacIntyre: Critical Perspectives on the Work of Alasdair MacIntyre,* edited by John Horton and Susan Mendes, 65-90. Notre Dame: University of Notre Dame Press, 1994.

Constable, Giles. *The Reformation of the Twelfth Century.* Cambridge: Cambridge University Press, 1996.

Cook, Martin. "Ways of Thinking Naturally." *Annual of the Society of Christian Ethics,* (1988): 161-78.

Cronin, Kieran. *Rights and Christian Ethics.* Cambridge: Cambridge University Press, 1992.

Crowe, Michael. *The Changing Profile of the Natural Law.* The Hague: Martinus Nijhoff, 1977.

Crysdale, Cynthia S. W. "Revisioning Natural Law: From the Classicist Paradigm to Emergent Probability." *Theological Studies* 56 (1995): 464-84.

Curran, Charles. *The Catholic Moral Tradition Today: A Synthesis.* Washington, D.C.: Georgetown University Press, 1999.

———. "Natural Law in Moral Theology." 1970. Reprinted in *Readings in Moral Theology No. 7: Natural Law and Theology,* edited by Charles E. Curran and Richard A. McCormick, 247-95. New York: Paulist, 1991.

Curran, Charles, with Richard McCormick. Introduction to *Readings in Moral Theology No. 7: Natural Law and Theology.* New York: Paulist, 1991.

D'Arcy, Eric. *Human Acts: An Essay in Their Moral Evaluation.* Oxford: Clarendon, 1963.

Davidson, Donald. *Essays on Actions and Events.* 2nd ed. Oxford: Clarendon, 2001.

Davies, Paul. *Norms of Nature: Naturalism and the Nature of Functions.* Cambridge: MIT Press, 2001.

Dawkins, Richard. "Accumulating Small Change." in *Philosophy of Biology,* edited by Michael Ruse, 62-68. Amherst: Prometheus Books, 1998. Reprinted from *The Blind Watchmaker: Why the Evidence of Evolution Reveals a Universe without a Design.* New York: Norton, 1986, 1987, 1996.

Dedek, John. "Premarital Sex: The Theological Argument from Peter Lombard to Durand." *Theological Studies* 41 (1980): 643-67.

Delhaye, Philippe. *Permanence du droit naturel.* Louvain: Editions Nauwelaerts, 1960.

de Lubac, Henri. *The Mystery of the Supernatural.* Translated by Rosemary Sheed. New York: Herder and Herder, 1967.

d'Entreves, A. P. *Natural Law: An Introduction to Legal Philosophy.* Rev. 2nd ed. London: Hutchinson, 1970.

de Sousa, Ronald. *The Rationality of Emotion.* Cambridge: MIT Press, 1987.

de Waal, Frans. *Good Natured: The Origins of Right and Wrong in Humans and Other Animals.* Cambridge: Harvard University Press, 1996.

Dickens, Charles. *A Christmas Carol* (1843). Various editions.

Donagan, Alan. *The Theory of Morality.* Chicago: University of Chicago Press, 1977.

Duffy, Stephen. *The Graced Horizon: Nature and Grace in Modern Catholic Thought.* Collegeville, Minn.: Liturgical Press, 1992.

Dupuis, Jacques. *Towards a Christian Theology of Religious Pluralism.* Maryknoll, N.Y.: Orbis, 1997.

Dworkin, Ronald. *Sovereign Virtue: The Theory and Practice of Equality.* Cambridge: Harvard University Press, 2000.

———. *Taking Rights Seriously.* Cambridge: Harvard University Press, 1977/1978.

Ehrenreich, Barbara, and Janet McIntosh. "The New Creationism." *The Nation,* June 9, 1997, 1-16.

Everard, William, Gerrard Winstanley, et al. *The True Levellers' Standard Advanced* (1649). In *The Puritan Revolution: A Documentary History,* edited by Stuart E. Prall, 174-81. New York: Doubleday/Anchor, 1968.

Farber, Paul Lawrence. *The Temptations of Evolutionary Ethics.* Berkeley: University of California Press, 1998.

Finnis, John. *Aquinas: Moral, Political, and Legal Theory.* Founders of Modern Political and Social Thought. Oxford: Oxford University Press, 1998.

———. *Natural Law and Natural Rights.* Oxford: Clarendon, 1980.

Flanagan, Owen, Jr. "Quinean Ethics." *Ethics* 93 (1982): 56-74.

———. *Varieties of Moral Personality: Ethics and Psychological Realism.* Cambridge: Harvard University Press, 1991.

Flannery, Kevin L., S.J. *Acts Amid Precepts: The Aristotelian Logical Structure of Thomas Aquinas's Moral Theory.* Washington, D.C.: Catholic University of America Press, 2001.

Foot, Philippa. *Moral Dilemmas and Other Topics in Moral Philosophy.* Oxford: Clarendon, 2002.

———. *Natural Goodness.* Oxford: Clarendon, 2001.

———. *Virtues and Vices and Other Essays in Moral Philosophy.* Berkeley: University of California Press, 1978.

Forsythe, David. *Human Rights in International Relations.* Cambridge: Cambridge University Press, 2000.

Fried, Charles. *Right and Wrong.* Cambridge: Harvard University Press, 1978.

Fuchs, Josef. "Is There a Specifically Christian Morality?" In *Readings in Moral Theology No. 2: The Distinctiveness of Christian Ethics,* edited by Richard McCormick and Charles Curran, 3-19. New York: Paulist, 1980; originally 1970.

———. *Moral Demands and Personal Obligations.* Washington, D.C.: Georgetown University Press, 1993.

Gaudium et Spes ("Pastoral Constitution on the Church in the Modern World"). In *The Documents of Vatican II,* Walter M. Abbott, S.J., general editor. London: Chapman, 1966.

George, Robert. *In Defense of Natural Law.* Oxford: Oxford University Press, 1999.

Gewirth, Alan. "Common Morality and the Community of Rights." In *Prospects for a Common Morality,* edited by Gene Outka and John Reeder, Jr., 29-52. Princeton: Princeton University Press, 1993.

———. *Reason and Morality.* Chicago: University of Chicago Press, 1978.

Gibbard, Allan. *Wise Choices, Apt Feelings: A Theory of Normative Judgment.* Cambridge: Harvard University Press, 1990.

Goodin, Robert. *Utilitarianism as a Public Philosophy.* Cambridge: Cambridge University Press, 1995.

Goodman, Lenn E., and Madeleine J. Goodman. "Creation and Evolution: Another Round in an Ancient Struggle." *Zygon* 18, no. 1 (March 1983): 3-43.

Gould, Stephen J. "Darwinism and the Expansion of Evolutionary Theory." In *Philosophy of Biology,* edited by Michael Ruse, 100-117. Amherst: Prometheus Books, 1998. Originally published in *Science* 216 (1982): 380-87.

Grabmann, Martin. "Das Naturrecht der Scholastik von Gratian bis Thomas von Aquin." In Vol. I of *Mittelalterliches Geistesleben: Abhandlungen zur Geschichte der Scholastik und Mystik,* 65-103. 3 vols. Munich: Hueber, 1926.

Gregory, Tulio. "The Platonic Inheritance." In *A History of Twelfth Century Western Philosophy,* edited by Peter Dronke, 54-80. Cambridge: Cambridge University Press, 1988.

Grene, Marjorie. "Hierarchies in Biology." *American Scientist* 75 (1987): 504-9.

Griffin, James. *Well-Being: Its Meaning, Measurement, and Moral Importance.* Oxford: Clarendon, 1986.

Grisez, Germain. "Natural Law, God, Religion, and Human Fulfillment." *American Journal of Jurisprudence* 46 (2001): 3-36.

———. *The Way of the Lord Jesus 1: Christian Moral Principles.* Chicago: Franciscan Herald Press, 1983.

———. *The Way of the Lord Jesus 2: Living a Christian Life.* Chicago: Franciscan Herald Press, 1993.

Gunnemann, Jon. "Human Rights and Modernity." *Journal of Religious Ethics* 16 (1988): 160-89.

Gustafson, James. *Ethics from a Theocentric Perspective,* vol. 1: *Theology and Ethics.* Chicago: University of Chicago Press, 1981.

———. *Ethics from a Theocentric Perspective,* vol. 2: *Ethics and Theology.* Chicago: University of Chicago Press, 1984.

———. "Nature: Its Status in Theological Ethics." *Logos* vol. E (1982): 5-23.

Haakonssen, Knud. *Natural Law and Moral Philosophy from Grotius to the Scottish Enlightenment.* Cambridge: Cambridge University Press, 1996.

Habermas, Jürgen. *Moral Consciousness and Communicative Action.* Translated by Christian Lenhardt and Shierry Weber Nicholsen. Cambridge: MIT Press, 1990.

Hacking, Ian. *The Social Construction of What?* Cambridge: Harvard University Press, 1999.

Hall, Pamela. *Narrative and the Natural Law: An Interpretation of Thomistic Ethics.* Notre Dame: University of Notre Dame Press, 1994.

Hallett, Garth L. *Greater Good: The Case for Proportionalism.* Washington, D.C.: Georgetown University Press, 1995.

———. *Priorities and Christian Ethics.* Cambridge: Cambridge University Press, 1998.

Hare, R. M. *Freedom and Reason.* Oxford: Oxford University Press, 1963/1965.

———. *The Language of Morals.* Oxford: Oxford University Press, 1952/1964.

———. *Moral Thinking: Its Levels, Method, and Point.* Oxford: Clarendon, 1981.

Häring, Bernard. *The Law of Christ: Moral Theology for Priests and Laity.* Vol. I. Translated by Edwin G. Kaiser. Westminster, Md.: Newman Press, 1965.

Hart, H. L. A. *The Concept of Law.* 2nd ed. Oxford: Clarendon, 1994. 1st ed. 1961.

Hart, H. L. A., with Tony Honoré. *Causation and the Law.* 2nd ed. Oxford: Clarendon, 1985.

Hauerwas, Stanley. *The Peaceable Kingdom: A Primer in Christian Ethics.* Notre Dame: University of Notre Dame Press, 1983.

———. *With the Grain of the Universe: The Church's Witness and Natural Theology.* Grand Rapids: Baker, 2001.

Haught, John. *God after Darwin: A Theology of Evolution.* Boulder, Colo.: Westview Press, 2000.

Hauser, Marc D. *Wild Minds: What Animals Really Think.* New York: Henry Holt, 2000.

Hefner, Philip. *The Human Factor: Evolution, Culture, and Religion.* Minneapolis: Fortress, 1993.

Himes, Michael J. "The Human Person in Contemporary Theology: From Human Nature to Authentic Subjectivity." 1983. Reprinted in *Introduction to Christian Ethics: A Reader,* edited by Ronald R. Hamel and Kenneth R. Himes, O.F.M., 49-62. New York: Paulist, 1989.

Hittinger, Russell. *The First Grace: Rediscovering the Natural Law in a Post-Christian World.* Wilmington: ISI Books, 2003.

Hobbes, Thomas. *Leviathan.* Edited with an introduction by C. B. MacPherson. 1651. Middlesex, U.K., and Baltimore: Penguin Books, 1968.

Hoffmann, Stanley. *Duties beyond Borders: On the Limits and Possibilities of Ethical International Politics.* Syracuse: Syracuse University Press, 1981.

Hollenbach, David. *Claims in Conflict: Retrieving and Renewing the Catholic Human Rights Tradition.* New York: Paulist, 1979.

———. *The Common Good and Christian Ethics.* Cambridge: Cambridge University Press, 2002.

Hollis, Martin. *Models of Man: Philosophical Thoughts on Social Action.* Cambridge: Cambridge University Press, 1977.

Hollis, Martin, and Steven Lukes, eds. *Rationality and Relativism.* Cambridge: MIT Press, 1982.

Horton, Robin. "Tradition and Modernity Revisited." In *Rationality and Relativism,* edited by Martin Hollis and Steven Lukes, 201-60. Cambridge: Massachusetts Institute of Technology Press, 1982.

Hume, David. *A Treatise of Human Nature.* Edited by L. A. Selby-Bigge. Oxford: Oxford University Press, 1888.

———. *An Enquiry Concerning the Principles of Morals* (1751). Edited by Thomas Beauchamp. Oxford: Clarendon, 1998.

Hursthouse, Rosalind. *On Virtue Ethics.* Oxford: Oxford University Press, 1999.

Hütter, Reinhard. "'God's Law' in *Veritatis splendor:* Sic et Non." In *Ecumenical Ventures in Ethics: Protestants Engage Pope John Paul II's Moral Encyclicals,* edited by Reinhard Hütter and Theodor Dieter, 84-114. Grand Rapids: Eerdmans, 1998.

———. "The Twofold Center of Lutheran Ethics: Christian Freedom and God's Commandments." In *The Promise of Lutheran Ethics,* edited by Karen Bloomquist and John Stumme, 31-54. Minneapolis: Fortress, 1998.

Hyams, Paul. "Due Process versus the Maintenance of Order in European Law: The Contribution of the *Jus Commune.*" In *The Moral World of the Law,* edited by Peter Coss, 62-90. Cambridge: Cambridge University Press, 2000.

Ignatieff, Michael. *Human Rights as Politics and Idolatry.* Princeton: Princeton University Press, 2001.

Ilesanmi, Simon. "Civil Political Rights or Social-Economic Rights for Africa? A Comparative Ethical Critique of a False Dichotomy." *Annual of the Society of Christian Ethics,* 1997, 191-212.

Jeater, Diana. "'Their Idea of Justice Is So Peculiar': Southern Rhodesia 1890-1910." In *The Moral World of the Law,* edited by Peter Coss, 178-95. Cambridge: Cambridge University Press, 2000.

Kagan, Shelly. *The Limits of Morality.* Oxford: Oxford University Press, 1989.

Kant, Immanuel. *The Groundwork of the Metaphysics of Morals.* Translated by H. J. Paton. 1948. Reprint, New York: Harper, 1964; 3rd ed. 1956.

Kass, Leon. *Toward a More Natural Science: Biology and Human Affairs.* New York: Macmillan, 1985.

Katz, Leo. *Ill-Gotten Gains: Evasion, Blackmail, Fraud, and Kindred Puzzles of the Law.* Chicago: University of Chicago Press, 1996.

Keenan, James. *Goodness and Rightness in Thomas Aquinas's "Summa Theologiae."* Washington, D.C.: Georgetown University Press, 1992.

———. "The Problem with Thomas Aquinas's Concept of Sin." *Heythrop Journal* 35 (1994): 401-20.

———. "Proposing Cardinal Virtues." *Theological Studies* 56 (1995): 709-29.

Keenan, James, and Thomas Shannon, eds. *The Context of Casuistry.* Washington, D.C.: Georgetown University Press, 1995.

Kekes, John. "Human Nature and Moral Theories." *Inquiry* 28 (1985): 231-45.

Kent, Bonnie. *Virtues of the Will: The Transformation of Ethics in the Late Thirteenth Century.* Washington, D.C.: Catholic University of America Press, 1995.

Kluxen, Wolfgang. *Lex naturalis bei Thomas von Aquin.* Wiesbaden: Westdeutscher, 2001.

Knauer, Peter. "La détermination du bien et du mal par le principe du double effect." *Nouvelle Revue Théologique* 87 (1965): 356-76.

Kovesi, Julius. *Moral Notions.* London: Routledge and Kegan Paul, 1967.

Krauz, Michael. *Relativism: Interpretation and Confrontation.* Notre Dame: University of Notre Dame Press, 1989.

Küng, Hans. *Global Responsibility: In Search of a New World Ethic.* New York: Continuum, 1996.

Küng, Hans, and Karl-Josef Kuschel, eds. *A Global Ethic: The Declaration of the Parliament of the World's Religions.* New York: Continuum, 1998.

Lambert, Malcolm. *Medieval Heresy: Popular Movements from the Gregorian Reform to the Reformation.* 2nd ed. Oxford: Blackwell, 1992.

Lennox, James. *Aristotle's Philosophy of Biology.* Cambridge: Cambridge University Press, 2001.

Lewis, Ewart. "Natural Law and Expediency in Medieval Political Theory." *Ethics* 50 (1940): 144-63.

Lewontin, Richard. *The Triple Helix: Gene, Organism, and Environment.* Cambridge: Harvard University Press, 2000.

Lisska, Anthony J. *Aquinas's Theory of the Natural Law: An Analytic Reconstruction.* Oxford: Clarendon, 1996.

Livingstone, David N. "The Idea of Design: The Vicissitudes of a Key Concept in the Princeton Response to Darwin." *Scottish Journal of Theology* 37 (1984): 329-57.

Locke, John. *Two Treatises of Government.* Edited with an introduction and notes by Peter Laslett. 1690. Cambridge: Cambridge University Press, 1963. 2nd ed. 1964; 3rd ed. 1968.

Long, Steven. "A Brief Disquisition regarding the Nature of the Object of the Moral Act according to St. Thomas Aquinas." *The Thomist* 67 (January 2003): 45-71.

———. "On the Possibility of a Purely Natural End for Man." *The Thomist* 64 (2000): 211-37.

Lottin, Odon. *Le droit naturel chez saint Thomas d'Aquin et ses prédécesseurs.* 2nd ed. Bruges: Beyart, 1931.

———. "Le problème de la moralité intrinsèque d'Abélard à saint Thomas d'Aquin." In *Psychologie et morale aux XIIe et XIIIe siècles,* vol. 2, 421-65. Louvain: Abbaye du Mont César, 1948.

———. "Synderese et conscience aux XIIe et XIIIe siècles." In *Psychologie et morale aux XIIe et XIIIe siècles,* vol. 2, 103-350. Louvain: Abbaye du Mont Cesar, 1948.

MacDonald, Margaret. "Natural Rights." *Proceedings of the Aristotelian Society,* 1947-48, 40-60.

MacDonald, Scott. "Aquinas' Ultimate Ends: A Reply to Grisez." *American Journal of Jurisprudence* 46 (2001): 37-50.

MacIntyre, Alasdair. *After Virtue: A Study in Moral Theory.* 2nd ed. Notre Dame: University of Notre Dame Press, 1984. 1st ed. 1981.

———. *Dependent Rational Animals: Why Human Beings Need the Virtues.* Peru, Ill.: Carus/Open Court, 1999.

———. *First Principles, Final Ends, and Contemporary Philosophical Issues.* Milwaukee: Marquette University Press, 1990.

———. *Three Rival Versions of Moral Enquiry: Encyclopedia, Genealogy, and Tradition.* Notre Dame: University of Notre Dame Press, 1990.

———. *Whose Justice? Which Rationality?* Notre Dame: University of Notre Dame Press, 1988.

Mahoney, John. *The Making of Moral Theology: A Study of the Roman Catholic Tradition.* Oxford: Clarendon, 1987.

Maritain, Jacques. *Man and the State.* Chicago: University of Chicago Press, 1951.

Martinez, German. "An Anthropological Vision of Christian Marriage." *The Thomist* 56, no. 3 (July 1992): 451-72.

Mayr, Ernst. "Species Concepts and Their Application." In *Philosophy of Biology,* edited by Michael Ruse, 136-45. Amherst: Prometheus Books, 1998. Originally published in *Populations, Species, and Evolution,* 10-20. Cambridge: Harvard University Press, 1963.

———. *Toward a New Philosophy of Biology: Observations of an Evolutionist.* Cambridge: Harvard University Press, 1988.

McCormick, Richard A. "Does Faith Add to Ethical Perception?" In *Readings in Moral Theology No. 2: The Distinctiveness of Christian Ethics,* edited by Richard McCormick and Charles Curran, 156-73. New York: Paulist, 1980. Originally published 1979.

———. "Human Sexuality: Towards a Consistent Ethical Method." In *One Hundred Years of Catholic Social Thought: Celebration and Challenge,* edited by John A. Coleman, S.J., 189-97. Maryknoll, N.Y.: Orbis, 1991.

McDowell, John. *Mind and World.* Cambridge: Harvard University Press, 1994.

McGrath, Alister E. *A Scientific Theology,* vol. 1: *Nature.* Edinburgh: T. & T. Clark; Grand Rapids: Eerdmans, 2001.

McInerny, Ralph. *Aquinas on Human Action: A Theory of Practice.* Washington, D.C.: Catholic University of America Press, 1992.

———. "Grisez and Thomism." In *The Revival of Natural Law: Philosophical, Theological, and Ethical Responses to the Finnis-Grisez School,* edited by Nigel Biggar and Rufus Black, 53-72. Aldershot: Ashgate Press, 2000.

McMullin, Ernan. "Cosmic Purpose and the Contingency of Human Evolution." *Theology Today* 55 (1998): 389-414.

———. "Evolution and Creation." In *Evolution and Creation,* edited by Ernan McMullin, 1-58. Notre Dame: University of Notre Dame Press, 1985.

Mead, George Herbert. *Mind, Self, and Society from the Standpoint of a Social Behaviorist.* Chicago: University of Chicago Press, 1934.

Meilaender, Gilbert. "*Eritis Sicut Deus:* Moral Theory and the Sin of Pride." *Faith and Philosophy* 3 (1986): 397-415.

Meron, Theodor. *Human Rights and Humanitarian Norms as Customary Law.* Oxford: Clarendon, 1989.

Midgley, Mary. *Beast and Man: The Roots of Human Nature.* New York: Meridian, 1978.

———. *The Ethical Primate: Humans, Freedom, and Morality.* London: Routledge, 1994.

Moore, G. E. *Principia Ethica.* Cambridge: Cambridge University Press, 1903.

Moss, Lenny. "Representational Preformationism to the Epigenesis of Openness to the World? Reflections on a New Vision of the Organism." *Annals of the New York Academy of Sciences* 981 (December 2002): 21-230.

———. *What Genes Can't Do.* Cambridge: MIT Press, 2003.

Murdoch, Iris. *The Sovereignty of Good.* London/New York: Routledge and Kegan Paul/Methuen, 1970.

Murray, John Courtney. *We Hold These Truths.* New York: Sheed and Ward, 1960.

Narcisse, Gilbert. "Le surnaturel dans la théologie contemporaire." *Revue Thomiste* 101, no. 1-2 (January/June 2001): 312-18.

Nederman, Cary. "Aristotelianism and the Origins of 'Political Science' in the Twelfth Century." *Journal of the History of Ideas* 52 (1991): 179-94.

———. "Nature, Sin and the Origins of Society: The Ciceronian Tradition in Medieval Political Thought." *Journal of the History of Ideas* 49 (1988): 3-26.

Nelson, Daniel Mark. *The Priority of Prudence: Virtue and Natural Law in Aquinas and the Implications for Modern Ethics.* University Park: Pennsylvania State University Press, 1992.

Niebuhr, Reinhold. "Christian Faith and Natural Law." 1940. Reprinted in *Love and Justice: Selections from the Shorter Writings of Reinhold Niebuhr,* 46-54. Louisville: Westminster/John Knox, 1957.

Northcott, Michael S. *The Environment and Christian Ethics.* Cambridge: Cambridge University Press, 1996.

Novak, David. *Natural Law in Judaism.* Cambridge: Cambridge University Press, 1998.

Nussbaum, Martha C. "Non-Relative Virtues: An Aristotelian Approach." In *Midwest Studies in Philosophy XIII: Ethical Theory: Character and Virtue,* edited by Peter French, Theodore E. Uehling, Jr., and Howard K. Wettstein, 32-53. Notre Dame: University of Notre Dame Press, 1988.

———. *Women and Human Development: The Capabilities Approach.* Cambridge: Cambridge University Press, 2000.

O'Donovan, Oliver. *The Desire of the Nations: Rediscovering the Roots of Political Theology.* Cambridge: Cambridge University Press, 1996.

———. *Resurrection and Moral Order: An Outline for Evangelical Ethics.* Grand Rapids: Eerdmans, 1986.

O'Meara, Thomas. "The Presence of Grace outside Evangelization, Baptism and Church in Thomas Aquinas' Theology." In *That Others May Know and Love,* 91-131. St. Bonaventure, N.Y.: St. Bonaventure University, 1997.

O'Neill, Onora. *Towards Justice and Virtue: A Constructive Account of Practical Reasoning.* Cambridge: Cambridge University Press, 1996.

O'Neill, William. "Babel's Children: Reconstructing the Common Good." *Annual of the Society of Christian Ethics,* 1998, 161-76.

———. "Ethics and Inculturation: The Scope and Limits of Rights Discourse." *Annual of the Society of Christian Ethics,* 1993, 73-92.

Padgen, Anthony. *The Fall of Natural Man: The American Indian and the Origins of Comparative Ethnology.* Cambridge: Cambridge University Press, 1982.

Parfit, Derek. *Reasons and Persons.* Oxford: Oxford University Press, 1984.

Pasnau, Robert. *Thomas Aquinas on Human Nature: A Philosophical Study of "Summa theologiae" Ia 75-89.* Cambridge: Cambridge University Press, 2002.

Pegis, Anton. "Nature and Spirit: Some Reflections on the Problem of the End of Man." *Proceedings of the American Catholic Philosophical Association* 23 (1949): 62-79.

Peterson, Gregory. "Whose Evolution? Which Theology?" *Zygon* 35 (2000): 221-32.

Pigden, Charles. "Logic and the Autonomy of Ethics." *Australian Journal of Philosophy* 67, no. 2 (1989): 127-51.

Pinches, Charles. *Theology and Action: After Theory in Christian Ethics.* Grand Rapids: Eerdmans, 2002.

Pinckaers, Servais. *Ce qu'on ne peut jamais faire: La question des actes intrinsèquement mauvais, Histoire et discussion.* Fribourg: Editions Universitaires Fribourg, 1986.

———. *L'Evangile et la morale.* Fribourg: Editions Universitaires Fribourg, 1990.

———. *Les sources de la morale chrétienne: Sa méthode, son contenu, son histoire.* Fribourg: Editions Universitaires Fribourg, 1985.

Pinker, Steven. *The Blank Slate: The Modern Denial of Human Nature.* New York: Viking Press, 2002.

Pope, Stephen. "The Evolutionary Roots of Morality in Theological Perspective." *Zygon* 33, no. 4 (December 1998): 545-56.

———. *The Evolution of Altruism and the Ordering of Love.* Washington, D.C.: Georgetown University Press, 1994.

———. "Scientific and Natural Law Analyses of Homosexuality: A Methodological Study." *Journal of Religious Ethics* 25, no. 1 (1997): 89-126.

Porter, Jean. "The Moral Act in *Veritatis Splendor* and in Aquinas's *Summa theologiae:* A Comparative Analysis." In *Veritatis Splendor: American Responses,* edited by Michael E. Allsopp and John J. O'Keefe, 278-95. Kansas City: Sheed and Ward, 1995.

———. *Natural and Divine Law: Reclaiming the Tradition for Christian Ethics.* Ottawa: Novalis; Grand Rapids: Eerdmans, 1999.

———. "Natural Equality: Freedom, Authority, and Obedience in Two Medieval Thinkers." *Annual of the Society of Christian Ethics* 21 (2001): 275-304.

———. "Natural Law as a Scriptural Concept: Theological Reflections on a Medieval Theme." *Theology Today* 59, no. 2 (July 2002): 226-41.

———. "Reason, Nature and the End of Human Life: A Consideration of John Finnis' *Aquinas.*" *Journal of Religion* 80, no. 3 (July 2000): 476-84.

———. "A Tradition of Civility: The Natural Law as a Tradition of Moral Inquiry." *Scottish Journal of Theology* 56, no. 1 (2003): 27-48.

———. "What the Wise Person Knows: Natural Law and Virtue in Aquinas's *Summa theologiae.*" *Studies in Christian Ethics* 12 (1999): 57-69.

Prior, A. N. *Logic and the Basis of Ethics.* Oxford: Oxford University Press, 1949.

Putnam, Hilary. *The Collapse of the Fact/Value Dichotomy and Other Essays.* Cambridge: Harvard University Press, 2002.

Quinn, Warren. "Actions, Intentions, and Consequences: The Doctrine of Doing and Allowing." *Philosophical Review* 48, no. 3 (July 1989): 287-312.

Rahner, Karl. *Foundations of the Christian Faith: An Introduction to the Idea of Christianity.* New York: Crossroad, 1985.

———. "On the Relationship between Nature and Grace." In *Theological Investigations,* 1:297-318. New York: Crossroad, 1961, 1965.

Rawls, John. *A Theory of Justice.* 2nd ed. Oxford: Oxford University Press, 1999. 1st ed., Cambridge: Harvard University Press, 1971.

Reeder, John, Jr. *Killing and Saving: Abortion, Hunger, and War.* University Park: Pennsylvania State University Press, 1996.

Rhonheimer, Martin. "The Cognitive Structure of Natural Law and the Truth of Subjectivity." *The Thomist* 67, no. 1 (January 2003): 1-44.

———. "The Moral Significance of Pre-rational Nature in Aquinas: A Reply to Jean Porter (and Stanley Hauerwas)." *American Journal of Jurisprudence* 48 (2003): 253-80.

———. *Natural Law and Practical Reason: A Thomist View of Moral Autonomy.* Translated by Gerald Malsbary. New York: Fordham University Press, 2000.

———. *Praktische Vernunft und Vernünftigkeit der Praxis: Handlungstheorie bei Thomas von Aquin in ihrer Entstehung aus dem Promelmkontext der aristotelischen Ethik.* Berlin: Akademie Verlag, 1994.

Rigali, Norbert. "Christ and Morality." In *Readings in Moral Theology No. 2: The Distinctiveness of Christian Ethics,* edited by Richard McCormick and Charles Curran, 111-20. New York: Paulist, 1980. Originally published 1978.

———. "Christian Morality and Universal Morality: The One and the Many." *Louvain Studies* 19 (1994): 18-33.

———. "Moral Pluralism and Christian Ethics." *Louvain Studies* 13 (1988): 305-21.

———. "The Uniqueness and Distinctiveness of Christian Morality and Ethics." In *Moral Theology: Challenges for the Future,* edited by Charles E. Curran, 74-93. New York: Paulist, 1990.

Rist, John. *Augustine: Ancient Thought Baptized.* Cambridge: Cambridge University Press, 1994.

Robertson, Geoffrey. *Crimes against Humanity: The Struggle for Global Justice.* 2nd ed. London: Penguin Books, 2000.

Rogoff, Barbara. *Apprenticeship in Thinking: Cognitive Development in Social Context.* Oxford: Oxford University Press, 1990.

Rolston, Holmes, III. *Genes, Genesis, and God: Values and Their Origins in Natural and Human History.* Cambridge: Cambridge University Press, 1999.

Rorty, Amélie, ed. *Essays in Aristotle's Ethics.* Berkeley: University of California Press, 1980.

Rose, Hilary, and Steven Rose, eds. *Alas, Poor Darwin: Arguments against Evolutionary Psychology.* New York: Random House, 2000.

Ruse, Michael. *Can a Darwinian Be a Christian? The Relationship between Science and Religion.* Cambridge: Cambridge University Press, 2001.

Sahaydachcy, Antonia Bocarius. "The Marriage of Unfree Persons: Twelfth Century Decretals and Letters." In *De Jure Canonico Medii: Festschrift für Rudolf Weigand, Studia Gratiana,* XXVII, 483-506. 1996.

Salzman, Todd. *What Are They Saying about Catholic Ethical Method?* Mahwah, N.J.: Paulist, 2003.

Schneewind, Jerome. *The Invention of Autonomy: A History of Modern Moral Philosophy.* Cambridge: Cambridge University Press, 1998.

———, ed. *Moral Philosophy from Montaigne to Kant.* Vol. 1. Cambridge: Cambridge University Press, 1990.

Schwarz, Hans. *Creation.* Grand Rapids: Eerdmans, 2002.

Searle, John. *The Construction of Social Reality.* New York: Free Press, 1985.

Sen, Amartya. *Development as Freedom.* New York: Random House, 1999.

Serene, Eileen. "The Interpretation of Aristotle's *Physics* and the Science of Motion." In *The Cambridge History of Later Medieval Philosophy from the Rediscovery of Aristotle to the Disintegration of Scholasticism, 1100-1600,* edited by Norman Kretzman, Anthony Kenny, and Jan Pinborg, 521-36. Cambridge: Cambridge University Press, 1982.

Shklar, Judith. *Ordinary Vices.* Cambridge: Harvard University Press, Belknap Press, 1984.

Shweder, Richard. *Why Do Men Barbecue? Recipes for Cultural Psychology.* Cambridge: Harvard University Press, 2003.

Sidgwick, Henry. *The Methods of Ethics.* 7th ed. New York: Macmillan, 1907. Republished with a new introduction by John Rawls (Indianapolis: Hackett, 1981).

Singer, Peter. "Famine, Affluence, and Morality." *Philosophy and Public Affairs* 1 (1972): 229-43.

———. *Rethinking Life and Death: The Collapse of Our Traditional Ethics.* New York: St. Martin's Press, 1994.

Smalley, Beryl. *The Study of the Bible in the Middle Ages.* 1952. Notre Dame: University of Notre Dame Press, 1964.

Smart, J. J. C. "An Outline of a System of Utilitarian Ethics." In J. J. C. Smart and Bernard Williams, *Utilitarianism For and Against,* 3-76. Cambridge: Cambridge University Press, 1973.

Smith, Janet E. "Natural Law and Personalism in *Veritatis Splendor.*" In *Veritatis Splendor: American Responses,* edited by Michael E. Allsopp and John J. O'Keefe, 194-207. Kansas City: Sheed and Ward, 1995.

Sorabji, Richard. "Aristotle on the Role of Intellect in Virtue." In *Essays in Aristotle's Ethics,* edited by Amélie Rorty, 201-19. Berkeley: University of California Press, 1980.

Southern, R. W. *Scholastic Humanism and the Unification of Europe,* vol. 1: *Foundations.* Oxford: Blackwell, 1995.

Spruyt, Hendrik. *The Sovereign State and Its Competitors.* Princeton: Princeton University Press, 1994.

Staley, Kevin. "Happiness: The Natural End of Man?" *The Thomist* 53, no. 2 (1989): 215-34.

Stevenson, Charles. *Ethics and Language.* New Haven: Yale University Press, 1944.

Stocker, Michael. *Plural and Conflicting Values.* Oxford: Clarendon, 1990.

Stout, Rowland. *Things That Happen Because They Should: A Teleological Approach to Action.* Oxford: Clarendon, 1996.

Tierney, Brian. *The Idea of Natural Rights: Studies on Natural Rights, Natural Law, and Church Law, 1150-1625.* Atlanta: Scholars Press, 1997.

Tkacz, Michael. "Neo-Darwinians, Aristotelians, and Optimal Design." *The Thomist* 62 (1998): 355-72.

Torrell, Jean-Pierre. "Nature et grâce chez Thomas d'Aquin." *Revue Thomiste* 101 (2001): 167-202.

Traina, Christine. *Feminist Ethics and Natural Law: The End of the Anathemas.* Washington, D.C.: Georgetown University Press, 1999.

———. "Oh Susanna: The New Absolutism and Natural Law." *Journal of the American Academy of Religion* 65, no. 2 (Summer 1997): 371-401.

Tuck, Richard. *Natural Rights Theories: Their Origin and Development.* Cambridge: Cambridge University Press, 1979.

Tweedale, Martin. "Universals and Laws of Nature." *Philosophical Topics* 13 (1982): 25-44.

Unger, Peter. *Living High and Letting Die: Our Illusion of Innocence.* Oxford: Oxford University Press, 1996.

Urmson, J. O. "Aristotle's Doctrine of the Mean." In *Essays in Aristotle's Ethics,* edited by Amélie Rorty, 157-70. Berkeley: University of California Press, 1980.

Vacek, Edward. "Divine-Command, Natural-Law and Mutual-Love Ethics." *Theological Studies* 57 (1996): 633-53.

Vandervelde, George. "The Grammar of Grace: Karl Rahner as a Watershed in Contemporary Theology." *Theological Studies* 49 (1988): 445-59.

Veritatis Splendor. Origins: CNS Documentary Service, 1993, 23.

Vogler, Candace. *Reasonably Vicious.* Cambridge: Harvard University Press, 2002.

Wallace, James. *Virtues and Vices.* Ithaca, N.Y.: Cornell University Press, 1978.

Watson, Gerard. "The Natural Law and Stoicism." In *Problems in Stoicism,* edited by A. A. Long, 216-38. London: Athlone, 1971.

Wawrykow, Joseph. *God's Grace and Human Action: Merit in the Theology of Thomas Aquinas.* Notre Dame: University of Notre Dame Press, 1995.

Weigand, Rudolf. *Die Naturrechtslehre der Legisten und Dekretisten von Irnerius bis Accursius und von Gratian bis Johannes Teutonicus.* Munich: Max Hueber, 1967.

Weiland, George. "Happiness: The Perfection of Man." In *The Cambridge History of Later Medieval Philosophy from the Rediscovery of Aristotle to the Disintegration of Scholasticism, 1100-1600,* edited by Norman Kretzman, Anthony Kenny, and Jan Pinborg, 675-86. Cambridge: Cambridge University Press, 1982.

Westberg, Daniel. "Did Aquinas Change His Mind about the Will?" *The Thomist* 58 (1994): 41-60.

———. *Right Practical Reason: Aristotle, Action, and Prudence in Aquinas.* Oxford: Clarendon, 1994.

Westin, Drew. *Self and Society: Narcissism, Collectivism, and the Development of Morals.* Cambridge: Cambridge University Press, 1985.

Williams, Bernard. "A Critique of Utilitarianism." In J. J. C. Smart and Bernard Williams, *Utilitarianism For and Against.* Cambridge: Cambridge University Press, 1973.

———. *Ethics and the Limits of Philosophy.* Cambridge: Harvard University Press, 1985.

———. *Moral Luck: Philosopical Papers, 1973-1980.* Cambridge: Cambridge University Press, 1981.

Xu, Xiaoqun. "Human Rights and the Discourse on Universality: A Chinese Historical Perspective." In *Negotiating Culture and Human Rights,* edited by L. Bell et al., 217-41. New York: Columbia University Press, 2001.

Yearley, Lee. "Conflicts among Ideals of Human Flourishing." In *Prospects for a Common Morality,* edited by Gene Outka and John P. Reeder, Jr., 233-53. Princeton: Princeton University Press, 1993.

———. *Mencius and Aquinas: Theories of Virtue and Conceptions of Courage.* New York: SUNY Press, 1990.

Index of Proper Names
(excluding Thomas Aquinas)

Index of Subjects